HISTORIC HO
CASTLES & GARDENS

THE ESSENTIAL REFERENCE GUIDE FOR VISITORS SINCE 1954

Athelhampton House & Gardens, Dorset
Winner Christie's / HHA Garden of the Year Award presented in 1998

a
JOHANSENS
publication

1

Knight Frank

KF

FOR SALE

0171-629 8171

Contents

Great Comp Garden

Raby Castle

Château de Valencay

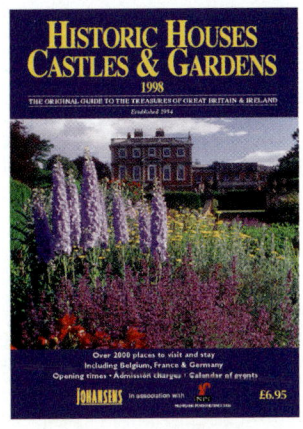

1998 Front Cover – Newby Hall, Yorkshire

Cover Picture: Belvoir Castle, Leicestershire, p99.

In association with

Chubb Insurance Company of Europe S.A.

3

First man, then machine.

When we first set out to design the CR-V, we approached it with the same philosophy that Sochiro Honda, our founder, encouraged.

He insisted that everything done in his name be done for a reason, rather than developing technology for technology's sake. Everything has to have a purpose, a relevance, a benefit.

For example, with the CR-V, we bore in mind that the vast majority of journeys it would undertake would be on tarmac. So instead of giving it permanent 4-wheel drive, we developed a system that could detect when 4-wheel drive was needed and immediately engage it.

It's this kind of thinking that's evident across the Honda range, whether in major pieces of technology, or in the more considered placing of switchgear.

For dealers and details, phone **0345 159 159** and find out why we try to follow our founder's example.

Technology you can enjoy, from Honda.

Some places are
more accessible
than others.

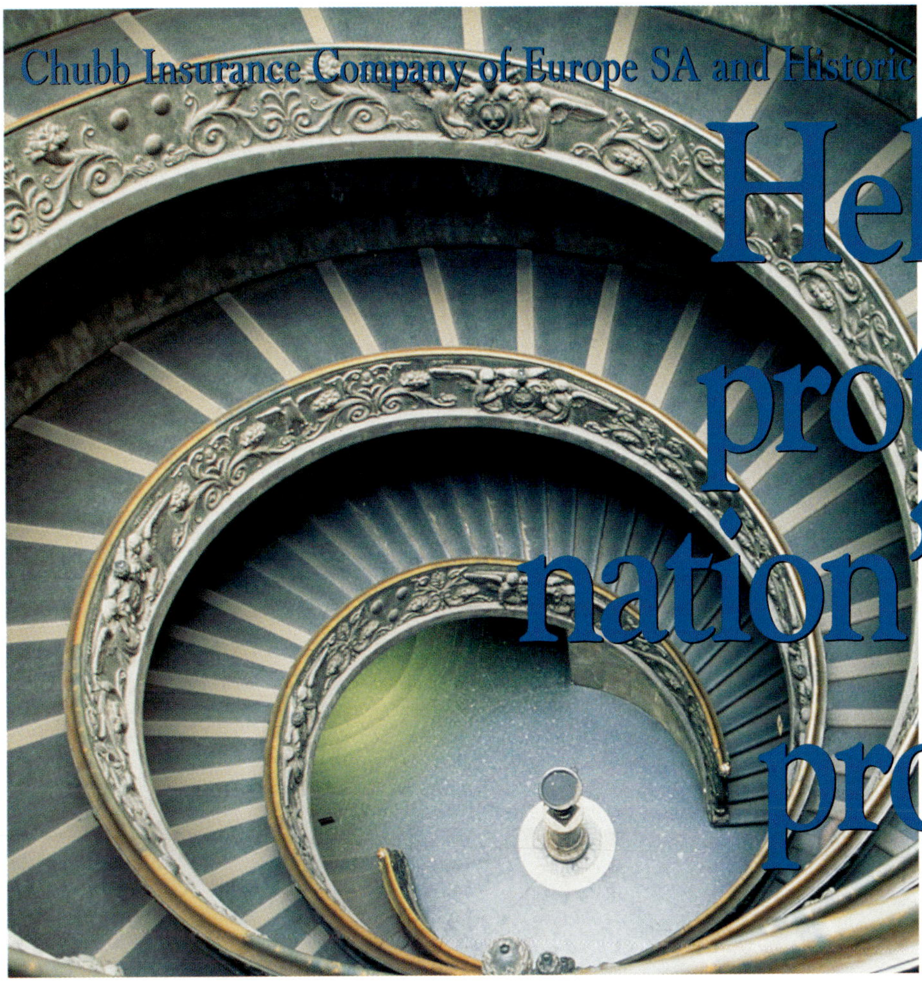

Helping to protect the nation's finest properties

Welcome to the 1999 edition of Historic Houses, Castles & Gardens. Chubb Insurance Company of Europe S.A. (Chubb) is delighted to be associated with this prestigious title published by Johansens.

Together, we aim to promote and protect the country's finest properties – for the generations of today and the future.

For 45 years, Historic Houses, Castles & Gardens has detailed the historic treasures which are an intrinsic part of our national heritage and play a valuable role in our leisure activities. The guide is not only used for choosing interesting places to visit but for arranging special occasions such as concerts and weddings. Since last year the guide has also included a selection of sites throughout continental Europe.

Like Johansens, Chubb has a wealth of experience in working with fine properties. For more than 116 years, members insurers of the Chubb Group of Insurance Companies have insured quality homes and contents. Today, the Chubb Group is one of the most innovative and successful global insurance organisations.

It's said that 'an Englishman's home is his castle' and at Chubb we appreciate that every home is unique. Whether you live in a suburban five bedroom detached or a rural manor house, our Masterpiece programme will provide your home and contents with the ultimate in insurance protection. We help protect homes and prevent under-insurance through our complimentary home appraisal service, which estimates full reconstruction costs and records special architectural features.

We're acknowledged as a leading insurer of jewellery and Masterpiece provides unrivalled cover for fine art, jewellery, collections and other personal treasures. Annual travel, personal liability, legal expenses and vacation homes cover can also be incorporated into one, easy to read policy.

Masterpiece was created for those who desire the best. With no restrictive warranties, worldwide cover and first class claims service, Masterpiece allows you to enjoy your lifestyle with total peace of mind. To discover more about a Chubb Masterpiece insurance programme, please call your broker or call Chubb free on 0800 111 511.

Or visit our web site: www.chubb.com

Proud sponsors of the 1999 Chubb Insurance Windsor International Horse Trials (27-30 May)

Chubb Insurance Company of Europe S.A.

Masterpiece®

THE GARDENS AT
HATFIELD HOUSE Hertfordshire

"There are nearly 14 acres of formal and informal gardens dating back to the late 15th century. From 1609 to 1611 John Tradescant the Elder laid out and planted the gardens for Robert Cecil, the builder of the House. Today the gardens, much embellished in the last years, contain many of the same plants growing in knot gardens typical of the period, arranged in the court of the 15th century Palace where Queen Elizabeth I spent much of her childhood. There are herb and sweet gardens, a parterre of herbaceous plants and roses, fountains, statuary and a foot maze or labyrinth, the whole enclosed in ancient rose-brick walls, topiaried yews, holly and pleached limes.

A wilderness garden, planted with forest and ornamental trees, blossoms in the spring with crabs, cherries, magnolias and rhododendrons underplanted with many flowers and bulbs, the whole providing colour and interest (for there are many rare and unusual plants) for all seasons."
"Photographs by Mick Hales, Garry Rogers and Jeremy Whitaker."

"I feel at home here as I gaze down and respond to the feeling of total delight which it gives me . . ."   Sir Roy Strong

"Hatfield's gardens are the most completely beautiful and fit for their purpose of any great house in England."   "Tradescant" of the RHS Journal.

FOR DETAILS SEE HERTFORDSHIRE SECTION

How to use this guide

If you want to identify a historic house, castle or garden, whose name you already know, look for it in the Index of all properties from page 299.

If you want to find a historic house, castle or garden in a particular county or area you can:
• Turn to the maps at the back of the book
• Look through the guide for the county you require
Each county is in alphabetical order. The properties are then listed alphabetically wherever possible. The maps cover the counties of England, Ireland, Scotland and Wales. Each historic house, castle and garden is clearly named and marked on these maps. Properties in Belgium, France, Germany and The Netherlands have their approximate positions labelled on the illustrated maps in their introductions.

Starting from page 259 there are a number of properties listed in certain categories: supplementary list by appointment only, Cambridge and Oxford Universities, film locations, garden specialists, plants for sale, art collections, weddings, top teas, open all year, conference facilities and accommodation.

To find somewhere local to stay, a full listing of Johansens recommended hotels, country houses and inns are included in county order on page 286.

Editorial Manager:	Yasmin Razak
Sales Executive:	Juliette Cutting
Production Manager:	Daniel Barnett
Production Controller:	Kevin Bradbrook
Senior Designer:	Michael Tompsett
Designer:	Sue Dixon
Special Promotions Editor:	Fiona Patrick
Sales & Marketing Manager:	Laurent Martinez
Marketing Executive:	Stephen Hoskin
Marketing–Sales Executive:	Babita Sareen
Map Illustrations:	Linda Clark
Publisher:	Phoebe Hobby
Managing Director:	Andrew Warren

Johansens Ltd, Therese House, Glasshouse Yard, London EC1A 4JN
Tel: 0171 566 9700 Fax: 0171 490 2538

Find Johansens on the Internet at: http://www.johansens.com

Copyright © 1999 Johansens Ltd.
a subsidiary of the Daily Mail and General Trust plc

ISBN 1 860 175945

Printed in England by St Ives plc
Colour origination by Catalyst Creative Imaging

Distributed in the UK and Europe by Johnsons International Media Services Ltd, London (direct sales) & Biblios PDS Ltd, West Sussex (bookstores). In North America by general sales agent: ETL Group, New York, NY (direct sales) and Hunter Publishing, New Jersey (bookstores). In Australia and New Zealand by Bookwise International, Findon, South Australia

Key to Symbols

🌿	The National Trust
	The National Trust for Scotland
	Historic Scotland
	English Heritage
	CADW
	Historic Houses Association
	HITHA
	Park
	Garden
	Refreshments
	Children's Playground
	Accommodation Available
	Meals Available
	Picnic Area
	Wedding Licence
♿	Disabled Access
	Guided Tours
	Gift Shop
	Nurseries – Plants for Sale
	Live Entertainment
	House by Appointment Only
	Haunted
C	Conference Facilities
	Used for Filming
	Special Group Rates

L'art de vivre
at every
Johansens
Recommended
Hotel

Behind the scenes at Blenheim

with His Grace the Duke of Marlborough

Blenheim was one of the stately homes featured in the first issue of Historic Houses, Castles & Gardens which was published back in 1954. The Palace was built by the architect Sir John Vanbrugh between 1705 and 1725 and has been home to 11 Dukes of Marlborough. The birthplace of Sir Winston Churchill, it attracts millions of visitors from all over the world. Now, in the Guide's 45th Anniversary Year, His Grace the 11th Duke of Marlborough talks to Rosanna Greenstreet about the magnificent stately home that he inherited in 1972 and reflects on the changes that have been made over the years to ensure that Blenheim Palace remains one of the world's most important historic sites.

"Blenheim was given as a gift to the first Duke by Queen Anne and Parliament in recognition of his victory over the French at the Battle of Blenheim. It is a very important part of our national heritage, and not only that, it's a World Heritage Site. I have the responsibility of ensuring that Blenheim is maintained for the future for everybody in the world, in addition to future generations of Churchills. Obviously, it is a burden, but it's a responsibility that I've readily accepted and a challenge that I have undertaken for an important heritage site.

A lot of changes have come over the years. When we originally opened, it was only four days a week and then, after I inherited, I put it up to seven. I thought that it was imperative – one, we needed the extra funds to keep the maintenance going and secondly it was always confusing to people when they turned up and didn't realise it wasn't open on a particular day. So I decided that it was a seven day a week business and we extended the season. We are now open from the middle of March to the end of October.

I think you've got to provide services for your visitors. There's a self-service restaurant and the Indian Room Restaurant for visitors on the Water Terraces and we have two different shops at the house – the Gift Centre in the Old Palace Dairy and the Book Shop in the Palace courtyard. Then down at the Pleasure Gardens we have the Butterfly House, the Herb and Lavender Garden and another shop with a cafeteria next door. There's the Marlborough Maze area where there's the world's largest symbolic hedge maze, the putting green and giant chess and draught boards. Over a period of time we've introduced different things – the boat ride on Blenheim Lake was one of the earliest things to be introduced, and the train ride – they are all part and parcel of the entrance ticket. Visitors can hire boats for rowing on the Queen's Pool, part of the lake.

We've got these different things so that when a family comes along, there's something for the children to be interested in as well as the grown ups, who probably appreciate the house and the art content more than the children. The children will enjoy the train

> ### "Obviously, it is a burden, but it's a responsibility that I've readily accepted"

The large and splendid Long Library

is an enormous room, but it's so well proportioned, you don't realise how big it is. I find that the general public seem to appreciate guided tours, though there are always one or two people who say they prefer to be left alone to go round on their own; but they much prefer guided tours than this modern business of listening to a tape recorder. We now have guide books in several different languages. We have quite a lot of overseas visitors in the summer, I would think over 30% of our visitors are foreign. The foreign element has increased in recent years, especially from Japan, although we haven't got as many Americans coming as we used to have – I think the reason for that is the strength of the pound.

There is a lot of competition now – I am fully aware that there are many more leisure activities available to people today. The one

> ## "there was very little the general public could do on a Sunday except go to a stately home – now there's all sorts of activities.."

and boat rides and the bouncy castle, the putting green and the Butterfly House – there is an adventure playground too. I know my young grandson goes on most of them!

I've got no additional plans at the moment. We have the horse trials regularly and we usually have a couple of craft fairs during the season and one or two other activities – a lot of corporate entertaining goes on and that has been growing recently. The new restaurant, The Orangery, is proving very popular – it is where a lot of wedding receptions take place and again, corporate entertaining. It used to be the conservatory where all the bedding plants for the Italian Garden were kept – but we've moved them down now to the gardens' area and it's been converted into a restaurant.

We have a very efficient lot of tour guides and they explain to the visitors about the various artefacts that are in the house. My personal favourite is the Long Library. It's got a fantastic organ at one end and the statue of Queen Anne by Rysbrack at the other. It

thing that's probably hitting us hardest at the moment and will continue to hit us, is Sunday opening. Many years ago there was very little that the general public could do on a Sunday except go to a stately home – now there's all sorts of activities available to them, including sport as well as shopping. I hope that with modern technology people will become more aware of the treasures that exist in houses and they will use them more and more for educational purposes. I think the education side is important and we have a full time education liaison officer who looks after the school parties when they turn up for an educational visit. We run

The "Blenheim" Tapestry – The 1st Duke (Hanovarian Grey Charger) receiving the surrender of Marshall Tallard

John Churchill, 1st Duke of Marlborough by Kneller

The north face of Blenheim

the Marlborough Heritage Educational Awards. When school children come round they are made aware of it and to enter they have to write about Churchill or Marlborough, or the house or the architecture. We have three different age categories and once a year I give prizes to the winners – usually a book about Blenheim or Marlborough. The Awards are known about far and wide and we've had children entering from the north and south, the east and west and sometimes from overseas as well.

When I was a child Blenheim was very different to what it is today. In those days we were only open on special occasions. My father inherited in 1934, so we didn't have many years here before the war, and of course once the war began a lot of dramatic changes took place. My father offered it to the nation to be used for some purpose or other as part of the war effort. Originally, Malvern College was evacuated here and they stayed for about a year: we still lived in the private wing. Then, after they left, we had MI5. I was at school most of the time, but I remember that there were about five hundred people working in the house and in the many Nissan huts which were scattered all over the courtyard.

After two World Wars there was a lot of maintenance that needed to be done. My hope is that we will be able to keep Blenheim going for a great many years. One can't foretell what's going to happen in the world, but I believe Blenheim's a very important part of world history. So we keep pressing on and hope that we will get the revenues required to maintain the place and do

"My hope is to keep Blenheim going for a great many years"

restoration work. My wife does a lot on the decorating side and the internal fabrics. My eldest son has started to get himself involved and my youngest son has provided some useful input, but he's very busy working on his own account in London as a business consultant. There are lots of things that I am desperate to get done but things have to be taken in order of priority. It just depends whether we're having a good year for visitors or a bad year, as to how many repairs and renewals can be done."

From Paper to Sapphire

45 years of Historic Houses, Castles & Gardens

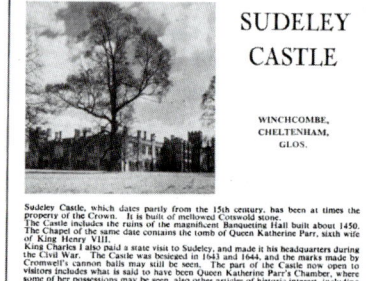

Historic Houses and Castles 1954

"Visiting historic houses is not an entirely new hobby". When the mysterious 'M.G.J.', editor of Historic Houses and Castles, penned those words in 1954 he may certainly have anticipated the rising interest in historic properties. It is unlikely, however, that he would have envisaged the increase in the number of properties from 250 houses and castles 45 years ago to over 2000 places to visit and stay today (fortunately the increase in the cost of the guide has not been quite so dramatic!). A further study of the editor's introduction reveals that much has changed since the first issue and references to the ease of travel such as "if you have no car do not be dismayed, since you can travel very comfortably by bus, coach or train" now appear dated.

The Orangery at Longleat, Wiltshire

However, whilst society has progressed, many of the original properties are still gracing the pages of the guide, 45 years later. Longleat House, a fine example of high Elizabethan architecture was listed in the first issue of the guide. This impressive stately home in Warminster is celebrating a special 50th anniversary as it was in 1949 that the Marquess of Bath opened Longleat to the public. Further attractions were added which included, in 1966, the first safari park in Europe and the famous lions of Longleat.

Recent additions include many family oriented activities, mazes and murals by the present Marquess of Bath, Alexander Thynn.

Another property from the original guide with a cause to celebrate this year is Hopetoun House, "Scotland's finest stately home". The Hope family commissioned Sir William Bruce to design their new home in South Queensferry 300 years ago. Construction began in 1699 and this year, the Trustees of the Hopetoun House Preservation Trust, who are now responsible for the house, are hosting a number of events to celebrate its Tercentenary. A series of concerts reflecting the changes during the centuries will be held amongst other highlights, such as a major conference which will be of interest to architectural historians and others interested in heritage.

In 1954, the entry for Sudeley Castle described a property "built of mellow Cotswold stone.... which dates back partly from the 15th century". Whilst the guide has developed over the years, the changes at the castle are also clearly evident. The castle now hosts a number of exhibitions each year including 'The Dent Glove Story' and the fascinating 'Emma Dent Exhibition'. The latter features geological items, jewellery, autographs of famous politicians and many other treasures, reflecting the various

A change in style – Sudeley Castle's entry 45 years ago (top) and today's entry (bottom)

Hopetoun House, Lothian

interests of the lady who exercised her creative influence over Sudeley from 1855 to 1900. The diverse calender of events has also grown over the years and highlights include the Sudeley Castle Autumn Rose and Garden Festival, popular with gardeners and floriculturists. One of the greatest changes at Sudeley Castle over the last 45 years is apparent when comparing the old entry against the current page. Whilst the original description of the castle omitted to refer to the gardens, the present entry places a great emphasis upon the attractive flower displays. Lady Ashcombe and her family have continued to add garden features such as a Buddleia Walk, designed to attract butterflies and the new Stone Garden.

Set in the heart of the New Forest, Beaulieu was one of the first Treasure Houses in England to open its doors to the public in 1952 and was one of the original properties featured in the guide. The house has remained a popular attraction but is being increasingly used for more versatile purposes. Many historic properties offer a comprehensive range of facilities for conferences, product launches and corporate entertainment and Beaulieu is no exception to this current trend. The house also provides a

Motors on show at Beaulieu

marvellous backdrop for films and dramas and "A Man for all Seasons" and Prince Edward's series "King and Country" are some of the many productions that have used Beaulieu as a film location.

A close inspection of the original front cover against that of the present guide reveals two of most significant changes that have been introduced since the first issue. The original title has evolved and now reflects the nation's growing interest in gardens. Special events are held throughout the spring and summer months and include garden festivals and flower shows such as the Rose Weekend at Borde Hill in Sussex.

Observant readers will also notice the second change detailed on the front cover. The properties featured are no longer from Great Britain alone, they are now complemented by an array of European châteaux, Schlösser, gardens and other historic monuments.

Historic Houses, Castles and Gardens has developed into a multi-national guide over the past 45 years and as the much discussed millennium approaches, it continues to encapsulate the changing demands and interests of visitors today.

Yasmin Razak

Nacqueville Château & Gardens, France

Boars, wars and decadence

An insight into the life of Sir Thomas Ingilby

R ipley Castle, with its magnificent vestiges of the country's historic past, stands imposingly in acres of beautiful grounds, just 10 minutes north of Harrogate. Ripley's name dates back to 500AD, evolving from Hrype-Leah, "the woodland clearing of the Hrype Tribe" who populated the area. The early part of the 13th century was particularly tempestuous with the villages surrounding the principal town of Knaresborough struck initially by an attack from the Scots and then by the bovine plague. Ripley was then under the ownership of the Thweng family and their sole survivor was a girl, Edeline. She met Thomas Ingilby during the early 1300s and their marriage was arranged. A most impressive dowry was offered and thus the possession of Ripley was acquired by the Ingilbys through marriage.

The castle has remained with the family for 26 generations and today is home to Sir Thomas and Lady Ingilby and their children. I asked Sir Thomas to recall his earliest memory of Ripley. "Playing hide and seek with friends in the castle and having to restrict our field of operations to two rooms because there were so many places to hide. If we didn't, we would never find each other and the game would go on rather longer than we expected".

Educated at Eton College, Sir Thomas inherited the Castle and the Estate in 1974 after the death of his father, Sir Joslan Ingilby. "My father died when I was 18 so I was still fresh from school. At the age of 18 you can take on the world, you don't see any of the pitfalls, you only see the opportunities. You think you can do anything and it has taken me about 20 years to learn that I can't. I was horribly green, extremely naïve, and I've learnt the hard way a good many times. I would have liked to have had the opportunity, with hindsight, to have worked within trade or commerce and form a bit more business experience, because I was trying to turn a very traditional business into a business of the 21st century and it was a very painful learning process. It has been hard, but no business man who has been successful has achieved those results without making a few mistakes and I've made my share".

Sir Thomas and Lady Emma have five children, four boys and a girl, and he considered their appreciation of the Castle. "Our children have always grown up here so they've never known any different and this to them is normal life. I think we only appreciate it more when we go away for the weekend to stay with friends and they can just open the French windows and run out into the garden which is the one thing they've never been able to do here. Firstly we live in a flat on the first floor of the castle from which we cannot get out without crossing a public route at some stage. Our garden is about 150 yards away from the castle so you can't actually go out and leave children alone in the house. It's a rather bizarre existence

Sir Thomas and Lady Ingilby with their children

and you can't pretend that its a normal family life when there are 300 people dancing the night away in a marquee just outside your bedroom window. The compensation is that from our flat we do have the most wonderful view across the deer park and lake. Indeed from our kitchen we have one of the finest kitchen sink views of any house in the world which is very therapeutic for washing up!"

"Whoever in their kindness brings me my pipe and slippers will be looked upon favourably!"

Sir Thomas continued "I don't want to put pressure on any of my children to take over the running of this place. Hopefully with luck, one of them will become so well-established in their own profession that they'll be making far more money than they ever could do here and they will make other arrangements to keep this place going in their absence. It doesn't bother me particularly which of them takes it on and if none of them wish to do so then it is time to call it a day. I certainly wouldn't hold it against them if they didn't want to take it on. They are all of quite a young age and I don't think any of them have their eyes on it already. Whoever in their kindness brings me my pipe and slippers will be looked upon favourably!".

I then asked if there was such a thing as a typical day in the life of Sir Thomas. "No! I think although our days should be planned and usually are at about 7 o' clock in the morning, generally by 9 o' clock, the order of battle is completely altered and we very seldom end up doing anything we planned to do that day at all. One of the great joys of this particular career is that you can never plan what you are doing. I like the phrase "If you want to hear God laugh just tell him your plans" because it's exactly like that here. That's what makes it such an exciting job and such fun. I would find it difficult to go back into normal employment again – it would seem terribly dull".

Sir Thomas explained the changes over the years regarding stately homes and discussed the popularity of the Castle with school groups and those seeking a weekend break. "School packages are a fairly well-established sideline of a stately home, but it's merely a question of how far you go down the road. We've tried to be professional in launching our package by preparing school educational packs to fit in with the NVQ National Curriculum so hopefully it's not just a visit to the Castle, it's actually part of the school's syllabus and they get good value for that. I don't think we've done anything especially new that other people haven't done but one of the things we've enjoyed doing most has been the development of the Murder Mystery Weekends between The Boar's Head Hotel and the Castle. We introduced these about 4 years ago and this has proved tremendously popular. It has even featured on The Holiday Programme and Jill Dando's legs will sell anything. After we'd been featured on that programme we received over 1000 enquiries and the weekends sold out for the next two years which was wonderful.

I think the biggest change regarding stately homes over the last few years has been the advent of the wedding licence. We have become a popular venue for weddings, having a church, castle and hotel all so close together. We held our first punk wedding last year, which was very exciting with a great deal of purple and black in evidence and a lot of that was on the bride's face! The cake was sort of semi-spherical with lots of black spikes sticking out of it and the costumes that turned up were quite amazing. They couldn't have been a nicer bunch of people, once you'd overcome the culture shock."

Ripley Castle and its glorious surroundings

He then described his plans for the future "We're working on plans to develop the coach house which we're hoping to turn into a banqueting suite. One of our main businesses, quite apart from the house, is that we do a tremendous number of corporate meetings and dinners, not to mention the weddings at weekends. At the moment we're living for 9 months of the year with a marquee outside our front door which isn't terribly aesthetically pleasing and it's also a bit noisy, so we decided that by moving it into the coach house it would solve a few problems. It's a huge project – over

£1 million pounds to complete, hopefully we shall get the bulk of it done next year (1999) and perhaps it will take a year or two to get a fully functioning unit. We're also planning to extend the hotel because that has gone very well."

Sir Thomas continued on the subject of the hotel. "The Boar's Head Hotel was an interesting experience – we always had been convinced that a hotel would be good as we host several events. The name of the hotel goes back to the 14th century story of Thomas Ingilby saving the life of King Edward III when he was attacked by a wild boar. We don't still have the boar but we do serve up one of its descendants every Sunday in our pies! Lady Emma runs The Boar's Head Hotel and makes all the decisions. She has a very good working relationship with the staff and an excellent eye for detail. I have a very minor input – just the wine list but someone has to do it!"

Preparing for a splendid banquet in the Tower Room

undertook for their final year theses. One year we sent them a marketing project and one of the ideas that they came up with was to form a consortium of stately homes, castles and gardens in the region. Without consulting us, they rang around quite a few of these properties and asked them if they would be interested. Much to our surprise, the feedback was incredibly positive. We got about 17 properties in the first year and there are now 35 properties. It has worked extremely well – we are all able to reach markets that we could not have reached individually. We are also able to attract commercial sponsors and we have been able to apply for European grant funding. There are many exciting prospects including a venture with KLM enabling travellers from Australia to fly to Europe, stay at The Boar's Head Hotel and tour all the castles, gardens and stately homes in the area. We do have a lot of interest from abroad and the Great Houses association allows us to attempt to open up the overseas market. We would like to develop Yorkshire as a major international tourist destination."

"There has to be a middle road between strict preservation and adaptation..."

I asked Sir Thomas about the funding available for historic properties and the information from the various associations. "I think that the funding available at the moment is probably at about the right level. In my opinion, the problem lies in the system for applying those funds which is becoming increasingly bureaucratic in terms of the amount of information required. The quality of advice from English Heritage is improving, I think there is a growing realisation that it is not good enough to just repair and restore a building, it must become functional and useful. There has to be a middle road between strict preservation and adaptation and in the discussions that we've had with English Heritage in the last 12 months, I've found that their attitude is extremely helpful.

The Historic Houses Association is a very important body in that it adds to the lobbying organisation and there is a lot of expertise, skill and professional knowledge in the membership. There are tax accountants and solicitors who also happen to be stately home owners and they are very good at giving their time to look at proposals made by the government or looking at the existing taxation system and trying to see how they can get the best deal for the stately homes.

'The Great Houses and Gardens of Yorkshire' developed originally out of a student project from the Leeds Metropolitan University. We used to give them projects which the students

Throughout the 700 years as the ancestral home of the Ingilbys there have been various occasions and events including the visit of the future king of England on the way to his coronation and two civil wars. I asked Sir Thomas if there was any event in the past that he wished he had witnessed. "I think it would have been fascinating to have been here during the Cromwellian Civil War, when so much was happening in the area. In fact if you could have been born around 1550 and lived for a century, you would have seen some amazing sights here. I think these years were some of the most turbulent periods of English history – particularly around this area which was a hotbed of recusancy. In two decades we experienced the Catholic persecutions with two members of the family being pursued like dogs across England and Europe and then found ourselves entertaining James I, the future king of England, on his way south to his coronation. Two years later, members of the family were part of the conspiracy that intended to blow him, his family and parliament sky high. Then within 35 years of that, there were the events of the Civil War when the family were divided in their opinions and whereas the father was a keen royalist, the son undoubtedly had strong parliamentary sympathies. The redoubtable 'Trooper' Jane Ingilby held Oliver Cromwell at gunpoint in the Castle Library to prevent him from searching the Castle for her brother, who was hiding in the Priest's Hole. The characters that

Sir Thomas' favourite room – The Knight's Chamber

were alive in the family at that time were so diverse that to have been a fly on the wall must have been incredible. It is a period of history that we cannot imagine now, living through such turbulence. They really were extraordinary times.

Sir Thomas continued to discuss the past centuries and the many vestiges of the Castle's history which are still visible today. He concluded by describing his favourite room. "The Knight's Chamber is the original medieval room in the Castle with all the 16th century panelling and the priest's hiding hole. I believe this room at Ripley is genuinely different from any other room in the world. It has such an extraordinary atmosphere. For sheer decadence it is hard to beat the carved oak wine cradle which is large enough to hold a magnum of wine and is shaped like a boat, hence the old English phrase "to push the boat out". Even though I go up there several times a week, I still feel that in spirit the room is still stuck in the 16th century. I always imagine that I am going to see someone in lace sitting in the corner – I never have done yet! That to me is the room that really brings me closer to my forbears here."

Interview by Yasmin Razak

The take charge card

With no pre-set spending limit you're always in charge. In the chaotic and unpredictable world of business travel, you need to be in control. The Diners Club Card gives you that control. The safety net of open ended spending*, backed up by the security of emergency assistance in over 175 countries worldwide. Give us a call on **0800 88 77 74** to find out how we can help you stay in charge. **Diners Club. The take charge card.**

Beautiful Britain with Rainbow Fair

Just some of the visitors on a beautiful day in May at The Gatcombe Craft Fair

Never in their wildest dreams did Shaun and Connie Duckworth imagine that founding Rainbow Craft Fairs would one day lead to a work schedule that would read like a royal progress of the Middle Ages.

In the early days of the late 70's and early 80's one day shows at civic and town halls throughout Lancashire and Cheshire was their forte, but they still felt that there was much more waiting out there for the development of the shows. It was Shaun who came up with the idea of developing two and three day shows but making them different by siting them at stately homes. In those far off days many homes were not interested until Rainbow proved itself. Faith was at hand in the persons of Sir Walter and Lady Bromley Davenport of Capesthorne Hall, Cheshire. Much has changed since those far off days of forty stands in a large marquee behind the house. Today, their 'oldest' stately home boasts in excess of one hundred and eighty stands at its twice a year show and it is still growing with the co-operation of the present day owners Mr and Mrs William Bromley Davenport.

Capesthorne was quickly joined with Newby Hall, home of the Gobelin tapestry and the magnificent gardens, Thoresby Park in the heart of Sherwood Forest, Arbury

Burghley House Stamford, Lincs. – Backdrop for the May Bank Holiday Rainbow Craft Fair

Hall, the Gothic gem of the Midlands and Rockingham Castle, scene of much activity in the English Civil War. In more recent times these were joined by Grimsthorpe Castle, whose rich forest provided timber for Henry VIII's fleet of the British Royal Navy.

Not only is Rainbow presenting ever bigger and better shows but also reviving interest in some of our historic gems. Many a visitor has been cajoled into following Rainbow Fair around beautiful Britain. It is quite a journey from Dalemain in the far north, a border stronghold famed for its beautiful gardens and Fell Pony Museums, to Sherborne Castle in the depths of Dorset. This ancient and historic site was one of the homes of Sir Walter Raleigh and is now the home of the Digby family. Then travel east to Burghley House at Stamford, home in its day of the powerful Cecil family, and now the residence of Lady Victoria Leatham and family.

What of the Royal connections? Rainbow have, for the past fourteen years, presented a large four day craft fair at Gatcombe Park, home of Her Royal Highness, The Princess Royal and Commodore T Lawrence. This long and happy association leads, in 1999; to the introduction of a second show each year in October.

This was joined some eight years ago by

*A still life in exotic woods by Ian Mennell,
well known Yorkshire woodturner and Rainbow Regular*

the originally three day, now four day, August Bank Holiday, show at Her Majesty, The Queen's Norfolk home, Sandringham. Set in the beautiful parkland overlooking the house and in view of the church, this huge event takes place each year with the coming together of over three hundred craft workers from all over Britain. Nowadays this is more like a festival of crafts. Due to this initial show's success, Rainbow now comes twice more in the year to this most royal and dignified setting in the April springtime and for a special Christmas show in the early days of December.

*Elizabeth Bailey, a regular exhibitor
at Rainbow Craft Fairs*

Now how does one join this merry band? Initially all craft workers are vetted for their originality and standards of work. Having passed this test they apply for the shows at which they wish to exhibit. Over the years the hard core of regulars has grown, many have become firm favourites with house owners and visitors alike. In fact, over many years deep friendships have been formed both by exhibitors and visitors because at Rainbow they are all considered to be our friends and greeted as such at every event!

By Connie Duckworth

*Janice Daughters, china painter,
demonstrates her craft at every show*

Historic properties teach us all a lesson

Sandford Awards for Heritage Education

Historic Houses, Castles and Gardens are joined by Cathedrals, museums and a famous ship to be rewarded for their commitment to heritage education in the 1998 national Sandford Awards, jointly sponsored by Johansens.

The awards were set up over twenty years ago to reward and encourage excellence in the field of historic education and interpretation and 1998 produced twenty winning properties nationwide in what the Heritage Education Trust, the organisers, called a 'record year for applications'.

A whole range of properties – from Canterbury and Chester Cathedrals and the Manchester Jewish Museum to the Ryedale Folk Museum and the World famous clipper ship the Cutty Sark, historic houses from Bowhill in the Scottish Borders to Boughton House in Northamptonshire – have been rewarded with either full Sandford awards or Quinquennial Review certificates, which are presented to properties five years after they received the full award for maintaining the high teaching and education standards.

A team of judges comprising ex-teachers, education inspectors and advisors, visit the prospective properties to review the following areas:

Boughton House

- Imaginative ways in which the property or site is being interpreted, particularly for young persons and students;
- Design of materials to aid interpretation;
- Quality of management before and during the visit;
- Development planning which acknowledges the use of new aids to learning;
- Ways in which the visit may encourage the study and use of different cross curricular links;
- Relevance to the National Curriculum, good liaison with teachers;
- Availability of facilities that enhance the quality of the student's visit;
- The recognition of the potential of appropriate new technology;

The Judges' reports on each property decides the final outcome on whether a property will receive an award or not. Canterbury Cathedral which attracts around 140,000 pupil visits each year was awarded a full Sandford Award in 1993 and received a Quinquennial certificate this year.

The Judge's report stated: *"Canterbury Cathedral is a World Heritage Site and a most beautiful building. The Education Services does justice in interpreting the Cathedral itself, its history, its Saints and its community. It provides high quality resources and support for visiting groups, both British and overseas, which related to the National Curriculum. Canterbury Cathedral has a dedicated team, which masters the logistics of the number of education visitors that would overwhelm any lesser prepared site and delivers an education experience of quality."*

All the properties who have been rewarded in the 1998 Sandford Awards will be presented with their awards in early spring at a prestigious national ceremony being held at Goodwood House, Chichester, West Sussex.

The Sandford Award is non competitive, recognising quality and excellence. There is no stipulation on the size of the property or the extent of the education service.

Entry is in the first place by the completion of a pro forma application, then, after consideration for qualification, a judge will be allocated to visit and report back to the main Judges Panel, whose recommendations are passed to the Directors for their decision.

For further information on the Sandford Awards, the new address for all communication to HET is: The Chief Executive, Heritage Education Trust, Boughton House, Kettering, Northamptonshire NN14 1BJ. Tel: 01536 515731 Fax: 01536 417255 E-mail: het@boughtonhouse.org.uk

Sandford Award Winners 1998

Full Awards: Cannock Chase Heritage Centre, Chester Cathedral, Clipper Ship Cutty Sark, Corfe Castle, The Goodwood Estate, Manchester Jewish Museum, St. Peter's Village Tour.

Quinquennial Review: Aston Hall, Avoncroft Museum, Bedford Museum and The Cecil Higgins Art Gallery, Blakesley Hall Museum, Boughton House, Bowhill House and Country Park, Canterbury Cathedral, The Heritage Centre – Macclesfield, Oakwell Hall Country Park, The Priest's House Museum, Rowley's House Museum, Ryedale Folk Museum, York Castle Museum.

Continued Listing (no certificate): Rockingham Castle, Sir Harold Hillier Gardens and Arboretum.

Heritage Education Trust

Sandford Award Holders

The following properties received Sandford Awards in the years in brackets after their names in recognition of the excellence of their educational services and facilities and their outstanding contribution to Heritage Education. Two or more dates indicate that the property has been reviewed and received further recognition under the system of quinquennial review introduced by the Heritage Education Trust in 1986.

The Argory, Co. Tyrone, Northern Ireland (1995)
Aston Hall, Birmingham (1993, 1998)
Avoncroft Museum of Buildings, Bromsgrove, Worcs. (1988, 1993, 1998)
Bass Museum Visitor Centre and Shire Horse Stables, Burton upon Trent, Staffs. (1990, 1995)
Beaulieu Abbey, Nr Lyndhurst, Hants. (1978, 1986, 1991)
Bede Monastery Museum, Jarrow, Tyne and Wear (1988)

Goodwood Estate

Bedford Museum and The Cecil Higgins Art Gallery, (1993, 1998)
Belton House, Grantham, Lincolnshire (1979)
Bewdley Museum, Worcs (1992, 1997)
Bickleigh Castle, Nr Tiverton, Devon (1983, 1988)
Blakesley Hall Museum, Birmingham (1993, 1998)
Blenheim Palace, Woodstock, Oxon (1982, 1987, 1992, 1997)
Boat Museum, Ellesmere Port, South Wirral (1986)
Bodiam Castle, East Sussex (1995)
Bolling Hall, Bradford, West Yorkshire (1978, 1987)
Boughton House, Kettering, Northants (1988, 1993, 1998)
Bowhill House & Country Park, Bowhill, Nr Selkirk, Borders, Scotland (1993, 1998)
Brontë Parsonage Museum, Haworth, Nr Keighley, West Yorks (1993)
Buckfast Abbey, Buckfastleigh, Devon (1985, 1990, 1995)
Buckland Abbey, Yelverton, Devon (1995, 1996)
Cannock Chase Heritage Centre, (1998)
Cannock Hall, Barnsley (1997)
Canterbury Cathedral, Canterbury, Kent (1988, 1993, 1998)
Castle Museum, York, North Yorks (1987, 1993, 1998)
Castle Ward, County Down, Northern Ireland (1980, 1987, 1994)
Cathedral & Abbey Church of St. Alban, St Albans, Herts (1986, 1991, 1996)
Chester Cathedral, Chester (1998)
Chiltern Open Air Museum, Chalfont St Giles, Bucks (1994)
Chirk Castle, Chirk, Clwyd, Wales (1994)
Clipper Ship Cutty Sark, Greenwich (1998)
Clive House Museum, Shrewsbury, Salop (1992, 1997)
Coldharbour Mill, Working Wood Museum, Cullompton, Devon (1989,1994)
Combe Sydenham, Nr Taunton, Somerset (1984, 1989, 1994)
Corfe Castle, (1998)
Crathes Castle and Gardens, Kincardineshire, Scotland (1992, 1997)
Croxteth Hall and Country Park, Liverpool, Merseyside (1980, 1989, 1994)
Culzean Castle and Country Park, Ayrshire, Scotland (1984, 1989, 1994)
Doddington Hall, Doddington, Lincolnshire (1978, 1986)
Dove Cottage and the Wordsworth Museum, Grasmere, Cumbria (1990, 1995)
Drumlanrig Castle and Country Park, Dumfriesshire, Scotland (1989)
Dulwich Picture Gallery, London (1990, 1995)
Dunham Massey, Altrincham, Cheshire (1994)

Erddig Hall, Nr Wrexham, Clwyd, Wales (1991, 1996)
Exeter Cathedral, Devon (1995)
Flagship Portsmouth, Portsmouth (1996)
Florence Courthouse, Co Fernanagh, Northern Ireland (1995)
Ford Green Hall, Stoke-on-Trent (1996)
Gainsborough Old Hall, Gainsborough, Lincs (1988, 1993)
Georgian House, Edinburgh, Lothian, Scotland (1978)
Gladstone's Land, Edinburgh, Scotland (1995)
Glamis Castle, Angus, Scotland (1997)
Godolphin, Helston, Cornwall (1993)
Goodwood Estate, Goodwood, West Sussex (1998)
Hagley Hall, Stourbridge, West Midlands (1981)
Harewood House, Leeds, West Yorks (1979, 1989, 1994)
Sir Harold Hillier Gardens and Arboretum, Ampfield, Nr Romsey, Hants (1993, 1998)
Heritage Centre, Macclesfield (1993, 1998)
Holdenby House, Northampton, Northants (1985, 1990, 1995)
Holker Hall, Cark-inCartmel, Cumbria (1982, 1988)
Hopetoun House, South Queensferry, Lothian, Scotland (1983, 1991)
Hornsea Museum, North Humberside (1987)
Ixworth Museum, Nr Bury St Edmunds, Suffolk (1982)
Jewellery Quarter Discovery Centre, Birmingham (1996)
Kingston Lacy House, Wimborne, Dorset (1990, 1995)
Lamport Hall, Northampton (1985)
Laundry Cottage, Normandby Hall Country Park, South Humberside (1994)
Leighton Hall, Carnforth, Lancashire (1982)
Lichfield Cathedral and Visitors' Study Centre, Lichfield, Staffs (1991, 1996)
Llancaiach Fawr Manor, Nelson, Mid Glamorgan (1994)
Macclesfield Museums, Macclesfield, Cheshire (1988, 1993)
Manchester Jewish Museum, Manchester (1998)
Margam Park, Nr Port Talbort, West Glamorgan (1981, 1986)
Moseley Old Hall, Wolverhampton, West Midlands (1984, 1989, 1994)
Museum of Kent Life, Cobtree, Kent (1995)
National Waterways Museums, Gloucester (1991, 1996)
Norton Priory, Cheshire (1992, 1997)
Oakwell Hall Country Park, Birstall, West Yorks. (1988, 1993, 1998)
The Old School, Bognor Regis (1996)
Penhow Castle, Nr Newport, Gwent, Wales (1980, 1986, 1991)
The Priest's House Museum, Wimborne Minster, Dorset (1993)
Quarry Bank Mill, Styal, Cheshire (1987, 1992, 1997)
The Queen's House, Greenwich (1995)
Ranger's House, Blackheath, London (1979, 1987)
Rockingham Castle, Nr Corby, Northants (1980, 1987, 1992)
Roman Baths Museum, Bath, Avon (1994)
Rowley's House Museum, Shrewsbury, Salop (1993, 1998)
Ryedale Folk Museum, (1993, 1998)
Sheldon Manor, Wilshire (1985)
The Shugborough Estate, Stafford, Staffs (1987, 1992, 1997)
South Shields Museum and Art Gallery, (Arbeia Roman Fort), Arbeia (1996)
Spring Hill, (1995)
St. Peter's Village Tour, (1998)
Sudbury Hall, Nr Derby, Derbyshire (1978)
Sutton House, Hackney (1996)
Tatton Park, Knutsford, Cheshire (1979, 1986, 1991, 1996)
Tenement House, Glasgow (1996)
Tower of London, Tower Bridge, London (1978, 1986, 1991, 1996)
Weald and Downland Open Air Museum, Chichester (1996)
Wigan Pier, Lancashire (1987, 1992, 1997)
Wightwick Manor, Wolverhampton, West Midlands (1986, 1991, 1996)
Wilberforce House and Georgian Houses, Hull, Humberside (1990)
Wimpole Hall, Near Cambridge, Cambs (1988, 1993)
York Minster, York (1984, 1989)

22

The British Isles

William Blake was right. England is a green and pleasant land. From the soaring medieval cathedrals, tributes to the faith of the churchmen and craftsmen who built them and grand country mansions of the aristocracy, filled with treasures, amongst them paintings, furniture and tapestries to the fortified castles, their grey stone walls still fronting a bygone hostile world and magnificent gardens with lilies, roses and other delights: the country is rich in history, tradition and both architectural and natural beauty. Great Britain and the islands around it are more than one vast historical theme park. Driving or walking through the countryside, during any season of the year, allows you to indulge in the changing landscape.

A short ride, for instance, from York, will take you through long stretches of wild, heather-covered moorland, ablaze with colour in the autumn, or past the sheep covered slopes of the Dales.

Further afield the glorious countryside will impress any traveller. Ireland, for example, with its wonderfully diverse landscape, has a seaside of outstanding beauty and a number of fine golf courses.

The hillside of the Cairngorms in Scotland, covered in bright purple heather, is a place where only game birds and deer are hardy enough to survive. The dramatic mountain peak of Snowdon, the tallest mountain in Wales – is a magnificent backdrop to the Snowdonia National Park –with its wooded valleys, mountain lakes, moors and estuaries, or the country lanes of the Lake District – a combination of peaks, rivers, waterfalls and glistening lakes.

The pages that follow for the British Isles go through the counties of England and the areas of Wales and Scotland, followed by Ireland. Details of all the properties and counties can be found on the maps which begin on page 305.

23

Bedfordshire

There is something gracious about the landscape of Bedfordshire, a quality which is apparent in all its four types of scenery – in the chalk hills in the south, in the green sand hills of the centre, in the broad basin of the Ouse and in the gently undulating countryside of the north.

Contrasts in the landscape of this home county, are in turn echoed to some extent in its town architecture. Bedfordshire plays host to two very different towns. Steeped in history, Bedford itself is a town of Anglo-Saxon origins and has a long standing association with John Bunyan, the rebellious and unconventional author of Pilgrim's Progress. Milton Keynes, the largest example of a new town in England, is almost beyond comparison due to its recent development.

Bedfordshire's gentle landscapes are easily accessed. A vast network of motorways leads out from the urban sprawl of London to this county of contrasts.

CECIL HIGGINS ART GALLERY

Castle Close, Castle Lane, Bedford
Tel: 01234 211222 Fax: 01234 327149

An unusual combination of recreated Victorian Mansion (originally the home of the Higgins family, wealthy Bedford brewers) and adjoining modern gallery housing an internationally renowned collection of watercolours, prints and drawings, ceramics, glass and lace. Room settings include many items from the Handley–Read Collection and furniture by Victorian architect William Burges. Situated in pleasant gardens near the river embankment. **Location:** Centre of Bedford, just off The Embankment, east of High Street. **Open:** Tues–Sat 11–5pm, Sun & Bank Holiday Mons 2–5pm (last admission 4.45pm). **Admission:** Free. Charge for guided tours & viewing of Reserve Collections. Disabled access.

SWISS GARDEN

Old Warden, Biggleswade, Bedfordshire
Tel: 01767 627666 (Bedfordshire County Council)

9 acre landscaped garden, set out in the 1830s, alongside a further 10 acres of native woodland with lakeside picnic area. Garden includes many tiny buildings, footbridges, ironwork features and intertwining ponds. Romantic landscape design highlighted by daffodils, rhododendrons and old rambling roses in season. **Location:** Signposted from A1 and A600. 2 miles W of Biggleswade, next door to the Shuttleworth Collection. **Open:** Please phone for opening times and prices. **Admission:** Charges apply. (Share to 'Friends of the Swiss Garden®'). Disabled access. Plants available for sale. No dogs except guide dogs.

map 5
S22

WOBURN ABBEY

Woburn, Bedfordshire,
Tel: 01525 290666 Fax: 01525 290271
(The Marquess of Tavistock and the Trustees of the Bedford Estates)

Woburn Abbey is the home to the Marquess and Marchioness of Tavistock and their family. The art collection, one of the most important in the country, includes paintings by Van Dyck, Gainsborough, Reynolds and Velasquez. In the Venetian Room there are 21 views of Venice by Canaletto. There is also French and English 18th century furniture, silver and gold and exquisite porcelain. There are 9 species of deer in 3,000 acre deer park including the Pere David deer, saved from extinction here at Woburn. The Flying Duchess Pavilion serves simple lunches, snacks and teas and there are gift shops and an Antiques Centre. Woburn Abbey and Safari Park has been named as the 1998 Good Guide to Britain Family Attraction of the Year.

map 4
E2

 ## WREST PARK

Silsoe, Beds
Tel: 01525 860152 (English Heritage)

Take a fascinating journey through a century and a half of gardening styles. Enjoy a leisurely stroll by the Long Wate, canals and Leg O'Mutton Lake and explore a charming range of garden buildings, including the baroque Archer Pavilion, Orangery and classical Bath House. Discover bridges and ponds, temples and altars, fountains and statues in over 90 acres of carefully landscaped gardens, laid out before a fabulous French-style Victorian Mansion. There is an informative audio-tour available. **Location:** 10 miles south of Bedford. **Open:** 1 Apr–1 Nov: 10–6pm, weekends and Bank Holidays only (or dusk if earlier in Oct). **Admission:** Adult £3.20, concs £2.30, child £1.60. (15% discount for groups of 11 or more).

map 4
E2

Berkshire

Berkshire is an unassuming county. Quiet and unpretentious – little concerned with outside approbation and making no effort to popularise its charms or to advertise its beauty and serenity. Whilst it is host to arguably the most famous castle in the kingdom and the school which is presently educating the future king of England and is graced with some of the most charming and unspoilt villages in the Thames Valley, it is reticent about its attractions. To the east of the county is Windsor, which is undoubtedly Berkshire's jewel. The town is dwarfed by the enormous castle on the hill above, which is surrounded by narrow streets, brimming with shops and old buildings.

Crossing over the Thames lies Eton and its famous public school, founded by Henry VI in 1440.

To the west of Berkshire lies Newbury, once a centre for the wool trade. Across the rolling Berkshire Downs is the Ridgeway, which was a vital trade route during the Bronze Ages and now offers wonderful walks across some of the highest points in the county.

The Savill Garden

BASILDON PARK

Lower Basildon, Reading RG8 9NR
Tel: 0118 984 3040 Fax: 0118 984 1267 (The National Trust)

Elegant classical 18th century house designed by Carr of York. Overlooking the River Thames is the Octagon drawing room containing fine furniture and pictures. The grounds include formal and terrace gardens, pleasure grounds and woodland walks. **Open:** 27 Mar –31 Oct, Wed–Sun & BH Mon 1–5.30pm. (Closed Good Friday). Park, garden & woodland walks as house. Note: House & grounds close at 5pm on 13–14 August. **Admission:** House, park & garden: Adult £4.10, child £2.05, family ticket £10.25. Park & garden only: Adult £1.80, child 90p, family ticket £4.50.

map 4
C4

ETON COLLEGE

Windsor, Berkshire SL4 6DW, UK
Tel: 01753 671177 Fax: 01753 671265

Founded in 1440 by Henry VI, Eton College is one of the oldest schools in the country. Visitors are invited to experience and share the beauty and traditions of the College. **Open:** Times are governed by both the dates for term and holidays on the school calendar, but the College will be open to visitors from the end of March until the beginning of October. Guided Tours during the season are available for individuals at 2.15 and 3.15pm daily. Guided Tours for groups by prior arrangement with the Visits Manager, Mrs Hunkin.

map 4
C4

DORNEY COURT

Dorney, Nr Windsor, Berkshire SL4 6QP
Tel: 01628 604638 Fax: 01628 665772 (Mrs Peregrine Palmer)

'One of the finest Tudor Manor Houses in England' – Country Life. Built about 1440 and lived in by the present family for over 450 years. The rooms are full of the atmosphere of history: early 15th and 16th century oak, 17th century lacquer furniture, 18th and 19th century tables, 400 years of portraits, stained glass and needlework. The 14th century church of St. James is a lovely, cool, cheerful and very English Church. **Location:** 2 miles W of Eton & Windsor in village of Dorney on B3026. From M4 use exit 7. **Open:** May: Bank Hol Mons & preceding Sun. July & Aug: Mon, Tues, Wed & Thurs, 1–4.30pm, Last adm. 4pm. Adults £4.50, children over 9 £2.80, 10% discount for Nat Trust, NADFAS and OAPSs. Parties by arrangement. **Refreshments:** Teas at the Plant Centre. Outstanding collection of plants for sale at Bressingham Plant Centre, PYO fruit from June–September.

map 4
E4

HIGHCLERE CASTLE

Nr Newbury, RG20 9RN
Tel: 01635 253210 Fax: 01635 255315

Designed by Charles Barry in the 1830s at the same time as he was building the Houses of Parliament. This soaring pinnacled mansion provided a perfect setting for the 3rd Earl of Carnarvon, one of the great hosts of Queen Victoria's reign. Old master paintings mix with portraits by Van Dyck and 18th century painters. Napoleon's desk and chair rescued from St. Helena sits with other 18th century furniture. The 5th Earl of Carnarvon, discovered the Tomb of Tutankhamun with Howard Carter. The castle houses a unique exhibition of some of his discoveries which were only rediscovered in the castle in 1988. The current Earl is the Queen's Horseracing Manager. In 1993 to celebrate his 50th year as a leading owner and breeder 'The Lord Carnarvon Racing Exhibition' was opened and offers a fascinating insight into a racing history that dates back three generations. The magnificent parkland, with its massive cedars, was designed by Capability Brown. The Secret Garden has a romance of its own with a beautiful curving lawn surrounded by densely planted herbaceous gardens. A place for poets and romantics. Guided tours are often provided, free of charge, to visitors. **Location:** 4.4 miles S of Newbury on A34, Jct 13 of M4 about 2 miles from Newbury. **Open:** 1 Jul–5 Sept, 7 days a week 11–5pm, last adm. 4pm, Sat last adm. 2.30pm. **Refreshments:** Lunches, teas, ices, soft drinks. **Conferences:** Business conferences, management training courses, film and photographic location. Licensed for civil weddings. Ample car park and picnic area adjacent to Castle. Suitable for disabled persons on ground floor only. One wheelchair available. Visitors can buy original items in Castle Gift Shop. No dogs are permitted in the house or gardens except guide dogs. No photography in the house. Occasionally subject to closure.

map 4 C5

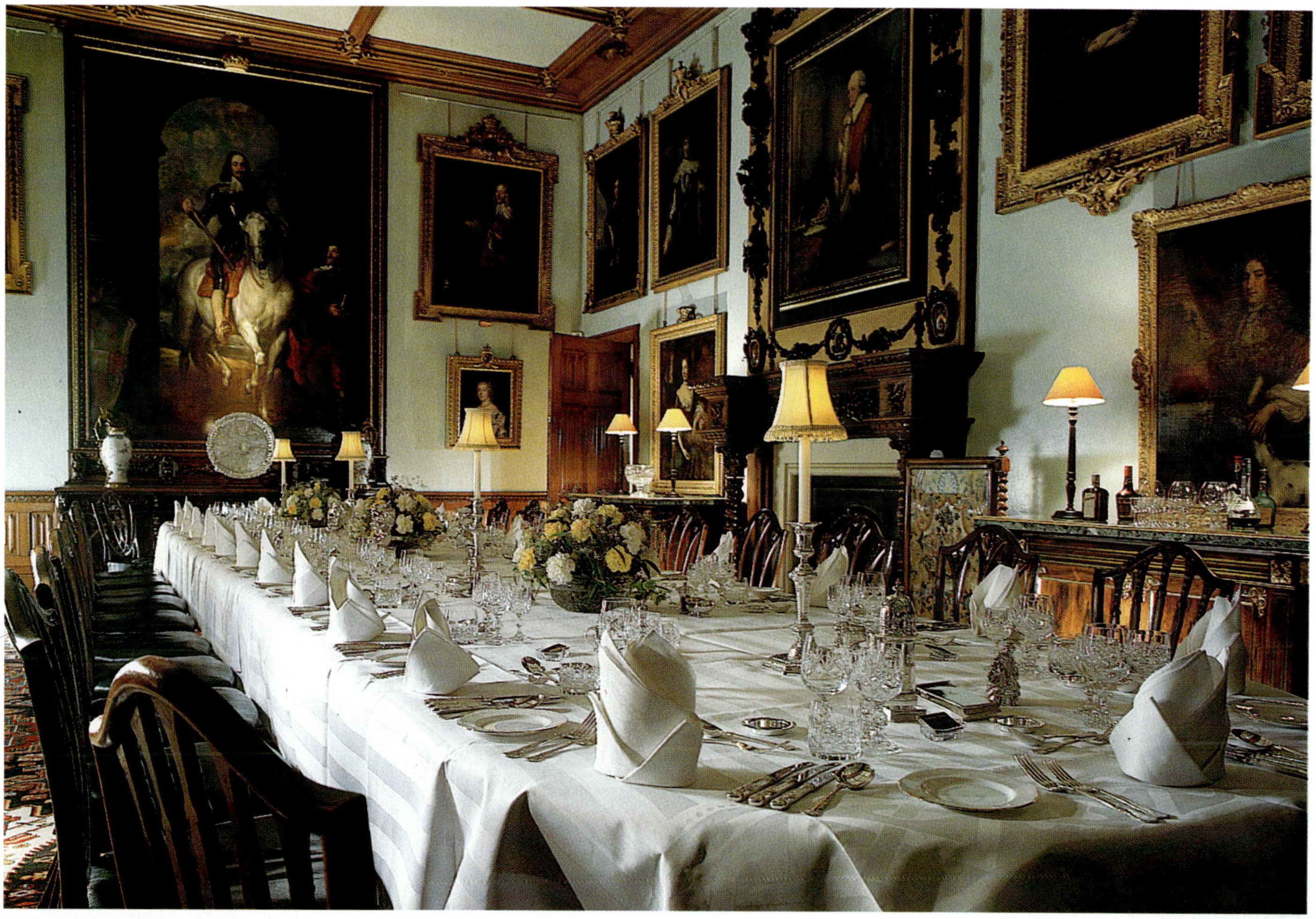

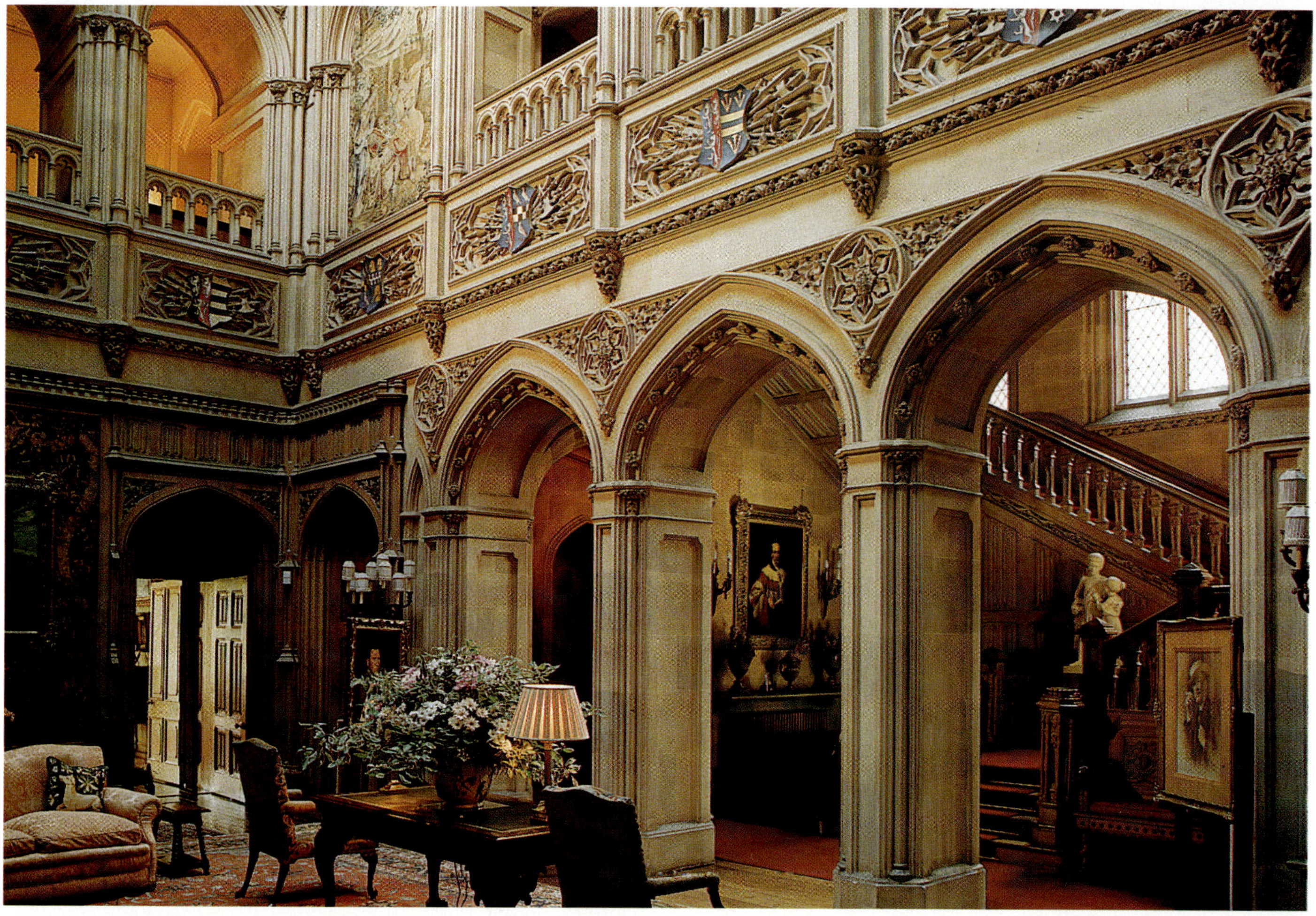

THE SAVILL GARDEN

Windsor Great Park
Tel: 01753 847518

World renowned woodland garden of 35 acres, situated in the tranquil surroundings of Windsor Great Park. The garden contains a fine range of rhododendrons, azaleas, camellias and magnolias; with adjoining rose gardens and herbaceous borders. Autumn provides a great feast of colour and the whole garden offers much of great interest and beauty at all seasons. Queen Elizabeth Temperate House. **Location:** To be approached from A30 via Wick Road and Wick Lane, Englefield Green. **Station(s):** Egham (3 miles). **Open:** Daily 10–6pm Mar–Oct, 10–4pm Nov–Feb (closed December 25/26). **Admission:** Adults £3.80, senior citizens £3.30, parties 20+ £3.30, accompanied children under 16 free of charge. **Refreshments:** Licensed self-service restaurant. Well stocked plant centre/gift shop. Ample parking.

ENGLEFIELD HOUSE

Englefield, Theale, Reading RG7 5EN
Tel: 01189 302221 Fax: 01189 303226 (Sir William Benyon)

A seven acre garden, herbaceous and rose borders, fountain, stone balustrades and staircases, woodland and water garden, set in Deer Park Location: 4m West of Reading off A4 11/4m of A4 at Theale. **Open:** Mondays throughout the year 10–6pm. 1st Apr–1 Oct, Mon–Thur, 10–6pm. **Admission:** Adults £2, children free.

SWALLOWFIELD PARK

Swallowfield, Berkshire RG7 1TG
Tel: 0118 9883815 Fax: 0118 9883930 (Country Houses Association)

Built by the Second Earl of Clarendon in 1678. **Location:** In the village of Swallowfield, 6 miles SE of Reading. **Open:** May–Sept, Wed– Thurs 2–5pm. Last entry 4pm. **Admission:** Adults £2.50, children £1. Free car park. No dogs admitted. Groups by arrangement.

TAPLOW COURT

Berry Hill, Taplow, Nr Maidenhead, Berks SL6 0ER
Tel: 01628 591215 Fax: 01628 773055 (SGI–UK)

Set high above the Thames affording spectacular views. A pre-Domesday manor. Remodelled mid-19th century by William Burn, retaining earlier neo-Norman Hall. 18th century home of Earls and Countesses of Orkney and more recently of Lord and Lady Desborough who entertained "The Souls" here. Tranquil gardens and grounds with Cedar Walk. Anglo-Saxon burial mound. Permanent and temporary exhibitions. Arts Festivals. **Location:** OS Ref. SU907 822. M4/J7 off Bath Road towards Maidenhead. 6m off M40/J2. **Open:** House and grounds: Easter Sunday, Monday and Sundays until the end of July, 2–6pm. **Admission:** No charge. Free parking.

ST GEORGE'S CHAPEL WINDSOR

Windsor, Berks SL4 1NJ
Tel: 01753 865538 Fax: 01753 620165 (The Dean & Canons of Windsor)

A fine example of perpendicular architecture. Begun in 1475 by Edward IV and it was completed in the reign of Henry VIII. Choir stalls dedicated to the order of the Knights of the Garter, founded by Edward III. **Location:** OS Ref: SU968 770. In Windsor town, just off the M4. **Open:** As Windsor Castle. Opening times are subject to change at short notice. Please call visitors office for further details. **Admission:** Free admission on payment of charge into Windsor Castle.

WELFORD PARK

Welford, Newbury RG20 8HU
Tel: 01488 608203 (J.H.L. Puxley)

Queen Anne house with later additions. Attractive gardens and grounds. **Location:** 6 miles NW of Newbury and 1 mile N of Wickham village off B4000. **Station:** Newbury. **Open:** Late spring and August Bank Holidays and 1–26 June inclusive from 2.30–5pm. **Admission:** Adults £3.50, OAPs and under 16s £2. Interior by prior appointment only.

WINDSOR CASTLE

Windsor, Berkshire SL4 1NJ
Tel: Visitor Office 01753 868 286 Fax: 01753 832 290

Windsor Castle, Buckingham Palace, and the Palace of Holyroodhouse are the Official residences of the Sovereign and are used by The Queen as both home and office. The Queen's personal standard flies when Her Majesty is in residence. Furnished with works of art from the Royal Collection, these buildings are used extensively by The Queen for State ceremonies and Official entertaining. They are opened to the public as much as these commitments allow. A significant proportion of Windsor Castle is opened to visitors on a regular basis including the Upper and Lower Wards, the North Terrace with its famous view towards Eton, Queen Mary's Dolls' House, the State Apartments including St. George's Hall, the Crimson Drawing Room and other newly restored rooms. **Open:** Everyday except Good Friday, from 12 noon on 25 April, 14 June, Christmas Day and Boxing Day and during any State visits. Nov–Feb 10–4pm (last admission 3pm) Mar–Oct 10–5.30pm (last admission 4pm). St. George's Chapel is closed to visitors on Suns as services are held throughout the day. Worshippers are welcome. <u>Admission:</u> Adult £10, children (under 17) £5, senior citizens (over 60) £7.50. Reduced charges apply if any part of the Castle is not open.

map 4
E4

Buckinghamshire

Henley on Thames officially rests in Buckinghamshire although three counties – Oxfordshire, Berkshire and Buckinghamshire meet there. Its historic buildings, including one of Britain's oldest theatres, are a fitting backdrop to the annual Royal Regatta week in July. Marlow is far less pretentious, set between the banks of the river Thames and the beautiful Chiltern Hills, but has as much character as its big cousin.

Buckingham, set in the northern part of the county, is home to the country's only private university. The town houses lots of lively small pubs and a market. Locally, there are many stately homes and gardens, including Stowe, which are all worth a visit.

Hughenden Manor

CHILTERN OPEN AIR MUSEUM

Newland Park, Gorelands Lane, Chalfont St. Giles, Buckinghamshire, HP8 4AD. Tel: Information Line: 01494 872 163 Office 01494 871 117 (Chiltern Open Air Museum Ltd)

A museum of historic buildings, rescued from demolition and re-erected in 45 acres of beautiful parkland, reflects the vernacular heritage of the Chilterns. You can explore barns, granaries, cartsheds and stables, a blacksmiths forge, a toll house, a 1940's prefab and more. Special events at weekends and daily in August include demonstrations and displays of traditional skills such as the pole-lathe, spinning and dyeing, spoon making and rag rug making. The working Victorian farm illustrates aspects of our rural past and is home to our animals. **Open:** 27 March–30 Oct 1999, Tues–Sun & Bank Holiday Mons, 10–5pm. Open daily in August. **Refreshments:** Tearooms, shop, playground, nature/seat trail.

map 4 D4

CLAYDON HOUSE

Middle Claydon, Nr Buckingham, Bucks MK18 2EY
Tel: 01296 730349 (The National Trust)

One of England's most extraordinary houses. In continuous occupation by the Verney family for over 350 years. Claydon was originally a Jacobean manor house, but was remodelled in the 1750s at a time when the craze for Chinoiserie was at its height. The result was the remarkable series of rooms we see today, lavishly decorated in intricately-carved white woodwork covered with motifs based on Oriental birds, pagodas and summer-houses. **Open:** 27 Mar–31 Oct: daily except Thur & Fri, 1–5pm. **Admission:** £4.10, family ticket £10.25. Tearoom: open 2–5pm (open at 1pm on Sun & Bank Hol Mon).

map 4 D3

CLIVEDEN

Taplow, Maidenhead, SL6 0JA, Bucks
Tel: 01628 605069 Fax: 01628 669461 (The National Trust)

Perched on cliffs above the Thames, this estate has magnificent views over the river. The great 19th century mansion (now let as a hotel) was once the home of Nancy, Lady Astor. There are a series of gardens, each with its own character and featuring roses, topiary, water gardens, statuary, and formal parterre. **Open:** Entire Estate: 13 Mar–31 Oct: daily 11–6pm. 1 Nov–31 Dec: daily 11–4pm. House (three rooms open): Apr–Oct: Thurs & Sun 3–6pm. Entry by timed ticket from information kiosk. **Admission:** Woodland Car Park only £3, family ticket £7.50. Grounds: £5, family ticket £12.50. House £1 extra. Licensed conservatory restaurant and shop.

map 4 D4

COWPER & NEWTON MUSEUM

Orchard Side, Market Place, Olney, MK46 4AJ
Tel: 01234 711 516 E-mail: museum@olney.co.uk

Once the home of the 18th century poet and letter writer William Cowper and now containing furniture, paintings and belongings of both Cowper and his ex-slave trader friend, Rev. John Newton (author of "Amazing Grace"). Attractions include re-creations of a Victorian country kitchen and wash-house, two peaceful gardens and Cowper's restored summerhouse, costume gallery, important collections of dinosaur bones and bobbin lace and local history displays. **Location:** 6 miles N of Newport Pagnell via A509. (Leave M1 at junction 14). **Station(s):** Milton Keynes or Bedford. **Open:** 1 Mar–23 Dec, Tue–Sat & Bank Hol Mons, 10am–1pm & 2–5pm. Closed Good Friday. **Admission:** Adults £2, children/students (with cards) £1, concs £1.50, family £5.

map 4 D2

HUGHENDEN MANOR

High Wycombe, Bucks HP14 4LA
Tel: 01494 532580 (The National Trust)

The home of Queen Victoria's favourite Prime Minister, Benjamin Disraeli. Much of his furniture, pictures and books remain and there are beautiful walks through the surrounding park and woodland. The garden is a recreation of the colourful designs of his wife, Mary Anne. **Open:** House: 1–30 Mar, Sat & Sun only, 31 Mar–31 Oct, daily except Mon & Tues (closed Good Fri, but open Bank Hol Mon) 1–5pm. Garden: same days as house 12–5pm. Park & Woodland: open all year. **Admission:** House & garden: £4.10, family ticket £10.20. Garden only £1.50, children 75p. Park & Woodland free. Tearoom and shop available.

map 4 D3/4

Nether Winchendon House

Aylesbury HP18 0DY
Tel: 01844 290199
(Robert Spencer Bernard Esq.)

Medieval and Tudor manor house with 18th century Strawberry Hill Gothic additions. Home of Sir Francis Bernard, Governor of New Jersey and Massachusetts, 1760. **Location:** 1 mile N of A418 Aylesbury/Thame Road, in village of Lower Winchendon, 6 miles SW Aylesbury. **Stations:** Aylesbury (7 miles). Haddenham and Thame Parkway (2 miles). **Open:** 4–31 May and 29/30 Aug, 2.30–5.30pm. Last party each day at 4.45pm. Parties at any time of year by written appointment. **Admission:** Adults £3, children (under 12) and OAPs £1.50 (not weekends or bank holidays). **Refreshments:** By arrangement. Correspondence to Robert Spencer Bernard Esq.

John Milton's Cottage

21, Deanway, Chalfont St Giles, HP8 4JH
Tel: 01494 872313 (Milton Cottage Trust)

The XVIth century cottage where John Milton lived and completed Paradise Lost and started Paradise Regained, contains many relics and exhibits of interest. Three museum rooms and attractive cottage garden open to the public. Free car park. **Location:** 1/2 m West of A413, 3m N of M40/J2 S side of street. **Open & Admission:** Please phone for details of opening times and admission charges.

Stowe (Stowe School)

Stowe, MK18 5EH
Tel: 01280 813650

Formerly the home of the Dukes of Buckingham it is a house adorned with the traditions of aristocracy and learning. For over one and a half centuries up to the great sale of 1848, the Temples and Grenvilles almost continuously rebuilt and refurbished it in an attempt to match their ever growing ambitions with the latest fashions. Around the mansion is one of Britain's most magnificent landscape gardens now in the ownership of the National Trust. **Location:** 4 miles N of Buckingham town. **Stations:** Milton Keynes. **Open:** 20 Mar–11 Apr, 5 Jul–5 Sept, daily 2–5pm. Sun 12–5pm. The house is closed, at times, for private functions. Please telephone first to check. **Admission:** Adults £2 children £1. Guide books and souvenirs available from Stowe Bookshop situated in the Menagerie on the South Front – open 10–5pm.

Stowe Landscape Gardens

Buckingham, Bucks MK18 5EH
Tel: 01280 822850. Fax: 01280 822437 (The National Trust)

One of the first and finest landscape gardens in Europe. Adorned with buildings by Vanbrugh, Gibbs and Kent, including arches, temples, a Palladian bridge and other monuments, the sheer scale of the garden must make it Britain's largest work of art. **Open:** 20 Mar–12 Apr: daily; 14 Apr–4 Jul: daily except Tues, Thurs, Sat; 5 Jul–4 Sept: daily; 5 Sept–31 Oct: daily except Tues, Thurs, Sat; 11–23 Dec 1999: daily 10–5pm or dusk if earlier. Last admission one hour before closing. **Admission:** Gardens £4.50. Family £11.50. Licensed tearoom.

Winslow Hall

Winslow, Buckinghamshire, MK18 3HL
Tel: 01296 712 323 (Sir Edward & Lady Tomkins)

Built 1698–1702. Almost certainly designed by Sir Christopher Wren. Has survived without any major structural alteration and retains most of its original features. Modernised and redecorated by the present owners. Good 18th century furniture, mostly English. Some fine pictures, clocks and carpets. Several examples of Chinese art, notably of the Tang period. Beautiful gardens with many unusual trees and shrubs. **Location:** At entrance to Winslow on A413, the Aylesbury road. **Station(s):** Milton Keynes or Aylesbury (both 10 miles). **Open:** All Bank Hol weekends (except Christmas), 2–5pm. July–Aug, Wed & Thur, 2.30–5.30pm or by appointment throughout the year. **Admission:** Adults £5.00, children free. **Refreshments:** Catering by arrangement.

WADDESDON MANOR

Nr. Aylesbury, Buckinghamshire, HP18 0JW
Tel: 01296 651211 Fax: 01296 651142

Waddesdon Manor was built at the end of the last century for Baron Ferdinand de Rothschild to entertain his guests and display his vast collection of art treasures. It has won many awards including Museum of the Year and Best National Trust Property 1997. The French Renaissance-style château houses one of the finest collection of French 18th century decorative arts in the world and an important collection of English portraits. The garden is famous for its landscape of specimen trees and seasonal bedding displays and the Rococo-style aviary houses a splendid collection of exotic birds. Thousands of bottles of vintage Rothschild wines are found in the wine cellars. There are gift and wine shops and a licensed restaurant. Many events are organised throughout the year including Collection study days, floodlit openings, wine tastings and garden workshops. **Location:** A41 between Aylesbury & Bicester. <u>**Open: Grounds, aviary, restaurant and shops:**</u> 3 Mar–24 Dec, Wed–Sun & Bank Hol Mons, 10–5pm. **House (including wine cellars):** 1 Apr–31 Oct, Thurs–Sun, Bank Hol Mons and Weds in Jul & Aug. 11–4pm. (Recommended last admission 2.30pm) Bachelors' Wing open Thurs & Fri & Weds in Jul & Aug. **Admission: House & grounds:** Adults £10, child £7.50. **Grounds only:** Adults £3, child £1.50. Bachelors' Wing £1. National Trust Members free. Timed tickets to the House can be purchased on site or reserved in advance by phoning 01296 651226, Mon–Fri 10–4pm. Advance booking fee: £3 per transaction.

map 4 D3

Cambridgeshire

Wansford

In Cambridge and Ely, this county has two of the most historic cities in England. Cambridge is an idyllic and irresistibly charming city, home to one of the oldest universities in the world. Some of the most ancient of Cambridge's thirty colleges adorn the timeless velvety green banks of the River Cam. Others, such as the ancient college of Gonville & Caius, one of Cambridge's oldest, lie grouped around squares known as courts and line the ancient streets of this busy market city. The bustling student community and their bicycles, create a wonderfully lively atmosphere in this collegiate city.

The ancient city of Ely is dominated by its wonderful cathedral, which overlooks the flat fens that surround it. Indeed, the city is reputed to take its name from the Saxon word "elig", meaning "Eel Island" and was once an island. Today, the drained fens form some of the most fertile agricultural land in England. It is also home, at Wicken Fen, to the oldest nature reserve in Britain.

ELTON HALL

Elton, Peterborough PE8 6SH
Tel: 01832 280468 Fax: 01832 280584 (Mr & Mrs William Proby)

This romantic house has been the home of the Proby family for over 350 years. Excellent furniture and outstanding paintings by Gainsborough, Reynolds, Constable and other fine artists. There are over 12,000 books, including Henry VIII's prayer book. Wonderful gardens, including restored Rose Garden, knot and sunken gardens and recently planted Arboretum. Stunning new Gothic Orangery. Bressingham Plant Centre is in the walled Kitchen Garden. **Location:** On A605, 8 miles W of Peterborough. **Open:** 2–5pm last Bank Hol in May (Sun/Mon 30/31 May) Weds in June, Weds, Thurs and Suns in July and Aug and Bank Hol Mon (30). **Admission:** Adults £4.50, accompanied children free. Garden only: Adults £2.50, accompanied children free. Private parties by appointment with Administrator. **Refreshments:** Home-made teas, lunches by arrangement.

ELY CATHEDRAL

The Chapter House, The College, Ely CB7 4DL
Tel: 01353 667735 Fax: 01353 665658

A wonderful example of Romanesque architecture. The Octagon and the Lady Chapel are of particular interest. There are superb medieval domestic buildings around the Cathedral. Stained glass museum, brass rubbing centre, shops and restaurants. **Location:** 15 miles N of Cambridge city centre via the A10. **Open:** Summer: 7–7pm. Winter: Mon–Sat, 7.30–6pm, Sun and week after Christmas, 7.30–5pm. Sun services: 8.15am, 10.30am and 3.45 pm. Weekday services: 7.40am, 8am & 5.30pm (Thurs only also 11.30am & 12.30pm). Admission charges apply.

DENNY ABBEY

Ely Road, Chittering, Waterbeach, CB5 9PQ
Tel: 01223 860489 (English Heritage)

What at first appears to be an attractive stone built farmhouse is actually the remains of a 12th century Benedictine abbey, which, at different times, also housed the Knights Templar and Franciscan nuns. Founded by the countess of Pembroke. **Location:** 6m North of Cambridge on the E side of the A10. **Open:** 1 Apr–31 Oct, 12–5pm. **Admission:** Adult £3.40, child £1.20, concession £2.40.

ISLAND HALL

Post Street, Godmanchester PE18 8BA
Tel: 0171 491 3724 (Mr Christopher & The Hon Mrs Vane Percy)

A mid 18th century mansion of great charm owned and restored by an award winning Interior Designer. This family home has lovely Georgian rooms, with fine period detail and interesting possessions relating to the owners' ancestors since their first occupation of the house in 1800. A tranquil riverside setting with formal gardens and ornamental island forming part of the grounds in an area of Best Landscape. **Location:** Centre of Godmanchester next to car park. 1 m S of Huntingdon. 15 m NW of Cambridge (A14). **Open:** Sundays: 4, 11, 18 & 25 July, 2.30–5pm. Last admittance is 4.30pm. **Admission:** House & Grounds: Adults £3.50, children 13–16 £2. Grounds only: Adults £2. Accompanied children under 13, grounds only £1. Group rate (by appt), May–Sept (except Aug) £3 per head (over 40 persons). Under 15 persons min charge £52.50 per group.

KIMBOLTON CASTLE

Kimbolton, Cambs
Tel: 01480 860505 Fax: 01480 861763 (Governors of Kimbolton School)

Tudor manor house associated with Katherine of Aragon, completely remodelled by Vanbrugh (1708–20); courtyard c.1694. Fine murals by Pellegrini in chapel, boudoir and on staircase. Gatehouse by Robert Adam. Parkland. **Location:** 8 miles NW of St Neots on B645; 14 miles N of Bedford. **Station(s):** St Neots (9 miles) **Open:** Easter Sun & Mon, Spring Bank Hol Sun & Mon, Summer Bank Hol Sun & Mon, also Sun 25 July, 1, 8, 15, & 22 Aug 2–6pm **Admission:** Adults £2.50, children & OAPs £1.50. **Conferences:** By negotiation. Guided tours for groups of 20 or more by arrangement on days other than advertised.

KING'S COLLEGE

King's Parade, Cambridge CB2 1ST
Tel: 01223 331212

Visitors are very welcome, but remember that this is a working College. Please respect the privacy of those who work, live and study here at all times. Recorded messages for services, concerts and visiting times: 01223 331155. **Open:** Out of term time – Mon–Sat, 9.30–4.30pm. Sun, 10–5pm. In term: Mon–Fri, 9.30–3.30pm. Sat, 9.30–3.15pm. Sun, 1.15–2.15pm, 5–5.30pm. **Admission:** Adults £3, children (12–17) £2, children under 12 free if part of a family unit, students £2. **Refreshments:** Meals by arrangement only. Guided tours are only available through Cambridge Tourist Office Tel: 01223 457574.

THE MANOR

Hemingford Grey, Huntingdon, Cambs PE18 9BN
Tel: 01480 463134 Fax: 01480 465026 (Mr & Mrs Peter Boston)

Built about 1130 and made famous as Green Knowe by the author Lucy Boston this house is reputedly the oldest continuously inhabited house in the country and much of the Norman house remains. It contains the Lucy Boston patchworks. The garden has topiary, one of the best collections of old roses in private hands, large herbaceous borders with many scented plants and a variety of Dykes Medal winner irises. **Open:** House all the year round but only by prior appointment. Garden open daily all year 10–6pm (dusk in winter). **Admission:** House and Garden: Adults £4, children £1.50. Garden only: Adults £1, children 50p.

OLIVER CROMWELL'S HOUSE

29 St. Mary's Street, Ely, Cambridgeshire
Tel: 01353 662062 Fax: 01353 668518 (East Cambridgeshire District Council)

Oliver Cromwell and his family moved to Ely in 1636 and lived in the city for some ten years. The house dates back to the 13th century. Eight period rooms contain sets, exhibitions and videos about Cromwell and the Fens Drainage story. There are helmets and costumes for children to try on. The house guide is available in five languages. Cromwell's old home is now open throughout the year and also houses the Ely Tourist Information Centre. A variety of guided tours of the city and Cromwell's House can be booked (costumed guides available). A Joint Ticket scheme operates through the four main attractions in Ely, including Cromwell's House and can be purchased here. Details on special events to commemorate the 400th anniversary of Oliver Cromwell's birth can be sent out on request at no charge. **Open:** Summer: 1 Apr–31 Oct, Daily, 10–5.30pm. Winter: 1 Nov–31 Mar, Mon to Sat, 10–5pm & Sun 10.15–3pm. **Admission:** Adult £2.70, concessions £2.20, family £7. Joint ticket Adults £8, concessions £6. Group prices on request.

map 4 F1

UNIVERSITY BOTANIC GARDEN

Cory Lodge, Bateman Street, CB2 1JF
Tel: 01223 336265 Fax: 01223 336278 (University of Cambridge)

Forty acres of outstanding gardens with lake, glasshouses, winter garden, chronological bed and nine National Collections, including Geranium and Fritillaria. **Location:** 1 mile S of Cambridge centre. Entrance on Bateman Street. **Stations:** Cambridge Railway Station 1/4 mile. **Open:** Open all year except Christmas Day and Boxing Day 10–6pm (summer), 10–5pm (autumn & spring), 10–4pm (winter). **Admission:** Charged weekends and Bank Holidays throughout the year and weekdays Mar 1–Oct 31. All parties must be pre-booked. Pre-booked school parties and disabled people free. No reductions for parties. **Refreshments:** Tearoom in the Gilmour Building. No dogs except guide dogs. Guided tours by the Friends of the Garden available by arrangement. **E-mail:** gardens@hermes .cam.ac.uk **Internet:** http://www.plantsci.cam.ac.uk/www/botgdn

map 4 F1

ANGLESEY ABBEY AND GARDEN

Lode, Cambridge CB5 9EJ Tel: 01223 811200

Open: House: 27 March to 17 Oct: daily except Mon & Tues (but open BH Mon) 1–5pm. Garden: 27 March to 4 July, 15 Sept to 17 Oct: daily except Mon & Tues (but open BH Mon); 5 July to 12 Sept: daily 11–5.30pm. Lode Mill: 27 March to 17 Oct:(telephone for details of winter opening): daily except Mon & Tues (but open BH Mon) 1–5pm. Last admission to house, garden and Lode Mill 4.30pm. New winter walk open in garden 21 Oct to 19 Dec & 6 Jan to March 2000: daily except Mon, Tues & Wed, 11–4pm. Note: Property closed Good Fri. Entry to the house is by timed tickets on Sun & BH Mons to ease overcrowding. At BH there maybe a long wait to enter the house and occasionally admission is not possible. **Admission:** £6, Sun & BH Mons £7; family discounts. Groups £5. Garden only £3.50 (groups £2.80). Lode Mill free on entry to garden. Group organisers send s.a.e. for information pack and booking form (no reductions Sun & BH Mons). **Events:** send s.a.e. for programme.

PECKOVER HOUSE & GARDEN

North Brink, Wisbech PE13 1JR Tel: 01945 583463 Fax: 01945 583463

Open: House & garden: 27 March to 31 Oct: Sat, Sun, Wed & BH Mon 12.30–5.30pm. Garden only: 27 March to 31 Oct: Mon, Tues & Thur 12.30–5.30pm. Groups welcome when house open and at other times by appointment. **Events:** telephone for details. Note: Members may, by written appointment with the tenants, view Nos. 14 and 19 North Brink. **Admission:** £3.50 (£2 on garden only days); family discounts. Groups £2.80.

WIMPOLE HALL

Arrington, Royston SG8 0BW Tel: 01223 207257 Fax: 01223 207838

Open: Hall: 13 March to 31 July, 1 Sept to 31 Oct: daily except Mon & Fri (but open Good Fri and BH Mons). Aug: daily except Mon (but open BH Mon) 1–5pm (but BH Suns & Mons 11–5pm). Garden: as Hall. Park: daily sunrise to sunset (closes at 5pm on concert nights). **Events:** 3/4 July, open-air concerts with fireworks; 14/15 Aug, garden concerts with fireworks; to book tel. 01223 207001. **Admission:** Hall & garden £5.70, child £2.50. Adult joint ticket with Home Farm £8, child £4. Adult party rate (12+ in group) £4.70, child group rate £2. Garden only £2.50. Car park 200m.

Cheshire

Chester

Known for its cats, its cheese, its excellent roads and surprisingly varied scenery, the county of Cheshire has retained its charming rural character throughout the centuries.

The county town of Chester comes from the Latin term 'Castra Devana', meaning 'camp on the Dee'. The town lies on an elbow of the River Dee and was founded by Romans during the first century AD. The town is surrounded by a medieval wall, packed with historic buildings, winding streets and a wealthy atmosphere. The picturesque Cheshire Plain is the home for a multitude of pretty villages and lush countryside.

Knutsford, with its black and white houses and winding streets, is typical of the towns clustered in the region. The whole area is a delight for the visitor.

ADLINGTON HALL

Nr Macclesfield, Cheshire SK10 4LF
Tel: 01625 820875 Fax: 01625 828756 (Mrs C Legh)

Adlington Hall is a Cheshire Manor and has been the home of the Leghs since 1315. The Great Hall was built between 1450 and 1505, the Elizabethan 'Black and White' in 1581 and the Georgian South Front in 1757. The Bernard Smith Organ was installed c1670. A 'Shell Cottage', Yew Walk, Lime Avenue, recently planted maze and rose garden. Recently restored follies include a Chinese bridge, Temple to Diana and T'ing House. Occasional organ recitals. **Location:** 5 miles N of Macclesfield on the Stockport/Macclesfield Road (A523). **Station(s)** Adlington (½m). **Open:** Throughout the year to groups by prior arrangement only. **Admission:** Hall and Gardens Adults £4, children £1.50 (over 25 people £3.50). **Refreshments:** At the Hall. Car park free.

ARLEY HALL AND GARDENS

Arley, Northwich Cheshire CW9 6NA
Tel: 01565 777353 Fax: 01565 777465 (Lord & Lady Ashbrook)

Arley Hall, built about 1840, stands at the centre of an estate which has been owned by the same family for over 500 years. An important example of the early Victorian Jacobean style, it has fine plaster work and oak panelling, a magnificent library and interesting pictures, furniture and porcelain. There is a private Chapel designed by Anthony Salvin and a 15th century cruck barn. The gardens overlooking parkland provide great variety of style and design, winning the Christies/HHA Garden of the Year Award in 1987. Features include the Double Herbaceous Border established in 1846, clipped Quercus Ilex avenue, pleached Lime avenue, Topiary, collections of shrub roses, exotic trees and shrubs and over 200 varieties of Rhododendron. **Location:** 5 m N Northwich; 6 m W of Knutsford; 7 m S of Warrington; 5 m off M6 at junctions 19 & 20; 5 m off M56 at junctions 9 & 10. Nearest main roads A49 and A50. **Open:** Easter- Sept inclusive. Gardens & Grounds, Tues-Suns & Bank Hol Mons 11-5pm. Guided tours and parties by arrangement. Hall open Tues and Sun only. **Admission:** Gardens £4, Hall £2.50 extra. Concessions and group bookings. **Refreshments:** Lunches and light refreshments in converted Tudor barn. **Events/Exhibitions:** Antique fairs, Garden Festival, Craft Shows, Fireworks & Laser Concert etc., Outdoor Theatre, Christmas Events. **Conferences:** Facilities available. Corporate activities, launches, filming, weddings, themed events, countryside days etc., Private & Corporate Dinners. Shop and Plant Nursery. Woodland Walk. Facilities for disabled. Dogs allowed in gardens on leads. Picnic area. Arley Garden Festival 26–27 June.

map 6 C1

BRAMALL HALL

Bramhall Park, Bramhall, Stockport, Cheshire, SK7 3NX
Tel: 0161 485 3708 Fax: 0161 486 6959 (Stockport Metropolitan Borough Council)

This magical Tudor manor house is set in 70 acres of parkland, with lakes, woods and gardens. The house contains 16th century wall paintings, Elizabethan fine plaster ceilings, Victorian kitchens and servant's quarters. Excellent stables, tearoom and gift shop. **Location:** 4 miles S of Stockport, off A5102. **Stations:** Cheadle Hulme. **Open:** Good Fri–30 Sept, Mon–Sat, 1–5pm. Sun & BHols, 11–5pm. 1 Oct–1 Jan, Tue–Sat, 1–4pm. Sun & BHols, 11–4pm. Closed 25–26 Dec. 2 Jan–Easter, Sat & Sun, 12–4pm. Parties by arrangement, including out of hours bookings. **Admission:** Adults £3.50, children/OAPs £2. **Refreshments:** Stables, tearooms. **Events/Exhibitions:** Full events programme. **Conferences:** Available for corporate entertaining and civil marriages. Disabled access on ground floor, shop and tearooms.

map 8
B4

CAPESTHORNE HALL

Nr. Macclesfield, Cheshire
Tel: 01625 861 221 Fax: 01625 861 619 (Mr & Mrs W. A. Bromley-Davenport)

Capesthorne Hall has been the home of the Bromley Davenport family and their ancestors since Domesday times. The present hall dates from 1719 and contains a great variety of paintings, sculptures and furniture. The gardens, lakes and park contain many interesting features including a Georgian Chapel and an old ice house. **Location:** 3½ miles south of Alderley Edge on A34. **Open:** Hall and Gardens: April–October, Wednesday, Sunday and Bank Holidays (afternoons). **Refreshments:** Butler's Pantry plus catering by arrangement. **Admission:** Adults £5.50, child £2.50. Special events throughout the year. Also available for corporate hospitality and wedding receptions.

map 8
B5

HOLEHIRD GARDENS

Patterdale Road (Kirkstone Pass Road), Windermere, Cumbria LA23 1NP
Tel: 01539 446008

5–acre garden of the Lakeland Horticultural Society. Open dawn to dusk throughout the year and attractive at all seasons. Wonderful views over the head of Lake Windermere to Langdale Fells beyond. Outstanding walled garden with well-stocked herbaceous borders, extensive rock gardens. Good collections of hostas, hellebores, geraniums and old roses. Specimen trees and mixed shrubberies. National Collections of astilbe, hydrangea and polystichum ferns. Maintained entirely by member volunteers. **Admission:** By donation (minimum £1 per head suggested), wardens on duty. Limited disabled access. Ample parking, coaches strictly by prior arrangement only.

CHOLMONDELEY CASTLE GARDEN

Malpas, Cheshire, SY14 8AH
Tel: 01829 720383/203 (The Marchioness of Cholmondeley)

Extensive pleasure gardens dominated by romantic Gothic Castle, built in 1801 of local sandstone. Imaginatively laid out with fine trees and water gardens, it has been extensively replanted from the 1960's with azaleas, rhododendrons, magnolias, cornus, acer and many other acid loving plants. As well as the beautiful water garden, there is a rose garden and many mixed borders. Lakeside picnic area, children's play area, rare breeds of farm animals, including llamas. Ancient private chapel in park. **Location:** Off A41 Chester/Whitchurch Road and A49 Whitchurch/Tarporley Road. **Station(s):** Crewe. **Open:** Good Fri 2 Apr–Thur 30 Sept, Wed, Thur, Sun & Bank Hols 11.30–5pm. **Enquiries to:** The secretary, Cholmondeley Castle (House not open to public). **Admission:** Adults £3, OAPs £2.50, children £1. Coach parties of 25 and over at reduced rates.

map 6
C/D1

 # DORFOLD HALL

Nantwich CW5 8LD

Tel: 01270 625245 Fax: 01270 628723 (Mr Richard Roundell)

Jacobean country house built 1616. Beautiful plaster ceilings and panelling. Interesting furniture and pictures. Attractive gardens including spectacular spring garden and summer herbaceous borders. Guided tours. **Location:** 1 mile W of Nantwich on A534 Nantwich/Wrexham Road. **Stations:** Nantwich (1½ miles). **Open:** Apr–Oct Tues and Bank Holidays Mons 2–5pm. At other times by appointment only. **Admission:** Adults £4, children £2.

map 6 D1

 # DUNHAM MASSEY HALL

Altrincham, Cheshire

Tel: 0161 941 1025 Fax: 0161 929 7508 (The National Trust)

18th century house containing the treasures of the 2nd Earl of Warrington who also laid out the formal parkland. The tranquil garden contains remnants from past layouts such as the moat, Elizabethan mount and Orangery, all set amongst sweeping lawns and waterside plantings. **Admission:** NT members free. House and Garden: Adult £5, child £2.50, family £12, booked parties £4.50 (min 15 paying adults). House only: Adult £3, child £1.50. Garden only: Adult £3, child £1.50. Car entry: £3 per car, £5 per coach/minibus (free to booked parties), £1 per motorcycle. **Open:** House and garden open 27 Mar–31 Oct. House, Sat to Wed 12–5pm (last entry 4.30pm, open at 11am Bank Hol Suns and Mons). Garden, shop and restaurant daily 11–5pm. Park open daily all year round.

NT Photographic Library, Nick Meers

map 6 B1

LITTLE MORETON HALL

Congleton, Cheshire CW12 4SD

Tel: 01260 272018 (The National Trust)

Begun in 1450, Little Moreton is regarded as the finest timber-framed moated manor house in England. The Chapel, Great Hall and Long Gallery, together with the Knot Garden, make Little Moreton a great day out. Location for TV films including Lady Jane and Moll Flanders. Try the local historic recipes in the restaurant and visit the shop with its extensive range of gifts. Parties welcome. Ghost Tour with supper for booked parties. Great Hall decorated for an Elizabethan Yuletide with Christmas Festivities, seasonal refreshments and shopping. Open Air theatre in July. **Admission:** Adult £4.20, child £2.10, family £10.50. **Open:** 20 Mar–31 Oct, Wed–Sun, Bank Holiday Monday 11.30–5pm. 6–28 Nov, Sat, Sun 11.30–4pm. 4–19 Dec, Sat, Sun 11.30–4pm Free entry. Tel: 01260 272018.

map 8 B5

NESS BOTANIC GARDENS

Ness, Neston, South Wirral, Cheshire L64 4AY

Tel: 0151 353 0123 Fax: 0151 353 1004

Pioneers in the world of plants since 1898. Beautiful Botanic Garden for all seasons with extensive displays of trees and shrubs, including Rhododendrons and Azaleas. Renowned heather, rock, terrace, water, rose and herb gardens. Visit our coffee shops which provide home-made cakes and light meals. Gift shop, plant sales area, visitor centre and picnic area. **Admission** Charge. **Location:** 6 miles from exit 4, M53, 5 miles from western end M56, off A540 Hoylake–Chester Road.

map 6 C2

NORTON PRIORY MUSEUM & GARDENS

Tudor Road, Manor Park, Runcorn, Cheshire WA7 1SX

Tel: 01928 569895 (The Norton Priory Museum Trust)

The beautiful 38 acre woodland gardens with an award winning walled garden are the setting for the now demolished mansion of the Brookes, built on the site of a former Augustinian priory. Excavated remains of the priory & the atmospheric 12th century undercroft can be found with displays on the medieval priory, the later houses and gardens in the museum. Contemporary sculpture is situated in the grounds. **Location:** From M56 (junction 11) turn towards Warrington and follow Norton Priory road signs. **Open:** Daily all year. Apr–Oct, Sat, Sun & Bank Hols 12–6pm; Mon to Fri 12–5pm; Nov–Mar, daily 12–4pm. Walled Garden open Mar–Oct, closed 24/25/26 Dec, 1 Jan. Special arrangements for groups. **Admission:** Adults £3.20, concs £1.90, family £8.50 (2 adults & up to 3 children under 16).

map 6 C1

PECKFORTON CASTLE

Stonehouse Lane, Nr. Tarporley CW6 9TN

Tel: 01829 260930 Fax: 01829 261230

An intact Norman style castle built by Lord Tollemache mid 1840, to design by Anthony Salvin. Situated on the Peckforton Hills, part of the dramatic sandstone trail. Come and discover the magic of Peckforton Castle. Our gossiping verger, the singing minstrel and the original talking Lord Tollemache to entertain you, our resident ghost tops the delight. Medieval re-enactments every Sunday in season weather permitting. **Refreshments.** Bar Curios. Setting for Robin Hood film 1991. **Open:** 2 April–12th September 10am–6pm. **Location:** 12 miles E Chester. **Admission:** Adults £2.50, child (5-14), students, seniors, disabled £1.50. Parties over 20 £1.00. Private hire functions available all year. Approved for Civil Marriages and official chapel blessings. Drivers and couriers N/C – Free Parking

map 6 C1

RODE HALL

Church Lane, Scholar Green ST7 3QP
Tel: 01270 873237 Fax: 01270 882962
(Sir Richard Baker Wilbraham Bt)

18th century country house with Georgian stable block. Later alterations by L Wyatt and Darcy Braddell. Repton landscape and formal gardens designed by Nesfield. Fully working walled kitchen garden. Icehouse. **Location:** 5 miles south west of Congleton between A34 and A50. **Open:** Easter–end Sept, Wednesdays and Bank Holidays and by appointment. Garden only: Tuesdays and Thursdays (and by Appointment from 2 Mar) 2–5pm. **Admission:** House, garden and kitchen garden £3.50. Garden and kitchen garden £2.00. (Senior citizens £2 and £1) **Refreshments:** Home-made teas.

map 8 B5

LYME PARK

Disley, Stockport, SK12 2NX
Tel: 01663 762023   Infoline: 01663 766492   Fax: 01663 765035

Legh Family home for 600 years, Part of the original Elizabethan house survives with 18th and 19th century additions by Giacomo Leoni and Lewis Wyatt. Four centuries of period interiors- Mortlake tapestries, Grinling Gibbons carvings, unique collection of English clocks.Historic gardens with conservatory by Wyatt, a lake and a 'Dutch'garden. A 1,400 acre park, home to red and fallow deer. Exterior featured as Pemberley in BBC's Pride and Prejudice. **Open & Admission:** Please phone for details of opening times and admission charges.

TABLEY HOUSE

Knutsford, Cheshire, WA16 0HB.
Tel: 01565 750 151 Fax: 01565 653 230
Owners: The Victoria University of Manchester

Fine Palladian mansion designed by John Carr of York for the Leicester family. The staterooms show family memorabilia, furniture by Gillow, Bullock and Chippendale and the first collection of English paintings ever made. **Location:** 2 miles W of Knutsford, entrance on A5033 (M6 Junction 19, A556). **Open:** Apr–end Oct: Thurs, Fri, Sat, Sun and Bank Hols, 2–5pm. (Last entry 4.30pm). Free car park. Main rooms and the Chapel suitable for the disabled. **Admission:** Adults £4. Child/student with card £1.50. **Refreshments:** Tearoom and shop facilities. ALL ENQUIRIES TO THE ADMINISTRATOR. **Conferences:** Small meetings, civil wedding licence.

map 6 C1

TATTON PARK

Knutsford, Cheshire WA16 6QN
Tel: 01625 534400 Fax: 01625 534403 (Cheshire County Council)

Large Regency mansion with extravagantly decorated staterooms, family rooms and servants workrooms. A superb collection of Gillow furniture, Baccarat glass and paintings by Italian and Dutch masters. Two exhibition rooms, one of which features personal memorabilia of the Egerton family. 1000 acres of deer park open to visitors with its lakes woods and open vistas, provide the setting for the magnificent mansion and help make Tatton one of England's most complete country estates. The Garden contains many unusual features and rare species of plants shrubs and trees. Considered to be one of the finest and most important gardens within the National Trust. Features include: Conservatory by Wyatt, Fernery by Paxton, Japanese, Italian and Rose gardens. The rare collection of plants including rhododendrons, tree ferns, bamboo and pines are the result of 200 years of collecting by the Egerton family. **Open: Park & Gardens:** open all year except Mondays but including Bank Holidays (Closed Christmas Day). **Farm:** Sundays only, Nov–Mar. Mansion Oldhall open Apr–Sept, phone for further details. Managed and Financed by Cheshire County Council.

map 6 C1

Cornwall

*I*t is usual to bracket Devon and Cornwall as if they shared many things in common. They share little except contiguity. Their scenery is vastly dissimilar – their speech and customs entirely different. Their climate is different. Even their cream is not the same.

Cornwall is far more rugged, its inland scenery barer. Devon wears an air of rich comfort. You feel in Cornwall the fierceness of man's struggle against nature. Yet on the south coast especially, man and nature have combined to create some of the most splendid gardens in Britain.

The place names of Cornwall sound foreign. Ventongimps, Trevisquite, Tol-Pedn-Penith, Lostwithiel, Menheniot, Chy-an-Drea, Tregeargate and Egloskerry. Cornwall is not English territory. The enchantment of Cornwall is legendary – Merlin, King Arthur,

Padstow

Tristan and Isolde – the magic lives on! The fortified headland of Tintagel, the picturesque fishing villages of St Ives, Port Gaverne and Port Isaac, the torrents and rock formations of Bodmin Moor and the clenched little harbour of Boscastle – are typical of Cornwall's craggy appeal, but the full elemental power of the ocean can best be appreciated on Cornwall's twin pincers of The Lizard point and Land's End, where the splintered cliffs resound to the constant thunder of the waves.

BOSVIGO

Bosvigo Lane, Truro, Cornwall
Tel: 01872 275774 Fax: 01872 275774 (Michael and Wendy Perry)

Unlike most Cornish Gardens, Bosvigo is a 'summer' garden. Shrubs take second place to herbaceous perennials, carefully planted to give a succession of colour from Jun through 'til Sept. The gardens comprise a series of walled or hedged 'rooms' all around the Georgian house (not open). Each room has its own colour theme. A Victorian conservatory houses a collection of semi-tender climbers and plants–a delightful place to sit and relax. This is a plantsman's garden–the harder you look, the more plants you will see. Featured in many books, magazines and on television. **Open:** Mar–end Sept, Thur–Sat, 11–6pm. **Admission:** Adults £2, children 50p (no concessions). Sorry, no dogs.

map 2
C6

BURNCOOSE NURSERIES & GARDEN

Gwennap, Redruth TR16 6BJ
Tel: 01209 861112 Fax: 01209 860011 (C H Williams)

The Nurseries are set in the 30 acre woodland gardens of Burncoose. Some 12 acres are laid out for nursery stock production of over 3000 varieties of ornamental trees, shrubs and herbaceous plants. Specialities include camellias, azaleas, magnolias, rhododendrons and conservatory plants. The Nurseries are widely known for rarities and for unusual plants. Full mail order catalogue £1.50 (posted). **Location:** 2 miles southwest of Redruth on the main A393 Redruth to Falmouth road between the villages of Lanner and Ponsanooth. **Open:** Mon–Sat 9–5pm, Sun 11–5pm. Gardens and tearooms open all year (except Christmas Day). **Admission:** Nurseries free, gardens £2.00.

map 2
C6

CAERHAYS CASTLE AND GARDENS

Gorran, St Austell PL26 6LY
Tel: 01872 501310 Fax: 01872 501870

One of the very few Nash built castles still left standing - situated within approximately 60 acres of informal woodland gardens created by J C Williams, who sponsored plant hunting expeditions to China at the turn of the century. Noted for its camellias, magnolias, rhododendrons and oaks. **English Heritage Listing:** Grade One, Outstanding. **Open:** Gardens 15th Mar–14 May 11–4pm. House 22 Mar–30 Apr, 2–4pm. Mon–Fri only. House closed on Bank Hol. Additional openings (Gardens only) Sat 17th & Sun 18th Apr, 11–4pm. **Admission:** House £3.50, Gardens £3.50, Children £1.50, House/Gardens £6. Guided Tour by head Gardener for groups can be arranged outside normal opening times, £4 each. Please contact for details of charity openings.

map 2
C6

GODOLPHIN HOUSE

Godolphin Cross, Helston, Cornwall TR13 9RE
Tel: 01736-762409 (Mrs M. Schofield)

Godolphin is of the Tudor and Stuart periods with Tudor stables. The garden retains its early raised walks. Elizabethan carp ponds are awaiting restoration. The Godolphins included Sidney, the Carolean poet and Sidney the 1st Earl, Lord High Treasurer, to Queen Anne. The 2nd Earl, Francis, owned the famous Godolphin Arabian horse, a painting of which hangs in the house. **Open:** Bank Hol Mon 2–5pm, May and Jun: Thurs 2–5pm, Jul and Sept: Tues and Thurs 2–5pm, Aug: Tues 2–5pm, Groups of 20 and over by arrangement: Thurs 10–1pm and 2–5pm. **Admission:** Adults £3, children £1, under 5s free. Garden: Adults 50p, children free, groups of 20 or over £2.

 map 2 B6

LANHYDROCK HOUSE

Bodmin, Cornwall
Tel: 01208 73320 Fax: 01208 74084 (The National Trust)

Lanhdrock, one of Cornwall's grandest houses, dates back to the 17th century but much was rebuilt after a fire in 1881 destroyed all but the north wing, which includes the magnificent Long Gallery with its extraordinary plaster ceiling. A total of 49 rooms are on show today, including servants' bedrooms, kitchens, the nursery suite and the grandeur of the dining-room. Surrounding the house are formal Victorian gardens, wooded higher gardens where magnolias, rhododendrons and camellias climb the hillside. **Open:** Gardens and Park only: 1 Mar–31 Oct 1999. House: 27 Mar–31 Oct 99 daily 11–5.30pm. Closes 5pm in October. House closed Mons (except Bank Hol Mons). **Admission:** House and gardens: Adult £6.40, child £3.20. Garden and grounds only: Adult £3.20, child, £1.60. Family ticket (2 adults + 3 children) £16. Pre-arranged parties £5.50.

 map 2 D5

PENCARROW

Washaway, Bodmin PL30 3AG
Tel: 01208 841369 (The Molesworth-St Aubyn Family)

Georgian house and listed gardens, still owned and lived in by the family. A superb collection of 18th century pictures, furniture and porcelain. Mile long drive and Ancient British Encampment. Marked walks through beautiful woodland gardens, past the great granite Victorian Rockery, Italian and American gardens, Lake and Ice House. Approximately 50 acres in all. Over 700 different rhododendrons, also an internationally known specimen conifer collection. **Open:** Easter–15 Oct, 1.30–5pm (1 June–10 Sept and Bank Hols 11am). **Admission:** Adults – House & Gardens £4.50, Gardens only £2. Children – House £2, Gardens: children and dogs very welcome and free. Group rate £4. NPI National Heritage Award Winner 1997 & 1998.

 map 2 D5

PENDENNIS CASTLE

Falmouth, Cornwall
Tel: 01326 316594 (English Heritage)

Facing the castle of St Mawes, with glorious views over the mile wide mouth of the River Fal, Pendennis Castle has stood in defence of our shores for almost 450 years. Take a guided tour through the tunnels to the Second World War Gun Battery. Explore the First World War Guardroom with its cells and see a Tudor gun deck in action complete with the sights and sounds of battle. A trip on the delightful ferry to St Mawes will make your day even more enjoyable. **Location:** On Pendennis Head 1m SE of Falmouth. **Open:** 1 Apr–31 Oct: daily, 10–6pm (5pm in October). Opens 9am July & Aug. 1 Nov–31 Mar: Wed–Sun, 10–4pm. **Admission:** Adult £3.80, conc £2.90, child £1.90. (15% discount for groups of 11 or more).

 map 2 C6

ST MAWES CASTLE

St Mawes, Falmouth, Cornwall
Tel: 01326 270526 (English Heritage)

Designed with three huge circular bastions resembling a clover leaf, Henry VIII's picturesque fort stands in delightful sub-tropical gardens. Here you can see a remarkable collection of plants from all corners of the world. Climb to the battlements and experience the breathtaking views across the bay to Falmouth and take a trip on the ferry across the estuary to Pendennis Castle. **Location:** In St Mawes on A3078. **Open:** 1 Apr–30 Sept: daily, 10–6pm, last admission 5.30pm. 1 Oct–31 Oct: daily, 10–5pm. 1 Nov–31 Mar: Fri–Tues, 10–4pm. (Closed 24–5 Dec). **Admission:** Adults £2.50, concs £1.90, child: £1.30. (15% discount for groups of 11 or more).

 map 2 C6

 ## ST MICHAEL'S MOUNT

Marazion, Nr Penzance, Cornwall
Tel: 01736 710507/01736 710 265 (The National Trust)

Home of Lord St Levan. Medieval and early 17th century with considerable alterations and additions in 18th and 19th century. **Location:** ½ mile from the shore at Marazion (A394), connected by causeway. 3 miles E Penzance. **Open:** 1 April–31 Oct, Mon–Fri, 10.30–5.30pm (last adm 4.45pm). **Weekends:** The castle and grounds are open most weekends during the season. Nov to end of Mar: Guided tours as tide, weather and circumstances permit. (NB: ferry boats do not operate a regular service during this period. **Admission:** Adults £4.40, children £2.20, groups £4, for 20 or more paying people. These are special charity open days when National Trust members are asked to pay.

 ## TRELOWARREN HOUSE & CHAPEL

Mawgan-in-Meneage, Helston, Cornwall, TR12 6AD
Tel: 01326 221366 Fax: 01326 221834 (Sir Ferrers Vyvyan, Bt.)

Home of the Vyvyan family since 1427. Part of the house dates from early Tudor times. The Chapel, part of which is pre-Reformation and the 17th century part of the house are leased to the Trelowarren Fellowship, an ecumenical charity, for use by them as a Christian residential healing and retreat centre. (Phone for details). The Chapel and main rooms containing family portraits are open to the public at certain times. Sunday services are held in the Chapel during the holiday season. **Location:** 6 miles S of Helston, off B3293 to St. Keverne. **Open:** House & Chapel: 2 Apr–27 Sept, Wed & Bank Hol Mons, 2.15–5pm. **Admission:** Adults £1.50, children 50p (under 12 free), including entry to various exhibitions of paintings. **Events/Exhibitions:** Exhibitions of paintings. Only the ground floor is suitable for disabled.

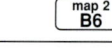

TREVARNO ESTATE & GARDENS

Trevarno Manor, Helston, Cornwall TR13 0RU
Tel: 01326 574274 Fax: 01326 574282 (Mr M. R. Sagin & Mr N. C. Helsby)

A historic and tranquil haven protected and unspoilt for 700 years. Experience the magical atmosphere of Trevarno, an original and fascinating Cornish Estate. Beautiful Victorian and Georgian gardens, extensive collection of rare shrubs and trees, numerous garden features and follies, fascinating Gardening Museum, Handmade soap workshop and pottery. Splendid Fountain Garden Conservatory tearoom. Walled gardens, woodland walks and abundant wildlife. Follow the progress of major restoration and conservation projects. **Location:** OS Ref SW642302. Leave Helston on Penzance road, signed from B3302 junction. **Open:** All year except Christmas Day 10.30–5pm. Groups welcome by prior arrangement. **Admission:** Gardens: Adult £3, OAP/disabled £2.50, children (5–14) £1.25. Museum: Adult £2, OAP/disabled £2, children (5–14) £1.

 ## TRERICE

Nr Newquay TR8 4PG Tel: 01637 875404 Fax: 01637 879300

Open: 28 March to 25 July, 6 Sept to 31 Oct: daily except Tues & Sat; 26 July to 5 Sept: daily. 27 March to 30 Sept, 11–5.30pm; (closes 5pm in Oct). Note: Solar Eclipse,11 Aug. Property closed all day. Events: send s.a.e. for programme. **Admission:** £4; family ticket £10. Pre-arranged parties £3.40. Restaurant: The Barn open as house, last serving 4.30pm (4pm in Oct). Organisers of groups should arrange for meals beforehand (tel. 01637 875404).

ANTONY

Torpoint, Plymouth PL11 2QA Tel: 01752 812191

Open: 1 April to 27 May, 1 Sept to 28 Oct: Tues, Wed, Thur & BH Mon; June, July & Aug: daily except Mon, Fri & Sat (but open BH Mon). 1.30–5.30pm; last admission 4.45. Bath Pond House can be seen by prior written application to Custodian and only when house is open. Woodland Garden (not NT – Carew Pole Garden Trust) open 1 March to 31 October,

daily 11–5.30pm. **Admission:** £4. Pre-arranged parties £3.40. £2.50 for access to Woodland Garden (NT members free on days when house open). Combined gardens-only ticket for Antony garden and adjoining woodland garden £3. Pre-arranged parties £2.40 per person. Note: Solar Eclipse,11 Aug. House closed all day, garden will open at later time of 1pm. **Restaurant:** Tea-room as house 12.30–5.30pm.

 ## COTEHELE

St Dominick, nr Saltash, PL12 6TA Tel: 01579 351346 Fax: 01579 351222

Open: House: 27 March to 31 Oct: daily except Fri (but open Good Fri). 11–5pm (11–4.30 in Oct). Mill: 27 March to 31 Oct: daily except Fri; July & Aug: daily.27 March to 30 June & 1 Sept, 1.30–5.30pm. 1–6pm in July & Aug; 1.30–4.30pm in Oct. Garden: open all year, daily 1–5.30pm. Note: Solar Eclipse,11 Aug. House closed all day, garden will open at later time of 1pm. **Admission:** £6; family ticket £15. Garden & mill only £3.20; family £8. All groups only by prior written arrangement with the Property Manager. £4.50. Coach group organisers will be sent a copy of the route when they book. No groups Sun or Bank Holidays.

Cumbria

Through the middle ages, successive kings and rulers fought over this territory. This has left the area with a multitude of Celtic monuments, Roman remains, stately homes and monastic ruins.

The Lake District dominates Cumbria, despite the attractions of other places of interest in the county. Windermere, Grasmere, Bowness, Ambleside, Kendal and Keswick are all best visited on foot. The lakes vary in character considerably, from the sombre Wastwater to the bright and breezy Windermere, the centre of most of the activities. Pastimes include hill-walking, windsurfing, rock climbing, cycling, canoeing and water-skiing.

Carlisle, set in the north of Cumbria, is a fine cathedral city which is steeped in the history of battle. The city stands imposingly as the gateway to the borders and Emporer Hadrian, Bonnie Prince Charlie and Robert the Bruce have all played a part in Carlisle's interesting past.

Loweswater

The rich land of the Eden Valley, popular with trout and salmon fishermen, complements the raw beauty of The North Pennines. Traditional sports such as Cumberland and Westmorland wrestling and fell racing are still practised and may be seen at many of the sports shows whilst the Egremont Crab Fair hosts the annual World Gurning Championship.

ABBOT HALL ART GALLERY

Kendal, Cumbria LA9 5AL
Tel: 01539 722464 Fax: 01539 722494 (Lake District Art Gallery & Museum Trust)

This elegant Georgian building provides a superb setting for its collection of fine art. Paintings by George Romney fill the walls of rooms furnished by Gillows of Lancaster. Touring exhibitions complement the permanent collection of 18th, 19th and 20th century British art. The gallery is situated by the banks of the River Kent overlooked by Kendal castle. The adjacent Museum of Lakeland Life looks at 300 years of local history. Exhibits include a Victorian street scene, reconstructed farmhouse rooms and a re-creation of Arthur Ransome's study. Also situated nearby is Kendal Museum of Natural History and Archaeology. **Open:** 7 days a week 12 Feb–24 Dec 1999 10.30–5pm (reduced hours in winter). **Admission:** Concessions, family tickets and season tickets available. Guided tours by appointment. **Directions:** 10 minutes drive from junctions 36 of the M6. Follow brown Museum signs to South Kendal.

map 11
F6

ACORN BANK GARDEN & WATERMILL

Temple Sowerby, Nr Penrith CA10 1SP
Tel: 017683 61893 (The National Trust)

A walled garden renowned for its impressive herb collection of culinary and medicinal plants. There are also mixed herbaceous and rose borders and orchards containing a wide range of northern varieties of fruit tree. There are circular walks on the estate, including a circular woodland route along the Crowdundle Beck to Acorn Bank Watermill which is open to the public. Refreshments kiosk in courtyard, together with a shop and plant sales. **Open:** 27 Mar–31 Oct: daily 10–5pm, last admission 4.30. **Admission:** Adults £2.30, children £1.20, family ticket £5.80, pre-arranged parties £1.70 per person. Car parking. **Events:** 17 Oct Apple Day.

map 11
F5

CASTLETOWN HOUSE

Rockcliffe, Carlisle, Cumbria CA6 4BN
Tel: 01228 74792 Fax: 01228 74464 (Giles Mounsey-Heysham, Esq)

Period House set in attractive gardens and grounds. **Location:** 5 miles NW of Carlisle on Solway coast, 1 mile W of Rockcliffe village and 2 miles W of A74. **Open:** House Only by appointment only.

map 10
E4

APPLEBY CASTLE

Appleby–In–Westmorland, Cumbria CA16 6XH
Tel: 017683 51402 Fax: 017683 51082 (Appleby Castle Limited)

Dominated by its impressive Norman Keep, the castle was a major stronghold of the powerful Clifford family, who helped to hold the northern Marches during medieval times and fought (and sometimes died) in most of the famous medieval battles, Bannockburn, Crecy, the Wars of the Roses and Flodden. Later the Castle was a favourite home of Lady Anne Clifford, the last in her line, who stubbornly held out for her heritage in the troubled years of the civil war and left an enduring legacy at the castle, which was further enhanced by her descendants, the Tufton family. Today visitors may enjoy a castle which has something to offer from each period of history. The Norman Keep has five floors and a dramatic view from the top. The curtain wall and defensive earthworks are amongst the most impressive in northern England. The Great Hall of the castle contains the famous Great Painting of Lady Anne and her family, together with other period pieces. In the grounds, the castle has a variety of birds and animals. The castle's stable block, built in the outer bailey is also of interest as is Lady Anne's 'Beehouse', actually a small oratory. **Open:** Daily, 27 Mar–31 Oct 1999. 10–5pm (last admissions) (closes 4pm October). **Admission:** Grounds, Keep & Great Hall: Adults £4, children under 5 years free, children 5–15 years £2, senior citizens £2, family tickets 2A + 2C £10. Parties of 20 or more: Adults: £3, children £1.50, senior citizens £1.50, bus driver: Further reductions for School Parties.

map 11
F5

DALEMAIN

Nr Penrith, Cumbria CA11 0HB
Tel: 017684 86450 Fax: 017684 86223 (Robert Hasell-McCosh)

Medieval Tudor and Georgian House and Gardens. Behind the impressive Georgian façade lies the real surprise of Dalemain–its sheer variety. There has been a settlement on this site since Saxon times. The House has evolved as dictated sometimes by domestic or agricultural demands or sometimes by the fashion of the day. As a result, parts of the house are a glorious confusion of winding passages, quaint stairways, unexpected rooms–the sort of house that children love to play in. Indeed, part of the charm of Dalemain is that it remains very much a family home still occupied by the same family who have lived here since 1679. The variety, extent and richness of the furniture portraits and contents at Dalemain is quite exceptional for a house of its size. Westmorland and Cumberland Yeomanry, Countryside, Agricultural and Fell Pony Collections. The delightful gardens have many rare plants and a collection of over 100 old-fashioned roses. Enjoy delicious home-made meals and teas beside the log fire in the medieval old hall. In LWT's recent production of Jane Eyre, Dalemains Medieval Courtyard and Great Barn provide the locations for Lowood Institution. **Open:** Sun 28 Mar–Sun 3 Oct. 1999 inclusive. Sun to Thur. Gardens, Gift Shop, Licensed Restaurant and Tearoom, and Agricultural and Countryside collections: 10.30–5pm (5pm Sun and Bank Hol. Mon). House: 11–4.30pm (Last entry 4pm). **Admission:** House & Gardens: Adult £5 child £3, family £13. Gardens: Adult £3, child free when accompanied. For further information or to discuss events, party visits and conferences please contact Bryan McDonald the Administrator. **Location:** A592 Penrith to Ullswater, M6 J40 2 miles.

map 10 E5

 ## HOLKER HALL AND GARDENS

Cark-in-Cartmel, nr Grange-over-Sands LA11 7PL
Tel: 015395 58328 Fax: 015395 58776 (Lord and Lady Cavendish)

Cumbria's premier Stately home has 25 acres of National Award winning gardens with water features, rare plants and shrubs, 'World Class ... not to be missed by foreign visitors' (Good Gardens Guide '98). Also exhibitions, deer park, adventure playground, motor museum. Home of the spectacular Holker Garden Festival 4–6 June '99. (Show Office 015395 58838). **Location:** N of Cark-in-Cartmel on B5278 from Haverthwaite; 4 miles W Grange-over-Sands. **Stations:** Cark-in-Cartmel. **Open:** Apr 1–Oct 31 every day excluding Sat, 10–6 last admission 4.30pm. **Admission:** Various prices depending on what you want to see and do. Reduction for groups of 20 or more. **Refreshments:** Home-made cakes, sandwiches, salads in the Coach House Cafe. Free car parking.

map 10 E6

 ## HUTTON-IN-THE-FOREST

Penrith
Tel: 017684 84449 Fax: 017684 84571 (Lord and Lady Inglewood)

The home of Lord Inglewood's family since 1605. Built around a medieval pele tower with 17th, 18th and 19th century additions. Fine English furniture and pictures, ceramics and tapestries. The lovely walled garden established in 1730 has an increasing collection of herbaceous plants, wall trained fruit trees and topiary. Also dovecote and woodland walk through magnificent specimen trees, identifiable from leaflet. **Location:** 6 miles NW of Penrith on B5305 Wigton Road (3 miles from M6 exit 41). **Stations:** Penrith. **Open:** House 1–4pm 29 Apr–3 Oct, Thurs, Fri and Sun, also Easter Fri, Sun, Mon and Bank Hols. Gardens 11–5pm everyday except Sat. Groups by arrangement from Apr–Oct. **Admission:** House and Gardens: Adult £4, child £2, family £10. Gardens only: Adult £2.50, children free. **Refreshments:** Home-made light lunches & teas in Cloisters when house is open, 12–4.30pm.

map 10 E4

ISEL HALL

Cockermouth, Cumbria CA13 0QG
(The Administrator)

Pele Tower with domestic range and gardens set on north bank of River Derwent. The house is small, so groups limited to 30. **Location:** 3½ miles N.E. of Cockermouth. **Station(s):** Aspatria 9 miles; Penrith 32 miles. **Open:** Mondays, 12 April–11 October, 2–4pm. Other times by written arrangement. **Admission:** £3. No dogs. No photography inside. It is regretted there is no disabled access upstairs.

map 10 D4

LEVENS HALL

Kendal LA8 0PD
Tel: 015395 60321 Fax: 015395 60669 (C H Bagot Esq)

Elizabethan house and home of the Bagot family containing fine furniture, the earliest English patchwork (c.1708) and the world famous Topiary Gardens (c.1694). NPI Heritage Award winners 1997/1998. In addition there is a collection of working model steam engines. **Location:** 5 minutes drive from exit 36 of the M6. 5 miles S of Kendal on the A6. **Station:** Oxenholme. **Open:** 1 Apr–14 Oct, Sun–Thurs (including Bank Hols). Garden & tearoom 10–5pm. House: noon–5pm. Last admissions 4.30pm. Closed Fri & Sat. **Admission:** House and Garden: Adults £5.30, children £2.80. Gardens only: Adults £3.90, children £2.10. **Refreshments:** Home-made light lunches & teas. We regret the house is not suitable for wheelchairs. **E-Mail:** levens.hall@farmline.com

MIREHOUSE

Mirehouse, Keswick CA12 4QE
Tel: 01768 772287 Fax: 01768 772287 (Mr & Mrs Spedding)

A regional winner in the 1998 NPI Heritage Awards. This house maintains its three hundred year tradition of welcome and peaceful enjoyment. Our visitors particularly appreciate the extraordinary literary and artistic connections, varied gardens and walks, natural adventure playgrounds, live classical music and the personal attention of members of the family. The Old Sawmill Tearoom is known for generous Cumbrian cooking. Catering for groups also available in the licensed Garden Hall. **Location:** A591 3½ miles N of Keswick. Good bus service. **Open:** 28 Mar–31 Oct. Gardens and tearoom: daily 10–5.30pm. Please telephone for winter opening times. House: Sun, Wed (also Fri in Aug) 2–4.30pm last entry. Also throughout the year by appointment for groups.

MUNCASTER WATER MILL

Ravenglass, Cumbria CA18 1ST
Tel: 01229 717232 (Lake District Estates)

Working old Manorial Mill with 13ft overshot wheel and all milling equipment. **Location:** 1 mile north of Ravenglass on A595. **Open:** Maundy Thursday–end Oct, daily, 10–5pm. Nov–March: weekends only, 11–4pm. **Admission:** Adult £1.60, child 80p, Family £4.

MUNCASTER CASTLE, GARDENS & OWL CENTRE

Ravenglass, Cumbria CA18 1RQ
Tel: 01229 717 614 Fax: 01229 717 010 (Mrs P. Gordon-Duff-Pennington)

Muncaster Castle, situated on the peaceful West Coast of Cumbria has been home to the Pennington family for 800 years. The treasures collected over this period give a unique insight into the life of the family. The Castle stands proudly in 77 acres of splendid woodland gardens, famed for rhododendrons and azaleas. The Terrace Walk boasts stunning views of the magnificent Lakeland fells and the two newly restored Victorian summer houses provide added interest. Over 40 species of birds are under the care of the World Owl Trust based at Muncaster. Daily at 2.30pm (during the season) a bird display and talk is given. Facilities include a new function room, café, gift shops, children's play area, plant centre and church, all with disabled access. The Castle is licensed for civil marriages. **Open:** Castle: Sun–Fri, 12.30–4pm, 21 Mar–7 Nov. Gardens & Owl Centre: 11–6pm, all year.

RYDAL MOUNT & GARDENS

Ambleside, Cumbria LA22 9LU
Tel: 01539 433002 Fax: 01539 431738 (Rydal Mount Trustees)

The historic house of William Wordsworth from 1813 until his death in 1850, now the family home of his descendants. It contains family portraits and his personal possessions. The extensive garden, landscaped by the poet, includes terraces, rare shrubs, trees and the poet's summerhouse which overlooks beautiful Rydal Water. **Location:** 1½ miles north of Ambleside on A591 Grasmere Road. **Open:** 1 Mar–31 Oct, 9.30–5pm, 7 days a week. 1 Nov–end Feb, 10–4pm. Closed on Tuesday. **Admission:** Adult £3.50, child £1, OAP/Student £3. Groups (min 10+) £2.50 per person. Garden only: £1.50.

STOTT PARK BOBBIN MILL

Low Stott Park, Ulverston, Cumbria LA12 8AX
Tel: 01539 531087 (English Heritage)

When this working mill was built in 1835 it was typical of the many mills in the Lake District which grew up to supply the spinning and weaving industry in Lancashire but have since disappeared. A remarkable opportunity to see a demonstration of the machinery and techniques of the Industrial Revolution. There is a working Static Steam Engine on Tuesday and Thursdays. **Location:** Near Newby Bridge on A590. **Open:** 1 Apr–31 Oct, daily, 10–6pm. Last tour 5pm.

NAWORTH CASTLE

Naworth Castle, Carlisle, Cumbria CA8 2HF
Tel: 016977 3229 Fax: 016977 3679 (Philip Howard)

Naworth Castle is now Cumbria's premier historic function. We offer exclusive use and outstanding personal service. We are licensed for Civil Ceremonies and in 1998 over 40 weddings took place. Our Great Hall can seat up to 200 people and we have Marquee facilities in our 17th century walled garden. Excellent car parking. Our large corporate clients include Rover, Honda, Ford U.K., British Telecom, Thorn Security, and Jaguar Cars. We have 13 double bedrooms all with their own bath/shower rooms which we can make available for residential conferences and parties although we do stress that we are NOT a hotel. We have outstanding retained caterers. We have horse riding stables, a clay pigeon shoot, river and lake fishing. 400 acres of woods for potential off road driving and a special 10.5 acre flat field for outdoor corporate events. We are flexible enough to cater for all clients requirements from conferences, corporate breaks, product launches, concerts, charity events and filming. Recent film credits include Catherine Cookson's "Black Candle", LWT's Jane Eyre (we were Thornfield) and Border's T.V.'s "Debatable Lands". **Open:** All year BY APPOINTMENT ONLY except Sats. All tours must be pre-booked minimum 15. We are ideal for specialist coach parties. Tours mostly conducted by owner. Lunches, teas and dinners can be provided and in certain circumstances accommodation. **1999 Special Events:** Fri 26–Sun 28th March: Galloway Antiques Fair. Thur 24 June: Thomson Roddick & Laurie Fine Pictures & Furniture Auction (viewing day Wed 23 June.) Fri 27–Mon 30 Aug: Galloway Antique Fair. 21 Oct: Thomson Roddick & Laurie Fine Art and Furniture Sale (viewing day on Wed 20 Oct).

map 11
F4

Derbyshire

Of all the English counties, this is probably the most traditional. Within its borders England passes from the plain country to the hill country, from the newer and softer rocks to the old and harder. As the Lake District dominates Cumbria, so the Peak District dominates Derbyshire.

Viaduct in Monsdale

The Peak District became Britain's first National Park in 1951. This vast rolling landscape stretches for an area of over five hundred square miles and is a favourite with walkers, climbers and pot-holers who congregate on the Pennine Way. The Tissington Trail is equally popular with walkers as it winds its spectacular way around this charming old village. Tissington was responsible for reviving the custom of well-dressing in the seventeenth century, as an act of thanksgiving for its deliverance from the deadly plague. Well-dressing continues to be a popular event in this area to this day.

At the Northern extremity of Derbyshire lies the former spa town of Buxton. This town is a rare gem where elegant sweeping terraces echo those found at Bath. To the southwest, the modern city of Derby is famed for its Crown Derby porcelain. Either of these towns would provide a welcome stopover point for energetic walkers to rest their weary feet.

Matlock is another fine Spa town, developed in the eighteenth century and home to some impressive buildings including the former hydrotherapy centre, perched on a hill above the town. Matlock is also an ideal base from which to venture out on the A6 as it makes its way through the stunning Derwent Gorge. Those travelling to the north of the county will be rewarded by the beauty of two great historic houses, Chatsworth and Haddon Hall.

BOLSOVER CASTLE

Bolsover, Derbyshire
Tel: 01246 823349 (English Heritage)

Winner of the 1995/6 NPI National Heritage Award, having been voted by the public as one of Britain's favourite national treasures. Bolsover has the air of a romantic story book castle. Visitors can explore the enchanting 17th century mansion and 'Little Castle' with its elaborate Jacobean fireplaces, panelling and wall paintings. Discover the mock-medieval fortifications, battlements, ruined staterooms where Charles I was entertained and indoor riding school, one of the oldest in Europe. An inclusive audio tour brings this magical castle to life. **Location:** Off M1 at junction 29, 6m from Mansfield. In Bolsover 6m E of Chesterfield on A632. **Open:** 1 Apr–30 Sept: daily, 10–6pm. 1 Oct–31 Oct: daily, 10–5pm. 1 Nov–31 Mar: Wed–Sun, 10–4pm. (Closed 24–26 Dec). Open 1 Jan 2000. **Admission:** Adults £3.10, concs £2.30, child £1.60. (15% discount for groups of 11 or more).

map 8 D5

CALKE ABBEY

Ticknall, Derby DE73 1LE
Tel: 01332 863822 Fax: 01332 865272

A great house with a big difference! A baroque mansion built 1701–3 for Sir John Harpur and set in a landscaped park. Little restored, Calke is preserved as a graphic illustration of the English country house in decline; contains the family's collection of natural history, a fine 18C state bed and interiors that are virtually unchanged since the 1880s. Walled garden, pleasure grounds and newly restored Orangery. Early 19C church. Historic parkland with Portland sheep and deer. **Open:** 27 Mar–31 Oct, daily except Thurs & Fri 12.45–5.30pm. Last entries 4.45pm. House & church: 1–5.30pm. Garden: 11–5.30pm. Last entries 5pm. House, church & garden closed 14 Aug. Park: open every day, all year, vehicle charge. Shop & restaurant: as house. Christmas shop & restaurant Nov & Dec weekends 11–4pm. **Admission:** £5, child £2.50, family ticket £12.50, gardens only £2.30. NT members free.

map 8 C6

CHATSWORTH

Chatsworth, Bakewell, Derbyshire, DE45 1PP
Tel: 01246 582204 Fax: 01246 583536 (Chatsworth House Trust)

Chatsworth, home of the Duke and Duchess of Devonshire, is one of the great treasure houses of England. Visitors see 26 richly decorated rooms furnished with an outstanding art collection. The 105 acre garden contains famous fountains, the Cascade, greenhouses and a maze. Children of all ages love the Farmyard and the new Adventure Playground. Shops, Restaurant and Bar. Guided tours and Behind the Scenes Day are available. New conference rooms in Stables. **Open:** Daily 17 Mar–31 Oct 1999, 11–4.30pm. **Events:** Angling Fair 8–9 May, International Horse Trials 22–23 May, Flower and Garden Show 26–27 June, Country Fair 4–5 Sept.

map 8 C5

EYAM HALL

Eyam, Hope Valley, Derbyshire, S32 5QW
Tel: 01433 631976 Fax: 01433 631603 E-mail: nicwri@globalnet.co.uk Internet: www.derbyshire.org/eyam-hall (Mr R H V Wright)

Built by the Wright family in 1671 in the famous "plague village" of Eyam and still their family home, Eyam Hall is a cosy and intimate house offering family portraits, costumes, tapestries and other fascinating artefacts collected over 3 centuries. **Location:** Approx. 10 miles from Sheffield, Chesterfield and Buxton and off the A623, Eyam Hall is in the centre of the village. **Open:** Apr–Oct incl. Wed, Thur, Sun & Bank Hol, 11–4pm. **Schools Programme:** phone for details. **Admission:** Adult £4, child £3, conc. £3.50, family £12.50. Party rates available with advance booking. **Craft Centre & Shops** in converted farm buildings; with crafts people at work and a selection of unusual products for sale. **Licensed Buttery** with delicious lunches, light snacks and home-made cakes. **Open:** All year daily except Mons 10.30–5.30pm. **Victorian Christmas Tours** in December – pre-booking essential. Events, concerts and private tours – please enquire.

map 8 C4

HARDSTOFT HERB GARDENS

Hall View Cottage, Hardstoft, Chesterfield, Derbyshire S45 8AH
Tel: 01246 854268

Consists of four display gardens with information boards and well labelled plants. **Location:** On B6039 between Holmewood & Tibshelf, 3m from J29 on M1. **Open:** Daily, 15 Mar–15 Sept, 10–5pm. Closed Tuesday (except Bank Hol). **Admission:** Adult £1, children free.

HARDWICK OLD HALL

Doe Lea, Nr Chesterfield S44 5QJ
Tel: 01246 850431 (English Heritage)

This large ruined house, finished in 1591, still displays Bess of Hardwick's innovative planning and interesting decorative plasterwork. The views from the top floor over the country park and 'New' Hall are spectacular. **Location:** 9½ miles SE of Chesterfield, off A6175, from Jct 29 / M1. **Open:** 1 Apr–31 Oct, Wed–Sun 10–6pm (5pm in October). Admission: Adult £2.50, concessions £1.90, child £1.30.

KEDLESTON HALL AND PARK

Kedleston Hall, Derby DE22 5JH
Tel: 01332 842191 Fax: 01332 841972 (The National Trust)

Experience the age of elegance in this neoclassical house built between 1759 and 1765 for the Curzon Family. Set in 800 acres of parkland with an 18 C pleasure ground, garden and woodland walks. Parties welcome. Introductory talks can be arranged. **Location:** 5m NW of Derby, signposted from roundabout where A38 crosses A52. **Open:** House: 27 Mar–31 Oct daily except Thurs and Fri (closed Good Fri) 12–4.30pm last admissions 4pm. Garden: same days as house 11–6pm. Park: 27 Mar–31 Oct: daily 11–6pm; Nov–Dec: Sat & Sun only 12–4pm. Events: concerts and theatre. Aug BH, Working Crafts Show: details from Property Manager. **Admission:** Adults £4.90, child £2.40, family £12.20. £1 reduction for pre-booked parties of 15+. Park & Garden only: Adults £2.10, child £1 (refundable against tickets for house); Thurs and Fri vehicle charge of £2 for park only.

map 8 C6

HADDON HALL

Bakewell (Derbyshire), Derbyshire
Tel: 01629 812855 Fax: 01629 814379 (The Duke of Rutland)

William the Conqueror's illegitimate son, Peverel and his descendants held Haddon for a hundred years before it passed into the hands of the Vernons. The following four centuries saw the development of the existing medieval and Tudor manor house from its Norman origins. In the late 16th century, it passed through marriage to the Manners family, later to become Dukes of Rutland, in whose possession it has remained ever since. Little has been added since the reign of Henry VIII, whose elder brother was a frequent guest and despite its time-worn steps, no other medieval house has so triumphantly withstood the passage of time. The terraced gardens, one of the chief glories of Haddon, were added during the 16th century. Now with roses, clematis and delphiniums in abundance, it is perhaps the most romantic garden in all England. A popular choice with film producers, Haddon Hall has recently appeared in: Elizabeth 1 (1997); Jane Eyre (1996); The Prince and The Pauper (1996); Moll Flanders (1996). **Location:** On the A6, 2 miles S of Bakewell. Open: 1 Apr–30 Sept, 1999. **Admission:** Adult £5.50, concession £4.75, child £3, family (2+3) £14.75. **Refreshments:** Licensed restaurant serving home-made food.

map 8
C5

LEA GARDENS

Lea, Matlock, Derbys DE4 5GH
Tel: 01629 534380 Fax: 01629 534260 (Mr & Mrs Jonathan Tye)

Visit Lea Gardens where you can see our highly acclaimed unique collection of rhododendrons, azaleas, kalmias and other plants of interest introduced from the far corners of the world. The gardens are sited on the remains of a medieval millstone quarry and cover an area of approximately four acres amidst a wooded hillside. The excellent rock gardens contain a huge variety of alpines with acers, dwarf conifers, heathers and spring bulbs. The teashop on site offers light lunches and home baking. A plant sales area reflects the contents of the garden offering up to 200 varieties of rhododendrons and azaleas. **Open:** Daily 10–7pm, 20 Mar–4 July. **Admission:** Adults £3, children 50p, season ticket £4.

map 8
C6

🏛 MELBOURNE HALL & GARDENS

Melbourne, DE73 1EN
Tel: 01332 862502 Fax: 01332 862263

This beautiful house of history is the home of Lord and Lady Ralph Kerr. Melbourne Hall was once the home of Victorian Prime Minister William Lamb who, as 2nd Viscount Melbourne, gave his name to the famous city in Australia. One of the most famous formal gardens in Britain featuring Robert Bakewell's wrought iron 'Birdcage'. **Location:** 7 m S of Derby off the A453 in village of Melbourne. **Open:** House open every day of Aug only (except first 3 Mons) 2–5pm. Garden open Apr–Sept Weds, Sats and Suns, Bank Hols Mons 2–6pm. **Refreshments:** Melbourne Hall Tearooms and Visitor centre and shops open at various times throughout the year. Car parking limited. Suitable for disabled persons. All enquiries 01332 862502.

map 8
C6

🏛 RENISHAW HALL

Near Sheffield, Derbyshire S21 3WB
Tel: 01777 860755 (Sir Reresby Sitwell)

Home of Sir Reresby and Lady Sitwell. Seven acres of Italian style formal gardens stand in 300 acres of mature parkland, encompassing statues, shaped yew hedges, a water garden and lakes. The Sitwell museum and art gallery (display of Fiori de Henriques sculptures) are located in the Georgian stables alongside craft workshops and café, furnished with contemporary art. Located 3 miles from exit 30 of the M1, equidistant from Sheffield and Chesterfield. Tours of house and gardens can be arranged. Telephone for details. **Open:** Easter to 12 September Fridays, Saturday, Sunday and Bank Holidays 10.30–4.30pm. Free car parking.

map 8
C4

🍂 HARDWICK HALL

Doe Lea, Chesterfield S44 5QJ Tel: 01246 850430 Fax: 01246 854200

Open: Hall: 27 March to 31 Oct: daily except Mon, Tues & Fri (but open BH Mons) 12.30–5pm. Garden: 27 March to 31 Oct: daily 12–5.30pm. Parkland: daily, 7am to 7pm. Old Hall (EH): 27 March to 31 Oct: daily: except Mon & Tues (but open BH Mons and closed Good Fri) 10–6pm. Events: send s.a.e. for details. **Admission:** £6; child £3; family £15. Garden only £3; child £1.50; family £7.50. Groups of 10+ (no reduction) only by written arrangement with Property Manager; Please send s.a.e Vehicles £1.50 (NT members free). Country Park car pak 50p for non-members. Joint ticket for Hall (NT) & Old Hall (EH): Adult £8; child £4; Children under 15 must be accompanied by an adult.

🍂 SUDBURY HALL

Sudbury, Ashbourne, Derbyshire DE6 5HT Tel: 01283 585305 Fax: 01283 585139

Open: 27 March to 31 Oct: daily except Mon & Tues (but open BH Mons & closed Good Fri). 1 April to 30 June, 1 Sept to 1 Nov, Wed to Fri, 1–5.30pm, Sat & Sun 12.30–5pm or sunset if earlier; July & Aug 12.30–5pm. Grounds: as Hall 12.30–6pm. Events: send s.a.e. for details. **Restaurant:** Coach House tea-room as house 12.30–5.30pm; Nov to 19 Dec: Sat & Sun 12–4pm. Coaches by appointment only, write (with s.a.e.) for booking form. **Admission:** £3.60; child £1.80; family £9. Groups £3.25. Joint ticket for Hall & Museum £5.70; child £2.80; family £14.20. Groups by arrangement with the Bookings Secretary.

Devon

There is beauty in Devon, whether inland or seaward. The colour of the soil is most unusual. Nowhere else will you find earth of quite such a rich hue. Nowhere else are the hedges of the fields quite so high or quite so thick.

Devon is a land of infinite variety - in its contours as well as in its colours. Level spaces are so uncommon, cricket pitches are hard to find. It is no place for cyclists, as the hills are ominous and well spread through the whole county. To see the region properly, you should travel on foot.

The varied scenery makes Devon the perfect holiday county. The climate is almost tropical for England – the sun shines warmly, and then the rain appears! This produces lush green beauty and stunning gardens.

Romantic moorland covers vast areas of inland Devon. Dartmoor covers 365 square miles in the south. This is the land of 'The Hound of the Baskervilles'. There are many rare birds that can be seen on the moor, as well as flocks of sheep who keep the undergrowth down and small groups of wild ponies.

The coastline is truly beautiful, with long stretches of sandy beaches. There is a constant reminder of Devon's seafaring history along both coasts. Exeter, Dartmouth and Torbay all offer excellent bases for touring the south of Devon. The varied attractions and beautiful scenery allow you to relax and unwind in this slow moving county.

Barnstaple, on the north coast, is steeped in history. In the centre of the town, on the Strand is a wonderful arcade topped with a statue of Queen Anne.

Don't miss the teas!

South Pool

BICKLEIGH CASTLE

Bickleigh, Nr. Tiverton, EX16 8RP, Devon.
Tel: 01884 855363 (M.J. Boxall)

A Royalist Stronghold with 900 years of history and still lived in. The 11th century detached Chapel, Armoury Guard Room with Tudor furniture and pictures, the Great Hall, Elizabethan bedroom, 17th century farmhouse. Museum of 19th century domestic and agricultural objects and toys. Picturesque moated garden, 'spooky' tower. **Location:** 4 miles south of Tiverton, A396. **Open:** Easter Week (Easter Sun–Fri), then Wed, Sun, Bank Hol Mons to late May Bank Hol; then to early Oct daily (except Sat) 2–5pm. (Last admission 4.30pm). Parties of 20 or more by prior appointment. **Admission:** Adults £4, children (5–15) £2, family ticket £10. Very popular for wedding receptions, civil wedding licence etc. For further details please telephone the Administrator.

map 3 F4

BUCKFAST ABBEY

Buckfastleigh, Devon, TQ11 OEE
Tel: 01364 642519 Fax: 01364 643891 (Buckfast Abbey Trust)

The monks of Buckfast welcome visitors to their famous Abbey–England's only medieval monastery to have been put back to its original use. The magnificent church was rebuilt by just four of the monks; today's activities include bee-keeping and making stained glass and tonic wine. **Location:** ½ mile from the A38 Plymouth to Exeter road at Buckfastleigh. **Open:** Daily all year, church and precinct 5.30–9.30pm; amenities 9–5.30pm (summer), 10–4pm (winter). **Admission:** Free. **Parking:** Free. **Refreshments:** Grange Restaurant serves refreshments and meals (all home-made) all day. Facilities: Exhibition, video, herb gardens, gift shop, bookshop and unique Monastic Shop selling products from Buckfast and many other European abbeys. **Internet:** http://www.buckfast.org.uk/homepage.htm **E-mail:** enquiries@buckfast.org.uk

map 3 F5

CADHAY
Ottery St Mary, EX11 1QT
Tel: 01404 812432 (Mr O William-Powlett)

Cadhay is approached by an avenue of lime-trees and stands in a pleasant listed garden, with herbaceous borders and excellent views over the original medieval fish ponds. Cadhay is first mentioned in the reign of Edward I. The main part of the house was built about 1550 by John Haydon who had married the de Cadhay heiress. He retained the Great Hall of an earlier house, the fine timber roof (about 1420) can be seen. An Elizabethan Long Gallery was added by John's successor in 1617, thereby forming a unique and lovely courtyard. Georgian alterations were made in the mid 18th century. **Location:** 1 mile NW of Ottery St Mary on B3176. **Open:** Late Spring & Summer Bank Hol Suns & Mons, also Tues, Weds, Thurs in July and Aug 2–6 (last adm. 5.30pm) **Admission:** Adults £4, children £2. Groups by arrangement only.

CASTLE DROGO
Drewsteignton, Exeter, Devon, EX6 6PB
Tel: 01647 433306 Fax: 01647 433186 (The National Trust)

This granite castle, built between 1910 and 1930, is one of the most remarkable works of Lutyens. It stands at over 900 feet overlooking the wooded gorge of the river Teign with beautiful views of Dartmoor. Spectacular walks through surrounding 600 acre estate. Formal garden with roses, flowering shrubs and herbaceous borders. **Open:** 1st Apr–1st Nov daily except Fri (open good Fri). Garden, shop, tearoom open daily, 11–5pm. **Admission:** Adults £5.30. Family ticket £13.20. Booked groups £4.40. Garden & Grounds only £2.50. Reduced rate for garden and grounds, Nov to Feb. National Trust members free. **Open:** Castle: 27 March to 31 Oct: daily except Fri (but open Good Fri) 11–5.30pm. Garden: all year: daily 10.30–dusk. Note: Solar Eclipse 11 August – Property will open at the later time of 12 noon.

map 3 F5

FLETE
Ermington, Ivybridge, Plymouth, Devon, PL21 9NZ.
Tel: 01752 830 308 Fax: 01752 830 309
(Country Houses Association)

Built around an Elizabethan manor, with alterations in 1879 by Norman Shaw. Wonderful II drop waterfall garden, designed by Russell Page ably assisted by Laurance of Arabia in the 1920's. **Location:** 11 miles E of Plymouth, at junction of A379 and B3121. **Station(s):** Plymouth (12 miles), Totnes (14 miles). **Bus Route:** No. 93, Plymouth–Dartmouth. **Open:** May–Sept. House and Garden: Wed & Thurs, 2–5pm. (Latest admission time 4.30pm) **Admission:** Adults £3.50, children £1. Garden only: open Sat & Sun 2–5pm. **Admission:** Adults £2.50, children free. Free car park. No dogs admitted.

 map 2 E6

HARTLAND ABBEY & GARDENS
Nr Bideford, North Devon EX39 6DT
Tel: 01237 441264/234 Fax: 01884 861134 (Sir Hugh and Lady Stucley)

Built 1157 in beautiful valley leading to Atlantic cove. Given by Henry VIII to Keeper of his Wine Cellar whose descendants live here today. Remodelled in 18-19th C, contains spectacular architecture and murals, fascinating collections of paintings, furniture, porcelain. Documents & seals from 1160AD; Victorian & Edwardian photographs; Museum; Dairy. Paths by Gertrude Jekyll lead to Bog Garden, Victorian Fernery opening 1999, woodland gardens of camellias, rhododendrons etc., secret 18th C walled gardens. Walk to beach with abundant wildflowers and wildlife. Peacock, donkeys, Jacob's sheep. Cream Teas. 1998 N.P.I. National Heritage Award Winner. **Location:** Off A39, between Hartland and Quay. **Open:** May–Sept incl. Easter Sun/Mon: Weds, Thurs, Suns & BHs, plus Tues in Jul & Aug. 2–5.30pm. **Admission:** House, gardens & grounds: Adults £4.25, child £1.50. Reduction for gardens etc only.

map 2 D3

KILLERTON HOUSE
Broadclyst, Exeter, Devon
Tel: 01392 881345 Fax: 01392 883112

Just 6 miles from Exeter, Killerton is Devon's most popular National Trust property. Elegant 18th century house designed by John Johnson with later additions, home of the Acland family. Also on display is costume from the Killerton Dress collection in a special exhibition for 1999 "Fin de Siècle" – costume from 1890's. Victorian laundry. 18 acre garden landscaped by Veitch with many original plantings of specimens collected by the plant hunters William and Thomas Lobb, Ernest 'Chinese' Wilson. Killerton also has a wonderful early 19th century rustic summer house and an ice house built in 1809. Excellent facilities for the less abled. Children quiz available.

map 3 F4

LYDFORD CASTLES & SAXON TOWN
Lydford, Okehampton, Devon
(site managed by The National Trust)

Standing above the lovely gorge of the River Lyd, this 12th century tower was notorious as a prison. The earthworks of the original Norman fort are to the south. A Saxon town once stood nearby and its layout is still discernible. **Location:** In Lydford off A386 8 miles southwest of Okehampton. **Open:** Any reasonable time.

RHS GARDEN ROSEMOOR
Great Torrington EX38 8PH
Tel: 01805 624067 Fax: 01805 624717 (Royal Horticultural Society)

A garden for all seasons. Lying in the wooded valley of the River Torridge, it includes an informal woodland area, mixed borders and intimate gardens close to the 18th century house. Within its original 8 acres, visitors will see a wide range of plants in a variety of beautiful settings and the Society is in the process of expanding the garden from 8 acres to 40. **Location:** 1 mile SE of Great Torrington on B3220 to Exeter. **Open:** Garden open all year from 10–6 Apr–Sept and 10–5 Oct–Mar. **Admission:** Adults £4, children under 6 yrs free, children 6–16 £1. Groups of more than 10 £3.25. One person accompanying a blind visitor or wheelchair user free. **Refreshments:** A restaurant provides home-made lunches and Devon Cream teas. Coaches welcome by appointment. Dogs are not admitted (except guide dogs).

 map 2 E4

KINGSTON HOUSE

Staverton, Totnes, Devon, TQ9 6AR
Tel: +44(0)1803 762 235 Fax: +44(0)1803 762 444 E-mail: kingston.estate.devon.co.uk (Michael, Elizabeth Corfield)

Kingston House, which was begun in 1726, was built for the wealthy wool merchant John Rowe, whose family had owned the Kingston Estate since 1502. John Rowe, nephew of William Rowe, appointed Lord High Sheriff of Devon by the ill-fated James II during his brief reign of 1685–1688, had a 'fine moderne built mansion' created to the north of the previous house, the ruins of which still survive in the gardens. Kingston House, now the home of the Corfield family, represents one of the finest surviving examples of early 18th century architecture in Britain today, possessing the finest marquetry staircase in England and a wealth of 18th century wall paintings. The Gardens at Kingston, following years of restoration, are approaching maturity and perfectly reflect the style of the period in a number of formal gardens as individual as the rooms of the house itself. **Open:** Gardens & Grounds: 16 May, 20 June & 11 July, in aid of NGS and by prior written agreement. **Dining:** for residents and their guests, the kitchens specialise in English haute cuisine with vegetables, fruit and herbs from the walled garden, to match an extensive cellar. **Accommodation:** Within the Kingston Estate grounds lie a variety of listed buildings built between 1650 and 1830, now sympathetically converted to provide period cottages for guests to stay on the estate. Each cottage has a four-poster bed in the master bedroom, is furnished in keeping and is equipped to an unusually high standard. Three exceptional period suites within the house are also available for visitors wishing to stay in this historic house. **E-mail:** info@kingston−estate.demon.co.uk **Internet:** www.kingston−estate.demon.co.uk

map 3
F5

POWDERHAM CASTLE

Kenton, Exeter EX6 8JQ
Tel: 01626 890243 Fax: 01626 890729 (Lord & Lady Courtenay)

Powderham Castle, the historic family home of the Earl of Devon, lies in an ancient and beautiful setting beside the Exe Estuary. There are regular guided tours of the magnificent State Rooms, beautiful gardens and grounds to explore, including the Children's Secret Garden, in the old Victorian walled garden. In springtime the Woodland Garden is full of colour and later in the summer The Rose Garden provides a fragrant home to Timothy Tortoise, at 155, the World's oldest pet! Powderham's new Farm Shop and Plant Centre open at Easter to provide an excellent new regional shopping centre. Courtyard Restaurant and Gift Shop. **Open:** Every day (except Sat) Grounds 1 March, Castle and grounds from 28 March–31 Oct. Guided tours every half an hour, last admission 5pm. Farm Shop at Powderham Castle – open seven days a week from March. **Admission:** Adult £5.45, Seniors £4.95, child £2.95 (5–16), family ticket £13.85 (2 Adults & 2 Children). **Location:** Signposted on A379 Exeter to Dawlish Road. Tel 01626 890243 for all information.

map 3
G5

TIVERTON CASTLE

Tiverton, Devon, Ex16 6RP. Tel: 01884 253200/255200
Fax: 01884 253200 (Mr & Mrs A. K. Gordon)

Few buildings evoke such an immediate feeling of history as Tiverton Castle. Originally built in 1106 by Richard de Redvers, Earl of Devon, on the orders of Henry I, it was then rebuilt in stone in 1293. Now many styles of architecture down the ages, from medieval to the present day can be seen. The magnificent medieval gatehouse and tower contain Civil War armoury. Furnishings and exhibits reflect the colourful history of the Castle and with continuing restoration there is always something new and interesting to see. Old walls, new gardens. **Open:** Easter–end of June and Sept. Sun, Thurs & Bank Hol Mon. July & Aug, Sun–Thurs, 2.30–5.30pm. Open at other times to parties of 12+ by prior arrangement. **Admission:** Adults £3, children (7–16) £2, (under 7) free. **Accommodation:** 4 superb self-catering holiday apartments. 4 keys, highly commended.

map 3
F4

TORRE ABBEY

The Kings Drive, Torquay TQ2 5JX
Tel: 01803 293593 Fax: 01803 215948 (Torbay Council)

For 800 years, Torre Abbey has been the home of Torquay's leading citizens. Founded as a monastery in 1196, the Abbey later became a country house and the Cary family's residence for nearly 300 years. As well as important monastic remains, you can see over twenty historic rooms, including the beautiful family chapel, a splendid collection of paintings and Torquay terracotta, colourful gardens and mementoes of crime writer Agatha Christie. Teas are served in the Victorian kitchen. **Open:** Daily, Easter to 1 Nov, 9.30–6pm. Last admission 5pm.

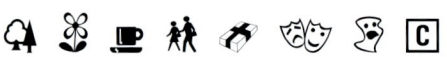

map 3
F5

UGBROOKE PARK

Chudleigh, Devon, TQ13 OAD
Tel: 01626 852179 Fax: 01626 853322 (Lord Clifford)

Beautiful scenery and quiet parkland in the heart of Devon. Original House and Church built about 1200, redesigned by Robert Adam. Home of the Cliffords of Chudleigh. Ugbrooke contains fine furniture, paintings, beautiful embroideries, porcelain, rare family military collection. Capability Brown Park with lakes, majestic trees, views to Dartmoor. Guided tours relate stories of Clifford Castles, Shakespeare's 'Black Clifford', Henry II's 'Fair Rosamund', Lady Anne Clifford who defied Cromwell, The Secret Treaty, the Cardinal's daughter, Clifford of the CABAL and tales of intrigue, espionage and bravery. **Location:** Chudleigh, Devon. **Open:** 11 July–2 Sept, Sun, Tues, Wed & Thurs. Grounds open 1–5.30pm. Guided tours of House 2pm and 3.45pm. **Admission:** Adults £4.50. Children (5–16) £2. Groups (over 20) £4. Private party tours/functions by arrangement.

map 3
F5

TOTNES CASTLE

Castle Street, Totnes TQ9 5NU
Tel: 01803 864406 (English Heritage)

By the North Gate of the hill town of Totnes you will find a superb motte and bailey castle, with splendid views across the roof tops and down to the River Dart. It is a symbol of lordly feudal life and a fine example of Norman fortification. **Location:** In Totnes, on the hill overlooking the town. Access in Castle Street off west end of High Street. **Open:** 1 Apr–end Sept: daily 10–6pm. Oct: daily 10–5pm. Nov–31 Mar: Wed–Sun 10–4pm. Closed 1–2pm in winter. **Admission:** Please call for admission charges.

YARDE

Yarde Farm, Malborough, Kingsbridge, Devon TQ7 3BY
Tel: 01548 842367 (John and Marilyn Ayre)

Grade I listed. An outstanding example of the Devon farmstead with a Tudor Bakehouse, Elizabethan farmhouse and Queen Anne mansion under restoration. Still a family farm. **Location:** On A381 ½ mile E of Malborough. 4 miles S of Kingsbridge. **Open:** Easter–31 Sept, Sun 11–5pm. **Admission:** Adults £2, children 50p, under 5s free.

map 3
F6

Dorset

The countryside of Dorset is bewitching. From dawn till dusk, through each season, the changing light reveals a new slant to the landscape. You could not describe the countryside as wild or grand, just charming and a little quaint, the home to beautiful thatched flint-and-chalk cottages.

Around Lyme Regis, which is at Dorset's western point, the cliffs are forbearing. The Purbeck Hills once linked the headlands of Brittany with the white cliffs of Dover.

The county town, Dorchester, is still recognized as the backdrop for Thomas Hardy's novel 'The Mayor of Casterbridge'. The high street is lined with 17th century and Georgian houses. The town has a wonderful feel to it, with many small and friendly places to eat.

North of Poole stands Wimbourne Minster, which was Thomas Hardy's home for many years. Comparisons are often drawn between Dorset and Hardy's 'Wessex' but many other authors such as Jane Austen and Sir Arthur Conan Doyle have their own connections with the area.

Cranborne, to the north of Wimbourne Minster, is a beautiful village on the edge of what used to be a royal forest and is now a stunning woodland.

The county holds a vast number of historic properties and some of the most beautiful gardens in England; they are well worth a visit.

Hardy's Cottage

ATHELHAMPTON HOUSE & GARDENS

Athelhampton, Dorchester
Tel: 01305 848363 Fax: 01305 848135 (Patrick Cooke)

Athelhampton House contains many finely furnished rooms including The Great Hall, Great Chamber, Wine Cellar and the Library & Billiard Room. The glorious Grade I garden, dating from 1891, is full of vistas and gains much from the fountains and River Piddle flowing through. The walled gardens include the world famous topiary pyramids and collections of tulips, magnolias, roses, clematis and lilies in season. Also 15th century Dovecote. **Location:** 5 miles east of Dorchester off A35(T) at Puddletown (Northbrook) junction. Follow brown signs for 1½ miles. **Open:** Mar–Oct daily (except Sat) 10.30–5pm. Nov–Feb, Sun 10.30–5pm. Restaurant serving lunches, cream teas and refreshments. Gift shop and free car park. Winner of the HHA/Christies Garden of the Year Award.

CHIFFCHAFFS

Chaffeymoor, Bourton, Gillingham, SP8 5BY, Dorset.
Tel: 01747 840841(Mr & Mrs K. R. Potts)

The garden surrounds a typical 400 year old stone Dorset cottage, which contains a very wide range of bulbs, alpines, herbaceous trees and shrubs, many of them unusual. It is planted for long periods of interest and divided into small individual gardens with many surprise views. In addition, we have a 1.5 acre woodland garden filled with azaleas, camellias, rhododendrons, bog primulas and daffodils, etc, and a host of unusual trees and shrubs. The bluebells are particularly beautiful in the spring. **Location:** 3 miles E of Wincanton, just off A303. **Open:** 30 Mar–30 Sept. Every Wed & Thurs and 1st & 3rd Sun each month and Bank Hol Weekends, 2–5.30pm. Also by appointment. Groups welcome. **Admission:** £2. **Refreshments:** By arrangement.

map 3
J3

CHRISTCHURCH PRIORY

Quay Road, Christchurch, Dorset BH23 1BU
Tel: 01202 485804 Fax: 01202 488645

A medieval monastic church begun in 1094. Famous for the "Miraculous Beam", Norman nave, turret, monks' quire, Jesse reredos to high altar, Lady Chapel, chantries, 15th century bell tower and St Michael's Loft, a former school, now a museum. Guided tours can be arranged. **Admission:** No charge, but donations invited of £1 per adult and 20p per student. Charge to ascend tower: adult 50p, child/student 30p; to visit museum: adult 50p, child/student 30p. **Open:** Every day except 25 Dec subject to church services: weekdays 9.30–5pm, Sun 2.15–5pm. Church Services: Sun: 8am Holy Communion, 9.45am Sung Eucharist, 11.15am Choral Matins & sermon, 6.30pm Choral Evensong & sermon. Weekdays: 7.30am morning prayer, 8am Holy Communion. Thurs 11 Holy Communion, 5.30 daily, evening prayer. **Internet:** http://www.resort–guide.co.uk/christchurch–priory

map 3
K4

COMPTON ACRES GARDENS

Canford Cliffs Road, Poole, Dorset
Tel: 01202 700778 Fax: 01202 707537 (Mr L. Green)

Compton Acres is set in a delightful area of Canford Cliffs in Poole, overlooking Poole Harbour and the Purbeck Hills beyond. Covering nearly ten acres, the nine gardens include an Italian Garden, an authentic Japanese Garden, a Rock and Water Garden and a Woodland Walk. The Tea Rooms and Terrace Brasserie serve a variety of food throughout the day, with our gift shop, ice cream parlour and well stocked Garden Centre. Compton Acres is one of the south's top attractions. **Location:** Off the B3065 onto Canford Cliffs Road. **Open:** 1 Mar–end Oct. **Admission:** Adult £4.95, senior citizen £3.95, child £1. Group rates 20+, adult £4.20, senior citizen £3.20, child 90p.

map 3
K5

CRANBORNE MANOR GARDEN

Cranborne, BH21 5PP
Tel: 01725 517248, Fax: 01725 517862
(The Viscount and Viscountess Cranborne)

Walled gardens, yew hedges and lawns; wild garden with spring bulbs, herb garden, Jacobean mount garden, flowering cherries and collection of old-fashioned and specie roses. Beautiful and historic garden laid out in the 17th century by John Tradescant and much embellished in the 20th century. **Location:** 18 miles N of Bournemouth B3078; 16 miles S of Salisbury A354, B3081. **Open:** Garden Centre open Mon–Sat 9–5pm, Sun 10–5pm. Something for every gardener, but specialising in old-fashioned and specie roses, herbs, ornamental pots and garden furniture. Garden only Mar–Sept, Wed 9–5pm. South Court occasionally closed. Free car park.

map 3
K5

HORN PARK GARDENS

Horn Park, Beaminster, Dorset
Tel: 01308 862 212 (Mr & Mrs John Kirkpatrick)

Large and beautiful garden. House built 1910 by a pupil of Lutyens – unique position, magnificent view to sea. Plantsman's garden, unusual trees, shrubs and plants in rock, water gardens terraces and herbaceous borders. Woodland Garden, Bluebell Woods, Wild flower meadow with over 160 species including orchids. Plants for sale. In RHS "Twelve Beautiful Gardens" calendar for 1998. Wedding receptions. **Location:** 1.5 miles N of Beaminster on A3066. **Station(s):** Crewkerne. **Open:** 1 Apr–31 Oct. Every Sun–Thur incl., 2–6pm & Bank Hol Mons. **Admission:** Adults £3. (Under 16 and wheelchair users free). Groups welcome any day or time, by prior arrangement, with teas if booked. Dogs on leads.

map 3
H4

DEANS COURT GARDEN

Deans Court, Wimborne, BH21 1EE, Dorset.
(Sir Michael & Lady Hanham)

Location: 13 peaceful acres few minutes walk from Minster. **Garden:** partly wild with specimen trees, peacocks, monastery fishpond, herb garden with over 200 species. Kitchen Garden with 18th century serpentine wall. **House:** Early Georgian with medieval origins and 19th century and later work. Free parking. Wholefood, home-made teas. Chemical–free plants and produce usually available. **Open:** Garden: Sun 4 Apr, 2 May, 29 Aug, 19 Sept, 2–6pm. Mon 5 Apr, 3 May, 30 Aug, 10–6pm. Organic Gardening Weekend Sat & Sun 7/8 Aug 2–6pm. Sculpture in the Garden Exhibition 30 May–30 June Fri 2–8pm; other days 2–6pm. Closed Mon 7, 14, 21 & 28 June. **Admission:** Adults £2; OAPs £1.50; children (5–15)50p. Different rates for Sculpture Exhibition. **House:** By written appointment–rates on application. Groups welcomed by prior written application.

map 3
K4

FORDE ABBEY AND GARDENS

Forde Abbey, Chard, Somerset TA20 4LU
Tel: 01460 221290, Fax: 01460 220296 (Mr M Roper)

Forde Abbey is the finest example of a Cistercian monastery still used as a family home today. The House contains a collection of magnificent Mortlake tapestries. The Abbey is surrounded by 30 acres of gardens with many unusual plants and shrubs. In the Spring, the garden is awash with spring bulbs and throughout the season there is always something of interest, including azaleas, magnolias, herbaceous borders, rock garden and bog garden. **Location:** 1 mile E of Chard Junction, 4 miles SE of Chard signposted off A30. **Open:** Gardens open daily throughout the year 10–4.30pm. House open April 1–end Oct, Sun, Wed & Bank Hols 1–4.30pm. Also open Thurs in June, July & August. **Admission:** House and gardens: Please telephone for details. **Refreshments:** Undercroft open for light lunches and teas 11–4.30 daily Easter – end Oct.

map 3
H4

KINGSTON LACY HOUSE, PARK & GARDEN

Wimborne, Dorset BH21 4EA
Tel: 01202 883402 Fax: 01202 882402 (The National Trust)

Beautiful 17th century house containing an outstanding collection of paintings, including works by Van Dyck, Titian and Brueghel. Fascinating interiors including the fabulous gilded leather Spanish Room. Exhibition of Egyptian artefacts from 3000BC. 250 acres of wooded parkland with splendid Red Devon cattle. New way marked walks now open. NT shop and restaurant. Dogs welcome in park and woods only. On B3082, Blandford Wimborne road. 1.5 miles from Wimborne. **Open:** House: 27 Mar–31 Oct 99, daily except Thur & Fri, 12–5.30pm (last admission 4.30) Garden and Park: 27 Mar–31 Oct 99, daily 11–6pm. For further information on events and winter openings please contact the House Manager, Kingston Lacy House, Wimborne, Dorset BH21 4EA. Tel No: 01202 883402. For an Events leaflet, please ring:– Kingston Lacy Estate Office on: 01202 882705.

map 3 K4

KINGSTON MAURWARD GARDENS

Dorchester, Dorset DT2 8PY
Tel: 01305 215000 Fax: 01305 215001

Kingston Maurward Gardens are set deep in Hardy's Dorset and are listed on the English Heritage register of Gardens. The 35 acres of classical 18th century parkland and lawns sweep majestically down to the lake from the Georgian House. The Edwardian Gardens include a croquet lawn, rose garden, herbaceous borders and large displays of tender perennials including the National Collections of Penstemons and Salvias. Stone terraces, balustrading and yew hedges have been used to create many intimate gardens and carefully planned vistas. The walled demonstration garden is planted with a superb collection of hedges and plants suitable for growing in Dorset. Lakeside Nature and tree trails, animal park, guided tours and lectures, conference centre, restaurant, visitor centre and plant sales. **Open:** 14 Mar–31 Oct, seven days a week from 10–5.30pm.

map 3 J5

LULWORTH CASTLE

The Lulworth Estate, East Lulworth, Wareham, Dorset BH20 5QS
Tel: 01929 400352

Lulworth Castle has been the home of the Weld family since 1641. Tragically the Castle endured a serious fire in 1929 but has been restored by English Heritage. In the Castle visitors can learn about the history of the Castle and the whole Estate. The Children's Farm gives the opportunity to meet a variety of animals and learn about rare breeds. The Courtyard Shop stocks a wide range of quality gifts and food and the Stable Café serves home-cooked meals all day with produce supplied from Mrs Weld's kitchen garden. A number of walks round the Estate are found within the guide books. Dogs welcome. **Open:** Summer 10–6pm, Winter 10–4pm.

map 3 J5

 # MAPPERTON

Mapperton, Beaminster, Dorset DT8 3NR
Tel: 01308 862645 Fax: 01308 863348 (Earl & Countess of Sandwich)

Terraced valley gardens surround charming Tudor/Jacobean manor house, stable blocks, dovecote and All Saints' Church. Pevsner's Dorset guide says, "There can hardly be anywhere a more enchanting manorial group than Mapperton". Above, the Orangery and Italianate formal garden with fountain court and topiary. Below, a 17th century summer house and fishponds. Lower garden with specimen shrubs and trees. Magnificent walks and views. Shop with plants, pots and gift items. Featured in Country Life, Country Living, Daily Telegraph and used as location in films, 'Emma', 'Restoration' and the BBC's 'Tom Jones'. **Location:** 1 mile off B3163, 2 miles off B3066. **Station:** Crewkerne. **Open:** Mar–Oct daily 2–6pm. **Admission:** Adults £3, under 18s £1.50, under 5s free. House open to group tours by appointment, adults £3.

map 3 H4

MINTERNE GARDENS

Minterne Magna, Nr Dorchester, Dorset, DT2 7AU
Tel: 01300 341 370 (The Lord Digby)

If you want a formal immaculate garden, do not come to Minterne, but if you want to wander peacefully through 20 wild woodland acres, where magnolias, rhododendrons, eucryphias, hydrangeas, water plants & water lilies, provide a new vista at each turn, and where ducks enhance the small lakes and cascades, then you will be welcome at Minterne, the home of the Churchill & Digby families for 350 years. **Location:** On A352 Dorchester/Sherborne Rd 2 miles N of Cerne Abbas. **Open:** Daily, 28 March–10 November 10–7pm. **Admission:** Adults £3 (Acc. children free).

map 3 J4

PARNHAM HOUSE & GARDENS

Parnham, Beaminster, Dorset
Tel: 01308 862 204 Fax: 01308 863 444 (John & Jennie Makepeace)

Tudor manor house built in 1540, enlarged by John Nash in 1810. Inspiring 20th century craftsmanship in the home of John and Jennie Makepeace, who have restored and enlivened this fascinating historic house and beautiful gardens into a world-renowned centre of excellence. Surrounded by 14 acres of formal and informal gardens, extensively restored and replanted by Jennie Makepeace. Parnham lies in a hidden valley, deep in the beautiful countryside of West Dorset. Furniture commissioned for public and private collections is designed by John Makepeace and can be seen in his studio. Pieces are available for sale or can be commissioned during your visit. **Location:** Take exit 25 from M5. From London take M3/A303 Crewkerne-Beaminster Road. Follow A3066. Parnham is ½ mile S of Beaminster. 5 miles N of Bridport. **Open:** 1 Apr–31 Oct, Sun, Tues, Weds, Thurs and Bank Holidays 10–5pm. **Admission:** Adults £5, children (5–15) £2, children (under 5) free, students £2. **Refreshments:** Licensed Buttery with delicious home-made food, tea and coffee. **John Makepeace Furniture Studio:** Unique furniture in the making. **Shop:** books and exciting work by British craftsmen and women in textiles, ceramics and wood. Available for weddings, film location and events.

map 3 H4

PURSE CAUNDLE MANOR

Purse Caundle, Nr. Sherborne, Dorset, DT9 5DY
Tel: 01963 250400 (Michael de Pelet Esq)

Interesting 15th/16th century Manor House. Lived in as a family home. Great Hall with minstrel gallery; Winter Parlour; Solar with oriel; bedchambers; garden. Not commercialised! Come and visit us. **Location:** 4 miles E of Sherborne; ¼ mile S of A30. **Open:** Easter Mon and May–Sept. Thurs, Sun & Bank Hol Mon 2–5pm showing every half hour. Coaches welcomed by appointment. **Admission:** £2.50. Children free. Free car park. **Refreshments:** Home-made cream teas by prior arrangement at £2 each for coach parties.

map 3 J4

MILTON ABBEY CHURCH

Milton Abbas, Nr. Blandford, Dorset, DT11 0BP
Tel: 01258 880489 (Organising Secretary)

A Church has stood here for over 1000 years. The present Abbey dates from the 14/15th century. The 18th century Gothic style house was built to compliment the Abbey & ancient Abbots Hall. Exterior by Sir William Chambers, interior in classic style by James Wyatt. Idyllic tranquil setting in the heart of Dorset, 1/2 mile from 200 year old 'new' village of Milton Abbas with its identical cottages. The Abbey is situated in grounds of Milton Abbey School and owned by diocese of Salisbury. **Location:** 3 1/2 from A354 (Puddletown to Blandford road). **Open:** Abbey Church throughout the year. House and grounds: Easter, Mid-July – End August, 10–6pm. **Admission:** Adults £1.75, Children free. when house and grounds are open. At other times donations are invited.

map 4 A6

SANDFORD ORCAS MANOR HOUSE

The Manor House, Sandford Orcas, Sherborne, Dorset DT9 4SB.
Tel: 01963 220206 (Sir Mervyn Medlycott, Bt.)

Tudor Manor House in remarkable original state of preservation, with gatehouse, spiral staircases and Tudor and Jacobean panelling. Fine collection of 14th–17th century stained glass, Queen Anne and Chippendale furniture, Elizabethan and Georgian needlework and 17th century Dutch paintings. Terraced gardens, with fine mature trees, topiary and herb garden. **Location:** 2 miles N or Sherborne, entrance next to church. **Open:** Easter Mon 10–6pm then May–Sept: Suns 2–6pm & Mons 10–6pm. **Admission:** £2.50, children £1. Pre-booked parties (of 10 or more) at reduced rates on other days if preferred.

map 3 J4

THE OLD RECTORY

Litton Cheney, Dorset
Tel: 01308 482 383 (Mr & Mrs Hugh Lindsay)

Greatly varied garden with small walled garden, partly paved with a prolific quince tree. A steep path leads to 4 acres of beautiful natural woodland on steep slope with springs, streams and ponds, primulas, native plants, wild flower lawn. (Stout shoes recommended). **Location:** 1 mile S of A35. 10 miles from Dorchester. 6 miles from Bridport. **Open:** For NGS. Also open with Little Cheney Gardens. Private visits also welcome by appointment, Apr–June. **Admission:** Charges apply. Please phone for details. Limited parking for infirm and elderly, otherwise park in village and follow signs. Plants available for sale.

map 3 H5

ST CATHERINE'S CHAPEL

Abbotsbury, Dorset
Tel: 01179 750700 (English Heritage)

A small stone chapel, set on a hilltop, with an unusual roof and small turret used as a lighthouse. **Location:** ½ mile S of Abbotsbury by pedestrian track to the hilltop. **Open:** Any reasonable times. For further information on admission please contact the S.W. regional office.

SHERBORNE OLD CASTLE

Castleton, Sherborne DT9 3SA
Tel: 01935 812730 (English Heritage)

The ruins of this 12th century castle are a testament to the 16 days it took Cromwell to capture it during the Civil War, after which it was abandoned. A gatehouse, some graceful arcading and decorative windows survive. **Location:** ½m E of Sherborne off B3145. ½m N of the 1594 castle. **Open:** 1 Apr–30 Sept, 10–6pm. 1–31 Oct, 10–5pm. 1 Nov–31 Mar, 10–4pm (but closed Mondays and Tuesdays). **Admission:** Adult £1.60, concessions £1.20, children (under 5's free) 80p.

SHERBORNE CASTLE

Sherborne DT9 3PY
Tel: 01935 813182, Fax: 01935 816727 (Sherborne Castle Estates)

Built by Sir Walter Raleigh in 1594. Home of the Digby family since 1617. The House contains fine furniture, porcelain and pictures. Set in 20 acres of lawns and pleasure grounds planned by 'Capability' Brown around the 50 acre lake. **Location:** 5 miles E of Yeovil off A30 to S, Station Sherborne. **Open:** 1 Apr–end Oct, Grounds open daily except Wed. Tues, Thurs, Sat, Sun and Bank Hol Mons. Castle open 1.30 – last admissions 5pm. Grounds and tearoom 12.30–6pm. Tearoom open for light lunches and teas. Well stocked gift shop. Other times by appointment (Party rates 25 or more). **Admission:** Charges on request, parties by arrangement. **Refreshments:** Tearoom. **Events/Exhibitions:** Various, telephone for details. Gift shop. Car parking on site.

map 3 J4

WOLFETON HOUSE

Dorchester, Dorset DT2 9QN
Tel: 01305 263 500 Fax: 01305 265090 (Capt. NTLL Thimbleby)

A fine medieval and Elizabethan Manor House lying in the water-meadows near the confluence of the Rivers Cerne and Frome. It was much embellished around 1580 and has splendid plaster ceilings, fireplaces and panelling of that date. See the Great Hall, stairs and chamber; parlour, dining room, chapel and cyder house. The medieval gatehouse has two unmatched and older towers. There are many fine works of art. **Location:** 1.5 miles from Dorchester on Yeovil road (A37); indicated by Historic House signs. **Station(s):** Dorchester South and West, 1.75 miles. **Open:** 1 May–30 Sept. Sun, Tues, Thurs & BHols. At other times throughout the year parties by arrangement. **Admission:** Charges not available at time of going to press. **Refreshments:** Ploughman's lunches, teas, evening meals for groups by arrangement. Cyder for sale. Available for weddings, parties etc.

map 3 J4

CLOUDS HILL

Wareham, Dorset BH20 7NQ Tel: 01929 405616

Open: 28 March to 31 Oct: daily except Mon, Tues & Sat (but open BH Mons) 12–5pm or dusk if earlier; no electric light. Groups wishing to visit at other times must tel. in advance. **Admission:** £2.30. No reduction for groups or children. Unsuitable for coaches or trailer caravans. No WC

HARDY'S COTTAGE

Higher Bockhampton, nr Dorchester DT2 8QJ Tel: 01305 262366

Open: 28 March to 31 Oct: daily except Fri & Sat (but open Good Fri) 11–5pm (or dusk if earlier). Cottage is 10min walk through woods from car park. **Admission:** £2.60. No reduction for children or parties. School parties and coaches by arrangement only. No WC. Hardy's works on sale.

CORFE CASTLE

Corfe Castle, Wareham BH20 5EZ Tel/fax: 01929 481294

Open: Daily, (closed 25, 26 Dec and for 2 days at end Jan). 1–27 March & 25–31 Oct: daily 10–4.30pm; 28 March to 24 Oct: 10–5.30pm; 1 Nov to 4 March 2000: 11–3.30pm. **Admission:** £4, children £2; family tickets £10 (2 adults & 3 children)/£6 (1 adult & 3 children). Groups £3.50, children £1.80. Car & coach-parking available at Castle View off A351; also at Norden park & ride and West St (not NT).

MAX GATE

Alington Avenue, Dorchester, Dorset Tel: 01305 262538 Fax: 01305 250978

Open: 28 March to 29 Sept: Mon, Wed & Sun 2–5pm. Note: Only dining and drawing room open. Private visits, tours and seminars by schools, colleges and literary societies by appointment with the tenants, Mr & Mrs Andrew Leah. **Admission:** £2.10, child £1.10. No reduction for groups. No WC

County Durham

A county of moors and rivers, County Durham is renowned for its fascinating heritage and magnificent scenery. One of the most famous of its vistas can be seen in the city of Durham itself, where the mighty towers of the cathedral stand silhouetted over the River Wear. Durham Cathedral has huge dimensions with 900 year old columns, piers and ribbed vaults.

The city was built in its entirety in the year 995 on 'Dunholm' or Island Hill, a rocky peninsula quite unique to Durham. To this day, the ancient centre of Durham is reached by a series of bridges that connect the older buildings with the modern town that has developed over the centuries.

Moving westwards from this historic city, the beautiful moorland scenery features a series of stunning Pennine valleys and spectacular waterfalls. Visit Teesdale's high force waterfall for a particularly splendid example of Durham's rugged beauty.

Barnard Castle, locally known as 'Barney', is a pretty little town, littered with cobble stone roads and a market place. The town is overlooked by the ruins of a Norman castle, hence its namesake.

The crumbly 'Cotherstone' sheep's cheese is a speciality of the dales surrounding Middleton-in-Teesdale.

Low Force Waterfall

AUCKLAND CASTLE

Bishop Auckland, Co Durham, DL14 7NR
Tel: 01388 601627

Principal country residence of the Bishops of Durham since Norman times and now the official residence of the present day Bishops. State Rooms, Chapel and Exhibition area available to visitors. Also access to the adjacent Bishop's park and 18th century Deerhouse. **Open:** 2–5pm May, June & September – Friday and Sunday; July – Thursday, Friday and Sunday; August – Wednesday, Thursday, Friday, Saturday and Sunday. Also the same hours on Bank Holiday Mondays. **Admission:** Adults £3, children over 12 and over 60's £2, children under 12 free. Excellent venues for concerts, exhibitions, conferences and meetings. **E-mail:** auckland.castle@zetnet.co.uk **Internet:** www.auckland–castle.co.uk

`map 11 H5`

⬚ AUCKLAND CASTLE DEER HOUSE

Bishop Auckland, Durham
Tel: 01912 611585 (English Heritage)

A charming building erected in 1760 in the park of the Bishops of Durham so that the deer could shelter and find food. Location: In Bishops Auckland Park, just north of town centre on A689. About 500 yards N of the castle. **Open:** Daily, May–Sept, 7am–sunset. **Admission:** Free. **Location:** In Bishop Auckland Park, just North of town centre on A689. About 500 yards North of the castle.

⬚ BARNARD CASTLE

Castle House, Durham DL12 9AT
Tel: 01833 638212 (English Heritage)

The substantial remains of this large Castle stand on a rugged escarpment overlooking the River Tees. Parts of the 14th century Great Hall and the cylindrical 12th century tower, built by the Baliol family can still be seen. **Location:** In Barnard Castle. No Parking. **Open:** 1 Apr–end Sept, 10–6pm. October, 10–5pm. 1 Nov–31 Mar, 10–4pm. Closed Mondays & Tuesdays. **Admission:** Adult £2.30, concesssions £1.70, children £1.20, under 5's free.

`map 11 G5`

DURHAM CASTLE
Durham, DH1 3RW
Tel: 01913 743 800 Fax: 01913 747 470 (The University of Durham)

Durham Castle, the former home of the Prince Bishop of Durham, was founded in the 1070s. Since 1832 it has been the foundation College of the University of Durham. With the Cathedral it is a World Heritage Site. Important features include the Norman Chapel (1072), the Great Hall (1284), the Norman Doorway (1540s). With its 14th century style Keep it is a fine example of a Motte and Bailey Castle. In vacations the Castle is a conference and holiday centre and prestige venue for banquets etc. **Location:** In the centre of the city (adjoining Cathedral).

Station(s): Durham (½ mile) **Open:** Guided tours only Apr–June daily 2–4pm. July–Sept daily 10–12 noon and 2–4pm. Oct–Mar Mon, Wed, Sat, Sun 2–4pm. **Admission:** £3 children £2, family ticket £6.50. Guide book £2.50. **Events/ Exhibitions:** Contact conference and accommodation secretary 0191 374 3863 **Accommodation:** Contact conference and accommodation secretary 0191 374 3863. **Conferences:** Contact conference and accommodation secretary 0191 374 3863 Fax 0191 374 7470.

map 11
H4

RABY CASTLE
Staindrop, Darlington, Co. Durham, DL2 3AY
Tel: 01833 660 202 Fax: 01833 660169 (The Lord Barnard, T.D.).

Principally 14th century, alterations made in 1765 and mid-19th century. The Castle is one of the largest 14th century castles in Britain and was built by the Nevills, although one of the towers probably dates back to the 11th century. Interior mainly 18th and 19th century; medieval kitchen and Servants' Hall. Fine pictures of the English, Dutch and Flemish Schools and good period furniture. Collection of horse-drawn carriages and fire-engines. Large walled gardens. **Location:** 1 mile N of Staindrop village, on the Barnard Castle-Bishop Auckland Road (A688). **Station(s):** Bishop Auckland & Darlington. **Open:** Easter Weekend (Sat–Wed). 1 May–30 June, Wed & Sun. 1

July–30 Sept, daily (except Sat). May & Spring & Summer Bank Hols, Sat–Wed. Castle: 1–5pm. Park & Gardens: 11–5.30pm. **Admission: Castle, Park & Gardens:** Adults £4.00, children £1,50, OAPs £3.00, Family (2 adults & 3 children) £10.00. **Park & Gardens only:** Adults £1.50, children/OAPs £1.00. Separate admission charge for Bulmer's Tower when open. Rates may vary when charity events are held. Special terms for parties of 25+ on above days by arrangement. (Tel. the Curator). **Refreshments:** Tea at the Stables. Picnic area. **E-mail:** admin@rabycastle.com

map 11
G5

Essex

Dedham

ssex is the most generous and least ambitious of the Home Counties. Rumour suggests that it is monotonous – and although it boasts no mountains nor hills, the chalk uplands of the north-west are compensation for the lack of sterner beauty.

True, the county is pancake flat in comparison to the neighbouring hump of Suffolk and hop fields of Kent. Yet this unwrinkled landscape favours Essex as a far more accessible and pleasurable place to explore on foot or bike. Visitors are able to truly appreciate its gentle patchwork countryside and experience its wider, soft-hued horizon.

Dotted between nature's mosaic, the inland towns of Essex, such as Coggeshall, Dedham and Ingatstone, wait patiently for visitors. Like old gentlemen bursting with incredible stories of battle, war and witchcraft to tell, they sit silently, anxious to be asked.

The towns on the coast have well defined characters of their own. The quayside of Maldon, locally known as the Hythe, is an ideal place to view the Thames sailing barges. Travel to Burnham-On-Crouch, which is the sailing home of Essex.

The last week in August is Burnham Sailing Week, when the whole place heaves with sailors and nautical groupies.

AUDLEY END HOUSE

Saffron Waldon, Essex
Tel: 01799 522842 (English Heritage)

"Too large for a King but might do for a Lord Treasurer", was how King James I described Audley End, built by his own Lord Treasurer Thomas Howard. Come and see its wonderful palatial interiors containing a famous picture collection and even an intriguing display of over 1,000 stuffed animals and birds. Then, stroll in 'Capability' Brown's fine landscaped parkland with its enchanting follies and see the colourful Parterre Garden. **Location:** 1m W of Saffron Walden on B1383 (M1 exits 8, 9 Northbound only & 10) **Open:** 1 Apr–30 Sept: Wed–Sun, 11–6pm. Last admissions 5pm. 1 Oct–31Oct: Wed–Sun, 10am–3pm: Guided tour only. (Closed 24–26 Dec). **Admission:** House & Grounds: Adult £6, concs £4.50, child £3, family £15. Grounds only: Adult £3.75, concs £2.80, child £1.90 (15% discount for groups of 11 or more).

map 5 **F2**

CHELMSFORD CATHEDRAL

New Street, Chelmsford, Essex CM1 1AT
Tel: 01245 294480

15th century building became a Cathedral in 1914. Extended in 1920's, major refurbishment in 1980's with contemporary works of distinction and a splendid new organ in 1994. **Location:** In Chelmsford. **Open:** Daily: 8–5.30pm. Sun services: 8am, 9.30am, 11.15am, and 6pm. Weekday services: 8.15am and 5.15pm.

GOSFIELD HALL

Halstead, Essex, CO9 1SF
Tel: 01787 472 914 Fax: 01787 479551(Country Houses Association)

Very fine Tudor gallery. **Location:** 2½ miles SW of Halstead on Braintree/Haverhill Road (A1017). **Stations(s):** Braintree. Bus route 352 Braintree-Halstead. **Open:** May–Sept, Weds and Thurs 2–5pm. House tours 2.30 and 3.15pm. Latest admission time 3.15pm. **Admission:** Adults £2.50, children 50p, groups £2.50 per head. Free car park. **Conferences:** By arrangement. No dogs admitted.

map 5 **G2**

HEDINGHAM CASTLE

Castle Hedingham, Nr. Halstead, Essex CO9 3DJ
Tel: 01787 460261 Fax: 01787 461473 (The Hon. Thomas Lindsay)

One of the finest and best preserved Norman keeps in England, it was built in 1140 by Aubrey de Vere. The keep walls are 12ft thick at the base, and is approached by a beautiful Tudor bridge which spans the dry moat surrounding the inner bailey. This was built in 1496 to replace the drawbridge, by the 13th Earl of Oxford, one of Henry VII's chief commanders at the battle of Bosworth. Visited by King Henry VII, King Henry VIII and Queen Elizabeth I and besieged by King John. Home of the de Veres, Earls of Oxford for 550 years, and still owned by their descendent, The Honourable Thomas Lindsay. The Banqueting Hall, reached from the first floor by a beautiful spiral staircase, 13ft wide in circumference and constructed round a central column, has a splendid Minstrels' Gallery and timbered ceiling supported by a magnificent central arch, 28ft wide, the finest Norman arch in England. Beautifully kept grounds with peaceful lakeside and woodland walks. Large picnic area. Light refreshments served inside the keep. Hog Roast on Bank Holiday weekends. **Location:** 40km (24 miles) SE of Cambridge, approached along the A1017 and B1058. Within easy reach of A12, M11 and M25. (60 miles from London). **Open:** Week before Easter to the end of Oct, Daily 10–5pm. Open all year round for private parties. **Admission:** Adults £3.50, children £2.50 (5–15), family £10.50 (2 adults & 5 children). Except for special events, please telephone for prices. **Events:** Grounds open to the public in Feb/March to view the snowdrops (please telephone to confirm opening times). Admission price includes entrance to the keep and a free glass of mulled wine! Various events planned throughout the year such as, Jousting Tournaments, Medieval Displays, with music and dance, including Falconry and historical drama.

map 5
G2

HYLANDS HOUSE, PARK & GARDENS

Hylands Park, Writtle, Chelmsford, Essex. CM2 8WF
Tel: 01245 606812

This beautiful villa, with its neoclassical exterior is surrounded by over 500 acres of parkland, including formal gardens. The house reopened at Easter 1999 after a period of restoration work. The Library, Drawing Room and Saloon have been restored to their appearance in the early Victorian period, whilst the Boudoir has been refurbished to match the Blue Room, refurbished in 1995. At the same time the Entrance Hall was the subject of work to restore it to its Georgian origins. It is possible to view the unrestored Ballroom on the ground floor. There is an exhibition detailing the restoration work and the history of the house. Please telephone for details on opening times and admission.

map 5 G3

RHS GARDEN HYDE HALL

Rettendon, Chelmsford, Essex CM3 8ET
Tel: 01245 400256 (Royal Horticultural Society)

A charming hilltop garden which extends to over 24 acres. Highlights include the spring bulbs, the modern all and intermediate bearded irises in late May and the rope walk of climbing roses and large beds ablaze with floribunda and hybrid tea roses in midsummer. There is also a small plant centre and delightful hot and cold meals are available in the Essex thatched barn when the garden is open. **Open:** 24 March–31 Oct. 24 March–August: 11–6pm & Sept–Oct: 11–5pm. **Admission:** Adults £3, children (6–16yrs) 70p. RHS Members free and one guest.

map 5 G3

INGATESTONE HALL

Hall Lane, Ingatestone, Essex CM4 9NR
Tel: 01277 353010, Fax: 01245 248979 (Lord Petre)

Tudor mansion in 11 acres of grounds, built by Sir William Petre, Secretary of State to four monarchs. The house continues to be the home of his descendants and contains furniture, pictures and memorabilia accumulated over the centuries. The house retains its original form and appearance including two priests' hiding places. **Location:** From London end of Ingatestone High Street, take Station Lane. House is half a mile beyond the level crossing. **Open:** Easter–end Sept. Sat, Sun and Bank Holidays. 1–6pm Plus school hols only, Wed, Thurs and Fri 1–6pm. **Admission:** Adults £3.50 OAPs/students £3, children 5–16 £2 (under 5s free) parties 20 or more 50p per head reduction. **Refreshments:** Tearoom. Car park adjacent to gates. 200m walk to house. Gift shop. No dogs (except guide dogs). The upper floor and some rooms downstairs are inaccessible to wheelchairs.

map 5 G3

LAYER MARNEY TOWER

Nr Colchester, Essex CO5 9US
Tel & Fax: 01206 330 784 (Mr Nicholas Charrington)

Lord Marney's 1520 masterpiece is the tallest Tudor gate house in the country. Visitors may climb the tower for excellent views of the Essex countryside. Explore the formal gardens and visit the Long Gallery, Corsellis Room and church. The Medieval Barn has rare breed farm animals and the deer are on the farm walk. Guided tours are available by arrangement (minimum of 25 people). The Long Gallery and Corsellis Rooms may be hired for corporate days, weddings, receptions, banquets or concerts. **Location:** 6 miles S of Colchester, signpost off the B1022 Colchester–Maldon Road. **Open:** 1 Apr–3 Oct 99 everyday except Saturday 12pm–5pm. Bank Holiday Sundays and Mondays 11–6pm. Groups anytime by arrangement. **Admission:** Adults £3.25, children £1.75, family ticket £9.00. **Refreshments:** Stable tearoom.

map 5 H3

THE SIR ALFRED MUNNINGS ART MUSEUM

Castle House, Dedham, CO7 6AZ, Essex.
Tel: 01206 322127 Fax: 01206 322127 (Castle House Trust)

Castle House and its collection is a fitting memorial to Sir Alfred Munnings who lived at Castle House from 1919 until his death. Castle House, a mixture of Tudor and Georgian periods, has been restored, with Munnings' original furniture, and stands in spacious well-maintained gardens. A collection representative of Munnings' life span of work. Special exhibition: A rare opportunity to see a unique collection of "Pencil Sketches & Drawings". **Location:** ¼ mile from Dedham Village. **Station(s):** Colchester, Manningtree, Ipswich. **Open:** May 2–Oct 3, Wed, Sun & Bank Hol Mons. Also Thurs and Sats in Aug, 2–5pm. **Admission:** Adult £3, conc £2, child 50p. Private parties by arrangement. Free car park.

map 5 H2

Gloucestershire

The picturesque honey coloured cottages of the Cotswolds are quite charming. It is easy to see why Gloucestershire attracts thousands of visitors every year, with its quaint blend of meandering lanes and fine churches.

Many Cotswold villages were established as early as the twelfth century, with money from the medieval wool trade. The landscape is breathtaking, with cottages built of mellow stone nestling in the rolling hills.

The cities of Gloucester and Cheltenham are well worth exploring. Situated on the River Severn, Gloucester is dominated by its imposing Norman Cathedral, the scene of the coronation of Henry III and famous for its wonderful early fan vaulting.

Bibury

Cheltenham is a city of elegance which becomes the centre of the horse racing world during Gold Cup week. In the 18th century, the high society flocked to the spa town to "take the waters". There are many fine examples of Regency-style architecture in and around the town.

To the south-east is the charming town of Cirencester, known as the capital of the Cotswolds.

The Forest of Dean, one of England's last remaining ancient woodlands, lies between the River Wye and the River Severn. For those interested in contemporary art, the Forest of Dean Sculpture Trail is a pleasant way in which to explore the surrounding woodland whilst admiring a number of creative artworks.

BERKELEY CASTLE
Gloucestershire, GL13 9BQ
Tel: 01453 810332 (Mr R J G Berkeley)

England's most Historic Home and Oldest Inhabited Castle. Completed in 1153 by Lord Maurice Berkeley at the command of Henry II and for nearly 850 years the home of the Berkeley family. 24 generations have gradually transformed a savage Norman fortress into a truly stately home. The castle is a home and not a museum. Enjoy the castle at leisure or join one of the regular one-hour guided tours covering the dungeon, the cell where Edward II was murdered, the medieval kitchens, the magnificent Great Hall and the State Apartments with their fine collections of pictures by primarily English and Dutch masters, tapestries, furniture of an interesting diversity, silver and porcelain. Splendid Elizabethan Terraced Gardens and sweeping lawns surround the castle, Tropical Butterfly House with hundreds of exotic butterflies in free flight – an oasis of colour and tranquillity. Facilities include free coach and parks, picnic lawn and two gift shops. Tearooms for refreshments, light lunches and afternoon teas. **Location:** Midway between Bristol and Gloucester, just off A38, M5 junctions 13 or 14. **Open:** April & May, Tues–Sun 1–5pm; June & Sept, Tues–Sat 11–5pm, Sun 1–5pm; Jul & Aug, Mon–Sat 11–5pm, Sun 1–5pm; Oct, Sun only 1–5pm; Bank Holiday Mondays 11–5pm. **Admission:** Adult £4.95, child £2.60, sen. citz £3.95. Pre-booked parties 25 or more: Adult £4.45, child £2.30, sen. citz £3.65, family ticket £13.50 (2 adults & 2 children). Gardens only: Adult £1.75, child 90p. Butterfly Farm: Adult £1.75, child/OAP 85p, school groups 50p.

BARNSLEY HOUSE GARDEN

Barnsley House, Nr. Cirencester, Glos GL7 5EE
Tel: 01285 740561 Fax: 01285 740628
(Charles & Denzil Verey)

Old garden re-planned since 1960 by Rosemary Verey inside 1770 wall. 4¹/₂ acres. **Special features:** Spring bulbs & blossom, laburnum walk (in flower late May–early June), mixed borders, autumn colour and berries, knot garden, decorative potager. Tuscan Temple & Gothick Summerhouse (both 1770's). House 1697 – not open. Plants, garden furniture & antiques for sale. **Location:** 4 miles northeast of Cirencester, on B4425. **Open:** 1 Feb–16 Dec, Mon, Wed, Thur & Sat 10am–5.30pm (Tues & Fri, shop and plant sales only). Barnsley village festival Sat May 15 1999. **Admission:** Garden £3.50, OAPs £2.50. Guided tour by appointment extra.

map 4
B3

BATSFORD ARBORETUM

The Estate Office Batsford, Moreton-in-Marsh, Gloucestershire.
Tel: 01608 650722 Fax: 01608 650290 (The Batsford Foundation)

The arboretum set in 55 acres of Cotswold countryside contains over 1500 trees with species from all over the world. The change in mood throughout the year never fails to seduce and excite the visitor with its tranquil beauty and Japanese influence. Spring carpets the ground with snowdrops. Narcissi and daffodils whilst the cherries and magnolias put on their finest display. In summer explore the bamboo groves, fine bronze statues and waterside planting. Experience the Autumn explosion when all the trees put on their finale display. **Location:** Off A44 Moreton-in-Marsh, Eversham Road. **Open:** Daily Mar–Nov. **Admission:** Adult £3.50, seniors £3, child free. Also: Cotswold Falcony Centre – Garden Centre – Tearooms.

map 4
B2

CHAVENAGE

Tetbury, Gloucestershire GL8 8XP
Tel: 01666 502329 Fax: 01453 836778 (David Lowsley-Williams, Esq.)

Elizabethan House (1576) set in the tranquil Cotswold countryside with Cromwellian associations. 16th and 17th century furniture and tapestries. Personally conducted tours, by the owner or his family. **Location:** 2 miles N of Tetbury, signposted off A46 (Bath–Stroud) or B4014. **Open:** Thurs, Sun and Bank Hols, 2–5pm. May – end Sept plus Easter Sun and Mon. **Admission:** Adults £3, children half-price. Parties by appointment as shown or other dates and times to suit. **Refreshments:** Catering for parties by arrangement. **Conferences:** Wedding receptions, dinners, corporate hospitality, also available for film and photographic location.

map 4
A3

CHEDWORTH ROMAN VILLA

Yanworth, Cheltenham
Tel: 01242 890256 Fax: 01242 840544 (The National Trust)

Chedworth Roman Villa is one of the finest Roman-period sites in Britain. Nestling in a wooded combe in the Cotswolds, it contains the ruins of a large, opulent country house of the 4th century. There are some very special features surviving–fine mosaics, a water shrine with running spring, two bath-houses, several hypocaust systems (Roman central heating) and many artefacts in the site museum. There is a ten minute video introduction to the site and a new audio tour which guides the visitor around the villa. There are various events and open days during the year and archaeological work continues. Visit Chedworth for a flavour of life in 4th century Britain. **Open:** Mar–Nov, Tues–Sun and BHols, 10–5pm (closes at 4pm after 25 Oct). **Admission:** Adult £3.40, child £1.70, family £8.50 (2 adults & 4 children). **Location:** 20 mins from Cirencester.

map 4
B3

FRAMPTON COURT

Frampton-on-Severn, Gloucester GL2 7EU
Tel: 01452 740267 Messages/Fax: 01452 740698 (Mrs H. Clifford)

Listed Grade I, by Vanbrugh. 1732. Stately family home of the Cliffords who have lived at Frampton since granted land by William the Conquerer, 1066. Fine collection of the original period furniture, tapestries, needlework and porcelain. Panelled throughout. Fine views over well kept parkland to extensive lake. A famous Gothic orangery stands in the garden reflected in a long Dutch ornamental canal similar to Westbury. The original well known floral water colours by the gifted 19th century great Aunts hang in the house. These inspired the book "The Frampton Flora". **Open:** All year by appointment £4.50. Tel: 01452 740267. Near jct. 13 of M5 motorway. Signposted.

map 4
A3

HARDWICKE COURT

Nr Gloucester, Glos
Tel: 01452 720212 (C G M Lloyd-Baker)

Late Georgian house designed by Robert Smirke, built in 1816–1817. Entrance Hall, Drawing Room, Library and Dining Room open. **Location:** 5 miles S of Gloucester on A38 (between M5 access 12 S only and 13). **Open:** Easter Mon–end Sept, Mon only 2–4pm other times by prior written agreement. **Admission:** £1, parking for cars only. Not suitable for disabled.

map 4
A3

HODGES BARN GARDENS

Shipton Moyne, Tetbury, Gloucestershire GL8 8PR
Tel: 01666 880202 Fax: 01666 880373 (Mrs Amanda Hornby)

Hodges Barn is a 15th century Cotswold stone dovecote converted into a charming family home surrounded by "one of the finest private gardens in England". Spring bulbs, magnolias and flowering trees are followed by a superb collection of old fashioned and climbing roses and many mixed shrub and herbaceous beds. **Open:** 1 Apr–19 Aug Mon, Tues, Fri 2–5pm. **Admission:** Adults £3, children free. Dogs on leads.

map 4
A4

HORTON COURT

Horton, Nr Chipping Sodbury B17 6QR
Tel: 01985 843600 (The National Trust)

A Cotswold manor house with 12th century Norman hall and early Renaissance features. Of particular interest is the late perpendicular ambulatory, detached from the house. Norman hall and ambulatory only shown. **Location:** 3 miles north-east of Chipping Sodbury. ¾ miles north of Horton, 1 mile west of A46. Open: 3 Apr–30 Oct, Wed & Sat, 2–6pm or dusk if earlier. **Admission:** Adult £1.80, child 90p.

KIFTSGATE COURT GARDENS

Chipping Campden, Gloucestershire, GL55 6LW
Tel: 01386 438 777 Fax: 01386 438 777 (Mr & Mrs J G. Chambers)

Garden with many unusual shrubs and plants including tree peonies, abutilons, etc, specie and old-fashioned roses. **Location:** 3 miles NE of Chipping Campden. **Open:** Apr–May & Aug–Sept; Wed, Thurs and Sun, 2–6pm. June–July; Wed, Thurs, Sat and Sun, 12noon–6pm. Bank Hols Mon 2–6pm. **Admission:** Adults £3.50, children £1. **Refreshments:** Whitsun – 1 Sept. Light lunches in June and July. Coaches by appointment only. Unusual plants for sale on open days.

map 4 B2

LYDNEY PARK SPRING GARDENS

Lydney, Gloucestershire GL15 6BU
Tel & Fax: 01594 842027 (Viscount Bledisloe)

Magnificent Woodland Garden in secluded valley with lakes and a wide selection of rhododendrons and azaleas, fine shrubs and trees. N.Z., Roman Museums & Roman Temple Site. Deer park, plants for sale. **Location:** ½ mile W of Lydney on A48 (Gloucester to Chepstow) **Open:** 11–6pm, Sun, Wed and Bank Hol from Easter–6 June. Every day 31 May–6 June. Parties by appointment. **Admission:** Adults £2.50, Wed £1.50. Accompanied children and car park free. **Refreshments:** Teas in dining room (house not otherwise open). Picnics in deer park. Dogs on lead. Taurus Café/Restaurant. Craft shop and Pottery at Old Park. Open all year (separate entrance when Gardens closed). Free car park.

MISARDEN PARK GARDENS

Miserden, Stroud, Gloucestershire
Tel: 01285 821303, Fax: 01285 821530 (Major M T N H Wills)

Spring flowers, shrubs, fine topiary (some designed by Sir Edwin Lutyens) and herbaceous borders within a walled garden, roses and specimen trees. 17th century manor house (not open), stunning position overlooking Golden Valley. New summerhouse and rill for 1999. **Location:** Miserden 7 miles from Gloucester, Cheltenham, Stroud & Cirencester; 3 miles off A417 (signed). **Open:** Every Tues, Wed & Thurs from 1 Apr–30 Sept, 10–5pm. Nurseries adjacent to garden open daily except Mons. **Admission:** Adults £3, (guided tour extra), children (accompanied) free. Reductions for parties (of 20 or more) by appointment.

map 4 A3

MILL DENE GARDEN

Old Mill Dene, Blockley, Moreton-in-Marxh GL56 9HU
Tel: 01386 700457 Fax: 01386 700526 (Mr & Mrs B S Dare)

In a naturally beautiful situation this 2½ acre Cotswold water-mill garden has been designed and planted by the owner. Steep lawned terraces rise from the mill-pool, stream and grotto; wander through a rose-walk to the cricket lawn, then to the potager at the top. All the garden has glimpses of the church as a back-drop and views over the Cotswold Hills. Plenty of seats encourage contemplation of tranquil water and vistas. **Location:** From A44 Bourton on the Hill, take turn to Blockley. 1½ miles down hill, turn left behind 30mph sign labelled cul-de-sac. Please telephone for opening details and admission charges.

OWLPEN MANOR

Owlpen, Nr Uley, Gloucestershire, GL11 5BZ
Tel: 01453 860261 Fax: 01453 860819 (Mr & Mrs C N Mander)

Romantic Tudor manor house (1450–1616), home of the Mander family. Magnificent Great Hall, Jacobean solar wing, unique painted textiles in a room haunted by Queen Margaret of Anjou (in 1471), and family and Cotswold Arts and Crafts collections. The formal terraced garden (1723) has fine yew topiary, parterres and mill pond walk. Medieval outbuildings include the Cyder House Restaurant (open daily), the Grist Mill and Court House (now holiday cottages) and a richly-detailed Victorian church. The house lies at the bottom of a picturesque wooded valley under the edge of the Cotswolds, with miles of walks. **House open:** 2–5pm, April 1–October 30, every day except Mondays (but open on Bank Holiday Mondays). *"Owlpen in Gloucestershire - ah what a dream is there!"* – Vita Sackville-West. **Internet:** http://www.owlpen.com/ **E-mail:** sales@owlpen.com

map 4 A3

ST MARY'S CHURCH

Kempley
Tel: 01179 750 700

A delightful Norman church with superb wall paintings from the 12–14th centuries which were only discovered beneath white wash in 1871. **Location:** On minor road. 1½ miles south–east of Much Marcle A449. **Open:** 1 Apr–30 Sept, open daily 10–6pm. 1 Oct–31 Mar, open daily 10–4pm. Closed 24–26 December and 1 January. **Admission:** Free.

RODMARTON MANOR

Cirencester, Gloucestershire GL7 6PF
Tel: 01285 841253 Fax 01285 841298 (Mr & Mrs Simon Biddulph)

The house is a unique example of the Cotswold Arts and Crafts and was built and furnished with local materials entirely by hand. The garden is a series of outdoor rooms. There are hedges, topiary, a troughery, a rockery, lawns, magnificent herbaceous borders and kitchen garden all in a romantic setting. **Location:** Off A433 6m west of Cirencester. **New details for 1999. Open:** The House and Garden open Wed, Sat and Bank Hol Mons 12 May–30 Aug 2–5pm. Groups please book. Guided tours of house can be booked for groups of 15 or more people at other times. Groups are welcome to visit the garden by appointment at other times. Guided tours of garden can also be booked. **Admission:** House and Garden £6 (children under 14 £3). Minimum group charge for house £90. Garden only £2.50 (accompanied children under 14 free).

 map 4 A3

PAINSWICK ROCOCO GARDENS

The Stables, Painswick House, Painswick, Gloucestershire GL6 6TH
Tel & Fax: 01452 813204 (Painswick Rococo Garden Trust)

Painswick Rococo Garden is a unique survivor from a brief period of 18th century garden design. It is set in a hidden Cotswold valley near the picturesque, historic wool town of Painswick. The garden boasts charming contemporary buildings, a large kitchen garden, herbaceous borders, woodland walks and wonderful views of the surrounding countryside. One of its most noted features is the magnificent carpet of snowdrops during late winter, early spring. Newly planted maze open for 1999. **Open:** Gardens from 13 Jan–30 Nov, Wed–Sun, plus Bank Hol Mons 11–5pm; daily in July and Aug. **Admission:** Adult £3, senior £2.70, child £1.60. The Coach House contains the restaurant/tearooms and gift shop is open Wednesday to Sunday. Ample car parking. The garden is a registered charity. **E-mail:** painsgard@aol.com **Internet:** www.beta.co.uk/painswick

 map 4 A3

STANWAY HOUSE

Cheltenham, Gloucestershire GL54 5PQ
Tel: 01386 584469 (Lord Neidpath)

The jewel of Cotswold Manor houses is very much a home rather than a museum and the centre of a working landed estate, which has changed hands once in 1275 years. The mellow Jacobean architecture, the typical squire's family portraits, the exquisite Gatehouse, the old Brewery, medieval Tithe Barn, the extensive gardens, arboretum pleasure grounds and formal landscape contribute to the timeless charm of what Arthur Negus considered one of the most beautiful and romantic houses in England. **Location:** 1 mile off B4632 Chelteham/Broadway road; on B4077 Toddington/Stow-on-the-Wold road; M5 junction 9. **Open & Admission:** Please phone for details of opening times and admission charges. **Refreshments:** Teas in Old Bakehouse in the village (01386 584204).

 map 4 B2

SEZINCOTE

Moreton-in-Marsh, Gloucestershire GL56 9AW
(Mr & Mrs D Peake)

Oriental water garden by Repton and Daniell with trees of unusual size. House in Indian style, inspiration of Royal Pavilion, Brighton. **Location:** 1 mile W of Moreton-in-Marsh on A44 to Evesham; turn left by lodge before Bourton-on-the-Hill. **Station(s):** Moreton-in-Marsh **Open:** Garden Thurs, Fri & Bank Hol Mons 2–6pm (or dusk if earlier) throughout the year, except Dec. House May, June, July and Sept, Thurs and Fri 2.30–6pm parties by appointment. Open in aid of National Gardens Scheme Sun July 4th 2–6pm. **Admission:** House and garden £4.50; garden only £3, children £1, under 5s free. **Refreshments:** Hotels and restaurant in Moreton-in-Marsh. No dogs.

 map 4 B2

WHITTINGTON COURT

Whittington, Nr Cheltenham, Gloucestershire GL54 4HF
Tel: 01242 820556 (Mrs J L Stringer)

Small Elizabethan stone-built manor house with family possessions. **Location:** 4 miles E of Cheltenham on A40. **Open:** Sat 3 Apr–Sun 18 Apr and Sat 14 Aug–Bank Hol Mon 30 Aug inclusive. **Admission:** Adults £2.50, OAPs £2, children £1. Open to parties by arrangement.

 map 4 B3

DYRHAM PARK

nr Chippenham SN14 8ER
Tel: Property Office 0117 937 2501; Warden's Office 01225 891364

Open: 27 March to 31 Oct: daily except Wed & Thur, 12–5.30pm. Garden as house: 11–5.30pm or dusk if earlier. Park: daily (closed 25 Dec) 12–5.30pm or dusk if earlier (opens 11 when garden open). Note: Propery closed 2, 3 July for jazz concerts. Events: 2, 3 July Jazz Festival.

HIDCOTE MANOR GARDEN

Hidcote Bartrim, nr Chipping Campden GL55 6LR
Tel: 01386 438333 Restaurant 01386 438703 Fax: 01386 438817

Open: 27 March to end of May, Aug to 31 Oct: daily except Tues & Fri; June & July: daily except Fri. March to end Sept 11–7pm, Oct 11–6pm; last admission 1hr before closing or dusk if earlier. Event: send s.a.e. for details. **Admission:** £5.60; family £14. Coach and groups by appointment only (tel. 01386 438333); no group reduction. No picnicking and no games in garden. Free car park 100m.

SNOWSHILL MANOR

Snowshill, nr Broadway WR12 7JU Tel: 01386 852410

Open: 27 March to 31 Oct: daily except Tues (closed Good Fri) 1–5pm; last admission 45 min before closing. Note: Entry to house is by timed ticket. Grounds: as house. April & Oct 12–5pm, May to end Sept 12–5.30pm. Tel. for details of special interest days. **Admission:** £5.60; family £14. Groups £4.60. Grounds, restaurant & shop only £2.50. Coach and school groups by written appointment only. Photography only by written arrangement with Curator.

WESTBURY COURT GARDEN

Westbury-on-Severn, Gloucestershire Tel: 01452 760461

Open: 27 March to 31 Oct: daily except Mon & Tues (but open BH Mons and closed Good Fri) 11–6pm. Other months by appointment. Events: send s.a.e. for details. **Admission:** £2.70. Free car park. Groups of 15+ by written appointment; no group reduction.

[Full-width photograph of Sudeley Castle reflected in water]

SUDELEY CASTLE

Winchcombe, Cheltenham, Gloucestershire GL54 5JD
Tel: 01242 602 308 (Lord & Lady Ashcombe)

Sudeley Castle, Winner of the 1996 HHA/Christie's Garden of the Year Award and the home of Lord and Lady Ashcombe, is one of England's great historic houses with royal connections stretching back 1000 years. Sudeley was the magnificent palace of Queen Katherine Parr, Henry VIII's sixth wife, who is buried in the Castle Church. Henry VIII, Elizabeth I and Charles I, amongst others, have all stayed here. A programme of reconstruction during the Victorian era enhanced Sudeley's earlier magnificence amongst the wealth of history on show, there is an impressive collection of masterpieces by Turner, Van Dyck and Ruebens. Visitors can enjoy the eight award-winning gardens surrounding the Castle. These enchanting gardens include the Queen's Garden, with its fine collection of old roses and the Victorian Kitchen Garden. **Open:** 6 Mar–31 Oct, Gardens, Exhibition Centre, Plant Centre and Shop: 10.30–5.30pm. Castle Apartments and Church: 11–5pm. 27 Mar–31 Oct, Restaurant: 10.30–5.30pm. Group and private tours out of season by arrangement. **Admission:** Castle and gardens: Adults £6, OAPs £5, children (5–13yrs) £3. Group rates (min 20): Adults £5, OAP's £4, children £3. Gardens and Exhibition Centre: Adults £4.50, OAP's £3.50, children (5–13yrs) £2.25. Other: Family ticket (2 adults and 2 children) £17, Adult season ticket £17, Family season ticket (2 adults and 2 children) £34, audio tour £2, Adventure playground (5–13yrs) £1. The Connoisseurs Choice: (Adult ticket, audio tour, castle guide book, free coffee in restaurant) £10. The Enthusiasts Choice: (Adult ticket, audio tour, free coffee in restaurant) £8.

map 4 B2

Hampshire

Curled in the semi circle formed by the Western Downs, the Hampshire Downs and the South Downs and sheltered from the Channel winds by the pearl and emerald hills of the Isle of Wight, the county of Hampshire basks in as mellow a climate as any part of the British Isles.

This is a land overflowing with incredible landscapes, charming villages, world-famous stately homes, forests, castles and manor houses. Its unassuming county town, Winchester, was the one time capital of England, and is home to a beautiful cathedral and many points of historic interest.

Hampshire's new forest, 145 square miles of heath and woodland, is the largest area of unenclosed land in Southern Britain. William the Conqueror's 'new' forest, despite its name, is one of the few primeval oak woods in England. The New Forest was a popular hunting ground for Norman kings and is the home of the Rufus Stone, where William II was shot dead. Numerous shaggy New Forest ponies and over 1,500 fallow deer may be seen rambling through the woodlands.

Chawton Church

New Forest Ponies

Once a vital naval port, Portsmouth today is a much quieter town, with a fascinating naval history from the 16th century to the Falklands war. The harbour is very busy and a mecca for day sailors with endless pubs and fish and chip bars.

AVINGTON PARK

Winchester, Hampshire SO21 1DB
Tel: 01962 779260 Fax: 01962 779864 (Mrs A M Hickson)

Avington Park is a Palladian mansion, where both Charles II and George IV stayed at various times. It was enlarged in 1670 with the addition of two wings and a classical portico surmounted by three statues. The State Rooms on view include the magnificent silk and gilded Ballroom, hand painted Drawing Room, Library and Hall. In a delightful parkland and lakeside setting, it adjoins an exquisite Georgian church, which may be visited. **Open:** May to September 2.30–5pm, Sundays and Bank Holiday Monday. Last tour 5pm. **Admission:** Adults £3, children £1.50. Coaches welcome by appointment all year.

JANE AUSTEN'S HOUSE

Chawton, Alton GU34 1SD
Tel/Fax: 01420 83262 (Jane Austin Memorial Fund)

17th century house where Jane Austen wrote or revised her six great novels. The house contains many items associated with her and her family, documents and letters, first editions of the novels, pictures, portraits and furniture. Pleasant garden, suitable for picnics, bakehouse with brick oven and wash tub, houses Jane's donkey carriage. **Location:** Just S of A31, 1 mile SW of Alton, signposted Chawton. **Open:** 1 Mar–1 Jan daily. Jan & Feb, Sat & Sun 11–4.30pm. Closed Christmas Day and Boxing Day. **Admission:** Adult £2.50, child (8–18) 50p, concessions £2.

BREAMORE HOUSE

Nr. Fordingbridge, Hampshire SP6 2DF
Tel: 01725 512468 (Sir Edward Hulse)

Elizabethan Manor House (1583) with fine collections of paintings, tapestries, furniture. Countryside Museum takes the visitor back to when a village was self-sufficient. Exhibition of Rural Arts and Agricultural machinery. **Location:** 3 miles N of Fordingbridge off the main Bournemouth Road (A338) 8 miles S of Salisbury. **Open:** 1 Apr–30 Sept 1998. House 2–5.30pm Countryside Museum 1–5.30pm. Other times by appointment. **Admission:** Combined ticket adults £5, children £3.50, reduced rate for parties and OAPs. **Refreshments:** Home-made snacks and teas available from midday.

BEAULIEU

Beaulieu, Brockenhurst, Hampshire SO42 7ZN
Tel: 01590 612345 Fax: 01590 612624 Internet: www.beaulieu.co.uk

Beaulieu is set in the heart of the New Forest and is a place that gives enormous pleasure to people with an interest in seeing history of all kinds. Overlooking the Beaulieu River, Palace House has been Lord Montagu's ancestral home since 1538. The House was once the Great Gatehouse of Beaulieu Abbey and its monastic origins are reflected in such features as the fan vaulted ceilings. Beaulieu Abbey was founded in 1204 and although most of the buildings have been destroyed, much of beauty and interest remains. The Domus, which houses an exhibition of monastic life, is home to beautiful wall hangings. Beaulieu is also home of the world famous National Motor Museum which traces the story of motoring from 1894 to the present day. 250 vehicles are on display including legendary World Record breakers such as Bluebird and Golden Arrow plus Veteran, Vintage and Classic cars and motorcycles.

The modern Beaulieu is very much a family destination where there are various free and unlimited rides and drives on a transportation theme to be enjoyed by everyone including a mile long monorail and replica 1912 London open topped bus. When visiting Beaulieu arrangements can be made to view the Estate's vineyards. Visits, which can be arranged between Apr–Oct, must be pre-booked at least one week in advance with the Beaulieu Estate office. Beaulieu also offers a comprehensive range of facilities for conferences, company days out, product launches, management training, corporate hospitality, promotions, film locations, exhibitions and outdoor events. **Open:** Daily 10–5pm except Easter–Sept 10–6pm. Closed Christmas Day. **Location:** By car take M27 to junction 2 then follow the Brown Tourist Signs. **Admission:** Please phone for details on 01590 612345.

map 4
C6

BROADLANDS

Romsey, Hampshire SO51 9ZD
Tel: 01794 505010

One of the finest examples of mid–Georgian architecture in England, Broadlands stands serenely in Capability Brown parkland on the banks of the River Test. Country residence of the famous Victorian Prime Minister, Lord Palmerston, and later home of Queen Victoria's great grandson, Earl Mountbatten of Burma. Visitors may view the House with its countless mementoes of the Mountbatten and Palmerston eras and its fine collection of art, furniture, porcelain and sculpture. History is brought vividly to life by means of the Mountbatten Exhibition and the audiovisual presentation. **Open:** Daily from 14 June–3 Sept, 12–5.30pm (last admission 4pm). **Admission:** Adults £5.50, senior citizens £4.70, students £4.70, disabled £4.70, children 12–16 £3.85 and children under 12 free. For group admission rate please call the number detailed above.

map 4 C6

EXBURY GARDENS

Nr Southampton SO45 1AZ, Tel: 01703 891203
Fax: 01703 243380 (E.L. de Rothschild, Esq.)

Described as 'Heaven with the gates open', this 200 acres garden, created by Lionel de Rothschild, contains magnificent displays of rhododendrons, azaleas and other woodland shrubs. Free 'Trail Guides' in Spring, Summer and Autumn to encourage the visitor to see newly planted areas, making this a beautiful day out any time. **Location:** Exbury village, south drive from Jct.2 M27 west of Southampton. Turn W off A326 at Didben Purlieu towards Beaulieu. **Open:** Daily, 27 Feb–31 Oct, 10–5.30pm (dusk if earlier). Free entry to Gift shop and Plant Centre. Please phone for admission charges.

map 4 C6

FAMILY TREES

Sandy Lane, Shedfield, Hampshire, SO32 2HQ
Tel: 01329 834 812
(Philip House)

Wide variety of fruit for the connoisseur. Trained tree specialists; standards, espaliers, cordons etc. Other trees, old roses and climbing roses. Free catalogue of trees of good size from Family Trees (as above). **Location:** See map in free catalogue. **Station(s):** Botley (2.5 miles). **Open:** Mid Oct–end Apr, Wed & Sat, 9.30am–12.30. **Admission:** No charge. No minimum order. Courier dispatch for next day delivery.

map 4 C6

GILBERT WHITE'S HOUSE & GARDEN & THE OATES MUSEUM

'The Wakes', Selborne, Nr. Alton, Hampshire, GU34 3JH
Tel: 01420 511275

Charming 18th century house and glorious garden, home of famous naturalist Rev. Gilbert White. Furnished rooms and original manuscript. Also fascinating museum depicting Capt. Lawrence Oates, hero of Scott's ill-fated Antarctic Expedition. Tea Parlour. Excellent shop. Plant sales. **Open:** 11–5 daily. 1 Jan–24 Dec. Groups welcome all year and summer evenings. **Admission:** Adults £4, OAPs £3.50, children £1, group rates also. **Events:** Unusual Plants Fair 19/20 June '99. Picnic to 'Jazz in June' 19 June '99. Mulled Wine & Christmas Shopping Day 28 November '99.

map 4 D5

HIGHCLERE CASTLE

Newbury RG20 9RN
Tel: 01635 253210

Designed by Charles Barry in the 1830s at the same time as he was building the Houses of Parliament. This soaring pinnacled mansion provided a perfect setting for the 3rd Earl of Carnarvon, one of the great hosts of Queen Victoria's reign. Old master paintings mix with portraits by Van Dyck and 18th century painters. The 5th Earl of Carnarvon, discovered the Tomb of Tutankhamun with Howard Carter.
FURTHER INFORMATION, OPENING TIMES AND DATES WITH PHOTOGRAPHY CAN BE SEEN UNDER THE COUNTY OF BERKSHIRE.

map 4 C5

HALL FARM HOUSE

Bentworth, Alton, Hampshire GU34 5JU
Tel: 01420 564010 (A.C & M.C Brooking)

map 4 D5

SIR HAROLD HILLIER GARDENS & ARBORETUM

Jermyns Lane Ampfield, Nr Romsey, Hampshire
Tel: 01794 368787 Fax: 01794 368027 (Hampshire County Council)

These beautiful 180 acre gardens are home to one of the best 20th century collections of plants to be found anywhere in the world. They were begun in 1953 by the famous nurseryman Sir Harold Hillier and since 1977 have been held in trust by Hampshire County Council, earning a reputation as a garden for all seasons. **Location:** The Gardens are 3 miles NE of Romsey. Signposted off the A3090 (A31). **Open:** Every day Apr–Oct 10.30–6pm (weekends and Bank Hols) Nov–Mar 10.30–dusk. Closed public holidays over Christmas. **Admission:** Adults £4.25 Apr–Oct, £3.25 Nov–Mar. OAP £3.75 Apr–Oct, £2.75 Nov–Mar. Children (5–16) £1. Under 5's Free. Discount for groups of 10 if booked in advance. Regret no dogs. **Refreshments:** Available in Jermyn's House every day from Easter–Oct and at weekends from Nov–Mar.

map 4
C6

HOUGHTON LODGE GARDENS

Stockbridge, Hampshire SO20 6LQ
Tel: 01264 810177 (Capt & Mrs M W Busk)

Landscaped pleasure grounds and fine trees surround unique 18th C 'Cottage Ornée' beside the River Test with lovely views over the tranquil and unspoilt valley. Featured in "The Buccaneers" (BBC TV) and the film "Wilde". Chalkcob walls shelter the 1 acre kitchen garden with ancient espaliered fruit trees, glasshouses and newly established herb garden. A GUIDED TOUR OF THE HYDROPONICUM SHOWS HOW TO GARDEN EASILY AT HOME WITHOUT SOIL OR PESTICIDES. **Location:** 1½ miles S of A30 at Stockbridge on minor road to Houghton village. **Station(s):** Winchester, Andover. **Open:** Mar–Sept, Sat, Sun & Bank Holidays 10–5pm, Mon, Tues, Thurs and Fri 2–5pm. **Admission:** Garden £3, Hydroponicum Tour £2. Visitor centre with hydroponics shop serves free refreshments. **E-mail:** T.Grimshaw@aol.com **Website:** www. hydroponicum.co.uk

map 4
C5

LANGLEY BOXWOOD NURSERY

Rake, Nr Liss, Hampshire GU33 7JL
Tel: 01730 894467 Fax: 01730 894703 (Elizabeth Braimbridge)

This small nursery, in a beautiful setting, specialises in box-growing, offering a chance to see together a unique range of old and new varieties, hedging, topiary, specimens and rarities. Some taxus also. Descriptive list available (4 x 1st class stamps). **Location:** Off B2070 (old A3) 3 miles south of Liphook. Ring for directions. **Open:** Mon–Fri 9–4.30pm, Sat – enquire by telephone first. National Collection – Buxus. **E-mail:** langbox@msn.com.uk

map 4
D6

MOTTISFONT ABBEY

Mottisfont, Nr Romsey, Hants, SO51 0LP
Tel: 01794 340757 Fax: 01794 341492 (The National Trust)

The abbey and garden form the central point of an 809 hectare estate which includes most of the village of Mottisfont, farmland and woods. It is possible to walk along a tributary of the River Test which flows through the garden, forming a superb and tranquil setting for a 12th century Augustinian priory, which, after the Dissolution, became a house. It contains the spring or 'font' from which the place-name is derived. The magnificent trees, walled garden and the national collection of old-fashioned roses combine to provide interest throughout the seasons. The abbey contains a drawing room decorated by Rex Whistler and the cellarium of the old priory. In 1996 the Trust acquired Derek Hill's 20th-century picture collection.

map 4
C6

ST AGATHA'S CHURCH

Market Way, Portsmouth, Hants
Tel & Fax: 01329 230330

A grand Italianate basilica of 1894, built for the famous Anglo Catholic priest, Fr R Dolling. Interior enriched with marble, alabaster, polished granite, carved stone and coloured glass. The apse displays a magnificent sgraffito mural c.1901, by Heywood Sumner, described by the late Sir Nikolaus Pevsner as "one of Portsmouth's few major works of art". Fine furnishings, many rescued from redundant churches. Guides available. **Location:** By Cascades Shopping Centre. On route for Historic Ships. **Open:** Sat, Sun, Wed Jun–Sept 10–3pm. Sat, Sun Oct–May 10–2pm. Other times by arrangement. **Admission:** Free. Nave available for hire subject to availability.

map 4
C6

SPINNERS GARDEN

Boldre, Lymington, Hants, SO41 5QE
Tel: 01590 673347 (P.G.G. Chappell)

A woodland garden on a slope overlooking the River Lymington Valley with rhododendrons, magnolias, Japanese maples, hydrangea species etc interplanted with a diversity of choice woodland and groundcover plants. Amongst a large collection of bog and woodland plants a NCCPG collection of Trilliums. Press mentions in '97 include a Roy Lancaster article in the July issue of 'The Garden'. The nursery contains as wide a selection of less common hardy plants, shrubs and trees as you will find anywhere. **Open:** Please telephone for details of opening times and admission charges.

map 4
C7

SOMERLEY

Ringwood, Hampshire BH24 3PL

Tel: 01425 480819 Fax: 01425 478613 E-mail: info@somerley.com

Somerley is the family home of the Sixth Earl and Countess of Normanton. Situated in 7,000 acres of meadows, woods and rolling parkland the house was designed by Samuel Wyatt in the mid 1700s. This magnificent Georgian family home, although not open to the public, is available on occasions for corporate functions, concerts, film work and outdoor activities. The estate boasts its own 4 x 4 off road driving course, a nine-hole golf course and five clay stands. Much of the food comes from the estate and the stunning Picture Gallery can seat 120 guests for dinner.

map 4 D7

STRATFIELD SAYE HOUSE

Stratfield Saye, Nr Reading, Hampshire RE7 2BT

Tel: 01256 882882 (The Duke of Wellington)

Home of the Dukes of Wellington since 1817. The house and exhibition pay tribute to Arthur Wellesley, the first and great Duke – soldier, statesman and victor of the Napoleonic wars. **House:** Contains a unique collection of paintings, furniture and personal effects of the Great Duke. **Wellington Exhibition:** Depicts the life and times of the Great Duke and features his magnificent funeral carriage. **Grounds:** Include gardens and the grave of Copenhagen, the Duke's favourite charger that carried him throughout the battle of Waterloo. **Location:** 1 mile W of A33 between Reading & Basingstoke (turn off at Wellington Arms Hotel); signposted. **Open:** House & Gardens May: Sat, Sun & Bank Hol Mon. Jun–Aug: daily except Fri. Sept: Sat & Sun. Grounds & Exhibition 11.30–6pm Last admission 4pm. House 12–4pm. **Admission:** Please telephone for charges.

map 4 D5

UPPARK

South Harting, Petersfield, Hampshire GU31 5QR

Tel: 01730 825415 Fax: 01730 825873 (The National Trust)

National Trust's most ambitious restoration project: Georgian interior, paintings, ceramics, textiles, furniture and dolls house rescued from 1989 fire. Multimedia exhibition of restoration. Interesting servants' rooms with H G Wells connections. Garden restored to Repton's design. **Location:** 5 miles SE of Petersfield on B2146. **Open:** Sun–Thurs (closed Fri and Sat) 28 Mar–28 Oct. Tickets, grounds, garden, shop and tearoom: 11.30–5.30pm. House: 1–5pm (4pm in Oct). **Admission:** Timed tickets in operation. Adults £5.50; family ticket £13.75. Parties (weekends only – no reduction) must book in advance.

map 4 D6

WINCHESTER COLLEGE

77 Kingsgate Street, Winchester SO23 9PE

Tel: 01962 868778   Fax: 01962 840207

This is one of the oldest public schools in the country. The college was founded by Bishop William of Wykeham in 1382. **Location:** In Winchester city centre, south of the Cathedral. **Open:** Apr–Sept, Mon–Sat, 10–1pm and 2–5pm. Oct–Mar, Mon–Sat, 10–1pm & 2–4pm. Closed on Sunday mornings. **Admission:** Charges apply. Guided tours may be booked for groups of 10+.

HINTON AMPNER GARDEN

Bramdean, nr Alresford SO24 0LA Tel: 01962 771305 Fax: 01962 771305

Open: Garden: 21 & 28 March, then 3 April to end Sept: daily except Mon, Thur & Fri (but open BH Mons) 1.30–5.30pm. House: 6 April to end Sept: Tues & Wed; Aug: daily except Mon, Thur & Fri 1.30–5.30pm. **Admission:** £4. Groups £3.50. Garden only £3.20. Special entrance for coaches; which must book in advance. No group bookings in Aug. **Restaurant:** Tea-room as garden 1.30–5pm (light lunches 1.30–2pm). Picnics in grass car park only.

SANDHAM MEMORIAL CHAPEL

Burghclere, nr Newbury RG20 9JT Tel: 01635 278394 Fax: 01635 278394

Open: March & Nov: Sat & Sun; April to end Oct: daily except Mon & Tues (but open BH Mons and closed Wed after BH Mons); Dec to Feb: by appointment only. March & Nov 11.30–4pm; April to end Oct

11.30–5pm. **Admission:** £2. No group reduction. Road verge parking. **Restaurant:** Picnicking on front lawn.

THE VYNE

Sherbourne St John, Basingstoke RG24 9HL

Tel: 01256 881337 Fax: 01256 881720

Open: House: 27 March to end Oct: daily except Mon & Tues 1.30–5.30pm (but open BH Mons 11–5.30pm). Grounds: weekends in March, then 27 March to end Oct: daily except Mon & Tues 12.30–5.30pm (but open BH Mons 11–5.30pm). **Events:** send s.a.e. for details or tel. Regional Box Office (tel. 01372 451596). **Admission:** £5; family £12.50. Groups (Wed to Fri only) £4. Grounds only £2.50. **Restaurant:** Licensed Old Brewhouse restaurant same days as grounds 12.30–2pm (opens 11 Good Fri & BH Mons), 2.30–5.30, last orders 5pm. Also open for booked Christmas lunches. Coach groups by arrangement only; tel. for details. Picnics in car park only.

Hereford & Worcester

Ross-on-Wye

Right against the Welsh border lies the old county of Herefordshire. The River Wye winds its way across this rugged land of pastoral landscapes, offering excellent salmon fishing. Situated along its meandering route is the city of Hereford with its beautiful Norman cathedral that towers above the River Wye. The spectacular Black Mountains lie to the South West along the Welsh borders, where trickling streams run through fertile valleys.

Worcester is famous for its fine timber buildings and its porcelain, particularly in Friar Street and New Street which houses the best examples of such architecture. Greyfriars and the Commandery are particularly worthy of a mention. Like Hereford, Worcester is dominated by a beautiful cathedral with an especially fine crypt. This wondrous place is also renowned for hosting a wide variety of musical events.

AVONCROFT MUSEUM OF HISTORIC BUILDINGS

Stoke Heath, Bromsgrove, Worcestershire B60 4JR
Tel: 01527 831363/831886 Fax: 01527 876934 (Council of Management)

25 buildings of historic, architectural and social value authentically restored and re-erected on 15-acre rural site. Covering 7 centuries, it ranges from the magnificently carved timber roof of the Priory of Worcester Cathedral, now gracing a fine new Guesten Hall, to a 1946 Pre-Fab, authentically furnished. English life over the centuries is illustrated – early agriculture by a range of timber-framed buildings, including a working windmill; the local 19th century industries of nail and chain-making; and many aspects of domestic social life. We also house the National Telephone Kiosk Collection. **Location:** At Stoke heath 2 miles south of Bromsgrove. **Open:** March–Nov from 10.30am. Some days closed. **Admission:** Adult £4.50, senior citizen £3.60, child £2.25. Group Rates: Adult £3.60, senior citizen £3, child £1.70.

PERHILL PLANTS

Perhill Nurseries, Worcester Road, Great Witley, Worcestershire
Tel: 01299 896 329 Fax: 01299 896 990 (Perhill Plants)

Specialist growers of 2,500 varieties of alpines, herbs and border perennials. Many rare and unusual. Specialties include penstemons, salvias, osteospermums, dianthus, alpine, phlox, alliums, campanulas, thymes, helianthemums, diascias, lavenders, artemesias, digitals and scented geraniums. **Location:** 10 miles NW of Worcester, on main Tenbury Wells Road (A443). **Open:** 1 Feb–15 Oct, daily, 9–5pm. Sun 10–4pm. Closed 16 Oct–31 Jan except by appointment.

BROBURY HOUSE & GARDEN

Brobury, Nr. Hereford, Herefordshire, HR3 6BS
Tel: 01981 500 229 (Mrs Leonora Weaver)

Brobury House is a magnificent Victorian Gentleman's country house which overlooks the beautiful Wye Valley at Bredwardine, famous for its Francis Kilvert connection. Brobury House is a private home open for functions and B&B. The 8 acres of beautifully landscaped grounds are a gardener's delight, since the owners have lavished 25 years of love and care into them! The internationally known art gallery has over 100,000 antique maps and prints for sale. All of Great Britain's counties, all the countries of the world and most subject matter are represented in our stock. So if you are looking for that unusual gift we could be of help. **Open:** Gardens and Gallery Mon–Sat 9–4.30pm, all year. Closed Sundays.

BURTON COURT

Eardisland, Nr Leominster, Herefordshire HR6 9DN
Tel: 01544 388231 (Lt. Cmdr. & Mrs. R. M. Simpson)

A typical squire's house, built around the surprising survival of a 14th century hall. The East Front re-designed by Sir Clough Williams-Ellis in 1912. Some European and Oriental costume, natural history specimens and models including a children's working model fairground. Pick your soft fruit in season. **Location:** 5 miles W of Leominster signposted on A44. **Open:** Spring Bank Holiday to end September, Wed, Thur, Sat, Sun, Bank Holiday Mon 2.30–6pm. **Admission:** Adults £2.50, children £2. **Refreshments:** Teas by arrangement. **Conferences:** Subject to availability.

BURFORD HOUSE GARDENS

Tenbury Wells, Worcestershire, WR15, 8HQ
Tel: 01584 810 777 Fax: 01584 810 673 (C. Chesshire)

The sweeping lawns and plantsman's paradise of Burford House Gardens are set in the picturesque valleys of the River Teme and Ledwyche Brook. The late Georgian bridge over the Ledwyche has been restored, leading to a new wildflower garden down to the heavenly spot where the two rivers meet. The grass garden has been redesigned, a bamboo collection planted and the National Collection of Clematis of over 200 varieties continues to grow. Also on site is **Treasures of Tenbury Plant Centre/Nursery** growing over 300 varieties of clematis and many of the unusual plants that can be seen in the gardens; specialising in quality plants for sale, pots, tools and friendly practical advice; **Burford House Gallery:** contemporary and one botanical art show annually; **Abode Gift Shop:** decorative and functional gifts, books and cards; **Burford Conservatories; Mulu** exotic plants; **Jungle Giants** bamboos. <u>Refreshments:</u> **Burford Buttery**, serving a wide selection of home-made cakes, pastries, hot and cold meals, teas and coffees. Seating 120 inside (including Buttery Marquee), 40 outside. <u>Location:</u> Tenbury Wells, Worcestershire, WR15 8HQ (off A456, 1 mile west of Tenbury Wells, 8 miles from Ludlow). <u>Car Parking:</u> Free parking for 120 cars, 10 coaches. <u>Open:</u> All year daily 10–6pm (last entry into gardens 5pm); evenings by arrangement. <u>Admission:</u> Adults £2.50, children £1.00; groups of 10+ £2.00. <u>E-mail:</u> treasures@burford.co.uk

map 7
F1

DINMORE MANOR & GARDENS

Nr Hereford HR4 8EE
Tel: 01432 830322 (Mr R G Murray, Dinmore Manor Estate Limited)

Spectacular hillside location. A range of impressive architecture dating from 14th to 20th century. Chapel, Cloisters, Great Hall, (Music Room) and extensive roof walk giving panoramic views of the countryside and beautiful gardens below. Large collection of stained glass. Interesting and unusual plants for sale in plant centre. <u>Location:</u> 6 miles N of Hereford on A49. <u>Open:</u> All the year daily 9.30–5.30pm. <u>Admission:</u> Adults £3, children (under 14) free when accompanied. <u>Refreshments:</u> Available in the Plant Centre most afternoons.

map 7
G1

HARTLEBURY CASTLE

Nr Kidderminster, Worcester, Hereford & Worcester DT11 7XX
Tel: 01299 250410 (Bishop's office) 01299 250416 (Museum)

Home of the Bishops of Worcester for over 1,000 years. Fortified in 13th century, rebuilt after sacking in Civil War and gothicised in 18th century. State Rooms include medieval Great Hall, Hurd Library and Saloon. Fine plaster work and collection of episcopal portraits. Also County Museum in North Wing. <u>Location:</u> In village of Hartlebury, 5 mile S of Kidderminster, 10 miles N of Worcester off A449. <u>Station:</u> Kidderminster 4 miles. <u>Open:</u> Country Museum: Mar–Nov, Mon–Thurs 10–5pm, Fri & Sun 2–5pm. Closed Good Friday. State rooms: Open by arrangement, please contact the museum for details. <u>Admission:</u> County Museum: Adults £2.20, concessions £1.10, family tickets £6.

map 4
A1

EASTNOR CASTLE

Eastnor, Ledbury, Herefordshire HR8 1RL
Tel: 01531 633160 Fax: 01531 631776 (Mr J. Hervey–Bathurst)

Home of the Hervey-Bathurst family, this magnificent Georgian Castle was built in 1812 and is dramatically situated in a 5000 acre estate in The Malvern Hills. Lavish Italianate and Gothic interiors recently restored to critical acclaim. Unique collection of armour, tapestries, furniture and pictures by Van Dyck, Kneller, Romney & Watts. Castellated terraces descend to a beautiful lake and the castle is surrounded by a famous arboretum and 300 acre Deer Park which can be used for large outdoor events. **Location:** 5 miles from junction 2 of M50. 2 miles east of Ledbury on A438 Tewkesbury Road. **Open:** 4 Apr–3 Oct on Sun and Bank Holiday Mon plus every day in Jul and Aug, except Sat. **Admission:** Castle and Grounds: Adults: £4.75, children £2.50. Reduced rates for groups, families and grounds only. Eastnor Castle is also available for exclusive corporate and private entertainment, activity and teambuilding days, wedding ceremonies, receptions and luxury accommodation for small groups.

map 7 G1

HARVINGTON HALL

Harvington, Kidderminster, Worcestershire DY10 4LR
Tel: 01562 777846 (the Roman Catholic Archdiocese of Birmingham)

Moated medieval and Elizabethan manor house containing secret hiding places and rare wall paintings. Georgian Chapel in garden with 18th century altar, rails and organ. **Location:** 3 miles SE of Kidderminster, ½ mile from the junction of A448 and A450 at Mustow Green. **Station(s):** Nearest Kidderminster. **Open:** Mar and Oct, Sat & Sun, Apr to Sept, Wed–Sun. All Bank Holidays. The Hall is available every day for pre-booked schools or groups and for meetings, conferences or wedding breakfasts. **Admission:** Adults £4, OAPs £3, children £2.50, family ticket £10, garden only £1. Free car parking. **Events:** Outdoor plays June and July. Craft Fair – April and Nov. Pilgrimage – early Sept. Wassail – December. Other events and reconstructions to be arranged. Occasionally the Hall may be closed for a private function, up to date information available by phone.

map 4 A1

HELLENS

Much Marcle, Ledbury, Herefordshire HR8 2LY
Tel: 01531 660 668 (The Pennington Mellor Munthe Charity Trust)

Built first as a monastery and then as a stone fortress in 1292 by Mortimer, Earl of March, with Tudor, Jacobean and Stuart additions, this manorial house has been lived in ever since by descendants of the original builder. Visited by the Black Prince, Bloody Mary and the family ghost (a priest murdered during the Civil War). Interesting family paintings relics and heirlooms from the Civil War and possessions of the Audleys, Walwyns and Whartons as well as Anne Boleyn. Also beautiful 17th century woodwork carved by the 'King's Carpenter' John Abel. All these historical stories incorporated into guided tours, revealing the loves and lives of those who lived and died here. Goods and chattels virtually unchanged and certainly not modernised. **Open:** Good Friday–2 Oct, Wed, Sat, Sun and Bank Hol Mons. Guided tours only on the hour 2–5pm (last tour 4pm). Other times by written appointment with the custodian. **Admission:** Adults £3.50, children £1.50 (must be accompanied by an adult).

map 7
G1

HERGEST CROFT GARDENS

Kington, Herefordshire HR5 3EG
Tel: 01544 230160 Fax: 01544 230160 (W.L. Banks, Esq.)

Spring bulbs to autumn colour, this is a garden for all seasons. Old-fashioned kitchen garden; spring and summer borders, roses. Over 59 champion trees and shrubs in one of the finest collections in the British Isles. National Collections of birches, maples and zelkovas. Rhododendrons up to 30ft. **Location:** On outskirts W of Kington off Rhayader Road (A44) (signposted to Hergest at W end of bypass). **Station(s):** Leominster – 14 miles. **Open:** 1 Apr–31 Oct 1.30–6pm. **Admission:** Adult £3.50, children under 16 free. Groups of 20+ by appointment anytime £2.75. Season tickets £12, access Apr–Mar. **Refreshments:** Home-made light lunches and teas. **Events:** Mon 3 May Flower Fair: plant stalls, special events. (£5 admission). Gift shop: Attractive gifts. Plant sales: Rare, unusual trees and shrubs. **Internet:** www.hergest.co.uk (W L Banks)

map 7
G2

HOPTON COURT

Hopton Court, Cleobury Mortimer, Kidderminister, DY14 OEF
Tel: 01299 270734 Fax: 01299 271132 (C. R. D Woodward)

Substantial changes were made to the house and grounds from 1798 to 1803. The works were supervised by John Nash and Humphrey Repton. Around 1820, a conservatory (graded II* in 1995) of cast-iron and glass was built. To the northeast of the house lies the stable block incorporating the Coach House. Both the Conservatory and the Coach House were renovated in 1997. Three rooms in the house and the Conservatory are licensed for civil ceremonies. The Conservatory is open four days a year without appointment, at other times by prior appointment. **Admission:** £3.50. The Coach House is available for receptions.

HOW CAPLE COURT GARDEN

How Caple, HR1 4SX, Hereford & Worcester.
Tel: 01989 740 612 Fax: 01989 740 611 (Mr & Mrs Roger Lee)

11 acres overlooking the River Wye. Formal Edwardian gardens; extensive plantings of mature trees and shrubs, water features and a sunken Florentine garden undergoing restoration. Norman church with 16th century Diptych. Specialist nursery plants and old variety roses for sale. **Location:** B4224, Ross-on-Wye (4.5 miles), Hereford (9 miles). **Open:** Daily 9–5pm, all year. **Admission:** Adults £2.50, children £1.25. Parties welcome by appointment. **Refreshments:** Teas and light snacks all year. Plant centre, dried flowers, gift shop. Car parking. Toilets.

map 7
G1

KENTCHURCH COURT

Nr Pontrilas, Hereford, Herefordshire, HR2 0DB
Tel: 01981 240 228 (Mr & Mrs John Lucas-Scudamore)

Fortified border manor house altered by Nash. Part of the original 14th century house still survives. Pictures and Grinling Gibbons carving. Owen Glendower's tower. **Location:** Off B4347, 3 miles SE of Pontrilas. Monmouth (12 miles). Hereford (14 miles). Abergavenny (14 miles). On left bank of River Monnow. **Open:** May–Sept. All visitors by appointment only. **Admission:** Adults £4, children £2. **Refreshments:** At Kentchurch Court by appointment. **Accommodation:** By appointment.

map 7 G2

LANGSTONE COURT

Llangarron, Ross on Wye, Herefordshire
Tel: 01989 770254 (R M C Jones Esq.)

Mostly late 17th century house with older parts. Interesting staircases, panelling and ceilings. **Location:** Ross on Wye 5 miles, Llangarron 1 miles. **Open:** Wednesdays & Thursdays 11–3pm between May 20–August 31, spring and summer bank holidays. **Admission:** Free.

map 7 H1

LITTLE MALVERN COURT

Nr Malvern, Hereford & Worcester, WR14 4JN
Tel: 01684 892988 Fax: 01684 893057 (Mrs Berington)

14th century Prior's Hall once attached to 12th century Benedictine Priory, with Victorian addition by Hansom. Family and European paintings and furniture. Collection of 18th and 19th century needlework. Home of the Berington family by descent since the Dissolution. 10 acres of former monastic grounds. Magnificent views, lake, garden rooms, terrace. Wide variety of spring bulbs, old fashioned roses, shrubs and trees. **Location:** 3 m S of Great Malvern on Upton-on-Severn Road (A4104). **Open:** 14 April–15 July, Wed and Thurs 2.15–5pm parties by prior arrangement. Guided tours – last admission 4.30pm. **Admission:** Adults: house and garden £4.50; house or garden only £3.50. Children: house and garden £2; house or garden only £1. **Refreshments:** Home-made teas only available for parties by arrangement. Partially suitable for wheelchairs in garden.

map 4 A2

MAWLEY HALL

Cleobury Mortimer, Nr. Kidderminster, Worcestershire, DY14 8PN

18th century house attributed to Francis Smith. Fine plasterwork and panelling. **Location:** 1 mile S of Cleobury Mortimer (A4117). 7 miles W of Bewdley. **Open:** 12 Apr–15 July, Mon & Thur, 2.30–5pm. Visitors are requested to give advanced notice to Mrs R Sharp, Bennet House, 54 St. James' Street, London SW1A 1JT. Tel: 0171 495 6702 **Admission:** £3.

map 4 A1

SPETCHLEY PARK GARDEN

Spetchley Park, Worcester, Hereford & Worcester WR5 1RS
Tel: 01905 345224 (Spetchley Gardens Charitable Trust)

This lovely 30 acre garden is a plantsman's delight, with a large collection of trees, shrubs and plants, many of which are rare or unusual. There is colour and interest throughout the months that the garden is open to visitors. The park contains red and fallow deer. **Location:** 3 miles E of Worcester on Stratford-upon-Avon Road (A422). **Open:** Gardens: 1 Apr–30 Sept. Tues–Fri 11–5pm, Suns 2–5pm. Bank Hols 11–5pm. Closed all Sats & all other Mons. **Admission:** Adults £3, children £1.50, concessions for pre-booked parties. **Refreshments:** Tea in the garden. Regret no dogs. House not open.

map 4 A2

MOCCAS COURT

Moccas, Herefordshire, HR2 9LH
Tel: 01981 500 381 (Trustees of Baunton Trust)

Built by Anthony Keck in 1775 overlooking the River Wye, decoration including the round room and oval stair by Robert Adam. Scene of famous 17th century romance and destination of epic night ride from London. Set in 'Capability' Brown parkland with an attractive walk to The Scar Rapids. **Location:** 10 miles E of Hay on Wye. 13 miles W of Hereford on the River Wye. 1 mile off B4352. **Station(s):** Hereford. **Open:** House & Gardens: Apr–Sept, Thurs, 2–6pm. **Admission:** £2.00. **Refreshments:** Food and drink available at the Red Lion Hotel, Bredwardine, by pre-booking only. **Accommodation:** Available at the Red Lion Hotel, Bredwardine. Disabled access in the garden only.

map 7 G2

WORCESTER CATHEDRAL

College Green, Worcester, Worcestershire, WR1 2LA
Tel: 01905 28854 Fax: 01905 611 139 (Dean & Chapter)

Beside the River Severn, facing the Malvern Hills. Built between 1084 and 1375. Norman Crypt and Chapter House. Early English Quire, Perpendicular Tower. Monastic buildings include the Refectory (now College Hall and open on request during August), Cloisters, remains of Guesten Hall and Dormitories. Tombs of King John and Prince Arthur. Elgar memorial window. Misericords. **Location:** Centre of Worcester. Main roads Oxford and Stratford to Wales. 3 miles M5, Junction 7. **Station(s):** Foregate Street (easier). Shrub Hill (taxi). **Open:** Every day, 7.30–6pm. Choral Evensong daily (except Thurs and school hols). **Admission:** Suggested donation £2. **Guided tours:** Visits Officer 01905 28854.

map 4 A2

Hertfordshire

Capel Manor

Aland of woods, streams and cornfields – a gracious countryside, undulating, varied, typically English, strangely remote and rich in historic monuments – Hertfordshire is a county which retains its ancient character in the midst of rapid development.

With the development of high speed trains, Hertfordshire has become a favourite area for commuters. Part of the county lies inside of the M25, down to Borehamwood, whilst the rest stretches up north into the open countryside.

St Albans today is a thriving market town, steeped in beauty and historic memories. It has seen more than its fair share of history through the years. St Albans was fought over twice during the War of the Roses and the area in front of the abbey's gate was a medieval meeting place and focus of rioting during the Peasant's Revolt of 1381. The cathedral, one of the longest in Britain, is an excellent example of medieval architecture. The town has an air of affluence best appreciated on foot.

Nearby, there are many vestiges of the country's heritage and architecture. Hatfield House is surrounded by beautiful parkland and is a fine example of a Jacobean house. The new towns of Welwyn Garden City and Hemel Hempstead are located close by and form a stark contrast to the many historical areas in this region.

ASHRIDGE

Berkhamsted, Hertfordshire HP4 1NS
Tel: 01442 843491, Fax: 01442 841209
(Governors of Ashridge)

150 acres of both parkland and intimate smaller gardens. The landscape influenced by Humphry Repton. Mature trees combined with unique features e.g. Beech Houses with windows and doors in a Pink and Grey Garden, Grotto – Ferns planted between Herts Pudding Stone. **Location:** 3½ miles N of Berkhamsted (A4251), 1 miles S of Little Gaddesden. **Station(s):** Berkhamsted. **Open:** Gardens open Easter, Apr–Sept Sat & Sun & B/Holidays 2–6pm. **Admission:** Gardens: Adults £2 Children/OAP £1. **Conferences:** For information please contact Carol Johnston, Conference Manager (01442 841027).

AYLETT NURSERIES LTD

North Orbital Road, St. Albans, Herts
Tel: 01727 822255 Fax: 01727 823024 (Mr and Mrs R S Aylett)

Aylett Nurseries of St Albans is a well-known family business with a reputation of high quality plants and service. Famous for dahlias– having been awarded a Gold Medal by the Royal Horticultural Society every year since 1961. In the spring our greenhouses are full of all popular bedding plants. Facilities also include spacious planteria, garden shop, coffee and gift shop, house-plants, florist, garden furniture. From the middle of October do not miss our Christmas Wonderland. **Location:** 2 miles out of St Albans, 1 mile from M10, M1, M25 & A1. **Open:** Daily (excl. Christmas and Easter day). Mon–Sat 8.30–5 Sun 10–4. **Admission:** Free. **Events:** Dahlia Festival–end Sept. **E-mail:** Aylett_Nurseries@compuserve.com **Internet:** www.martex.co.uk/hta/aylett

---

CATHEDRAL AND ABBEY CHURCH OF SAINT ALBAN

St Albans, Hertfordshire AL1 1BY.
Tel: 01727 860780 Fax: 01727 850944 (Dean and Cathedral Council of St Albans)

Standing in the centre of the historic city of St Albans, the Cathedral is the imposing and beautiful abbey church of a Benedictine monastery founded by King Offa in 793 on the site of execution of St Alban, first British martyr (died c.250). The present church was built in 1077 using Roman brick from nearby Verulamium. Became the parish church of St Albans in 1539 and a cathedral in 1877. **Admission:** Free. Spectacular multi-image audiovisual show 'The Martyr's Cathedral' (£1.50 adults/£1 children). Shop and Refectory Restaurant. Guided Tours available. All enquiries 01727 860780. **E-mail:** cathedra@alban.u-net.com. **Internet:** www.stalbansdioc.org.uk/cathedral/

CROMER WINDMILL

Ardeley, Stevenage SG2 7QA
Tel: 01279 843301 (Hertfordshire Building Preservation Trust)

Hertfordshire's last surviving Post Mill now fully restored, with grants from English Heritage and Heritage Lottery Fund. Short video for visitors showing method of working. ½ hour video available on loan, with brochure giving history of Mill. Disabled access, adequate parking, no lavatories, literature and tea towels on sale. **Open:** Sundays, Bank Holidays, 2 and 4 Saturday 2.30–5pm mid May–mid Sept. Special parties by arrangement. Cristina Harrison 01279 843301. **Admission:** Adults £1.25, children 25p. **Location:** OSS TL304287. On the B1037 between Stevenage and Cottered.

THE GARDENS OF THE ROSE

Chiswell Green, St Albans, Herts AL2 3NR
Tel: 01727 850461, Fax: 01727 850360 (The Royal National Rose Society)

The Royal National Rose Society's Gardens provide a wonderful display of one of the best and most important collections of roses in the world. There are some 30,000 roses in 1800 different varieties. The Society has introduced many companion plants which harmonise with the roses including over 100 varieties of clematis. The garden, named for the Society's Patron HM The Queen Mother, contains a fascinating collection of old garden roses. Various cultivation trials show just how easy roses are to grow and new roses can be viewed in the International Trial Ground. **Open:** Spring season: 4 Apr–30 May, Sun & Bank Hols. only 10–4pm. Summer season: 5 June–26 Sept, Mon–Sats 9–5pm. Sun & Bank Hols. 10–6pm. **E-mail:** mail@rnrs.org.uk **Internet:** r oses.co.uk

map 4
E3

GORHAMBURY

St Albans, Hertfordshire AL3 6AH
Tel: 01727 854051 Fax: 01727 843675 (The Earl of Verulam)

Mansion built 1777–84 in classical style by Sir Robert Taylor, 16th century enamelled glass and historic portraits. **Location:** 2 miles W of St Albans, entrance off A4147 at Roman Theatre. **Station(s):** St Albans **Open:** May–Sept, Thurs 2–5. Gardens open with the house. **Admission:** Adults £4, children £2.50, OAPs £2. Guided tours only. Parties by prior arrangement, Thurs £3.50, other days £5.

map 4
E3

ST. PAULS WALDEN BURY

Hitchin, Herts. SG4 8BP
Tel: 01438 871218/871229. Fax: As telephone. (Bowes Lyon)

Formal landscape garden, laid out around 1730, covering about 40 acres. Listed Grade I. Avenues and rides span woodland gardens leading to temples, statues, lake and ponds. There are also more recent flower gardens, best from Apr–Jul. This is the childhood home of Queen Elizabeth, the Queen Mother. **Open:** Suns, 18 Apr, 16 May, 13 Jun 2–7pm. Adults £2.50, children 50p. Home-made teas. Lakeside Concert Jul to be announced. Also by appointment, £5 entry. Proceeds go to charity. **E-mail:** Boweslyon@aol.com

map 4
E2

CAPEL MANOR

Bullsmoor Lane, Nr Enfield, Hertfordshire EN1 4RQ
Tel: 0181 366 4442 Fax: 01992 717544 (Capel Manor Charitable Corporation)

Capel Manor Gardens provide a colourful and scented Oasis surrounding a Georgian Manor House, headquarters of Greater London's specialist College of Horticulture studies. The attractions include 30 acres of richly planted theme gardens including the Italianate Maze, Japanese Garden and many others. Garden Which? Magazine demonstration and model gardens. The National Gardening Centre with specially designed gardens. The Hessayon Centre (our visitor's centre) with garden gift shop and floristry training shop *Animal World and Victorian Stables and Clydesdale Horses. FURTHER INFORMATION, OPENING TIMES AND DATES WITH PHOTOGRAPHY CAN BE SEEN UNDER THE LONDON SECTION.

map 5
F3

BENINGTON LORDSHIP

Benington
Tel: 01438 869668 Fax: 01438 869622 (Mr & Mrs C.H.A Bott)

Hilldrop garden on castle ruins overlooking lakes. Amazing April display of Scillas, scented rose garden, hidden rock/water garden, spectacular borders, ornamental kitchen garden, nursery. **Location:** 5m E of Stevenage, in Benington Village. **Open:** Please phone to confirm times, dates and prices.

BERKHAMSTED CASTLE

Berkhamsted, St Albans, Hertfordshire
Tel: 01442 871737 (English Heritage)

The extensive remains of a large 11th century motte and bailey castle which held a strategic position on the road to London. **Location:** Adjacent to Berkhamsted railway station. **Open:** British Summer time: 10–6pm. During the winter: 10–4pm. **Admission:** Free.

COCKHAMSTED

Braughing
(Mr & Mrs David Marques)

2 acres of informal gardens. Shrub roses surrounded by open country. Island with trees surrounded by water filled 14th century moat. Teas in aid of Leukaemia Research. **Location:** 2m E of village towards Braughing Friars. **Open:** Please contact to confirm times, dates and prices.

HATFIELD HOUSE

Hatfield, Hertfordshire AL9 5NQ
Tel: 01707 262823, Fax: 01707 275719 (The Curator)

Hatfield House was built by Robert Cecil, 1st Earl of Salisbury and Chief Minister to King James I, in 1611. This celebrated Jacobean house, which stands in its own Great Park, has been in the Cecil family ever since. The staterooms are rich in world famous paintings, exquisite furniture, rare tapestries and historic armour. Within the delightful garden stands the surviving wing of the Royal Palace of Hatfield (1497), were Elizabeth I spent much of her childhood and first heard of her accession to the throne. Today, the Marchioness of Salisbury continues to recreate and maintain the grounds and beautiful gardens in a style that reflects their Jacobean history. **Location:** 21 miles N of London – A1(M) Junction 4, 2m. Signed off A414 & A1000. Opposite Hatfield railway station (Kings Cross 29mins). **Open:** 25 Mar–26 Sept (closed Good Friday, but open Bank Hol Mons) House: Tues–Thurs, guided tours only, 12–4pm, Sat and Sun, no tours, 1–4.30pm. Bank Hols, no tours, 11–4.30pm. Park: daily, except Fri,10.30–8pm (West Gardens: 11–6pm, closed Mon). Connoisseurs' Day (every Fri): Park & all Gardens, 11–6pm and extended house tours for booked parties (20+). Last Admissions to park 5pm. **Admission:** (except for major events see below) House, park and west garden: adult £6, child £3, booked party (20+) £5. Park: £1.50, child 80p. Connoisseurs' Day (FRIDAY ONLY) Park & all gardens: £5, house tour: booked party (20+), £4 extra. **Events:** Living Crafts (25th year) 6–9 May, Festival of Gardening 19/20 June, A Tudor Revel 17/18 July, Art in Clay 6–8 August, Country Lifestyle Fair 10–12 Sept. Functions, weddings and banqueting: Tel: 01707 262055.

map 4 E/F3

KNEBWORTH HOUSE

Knebworth, Hertfordshire
Tel: 01438 812661 (The Lord Cobbold)

Home of the Lytton family since 1490 and still a lived-in family house. Transformed in early Victorian times by Edward Bulwer–Lytton, the author, poet, dramatist and statesman, into the unique High Gothic fantasy house of today, complete with turrets, griffins and gargoyles. Home of Constance Lytton, the Suffragette, and Robert Lytton, the Viceroy of India who proclaimed Queen Victoria Empress of India at the Great Delhi Durbar of 1877. Visited by Queen Elizabeth I, Charles Dickens and Sir Winston Churchill. The interior contains many different styles, including the Jacobean Banqueting Hall, the Regency elegance of Mrs Bulwer–Lytton's bedroom, the Victorian State Drawing Room and the Edwardian designs of Sir Edwin Lutyens in the Entrance Hall, Dining Parlour and Library. 25 acres of beautiful gardens, simplified by Lutyens, including pollarded lime avenues, formal rose garden, maze and Gertrude Jekyll herb garden. 250 acres of gracious parkland, with herds of red and sika deer, includes extensive children's adventure playground and miniature railway. Special events staged throughout the summer. World famous for its huge open-air rock concerts, and used as a film location for Batman, the Shooting Party, Wilde, Jane Eyre and the Canterville Ghost, amongst others. **Location:** Direct access off A1(M) junction 7 (Stevenage South A602). 28 miles N of London. 12 miles N of M25 junction 23. **Open:** Daily: 27 Mar–11 Apr, 29 May–5 Sept (exc. 6 June). Weekends & Bank Hols: 17 April–23 May, 11 Sept–26 Sept. **Times:** Park, Gardens & Playground 11–5.30pm. House & Indian Exhibition 12–5pm. (last admission 4.30pm).

map 4
E3

SCOTT'S GROTTO

Scott's Road, Ware, Herts SG12 9SQ
Tel: 01920 464131, 01992 584322 (East Hertfordshire District Council)

Grotto, summerhouse and garden built 1760–73 by Quaker poet John Scott. Described by English Heritage as 'one of the finest grottos in England.' Now extensively restored by The Ware Society. **Location:** Scott's Road, Ware (off A119 Hertford Road). **Station:** Ware/Liverpool Street line. **Open:** Every Sat beginning of Apr–Sept and Easter, Spring and Summer Bank Hol Mons 2–4.30pm. **Admission:** Free but donation of £1 requested. Please park in Amwell End car park by level crossing (300 yards away) and walk up Scott's Road. Advisable to wear flat shoes and bring a torch. Parties by prior arrangement.

map 5
F3

SHAW'S CORNER

Ayot St Lawrence, Nr Welwyn, Herts AL6 9BX
Tel: 01438 820307 (The National Trust)

The home of George Bernard Shaw from 1906 until his death in 1950. The rooms remain much as he left them, with many literary and personal effects evoking the individuality and genius of this great dramatist. The garden has richly planted borders and views over the Hertfordshire countryside. **Open:** 1 Apr–1 Nov: daily except Mon & Tues (but closed Good Fri and open Bank Hol Mon) 1–5pm. **Admission:** £3.30, family ticket £8.25. **Location:** At SW end of village, 2 miles NE of Wheathampstead: approx. 2 miles from B653.

map 4
E3

OLD GORHAMBURY HOUSE

St Albans, Hertfordshire
Tel: 01604 730320 (English Heritage)

The remains of this Elizabethan mansion, particularly the porch of the Great Hall, illustrate the impact of the Renaissance on English architecture. **Location:** ¼ mile west of Gorhambury House and accessible only through private drive from A4147 at St Albans (2 miles). **Open:** May–Sept, Thursday only, 2–5pm. At any other times by appointment only. **Admission:** Free.

Isle of Wight

Nunwell House

The Isle of Wight is an extremely popular destination. Its magnificent landscape is complemented by some unique scenery, such as the stunning Needles. The old capital of Carisbrooke is home to the 11th century Norman castle where Charles I was imprisoned in 1647. Visitors will be fascinated by the history and splendour of Osborne House, designed by Prince Albert.

The Isle of Wight's popular resorts are Sandown, Shanklin and Newport, renowned for their golden beaches. The quaint village of Godshill is often frequented by day-trippers as it offers pleasant tearooms, a model village and other attractions. The island is a famous base for sailing, the big highlight of the sailing calendar being Cowes Week.

CARISBROOKE CASTLE

Newport, Isle of Wight
Tel: 01983 522107 (English Heritage)

Royal fortress and prison to King Charles I, Carisbrooke is set dramatically on a sweeping ridge at the very heart of the Isle of Wight. One of the most popular attractions are the famous Carisbrooke donkeys. See them tread the huge wheel in the medieval well house, much as donkeys would have done in the 18th century. Discover the popular interactive exhibitions and museum, which trace the history of the castle. The island's World War I Memorial chapel offers a moment of contemplation before admiring the breathtaking views from the castle walls. **Location:** 1¼ m SW of Newport. **Open:** 1 Apr–30 Sept: daily, 10–6pm, 1 Oct–31 Oct: daily, 10–5pm, 1 Nov–31 Mar: 10–4pm. (Closed 24–5 Dec) **Admission:** Adults £4.50, concs. £3.40, child £2.30, family £11.30 (15% discount for groups of 11 or more).

map 4
C7

DEACONS NURSERY (H.H)

Moor View, Godshill, PO38 3HW, Isle of Wight
Tel: 01983 840 750 Fax: 01983 523 575 (G. D. Deacon & B. H. Deacon)

Specialist national fruit tree growers. Trees and bushes sent anywhere so send NOW for a FREE catalogue. Over 250 varieties of apples on various types of root stocks from M27 (4ft), M26 (8ft) to M25 (18ft). Plus pears, peaches, nectarines, plums, gages, cherries, soft fruits and an unusual selection of family trees. Many special offers. Catalogue always available (stamp appreciated). Many varieties of grapes; dessert and wine, plus hybrid hops and nuts of all types. **Location:** The picturesque village of Godshill. Deacons Nursery is in Moor View off School Crescent (behind the only school). **Open:** Winter – Mon–Fri, 8–4pm. Summer – Mon–Fri, 8–5pm. Sat, 8–1pm.

map 4
C7

NUNWELL HOUSE & GARDENS

Coach Lane, Brading, Isle of Wight
Tel: 01983 407240 (Col. & Mrs J A Aylmer)

Nunwell House has been a family home for 5 centuries and reflects much island and architectural history. Finely furnished with Jacobean and Georgian wings. Lovely setting with Channel views and 5 acres of tranquil gardens. Special family military collections. **Location:** 1 mile from Brading turning off A3055 signed; 3 mile S of Ryde. **Station:** Brading. **Open:** 30/31 May then 28 Jun–8 Sept, Mon, Tues & Weds 1–5pm with House tours at 1.30, 2.30 and 3.30pm. **Admission:** £4 (includes guide book) – reductions for senior citizens, children and parties. Gardens only £2.50. **Refreshments:** Picnic areas: large parties may book catering in advance. Parties welcome out of season if booked. Large car park. Regret no dogs.

map 4
C7

OSBORNE HOUSE

East Cowes, Isle of Wight
Tel: 01983 200022 (English Heritage)

Visit the magnificent Osborne House, the beloved seaside retreat of Queen Victoria and gain insight into the private family life of Britain's longest reigning monarch. The Royal Apartments, have been preserved almost unaltered since Victoria died here in 1901. The Swiss Cottage, a chalet built in the grounds for the children gives a fascinating insight into their lives and there is an authentic Victorian carriage to take visitors between house and cottage. **Location:** 1m SE of East Cowes. **Open:** 1 Apr–30 Sept: House daily, 10–5pm. Grounds daily, 10–6pm. 1 Oct–31 Oct: House & Grounds daily, 10–5pm. 1 Nov–12 Dec: Sun, Mon, Wed, Thur, 10–2.30pm by pre-booked guided tour only. **Admission:** House & Grounds: Adults £6.90, concs £5.20, child £3.50, family £17. Grounds only: Adults £3.70, concs £2.80, child £1.90. (15% discount for groups of 11 or more).

map 4
C7

Kent

The fruitful fields of the lowlands and the inspiring contours of the downland ridges present a typical picture of England, as the idealist would have it. The county boasts fine countryside, picturesque villages, an elegant spa town, the white cliffs and a county town which is one of the most venerable in England.

Canterbury, on the River Stour, is the centre of the Anglican church and seat of the Archbishop of Canterbury. The cathedral houses a magnificent collection of twelfth and thirteenth century stained glass and the tomb of the Black Prince.

Kent's seaside towns of Whitstable, Margate and Broadstairs are an odd combination of the nostalgic and frivolous. Viking Bay is just one of several sandy coves that dent Thanet's eastern shore. Between Broadstairs and Margate you'll find Stone, Joss, Kingsgate and Botany Bay, with Louisa Bay to the south – all quiet gems.

Matfield Village Green

BELMONT

Belmont Park, Throwley, Faversham, Kent ME13 0HH
Tel: 01795 890202 (Harris (Belmont) Charity)

Charming late 18th century mansion by Samuel Wyatt set in fine parkland. Seat of the Harris family since 1801 when it was acquired by General George Harris, the victor of Seringapatam. The delightfully furnished house contains interesting mementoes of the family's connections with India and colonies, plus the fifth Lord Harris's fine clock collection. Tearoom and gifts. **Location:** 4½ miles south-southwest of Faversham, off A251 (signed from Badlesmere). **Open:** 4 Apr–26 Sept 1999, Sat, Sun & Bank Hols from 2–5pm. (Last admission 4.30pm) Groups on Tue & Thur by appointment. **Admission:** House & garden: Adult £5.00, OAP £4.50, child (2–16 yrs) £2.50. Garden: Adult £2.75, OAP £2.75, child £1.

COBHAM HALL

Cobham, Nr Gravesend, Kent DA12 3BL
Tel: 01474 823371 Fax: 01474 822995/824171

Cobham Hall is an outstandingly beautiful, red brick mansion in Elizabethan, Jacobean, Carolian and 18th century styles. Former home of the Earls of Darnley, set in 150 acres of parkland. Charles Dickens used to walk through the grounds from his house to the Leather Bottle in Cobham Village. There are many fine 17th century marble fireplaces and an 18th century historic snetzler organ in the magnificent Gilt Hall. Cobham Hall is now an independent, international school for girls. **Location:** By A2/M2, between Gravesend & Rochester, 8 miles from Jct 2 on the M25. **Open** March, April, July & August most Wednesdays & Sundays and Easter Weekend, 2–5pm each day. All tours guided. Please call to check dates & times. **Admission:** £3.50/£2.50. **Events/Exhibitions:** Many through year, please phone for details. **Excellent venue for conferences.**

DODDINGTON PLACE GARDENS

Sittingbourne, Kent ME9 0BB
Tel/Fax: 01795 886101 (Mr and Mrs Richard Oldfield)

10 acres of landscaped gardens in an area of outstanding natural beauty. Woodland garden (spectacular in May/June), an Edwardian rock garden, formal terraces with mixed borders, impressive clipped yew hedges, a new folly, fine trees and lawns. **Location:** 4 miles from A2 and A20. 5 miles from Faversham. 6 miles from Sittingbourne, 9 miles from Canterbury. **Station(s):** Sittingbourne, Faversham. **Open:** May–Sept: Suns 2–6pm Weds and Bank Hol Mons 11–6pm. Groups also on other days by prior arrangement. **Admission:** Adults £2.50, children £0.25p, group rate £2 coaches by prior arrangement. Restaurant serving morning coffee, lunches, afternoon teas. Gift shop and restaurant open to non garden visitors.

map 5 H5

DOVER CASTLE

Dover, Kent
Tel: 01304 211067 (English Heritage)

The special highlight of a visit to Dover Castle is the recently opened network of secret wartime underground tunnels which functioned as the nerve centre for the evacuation of Dunkirk. There is even an underground hospital where visitors can experience the sights, sounds and smells of life underground. However, there's as much to see above ground as there is below. Visitors will unlock over 2,000 years of history when they explore Henry II's Keep, the Royal apartments, the 'Live & Let Spy' Exhibition, the Royal Regiment Museum, Saxon Church and Roman lighthouse – the tallest Roman structure still standing in Europe. **Location:** On East side of Dover. **Open:** 1 Apr–30 Sept: daily 10–6pm, 1 Oct–31 Oct: daily, 10–5pm, 1 Nov–31 Mar: 10–4pm. (closed 24–5 Dec) **Admission:** Adult £6.90, concs £5.20, child £3.50, family £17. (15% discount for groups of 11 or more).

map 5 J5

DOWN HOUSE

Downe, Kent, BR6 7JT
Tel: 01689 859119 (English Heritage)

Explore the home of the 19th century's most influential scientist, Charles Darwin. It was from his study that he worked the scientific theories that scandalised and revolutionised the Victorian World, culminating the publication of the most significant book of the century *On the Origin of Species by means of Natural Selection, in 1859.* Down House was his family home for 40 years. It was the centre of intellectual world and even now his study remains full of his notebooks and journals from his epic voyage of discovery that took him most famously to the Galapagos Islands. **Location:** In Luxted Road, Downe off A21 near Biggin Hill. **Open:** 1 Apr–30 Sept: Wed–Sun, 10–6pm. 1 Oct–31 Oct: Wed–Sun, 10–5pm. 1 Nov–31 Jan: Wed–Sun, 10–4pm. (Closed 24–26 Dec & 1–28 Feb). **Admission:** Adults £5.50, concs £4.10, child £2.80 (15% discount for groups of 11 or more).

map 5 F5

FINCHCOCKS

Goudhurst, Kent TN17 1HH
Tel: 01580 211702, Fax: 01580 211007 (Mr & Mrs Richard Burnett)

Georgian manor in beautiful garden, housing a magnificent collection of ninety historical keyboard instruments. Many of these are fully restored and played whenever the house is open in entertaining musical tours. Pictures, prints and exhibition 'The Lost Pleasure Gardens'. **Location:** Off A262 1½ west of Goudhurst, 10 miles from Tunbridge Wells. **Open:** Easter–end of Sept, Suns and BH Mons and Wed and Thurs in Aug: 2–6pm. **Admission:** Adult £6, children £4, family ticket £13. **Garden only:** £2. Free parking. **Refreshments:** Teas. **Reserved Visits:** Groups and individuals most days April–October. **Events:** Finchcocks Festival: weekends in September. Craft & Garden Fairs: end of May–October. **Civil Marriages and Receptions:** Available for functions.

map 5 G5

GAD'S HILL PLACE

Rochester, Kent ME3 7PA
Tel: 01474 822366 (Gad's Hill School Ltd)

Grade 1 listed building, built in 1780. Home of Charles Dickens from 1857 to 1870. **Location:** On A226; 3 miles from Rochester, 4 miles from Gravesend. **Station:** Higham (1½ m) **Open:** 1st Sun in month Apr–Oct and Bank Hol Sun (incl. Easter) 2–5pm. During Rochester Dickens Festivals (June and Dec) 11–4pm. At other times by arrangement. Parties welcome. Rooms, including newly restored conservatory, can be hired for weddings/parties (wedding licence). Free coach/car parking. **Admission:** £2.50, child £1.50 parties by arrangement. Proceeds to restoration fund. **Refreshments:** Sundays, cream teas; Dickens Weekends, Dickensian refreshments; other catering by arrangement.

map 5 G4

GOODNESTONE PARK GARDENS

Goodnestone Park, Canterbury, Kent CT3 1PL
Tel & Fax: 01304 840107

The home of Lord and Lady FitzWalter, Goodnestone Park Gardens covers approximately fourteen acres. The formal area around the house with fine old specimen trees, leads into a small arboretum with an avenue of limes. This adjoins a mature woodland area, with a 1920's rockery and pond. Finally, the walled garden; with some of the walls dating back to the 17th century. This area has been redesigned and planted during the last 30 years, with changes and new plantings continuing all the time. Jane Austen was a frequent visitor, her brother marrying a daughter of the house. **Open:** 29 Mar–22 Oct: weekdays 11–5pm, Sun 12–6pm. Closed Tues & Sat. **Admission:** Adults £2.50, child (under 12) 20p, Family Ticket (2 Adults & 2 children under 12) £4.50. Disabled in wheelchair £1. Season ticket £12.50. Parties of 20+: (unguided) £2.30, (guided) £3.

map 5 J5

GREAT COMP GARDEN

Comp Lane, St. Mary's Platt, Borough Green, Sevenoaks, Kent TN15 8QS.
Tel: 01732 886 154/882 669 (Great Comp Charitable Trust)

Skilfully designed 7 acre garden of exceptional beauty, surrounding a fine early 17th century manor house. Sweeping lawns, romantic ruins and tranquil woodland walks guide the visitor through areas of different character. The extensive collection of trees, shrubs and perennials offer inspiration and pleasure and include many which are rarely seen. The Italian Garden, completed in 1994 offers shelter to the more tender species of plants including Salvias, Bottlebrushes and Cordelines and is at its most colourful during the summer months. The nursery offers a wide and unusual range of plants, most of which can be seen growing in the garden. **Open:** Apr–Oct, daily, 11–6pm. **Admission:** Adults £3, children £1. **Refreshments:** Teas at weekends and Bank Hols. **Special Events:** Festival of Chamber Music takes place annually between July and September in the converted stable. Disabled access.

map 5 G5

GREAT MAYTHAM HALL

Rolvenden, Cranbrook, Kent, TN17 4NE.
Tel: 01580 241 346 Fax: 01580 241 038
(Country Houses Association)

Built in 1910 by Sir Edwin Lutyens. **Location:** Half a mile S of Rolvenden Village, on road to Rolvenden Layne. **Station(s):** Headcorn (10 miles), Staplehurst (10 miles). **Open:** May–Sept, Wed & Thurs, 2–5pm. (Last entry 4.30pm). **Admission:** Adults £3.50, children £1.75. Free car park. No dogs admitted. Groups by arrangement. Up to 20 £3.50pp, over 20 £4pp, including tea & biscuits.

map 5 G6

GROOMBRIDGE PLACE

Groombridge Place, Groombridge, Nr. Royal Tunbridge Wells, Kent TN3 9QG
Tel: 01892 863999 Fax: 01892 863996 (Blenheim Asset Management Ltd)

Winner of South East England Tourist Board Visitor Attraction of the Year 1997. Surrounded by acres of breathtaking parkland, Groombridge Place has an intriguing history stretching back to medieval times. Flanked by a medieval moat, with a classical 17th century manor as its backdrop, the beautiful formal gardens boast a rich variety of "rooms", together with extensive herbaceous borders. High above the walled gardens and estate vineyard, hidden from view, lies The Enchanted Forest, where magic and fantasy await discovery. Here are secret mysterious gardens to challenge and delight your imagination and reward your mind's ingenuity. <u>Location:</u> On B2110, (off A264), 4 miles south west of Tunbridge Wells, 9 miles east of East Grinstead. <u>Open and Admission:</u> 31 March–31 October 1999 Daily 9–6pm. Adults: £6.50, Children: £5.50, Senior Citizens: £5.50.

map 5
F5

HEVER CASTLE AND GARDENS

Nr Edenbridge, Kent TN8 7NG
Tel: 01732 865224 Fax: 01732 866796 (Hever Castle Ltd)

Hever Castle is a romantic 13th century moated castle, once the childhood home of Anne Boleyn. In 1903, William Waldorf Astor bought the castle and created beautiful gardens. He filled the castle with wonderful furniture, paintings and tapestries which visitors can enjoy today. The spectacular award-winning gardens include topiary, Italian and Tudor gardens, a 110 metre herbaceous border and a lake. A yew maze (open May–Oct) and a unique water maze (open April–Oct) are also in the gardens. The Miniature Model Houses Exhibition must also be seen. **Location:** Hever Castle is 30 miles from London, 3 miles SE of Edenbridge. Exit M25 junctions 5 or 6. Stations: Edenbridge Town 3 miles (taxis available), Hever 1 mile (no taxis).

Open: Daily 1 Mar–30 Nov. Gardens open 11am. Castle opens 12 noon. Last admission 5pm. Final exit 6pm. Mar & Nov 11–4pm. **Admission:** Castle and garden ticket, Gardens only ticket and family ticket. Group discounts also available (minimum 15). Pre-booked guided tours of the castle available for groups. **Refreshments:** Two licensed self-service restaurants serving hot and cold food throughout the day. Picnics welcome. **Events:** Special events includes May Day Music and Dance 1–3 May, Merrie England Weekend (29–31 May) and the Patchwork & Quilting exhibition (10–12 Sept). **Conferences:** Exclusive luxury conference facilities available in the Tudor Village.

map 5 F5

HALL PLACE

Bourne Road, Bexley, DA5 1PQ, Kent
Tel: 01322 526 574 Fax: 01322 522 921
(Bexley Council)

Historic house built in 1540, with additions c.1650. Museum and other exhibitions. Outstanding rose, rock and herb gardens and floral bedding displays. Conservatories, parkland and topiary. **Location:** Near the junction of A2 and A223. **Station(s):** Bexley (half a mile). **Open:** House: Mon–Sat, 10–5pm (4.15pm in winter). British Summer Time only – Suns, 2–6pm. Park & Grounds: Daily during the daylight during the year. **Admission:** Free. **Refreshments:** At café & restaurant.

LADHAM HOUSE

Ladham Road, Goudhurst, Kent
Tel: 01580 211203 Fax: 01580 212596
(Mr and Mrs Alastair Jessel)

Privately owned family house set in 10 acres of rolling lawns, fine specimen trees, rhododendrons, azaleas, camellias, shrubs and magnolias. Arboretum and newly cleared woodland walk; spectacular twin mixed borders. Fountain garden and bog garden. Fine views. Restored old rock garden with waterfall. **Location:** 10 miles east of Tunbridge Wells, 1 mile east of Goudhurst off A262 Goudhurst–Ashford road, signposted from B2079 Marden–Horsmonden road. **Open:** For NGS Sun 4 May, 16 May and 3 Oct, 2–5.30pm. At all other times by appointment. Coach parties welcomed. Superb marquee site for weddings and private parties. **Admission:** Adults £3, children under 12 50p. Free parking. **Refreshments:** Available on NGS open days and at other times by arrangement.

LULLINGSTONE CASTLE

Eynsford, Kent DA14 0JA
Tel: 01322 862114 (Guy Hart Dyke, Esq) Fax: 01322 862115

Family portraits, armour, Henry VII gatehouse, church, herb garden. **Location:** In the Darenth valley via Eynsford on A225. **Station:** Eynsford (½ m) **Open:** Castle and grounds Apr–June, Sun & Bank Hols only. July–Sept Sat, Sun & Bank Hols. Wed, Thurs and Fri by arrangement (2–6pm). Telephone for enquiries or bookings. **Admission:** Adults £3.75, children £1.50, OAPs £3. Free car parking. **Refreshments:** In the gatehouse tearooms.

LYMPNE CASTLE

Nr Hythe, Kent CT21 4LQ
Tel: 01303 267571

This romantic medieval castle with an earlier Roman, Saxon and Norman history was once owned by the Archdeacons of Canterbury. It was rebuilt about 1360 and restored in 1905, 300 feet above the well known Roman Shore Fort – Stutfall Castle. Four miles from the ancient Cinque Port of Hythe, it commands a tremendous view across Romney Marshes to Fairlight over the great sweep of the coast from Dover to Dungeness and across the sea to France. Terraced gardens with magnificent views out to sea. **Location:** 3 miles NW of Hythe off B2067, 8 miles W of Folkestone. **Conferences:** Conferences, licensed for civil weddings. Reception facilities.

Due to unforeseen circumstances the castle will remain closed in 1999.

MOUNT EPHRAIM GARDENS

Hernhill, Nr Faversham, Kent
Tel: 01227 751496 Fax: 01227 750940 (Mr & Mrs E S Dawes & Mrs M N Dawes)

8 acres of superb gardens set in the heart of family run orchards. The gardens offer an attractive balance of formal and informal with a herbaceous border, a topiary, a Japanese style rock garden, a water garden, rose terraces and a lake. Vineyard and orchard trails to follow. **Location:** 1 mile off M2, A2 or A299. **Open:** Easter–Sept. Mon, Wed, Thurs, Sat & Sun, 11–6pm. Bank Holidays 11–6pm. Groups at all times by arrangement. House open by appointment for groups of approximately 20–25.

LEEDS CASTLE

Maidstone, Kent ME17 1PL.
Tel: 01622 765400 Fax: 01622 735616 (Leeds Castle Foundation)

Standing majestically on two islands in the middle of a natural lake, Leeds Castle is one of England's oldest and most romantic stately homes. Known as "the loveliest Castle in the world", Leeds was home to six of the medieval Queens of England, and most famous of monarchs, King Henry VIII. It now contains a magnificent collection of furnishings, tapestries and paintings. Leeds Castle is surrounded by 500 acres of rolling parkland and superb gardens which include a Wood Garden with meandering streams and the Culpeper Garden – many people's idea of the perfect English country garden. Opening in May 1999, the Lady Baillie Garden, with its terraced, Mediterranean style overlooking the Great Water, is a major new addition planted in memory of the last private owner, Olive, Lady Baillie. Other attractions at the Castle include a unique Dog Collar Museum, a maze and secret underground grotto and an exotic bird aviary housing more than 100 species of rare and endangered birds. **Events:** An extensive programme of events include Open Air Concerts on 26th June and 3rd July, the Balloon & Vintage Car Weekend on 11th and 12th September and the Leeds Castle Flower Festival from 3rd to 6th June. **Location:** 4 miles east of Maidstone, M20/A20 Junction 8. **Open:** All year (except 26 June, 3 July and 25 Dec 1999). **Admission:** Please phone 01622 765400 for details.

map 5
G5

OWL HOUSE GARDENS
Lamberhurst, Kent
Tel: 01892 890230 (Maureen, Marchioness of Dufferin & Ava)

13 acres of romantic gardens surround this 16th century timber framed wool smuggler's cottage. Spring flowers, roses, rare flowering shrubs and ornamental fruit trees. Expansive lawns lead to leafy woodland walks graced by English and Turkish oaks, elm, birch and beech trees. Rhododendrons, azaleas and camellias encircle peaceful informal sunken water gardens. **Location:** 8 miles SE of Tunbridge Wells; 1 mile from Lamberhurst off A21. **Station(s):** Tunbridge Wells or Wadhurst. **Open:** GARDENS ONLY. All the year – daily and weekends including all Bank Hol weekends 11–6pm. **Admission:** £4, children £1. Free parking. Dogs on lead. Coach parties welcome.

map 5
G5

PATTYNDENNE MANOR
Goudhurst, Kent TN17 2QU
Tel: 01580 211361 (Mr & Mrs D C Spearing)

One of the great timber houses of England, built of oak trees before Columbus discovered America. Special architectural features include banqueting hall, dragon beams, upturned oak trees, enormous fireplaces, 13c prison, pleasant gardens. Connected with Henry VIII. Lived in as a family house, furnished, lecture tour by owner. Ghosts (occasionally). **Location:** 1 miles S of Goudhurst on W side of B2079. **Open:** Open to groups by prior appointment (Groups 20–55 people). Connoisseur's tour also possible. **Admission:** £4.50 **Refreshments:** Light refreshments available.

map 5
G5

PENSHURST PLACE AND GARDENS
Penshurst, Nr Tonbridge, Kent TN11 8DG
Tel: 01892 870307 Fax: 01892 870866 (Viscount & Viscountess De L'Isle)

The Ancestral home of the Sidney Family since 1552, with a history going back six and a half centuries, Penshurst Place has been described as "the grandest and most perfectly preserved example of an fortified manor house in all England". See the awe-inspiring medieval Barons Hall with its 60ft high chestnut beamed roof, where Kings, Queens, noblemen, poets and great soldiers have all dined. The Staterooms contain fine collections of tapestries, furniture, portraits, porcelain and armour from the 15th, 16th, 17th and 18th centuries. The Gardens, first laid out in the 16th century have remarkably remained virtually unaltered during 400 years. A network of trimmed yew hedges and flower terraces make up the 10 acre patchwork of individual garden rooms designed to give colour all year round. Other features include a toy museum, adventure playground, shop, plant centre, restaurant, 200 acre park with lakes and a nature trail. Penshurst Place offers an exquisite arena for corporate and private entertainment amidst beautiful Kent countryside. **Open:** Weekends from 27 Feb, daily from 27 Mar–31 Oct. **Admission:** House & Gardens: Adults £5.70, students/OAPs £5.30, children (5–16) £3.20, family ticket £15. Adult party (20+) £5.10. Gardens only: Adults £4.20, students/OAPs £3.70, children (5–16) £2.80, family ticket £12. Garden season ticket £20. **E-mail:** penshurst@pavilion.co.uk. **Internet:** www.seetb.org.uk

map 5
F5

THE NEW COLLEGE OF COBHAM

Cobham, Nr Gravesend, Kent DA12 3BX
Tel: 01474 812503 (The New College of Cobham Trust)

Almshouses based on medieval chantry built 1362, part rebuilt 1598. Originally endowed by Sir John de Cobham and descendants. **Location:** 4 miles W of Rochester; 4 miles SE of Gravesend; 1½ miles from junction Shorne-Cobham (A2). In Cobham rear of Church of Mary Magdelene. **Station(s):** Sole St (1 mile). **Open:** Apr–Sept, daily 10–7pm. Oct–Mar, daily 10–4pm. **Refreshments:** Afternoon teas by prior arrangement. Guided tours by prior arrangement.

map 5 G4

RIVERHILL HOUSE GARDENS

Riverhill, Sevenoaks, Kent TN15 0RR
Tel 01732 458802 (The Rogers Family)

A lived in family home. Panelled rooms, portraits and interesting memorabilia. Historic hillside garden with sheltered terraces. Rhododendrons, azaleas and bluebells in woodland setting. **Location:** 2 miles S of Sevenoaks on road to Tonbridge (A225). **Station(s):** Sevenoaks. **Open:** Gardens: April, May and June only. Every Wed, Sun and all Bank Holiday weekends during this period. 12–6pm. The House is also open for party bookings of 20 upwards, (adults only) in above period. **Admission:** Gardens: Adults £2.50, children 50p. House and Garden: £3.50. **Refreshments:** Home-made teas in the Old Stable. Catering for booked parties. Ploughmans lunches, teas etc by arrangement. Unsuitable for wheelchairs. No dogs. All enquiries to Mrs Rogers (01732 458802/452557).

map 5 F5

SQUERRYES COURT

Manor House & Gardens, Westerham, Kent TN16 1SJ
Tel: 01959 562345, Fax: 01959 565949 (Mr J St. A Warde)

Squerryes Court is a beautiful, privately owned Manor House built in 1681 in a parkland setting. The house was acquired by the Warde family in 1731 and is lived in by the same family today. The Old Master paintings, furniture, porcelain and tapestries were collected by the Wardes in the 18th century. The lovely gardens, landscaped in the 18th century, are interesting throughout the year with a lake, spring bulbs, borders, recently restored formal garden, topiary and 18th century dovecote. **Location:** Western outskirts of Westerham signposted from A25. Junctions 5 & 6 M25 10 mins. **Station(s):** Oxted or Sevenoaks. **Open:** 1 Apr–30 Sept. Wed, Sat, Sun & BH Mon. Garden: 12–5.30pm. House 1.30–5.30pm (last entry 5pm). **Admission:** House/Grounds:

Adults £4, OAPs £3.60, children (14 and under) £2.30. Grounds only: Adults £2.40, OAPs £2.10, children (14 and under) £1.40. Parties over 20 (any day) by arrangement. House & Garden £3.40. Garden only £2.10. Guided (small extra charge). Pre-booked lunches/teas. Restaurant licence. **Refreshments:** Home-made teas served in Old Library from 2–5pm on open days. **Conferences:** House and Grounds are available for private hire all year e.g. marquee wedding receptions, corporate conferences, luncheons, dinners, promotions, launches, clay pigeon shoots. Dogs on leads in grounds only. Free parking at house.

map 5 F5

SMALLHYTHE PLACE

Smallhythe, Tenterden, Kent TN30 7NG
Tel/Fax: 01580 762334 (National Trust)

Home of Shakespearean actress Dame Ellen Terry, containing personal and theatrical memories. Also garden and barn theatre. **Location:** OS Ref. TQ893 300. 2 miles south of Tenterden on east side of Rye road B2082. **Open:** 12 Apr–31 Oct 1999, 1.30–5.30pm. **Admission:** Adult £3, child £1.50, family £7.50.

map 5 H6

THE THEATRE ROYAL

102 High Street, Chatham, Kent ME4 4BY
Tel: 01634 831028 (Chatham Theatre Royal Trust Ltd)

The Theatre Royal, built in 1899 to accommodate 3000 people, is Kent's finest surviving Victorian Theatre. No expense was spared in its construction or furnishing and it played host to many top stars of their day. In 1955 the curtain finally fell and the building converted to shops and warehousing. Threatened with demolition in the early 1990s the near derelict building was listed and purchased by a charitable trust who are working to reopen it as a first class venue. This gives the public an ideal opportunity to see restoration work in progress. The theatre is open for guided tours most weekdays and groups are welcome any day or time by appointment. Admission is by donation.

map 5 G4

TONBRIDGE CASTLE

Tonbridge, Kent TN9 1BG

Tel: 01732 770929 Fax: 01732 770449 (Tonbridge & Malling Borough Council)

A fine example of the layout of a Norman Motte and Bailey Castle set in landscaped gardens overlooking the River Medway. The site is clearly interpreted and the exhibition in the Castle Gatehouse depicts life as it was 700 years ago. Tours are available from the Tourist Information Centre. **Location:** In town centre off High Street. **Station(s):** Tonbridge (Main line Charing Cross). **Open:** Apr–Sept Mon–Sat 9–5pm, Sun and BH 10.30–5pm; Oct–Mar, Mon–Fri 9–5pm, Sat 9–4pm, Sun 10.30–4pm. Last tours 1 hr before closing time. Self guided headset tours, guided tours by arrangement. **Admission:** Adults £3.45, child/snr citizens £1.70, family £8. **Refreshments:** Nearby. **Accommodation:** Nearby. **Conferences:** Room for hire. Approved for civil marriages. **Please ring for opening times after September 1999.**

map 5 G5

⊞WALMER CASTLE & GARDENS

Kingsdown Road, Walmer, Deal, Kent
Tel: 01304 364288 (English Heritage)

Walmer Castle was originally built by Henry VIII to defend the south coast but has since been transformed into an elegant stately home. As the residence of the Lords Warden of the Cinque Ports, Walmer was used by the Duke of Wellington, (don't miss the Duke's famous 'Wellington boots') and is still used today by HM the Queen Mother. Many of her rooms are open to view. Recently opened is the Queen Mother's Gardens that commemorate her 95th birthday. The gardens are stunning in summer and the herbaceous borders are exceptional. **Location:** On coast S of Walmer on A258. **Open:** 1 Apr–30 Sept: daily, 10–6pm. 1 Oct–31 Oct: daily, 10–5pm. 1 Nov–31 Mar: Wed–Sun 10–4pm. Closed 1–18 Jan. **Admission:** Adults £4.50, concs £3.40, child: £2.30. (15% discount for groups of 11 or more).

map 5 J5

CHARTWELL

Westerham TN16 1PS Tel: Information 01732 866368

Open: House, garden & studio: 27 March to 30 June: daily 11–5 (except Mon & Tues, but open BH Mon and see What's new above); last admission 4.30.

EMMETTS GARDEN

Ide Hill, Sevenoaks TN14 6AY Tel: 01732 750367 Enquiries 01732 868381

Open: 27 March to 30 May: Sat, Sun & Wed, plus BH Mon & Good Fri 11–5.30. Last admission 4.30. Events: for details of concerts and other events tel. 01892 891001.

IGHTHAM MOTE

Ivy Hatch, Sevenoaks TN15 0NT Tel: 01732 810378 Fax: 01732 811029

Open: 28 March to 31 Oct: daily except Tues & Sat 11–5.30. Last admission 4.30pm. Car park open dawn to dusk throughout the year. Estate walks leaflet available. Events: for details tel. 01892 891001

KNOLE

Sevenoaks TN15 0RP Tel: 01732 462100 Infoline: 01732 450608

Open: House: 27 March to 31 Oct: Wed, Thur, Fri & Sat 12–4; Sun, Good Fri & BH Mon 11–5. Pre-booked groups on Thur, Fri & Sat 12–3. Park: open daily to pedestrians by courtesy of Lord Sackville. Garden: May to Sept: first Wed in each month only, by courtesy of Lord Sackville, 11–4; last admission 3. Events: programme of concerts and lectures; for details tel. 01892 891001.

QUEBEC HOUSE

Westerham TN16 1TD Tel: (Regional Office) 01892 890651

Open: 28 March to 26 Oct: Tues & Sun only 2–6. Parties by arrangement; please write to tenant.

SCOTNEY CASTLE GARDEN

Lamberhurst, Tunbridge Wells TN3 8JN Tel: 01892 891081

Open: Garden: 27 March to 31 Oct: (Old Castle: May to 12 Sept) Wed to Fri 11–6; Sat & Sun 2–6, or sunset if earlier; BH Sun & BH Mon 12–6 (closed Good Fri). Last admission 1hr before closing. Events: tel. 01892 891001 for details.

SISSINGHURST CASTLE GARDEN

Sissinghurst, nr Cranbrook TN17 2AB

Tel: 01580 715330 Infoline: 01580 712850

Open: 27 March to 15 Oct: Tues to Fri 1–6.30; Sat, Sun & Good Fri 10–5.30. Closed Mon, incl. BH. Ticket office & exhibition open at 12 on Tues–Fri. (The garden is less crowded in April, Sept & Oct, also Wed to Fri after 4pm).

SMALLHYTHE PLACE

Smallhythe, Tenterden TN30 7NG Tel: 01580 762334

Open: 27 March to 31 Oct: daily except Thur & Fri (but open Good Fri) 1.30–6pm, or dusk if earlier. (The Barn Theatre may be closed some days at short notice).

STONEACRE

Otham, Maidstone ME15 8RS Tel: 01622 862871

Open: 27 March to 30 Oct: Wed & Sat 2–6. Last admission 5pm.

Lancashire

Ribble Valley

Lancashire is well endowed with beauty, charm and even grandeur – and much maligned by its image of dreary industrial mines, mills, ugly towns and smoke blackened countryside. There is farming land with great expanses of cornfields, meadows, pleasant vales and bare moorlands, whilst in the north it shares some of the finest mountain and lake scenery in Britain. Inland, the Forest of Bowland and the Ribble Valley both offer fantastic views.

Southport, a beautiful seaside resort, is famous for its annual international flower show. It is a lively and cosmopolitan town.

The historic county town of Lancaster is tiny when compared to Liverpool and Manchester, but it boasts a long history. The Romans named it after their camp over the River Lune.

Today, its university and cultural life still thrive and the Norman castle, Georgian streets, Lune Aqueduct and a smattering of museums will fascinate the traveller.

BROWSHOLME HALL

Nr Clitheroe, Lancashire BB7 3DE
Tel: 01254 826719 Fax: 01254 826739 (Robert Redmayne Parker)

Built in 1507 and set in a landscaped park, the Ancestral home of the Parker family, with an Elizabethan façade and Regency West Wing recast by Sir Jeffrey Wyatville. Portraits (incl. Devis & Romney), a major collection of furniture, arms, stained glass and other strange antiquities from stone age axes to fragment of a zepellin. **Location:** 5 miles NW of Clitheroe: off B6243; Bashall Eaves–Whitewell signposted. **Open:** 2–4pm Good Fri, Easter Weekend and Spring Bank Hol Weekend. Fri, Sat and Sun in Aug and Aug Bank Hol Mon. **Admission:** Adults £3.50, children £1. **Coach parties particularly welcome by appointment.**

map 11
F7

BLACKBURN CATHEDRAL

Blackburn BB7 3DG
Tel: 01254 51491 Fax: 01254 667309

Blackburn Cathedral is set on a historic Saxon site in the town centre. Built as the Parish Church in 1826, subsequent extensions give a uniqueness to both interior and exterior. Features including the lantern tower, central altar with corona above, fine Walker organ, stained glass from medieval period onwards. Recent restoration work gives a new magnificence. **Location:** 9 miles E of M6 / Jct 31, via A59 and A677, city centre. **Open:** Mon–Fri 9–5.30pm. Sat 9.30–4pm. Sun 8–5pm. **Admission:** Donations.

GAWTHORPE HALL

Padiham, Nr Burnley, Lancashire BB12 8UA
Tel: 01282 771004 Fax: 01282 770178 (The National Trust)

An Elizabethan gem in the heart of industrial Lancashire. The Rachel Kay-Shuttleworth textile collections exhibited. Portrait collection loaned by National Portrait Gallery. Events and exhibitions during high season. **Open:** Hall 27 Mar–7 Nov: daily except Mon and Fri, open Good Fri & BH Mon. 1–5pm. Last admission 4.30pm. Garden: all year, daily 10–6pm. Tearoom open as Hall 12.30–4.30pm. **Admission:** Hall: adults £2.90, children £1.30, family ticket £8, concessions £1.45. Garden: free. Parties by prior arrangement. Free parking 150m. Hall not suitable for baby-packs or pushchairs. **Location:** ¼ mile out of Padiham on A671 to Burnley. Bus services from Burnley (Barracks & Manchester Road Tel: 01282 423125.) Railway station 2m (Rose Grove). Managed by Lancashire County Council. Free to NT members.

map 8
B3

HEATON HALL

Heaton Park, Prestwich, Manchester, Lancashire, M25 2SW
Tel: 0161 773 1231/236 5244 Fax: 0161 236 7369
(Manchester City Art Galleries)

Set in 650 acres of rolling parkland, Heaton Hall is a magnificent Grade I listed building described as 'the finest house of its period in Lancashire and one of the finest in the country'. Designed by James Wyatt in 1772, the building's beautifully restored 18th century interiors are furnished with fine paintings and furniture of the period. A superb collection of Wyatt furniture from Heveningham Hall in Suffolk is a new highlight this year. The unique circular Pompeiian Room, elegant Music Room and Annual art exhibition are also not to be missed. **Open:** Easter–Sept. **Admission:** free. Please call for details.

map 8
B4

HOGHTON TOWER

Nr Preston PR5 OSH
Tel: 01254 852986 Fax: 01254 852109

Hoghton Tower is the home of the 14th Baronet Sir Bernard de Hoghton. It is one of the most dramatic looking houses in Lancashire. There have been 3 houses on the present site stretching back to 1100 AD whilst the estates have remained in unbroken succession since the Norman conquest. The grounds are sited on the hill commanding extensive views of the sea, the Lakes and north Wales. There are also some walled gardens. Location: M6 Jct 28, 10 mins. 6 miles SE of Preston, E of A675. **Open:** All Bank Hols & July, Aug & Sept, Mon–Thur, 11–4pm & Sun, 1–5pm. **Admission:** House only: Adults £2.50, child £1.25, conc. £2. Pre-arranged groups: Adult £3.50. Gardens, shop & tearoom only £1.

LEIGHTON HALL

Carnforth LA5 9ST
Tel: 01524 734474 Fax: 01524 720357

The Hall's neo–Gothic façade was superimposed on an 18th century house, which in turn, had been built on the ruins of the original medieval house. Leighton Hall is situated in a bowl of parkland, with a panoramic view of the Lakeland fells rising behind it. Connoisseurs of furniture will enjoy the 18th century pieces by Gillow of Lancaster. The main garden has a continuous herbaceous border and rose covered walls. **Location:** 3 miles N of Carnforth. 1½ mile W of A6. **Open:** May–September, Tue–Fri & Sun 2–5pm and BH Mons. Groups 25+ may be pre–booked at any time. **Admission:** Charges apply.

RUFFORD OLD HALL

Rufford, Nr Ormskirk, L40 1SG
Tel: 01704 821254 Fax: 01704 821254 (The National Trust)

Come and enjoy the former ancestral home of the Lords of the Manor of Rufford, one of Lancashire's finest 16th century buildings. There's a glorious garden, kitchen restaurant and shop and within the House, a wide variety of tapestries, arms, armour and paintings. The Great Hall has an intricately carved movable wooden screen and dramatic hammerbeam roof. **Location:** 7 miles N of Ormskirk, in the village of Rufford on E side of A59. **Open:** 27 Mar–31 Oct, Sat–Wed 1–5pm. Also open Thurs 8 April, 3 Jun, and all Thurs in Aug. Garden: same days 12–5.30pm. **Admission:** House and garden £3.80, children £1.90, family ticket £9.50. Garden only: £2. Gift shop, wheelchair, food, picnic site.

`map 6 B2`

SAMLESBURY HALL

Preston, New Road, Preston PR5 0UP
Tel: 01254 812010 Fax: 01254 812174 (Samlesbury Hall Trust)

Built in 1325, the hall is an attractive black and white timbered manor house set in extensive grounds. Relax in pleasant surroundings and enjoy a superb selection of antiques, collectors items, crafts and exhibitions. **Location:** N side of A677, 4m WNW of Blackburn. **Open:** All year everyday except Mon: 11–4.30pm. Closed over Christmas and New Year. **Admission:** Adult £2.50, Child £1. Parking for 70 cars.

STONYHURST COLLEGE

Stonyhurst, Clitheroe. Lancashire BB7 9PZ
Tel: 01254 826345 Fax: 01254 826732

The original house (situated close to the picturesque village of Hurst Green in the beautiful Ribble Valley) dates from the late 16th century. Set in extensive grounds which include ornamental gardens. The College is a Catholic boarding & day school, founded by the Society of Jesus in 1593. **Location:** Just off the B6243 (Longridge–Clitheroe) on the outskirts of Hurst Green. 10 miles from junction 31 on M6. **Station(s):** Preston. **Open:** House weekly 19 July–30 Aug, daily except Fri (incl. Aug Bank Hol Mon) 1–5pm. Grounds and Gardens weekly 1 July–30 Aug, daily except Fri (incl. Aug Bank Hol Mon) 1–5pm. **Admission:** House and Grounds £4, children (4–14) £3 (under 4 free), senior citizens £3. Grounds only £1. **Refreshments:** Refreshments/Gift shop: Limited facilities for disabled. Coach parties by prior arrangement. No dogs permitted.

`map 8 A3`

TOWNELEY HALL ART GALLERY & MUSEUMS

Burnley, Lancashire, BB11 3RQ
Tel: 01282 424213 Fax: 01282 436138 (Burnley Borough Council)

The former home of the Towneley family, dating originally from the 14th century, has been an Art Gallery and Museum since 1903. Collections include oak furniture, 18th and 19th century paintings and decorative arts. Major summer exhibitions and temporary loan exhibitions. There is a Natural History Centre with aquarium and nature trails in the grounds. A separate museum of Local Crafts and Industries is housed in the former brew-house. **Location:** ½ mile SE of Burnley on the Burnley/Todmorden Road (A671). Station(s): Burnley Central (1½ miles). **Open:** All the year Mon–Fri 10–5pm, Sun 12–5pm, closed Sat throughout year and Christmas–New Year. **Admission:** Free. **Refreshments:** At cafe on grounds.

`map 8 B3`

TURTON TOWER

Chapeltown Road, Turton, Bolton, Lancashire, BL7 0HG
Tel: 01204 852 203 Fax: 01204 853 759
(Lancashire County Museum Service)

A Lancashire country house dating from medieval times incorporating reconstructed period rooms and a substantial collection of English and Continental domestic wood furniture complemented by an exhibition gallery, tearoom, gift shop, outdoor theatre and other events. Demonstration workshops. Organised guided tours and school tours available. Woodland gardens. **Open:** May–Sept: Sat/Sun 1–5pm, Mon–Thur 10–12pm, 1–5pm. Oct–Mar: Sat–Wed 1–4pm. Apr: Sat–Wed 2–5pm. Nov–Feb: Sun 1–4pm.

`map 6 A1`

Leicestershire

Within its borders, the Midland plain falters and dies and the level stretches of East Anglia merge into gentle, undulating countryside. This is the charm of Leicestershire – simplicity of landscape, a green and pleasant land with few industrial blots to mar its peaceful expanse.

Of the many picturesque and interesting corners of Leicestershire, two are frequently overlooked. The first is linked with a date almost as well known as 1066. In 1485, Richard III was defeated and slain by Henry of Richmond at Bosworth Field. The actual site of the battle is not the little town of Market Bosworth – but between Shenton and Sutton Cheney.

The other is Charnwood Forest. Compared with the mountains of Cumbria, these hills are insignificant, but the eyes delight at the scraggy rocks jutting out abruptly through the fern clad miniature mountains. Picturesque

Town Hall Square, Leicestershire

villages nestle into the countryside, such as Woodhouse Eaves, Newtown Linford and Swithland, with its world famous quarry of blue slate.

Leicester, one of England's cleanest cities, is home to great antiquity. The Old Town Hall is one of Britain's oldest buildings. Here, under the magnificent oak beamed roof, Shakespeare recited his verses to Queen Elizabeth. Traditionally the home of King Lear, with the old Roman walls still standing, the city during Saxon times was the seat of East Mercian Bishops and during the reign of the House of Lancaster, possessed a royal castle. But of Leicester's greatest pride, only the outer walls remain of the abbey where Wolsey came to lay his bones.

If you like to walk, the wolds around Melton Mowbray offer wonderful opportunities. Melton Mowbray is a very pretty market town, offering many interesting little shops and cosy places to eat.

BELVOIR CASTLE
Nr Grantham, Lincolnshire NG32 1PD
Tel: 01476 870262 (Duke of Rutland)

Seat of the Dukes of Rutland since Henry VIII's time and rebuilt by Wyatt in 1816. A castle in the grand style, commanding magnificent views over the Vale of Belvoir. The name dates back to the famous Norman Castle that stood on this site. Many notable art treasures, and interesting military relics. The Statue gardens contain many beautiful 17th century sculptures. Flowers in bloom throughout most of the season. Medieval Jousting Tournaments. Conference and filming facilities. Banquets, school visits, private parties. **Location:** 7 m WSW of Grantham, between A607 (to Melton Mowbray) and A52 (to Nottingham). **Open:** 30 Mar–30 Sept, Tues, Wed, Thurs, Sat, Sun and Bank Hols. Suns only in Oct 11–5. Other times for groups by appointment. **Admission:** Adults £5, children £3, seniors £4. Parties 20+: Adults £4, Seniors £3.50. School parties £2.50. Privilege Card holders – party rate. On Jousting Tournament days an extra charge of 50p per person will apply. Ticket office and catering facilities in the Castle close approximately 30 mins before the Castle. Books are on sale at the ticket office or inside the Castle, or by post £3.50 include. post and packing. We regret that dogs are not permitted (except guide dogs).

map 8 E6

99

KAYES GARDEN NURSERY

1700 Melton Road, Rearsby, Leicester, Leicestershire LE7 4YR
Tel: 01664 424578 (Mrs Hazel Kaye)

Set in the lovely rural Wreake Valley, the garden houses an extensive collection of interesting and unusual hardy plants. A long pergola leads the visitor into the garden and forms a backdrop to the double herbaceous borders. Mixed beds beyond are filled with a wide range of herbaceous plants, shrubs and shrub roses in subtle colour coordinated groups. A stream dissects the garden and ends in a large wild life pond alive with a myriad of dragonflies. Aromatic herbs surround a much favoured seat which looks out across one of the garden ponds towards flower beds shaded by old fruit trees, where hellebores, ferns and many other shade loving plants abound. **Open:** Mar–Oct inclusive Tues–Sat 10–5pm Sun 10am–noon. Nov–Feb inclusive Fri and Sat 10–4.30. Closed Dec 25–Jan 31 inclusive. **Admission:** Entrance to garden £2. Coach parties welcome by appointment.

`map 8 D6`

 # THE MANOR HOUSE

Manor Road, Donington-Le-Heath, Coalville, Leicestershire LE67 2FW
Tel: 01530 831259 (Leicestershire Museums, Arts and Records Service)

A fine Medieval Manor House dating back to about 1280. The house has fascinating grounds surrounding the house including period herb gardens and a miniature maze. The adjoining Barn Tea Room serves tempting home-made delights and light lunches. A programme of special events and exhibitions for all ages runs throughout the season. Admission to the Manor House is free. There is plenty of free parking. Disabled access is on the ground floor of the Manor House, the gardens and Barn Tea Room. **Open:** Wed before the Easter Bank Holiday, then daily until 30 Sept inclusive, 11–5pm. Oct–Mar, 11–3pm.

`map 8 C/D7`

LYDDINGTON BEDE HOUSE

Blue Coat Lane, Lyddington, Uppingham LE15 9LZ
Tel:01572 822438 (English Heritage)

Set among golden–stone cottages, the Bede House was originally a medieval palace of the Bishop of Lincoln. It was later converted into an alms house. **Location:** In Lyddington, 6 miles N of Corby, 1 mile E of A6003. **Open:** Please phone for opening times and admission charges.

STANFORD HALL

Lutterworth, Leicestershire, LE17 6DH
Tel: 01788 860250, Fax: 01788 860870 (The Lady Braye)

William and Mary house, fine pictures (including the Stuart collection), furniture and family costumes. Replica 1898 flying machine, motorcycle museum, rose garden, nature trail. Craft centre (most Sundays). **Location:** M1 exit 18, M1 exit 19 (from/to North only); M6 exit at A14/M1(N) junction. **Open:** Easter–end Sept, Sats, Suns, Bank Hol Mons and Tues following 2.30–5.30pm (last admission 5pm). On Bank Hols and event days open 12 noon (house 2.30pm). **Admission:** House and grounds: Adult £4, child £2. Grounds only: Adult £2.20, child £1. Prices subject to increase on some event days. Parties (min 20): Adult £3.60, child £1.80. Museum: Adult £1, child 35p. **Refreshments:** Home-made teas. Light lunches most Sundays. Suppers, teas, lunches for pre-booked parties any day during season.

`map 4 C1`

WARTNABY

Wartnaby, Leicestershire
Tel: 01664 822 296 (Lord & Lady King)

Medium sized garden, shrubs, herbaceous borders, newly laid out rose garden with good collection of old-fashioned roses and others. Small arboretum. Formal vegetable garden. **Location:** 4 miles NW of Melton Mowbray. From A606, turn W in Ab Kettley. From A46 at Six Hills Hotel, turn E on A676. **Open:** For NGS: **Admission:** Charges apply. (Share to Wartnaby Church®). Disabled access. Plants available for sale.

`map 8 D6`

Lincolnshire

In this county the fens and the great stretches of southern waterways come into their own, revealing a land where field upon field extends over unending acres of plain, to a distant skyline tinged to deepest red by the setting sun. The Spalding Fens, where the endless acres of red, white, blue and variegated yellow tulips wave majestically under the

The view from Bluestone Heath Road

power of stiff breezes and the mixed holdings of daffodils, narcissi and hyacinths have an intoxicating effect, mingle like an eastern carpet at your feet.

The windmills of England are fast disappearing but many are still to be found in the Lincolnshire fens. A visit to the old town of Boston, with its magnificent parish church and a well rounded climb to the top of the 272 foot high lantern tower, reveals the splendour of the fens and the array of ancient windmills dotting a landscape which is forever divided into long straight fields of varying colours.

During the middle ages profits from the wool industry

enabled the development of towns such as Lincoln, the county town, which still houses many fine, historic buildings. Lincoln sits on a cliff above the River Witham. The whole city seems to rise out of the flat fens, with the towers of Lincoln Cathedral being visible for many miles around. The Romans first settled here in AD48 and the historic flavour of the city still remains.

There are many pretty towns in Lincolnshire: Grantham is the site of a wonderful medieval church and an alternative shrine is to the place where Margaret Thatcher was born! Stamford, in the very southern point, is a beautiful little town, with spires, antique shops, splendid churches and a quarry of little lanes and cobbled alleys.

Lincolnshire is also home to a large coastline. It shares The Wash with Norfolk and houses the popular seaside resort of Skegness, which attracts many holidaymakers in the height of the season.

AUBOURN HALL

Aubourn, Nr. Lincoln, Lincolnshire, LN5 9DZ
Tel: 01522 788 270 (Lady Nevile)

Late 16th century house attributed to J. Smythson (Jnr). Important carved staircase and panelled rooms. Lovely garden with deep borders, roses, pond and lawns. **Open:** For charity July–Aug, Wed, 2–5pm. Garden only open Sun 16 May, 6 June, 4 July, 19 Sept. **Admission:** £3, OAPs £2.50. Disabled access to gardens only.

♣ ♿ 👫 map 9 E5

AYSCOUGHFEE HALL MUSEUM & GARDENS

Churchgate, Spalding, Lincolnshire.
Tel: 01775 725468 Fax: 01775 762715

Ayscoughfee Hall is a late-Medieval wool merchants house set in five acres of walled gardens. The Hall is on the east bank of the River Welland five minutes walk from Spalding town centre. The fully Registered 'Museum of South Holland Life' is housed within the Hall and has galleries on local villages, the history of Spalding, agriculture and horticulture. The Museum also includes a gallery dedicated to Matthew Flinders, the District's most famous son, and many specimens from the important Ashley Maples bird collection are on display. **Open:** Garden cafe open seasonally, Mar–Sept. Spalding Tourist Information Centre is also housed within Ayscoughfee Hall. Hall closed winter weekends (Nov–Feb).

♣ ☕ 🍴 🎠 ♿ 👫 🎁 map 9 6F

BURGHLEY HOUSE

Stamford
Tel: 01780 752451 Fax: 01780 480125 (Burghley House Trustees)

The finest example of later Elizabethan architecture in England, built (1565–1587) by William Cecil, the most able and trusted adviser to Queen Elizabeth I. Eighteen magnificent staterooms are open to visitors. Those painted by Antonio Verrio in the late 17th century form one of the greatest decorated suites in England. Burghley is a sumptuous Treasure House and contains one of the finest private collections of 17th century Italian paintings in the world. **Location:** 1 m SE of Stamford, clearly signposted from the A1 and all approaches. Station(s): Stamford (1 mile) Peterborough (10 miles). **Open:** 1 Apr–3 Oct daily, 11 4.30pm except 4 Sept. **Admission:** Adults £6.10, OAPs £5.85. 1 Child per full paying adult, free of charge. Additional children £3. Party rates available.

☕ 🍴 👫 🎁

DODDINGTON HALL

Doddington, Lincoln LN6 4RU
Tel: 01522 694308 (A Jarvis)

Doddington Hall is a superb Elizabethan Mansion surrounded by walled gardens and courtyards and entered through a Tudor Gate House. It stands today as it was built, and its fascinating contents reflect 400 years of unbroken family occupation with fine china, textiles, furniture and family portraits. The gardens contain magnificent box-edged parterres, sumptuous borders and a wonderful succession of spring flowering bulbs that give colour in all seasons. **Open:** Gardens only: Sundays 2–6pm March and April. House and Gardens: Weds, Suns and Bank Hol Mons 2–6pm May–Sept. Parties and school parties at other times by appointment. **Admission:** Adults: house and gardens £4.20, gardens only £2.10. Children: house and gardens £2.10, gardens only £1.05, family ticket £11.50.

map 8 E5

GRIMSTHORPE CASTLE

Grimsthorpe, Bourne, Lincolnshire PE10 0NB. Tel: 01778 591205, Fax: 01778 591259 (Grimsthorpe & Drummond Castle Trust)

The home of the Willoughby de Eresby family since 1516. Examples of early 13th century architecture, the Tudor period of the reign of Henry VIII and work by Sir John Vanburgh. State Rooms and Picture Galleries open to the Public. **Location:** 4 miles NW of Bourne on A151. **Open:** Sun, Thur and Bank Hols from Easter Sun until 26 Sept. Also daily in Aug except Fri and Sats. Park: open 11–6pm. Castle and Gardens: open from 1pm. **Admission:** Adults £3, Concession £2, child £1.50. Additional separate charge for Castle – Adults £2, Concession £2.50. Combined Ticket: Adults £6, Concession £4.50 child £3. **Refreshments:** The Coach House serves light lunches, teas and refreshments 11.15, last orders 5.30 – licensed. **Events/Exhibitions:** For special major events alternative charges may operate. Conference room. Nature trail. Adventure playground. Red deer herd. Cycle trail. Ornamental vegetable garden.

map 8 E6

LINCOLN CASTLE

Castle Hill, Tel: 01522 511068
(Recreational Services Dept., Lincolnshire County Council)

Built by William the Conqueror in 1608, the Castle with its towers, walls and gatehouses, dominates the bail, alongside Lincoln's great Cathedral. The 1215 Magna Carta, sealed by King John at Runnymeade, is set in an informative exhibition. The administration of law and order is well established here with a history stretching back over 900 years. Visitors may attend Crown Court sittings on most weekdays. Encompassed within the walls is a unique Victorian prison chapel where incarceration can be 'experienced'. Events throughout the year. **Location:** Opposite west front of Lincoln Cathedral in the centre of Historic Lincoln. **Open:** Winter: Mon–Sat 9.30–last admission 3.30pm. British Summer Time: as winter but last admission 4.30pm. Closed Christmas Day, Boxing Day and New Year's Day. **Admission:** Adults £2.50, children 16 & under £1, family ticket £6.50.

map 8 E5

MARSTON HALL

Grantham
Tel: 01400 250225 (The Rev Henry Thorold, FSA) or 01400 250167 (Mrs Balham)

Tudor manor house with Georgian interiors, held by Thorold family since 14th century. Interesting pictures and furniture. Romantic garden with long walks and avenues, high hedges enclosing herbaceous borders and vegetables. Gothick gazebo and ancient trees. **Open:** Suns, 13 & 20 June, 25 July 1999, 2–6pm and by appointment. **Admission:** House & garden £2.50. **Refreshments:** Home-made cream teas. In aid of local causes. **Location:** 6 miles NW of Grantham.

map 8 E6

NORMANBY HALL

Normanby, Scunthorpe, North Lincolnshire DN15 9HU
Tel: 01724 720588 Fax: 01724 721248 (North Lincolnshire Council)

The restored working Victorian Walled Garden is growing produce for the 'big house', as it would have been done 100 years ago. Set in 350 acres of park, visitors can also see the Regency Mansion, designed by Sir Robert Smirke, which the Garden was built to serve. The rooms of the Hall are displayed in styles depicting the Regency, Victorian and Edwardian eras. Costume from the Museum Service's collections is also exhibited. **Location:** OS Ref. SE886 166. 4 miles North of Scunthorpe off B1430. Tours by arrangement. **Open:** Hall & Farming Museum: 29 Mar–3 Oct, daily, 1–5pm. Park: All year, daily, 9am–dusk. Walled Garden: All year, daily, 11–5pm (4pm winter). **Admission:** Summer Season: Adults £2.50, concs £1.50, family ticket (2 adults, 3 children) £6.50, half price for North Lincolnshire residents. Winter Season: £2 per car.

BELTON HOUSE

Grantham NG32 2LS
Tel: 01476 566116 Fax: 01476 579071

Admission: £5.20 adults, £2.60 child, £13 family, groups £4.20. **Open:** 27 March to 31 Oct: daily except Mon & Tues (but closed Good Fri and open BH Mon) House: 1–5.30pm; Garden & park (incl. adventure playground): 11–5.30pm (closes 4.30pm on 24 July). Park only: all year on foot only from Lion Lodge gates. Note: No access from this entrance to house, garden or adventure playground. Park may occasionally be closed for special events. Bellmount Woods: daily, access from a separate car park. **Events:** send a s.a.e. for details. **Restaurant** Licensed restaurant as house 12–5pm. 6 Nov to 19 Dec: Sat & Sun 12–4pm. Open for functions and booked groups throughout year; write (with s.a.e.) for details.

TATTERSHALL CASTLE

Tattershall, Lincoln LN4 4LR
Tel: 01526 342543

Admission: £3 adults, £1.50 child, £7.50 family, but accompanied children free in July & Aug. Groups £2.60. Coach groups must book. **Open:** House: 3 April to 31 Oct: daily except Thur & Fri; 6 Nov to 19 Dec: Sat & Sun. 3 April to 31 Oct: 10.30–5.30pm; 6 Nov to 19 Dec: 12–4pm. Ground floor of castle may occasionally be closed for functions or events, tel. to check. Events: 30/31 May medieval living history weekend; send s.a.e. for details. **Restaurant:** Some drinks and ice-creams available in shop (open as castle). Picnicking welcome in grounds.

London

L ondon is beautiful even when the sky is grey. St Paul's, rising above the drabness of Victorian warehouses and offices, adorns a city where Wren churches tucked away in odd corners and the halls of city companies are exquisite gems of craftsmanship.

Johnson declared that someone who is tired of London must be tired of life. The social and cultural heart of the city has long been the bustling West End, where

Regents Park and Lake

the contagious lively ambience lasts long into the night in the street cafés and restaurants.

It is also possible to snatch a moment's reflection in one of London's great parks such as Hyde Park, Regents Park or Richmond Park. It is sometimes easy to forget that these verdant glades are just a stone's throw from the bustle of a capital city.

Today more than ever, London whets the appetite for living.

APSLEY HOUSE, THE WELLINGTON MUSEUM

149 Piccadilly, Hyde Park Corner, London, W1V 9FA
Tel: 0171 499 5676 Fax: 0171 493 6576

Apsley House was designed by Robert Adam and built between 1771 and 1778 for Baron Apsley. It was the first house to be encountered after passing a toll gate from the West, hence its name 'No. 1 London'. In 1817, Apsley House was bought by the first Duke of Wellington. The palatial interiors provide a magnificent setting for the Duke's outstanding collection of paintings, including works by Velasquez, Goya, Rubens, Wilkie, Dutch and Flemish masters; porcelain, silver, sculpture, furniture, swords, medals and memorabilia. **Open:** Tue–Sun 11–5pm. **Admission:** Adults £4.50, concessions £3 both including soundguide, pre-booked groups £2.50, children under 12 free.

map 5
J6

BANQUETING HOUSE

Whitehall Palace, London
Tel: 0171 930 4179

From the days of Henry VIII until its destruction by fire in 1698, the Palace of Whitehall was the Sovereign's main London residence. The only part to survive that fire was the Banqueting House. It is also the only building in Whitehall that is open to the public and it offers an oasis of peace and tranquillity amidst the bustle of Westminster. The Banqueting House was built in 1622 from a design by Inigo Jones, the leading architect of the time. The beautiful vaults beneath are known as the Undercroft–a favourite haunt of James I. When Charles I came to the throne, he further enhanced the building's interior by commissioning the Flemish painter, Rubens, to paint the ceiling. In 1635 Ruben's nine canvasses, including two measured 28x20 feet and two measuring 40x10 feet, were finally put in place. These exquisite

paintings are still intact and provide a spectacular sight for today's visitors. Just as the Banqueting House featured in his early career as King, so it was to feature at the end of Charles I's reign. On 30 January 1649 on a high platform outside the north end of the building, Charles was beheaded, the only British Monarch ever to suffer such a fate. **Location:** London underground–Westminster (District/Circle line) Embankment (District/Circle, Northern & Bakerloo lines), Charing Cross (Northern, Bakerloo & Jubilee lines). BR–Charing Cross. **Open:** Mon–Sat 10–5pm. Closed Suns, 24–26 Dec, 1 Jan, Good Friday & other public holidays & at short notice for Government Functions. **Admission:** Adults £3.60, senior citizens £2.80, child under 16 yrs £2.30, under 5s free. **Internet:** www.hrp.org.uk

map 5
J6

BOSTON MANOR HOUSE

Boston Manor Road, Brentford, Middlesex, TW8 9JX
Tel: 0181 560 5441 Fax: 0181 862 7602 (Hounslow Cultural and Community Services)

Boston Manor House is a fine Jacobean Manor built in 1623, extended in 1670 when the Clitherow family bought the house. It was their family home until 1924. Boston Manor is renowned for its fine English Renaissance plaster ceilings in the State Rooms on the first floor. The Drawing Room has a magnificent ceiling divided into panels representing the senses, the elements, peace, plenty, war and peace and faith, hope and charity. These rooms are furnished with items on loan from Gunnersbury Park Museum. The ground floor rooms date from the early 19th century and house part of the local collection of paintings. The ground floor dining room and library are available for letting for small wedding receptions and seminars. When not in use they may be viewed by visitors. <u>Station(s):</u> Underground Boston Manor, Piccadilly Line 200 yards north of House. <u>Open:</u> Sat, Sun, Bank Hol Mons and from the first Sat in April to the last Sun in October, 2.30-5pm. Children must be accompanied by an adult. <u>Admission:</u> Free. Parking in Boston Manor Road.

map 4
E4

CAPEL MANOR

Bullsmoor Lane, Nr Enfield, Hertfordshire EN1 4RQ
Tel: 0181 366 4442 Fax: 01992 717544 (Capel Manor Charitable Corporation)

Capel Manor Gardens provide a colourful and scented Oasis surrounding a Georgian Manor House, headquarters of Greater London's specialist College of Horticulture studies. The attractions include 30 acres of richly planted theme gardens including the Italianate Maze, Japanese Garden and many others. Garden Which? Magazine demonstration and model gardens. The National Gardening Centre with specially designed gardens. The Hessayon Centre (our visitor's centre) with garden gift shop and floristry training shop *Animal World and Victorian Stables and Clydesdale Horses. A full and varied programme of shows and events. Free car parking. Group visits with special rates. <u>Refreshments:</u> By the "Refectory by the Lake". Disabled facilities including toilets and access around most parts of the Estate. Free wheelchair loan and free entry for wheelchair assistants. Sensory garden and gardens designed for wheelchair users. <u>Admission:</u> Mar–Oct: Adults £4, concessions £3.50 (including senior citizens, disabled etc.), children £2 (3–16 years), family ticket £10 (2 adults and 2 children). Nov–Feb: Special Winter Rates, please telephone for details.

map 5
F3

BUCKINGHAM PALACE

London, SW1A 1AA
Tel: The Visitor Office 0171 839 1377 Fax: 0171 930 9625

Buckingham Palace, Windsor Castle and the Palace of Holyroodhouse are the Official residences of the Sovereign and are used by The Queen as both home and office. The Queen's personal standard flies when Her Majesty is in residence. Furnished with works of art from the Royal Collection, these buildings are used extensively by The Queen for State ceremonies and official entertaining. They are opened to the public as much as these commitments allow. **THE STATE ROOMS:** Are opened daily from 6 Aug –3 Oct 9.30–4.30pm. Tickets can be obtained during Aug–Sept from the Ticket Office in Green Park but are subject to availability. <u>Admission:</u> Adult £10, children (under 17) £5, senior citizens (over 60) £7.50. To pre book your tickets telephone the Visitor Office 0171 839 1377. All tickets booked in advance are £10 and are subject to a small transaction fee. Disabled visitors are very welcome and should telephone in advance for information on access. **THE QUEEN'S GALLERY:** Has a diverse programme of exhibitions. <u>Exhibitions:</u> Mark Catesby's Natural History of America until 10 Jan, 30 Jan–11 Apr, The Kings Head, Portraits of Charles 1, followed by an exhibition dedicated to the work of Raphael 21 May–10 Oct. <u>Open:</u> 9.30–4.30pm, (last admission 4pm) every day during exhibitions, except 10 Apr, 25 and 26 Dec. In the autumn The Queen's Gallery will close for refurbishment and will reopen in 2002, the Golden Jubilee year. **THE ROYAL MEWS:** Is one of the finest working stables in existence. It is a unique opportunity for visitors to see a working department of the Royal Household. The Monarch's magnificent Carriages and Coaches including the Gold State Coach are housed here, together with their horses and State liveries. <u>Open:</u> All year Tues, Wed, Thurs 12–4pm. Last admission 3.30. Extra days and hours are added in the summer months.

map 5
J6

BURGH HOUSE

New End Square, Hampstead, London, NW3 1LT
Tel: 0171 431 0144 Fax: 0171 435 8817 (London Borough of Camden)

A Grade I listed building erected in 1703, in the heart of old Hampstead. Home to many notable professional people before the war. Re-opened in 1979, it houses the Hampstead Museum, an Art Gallery with regularly changing exhibitions and a panelled Music Room popular for weddings, (the house is now licensed), wedding receptions, seminars and conferences. Also used for recitals, talks, local society meetings, book fairs and other events. Licensed basement Buttery and award-winning Gertrude Jekyll-inspired terrace garden. Buttery reservations on 0171 431 2516. **Station(s):** Underground, Hampstead. Rail, Hampstead Heath. **Buses:** 24, 46, 168, 210, 268, C11. **Open:** Wed–Sun, 12noon–5pm. Bank Hols & Good Friday, 2–5pm. Buttery: 11–5.30pm. Closed Christmas/New Year. **Admission:** Free to House/Museum. **Refreshments:** The Buttery.

map 5 F4

CARLYLE'S HOUSE

24 Cheyne Row, Chelsea, London SW3 5HL
Tel: 0171 352 7087 (The National Trust)

Part of a terrace in a quiet backwater of Chelsea, this Queen Anne house was the home of writer and historian Thomas Carlyle from 1834 until his death. The house, which contains the original furniture and many books, portraits and relics of his day, was visited by many illustrious Victorians, including Chopin, Dickens, Tennyson and George Eliot. The restored Victorian walled garden also reflects the Carlyle's life here. **Open:** 27 Mar–31 Oct: Wed to Sun (but open Bank Hol Mon) 11–5pm. Last admission 4.30pm. Closed Good Fri. Price: £3.30; child £1.65.

map 5 J7

CHELSEA PHYSIC GARDEN

66 Royal Hospital Road, London, SW3 4HS
Tel: 0171 352 5646 (The Chelsea Physic Garden Company)

The second oldest botanic garden in the country, founded in 1673 including notable collection of medicinal plants, comprises 4 acres densely packed with c. 6,500 plants, many rare and unusual. **Location:** Swan Walk, off Royal Hospital Road, Chelsea; near junction of Royal Hospital Road and Chelsea Embankment. **Station(s):** Sloane Square – underground. **Open:** Apr–end Oct, Suns, 2–6pm, Wed 12–5pm. Also 12–5pm in Chelsea Flower Show Week and Chelsea Festival Week. Open at other times for subscribing friends and groups by appointment. **Admission:** Adults £4, children/students/unemployed £2. Garden accessible for disabled and wheelchairs via 66 Royal Hospital Road. Parking in street on Sun and on other days across Albert Bridge in Battersea Park. **Refreshments:** Home-made teas. No dogs (except guide dogs).

map 5 J7

CHISWICK HOUSE

Burlington Lane, Chiswick, London, W4
Tel: 0181 995 0508 (English Heritage)

Lord Burlington's internationally celebrated villa never fails to inspire a sense of awe in all who visit. An exhibition on the ground floor reveals why this villa and its gardens are so important to the history of British architecture and an audio-tour will escort you through the fine interiors, including the lavish Blue Velvet Room. The Italianate grounds are equally impressive and have, at every turn, something to surprise and delight – including statues, temples, obelisks and urns. **Location:** Burlington Lane, W4. **Open:** 1 Apr–30 Sept: daily 10–6pm. 1–31 Oct: daily, 10–5pm. 1 Nov–31 Mar: Wed–Sun, 10–4pm. (Closed 24–25 Dec & 1–18 Jan 2000). **Admission:** Adults £3, concs £2.30, child £1.50 (15% discount for groups of 11 or more).

map 5 H7

COLLEGE OF ARMS

Queen Victoria Street, London, EC4V 4BT
Tel: 0171 248 2762 Fax: 248 6448 (College of Arms)

Mansion built in 1670s to house English Officers of Arms and panelled Earl Marshal's Court. Official repository of Armorial Bearings and Pedigrees of English, Welsh, Northern Ireland and Commonwealth families, with records covering 500 years. **Location:** S of St. Paul's Cathedral **Station(s):** Blackfriars or St Pauls. **Open:** Earl Marshal's Court: All year (except public holidays and State and special occasions), Mon–Fri, 10–4pm. Record Room: Open for tours (groups of up to 20) by special arrangement in advance with Officer in Waiting. (Fee by negotiation). **Admission:** Free. Officer in Waiting available to take enquiries concerning grants of Arms and genealogy.

map 5 J6

FENTON HOUSE

Windmill Hill, Hampstead, London NW3 6RT.
Tel: 0171 435 3471 (The National Trust)

A late 17th century house with an outstanding collection of porcelain and early keyboard instruments, most of which are in working order. The delightful walled garden includes fine displays of roses, an orchard and vegetable garden. **Open:** 1 Mar to 3 Apr: Sat & Sun only 2–5pm. 3 Apr–1 Nov: Sat, Sun & Bank Hol Mon 11–5pm; Wed, Thurs & Fri 2–5pm; last admission 30 minutes before closing. **Admission:** £4.10; family ticket £10.25. **Location:** Visitor's entrance on W side of Hampstead Grove.

map 4 E4

THE DE MORGAN FOUNDATION

Old Battersea House, 30 Vicarage Crescent, Battersea, SW11 3LD

A substantial part of The De Morgan Foundation collection of ceramics by William De Morgan and paintings and drawings by Evelyn De Morgan (née Pickering), her uncle Roddam Spencer Stanhope, J. M. Strudwick and Cadogan Cowper are displayed on the ground floor of Old Battersea House – a Wren-style building which is privately occupied. **Location:** 30 Vicarage Crescent, Battersea. **Open:** Admission by appointment only, usually Wed afternoons. All visits are guided. **Admission:** £2 (optional catalogue £1.50). Parties – max. 30 (split into two groups of 15). Admission by writing in advance to The De Morgan Foundation, 56 Bradbourne Street, London, SW6 3TE.

map 5 **J7**

GREENWICH – OBSERVATORY

National Maritime Museum, Romney Road, Greenwich, SE10 9NF
Tel: 0181 312 6565 (24hr infomation line) Fax: 0181 312 6632

The Millennium starts here on the Greenwich Meridian. See the Astronomer Royal's apartments. Charming Wren building. Watch the time ball fall at 1 o'clock. Harrison's amazing clocks. The nearby National Maritime Museum's modern new extension opens Easter 1999 with features on exploration, Nelson, trade and empire, passenger liners and the global garden. *Note: The Queen's House is closed until 30 November 1999.* **Location:** Off A2. River boats from central London. **Station(s):** Maze Hill. **Open:** Daily (except 24–26 Dec) 10–5pm. **Admission:** Price not available at time of publication. **Internet:** www.nmm.ac.uk

map 5 **J6**

HOGARTH'S HOUSE

Hogarth Lane, Great West Road, Chiswick, London, W4 2QN
Tel: 0181 994 6757 Fax: 0181 862 7602 (Hogarth House Foundation)

Just 50 yards away from the busy Hogarth Roundabout lies this charming early 18th century house, which was the country home of William Hogarth, the famous painter and engraver. He lived here from 1749 until 1764, the year of his death. The house is now a gallery, describing the life and works of Hogarth and his various interests, as well as showing his famous engravings. **Location:** 50 yards W of Hogarth Roundabout, on A4 Great West Road. **Station(s):** BR Chiswick (from Waterloo) – ½ mile. Turnham Green Underground, District Line – 1 mile. **Open:** Tue–Fri: Apr–Oct, 1–5pm. Nov–Mar, 1–4pm. Sat & Sun: Apr–Oct, 1–6pm. Nov–Mar, 1–5pm. Closed Mondays (excluding Bank Hols), Good Friday, 25 & 26 Dec, and the month of January. **Admission:** Free. Parties by arrangement. Parking as for Chiswick House Grounds – signed and also named spaces in Axis Business Centre behind house.

map 5 **H7**

KEATS HOUSE

Keats Grove, Hampstead, London, NW3 2RR
Tel: 0171 435 2062 Fax: 0171 431 9293 (Corporation of London)

Keats House was built in 1815–1816. John Keats, the poet, lived here from 1818 to 1820; here he wrote 'Ode to a Nightingale' and met Fanny Brawne, to whom he became engaged. It houses letters, books and other personal relics of the poet and his fiancée. **Location:** S end of Hampstead Heath, near South End Green. **Station(s):** BR – Hampstead Heath. Underground – Belsize Park or Hampstead. Bus: 24, 46, C11, C12 (alight South End Green), 268 (alight Downshire Hill). **Open:** Keats House will be closed from time to time for ongoing repairs. Please telephone for details of current opening times. **Admission:** Free.

map 5 **F4**

HAMPTON COURT PALACE

East Molesey, Surrey KT8 9AU
Tel: 0181 781 9500

With its 500 years of royal history Hampton Court Palace has been home to some of Britain's most famous kings and queens and also the setting for many great historical events. When viewed from the west, Hampton Court is still the red brick Tudor palace of Henry VIII, yet from the east it represents the stately Baroque façade designed by Sir Christopher Wren for William III. The sumptuous interiors reflect the different tastes of its royal residents and are furnished with great works of art, many still in the positions for which they were originally intended. Discover the delights that this marvellous palace has to offer – the recently restored Privy Garden, the 16th century Tudor kitchens and the Mantegna's, a series of nine paintings that represent some of the most important Italian Renaissance works of art in the world. Costumed guides give lively and informative tours of the stunning interiors of the King's Apartments, giving a unique insight into the daily lives of the kings and their courtiers. **Location:** Take Exit 12 & A308 from M25 or Exit 10 onto the A307. **Station:** Hampton Court 32 minutes from London Waterloo via Clapham Junction. **Open:** Mid Mar–Mid Oct, Tue–Sun 9.30–6pm, Mon 10.15–6pm. Mid Oct–Mid Mar, Tue–Sun 9.30–4.30pm, Mon 10.15–4.30pm. Closed 24–26 Dec inclusive. **Admission:** Adults £9.25, senior citizens/students: £7, child under 16yrs £6.10, child under 5yrs free, family ticket (up to 2 adults & 3 children): £27.65. **Events/Exhibitions:** Half-term activities include storytelling for children, young and old and at Christmas time, the palace is a hive of activity with preparations for a banquet fit for Henry VIII along with a myriad of 16th century entertainments. **Internet:** www.hrp.org.uk

map 4
E4

 # KENWOOD HOUSE

Hampstead, London
Tel: 0181 348 1286 (English Heritage)

Discover a true hidden gem amongst the multitude of attractions in London and visit Kenwood, a neoclassical house containing the finest private collection of paintings ever given to the nation, all set in 112 acres of landscaped parkland. With important works by many world-famous artists, including Rembrandt, Vermeer, Turner, Reynolds and Gainsborough, a visit to Kenwood is a must for art lovers. In the 1760s the house was re-modelled by Robert Adam and the breathtaking library is one of his finest achievements. Outside, the sloping lawns and ornamental lake form a wonderfully atmospheric backdrop for our programme of hugely popular lakeside concerts with their dramatic firework finales. **Location:** Hampstead Lane NW3 **Open:** 1 Apr–30 Sept: daily, 10–6pm, 1 Oct–31 Oct: daily, 10–5pm. 1 Nov–31 Mar: daily, 10–4pm (closed 24–25 Dec). Open 1 Jan 2000. **Admission:** Free.

KEW GARDENS, ROYAL BOTANIC GARDENS

Kew, Richmond, Surrey, TW9 3AB
Tel: 0181 940 1171 Fax: 0181 332 5197 (Royal Botanic Gardens)

At any time of the year, Kew's 300 acres offer many special attractions: bluebells in the spring; colourful displays in the summer; beautiful autumnal tints. With some of the largest glasshouses in the world displaying thousands of exotic plants, there is always something to enjoy. The Palm House simulates the multi-layered nature of a tropical rainforest with a canopy of palms and climbers. The Princess of Wales Conservatory under one roof, ranging from cacti in hot desert to orchids in steamy rainforest. The blooms of South Africa, the Caribbean and the Mediterranean can be found in the Temperate House, while the Alpine House, the Waterlily House and the Evolution House contain much to fascinate and delight. The newly opened exhibition 'Plants & People' which displays superb artefacts from Kew's collections and celebrates mankind's ingenious and effective use of plants, is proving to be a big success with all age ranges. Kew also has two art galleries, provides guided tours, excellent variety of catering facilities and shops which offer a wide range of books and gifts with a botanical theme. **Station(s):** Kew Gardens District Line, Kew Bridge British Rail. **Open:** Kew: Daily (except Christmas Day & New Years Day) 9.30am. Tel: 0181 940 1171. Wakehurst Place: Daily (except Christmas Day & New Years Day), 10.00am. Tel: 01444 894066. Closing times for both properties vary according to season; ring for details. **Admission:** Adult £5, concession £3.50, children (5–16) £2.50, Under 5's free. Discount for group bookings 10+ people. Please ring. Tel. No's: 0181 332 5622 Kew 01444 894066 Wakehurst

---

 # LEIGHTON HOUSE MUSEUM & ART GALLERY

12 Holland Park Road, London, W14 8LZ
Tel: 0171 602 3316 Fax: 0171 371 2467

Leighton House was the first of the magnificent Studio Houses to have been built in the Holland Park area and today is open to the public as a museum of High Victorian Art. The home of the great classical painter and President of the Royal Academy, Frederic Lord Leighton, was designed by George Aitchison. The Arab Hall, is the centrepiece of Leighton House with dazzling gilt mosaics and authentic Isnik tiles. Temporary exhibitions are held throughout the year. **Nearest Underground:** High Street Kensington. **Buses:** 9, 9a, 10, 27, 28, 49. **Open:** All year, Mon–Sat, 11–5pm. Closed Sun & Bank Hols. **Admission:** Free. Donations welcome. The house may be booked for concerts, lectures, receptions and private functions.

LINLEY SAMBOURNE HOUSE

18 Stafford Terrace, London, W8 7BH
Tel: 0171 937 0663 Fax: 0171 371 2467 (The Royal Borough of Kensington & Chelsea)

The home of Linley Sambourne (1844–1910), chief political cartoonist at 'Punch' Magazine. A unique survival of a late Victorian town house. The original decoration and furnishings have been preserved together with many of Sambourne's own cartoons and photographs, as well as works by other artists of the period. **Location:** 18 Stafford Terrace. **Station(s):** London Underground – Kensington High St. **Buses:** 9, 10, 27, 28, 31, 49, 52, 70. **Open:** 1 Mar–31 Oct. Wed, 10–4pm (Last entry 3.30pm). Sun, 2–5pm (Last entry 4.30pm). Groups of 15 or more at other times by prior arrangement. Apply to The Victorian Society, 1 Priory Gardens, London, W4. Tel: 0181 994 1019. **Admission:** Adults £3, children (under 16) £1.50, OAPs £2.50.

KENSINGTON PALACE STATE APARTMENTS

Kensington, London
Tel: 0171 937 9561

Situated in the peaceful surroundings of Kensington Gardens, Kensington Palace State Apartments are open to the public. The history of the Palace dates back to 1689 when the newly crowned William III and Mary II commissioned Sir Christopher Wren to convert the then Nottingham House into a Royal Palace. The palace was again altered when George I had the artist William Kent paint the magnificent trompe l'oeil ceilings and staircases which can still be enjoyed at this most intimate of Royal Palaces. Other highlights include the Cupola room where Queen Victoria was baptised and the recently restored King's Gallery. The State Apartments are home to 'Dressing for Royalty' – a stunning presentation of Royal Court and Ceremonial Dress dating from the 18th century, which for the first time allows visitors to experience the excitement of preparing for Court – from invitation to presentation. There is also a dazzling selection of 16 dresses owned and worn by HM Queen Elizabeth II. **Location:** On the edge of Hyde Park, just off Kensington High Street. **Open:** Summer; 10–last entry 5pm. Open every day. Winter; 10–last entry 3pm. Wednesday to Sunday. **Refreshments:** Available all day in the Orangery. **Internet:** www.hrp.org.uk

map 5
J6

MARBLE HILL HOUSE

Twickenham, London
Tel: 0181 892 5115 (English Heritage)

Explore this magnificent Palladian Thames-side villa with its 66 acres of parkland. Admire the Great Room with its lavishly gilded decoration and architectural paintings by Pannini. See the important collection of early Georgian paintings and furniture and the Lazenby Bequest Chinoiserie display. The inclusive audio tour, exhibition and film will reveal the history of this beautiful house and its residents. Marble Hill House was originally built for the Countess of Suffolk, mistress to King George II. Today it offers a wonderful riverside backdrop for a programme of spectacular open-air concerts. **Location:** Richmond Road, Twickenham. **Open:** 1 Apr–30 Sept: daily, 10–6pm. 1–31 Oct: daily, 10–5pm. 1 Nov–31 Mar: Wed–Sun, 10–4pm. (Closed 24–5 Dec & 1–18 Jan 2000). **Admission:** Adult £3, concs £2.30, child £1.50. (15% discount for groups of 11).

map 4
E4

MUSEUM OF FULHAM PALACE

Bishops Avenue, Fulham, London SW6 6EA
Tel: 0171 736 3233 (Museum & Tours) 0181 748 3020 x4930 (Functions)
(L.B. of Hammersmith & Fulham & Fulham Palace Trust, Reg Charity No 1020063)

A Tudor courtyard, a herb garden and a history going back 5000 years. You can find all these at Fulham Palace, once the home of the Bishop of London. The building is a charming mixture of periods (Tudor with Georgian additions and Victorian chapel). Three rooms available for functions. The museum in part of the Palace tells the story of this ancient site; the displays include paintings, archaeology, garden history and a fascinating scale model of the building. The gardens, famous in the 17th century under Bishop Compton who introduced plants from Virginia, now contain over 40 specimen trees and a knot garden of herbs. **Open:** Gardens open daylight hours. Museum open Mar–Oct: Wed–Sun 2–5pm; Nov–Feb: Thurs–Sun 1–4pm. **Admission:** Gardens free. Museum: Adults 50p, concs 25p. Tour of 4 rooms & garden every 2nd Sun all year at 2pm (£2). Private tours by appointment (£5 per head incl. tea). Plant and Produce Sale April 25th 11–4pm. Fulham Pottery exhibition Aug–Sept. **Christmas Bazaar Nov 17th. Education Service available. Ring for details of current events.**

map 5
J6

MUSEUM OF GARDEN HISTORY

Lambeth Palace Road, London SE1 7LB
Tel: 0171 401 8865 Fax: 0171 401 8869 (The Tradescant Trust)

Fascinating permanent exhibition of the history of gardens, collection of ancient tools and re-created 17th century garden displaying flowers and shrubs of the period – seeds of which may be purchased in the Garden Shop. Plus knowledgeable staff, gift shop, café and tombs of the Tradescants and Captain Bligh of the Bounty. Lectures, courses, concerts and art exhibitions held regularly throughout the year. **Location:** Lambeth Palace Road. **Station(s):** Waterloo or Victoria, then 507 Red Arrow bus, alight Lambeth Palace. **Open:** Mon–Fri, 10.30–4pm. Sun 10.30–5pm. Closed Sat. Closed 2nd Sun in Dec to 1st Sun in Mar. **Admission:** Free. Donations appreciated. **Refreshments:** Tea, coffee, light lunches. Parties catered for but prior booking essential. Literature sent on request with SAE. **Internet:** http://www.compulink.co.uk/~museumgh

map 5
J7

ORLEANS HOUSE GALLERY

Riverside, Twickenham, Middlesex
Tel: 0181 892 0221 Fax: 0181 744 0501 (London Borough of Richmond-upon-Thames)

Stroll along a peaceful riverside road into secluded woodland gardens, to find stunning 18th century interior design and an excellent public art gallery. Visitors of all ages can try out their own artistic talents in a pre-booked workshop at Orleans House, or to soak up more history, Marble Hill Park and Ham House are nearby. Finish off with great pub grub around the corner from the Gallery, which is reached easily from London and the south east by road, rail, or even by boat. **Station(s):** St. Margarets Station, overland from Waterloo / Richmond, District Line. **Admission:** Free. **Open:** Tues–Sat, 1–5.30pm; Sun & Bank Holidays 2–5.30pm. Oct–Mar, 4.30pm closing. **E-mail:** jane.dalton@ virgin.net **Website:** www.guidetorichmond.co.uk/orleans.html

PITSHANGER MANOR & GALLERY

Mattock Lane, Ealing, London W5 5EQ
Tel: 0181 567 1227 Fax: 0181 567 0595

Pitshanger Manor and Gallery is set in the beautiful surroundings of Walpole Park, Ealing in West London. The Manor's most illustrious owner was the architect Sir John Soane (1753–1837), 'Architect and Surveyor' to the Bank of England. He rebuilt most of the house to create a Regency villa using highly individual ideas in design and decoration. The house is continually being restored and refurbished to its early 19th century style. A Victorian wing houses a large collection of Martinware pottery. Pitshanger Manor and Gallery is open to the public as a historic house and cultural centre. Adjacent to the manor is a newly refurbished contemporary art gallery – Programming a wide range of changing exhibitions. Please phone for current exhibition programme. **Open:** Tues–Sat 10–5pm. Closed Sun and Mon. Also closed Christmas, Easter and New Year. **Admission:** FREE Parties by arrangement.

ST. JOHN'S GATE
(MUSEUM OF THE ORDER OF ST. JOHN)
St. John's Lane, Clerkenwell, London, EC1M 4DA
Tel: 0171 253 6644 Fax: 0171 336 0587 (The Order of St. John)

Tudor Gatehouse, Grand Priory Church, 12th century Crypt and Museum. Fascinating insight into religious, medical and military history of the Hospitaller Knights of St. John, from the crusades to present day. Includes Maltese silver, furniture, paintings, prints, armour, and pharmacy jars. St. John's Gate also has historic associations with Shakespeare, Hogarth, Cave and Dr. Johnson. Collections include Order's modern work – St. John Ambulance, on which there is a new multimedia interactive exhibition opening Spring 1999, and the St. John Ophthalmic Hospital in Jerusalem. **Location:** St. John's Lane. **Station(s):** London Underground - Farringdon, **Open:** Museum: Mon–Fri, 10–5pm. Sat, 10–4pm. Tours of Gate, Church & Crypt: 11am & 2.30pm, Tue Fri & Sat. **Admission:** Free. (Donations for tours requested). Charity Reg No: 235979.

map 5
J6

OSTERLEY PARK

Jersey Road, Isleworth, Middlesex, London TW7 4RB
Tel: 0181 568 7714 (The National Trust)
Recorded Visitor Information 01494 755566

Although originally a Tudor house, Osterley was transformed into what we see today by Robert Adam in 1761. The spectacular interiors contain one of Britain's most complete examples of his work and include exceptional plasterwork, carpets and furniture. The house also has an interesting kitchen. The house is set in extensive park and farmlands. **Open:** House: 1 Apr–31 Oct; Wed to Sun 1–4.30pm but open Bank Hol Mon. Closed Good Fri. Last admission 4.30. Park and Pleasure grounds open all year 9–7.30pm or sunset if earlier. **Admission:** £4.10; family ticket £10.25. Tearoom and shop available.

map 4
E4

SIR JOHN SOANE'S MUSEUM

13 Lincoln's Inn Fields, London WC2A 3BP
Tel: 0171 430 0175 Fax: 0171 831 3957
(Trustees of Sir John Soane's Museum)

Built by the leading architect Sir John Soane, RA, in 1812–1813, as his private residence. Contains his collection of antiquities and works of art. **Stations(s):** London Underground – Holborn. **Open:** Tues–Sat, 10–5pm. Lecture tours, Sat 2.30pm, Max. 22 people. Tickets £3, on a first come, first served basis from 2pm, no groups. Groups welcome at other times by prior arrangement (Tel: 0171 405 2107). Late evening opening on first Tue of each month, 6–9pm. Also library and architectural drawings collection by appointment. Closed Bank Hols. **Admission:** Free but donations welcome. **Events/Exhibitions:** Changing exhibitions of drawings in the 'Soane Gallery'. Jan–Apr 1999 'Primitive Types: The Sans Serif Alphabet from Sir John Soane to Eric Gill'; Jun–Aug 1999 'Soane and the Ruin'.

map 5
J6

SOUTHSIDE HOUSE

Woodhayes Road, Wimbledon, SW19 4RJ
Tel: 0181 946 7643 (The Pennington Mellor Munthe Charity Trust)

Built by Robert Pennington in 1665 after the death of his first born in the Plague. The family befriended or were related to many distinguished names through the centuries; amongst others Ann Boleyn's descendants, Nelson and the Hamiltons, the infamous "Hellfire Duke of Wharton" and Natalie, the widowed Queen of Serbia. Family portraits and possessions of theirs are on show. Bedroom prepared for Prince of Wales in 1750 and gifts to John Pennington–family 'Scarlet Pimpernel'. In 1907 the heiress, Hilda Pennington Mellor married Axel Munthe the Swedish doctor and philanthropist. After the Second World War Hilda and her sons Viking and Malcolm restored the house. Haunted by his vision of a bombed out Europe, Malcolm who had lived extraordinary adventures during the war, determined to make a cultural ark of the family inheritance, and with minimal resources but fine aesthetical sense made good the war damage. Guided tours give reality and excitement to the old family histories. **Location:** On S. Side of Wimbledon Common (B281) Opposite Crooked Billet Inn. **Open:** 2 Jan–Jun 24, Tues, Thurs, Sat & Bank Holiday Mons. Guided tours only on the hour 2–5pm (last tour 5pm). Also open for private parties by special arrangement only with the Administrator from 1 Dec–24 Jun. **Admissions:** Adults £5, (child accompanied by adult £2).

map 5
F4

SPENCER HOUSE

27 St James's Place, London, SW1A 1NR
Tel: 0171 514 1964 Fax: 0171 409 2952

Spencer House, built 1756–1766, for the first Earl Spencer, an ancestor of Diana, Princess of Wales (1961–97) is London's finest surviving 18th century private palace. The construction of the House involved some of the greatest artists and craftsmen of the day, including the Palladian architect John Vardy and James 'Athenian' Stuart. The House has now regained the full splendour of its 18th century appearance after a ten year programme of restoration undertaken by RIT Capital Partners plc, under the Chairmanship of Lord Rothschild. Spencer House is now partly used as offices and as a place where entertainments can be held in the historic setting of the state rooms, where the remarkable restoration is complemented by a magnificent collection of paintings and furniture. The House is open to the public on Sun and is available for private and corporate entertaining during the rest of the week. **Station(s):** Green Park. **Open:** Every Sun, except during Jan & Aug, 10.30am–5.30pm. Tours last approx. 1 hour (Last tour 4.45pm). Tickets available at door from 10.30 on day. Enquiry Line: 0171 499 8620. **Admission:** Adults £6, concessions £5 (students/Friends of the Royal Academy, Tate and V&A, all with cards/children 10–16; under 10 not admitted). Prices valid until end 1999.

map 5
J6

STRAWBERRY HILL HOUSE

Waldegrave Road, Strawberry Hill, Twickenham, Middlesex.
Tel: 0181 240 4114 Fax: 0181 255 6174 (St. Mary's University College):

Horace Walpole converted a modest house into a fantasy villa. It is widely regarded as the first substantial building of the Gothic Revival, and as such internationally known and admired. A century later Lady Waldegrave added a magnificent wing to Walpole's original structure. Guided tours take approximately 75 minutes and it is worth coming to see this unique house. These magnificent rooms can also be hired for corporate events, wedding receptions and conferences both day and residential. **Open:** Advance group bookings by appointment only are taken throughout the year and the House is open to the general public on Suns from Easter to Mid October, between 2pm and 3.30pm. This information was correct at the time of going to print, please phone 0181 240 4224 for up to the minute information. **Admission:** The ticket price is £4.75 concessions for OAP's, a maximum of 20 people per tour, the house is not suitable for disabled or children under 14 years of age. For information regarding advance group bookings or functions, please call the conference office on 0181 240 4114/0181 240 4311 or 0181 240 4044.

map 4 E4

ENTRY TO THE TRAITORS' GATE

TOWER OF LONDON

Tower Hill, London
Tel: 0171 709 0765

Begun by William the Conqueror in 1078 to help secure London, the chief city of his new realm, the Tower of London has served as a royal residence, fortress, mint, armoury and more infamously a prison and place of execution. Since the seventeenth century, the Crown Jewels have been on public display at various locations in the Tower; today visitors can see them in all their glory in the magnificent new Jewel House. Not to be missed is the new 'Crowns and Diamonds' exhibition which charts the evolution of English royal crowns and tells the story of some of the most famous stones set in them. Take time to explore the newly refurbished White Tower, the original Tower of London, with the Royal Armouries' recently re-presented collections of arms and armour. Once inside, the Yeomen Warder 'Beefeaters' give free guided tours providing an unrivalled insight into the dark secrets of the Tower's history. They will tell the legend of the ravens,

resident for over 900 years, without whom the Tower and the Kingdom would fall. Above the notorious Traitor's Gate, costumed guides evoke life at the court of King Edward I in the recently restored chambers of the Medieval Palace. Visitors can stand on Tower Green where three queens of England lost their heads, enter the Bloody Tower where Sir Walter Raleigh was imprisoned and then stroll along the Wall Walk with its panoramic views of the River Thames. With its state parades, gun salutes and pomp and circumstance, the Tower really is London. **Location:** Underground to Tower Hill or buses 15, 25, 42, 78, 100, D1. Included on all major sightseeing tours. **Open:** 9–5pm, Mar–Sept. 9–4pm, Oct–Feb. The Tower opens at 10 am on Sundays throughout the year. **Admission:** Adults £9.50, child £6.25, concs £7.15, family £28.40. Groups: Call 0181 781 9540 for special features and rates. Further information: Call 0171 709 0765.

map 5
J7

SYON PARK

Syon Park, Syon House & Gardens, Brentford, Middlesex TW8 8JF
Tel: 0181 560 0883 Fax: 0181 568 0936 (Syon Park Ltd)

Sir John Betjeman described Syon House as "The Grand Architectural Walk". Syon House is the London home of the Duke of Northumberland, whose family have lived here since the late 16th century. The present house is Tudor in origin, having been built by Lord Protector Somerset on the site of a medieval Abbey. It was in the Long Gallery that Lady Jane Grey was offered the Crown and at Syon where some of Charles 1st's children were imprisoned during the Civil War. The first Duke of Northumberland commissioned Robert Adam to remodel the interior into the magnificent suite of State rooms on view today. The parkland was landscaped by Capability Brown. Within it there are 30 acres of gardens which incorporate 'The Great Conservatory', (shown above) designed by Charles Fowler in the 1820s, the Rose Garden and over 200 species of rare trees. Housed in the former stables is one of the country's best known garden centres. Patio Cafeteria, National Trust Gift Shop. **Open:** House 11–5pm, Wed, Thurs, Suns and Bank Hols, 17 Mar–31 Oct. Gardens open daily 10–5.30pm or dusk except 25–26 Dec. Party rates, guide service if required.

map 4
E4

THE WALLACE COLLECTION

Hertford House, Manchester Square, London
Tel: 0171 935 0687 Fax: 0171 224 2155

The Wallace Collection is a national museum located in Hertford House, which was built in 1776. Within the superb range of fine and decorative arts are magnificent 18th century French paintings, furniture and porcelain, paintings by Titian, Rembrandt and Rubens and opulent displays of gold boxes, sculpture, miniatures and Renaissance works of art. **Location:** Manchester Square (behind Selfridges). **Station(s):** London Underground Bond Street. **Open:** Mon–Fri, 10–5pm. Sun, 2–5pm. Free lectures on the collection, daily. All of the galleries are accessible to wheelchair users, who are advised to telephone before their visit (ext.23). Wheelchairs available on request. **Admission:** Free (donations). **Internet:** www.demon.co.uk/heritage/wallace

THE TRAVELLERS CLUB

106 Pall Mall, London, SW1Y 5EP
Tel: 0171 930 8688 Fax: 0171 930 2019

The Club House was designed by 34 yr. old Charles Barry. His design broke architectural precedent, the Pall Mall façade being derived from the Palazzo Pandolfino in Florence, causing considerable comment in its day. Barry went on to design the Houses of Parliament. **Location:** 106 Pall Mall. **Station(s):** London Underground: Piccadilly Circus, Charing Cross. **Open:** By prior appointment only, Mon–Fri, 10–12noon. Closed Bank Hols, August and Christmas. **Admission:** Adults £8 by prior appointment. **Refreshments:** Included.

2 WILLOW ROAD

2 Willow Road, Hampstead, London NW3 1TH
Tel: 0171 435 6166 (The National Trust)

The former home of Erno Goldfinger, designed and built by him in 1939. One of Britain's most important examples of modernist architecture, the house is filled with furniture also designed by Goldfinger. The interesting art collection includes work by Henry Moore and Max Ernst. **Open:** 1 Apr–30 Oct: Thurs, Fri & Sat 12–5pm. Last admission 4pm. Guided tours every 45 minutes from 12.15 until 4pm. **Admission:** £4.10. No parking at house. Limited on-street parking.

map 5
J6

map 4
E4

(don't keep 'em waiting)

AT&T Direct® Service

AT&T Direct is a great way to reach those you care about back home. It provides quick access to English-speaking operators and fast connections with clear sound quality.

For easy dialing instructions and access numbers, please find a wallet guide in the back of this publication.

For more information, check out the AT&T Worldwide Traveler Web Site at http://www.att.com/traveler

©1998 AT&T. All Rights Reserved.

AT&T

It's all within your reach.

Greater Manchester

Manchester houses a buzzing cultural scene. Museums, classical concerts, ballet, theatre, ethnic festivals and clubs famous for footballers, test cricketers and other sportsmen are all part of its legend.

As the millennium approaches, historic edifaces are being spruced up, architects are transforming the old mills, new buildings are springing up and the canals have been cleared and are attracting the colourful barges and small boats again.

In 1830, the railway to Liverpool was opened and carried the first passenger trains in the world. Over a century later, the Victorian Gothic architecture still dominates the city.

SMITHILLS HALL

Off Smithills Dean Road, Bolton, BL1 7ND
Tel: 01204 841265 (Bolton Museum, Art Gallery & Aquarium)

14th century manor house. Highlights include the Great Hall with its open timber roof, and Tudor linenfold panelling in the withdrawing room. **Open:** Apr–Sept, Tues–Sat 11–5pm, Sun 2–5pm. Closed: Mondays except Bank Holidays. Oct–March, closed to the general public. Open to pre-booked party tours. **Admission:** Adults £2, concs £1, groups £1.50.

HALL I'TH' WOOD

GREEN WAY, OFF CROMPTON WAY, BOLTON BL1 8UA TEL: 01204 301159
Late Medieval Merchants House which became the home of Samuel Crompton in 1779 where he invented the Spinning Mule. **Open:** Apr–Sept, Tues–Sat 11–5pm, Sun 2–5pm. Closed: Mondays except Bank Holidays. Oct–March, closed to the general public. Open to pre-booked party tours. **Admission:** Adults £2, concs £1, groups £1.50.

Merseyside

Liverpool stands majestically on the estuary of the River Mersey and used to be England's second greatest port. Many of the old docks have been renovated, such as the Albert Dock, designed by Jesse Hartley in 1846, which has been transformed into shops and cafés and houses an offshoot of the London Tate Gallery, 'The Beatles Story' and the sight and sound show.

Merseyside also has an expanse of coastline, facing the Irish Sea. To the north is Southport which overlooks this often rough stretch of water. Situated close to Liverpool, is the appealing seaside resort of Wallasey, which sits on the peninsular of the Wirral, with fantastic sandy beaches. The Wirral used to be a royal game reserve; it is now a wonderful haven for waders and waterfowl. The salt marshes of the Dee estuary produce an area that attracts these feathered delights, perfect for bird-watchers.

Liverpool

LIVERPOOL CATHEDRAL

Liverpool L1 7AZ
Tel: 0151 709 6271 Fax: 0151 709 1112

Sir Giles Gilbert Scott's greatest creation. Built this century from local sandstone with superb glass, stonework and major works of art, it is the largest Cathedral in Britain with a fine musical tradition, a tower offering panoramic views and award-winning refectory. There is a unique collection of church embroidery, a full range of souvenirs, cards and religious books. **Location:** Central Liverpool, 1/2 mile south of Lime Street station. Open: 8–6pm. **Admission:** Donations please.

SPEKE HALL

The Walk, Liverpool L24 1XD
Tel:0151 427 7231 Infoline: 0345 585702Fax: 0151 427 9860 (The National Trust)

One of the most famous half–timber houses in the country, set in varied gardens and attractive wooded estate. Tudor Great Hall, Victorian interiors, William Morris wallpapers. There is a Rose and Stream Gardens. Woodland walks and stunning views of the Mersey estuary. **Location:** North bank of the Mersey, 6m SE of city centre. Follow signs for Liverpool airport. Please phone for details of opening times and admission charges.

MEOLS HALL

Southport PR9 7LZ
Tel: 01704 228326 Fax: 01704 507185 (R Hesketh Esq.)

A 17th century manor house, with subsequent additions, containing an interesting collection of pictures, furniture, china etc. **Location:** 1 mile N of Southport: 16 miles SW of Preston: 20 miles N of Liverpool; near A565 and A570. **Station(s):** Southport. **Open:** 14 Aug–14 Sept, 2–5pm. **Admission:** Adults £3, children £1, those under 10 accompanied by adult free. **Refreshments:** Available in local village 200 yards. Afternoon teas available for group bookings. Tithe Barn available for weddings and corporate hospitality. **Events:** For 1999 include Musical Weekend, Churchtown Country Show and Bonfire Party.

Norfolk

Kings Lynn

Norfolk is one of England's most peaceful counties. This flat county boasts some of the most glorious coastline which has a unique network of inland waterways, tranquil heaths, woodland and hedgerows.

Norfolk remains unspoilt by man or time. This reflects in the county town, Norwich, which to this day is one of the best preserved towns in England. In the 9th century, Norwich was fortified by the Saxons and the medieval street plan remains.

The Norfolk Broads National Park attracts birdwatchers and boaters from around the country. The Broads to the east, best seen on a boat, contain many slow moving shallow rivers which meander through the countryside, until they join the coast around the popular holiday resort of Great Yarmouth.

THE FAIRHAVEN WOODLAND & WATER GARDENS

South Walsham, Nr Norwich, Norfolk NR13 6EA
Tel & Fax: 01603 270449 (G.E. Debbage)

170 acre Woodland & Water Garden and Bird Sanctuary in the beautiful Norfolk Broads. Largest collection of naturalised Candelabra Primula in England. Over 90 recorded species of birds, many rare plants and shrubs. Special times to visit the Gardens include, 'Primrose Weeks' during April, 'Candelabra Primula Weeks' May–early June, 'Autumn Colours October'. A different flowering almost every month gives visitors something special to see every time they visit. Children's nature trail, boat trips, plant sales restaurant, gift shop. **Location:** Nine miles NE of Norwich on the B1140. **Open:** 1 Apr–31 Oct, 11–5.30pm Closed Mon except Bank Hol. **Admission:** Adults £3, OAPs £2.70, children £1. Under 5s free. Group bookings: Please contact in advance. Free guided tours available, group discounts. The Fairhaven Garden Trust is a Registered Charity No 265686.

map 9 K6

HOLKHAM HALL

Wells-next-the-Sea, Norfolk NR23 1AB
Tel: 01328 710227, Fax: 01328 711707 (The Earl of Leicester)

One of Britain's most majestic stately homes, situated in a 3,000 acre deer park, on the beautiful north Norfolk coast. This celebrated Palladian style mansion, based on designs by William Kent, was built between 1734 and 1762 by Thomas Coke, 1st Earl of Leicester. The magnificent alabaster entrance hall rises the full height of the building and in the richly and splendidly decorated Staterooms are Greek and Roman statues, brought back by the 1st Earl from his Grand Tour of Europe, fine furniture by William Kent and paintings by Rubens, Van Dyck, Claude, Poussin and Gainsborough. In addition to the Hall there is a Bygones Museum in the original stable block, History of Farming

Exhibition in the porters' lodge and Holkham Nursery Gardens in the 18th century walled kitchen garden. **Location:** 2 miles W of Wells-next-the-Sea. S off the A149. **Open:** Suns–Thurs (incl.) 30 May–30 Sept 1–5pm. Plus Easter, May, Spring & Summer Bank Hols. Sun & Mon 11.30–5pm. (last admission 4.45pm). **Admission:** Hall: Adults £4, children £2. Bygones: Adults £4, children £2. Combined ticket: Adults £6, children £3. Reduction on parties of 20 or more. Private tours of the Hall by arrangement. **Refreshments:** Restaurant. **Events:** Holkham Country Fair, Sat 17 & Sun 18 July. NB: Hall & Museum Closed. Gift shop and pottery.

map 9 H6

HOUGHTON HALL

Kings Lynn
Tel: 01485 528569 (The Marquess of Cholmondeley)

The Home of the Marquess of Cholmondeley, Houghton Hall was built in the 18th century for Sir Robert Walpole by Colen Campbell and Thomas Ripley, with interior decoration by William Kent and is regarded as one of the finest examples of Palladian architecture in England. Houghton was later inherited by the 1st Marquess of Cholmondeley through his grandmother, Sir Robert's daughter. Situated in beautiful parkland, the house contains magnificent furniture, pictures and china. Pleasure grounds. A private collection of 20,000 model soldiers and militaria. Newly restored walled garden. **Location:** 13 miles E of King's Lynn; 10 miles W of Fakenham off A148. **Open:** Thurs, Sun and Bank Hol. Mon from 4 April–26 September 2–5:30pm, last admission 5pm. **Admission:** House, park and grounds: (include soldier museum, walled garden, tearoom and gift shop) Please telephone for details.

map 9 H6

EUSTON HALL

(Nr.Thetford), Suffolk
Tel: 01842 766366 (The Duke and Duchess of Grafton)

Euston Hall – Home of the Duke and Duchess of Grafton. The 18th century country house contains a famous collection of paintings including works by Stubbs, Van Dyck, Lely and Kneller. The pleasure grounds were laid out by John Evelyn and William Kent, lakes by Capability Brown. 17th century parish church in Wren style. Watermill, craft shop, picnic area. **Location:** A1088; 3 miles S Thetford. **Open:** June 3–Sept 30 Thurs only 2.30–5pm, also Sun June 27 and Sept 5, 2.30–5pm. **Admission:** Adults £3, children 50p, OAPs £2.50. Parties of 12 or more £2.50 per head. **Refreshments:** Teas in Old Kitchen.

map 5 H1

HOVETON HALL GARDENS

Hoveton Hall, Norwich, Norfolk.
Tel: 01603 782798 Fax. 01603 784564

Hoveton Hall Gardens – 15 acres of rhododendron and azalea filled woodland, laced with streams leading to a lake. Daffodils galore in Spring. Formal walled herbaceous and vegetable gardens. Morning coffee, light lunches and delicious home-made teas. **Open:** Easter Sun to mid Sept, Wed, Fri, Sun and Bank Hol Mons 11–5.30pm. Coaches welcome by appointment.

map 9 J6

MANNINGTON HALL

Saxthorpe, Norfolk
Tel: 01263 584175, Fax: 01263 761214 (Lord and Lady Walpole)

15th century moated house and Saxon church ruins set in attractive gardens. Outstanding rose gardens. Extensive walks and trails around the estate. **Location:** 2 miles N of Saxthorpe, near B1149; 18 miles NW of Norwich; 9 miles from coast. **Open:** Walks daily all year; Garden May–Sept Sun 12–5pm. Also June–Aug Wed, Thurs and Fri 11–5. **Admission:** Adults £3, children (accompanied children under 16) free OAPs/students £2.50. House open by prior appointment only. **Refreshments:** Coffee, salad lunches and home-made teas.

WOLTERTON PARK

Erpingham, Norfolk
Tel: 01263 584175, Fax: 01263 761214 (Lord and Lady Walpole)

Extensive historic park with lake and 18th century Mansion house. **Location:** Near Erpingham, signposted from A140 Norwich to Cromer Road. **Station(s):** Gunton. **Open:** Park open all year, daily 9–5pm or dusk if earlier. 1999 Hall: Fridays from April 30, 2–5pm (last entry 4pm). For Sundays and events see local press. **Admission:** Park £2 per car. Hall: £5. **Refreshments:** Pub at drive gate. **Events/Exhibitions:** Yes. **Accommodation:** Limited. **Conferences:** Yes.

map 9 J6

map 9 J6

SANDRINGHAM HOUSE, MUSEUM AND GROUNDS

Estate Office, Sandringham, Norfolk PE35 6EN
Tel: 01553 772675 (Her Majesty The Queen)

Sandringham is the charming country retreat of Her Majesty The Queen hidden in the heart of sixty acres of beautiful wooded grounds. All the main ground floor rooms used by The Royal Family, full of their treasured ornaments, portraits and furniture, are open to the public. More Royal possessions dating back more than a century are displayed in the Museum housed in the old stable and coach houses. Glades, dells, lakes and lawns are surrounded by magnificent trees and bordered by colourful shrubs and flowers. A free Land Train from within the entrance will carry passengers less able to walk through the grounds to the House and back. All areas are fully accessible by wheelchair.

Location: 8 m NE of King's Lynn (off A148). **Open:** House: from 1 April–20 July 1999 daily 11–4.45pm (Grounds and Museum 24 July), reopens 5 August–3 October, daily 10.30 (Museum 11am) to 5pm. Grounds and Museums open weekends in October. **Admission:** House, Grounds & Museum: Adults £5, seniors/students £4, children (5–15) £3. Grounds & Museum: Adults £4, seniors/students £3.50, children (5–15) £2.50. **Refreshments:** Air-conditioned restaurant and waitress service tearoom open daily Easter–Oct. Visitor Centre with gift shop, plant stall and country park open daily Easter to October and weekends November–March.

map 9
G6

WALSINGHAM ABBEY GROUNDS & SHIREHALL MUSEUM

Walsingham, Norfolk NR22 6BP
Tel: 01328 820259 Fax: 01328 820098 (Walsingham Estate Co.)

Set in Walsingham, a picturesque medieval village, the grounds contain the remains of an Augustinian Priory founded in 1153 on a site next to the Holy House and provide pleasant river and woodland walks. Famous for the snowdrop walks during Feb/Mar. Open to the public daily 10–4pm, entry through Museum or Estate Office when High Street gate closed. Telephone for more details. **Refreshments/Accommodation:** Wide range available in the village. Car park: Pay and display 50 yards.

map 9
H6

BLICKLING HALL, GARDEN & PARK

Blickling, Norwich NR11 6NF Tel: 01263 738030 Fax: 01263 731660

Open: House: 27 March to 31 Oct: daily except Mon & Tues (but open BH Mons) 1–4.30pm. Garden: 27 March to end July, Sept to 31 Oct as house. Aug daily; 1 Nov to 31 March 2000: Sat & Sun. 27 March to 31 Oct 10.30–5.30pm; Nov to March 2000 11–4pm. Park and woods: daily dawn to dusk. **Events:** tel. or send s.a.e. for details. **Admission:** £6.20. Groups £5.20. Groups must book with s.a.e. to Property Manager. Garden only: £3.50. Free access to South Front, shop, restaurant and plant centre. Coarse fishing in lake; permits from Warden, tel. 01263 734181.

FELBRIGG HALL, GARDEN & PARK

Felbrigg, Roughton, Norwich NR11 8PR Tel: 01263 837444

Open: House: 27 March to 31 Oct: daily except Thur & Fri 1–5pm; BH

Mons & BH Suns 11–5pm. Garden: as house 11–5.30pm. Woodland, lakeside walks and parkland: daily (closed Christmas Day) dawn to dusk. **Events:** send s.a.e. for details or contact Events Box Office (tel. 01263 838297). **Admission:** House & garden: Adult £5.50, child £2.70, family £13.70. Groups (except Sun) £4.50; book with s.a.e. to Property Manager. Garden only £2.20. **Restaurant.**

OXBURGH HALL, GARDEN & ESTATE

Oxborough, King's Lynn PE33 9PS Tel: 01366 328258 Fax: 01366 328066

Open: House: 27 March to 31 Oct: daily except Thur & Fri 1–5pm; BH Mon 11–5pm. Garden: 6–21 March: Sat & Sun; 27 March to 31 July, 1 Sept to 31 Oct: daily except Thur & Fri; Aug daily. 6 to 21 March 11–4pm, 27 March to 31 Oct 11–5.30pm. **Events:** send s.a.e. for full details. **Admission:** House, garden & estate: £5, booked groups £4; book with s.a.e. to Administrator. Garden & estate only: £2.50.

Northamptonshire

Oundle

Cottesbrooke Hall

Northamptonshire is a gently undulating county where church spires and grand estates nestle amongst rolling hills rising to a lofty height of seven hundred feet above sea level in places. Its beautiful landscape comprises waterways, ancient woodlands and rivers. Visitors can enjoy a hearty pub lunch after a morning of guided walks or cycling through the meandering valleys.

The impressive town of Northampton is the setting for Holy Sepulchre, one of only four surviving round Norman churches in England. A fine display of works of art by Henry Moore and Graham Sutherland may be seen at St Matthew's church in Kingsley.

As you walk around, it is easy to appreciate the spacious, ordered layout of this town, created after Northampton was destroyed by a huge fire in the seventeenth century.

Travelling further east, St James' Church in Thrapston is often frequented by historians as the family coat of arms of Sir John Washington, relative of the first American president, is depicted.

Those wishing to explore the county's national treasures must visit the many historic properties in the area. Althorp, the home of the Spencer family, Holdenby House with its magnificent gardens and Rockingham Castle, built by William the Conqueror are all fine examples of Northamptonshire's rich heritage.

BOUGHTON HOUSE

Boughton House, Kettering, Northamptonshire.
Tel: 01536 515731 Fax: 01536 417225 E-mail: llt@boughtonhouse.org.uk (Duke of Buccleuch)

Northamptonshire home of the Duke of Buccleuch and his Montagu ancestors since 1528. A 500 year old Tudor Monastic building, gradually enlarged until French style addition of 1695 led the sobriquet "The English Versailles". Outstanding collection of fine arts from the world renowned Buccleuch Collection including 16th century carpets, 17th, 18th century French and English furniture, tapestries, porcelain and painted ceilings and notable works of art including works by El Greco, Murillo, Caracci and over 40 Van Dyck paintings. There is an incomparable Armoury and Ceremonial Coach. Extensive parkland with historic avenues of trees, woodlands, lakes and riverside walks. There is a Plant Centre in attractive old walled garden and tearooms in the attractively refurbished Stable Block adjacent to the House, which together with the Adventure

Woodland Play area and Gift Shop are open weekends and daily throughout August. **Internet:** Award winning site gives full information, a 'virtual' tour of House and details of our group visits and educational facilities (Heritage Education Trust, Sandford Award Winner 1988, 1993 and 1998) www.boughtonhouse.org.uk. **Open: House and Park:** Daily (including Fri) 1 Aug–1 Sept. Park from 1pm, House 2pm, last entry 4.30pm. Staterooms strictly by pre-booked appointment, telephone 01536 515731 for details. **Park:** Daily (except Fri) 1 May–1 Sept, 1–5pm Plant Centre, Adventure Play area, tearoom open daily in Aug and weekends during park opening. Educational groups throughout the year, by prior appointment. **Admission:** House and Park: Adults £6, OAP/child £5. Park only: Adults £1.50, OAP/child £1. Wheelchair visitors free.

map 4
D1

ALTHORP

The history of Althorp is the history of a family. The Spencers have lived and died here for nearly five centuries and twenty generations.

Since the death of Diana, Princess of Wales, Althorp has become known across the world, but before that tragic event, connoisseurs had heard of this most classic of English stately homes on account of the magnificence of its contents and the beauty of its setting.

Next to the mansion at Althorp lies the honey-coloured stable block, a truly breathtaking building which at one time accommodated up to 100 horses and 40 grooms. The stables are now the setting for the Exhibition celebrating the life of Diana, Princess of Wales and honouring her memory after her death. The freshness and modernity of the facilities are a unique tribute to a woman who captivated the world in her all-too-brief existence.

All visitors are invited to view the House, Exhibition and Grounds as well as the Island in the Round Oval where Diana, Princess of Wales is laid to rest.

Althorp is clearly signed from junction 16 of the M1. The Park is located 5 miles west of Northampton off the A428.

Open daily, 1st July to 30th August 1999, 9am to 5pm. Last admission at 4pm.
At the time of booking visitors will be asked to state a preference for a morning or an afternoon visit.

All visitors are requested to book in advance to visit Althorp. This is necessary in order to preserve the dignity and tranquillity of every visit.

Adults £9.50
Senior Citizens £7
Children (5–17) £5
Children under 5 free
All the profits from visitor activity at Althorp are donated to the **Diana, Princess of Wales Memorial Fund,**
a registered charity, subject to a minimum donation of 10% of the admission fee.

Group visits by arrangement only.

Please contact our dedicated booking line (24 hour service)
Tel: +44 (0)1604 592020

Althorp, Northampton NN7 4HQ Tel: +44 (0)1604 770107 Fax: +44 (0)1604 770042
http://www.althorp.com

CASTLE ASHBY

Castle Ashby House, Castle Ashby, Northampton NN7 1LQ
Tel: 01604 696696 Fax: 01604 696516

The lands at Castle Ashby were given to the Compton family in 1512 by Henry VIII. In 1574 Queen Elizabeth 1 gave William, Lord Compton, permission to demolish the derelict 13th century castle and build the present House on this site. The original plan of the House was in the shape of an 'E' in honour of Queen Elizabeth and in 1625 the courtyard was enclosed by a screen designed by Inigo Jones. Castle Ashby is still the home of the Compton family, the 7th Marquess of Northampton being the 27th generation. The Castle and the Compton family have a fascinating history; related by marriage to most of the aristocratic families in this country. These liaisons are still remembered in the names given to each of the bedrooms. Castle Ashby stands at the heart of a 10,000 acre working estate, surrounded by 200 acres of beautiful parkland. It is not open to the public and is the only Stately

Home available on an exclusive basis with 26 exquisitely refurbished bedrooms, in addition to the recently restored State Suite which is absolutely unique in the country. Despite its seclusion and tranquillity, Ashby is capable of hosting the most sophisticated event, whilst clients are cared for by experienced professionals. Our aim is to provide discreet service with a touch of informality to allow guests to experience the enjoyment of using the house as if it were their own. Located 55 miles from London the Capability Brown landscape contains many superb walks and lakes for fishing. Horse-riding, clay shooting and carriage driving are also accessible. The vast gardens incorporate a Triumphal Arch, Orangery, Italian Gardens and Camellia Houses.

map 4
D2

COTTESBROOKE HALL AND GARDENS

Nr Northampton, Northants NN6 8PF
Tel: 01604 505808 Fax: 01604 505619 (Captain & Mrs John Macdonald-Buchanan)

Architecturally magnificent Queen Anne house commenced in 1702. Renowned picture collection, particularly of sporting and equestrian subjects. Fine English and Continental furniture and porcelain. Main vista aligned on celebrated 7th century Saxon church at Brixworth. House reputed to be the pattern for Jane Austen's 'Mansfield Park'. Celebrated gardens of great variety including herbaceous borders, water and wild gardens, fine old cedars and specimen trees. The magnolia, cherry and acer collections are notable, as also are the several fine vistas across the park. **Location:** 10 miles N of Northampton (A14–A1/M1 Link Road), near Creaton on A5199, near Brixworth on A508. **Open:** Easter to end Sept. **House and Gardens:** Thurs and Bank Hol Mon afternoons, plus all Sat and Sun afternoons in Sept 2–5.30pm. Last admission 5pm. **Gardens Only:** Tues, Wed and Fri afternoons 2–5.30pm. Last admission 5pm. **Admission: House and Gardens:** Adults £4. **Gardens Only:** £2.50; children half price. **Refreshments:** Tearoom open 2.30–5pm. Gardens, but not house, suitable for disabled. Car park. Plants for sale. No dogs. **PRIVATE BOOKINGS:** Available for group visits to the house and gardens, or gardens only, on any other day during the season, except weekends, by prior appointment. **Lunches/refreshments** Available for groups by prior arrangement. Please telephone for information.

map 4 D1

COTON MANOR GARDEN

Nr Guilsborough, Northamptonshire NN6 8RQ
Tel: 01604 740219 Fax: 01604 740838 (Mr & Mrs I Pasley-Tyler)

Traditional old English garden set in unspoilt countryside, with yew and holly hedges, extensive herbaceous borders, rose garden, water garden, herb garden, woodland garden, famous bluebell wood (early May) and recently established wild flower meadow. **Location:** 10 miles N of Northampton and 11 miles SE of Rugby. Follow tourist signs on A428 and A5199 (formerly A50). **Station(s):** Northampton, Long Buckby. **Open:** 1 Apr–30 Sept daily Wed-Sun and Bank Hol Mons 12–5.30pm. **Admission:** Adults £3.50, senior citizens £3, children £2. **Refreshments:** Restaurant serving home-made lunches and teas. **Events/Exhibitions:** Unusual plants propagated from the garden for sale during season.

map 4 D1

HADDONSTONE SHOW GARDEN

The Forge House, Church Lane, East Haddon, Northampton, NN6 8DB
Tel: 01604 770711 Fax: 01604 770027 (Haddonstone Limited)

See Haddonstone's classic garden ornaments in the beautiful setting of the walled manor gardens – including urns, troughs, fountains, statuary, bird baths, sundials and balustrading. Featured on BBC Gardeners' World, the garden is on different levels with shrub roses, ground cover plants, conifers, clematis and climbers. As part of Haddonstone's Silver Jubilee Celebrations, the garden was substantially expanded to allow a temple, pavilion and Gothic Grotto to be displayed. **Location:** 7 miles NW of Northampton off A428. **Open:** Mon–Fri 9–5.30pm closed weekends, Bank Hols and Christmas period. **Admission:** Free. Groups must apply in writing for permission to visit.

map 4 D1

LAMPORT HALL & GARDENS

Lamport, Northamptonshire, NN6 9HD
Tel: 01604 686 272 Fax: 01604 686 224

Built for the Isham family. The South West front is a rare example of John Webb, pupil of Inigo Jones and was built in 1655 with wings added in 1732 and 1740. The Hall contains a wealth of outstanding books, paintings, furniture and china. Set in spacious wooded parkland with tranquil gardens including a remarkable rock garden. **Location:** 8 miles N of Northampton on A508. **Open:** Easter–3 Oct, Sun & Bank Hol Mons, 2.15–5.15pm. 23–24 Oct, 2.15–5.15pm. Last tour/admission 4.00pm. Aug, Mon–Sat one tour at 3.30pm. **Group Visits:** Welcome at anytime by prior arrangement. **Admission:** Adults £3.80, senior citizens £3.30, children £2. **Refreshments:** Home-made teas in the Victorian Dining Room. **Events:** Telephone for a free brochure. **Conferences:** Available for conferences/corporate hospitality.

   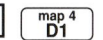

map 4 D1

HOLDENBY HOUSE GARDENS & FALCONRY CENTRE

Holdenby, Northampton, Northants NN6 8DJ
Tel: 01604 770074 Fax: 01604 770962 (Mr & Mrs James Lowther. Administrator: Sarah Maughan)

Situated just two miles across the fields from Althorp, few places have played such a pivotal role in our history as Holdenby House. Built by Queen Elizabeth's Chancellor as a place in which to entertain the Queen, it became by an ironic twist of fate first the Palace and then the prison of her successor, Charles I, after his defeat in the Civil War. Today, Holdenby, though no longer the largest House in England, provides a splendid backdrop to beautiful grounds, with many features designed to evoke Holdenby's historic past. There is a Falconry Centre, where you can see this traditionally royal pursuit demonstrated and even try it yourself. Rosemary Verey's Elizabethan Garden is a reconstruction in small scale of Sir Christopher Hatton's magnificent garden while Rupert Golby has recently replanted the Fragrant Border.

There is a full working Armoury, where suits of armour are still made using traditional methods, as well as makers of historic costumes and pine furniture. Our 17th century Farmstead powerfully evokes the sights and smells of 17th century life. For the children there are lakeside train rides, a play area and children's farm. **Location:** 7 miles NW of Northampton, off A428 & A50. M1 exit 15a or 18. **Station:** Northampton. **Open:** Easter Sun–end Sept. Gardens and Falconry, daily (excluding Saturday) 2–6pm. Bank Hol Sun and Mon 1–6pm. House open 5 Apr, 31 May, 30 Aug or by appointment. **Admission:** Gardens & Falconry Centre: Adults £3, children £1.75. House, Garden & Falconry Centre: Adults £4, children £2. Refreshments, teas and shop (Sun only).

map 4 D1

THE MENAGERIE, HORTON

Horton, Northampton, NN7 2BX, Northamptonshire.
Tel: 01604 870 957 (Mr A Myers)

A garden of the 1990s, designed by the late Ian Kirby and surrounding a folly built by Thomas Wright of Durham for the 2nd Earl of Halifax, c.1754–1757. Spiral mount, hornbeam alleys, formal ponds with fountains and exotic and native bog gardens, thatched arbours in the classical and gothic styles. Plant sales. Teas. **Location:** 6 miles S of Northampton, 1 mile S of Horton, on B526. Turn left immediately after lay-by. **Open:** Apr–end Sept. Garden only, Mon and Thurs 2–5pm and last Sun each month 2–6pm. House, garden and Shell Grotto open to groups of 20 or more by appointment at other times. **Admission:** Garden: Adults £3.50, children £1.50.

map 4 D1

THE PREBENDAL MANOR HOUSE

Nassington, Nr. Peterborough, Northamptonshire, PE8 0QG
Tel: 01780 782 575 (Mrs J. Baile)

Grade 1 listed and dating from the early 13th century the Prebendal Manor is the oldest house in Northamptonshire, steeped in history and still retaining many architectural features. Unique to the region are the 14th century re-created medieval gardens which include a rose arbour, herber, flowery mead, and medieval fish ponds. Also included are the 15th century dovecote and tithe barn museum. Home-made teas. Lunches to order. **Location:** 6 miles N of Oundle, 7 miles S of Stamford, 8 miles W of Peterborough. **Open & Admission:** Please telephone for details of opening times and admission charges.

map 8 E7

SOUTHWICK HALL

(Christopher Capron)
Southwick, Peterborough, Northants PE8 5BL
Tel: 01832 274064 (W.J. Richardson)Manager

A family home since 1300, retaining medieval building dating from 1300, with Tudor rebuilding and 18th century additions. Exhibitions: Victorian and Edwardian life; collections of agricultural and carpentry tools, named bricks and local archeological finds and fossils. **Location:** 3 miles N of Oundle; 4 miles E of Bulwick. **Open:** Bank Holidays (Sunday & Monday) Apr 4–5, May 2–3, 30–31, Aug 29–30 and Weds May–Aug, 2–5pm. Parties at other times (Easter–Aug) by arrangement with the Manager. **Admission:** Adults £3, OAPs £2.50, children £1.50 (all inclusive). **Refreshments:** Teas available.

map 8 E7

Northumberland

Northumberland is steeped in the past; with its boundaries on two sides – the River Tweed and the Cheviot Hills separating it from Scotland – it was the scene of many fierce battles as armies came along the original route of today's A1.

Parts of Hadrian's Wall, built by the Roman emperor of that name, still straddle the wild, undulating moorland. Romans would have difficulty in recognising some of the terrain today, modern man having planted large pine forests and built an artificial lake.

Northumberland has glorious scenery – The National Park is famous for its unspoilt rugged beauty and its stark, dramatic coastline is spectacular. Viking invasions drove the monks from Holy Island (Lindisfarne). The Farne Islands are now a nature reserve for seals and seabirds. Villages with fascinating names cluster round ancient crosses, runic inscriptions still visible; water mills and old smithies are reminders of past trades.

Lindisfarne Castle

However, every century is represented – the Norman Churches, Saxon towers, Hexham Abbey, Alnwick Castle and the magnificent manor houses, still with topiary and knotted herb gardens, through to the traditional fishing quays and 19th century corn mills. Newcastle-Upon-Tyne, (now in the county of Tyne and Wear) once a giant in the ship building industry and home of the first railway, has always been the hub of Northumberland's commerce and today its cultural activities span the arts.

BAMBURGH CASTLE

Bamburgh ME69 7DF
Tel: 01669 620314

Bamburgh Castle is the home of Lady Armstrong and her family. The earliest reference to Bamburgh shows the craggy citadel to have been a royal centre by AD 547. The public rooms contain many exhibits, including the collections of armoury on loan from HM Tower of London. Porcelain, china , jade, furniture from many periods, oils, water – colours and a host of interesting items are all contained within one of the most important buildings of Britain's national heritage. **Location:** 42m N of Newcastle–upon–Tyne. 6m E of Belford by B1342 from A1 at Belford. **Open:** April–October daily 11–5pm. Last entry 4.30pm. **Admission:** Adult £4, child £1.50, OAP £3. Groups: Adult £3, child £1, OAPs £2. Groups up to 16 – min. payment £30.

❖ BELSAY HALL, CASTLE & GARDENS

Northumberland
Tel: 01661 881636 (English Heritage)

Explore a ruined castle, manor house and neoclassical hall all set amidst 30 acres of magnificent landscaped grounds – a great and varied day out for all who visit. The beautiful honey-coloured stone from which the Belsay Hall is built came from its own quarries which have since become the unusual setting for one of the series of spectacular gardens, deservedly listed Grade I in the Register of Gardens. Enjoy the mix of formal and informal; rhododendrons, magnolias, ornate terraces and even a winter garden are among Belsay's special features. **Location:** In Belsay, 14m NW of Newcastle on A696. **Open:** 1 Apr–30 Sept: daily, 10am-6pm. 1 Oct–31 Oct: daily, 10–5pm. 1 Nov–31 Mar: daily 10–4pm. (Closed 24–5 Dec). Open 1 Jan 2000. **Admission:** Adults £3.80, concs £2.90, child £1.90 (15% discount for groups of 11 or more).

ALNWICK CASTLE

Alnwick, Northumberland NE66 1NQ
Tel: 01665 510777 Fax: 01665 510876 (His Grace the Duke of Northumberland)

Described by the Victorians as 'The Windsor of the North', Alnwick Castle is the home of the Duke of Northumberland whose family, the Percys, have lived here since 1309. This border stronghold has survived many battles, but now peacefully dominates the picturesque market town of Alnwick, overlooking landscape designed by Capability Brown. The stern, medieval exterior belies the treasure house within, furnished in palatial Renaissance style, with paintings by Titian, Van Dyck and Canaletto, fine furniture and an exquisite collection of Meissen china. Other attractions include the Regimental Museum of Royal Northumberland Fusiliers, Museum of early British and Roman relics as well as the Museum of PercyTenantry volunteers, Coach House, Dungeon, Gun Terrace and Grounds, which offer peaceful walks and superb views over the surrounding countryside. Children's playground. Gift shop. **Location:** Just off the town centre on the northern side of Alnwick. **Station:** Alnmouth (5m) **Open:** Daily Maundy Thursday–end September 11–5pm (last admission 4.15pm). Open all Bank Holidays. Private tours and functions by arrangement. Address: Estate Office, Alnwick Castle, Alnwick, Northumberland NE66 1NQ. Free parking for cars and coaches. **Refreshments:** Tearoom serving home-made fare. **Events/Exhibitions:** For details, contact the Castle Administrator, Alnwick Castle, Alnwick, Northumberland, NE66 1NQ. Tel: 01665 510777. Mon-Fri and weekends during season only (01665 603942). Disabled please enquire.

map 11 H2

CHILLINGHAM CASTLE & GARDENS

Chillingham, Northumberland NE66 5NJ
Tel: 01668 215359 Fax: 01668 215463 (Sir Humprey Wakefield Bt)

This medieval family fortress remains home since the 1200's to the same family including the Earls Grey and Tankerville. Complete with jousting course, alarming dungeon and even a torture chamber, the castle displays many remarkable restoration techniques in action alongside antique furnishings, paintings, tapestries, arms and armour. Wrapped in the nation's history it occupied a strategic position as fortress during Northumberland's bloody border feuds, often besieged and at many times enjoying the patronage of royal visitors. The Italian ornamental garden, landscaped avenues and gate lodges were created by Sir Jeffrey Wyatville, fresh from his triumphs at Windsor Castle. The castle grounds command breathtaking views of the surrounding countryside. As you walk to the lake you will see, according to the season, drifts of snowdrops, daffodils or bluebells and an astonishing display of rhododendrons. **Location:** 12 miles N of Alnwick, signposted from A1 and A697. **Open:** Good Fri–Easter Mon & 1 May–30 Sept, 12–5pm. Open 7 days a week July & Aug. Closed Tue–May, Jun–Sept. All year for groups by arrangement. **Admission:** Adults £4.30, OAPs £3.80. Children free when accompanied. Parties (10 +) £3.50. Coaches welcome. **Refreshments:** Tearoom within the castle. Restaurant facilities available to groups by prior arrangement. **Events/Exhibitions:** Musical and theatrical events regularly planned. **Accommodation:** Private family suites of rooms available at times within the castle. Coaching rooms available for let in original stable buildings. **Conferences:** Facilities within castle or theatre for presentations. Access for disabled may be difficult due to number of stairs.

map 11 G2

 # CHIPCHASE CASTLE & GARDENS

Wark on Tyne, Hexham, Northumberland
Tel: 01434 230203, Fax: 01434 230740 (Mrs P J Torday)

An imposing 17th and 18th century Castle with 14th century Pele Tower set in formal and informal gardens. A chapel stands in the park. One walled garden is now a nursery specialising in unusual perennials. **Location:** 2 miles S of Wark on the Barrasford Road **Open:** Castle: 1-28 June, daily 2-5pm. Tours by arrangement at other times. Gardens and Nursery: Easter-31 July, Thurs to Sun and Bank Hols 10-5. **Admission:** Castle £3, gardens £1.50, nursery free.

map 11 G3

HOWICK HALL GARDENS

Alnwick NE66 3LB
Tel/Fax: 01665 577285 (Howick Trustees Ltd)

Extensive grounds including a natural woodland garden in addition to the formal gardens surrounding the Hall. **Location:** 6 m NE of Alnwick, nr Howick village. **Open:** Apr–Oct daily 1–6pm. **Admission:** Adult £2, children and pensioners £1. Season tickets are available.

 # LINDISFARNE PRIORY

Holy Island, Berwick–upon–Tweed TD15 2RX
Tel: 01289 389200 (English Heritage)

The site of one of the most popular early centres of Christianity in Anglo–Saxon England. St Cuthbert converted pagan Northumbria and miracles occurring at his shrine established this 11th century priory as a major pilgrimage centre. The evocative ruins, with the decorated 'rainbow' arch curving dramatically across the nave of the church, are still the destination of pilgrims today. **Location:** On Holy Island, check tide times. **Open:** 1 April–30 Sept: daily, 10–6pm. 1 Oct–31 Oct: daily, 10–5pm. 1 Nov–31 March: daily, 10–4pm. **Admission:** Adult £2.80, children £1.40, concessions £2.10.

MELDON PARK

Morpeth, NE61 3SW
Tel: 01670 772661 (M Cookson)

Isaac Cookson III purchased the Meldon land in 1832. John Dobson, the famous architect, was commissioned to build the house. The entrance is through an Ionic porch having two rows of columns to the front door. Once inside, there is an enormous staircase lit by an outstanding window facing the north. Between the two wars Edwin Lutyens was employed to enrich the Hall, which included mahogany balustrades and 18th century decorations. The garden has a wonderful collection of rhododendrons best seen in early June, an old fashioned Kitchen gardens and many greenhouses. **Location:** 7m west of Morpeth on the B6343. 5m north of Belsay. **Open:** Please call for details, opening times and admission charges.

PRUDHOE CASTLE

Prudhoe NE42 6NA
Tel: 01661 833459 (English Heritage)

Set on a wooded hillside overlooking the River Tyne are the extensive remains of this 12th century castle including a gatehouse, curtain wall and keep. There is a small exhibition and video presentation. **Location:** In Prudhoe, on a minor road north from A695. **Open & Admission:** Please call for details of times and admission charges.

WARKWORTH CASTLE

Warkworth, Morpeth, Northumberland NE66 0UJ
Tel: 01665 711423 (English Heritage)

The great towering keep of this 15th century castle, once the home of the mighty Percy family, dominates the town and River Coquet. **Location:** 7 miles south of Alnwick on A1068. **Open:** 1 Apr–end Sept, 10–6pm. In October 10–6pm or dusk if earlier. 1 Nov–31 Mar, 10–4pm. Closed Christmas eve, Christmas day, Boxing day and New Years day. **Admission:** Adult £2.40, concessions £1.80, children £1.20. 15% discount on groups of 11 or more.

CHERRYBURN

Station Bank, Mickley, Nr Stocksfield NE43 7DB Tel: 01661 843276

Open: 1 April to 31 Oct: daily except Tues and Wed 1–5.30pm. **Events:** 3 May, May Day celebration traditional music, dance and the Bewick Whistling competition, as well as wood engraving and printing, send s.a.e for details. Restaurant.

LINDISFARNE CASTLE

Holy Island, Berwick-upon-Tweed TD15 2SH Tel: 01289 389244

Open: 1 April to 31 Oct: daily except Fri (but open Good Fri). As Lindisfarne is a tidal island, times vary so that visitors may reach the castle at low tide. On open days the castle will open for 41/2hrs, which will always include 12–3pm. It will either open earlier or later, depending on the tide; please tel. for details. Garden open only when gardener is present, usually Fri but tel. in advance.

CRAGSIDE HOUSE, GARDEN & ESTATE

Rothbury, Morpeth NE65 7PX Tel: 01669 620150/620333

Open: House: 1 April to 31 Oct: daily except Mon (but open BH Mons) 1–5.30pm; last admission 4.45pm. Estate: as house 10.30–7pm; last admission 5pm. (also Mons in June and some days in Nov & Dec). **Events:** send s.a.e. for details. Property available for weddings. Restaurant.

WALLINGTON

Cambo, Morpeth NE61 4AR Tel: 01670 774283

Open: House: 1 April to 31 Oct: daily except Tues. April to 30 Sept 1–5.30pm, Oct 1–4.30pm. Walled garden: daily. April to end Sept 10–7pm, Oct 10–6pm, Nov to March 2000 10–4pm or dusk if earlier. Grounds: Daily in daylight. **Events:** varied programme, send s.a.e for full programme. Wallington is available for weddings, corporate bookings and special events. Restaurant.

Nottinghamshire

The river Trent and its tributaries are the determining factors to the scenery of Nottinghamshire. The county is shaped like an elongated oval, through the eastern half of which the broad sleepy Trent flows without haste in a placid pastoral landscape – a county fertile in crops and fields of thousands of head of cattle.

Nottinghamshire is perhaps most famous for the traditions surrounding Robin Hood and Sherwood forest. Indeed the entire county was once swathed in this dense forest which is now confined to an area of some twenty miles. The tree alleged to have been frequented by Robin Hood and his merry men, still stands (albeit on crutches!) in Sherwood Forest Country Park. This part of the forest has survived almost untouched for centuries and it is easy to conjurer up images of this thirteenth century rogue astride his trustworthy stead.

To the South of Sherwood Forest lies the city of Nottingham, which once commanded a ford over the river. Famous for centuries for its lace and textiles, Nottingham today is a lively and thriving city where life congregates at Market Square or at the annual Goose Fair held each October. Nottingham also has one of the most successful of the new universities established after World War II.

Nottingham

NEWARK TOWN HALL

Market Place, Newark, Nottinghamshire
Tel: 01636 680 333 Fax: 01636 640 967 (Newark Town Council)

One of the finest Georgian Town Halls in the country, the building has recently been refurbished in sympathy with John Carr's original concept. On display is the Town's collection of Civic Plate, silver dating generally from the 17th and 18th century, including the 'Newark Monteith' and the Newark 'Siege Pieces'. Other items of interest are some early historical records and various paintings including a collection by the artist Joseph Paul. **Location:** Market Place, Newark. Located on A1 and A46. **Station(s):** Newark Castle. Northgate (½ mile). **Open:** All year, Mon–Fri, 10–12noon & 2–4pm. Open at other times for groups by appointment. Closed: Sat, Sun, Bank Hol Mons & Tue following and Christmas week.

NORWOOD PARK

Norwood Park, Southwell, Nottinghamshire NG25 OPF
Tel/Fax: 01636 815649 (Sir John and Lady Starkey)

Norwood Park is situated on the edge of the picturesque Minster town of Southwell. The estate combines the delightful Georgian country house and stables, set in a medieval deer Park with ancient oaks, fishponds and eyecatcher Temple overlooking apple orchards and the cricket ground. The house offers comfortable reception rooms, while the Gallery complex is a unique and versatile setting for any event. Norwood Park is perfect for any business or social occasion, from conferences and activity days to civil marriages, fairy tale wedding receptions and dinner/dances. The estate is also ideal for film work. First 9–holes of USA designed golf course and practice area, opens Spring '99. **Contact:** Sarah Dodd – Events Manager. **E-mail:** Starkey@farmline.com

 map 8 D5

PAPPLEWICK HALL

Nr. Nottingham, NG15 8FE, Nottinghamshire
Tel: 0115 963 3491 Fax: 0115 964 2767 (Dr R. Godwin-Austen)

Fine Adam house built 1784 with lovely plasterwork ceilings. Park and woodland garden, particularly known for its rhododendrons. **Location:** 6 miles N of Nottingham, off A69. 2 miles from Junction 27, M1. **Open:** 1st, 3rd & 5th Weds in the month. **Refreshments:** By arrangement. **Events/Exhibitions:** 3rd Sat in June – annual fête and maypole dancing. **Conferences:** Up to 30 people. **Admission:** £5.

map 8 D6

Oxfordshire

Oxfordshire will appeal to the lover of noble architecture. The churches stand out as the most consistently handsome of any county of England. The manor houses which represent every period of architecture, cry out to be discovered. And then there is Oxford – the city of dreaming spires which still maintain a medieval character.

Oxford's architectural beauty is best appreciated on foot. Some of the best examples of college architecture are to be found around Radcliffe Square and the Bodelian Library, crowned by its famous domed Baroque rotunda.

Oxford's college buildings are quite unique, and many of them have retained their original features over many centuries. Oxford is a wonderful place in which to spend a few relaxing hours. Once you have taken your fill of wondrous architecture, why not take a riverside walk, or, if the sun shines, go punting on the river.

Around Oxford, the Vale of the White Horse, White Horse Hill and Uffington are all worth visiting. Standing in the heart of the Vale, the village of Uffington provides a good vantage point, overlooking this great prehistoric horse.

Oxford Botanic Garden

ARDINGTON HOUSE

Ardington House, Wantage, Oxfordshire
Tel: 01235 821566 Fax: 01235 821151 (The Baring Family)

Home of the Baring family. Early 18th century beautifully symmetrical house with exceptionally fine brickwork. The entrance is dominated by the Imperial Staircase – two flights of stairs coming back into one. These are very rare and the Ardington Staircase is a magnificent example. The Hall and Dining Room have original panelling. Cornices and woodwork in the Hall are beautiful and the Dining Room has a plaster work ceiling. Attractive garden, river and stable yard. Weddings, dinner parties. **Open:** 2.30–4.30pm.

| map 4 |
| C4 |

AYNHOE PARK

Suite 10, Aynho, Banbury, Oxfordshire, OX17 3BQ
Tel: 01869 810 636 Fax: 01869 811 054
(Country Houses Association)

17th century mansion. Alteration by Soane. **Location:** Junction 10 M40, then 3 miles W on B4100. **Station(s):** Banbury (7.5 miles), Bichester (8 miles). **Open:** May–Sept, Wed & Thurs, 2–5pm. (Last entry 4.45pm). **Admission:** Adults £2.50, children £1. Free car park. No dogs admitted. Groups by arrangement.

| map 4 |
| C2 |

BROUGHTON CASTLE

Banbury, Oxfordshire OX15 5EB
Tel & Fax: 01295 276070 (the Lord Saye and Sele)

The home of the family of Lord and Lady Saye & Sele for 600 years. Surrounded by a moat, it was built in 1300 and greatly enlarged in 1550. It contains fine panelling and fireplaces, splendid plaster ceilings and good period furniture. Civil War Parliamentarian connections. Beautiful walled gardens, with old roses, shrubs and herbaceous borders. **Location:** 2 miles W of Banbury on the B4035 Shipston-on-Stour Road. **Open:** Weds and Suns 19 May–12 Sept. Also Thurs in July and August. Bank Hol Suns and Bank Hol Mons (including Easter) 2–5pm. Groups welcome on any day and at any time during the year, by appointment. Telephone 01295 276070 or 01869 337126. **Admission:** Adult £4, senior citizens £3.50, students £3.50, children £2. Groups reduced rates. Tearoom and shop.

| map 4 |
| C2 |

DITCHLEY PARK

Enstone, Chipping Norton, Oxfordshire OX7 4ER
Tel: 01608 677346, Fax: 01608 677399 (Ditchley Foundation)

Third in size and date of the great 18th century houses of Oxfordshire, Ditchley is famous for its splendid interior decorations (William Kent and Henry Flitcroft). For three and a half centuries the home of the Lee family and their descendants – Ditchley was frequently visited at weekends by Sir Winston Churchill during World War II. It has now been restored, furnished and equipped as a conference centre devoted to the study of issues of concern to the people on both sides of the Atlantic. **Location:** 1½ miles W of A44 at Kiddington; 2 miles from Charlbury (B4437). **Station(s):** Charlbury (2 miles) **Open:** Group visits by prior arrangement with the Bursar, Mon, Tues and Thurs afternoons only. Closed July-mid Sept. **Admission:** House opening fee £30. Entry fee £4 per person.

| map 4 |
| C3 |

BLENHEIM PALACE

Woodstock, OX20 1PX
Tel: 01993 811325 (24hrs information) Fax: 01993 813527 (His Grace the Duke of Marlborough)

Blenheim Palace, home of the 11th Duke of Marlborough and birthplace of Sir Winston Churchill, was built for John Churchill, 1st Duke of Marlborough in recognition of his great victory over the French at the Battle of Blenheim, 1704. The Palace, designed by Sir John Vanbrugh, is set in 2,100 acres of parkland landscaped by "Capability" Brown and is one of the finest examples of English Baroque. The collection comprises tapestries, paintings, sculpture and fine furniture set in magnificent gilded staterooms. The Gardens are renowned for their beauty and include the formal Water Terraces, Italian Garden, Rose Garden and Arboretum. In the Pleasure Gardens are the Butterfly House, adventure play area, cafeteria and a shop, as well as the Marlborough Maze, the world's largest symbolic hedge maze. An inclusive ticket covers the Palace Tour, park, gardens, launch, train, nature trail and car parking. Close to Oxford and next to the historic town of Woodstock, the Palace is easily accessible by car, train and coach. In 1998, events include Craft Fairs at the May Day and August Bank Holiday weekends, Firework Concerts, and the Blenheim International Horse Trials (9–12 Sept). **Open:** 15 March–31 Oct 10–5.30pm (last admission 4.45pm) Licensed Restaurant and self-service Cafeterias. **Conferences:** The Orangery and Spencer Churchill Rooms offer luxurious conferences and corporate hospitality facilities overlooking the Italian Garden, throughout the year. **Education:** A Sandford Award holder since 1982. **Admission:** Please phone for details. **Internet:** www.blenheimpalace.com **E-mail:** administration@ blenheimpalace.com

map 4
C3

BUSCOT PARK
Faringdon, Oxfordshire SN7 8BU
Tel: 01367 240786 Fax: 01367 241794 (Lord Faringdon)

The late 18th century neoclassical house contains the Faringdon Collection of paintings and furniture. The park features a water garden, designed in the early 20th century by Harold Peto. **Open:** House & grounds: 1 Apr–end Sept, Wed–Fri 2–6pm (incl. Good Fri and also open Easter Sat & Sun). Also open every Second & fourth Sat and immediately following Sun 2–6pm. Last admission to house 5.30pm. Grounds only: 1 Apr–end Sept: open as house but also Mon (but not Bank Hol. Mon) & Tue 2–6pm. **Admission:** House and grounds £4.40. Grounds only £3.30. Children half price. Parties must book in writing or by fax to the Estate Office. Unsuitable for wheelchair users due to gradients, gravel paths and steps to house. Tearoom open same days as house 2.30–5.30pm. No dogs allowed. **Location:** Between Lechlade and Faringdon, on A417.

FAWLEY COURT
Henley-on-Thames, Oxon RG9 3AE
Tel: 01491 574917 Fax: 01491 411587 (Congregation of Marian Fathers)

Designed by Sir Christopher Wren, built in 1684 for Col W Freeman, decorated by Grinling Gibbons and by James Wyatt. The Museum consists of a library, various documents of the Polish kings, a very well preserved collection of historical sabres and many memorable military objects of the Polish army. Paintings, early books, numismatic collections, arms and armour are also housed in a part of 12th century manor house. **Location:** 1 mile north of Henley-on-Thames east to A4155 to Marlow. **Open:** Mar–Oct Wed, Thurs & Sun, 2–5pm. Other dates by arrangement. Closed Easter and Whitsuntide weeks and Nov–Feb. **Admission:** House, museum and grounds: Adults £4, OAPs £3, child £1.50, groups (min 12) £3.

KELMSCOTT MANOR
Kelmscott, Nr. Lechlade, Oxfordshire, GL7 3HJ.
Tel: 01367 252 486 Fax: 01367 253 754 (Society of Antiquaries)

Kelmscott Manor was the country home of William Morris – poet, craftsman and socialist – from 1871 until his death in 1896. It is the most evocative of all his houses and continues to delight with the charm of its architecture, the fascination of its contents and the charm of its garden, which has recently undergone extensive restoration and now contains many fine examples of plants and flowers which would have been an inspiration to Morris. **Location:** 2 miles SE of Lechlade, on the Lechlade/Faringdon Road. **Open:** Apr–Sept, Wed 11am–1pm, 2–5pm. The 3rd Sat in Apr, May, June and Sept, 2–5pm. The 1st and 3rd Sat in July & Aug, 2–5pm. Thurs & Fri – private group visits. **Admission:** Adults £6, Children £3, Students £3. **Events/Exhibitions:** Centenary exhibition "William Morris at Kelmscott". Gift shop and bookshop.

KINGSTON BAGPUIZE HOUSE
Nr Abingdon, Oxfordshire OX13 5AX
Tel: 01865 820259 Fax: 01865 821659 (Mr and Mrs Francis Grant)

Beautiful 1660's manor house remodelled in early 1700's in red brick with stone facings. Cantilevered staircase and finely proportioned panelled rooms. Set in mature parkland, the gardens contain a notable collection of plants including rare trees, shrubs, perennials and bulbs. Available for functions. **Location:** In Kingston Bagpuize village, S of A420/A415 intersection. Abingdon 5 miles, Oxford 9 miles. **Station(s):** Oxford or Didcot. **Open:** Mar 7, 21; Apr 3,4,5, 17, 18; May 1, 2, 3, 29, 30, 31; Jun 19, 20; Jul 10, 11, 21, 24, 25; Aug 11, 14, 15, 28, 29, 30; Sept 8, 11, 12, 22, 25, 26; Oct 10. 2.30–5.30pm. Garden: Last entry 5pm. House: Guided tours only, last tour 4.45pm. **Admission:** House & Garden: Adult £3.50, OAP £3, child £2.50 (under 5s not admitted to house but free to garden). Groups welcome by appointment. Wheelchairs garden only. No dogs. **Refreshments:** Home-made teas.

NUFFIELD PLACE
Huntercombe, Henley-on-Thames, Oxon RG9 5RY
Tel: 01491 641224 (Nuffield College/Friends of Nuffield Place)

Home from 1933–63 of William Morris, Lord Nuffield, car manufacturer and philanthropist. A rare survival of a complete upper-middle class home of the 1930's, retaining majority of furniture and contents acquired on taking up residence. Fine quality rugs, clocks, tapestries and custom-made furniture. Four acre gardens, laid out around 1914 when house was built, contain mature trees, yew hedges, rose pergola, rockery and pond. **Location:** Approximately 7 miles Henley-on-Thames just off A4130 to Oxford. Coach service X39 Oxford/ Heathrow. **Open:** May–Sept every 2nd and 4th Sun 2–5pm. **Admission:** Adults £3, concession £2, children 50p. Garden only £1. Parties by arrangement. **Refreshments:** Home-made teas. Ground floor and gardens suitable for disabled. No disabled lavatory.

MAPLEDURHAM HOUSE & WATERMILL

Nr. Reading, Oxfordshire, RG4 7TR Tel: 01189 723 350
Fax: 01189 724 016 (The Mapledurham Trust)

Late 16th century Elizabethan home of the Blount family. Original plaster ceiling, great oak staircase, fine collection of paintings and private chapel in Strawberry Hill Gothic added in 1797. The 15th century Watermill is fully restored and producing flour and bran which are sold in the gift shop. **Location:** 4 miles NW of Reading on North bank of River Thames. Signposted from A40704. **Open:** Easter–end Sept. Midweek parties by arrangement. **Admission:** Please phone for details. **Refreshments:** Tearooms serving cream teas. **Events/Exhibitions:** By arrangement. **Conferences:** By arrangement. **Accommodation:** 11 self-catering holiday cottages. Wedding receptions by arrangement. Car parking and picnic area.

map 4
D4

ROUSHAM HOUSE

Rousham, Steeple Aston, Oxfordshire OX6 3QX
Tel: 01869 347110 or 0860 360407 (C Cottrell-Dormer Esq.)

Rousham House was built by Sir Robert Dormer in 1635 and the shooting holes were put in the doors while it was a Royalist garrison in the Civil War. Sir Robert's successors were Masters of Ceremonies at Court during eight reigns and employed Court artists and architects to embellish Rousham. The house stands above the River Cherwell one mile from Hopcrofts Holt, near the road from Chipping Norton to Bicester. It contains 150 portraits and other pictures and much fine contemporary furniture. Rooms were decorated by William Kent (1738) and Roberts of Oxford (1765). The garden is Kent's only surviving landscape design with classic buildings, cascades, statues and vistas in thirty acres of hanging woods above the Cherwell. Wonderful herbaceous borders, pigeon house and small parterre. Fine herd of rare Long-Horn cattle in the park. Wear sensible shoes and bring a picnic and Rousham is yours for the day. **Location:** 12 miles N of Oxford; E of A4260; S of B4030. **Station:** Heyford (1 mile). **Open:** Apr–Sept inclusive Wed, Sun & Bank Hols 2–4.30pm. Gardens only every day all year 10–4.30pm. No children under 15. No dogs. Groups by arrangement on other days. **Admission:** House: Adults £3. Garden £3.

map 4
C3

UNIVERSITY OF OXFORD BOTANIC GARDEN

Rose Lane, Oxford, Oxfordshire
01865 276920 Fax: 01865 276920 (University of Oxford)

The University of Oxford Botanic Garden is the oldest botanic garden in Britain. For more than 375 years this Walled Garden, built before the English Civil War, has stood on the bank of the River Cherwell in the centre of Oxford. It has evolved from a seventeenth century collection of medical herbs to the most compact yet diverse collection of plants in the world. In addition to the botanical family beds and the National Collection of Euphorbias, there is a range of glasshouses including a Tropical Lily House, Palm House and Arid House. Outside the original Walled Garden there are herbaceous borders, a newly restored bog garden and a rock garden. **Open:** Open all year (except Good Fri and Christmas Day). Apr–Sept 9–5pm. Oct–Mar 9–4.30pm. Last admission 4.15pm. **Admission:** £2: Apr–Aug.

map 4
C3

STONOR PARK

Nr Henley-on-Thames, Oxfordshire RG9 6HF
Tel: 01491 638587, Fax: 01491 638587 (Lord and Lady Camoys)

Ancient home of Lord and Lady Camoys and the Stonor family for over 800 years and centre of Catholicism throughout the Recusancy Period, with its own medieval Chapel where mass is still celebrated today. Sanctuary for St. Edmund Campion in 1581. An exhibition features his life and work. The house is of considerable architectural interest, built over many centuries from c.1190 and the site of prehistoric stone circle, now recreated within the grounds. A family home containing fine family portraits and rare items of furniture, paintings, drawings, tapestries, sculptures and bronzes from Britain, Europe and America. Peaceful hillside gardens with magnificent roses and ornamental ponds. Souvenir gift shop and afternoon tearoom serving home-made cakes. Parties welcome, lunches available by prior arrangement. John Steane says of Stonor " If I had to suggest to a visitor who has only one day to sample the beauties of Oxfordshire I would suggest a visit to Stonor and a walk through its delectable park". **Location:** On B480; 5 miles N of Henley-on-Thames, 5 miles S of Watlington. **Station(s):** Henley-on-Thames. **Open:** Apr–Sept, Suns & Bank Hol Mons 2–5.30pm, but closed 13 June 1999. Wed (July–August) 2–5.30pm. Sats (29 May & 28 Aug only) 2–5.30pm. Groups welcome (by appointment) on any day (at any time) between Apr–Sept when the house is not open to the public. Min. number 12 persons on public days, 20 for private visits. **Admission:** House & Gardens: Adults £4.50, child (under 14 with adult) free. Adults (Group) £4 subject to group payment on arrival. Private tours £5 per person subject to group payment. Gardens only: Adults £2.50. **Refreshments:** Tearoom. Group lunches and suppers by arrangement.

map 4 D4

WALLINGFORD CASTLE GARDENS

Castle Street, Wallingford, Oxfordshire.
Tel: 01491 835 373 Fax: 01491 826 550
(Wallingford Town Council)

These gardens are situated on part of the site of Wallingford Castle, which was built by William the Conqueror and demolished by Oliver Cromwell in 1652. The remains of St. Nicholas Priory are a feature of the Gardens, which is a haven of beauty and tranquillity and has a well-established wildlife area. **Location:** Bear Lane, Castle Street, Wallingford, Oxfordshire. **Open:** Apr–Oct, 10–6pm. Nov–Mar, 10–3pm. **Admission:** Free. **Events/Exhibitions:** Band concerts some Sundays in summer. Telephone for details. 'Britain in Bloom' winner 1993, 1996, 1997 and 1998. Car parking in the town. **Tourist Information Office:** 01491 826 972.

map 4 C4

ASHDOWN HOUSE

Lambourn, Newbury RG16 7RE Tel: 01488 72584

Open: Hall, stairway, roof and grounds only: April to end Oct: Wed & Sat. Guided tours only; at 2.15pm, 3.15pm & 4.15pm from front door. Woodland: all year: daily except Fri, dawn to dusk. **Restaurant. Admission:** £2.10. Woodland free. No reduction for groups, which must book in writing. Car park 250m. No WC.

GREYS COURT

Rotherfield Greys, Henley-on-Thames RG9 4PG
Tel: 01491 628529 or (Infoline)01494 755564

Open: House (part of ground floor only): 2 April to end Sept: Mon, Wed & Fri (closed Good Fri) 2–6pm. Garden: 2 April to end Sept: daily except Thur & Sun (closed Good Fri) 2–6pm. **Admission:** £4.50. child £2.20; family £11.20. Garden only £3.20; family £8. Parking 220m. No reduction for coach groups, which must book in advance. **Events:** for details send s.a.e. to The Box Office, PO Box 180, High Wycombe, Bucks HP14 4XT. **Restaurant.**

CHASTLETON HOUSE

Chastleton, Moreton-in-Marsh GL56 0SU

Tel: 01608 674355 or 01608 674284 (Bookings) 01494 755560 (Infoline)

Open: 1 April to end Oct: daily except Sun, Mon & Tues 12–4pm. Last admission 3pm. Note: Admission for all visitors (incl. NT members) by timed ticket, which must be booked in advance; write to the ticket office (do not include payment) or tel. 01608 674284, Mon to Fri 10–1pm from 1 Feb 1999. **Admission:** Adult £5, child £2.50, family £12.50. Groups (min 11, max. 25) by written arrangement only. No group reduction. No access for coaches. Car park on hill 270m from house; return walk includes a short but steep hill.

GREAT COXWELL BARN

Great Coxwell, Faringdon, Oxfordshire Tel: 01793 762209

Open: Daily at reasonable hours. **Admission:** 50p. No WC.

WATERPERRY GARDENS

Nr Wheatley, Oxfordshire OX33 1JZ
Tel: 01844 339226/254 Fax:01844 339883

The peaceful gardens at Waterperry feature a magnificent herbaceous border, shrub and heather borders, alpine and rock gardens, a formal garden and a new rose garden. Together with stately trees, a river to walk by and a quiet Saxon Church to visit – all set in 83 acres of unspoilt Oxfordshire. The long established herbaceous and alpine nurseries provide year round interest. For the experienced gardener, the novice, or those who have no garden of their own, here is a chance to share, enjoy and admire the order and beauty of careful cultivation. Garden Shop and Plant Centre with exceptionally wide range of plants, shrubs etc produced in the nurseries for sale. Main agents for Haddonstone, Pots and Pithoi and Whichford Pottery. The Pear Tree Teashop provides a delicious selection of freshly prepared food made on the premises. Serving hot and cold light lunches, morning coffee, cream teas etc. Wine licence. The Art in Action Gallery exhibits and sells quality ceramics, wood, glass, paintings, jewellery, textiles, etchings and engravings. <u>Location:</u> 9 miles from Oxford, 50 miles from London, 42 miles from Birmingham, M40 Junction 8. Well signposted locally with Tourist Board symbol. <u>Station(s):</u> Oxford & Thame Parkway. **Open:** Gardens & Shop: Apr–Oct 9–5.30pm, Nov–Mar 9–5pm. Pear Tree Teashop: Apr–Oct 10–5pm, Nov–Mar 10–4pm. Art in Action Gallery: Apr–Oct 9–5pm, Nov–Mar 9–4.30pm. **Open Daily** except Christmas and New Year Holidays. Open only to Art in Action visitors (enquiries 0171 381 3192) 15–18 July. The Pear Tree Teashop will close from 14 July–19 July incl. <u>Admission:</u> Apr–Oct Adults £3.25, senior citizens £2.75, parties (20+) £2.75. Nov–Mar £1.50 all categories. Coaches by appointment only.

map 4 D3

Shropshire

This county is a hidden treasure, a real gem for visitors although it remains off the main tourist routes. The hills and mountains to the west separate Shropshire and Wales. The north of the county is home to seven beautiful lakes, which are wonderful for walking and home to a large number of birds.

Shrewsbury sits in a large loop of the River Severn. This made an excellent defence system during the frontier battles between England and Wales. Within the town is a wealth of medieval buildings and monuments. There are many timber framed buildings, narrow streets and a charming old market square.

Ludlow retains a huge amount of geological interest, with several fossils having been found around there, that are now on display in the museum. Many pretty shops and half-timbered Tudor buildings are located in the town.

Above: Old Market Hall, Shrewsbury

BOSCOBEL HOUSE & THE ROYAL OAK

Shifnal, Shropshire
Tel: 01902 850244 (English Heritage)

Discover the fascinating history of the fully restored and refurbished lodge and famous 'Royal Oak' tree where the future King Charles II hid from Cromwell's troops in 1651. The panelled rooms, secret hiding places and pretty gardens lend a truly romantic character. A fascinating guided tour and an award winning exhibition also cover the later additions to the site – a Victorian farmhouse, dairy, smithy and farmyard complete with resident ducks and geese. **Location:** On classified road between A41 and A5, 8m NW of Wolverhampton. **Open:** 1 Apr–30 Sept: daily, 10–6pm, last admission 5.30pm. 1 Oct–31 Oct: daily, 10–5pm. 1 Nov–31 Dec: Wed–Sun, 10–4pm & 1 Feb–31 Mar: Wed–Sun, 10–4pm, last admission 3.30pm. House will be closed 24–25 Dec & 1–31 Jan. **Admission:** Adults £4, concs £3, child £2. (15% discount for groups of 11 or more).

map 8 B7

BURFORD HOUSE GARDENS

Tenbury Wells, Worcestershire, WR15, 8HQ
Tel: 01584 810 777 Fax: 01584 810 673 (C. Chesshire)

The sweeping lawns and plantsman's paradise of Burford House Gardens are set in the picturesque valleys of the River Teme and Ledwyche Brook. The late Georgian bridge over the Ledwyche has been restored, leading to a new wildflower garden down to the heavenly spot where the two rivers meet. The grass garden has been redesigned, a bamboo collection planted and the National Collection of Clematis of over 200 varieties continues to grow. Also on site is **Treasures of Tenbury Plant Centre/Nursery** growing over 300 varieties of clematis and many of the unusual plants that can be seen in the gardens; specialising in quality plants for sale, pots, tools and friendly practical advice; **Burford House Gallery:** contemporary and one botanical art show annually; **Abode Gift Shop:** decorative and functional gifts, books and cards; **Burford Conservatories; Mulu** exotic plants; **Jungle Giants** bamboos. **Refreshments: Burford Buttery,** serving a wide selection of home-made cakes, pastries, hot and cold meals, teas and coffees. Seating 120 inside (including Buttery Marquee), 40 outside. **Location:** Tenbury Wells, Worcestershire, WR15 8HQ (off A456, 1 mile west of Tenbury Wells, 8 miles from Ludlow). **Car Parking:** Free parking for 120 cars, 10 coaches. **Open:** All year daily 10–6pm (last entry into gardens 5pm); evenings by arrangement. **Admission:** Adults £2.50, children £1.00; groups of 10+ £2.00. **E-mail:** treasures@burford.co.uk

map 7 F1

HAWKSTONE HISTORIC PARK & FOLLIES

Weston-under-Redcastle, Nr Shrewsbury, Shropshire, SY4 5UY
Tel: 01939 200 611 Fax: 01939 200 311 (Hawkstone Park Leisure Ltd.)

Few places in the world can claim to be truly unique. However, Hawkstone Park with its well hidden pathways, concealed grottoes, secret tunnels and magical collection of follies earns that right. It is an ideal day out for both the young and old. A giant theatre in landscape - it was originally one of the most visited landscapes in Britain and is the only Grade I landscape in Shropshire. Work to restore the Park to its former glory began in April 1991 after a 100 year closure. Visitors are once more privileged to enter the Hawkstone Labyrinth. Folly buildings, it has been said 'indulge a natural urge to express eccentricity with the resources of wealth and imagination". It is a description which sits perfectly on the shoulders of the hills of Hawkstone. Sir Roland Hill started it all in the 18th century with his son Richard "The Great Hill", not only taking over but also increasing the tempo and arranged for some 15 miles of paths and some of the best collections of follies in the world to be constructed in the grounds of their ancestral home. At the turn of the 19th century the Hills could no longer accommodate the growing number of sightseers to the Hall. As a result an inn, now the Hawkstone Park Hotel, was opened and guided tours were organised. Hawkstone, according to one top writer, became "the inspiration for Longleat, Wombourne and other stately homes which attract visitors". Little has changed since then. The Park is full of attractions, surprises and features. You can, for example, tread the timeless stone steps, see the dramatic cliffs and rocks, towers, monuments, tunnels, passageways, precipice rocks, paths, rustic sofas and romantic secret valleys. Even the Duke of Wellington was a regular visitor. It takes about 3 hours to complete the whole tour of the Park. **Location:** 8 miles N of Shrewsbury, off A49. **Open:** 1 Apr–31 Oct, daily from 10am, Sat & Sun Nov–28 Feb. **Admission:** Adults £4.75, child £2.75, senior citizen £3.75. Family £12.50. Small additional charges apply on Bank Holidays and special events. Special reduced rates for coaches. Gift shop, tearoom and hotel & golf course adjacent. Please wear sensible shoes. Dogs admitted on leads. Guided tours by arrangement.

map 6
D1

HAWKSTONE HALL & GARDENS

Marchamley, Shrewsbury, Shropshire, SY4 5LG
Tel: 01630 685 242 Fax: 01630 685 565 (The Redemptorists)

Grade I Georgian mansion and gardens set in spacious parkland. From 1556–1906, Hawkstone was the seat of the distinguished Hill family of Shropshire. The principal rooms include the Venetian Saloon, the Ballroom, the Refectory Gallery, the Billiard Room, the Drawing Room and the Winter Garden. The gardens, which have been fully restored over the past 8 years, comprise terraces and lawns, a rose garden, a lily pool and woodland with a magnificent collection of trees. <u>Location:</u> Entrance at Marchamley on A442, 2 miles N of Hodnet. <u>Open:</u> 5–31 Aug, 2–5pm. <u>Admission:</u> £2.50.

map 6 D1

 # HODNET HALL GARDENS

Hodnet, Market Drayton, Shropshire TF9 3NN
Tel: 01630 685202 Fax: 01630 685853 (Mr & Mrs A.E.H. Heber-Percy)

60+ acres of landscaped gardens, renowned to be amongst the finest in the country. Woodland walks amidst forest trees, shrubs and flowers alongside a daisy chain of ornamental pools. Light lunch or afternoon tea in the 17th century tearooms, adjacent to which is a gift shop. The walled Kitchen Garden grows a wide range of flowers and produce which are available for sale during the appropriate season. Disabled visitors are especially welcome. Guided tours and evening parties by appointment. <u>Location:</u> A53 (Shrewsbury–Market Drayton): A442 (Telford–Whitchurch): M6 exits 12 & 15: M54 exit 3. <u>Open:</u> 1 April–30 Sept. Tues–Sun & Bank Holiday Mons 12–5pm. <u>Admission:</u> Adult £3, OAPs £2.50, child £1.20. Special rates for parties (prebook please).

map 6 D1

HOPTON COURT

Hopton Court, Cleobury Mortimer, Kidderminister, DY14 OEF
Tel: 01299 270734 Fax: 01299 271132 (C. R. D Woodward)

Substantial changes were made to the house and grounds from 1798 to 1803. The works were supervised by John Nash and Humphrey Repton. Around 1820, a conservatory (graded II* in 1995) of cast-iron and glass was built. To the northeast of the house lies the stable block incorporating the Coach House. Both the Conservatory and the Coach House were renovated in 1997. Three rooms in the house and the Conservatory are licensed for civil ceremonies. The Conservatory is open four days a year without appointment, at other times by prior appointment. <u>Admission:</u> £3.50. The Coach House is available for receptions.

LUDFORD HOUSE

Ludlow, Shropshire, SY8 1PJ
Tel: 01584 872542 Fax: 01584 875662 (D. F. A. Nicholson)

A historic house, in part dating back to the 11th century, with later additions. Standing in 6 acres of well-maintained gardens and grounds. <u>Location:</u> ½ mile S of Ludlow, B4361. <u>Station(s):</u> Ludlow. <u>Open:</u> Spring & summer by written appointment only, with limited inspection of the interior. <u>Admission:</u> £3.00. <u>Refreshments:</u> Hotels and restaurants in Ludlow. Unsuitable for disabled.

map 7 F1

IRONBRIDGE GORGE MUSEUMS

Ironbridge, Telford, Shropshire TF8 7AW
Tel: 01952 433522/0800 590258 Fax: 01952 432204 (Independent Museum Trust)

Stunning Ironbridge Gorge, World Heritage Site, Birthplace of the Industrial Revolution, is home to a unique series of museums in the Valley. Coalport China Museum, Jackfield Tile Gallery, Broseley Tobacco Pipe Museum, Rosehill and Dale House, homes of the Ironmasters, the Museum of Iron as well as Blists Hill Victorian Town. <u>Open:</u> 10–5pm with seasonal variations of time and closure. Please telephone for 'Winterval' information. <u>Admission:</u> Passport tickets to all museums; Adult £9.50, senior £8.50, family (2 adults + 5 children) £29. <u>Internet:</u> www.vtel.co.uk/igmt

map 6 E1

OLD COLEHURST MANOR

Colehurst, Market Drayton, Shropshire TF9 2JB
Tel: 01630 638833 Fax: 01630 638647 (Bjorn Teksnes Lord of the Manor)

Undoubtedly one of the best period houses you will ever have the pleasure of visiting. The reasons... Perhaps because we are a living home where visitors are welcomed as guests. There is no staid formality here. The rooms seen are all used by the family and their pets. Even the animals themselves greet you and often accompany the tour. The beautiful timber frame house, lovingly restored by the present Lord of the Manor and his lady has a warmth and a tactile quality, which we encourage by having no roped off areas or 'private' signs. During your personal tour you will see priest holes and beautiful period furniture blending with our family belongings. Tales will be told of the history, restoration and the spirits of the house. Come back in time with past and present occupants. For those who enjoy gardens, Bjorn's rose, clematis, herb and knot gardens are a delight, and not to forget Juliet's animal corner. Our dining room and old library make an atmospheric setting for one of Maria, Lady of the Manor's teas or light lunches, all home baked in our 17th century kitchens, and not forgetting our speciality dishes from the past and the unique 17th century experience. **Location:** Follow brown signs on A41–A53 and A529. Stations: Stoke–on–Trent 12 miles, Shrewsbury 17 miles, Air: Manchester airport, 1½ hours. **Conference/Function Room:** Library capacity 70, Dining Room capacity 14. **Open:** 1 Apr–30 Sept, every day 11–5pm. Mon and Sat by appt only. Last entrance 1 hour before last tour. 1 Oct–31 Mar by appt only. **Admission:** Adult £4, child £2.75, Family Ticket £11.50. Group min 20 max 50: Adult £3.50, child £2.75, student £3.50, OAP £4 No photography in house. Restaurant by appt only. Guided tours obligatory. Limited parking for cars.

map 6 D1

ROWLEY'S HOUSE MUSEUM

Barker Street, Shrewsbury, Shropshire
Tel: 01743 361196 Fax: 01743 358411 (Shrewsbury and Atcham Borough Council)

Major regional museum displaying varied collections in timber-framed 16th century warehouse and adjoining 17th century brick mansion. Archaeology, including Roman Wroxeter; geology; costume; natural and local history; temporary exhibitions including contemporary arts and crafts. **Open:** Tue–Sat 10–5pm; Summer Suns and Bank Hol Mons 10–4pm. Closed Christmas/New Year period.

map 6 E1

SHIPTON HALL

Much Wenlock, Shropshire, TF13 6JZ.
Tel: 01746 785 225 Fax: 01746 785 125 (J. N. R. N. Bishop)

Delightful Elizabethan stone manor house c.1587 with Georgian additions. Interesting Rococo and Gothic plaster work by T. F. Pritchard. Stone walled garden, medieval dovecote and parish church dating from late Saxon period. Family home. **Location:** In Shipton, 6 miles SW of Much Wenlock near junction B4378 & B4368. **Station(s):** Craven Arms (10 miles), Telford (14 miles), Ludlow (14 miles). **Open:** Easter–end Sept, Thurs. Not Sun, except Bank Hol Suns & Mons (except Christmas & New Year) 2.30–5.30pm. Also by appointment throughout the year for parties of 20+. **Admission:** House & Garden: Adults £3, children £1.50, parties of 20+ less 10%. **Refreshments:** Teas/buffets by prior arrangement.

map 6 E1

SHREWSBURY CASTLE & SHROPSHIRE REGIMENTAL MUSEUM

Castle Street, Shrewsbury, Shropshire
Tel: 01743 358516 Fax:01743 358411

Norman castle with substantial alterations by Thomas Telford in the eighteenth century. The Great Hall now houses the collections of the Shropshire Regimental Museums plus graphic displays on the history of the castle. **Open:** Museum, Tue–Sat & summer Suns, 10–4.30pm. Closed Dec–Jan. Please phone for details. Free admission to the grounds Mon–Sat (and summer Suns).

PREEN MANOR

Church Preen, Nr. Church Stretton
Tel: 01694 771 207 (Mr & Mrs P Trevor-Jones)

6 acre garden on site of Cluniac monastery and Norman Shaw mansion. Kitchen, chess, water and wild gardens. Fine trees in park and woodland walks. Featured in NGS video 1. Replanning still in progress. **Location:** Wenlock-Church Stretton road. **Open:** Please phone for details. Private visits of 15+ groups and coach parties by appointment, June & July only. **Admission:** Charges apply. **Refreshments:** Tea and home-made cakes available. (Oct – tea only). Not suitable for wheelchairs. Plants available for sale. No dogs except guide dogs.

STOKESAY CASTLE

Craven Arms, Salop
Tel: 01588 672544 (English Heritage)

A visit to Stokesay guarantees a day out to remember. Take a trip back in time with our free audio tour or relax in the charming 'cottage' style garden framed by the tranquil Welsh borders scenery. Historically the castle represents the country's finest example of a fortified manor house built in a style that owes more to fashion than to fortification. The solid walls and crenellated battlements form part of an ostentatious building programme begun by the wool merchant. Lawrence of Ludlow in 1281. The majority of features familiar to the original owner can still be seen including the Great Hall that once echoed to the sounds of feasts and banquets. **Location:** 7m NW of Ludlow off A49. **Open:** 1 April–30 Sept: daily, 10–6pm. 1 Oct–31 Oct: daily, 10–5pm. 1 Nov–31 Mar: Wed–Sun, 10–4pm. (Closed 24–25 Dec). Open 1 Jan 2000. **Admission:** Adults £3.20, concs £2.40, child £1.60. (15% discount for groups of 11 or more).

map 7 F2

WALCOT HALL

Lydbury North, Nr. Bishops Castle, SY7 8AZ, Shropshire.
Tel: 0171 581 2782 Fax 0171 589 0195 (C. R. W. Parish)

Built by Sir William Chambers for Lord Clive of India, Walcot Hall possesses a free-standing Ballroom; stable yard with twin clock towers; extensive walled garden and wonderful arboretum noted for its rhododendrons, azaleas and specimen trees. **Location:** 3 miles E of Bishops Castle, on B4385, half a mile outside Lydbury North. **Station:** Craven Arms. **Open:** Arboretum open 12–4.30pm, Fri, Sat and Sun, Apr 1–Oct 31. House by appointment except National Garden scheme open day 30–31 May 1999, 2–6pm. **Admission:** Adults £3, children (under 15) free. Collect tickets from Powis Arms, beside main gate. **Accommodation:** All year holiday flats. Estate suitable for film and photographic locations, marriage licence, Ballroom available for receptions and conferences.

map 7 F2

WOLLERTON OLD HALL GARDEN

Wollerton, Market Drayton, Shropshire TF9 3NA
Tel: 01630 685760 Fax: 01630 685583 (John & Lesley Jenkins)

A delightful award-winning 20th century formal garden surrounding a 16th century house. A profusion of imaginatively planted borders combine to create small separate gardens each with its own character. Knot garden, lime allée, old roses and collection of clematis feature predominantly. Unusual plants for sale. **Location:** Brown signed off Shrewsbury to Market Drayton A53. **Open** garden only: 2 May–30 Aug every Fri, Sun and Bank Hol. 12–5pm. **Admission:** Adults £3, senior citizens £2.80, children £1. Parties by appointment, special rates (min 25). **Refreshments:** Tearoom serving home-cooked lunches and teas.

map 6 D1

ATTINGHAM PARK

Shrewsbury SY4 4TP Tel: 01743 708123 Fax: 01743 708150

Open: House: 26 March to 31 Oct: daily except Wed & Thur 1.30–5pm; (BH Mon 11–5pm). Deer park & grounds: Daily (closed 25 Dec). March to end Oct: daily 8–9pm; Nov to Feb 2000 daily 8–5pm. **Events:** Send s.a.e. for programme. **Admission:** House & park: £4; family ticket £10. Booked groups £3.50. Park & grounds only: £1.80. **Restaurant.**

BENTHALL HALL

Broseley TF12 5RX Tel: 01952 882159

Open: 4 April to 29 Sept: Wed, Sun & BH Mon 1.30–5.30pm. House and/or garden for groups by prior arrangement: Tues & Wed am.

Events: church services most Suns 3.15pm; visitors welcome. **Admission:** £3, children £1. Garden only £2. Booked groups £2.50 (min 22 people/£55). Parking 150m. Coaches by appointment. **Restaurant.**

DUDMASTON

Quatt, nr Bridgnorth WV15 6QN Tel: 01746 780866 Fax: 01746 780744

Open: 28 March to 29 Sept: Wed & Sun plus BH Mons 2–5.30pm. Garden: as house 12–6pm. Booked groups Thur 2–5.30pm. **Events:** send s.a.e. for details. **Admission:** House & garden £3.50, children £2; family ticket £8. Booked Groups £2.90. Garden only £2.50. Parking 100m. **Restaurant.**

WESTON PARK

Weston-U-Lizard, Nr Shifnal, Shropshire
Tel: 01952 850207 Fax: 01952 850430 (Weston Park Foundation)

Nestled in 1,000 acres of "Capability" Brown Parkland and formal gardens this superb Stately Home, built in 1671 and designed by Lady Wilbraham, contains a magnificent collection of treasures, including work by Van Dyck, Lely and Gainsborough. The house has 28 historic bedrooms, available on an exclusive basis for conferences and private parties. An extensive event programme available during the summer, including a balloon festival, outdoor symphony firework concert and a game and country sports fair. The Parkland includes a deer park, woodland adventure playground, pets corner and miniature railway.

The Old Stables, now renovated into a tearoom and licensed bar, serves lunch and afternoon tea. **Location:** Situated on A5, 8 miles M6 Junction 12 and 3 miles M54 Junction 3. **Open:** Easter Weekend. May & June – every weekend (inc. Bank Hols). July & Aug – every day. Sept – first three weekends. (Dates subject to change). **Admission:** House, park and gardens: Adults £5.50, OAP's £4.30, children £3.40. Park and gardens only: Adults £3.80, OAP's £2.80, children £2.20. Group rates available. Dogs (on leads) welcome.

map 8 B7

143

Somerset

Glastonbury Tor

There is more scenic variety in Somerset than in any other part of the West Country – impressive moorland, verdant hills, romantic coastal reaches, combes, woodlands and flats. Two towns in Somerset – Taunton and Wells – dominate the county. Both are set in a time lock which tourists and developers thankfully fail to crack.

The nearby Mendip Hills are characterised by chasms and caverns while the neighbouring Quantock Hills with their clear streams and grazing deer are the heartlands of Somerset. This is a region of verdant glens, thatched pubs and village greens.

The mood changes dramatically at Exmoor, a protected wilderness which extends as far as the coast, where the cliffs and sea create a perfect setting. Bath was transformed by the Romans. It was the first spa town in the 18th century. Today it remains ever popular.

BARFORD PARK

Enmore TA5 1AG
Tel: 01278 671269

Set in a large garden and looking out across a ha-ha to a park dotted with fine trees, it presents a scene of peaceful domesticity, a miniature country seat on a scale appropriate today. The well-proportioned rooms, with contemporary furniture, are all in daily family use. The walled flower garden is in full view from the house, and the woodland and water gardens and archery glade with their handsome trees form a perfect setting for the stone and red-brick Queen Anne building. **Location:** 5m W of Bridgwater. **Open:** May–Sept by appointment. **Admission:** Charges not available at the time of going to press. **Refreshments:** Teas and buffet luncheons for groups, by appointment.

map 3
G3

 JOHN BARSTAPLE ALMSHOUSE

Old Market St, Bristol, BS2 0EU
Tel: 01179 265 777 (Bristol Municipal Charities)

Victorian almshouse with garden courtyard. Location: Half a mile from Bristol city centre, on A4. **Station(s):** Bristol Temple Meads. **Open:** Garden & Exterior buildings only (now extensively renovated): Weekdays all year, 10am–1pm. By appointment only telephone 0117 9265777. **Admission:** Free. The almshouses are occupied mainly by elderly residents and their rights for privacy should be respected.

map 3
H2

THE BISHOP'S PALACE

Wells, Somerset, BA5 2PD
Tel: 01749 678 691 (The Church Commissioners)

The fortified and moated medieval palace unites the early 13th century first floor hall (known as The Henderson Rooms), the late 13th century Chapel and the now ruined Great Hall, also the 15th century wing which is today the private residence of the Bishop of Bath and Wells. The extensive grounds, where rise the springs that give Wells its name, are a beautiful setting for borders of herbaceous plants, roses, shrubs, mature trees and the Jubilee Arboretum. The Moat is home to a collection of waterfowl and swans. **Location:** City of Wells: enter from the Market Place through the Bishop's Eye or from the Cathedral Cloisters, over the Drawbridge. **Station(s):** Bath and Bristol. **Open:**

The Henderson Rooms, Bishop's Chapel and Grounds: 1 Apr–31 Oct, Tues, Wed, Thurs, Fri 11–6pm and Sun 2–6pm and daily in Aug, 10–6pm. Also for exhibitions as advertised. As this is a private house, the Trustees reserve the right to alter these times on rare occasions. **Admission:** As advertised – guided and educational tours by arrangement with the Manager. **Refreshments:** A limited restaurant service is available in the Undercroft, unless prior bookings are made. **Events/Exhibitions:** Wedding receptions. Open air theatre. **Conferences:** Conferences and special events by arrangement with the manager.

map 3
H3

COMBE SYDENHAM COUNTRY PARK

Monksilver, Taunton, Somerset, TA4 4JG
Tel: 01984 656 284 Fax: 01984 656 273

Built in 1580 on the site of the monastic settlement, home of Elizabeth Sydenham, wife of Sir Francis Drake. Beautifully restored Courtroom and Cornmill. Elizabethan-style gardens. Deer park. Play area, Woodland walks with the 'Alice' Trail and the 'Ancient' Trail of Trees. Fish farm. Picnic area. **Open:** Country Park Walks, play area & woods: 1 Apr–30 Sept everyday. Guided tour of West wing of House, Gardens and Cornmill 31 May–28 Sept, Mon, Thurs and Fri at 2pm. Booklets for Self guided 'Alice' Trail and the 'Ancient' Trail of Trees available for sale 1.30–2pm on tour days. Group bookings available (min 20). **Admission:** Country Park £3 per vehicle. Guided tour, adults £5, children £2.

map 3 G3

CROWE HALL

Widcombe Hill, Bath, Somerset, BA2 6AR
Tel: 01225 310322 (John Barratt)

Elegant George V classical Bath villa, retaining grandiose mid-Victorian portico and great hall. Fine 18th century and Regency furniture: interesting old paintings and china. 10 acres of romantic gardens cascading down hillside. Terraces, Victorian grotto, ancient trees. **Location:** Approx. ¼ mile on right up Widcombe Hill, 1 mile from Guildhall. **Open: Garden:** 21 March, 18 April, 9 & 23 May, 13 June, 11 July and groups by appointment. **House:** By appointment only, £2. **Admission:** Adults £2, children £1. **Refreshments:** Teas on opening days and by appointment. Dogs welcome.

map 3 V16

DODINGTON HALL

Nr. Nether Stowey, Bridgwater, Somerset
Tel: 01278 741 400
(Lady Gass, Occupiers Mr & Mrs P.Quinn)

Small Tudor manor house on the lower slopes of the Quantock Hills. Great hall with oak roof. Carved stone fireplace. Semi-formal garden with roses and shrubs. **Location:** ½ mile from A39, 11 miles from Bridgwater. 7 miles from Williton. **Open:** Sat & Sun May 29, 30; June 5, 6; 12, 13; 19, 20; 26, 27. **Admission:** Donations for charity. Parking for 15 cars. Regret unsuitable for disabled.

map 3 G3

EAST LAMBROOK MANOR GARDEN

South Petherton, Somerset Tel: 01460 240 328
Fax: 01460 242 344 (Mr & Mrs Andrew Norton)

This Grade I listed garden is one of the best loved in Britain. It was the home of the late Margery Fish. It is also the subject of many books, articles and television and radio programmes. The 17th century malthouse has been developed to provide modern facilities for visitors retaining its unique character. During the summer months there are exhibitions of paintings by local artists. The garden also contains the National Collection of Geraniums. **Location:** Off A303. 2 miles N of South Petherton. **Open:** 1 Mar–30 Sept, Tues, Wed, Thurs, Sat and by appointment, 10–5pm. **Admission:** Adults £2.50, students/children 50p, OAPs £2.

map 3 H4

FAIRFIELD

Stogursey, Bridgwater, Somerset
Tel: 01278 732251 Fax: 01278 732277 (Lady Gass)

Elizabethan House of medieval origin, undergoing extensive repairs. Woodland garden. Location: 11 miles W of Bridgwater, 8 miles E of Williton. From A39 Bridgwater/Minehead turn N; house 1 mile W of Stogursey. **Open:** House open in summer (when repairs allow) for groups by appointment only. Garden open for NGS and other charities on dates advertised in spring. **Admission:** Donations for charity. Disabled access. No dogs, except guide dogs.

map 3 G3

GAULDEN MANOR

Tolland, Lydeard St Lawrence, Nr Taunton, Somerset TA4 3PN
Tel: 01984 667213 (James Le Gendre Starkie)

Small historic red sandstone Manor House of great charm. A real home lived in and shown by the owners. Past seat of the Turberville family immortalised by Thomas Hardy. Great Hall has magnificent plaster ceiling and oak screen to room known as the chapel. Fine antique furniture and many hand embroideries worked by the wife of owner. Interesting grounds include rose gardens, bog garden with primulas and moisture loving plants, butterfly and herb garden. Visitors return year after year to enjoy this oasis of peace and quiet set amid superb countryside. **Location:** 9 miles NW of Taunton signposted from A358 and B3224. **Open:** June 6–Aug 30 on Thurs, Sun & Summer Bank Hols, 2–5pm. Parties on other days by prior arrangement. **Admission:** Adults: house and garden £3.80. Garden only £2, children £2.

map 3 G3

HESTERCOMBE GARDENS

Hestercombe, Cheddon Fitzpaine, Taunton, Somerset TA2 8LG
Tel: 01823 413923 Fax: 01823 413747

Over three centuries of garden history are encompassed in Hestercombe's fifty acres of formal gardens and parkland near Cheddon Fitzpaine, Taunton. The unique Edwardian gardens, designed by Sir Edwin Lutyens and planted by Gertrude Jekyll, were completed in 1906. With terraces, pools and an orangery, they are the supreme example of their famous partnership. These gardens are now reunited with Hestercombe's secret Landscape Garden, which opened in Spring '97 for the first time in 125 years. Created by Coplestone Warre Bampfyide in 1750s, these Georgian pleasure grounds comprise forty acres of lakes, temples and delightful woodland walks. **Location:** 4m NE of Taunton off A361. **Open:** Daily 10–last admission 5pm. **Admission:** Adults £3.50, children (5–15) £1. Groups and coaches by prior arrangement only.

map 3 G3

MAUNSEL HOUSE

North Newton, Nr Bridgwater, Somerset TA7 0BU
Tel: 01278 663413 / 661076 (Sir Benjamin Slade)

Imposing 13th century manor house, partly built before the Norman Conquest but mostly built around a Great Hall erected in 1420. Geoffrey Chaucer wrote part of The Canterbury Tales whilst staying at the house. Maunsel House is the ancestral seat of the Slade family and is now the home of the 7th baronet, Sir Benjamin Slade. Wedding receptions, private and garden parties, conferences, functions, filming, fashion shows, archery, clay pigeon shooting, equestrian events. **Location:** OS Ref: ST302 303, Bridgwater 4m, Bristol 20 miles, Taunton 7 m, M5/J24, turn left North Petherton 2½ m SE of A38 at North Petherton. Gardens only 1 Apr–1 Oct (to include Easter). £2 (Honesty Box) Suns 2–5.30pm. **Open:** Coach and group parties welcomed by appointment. **Admission:** For further info tel: 0171 352 1132 (office hrs). **E-mail:** shirlstar@clara.net

map 3
G3

HATCH COURT

Hatch Beauchamp, Taunton, Somerset, TA3 6AA
Tel: 01823 480 120 Fax: 01823 480 058 (Dr & Mrs Robin Odgers)

A most attractive and unusual Grade I listed Bath stone Palladian mansion, surrounded by extensive gardens, beautiful parkland with a herd of fallow deer and stunning views over the Somerset countryside. A much loved and lived-in family home, shown by present members of the family (youngest aged 10), containing fine furniture, paintings and a unique semicircular china room and a small private military museum. **Location:** 6 miles SE Taunton, off A358. **Open & Admission:** Please phone for details, opening times and admission charges. **Refreshments:** Full catering available. **Conferences:** Functions, promotions, etc. Full facilities and experienced staff. Entire gardens – wheelchair accessible.

map 3
H4

MILTON LODGE GARDENS

Old Bristol Road, Wells, Somerset
Tel: 01749 672168 (Mr D C Tudway Quilter)

Grade II listed terraced garden dating from 1906, with outstanding views of Wells Cathedral and Vale of Avalon. Mixed borders, roses, fine trees. Separate 8 acre early XIX century arboretum. **Location:** ½m N of Wells. From A39 Bristol-Wells turn N up Old Bristol Road; free car park first gate on left. **Open:** Garden and arboretum only Easter–end Oct daily (except Sat) 2–6pm. Parties and coaches by prior arrangement. **Admission:** Adults £2, children (under 14) free. Open on certain Suns in aid of National Gardens Scheme. **Refreshments:** Teas available Suns and Bank Hols Apr-Sept. No dogs.

map 3
H3

 MUSEUM OF COSTUME & ASSEMBLY ROOMS

Bennett Street, Bath, Somerset
Tel: 01225 477789 Fax: 01225 477743 (National Trust)

The Assembly Rooms in Bath are open to the public daily (admission free) and are also popular for dinners, dances, concerts and conferences. The magnificent interior consists of a splendid Ball Room, Tea Room and Card Room, connected by two fine octagonal rooms. They are now owned by the National Trust and managed by Bath and North East Somerset Council, which runs a full conference service. The building houses one of the largest and most comprehensive collections of fashionable dress in the country, the Museum of Costume (admission charge). Its extensive displays cover the history of fashion from the late 16th century to the present day, interpreted by hand-held audio guides at no extra charge. The shop sells publications and gifts associated with the history of costume to all visitors. **Open:** All year, 10–5pm. Closed 25/26 Dec. Last admission ½ hour before closing.

map 3
J2

 NUMBER ONE, ROYAL CRESCENT

Bath, Avon.
Tel: 01225 428 126 Fax: 01225 481 850 (Bath Preservation Trust)

Number One was the first house built in the Royal Crescent in 1767 and is a fine example of John Wood the Younger's Palladian architecture. Visitors can see a grand town house of the late 18th century with authentic furniture, paintings and carpets. There is a study, dining room, lady's bedroom, drawing room, kitchen and museum shop. **Location:** Bath, upper town, close to the Assembly Rooms. **Open:** Mid Feb–end Oct, Tues–Sun, 10.30–5pm. Nov, Tue–Sun, 10.30–4pm. Last admission 30 mins before closing. Private tours out of hours if required by arrangement with the Administrator. Open Bank Hols and Bath Festival Mon. Closed Good Fri. **Admission:** Adults £4, children/students/OAPs £3, all groups £2.50, family ticket £8.

map 4
A4

KENTSFORD HOUSE

Washford, Watchet, Somerset.
(Mrs Wyndham)

House open only by written appointment with Mr R. Dibble. **Open:** Gardens Tues and Bank Hols. 16 Mar–31 Aug. **Admission:** Donations towards renovation of fabric.

ORCHARD WYNDHAM

Williton, Taunton, Somerset TA4 4HH
Tel: 01984 632309 Fax: 01984 633526 (Wyndham Est Office)

English Manor House. Family home for 700 years encapsulating continuous building and alteration from 14th to 20th centuries. **Location:** 1 mile from A39 at Williton. **Open:** House and gardens Thurs, Fri and Bank Hol Mon 30 Jul–30 Aug 1999 2–5pm. Guided tours only, last tour 4pm. Limited showing space within the house. To avoid disappointment please advance book places on tour by telephone or fax. House unsuitable for wheelchairs. Narrow road suitable for light vehicles only. **Admission:** Adults £4. Children under 12 £1.

SHERBORNE GARDEN (PEAR TREE HOUSE)

Litton, Bath BA3 4PP
Tel: 01761 241220 (Mr & Mrs J Southwell)

4 acre garden of considerable horticultural interest. Collections of hollies (150), ferns (250), hostas, hemerocallis, rose species, giant and small grasses, all well labelled. Ponds and bridges, small pinetum, plantation with young collection of oak trees. T.V. Gardeners' World and Garden Club. **Location:** Litton, 7 miles N of Wells, Somerset, on B3114 off A39. 15 miles from Bath & Bristol. **Open:** Suns & Mons, Jun–Oct. Other times by appointment. **Admission:** £2, children free. Tea/coffee available. Suitable for disabled. Dogs on leads. Parties by arrangement. Picnic area. Free car parking.

BARRINGTON COURT

Barrington, nr Ilminster TA19 0NQ Tel: 01460 241938

Admission: Adults £4, children £2. Groups £3.50, children £1.75. **Open:** 27 Feb to 14 March: Sat & Sun 11–5.30pm; 20 March to 31 Oct: daily except Fri 11–5.30pm. Coach groups by appointment only. Note: Although the garden is open as usual, access to the Court House is limited during 1999 because of essential safety work. For further information, please tel. 0891 33525. **Events:** 4 April Easter Egg Hunt; for details tel. 01985 843601.

CLEVEDON COURT

Tickenham Road, Clevedon, North Somerset BS21 6QU Tel: 01275 872257

Admission: Adults £4, children £2. Groups of 20+ by arrangement; no reduction. Coaches by appointment. Unsuitable for trailer caravans or motor caravans. **Open:** 28 March to 30 Sept: Wed, Thur, Sun & BH Mons 2–5pm. **Restaurant.**

COLERIDGE COTTAGE

35 Lime Street, Nether Stowey, Bridgwater TA5 1NQ Tel: 01278 732662

Admission: Adults £2.50, children £1. No reduction for groups which must book. **Open:** 1 April to 30 Sept: daily except Mon, Fri & Sat 2–5pm. In winter by written application to the Custodian.

DUNSTER CASTLE

Dunster, nr Minehead TA24 6SL Tel: 01643 821314

Admission: Castle, garden & park: £5.40, children (under 16) £2.80; family ticket £13.80 (2 adults & 3 children). Booked groups £4.70. Garden & park only £2.90, children (under 16) £1.30; family ticket £6.90. Castle is a 10min steep climb from car park, but electrically powered vehicle available to give lifts when necessary. Car park in grounds. **Open:** Castle: 27 March to 31 Oct: daily except Thur & Fri. March to Sept 11–5pm; Oct 11–4pm. Garden and park: daily (closed 25 Dec). Jan to March, Oct to Dec 11–4pm; April to Sept 10–5pm. **Events:** very varied programme; for full details tel. 01985 843601. **Restaurant.**

LYTES CARY MANOR

Nr Charlton Mackrell, Somerton TA11 7HU Tel: Regional Office 01985 843600

Admission: Adult £4, children £2. No group reduction. Coaches only by appointment; large ones cannot get through gates so must stop in narrow road, ¼ mile walk. **Open:** 27 March to 30 Oct: Mon, Wed & Sat 2–6 or dusk if earlier.

MONTACUTE HOUSE

Montacute TA15 6XP Tel: 01935 823289

Admission: Adults £5.40, children £2.70; family ticket £13.40. Booked groups (15+) £4.90, children £2.40. Limited parking for coaches which must be booked in advance. Garden and park only: 24 March to 31 Oct: Adults £3, children £1.30; 4 Nov to March 2000: £1.50. No reduction for groups; group organisers must book in writing to House Manager with s.a.e. **Open:** House: 24 March to 31 Oct: daily except Tues 12–5.30pm. Garden & park: 24 March to 31 Oct: daily except Tues; 4 Nov to March 2000: daily except Mon & Tues . March to Oct 11–5.30pm; Nov to March 11.30–4pm. **Events:** for details of all events tel: 01985 843601. Restaurant.

TINTINHULL HOUSE GARDEN

Farm Street, Tintinhull, Yeovil, Somerset BA22 9PZ Tel: 01935 822545

Admission: Adult £3.70, children £1.80. No group reduction. Coach groups by arrangement in advance with the Gardener; tel. for details. No WC. **Open:** 27 March to 30 Sept: daily except Mon & Tues 12–6pm (but open BH Mons). **Restaurant:** Tea Room as property 12–5.30pm.

TREASURER'S HOUSE

Martock, Somerset TA12 6JL Tel: 01935 825801

Admission: Adult £1.70. No reduction for children. Parties (no reduction) only by arrangement with tenant; tel. for details. No WC. **Open:** 28 March to 28 Sept: Sun, Mon & Tues 2–5pm. Note: Only medieval hall, wall-painting and kitchen are shown. Parking is limited and unsuitable for coaches and trailer caravans.

Staffordshire

*I*f there is a Cinderella of the shires with beauty undiscovered, it is Staffordshire. Large numbers of people still cherish an utterly wrong impression of the county because of its famous "potteries" and industrial towns. It contains some of Britain's fairest treasures.

The Dove flows beside a string of market towns and hamlets; gems of lovely unspoiled England. Picturesque Ellastone, which lies below the lofty limestone ridge of the Weaver Hills was George Eliot's scene for 'Adam Bede' – high above is the quaint Wooton with its great park.

The capital of North Staffordshire is the town of Stoke-on-Trent, immortalised in the work of Arnold Bennett. Some of the finest porcelain in the world originates from this area and there are plenty of museums devoted to the development of this craft. For those interested in more energetic pastimes, the theme park at Alton Towers lies just fifteen miles to the east.

Lichfield, the birthplace of Dr. Samuel Johnson, is famous for its distinctive, three-spired cathedral, built in the thirteenth century and housing some magnificent Belgian stained glass.

ANCIENT HIGH HOUSE

Greengate Street, Stafford, Staffordshire, ST16 2HS
Tel: 01785 240204 (Stafford Borough Council)

The Ancient High House is the largest timber-framed town house in England. It was built in 1595 by the Dorrington family. Its most famous visitor was King Charles 1, who stayed here in 1642. Now a registered museum, the fascinating history of the house is described in a series of displays. The top floor contains the Museum of the Staffordshire Yeomanry. Stafford's Tourist Information Centre is on the ground floor. An attractive gift shop is on the first floor, adjacent to the temporary exhibition area. **Location:** Town centre. **Admission:** Phone for prices. **E-mail:** RHalliwell@compuserve.com **Internet:** staffordbc.gov.uk

BARLASTON HALL

Barlaston, Staffs ST12 9AT
Tel: 01782 372749 Fax: 01782 372391 (Mr and Mrs James Hall)

Barlaston Hall is a mid-eighteenth century palladian villa, attributed to the architect Sir Robert Taylor, extensively restored during the 1990s with the support of English Heritage. The four public rooms, open to visitors, contain some fine examples of eighteenth century plaster work. **Open:** By appointment to groups of 10–30. **Admission:** £3.50 per head including refreshments. If you wish to visit the hall, please write or fax giving details of your group including numbers, range or possible dates and a telephone contact. Recorded message with other opening times on above number.

DUNWOOD HALL

Longsdon, Nr Leek, Staffordshire ST9 9AR
Tel: 01538 385071

Dunwood Hall is a private lived-in country house on the Staffordshire, Cheshire, Derbyshire borders near the Peak District. It is a listed building, recorded in Pevsner and is an unspoiled example of the Victorian neo-Gothic period, both the interior and the exterior influenced by Pugin. Outstanding is the large high–galleried hall, with the original Minton-tiled floor. The unique architecture, period décor, secluded gardens and the steepled stable–block (listed), all make a venue with authentic Victorian ambience. Interested societies or groups are welcome by arrangement for private visits. Dunwood Hall is in Longsdon, 3 miles west of Leek on the A53 to Stoke-on-Trent. **Open:** All year. **Accommodation:** Available. **Admission:** £3–£5 (garden/house/guided tours) Home–made teas by agreement.

CHILLINGTON HALL

Nr Wolverhampton, Staffordshire WV8 1RE
Tel: 01902 850236 (Mr & Mrs John Giffard)

Georgian house. Part 1724 (Francis Smith); part 1785 (Sir John Soane). Fine saloon. The lake in the park was created by 'Capability' Brown. The bridges by Brown and Paine and the Grecian and Roman Temples, together with the eye-catching Sham House, as well as many fine trees add great interest to the four mile walk around the lake. Dogs welcome in grounds if kept on lead. **Location:** 4 miles SW of A5 at Gailey; 2 miles Brewood. Best approach is from A449 (Jct 12, M6 Jct 2, M54) through Coven (no entry at Codsall Wood). **Open:** June–Sept 14 Thurs (also Suns in Aug) 2.30–5.30pm open Easter Sun & Suns preceding May and late Spring Bank Holidays 2.30–5.30pm. Parties of at least 15 other days by arrangement. **Admission:** Adults £3, (grounds only £1.75) children half-price.

THE DOROTHY CLIVE GARDEN

Willoughbridge, Market Drayton, Shropshire, TF9 4EU
Tel: 01630 647237 Fax: 01630 647902 (Willoughbridge Garden Trust)

The garden is known for its woodland plantings, established in a disused gravel quarry. A spectacular waterfall cascades between mature rhododendrons, azaleas and choice woodland plants. A south facing hillside garden provides views of surrounding countryside. A scree garden, water features and colourful summer borders are among the many delights. **Location:** A51, midway between Nantwich and Stone, 3 miles S of Bridgemere Garden World. **Open:** Garden only: 1 Apr–31 Oct, daily 10– 5.30pm. **Admission:** Adults £3, senior citizens £2.50, children up to 11 yrs free, 11–16 yrs £1. Free car park. **Refreshments:** Tearoom open daily. Beverages, home baking and light snacks.

map 8
A6

FORD GREEN HALL

Ford Green Road, Smallthorne, Stoke-on-Trent, Staffordshire.
Tel: 01782 233 195 Fax: 01782 233 194
(Stoke-on-Trent City Council)

A timber-framed farmhouse built for the Ford family in 1624, with eighteenth century brick additions. The house is furnished according to inventories of the 17th and 18th century to give a flavour of the domestic life of the Ford family. **Location:** Smallthorne on B5051 Burslem-Endon Road. **Station(s):** Nearest Stoke-on-Trent. **Open:** Sunday–Thursday 1–5pm. Closed 25 Dec–1 Jan. **Admission:** Adult £1.50, concessions £1.00. Group/Coach parties by appointment. **Refreshments:** Small tearoom. Events/Exhibitions: Wide variety of events held throughout the year. Small parties by prior arrangement.

map 8
B5

SANDON HALL

Sandon, Stafford, Staffordshire
Tel: 01889 508004, Fax: 01889 508586 (The Earl of Harrowby)

Situated in the heart of Staffordshire and surrounded by 400 acres of parkland, this elegant neo-Jacobean house is a superb venue for a wide range of functions and for visits. Sandon Hall, ancestral home of the Earl of Harrowby, is steeped in history and contains many letters, clothes and furnishings of national importance which can be viewed in the museum. The 50 acre garden is landscaped and is especially beautiful in May/June, while the rolling parkland, laid out in the mid-18th century, is a visual delight throughout the seasons. **Location:** 5 miles NE of Stafford on A51, 10 mins from Jct 14, M6. **Open:** Throughout the year in booked groups only. **Admission:** Guided Tour £4 (concessions £3.50). Gardens £1.50 (concessions £1). **Refreshments:** Tea and cakes or Ploughman's Lunch – advance booking essential.

map 8
B6

IZAAK WALTON'S COTTAGE

Worston Lane, Shallowford, Nr. Great Bridgeford,
Stafford, Staffordshire, ST15 0PA
Tel: 01785 760 278 (Stafford Borough Council)

Izaak Walton's Cottage was bequeathed to Stafford by this famous author of the 'Compleat Angler'. It is a delightful timber-framed, thatched cottage and registered museum. It has a series of angling displays showing how the equipment for this sport developed over the years. The events programme takes place each summer, both in the cottage and within its' beautiful garden. It has facilities for disabled visitors, although gravel paths can make access difficult. There are refreshment facilities. **Open:** Apr – Oct.

map 8
B6

🌿 THE SHUGBOROUGH ESTATE

Milford, Nr. Stafford, ST17 0XB, Staffordshire.
Tel: 01889 881 388 Fax: 01889 881323 (Staffordshire County Council)

Magnificent 900 acre seat of the Earls of Lichfield. Architecture by James Stuart and Samuel Wyatt. Rococo plasterwork by Vassalli. Extensive parkland with neoclassical monuments. Beautiful formal garden with Edwardian terrace and rose garden. Working rare breeds farm with restored mill. County museum with Victorian working kitchens and laundry. **Location:** 6 miles E of Stafford on A513. 10 mins from M6, Junction 13. **Station(s):** Stafford. **Open:** Daily 27 Mar–26 Sept, 11–5pm, Oct – Suns only. All year to booked parties. A superb range of tours and packages for schools and adult groups. For further information, please contact the Bookings Officer. **Admission:** Adults £4, concs £3. All-in-Ticket (house, farm & museum) Adults £8, concs £6. Site entry £2 per vehicle. **Conferences:** Facilities available. Please contact Mrs Anne Wood.

map 8
B6

STAFFORD CASTLE & VISITOR CENTRE

Newport Road, Stafford, Staffordshire, ST16 1DJ
Tel: 01785 257 698 (Stafford Borough Council)

Stafford Castle is the impressive site of a Norman motte and bailey fortress. A later stone castle was destroyed during the Civil War, after being defended by Lady Isabel Stafford. It was partly rebuilt in the early 19th century and although now a ruin, is an important example of Gothic Revival architecture. A series of trail boards tell the story of the site. The Visitor Centre displays artefacts from a series of archaeological excavations. An audiovisual presentation narrated by Robert Hardy sets the scene. A collection of chain mail and other objects are fun to try on. A herb garden and attractive gift shop complete this interesting corner of Staffordshire. Picnic area, disabled access and guided tours available.

TAMWORTH CASTLE

The Holloway, Tamworth, Staffordshire B79 7LR
Tel: 01827 709626 Fax: 01827 709630 (Tamworth Borough Council)

Dramatic Norman castle with 15 rooms open to the public, set in attractive town centre park noted for its floral terraces. Includes Great Hall, Dungeon and Haunted Bedroom featuring *Living Images*. "The Tamworth Story" – interactive exhibition telling the town's history from Roman times to the present day. Tamworth Castle celebrates its Centenary in 1999. **Location:** Town centre, in Castle Pleasure Grounds; 15 miles NE of Birmingham. **Station:** Tamworth. **Open:** All year Mon–Sat 10–5.30pm and Sun 2–5.30pm (last admission 4.30pm). Closed Christmas Eve, Christmas Day, Boxing Day. **Admission:** Adults £4, OAP £3, children £2 and family ticket £11. **Events:** Approx 12 special events are held annually. Many are on Bank Holidays.

WHITMORE HALL

Whitmore, Nr Newcastle-under-Lyme, Staffordshire ST5 5HW.
Tel: 01782 680478 Fax: 01782 680906 (Guy Cavenagh-Mainwaring Esq)

Whitmore Hall is a Grade 1 listed building, designated as a house of outstanding architectural and historical interest, and is a fine example of a small Carolinian Manor House, although parts of the Hall date back to a much earlier period. It has been the owner's family home for over 950 years and has continuous family portraits dating back to 1624. A special feature of Whitmore is the extremely rare example of a late Elizabethan stable block. The exterior grounds include a beautiful home park with a lime avenue leading to the house. **Location:** 4 miles from Newcastle-under-Lyme, on A53 to Market Drayton. **Open:** 1 May–31 August, Tues, Wed and Bank Hols, 2–5.30pm. **Admission:** Adult £3, child 50p.

BIDDULPH GRANGE GARDEN

Biddulph Grange, Biddulph, Stoke-on-Trent ST8 7SD

Tel: 01782 517999 Fax: 01782 510624

Open: 27 March to 31 Oct: daily except Mon and Tues (but open BH Mons, closed Good Fri); 6 Nov to 19 Dec: Sat & Sun. 27 March to 31 Oct: Wed to Fri 12–6pm, Sat, Sun & BH Mons 11–6pm; last admission 5.30pm or dusk if earlier; 6 Nov to 19 Dec: 12–4pm or dusk. **Events:** send s.a.e. for details. **Admission:** 27 March to 31 Oct: £4.20; child £2.10; family £10.50. Group rate £3 (15+ must book). Free car park 50m. **Restaurant:** Tea-room as property 12–5.30pm (last admission). Picnics in car park only.

MOSELEY OLD HALL

Moseley Old Hall Lane, Fordhouses, Wolverhampton WD10 7HY

Tel & Fax: 01902 782808

Open: 20 March to end May: Sat & Sun, BH Mon and following Tues (except 4 May); June, Sept & Oct: Wed, Sat & Sun; July & Aug: daily except Mon, Thur & Fri (but open BH Mon); Nov to 19 Dec: Sun (guided tours only). March to end Oct 1.30–5.30pm (BH Mons 11–5pm) Nov & Dec 1.30–4pm. Booked groups at other times, inc. evening tours. **Events:** send s.a.e. for full programme. **Admission:** £3.90; family ticket £9.75. Booked groups £2.50 (out of hours only). **Restaurant.**

Suffolk

*T*hose who delight in wide open spaces, blowing winds and delicate, shifting colour will find their paradise in Suffolk. There is a lyrical, quirky quality to the names of streets, villages and towns in Suffolk. The charmed villages and seaside towns of Orford, Somerleyton, Walberswick, Southwold and Aldeburgh remain resolutely unspoilt and almost Dickensian in appearance despite their seasonal popularity. Aldeburgh wakes up for three weeks in June to play host to East Anglia's most compelling cultural gathering, the Aldeburgh Festival, and then promptly falls back to sleep again.

Southwold, lying in the middle of this aptly named "heritage coast" retains all the charm of a bygone age. There is an impression that the whole of East Anglia is a flat and unrelieved landscape, but in fact it is alive with undulating hills, completely gold with corn in the summer, interspersed with dark, dense copses of trees and sprinkled all over this, the large pink Suffolk farmhouses.

The county has suffered changing fortunes,

Snape Maltings

but a testament to former immense wealth can be seen in the huge churches, which dwarf all that now surrounds them. The town of Dunwich used to have thirteen of these mini-cathedrals, but due to fierce erosion they, along with the entire town and its once great port, have been lost.......to the sea!

CHRISTCHURCH MANSION
Christchurch Park, Ipswich, Suffolk
Tel: 01473 253 246 Fax: 01473 281 274 (Ipswich Borough Council)

A fine tudor house set in beautiful parkland. Period rooms furnished in styles from 16th to 19th centuries. Outstanding collections of china, clocks and furniture. Paintings by Gainsborough, Constable and other Suffolk artists. Attached, the Wolsey Art Gallery shows a lively temporary exhibition programme. **Location:** Christchurch Park, near centre of Ipswich. **Station(s):** Ispwich (1.25 miles). **Open:** From Easter, Tues–Sat, 10–5pm (dusk in winter). Sun 2.30–4.30pm (dusk in winter). Also open Bank Hol Mons. Closed 24–26 Dec, 1–2 Jan & Good Fri. **Admission:** Free.

map 5
H2

EUSTON HALL

(Nr.Thetford), Suffolk
Tel: 01842 766366 (The Duke and Duchess of Grafton)

Euston Hall – Home of the Duke and Duchess of Grafton. The 18th century country house contains a famous collection of paintings including works by Stubbs, Van Dyck, Lely and Kneller. The pleasure grounds were laid out by John Evelyn and William Kent, lakes by Capability Brown. 17th century parish church in Wren style. Watermill, craft shop, picnic area. **Location:** A1088; 3 miles S Thetford. **Open:** June 3–Sept 30 Thurs only 2.30–5pm, also Sun June 27 and Sept 5, 2.30–5pm. **Admission:** Adults £3, children 50p, OAPs £2.50. Parties of 12 or more £2.50 per head. **Refreshments:** Teas in Old Kitchen.

map 5
H1

HAUGHLEY PARK

Nr Stowmarket, Suffolk IP14 3JY
Tel: 01359 240701 (Mr & Mrs R J Williams)

Imposing red-brick Jacobean manor house of 1620, set in gardens, park and woodland. Unaltered three storey east front with five gables topped with crow steps and finials. North end rebuilt in Georgian style, 1820. Six acres of well-tended gardens including walled kitchen garden. Nearby 17th century brick and timber barn restored as meeting rooms. Three woodland walks (1.5 to 2.5 miles) through old broadleaf and pine woodland with bluebells and lily of the valley (May) and rhododendron, azaleas, camellias (June). **Location:** 4 miles W of Stowmarket signed off A14 (Haughley Park, not Haughley). **Open:** Gardens: May–Sept, Tues and first two Sundays in May 2–5.30pm. House: by appointment (01359 240701) May–Sept, Tues 2–5.30pm. **Admission:** Adults £2, children £1.

map 5
H1

HENGRAVE HALL CENTRE

Hengrave Hall, Bury St Edmunds, Suffolk
Tel: 01284 701561 Fax: 01284 702950 (Religious of the Assumption)

Hengrave Hall is a Tudor mansion of stone and brick built between 1525 and 1538. Former home to the Kytson and Gage families, it was visited by Elizabeth I on her Suffolk Progress. Set in 45 acres of cultivated grounds, the Hall is now run as a Conference and Retreat Centre by the Hengrave Community of Reconciliation. The ancient church with Saxon tower adjoins the Hall and continues to be used for daily prayer. **Location:** 3.5 miles NW of Bury St Edmunds on the A1101. Enquire: The Warden for: tours (by appointment); conference facilities (day/ residential); retreats, programme of events; school's programme.

map 5 G1

HELMINGHAM HALL GARDENS

The Estate Office, Helmingham Hall, Stowmarket, Suffolk IP14 6EF
Tel: 01473 890363 Fax: 01473 890776

Completed in 1510, the Hall has been the home of the Tollemache family continuously to the present day. There are two superb gardens that extend to several acres set in 400 acres of ancient parkland containing herds of Red and Fallow deer and Highland cattle. The main garden is surrounded by its own Saxon moat and 1740 wall, with wide herbaceous borders and planted tunnels intersecting an immaculate kitchen garden; the second is a very special rose garden enclosed within high yew hedges with a herb and knot garden containing plants grown in England before 1750. Listed Grade I by English Heritage. **Open:** 25 Apr–5 Sept, Sun only 2–6pm. Also by appointment only for groups, Wed 2–5pm. **Admission:** Adults £3.50, senior citizens £3, children £2, groups 30+ £3 (£3.50 on Wed). Please call 01473 890363 to make an appointment.

map 5 H2

IPSWICH MUSEUM

Ipswich, Suffolk, IP1 3QH.
Tel: 01473 213 761 (Ipswich Borough Council)

Geology and natural history of Suffolk; Mankind galleries covering Africa, Asia, America and the Pacific. 'Romans in Suffolk' and 'Anglo-Saxons in Ipswich' exhibitions. **Location:** High Street in Ipswich town centre. **Station(s):** Ipswich. **Open:** Tues–Sat, 10–5pm. Closed Dec 24, 25 & 26, Jan 1 & 2. Closed Bank Holidays. Temporary exhibition programme. **Admission:** Free.

map 5 H2

EAST BERGHOLT PLACE GARDEN

East Bergholt
Tel: 01206 299 224 (Mr & Mrs R. L. C. Eley)

15 acres of garden and arboretum, originally laid out at the beginning of the century by the present owner's great grandfather. A wonderful collection of fine trees and shrubs, many of which are rarely seen growing in East Anglia and originate from the famous plant hunter George Forrest. Particularly beautifully in the spring when the rhododendrons, magnolias and camellias, are in bloom. A specialist plant centre has been set up in the Victorian Walled Garden, **Location:** 2 miles E of A12, on B1070 Manningtree Road, on the edge of East Bergholt. **Open:** Mar–Sept, Tue–Sun & Bank Hols, 10–5pm. Also open on extra dates for the NGS. Please phone for details. **Admission:** Adults £2, Children free. **Refreshments:** Teas on NGS days and on other days by application. No dogs.

map 5 H2

KENTWELL HALL

Long Melford, Suffolk, CO10 9BA,
Tel:01787 310207. Fax: 01787 379318 (Mrs Phillips)

A mellow redbrick Tudor Mansion in its own broad moat. An oasis of tranquillity. Exterior little changed from when it was built. Interior shows changes of successive family occupiers. Moat House of c.1500 is a fine service building rising sheer from Moat with dairy, bakehouse and brewhouse. Moated Walled Garden with potager and herb garden. Lived in family home. Famous for RECREATIONS OF DOMESTIC TUDOR LIFE on selected weekends throughout season. Also Farm with Rare Breed Farm animals. **Open:** March; Suns only for Gardens and Farm; Apr–19 June Suns only & selected weekdays; June 20–July 11 Sats & Suns for Great Annual Re-Creations of Tudor Life; July 14–Sept 5 daily; Sept 6–Oct 31 Suns only, usually 12–5pm, but Re-Creations weekends from 11am. Telephone for details of Re-Creation weekends.

map 5 G2

OTLEY HALL

Otley, Nr Ipswich IP6 9PA
Tel: 01473 890264 Fax: 01473 890803 (Mr Nicholas & Mrs Ann Hagger)

A stunning medieval moated hall, grade 1 listed and a family home. Rich in history and architectural detail: ornately carved beams, superb linenfold panelling and 16 C wall paintings. Home of the Gosnold family for some 300 years from 1401. Bartholomew Gosnold voyaged to the New World in 1602 and named Cape Cod and Martha's Vineyard. He returned in 1606/7 to found the Jamestown colony, the first English-speaking settlement in the US, 13 years before the *Mayflower* landed. He is also linked to Shakespeare. The house is set in 10 acres of gardens which include a knot and herb garden. **Open:** Bank Hol Suns and Mons, 12.30–6pm; Gardens only Mons from 12 Apr–20 Sept, 2–5pm. **Admission:** Adult £4, child £2.50. Garden Days: Adult £2.50, children £1. Coach parties welcome by appointment for private guided tours. Receptions and corporate entertaining.

map 5 H2

SOMERLEYTON HALL & GARDENS

Somerleyton, Lowestoft, Suffolk NR32 5QQ
Tel: 01502 730 224 Fax: 01502 732 143 (The Rt. Hon. Lord Somerleyton KCVO)

Home of Lord and Lady Somerleyton, Somerleyton Hall is a splendid early Victorian mansion built in Anglo-Italian style with lavish architectural features, magnificent carved stonework and fine state rooms. Paintings by Landseer, Wright of Derby and Stanfield, wood carvings by Willcox of Warwick and Grinling Gibbons. The justly renowned 12 acre gardens feature an 1846 yew hedge maze, glasshouses by Paxton, fine statuary, pergola, walled garden, Vulliamy tower clock, magnificent specimen trees and beautiful borders. Also Loggia Tea Rooms and miniature railway. **Location:** 5 miles NW Lowestoft B1074. **Open:** Easter Sunday to end September, Thursdays, Sundays and Bank Holidays plus Tuesdays and Wednesdays during July and August. Gardens 12.30–5.30pm, Hall 1–5pm. Coach parties welcome, private tours and functions by arrangement.

map 9 K7

SHRUBLAND PARK GARDENS

Shrubland Park, Coddenham, Ipswich, Suffolk
Tel: 01473 830221 Fax: 01473 832202 (Lord De Saumarez)

The extensive formal garden of Shrubland Park is one of the finest examples of an Italianate garden in England. Much use is made of evergreens clipped into architectural shapes to complement the hard landscaping of the masonry. Pines, cedars, holly and holm oak soften this formal structure and add to the Italian flavour. Sir Charles Barry exploited the chalk escarpment overlooking the Gipping Valley to create one of his famous achievements, the magnificent 'Grand Descent' which links the Hall to the lower gardens through a series of terraces. **Location:** 6 miles north of Ipswich to the east of A14/A140 Beacon Hill junction. **Open:** Suns 2–5pm from 4 Apr–12 Sept inclusive, plus Bank Hol Mons. **Admission:** Adults £2.50, children and seniors £1.50. Guided tours by arrangement. Toilet facilities but no refreshments. Limited suitability for wheelchairs.

map 5 H2

ST EDMUNDSBURY CATHEDRAL

Angel Hill, Bury St Edmunds, Suffolk IP33 1LS
Tel: 01284 754933 Fax: 01284 768655 (The Church of England)

Set in the renowned gardens of the ruined abbey, ancient and modern combine in harmony in Suffolk's Cathedral. Visitors commend the tranquil atmosphere of prayer and worship combined with a real sense of welcome. The 16th century nave, by the same builder as King's College, Cambridge, was enhanced with the addition of Quire and Crossing in present times by architect, Stephen Dykes Bower. The Cloisters Gallery has regular exhibitions and the treasury houses church plate from the Diocese. **Location:** Bury St Edmunds town centre. **Open:** Daily, 8.30–6pm, except in British Summer Time (July, Aug, Sept) 8.30–8pm. **Admission:** Donation of £2 is suggested.

WINGFIELD OLD COLLEGE & GARDENS

Wingfield, Nr Stradbroke, Suffolk IP21 5RA
Tel: 01379 384888 Fax: 01379 384034 (Mr & Mrs Ian Chance)

This delightful medieval house with walled gardens offers a unique Arts and Heritage experience. Spectacular medieval Great Hall. Exhibitions of contemporary art in the newly converted Great Barn creative centre plus permanent collections of textiles, ceramics and garden sculpture. Discover the exploits of history's colourful characters associated with the Old College – the Black Prince – William de la Pole – Mary Tudor. Walled Gardens, Old Roses and Topiary. **Location:** Signposted off B1118 (Off the A140 Ipswich/Norwich trunk road) and the B1116 (Harleston–Fressingfield). **Open:** Easter Sat–end Sept Sats, Suns, Bank Hol Mons 2–6pm. **Admission:** Adults £3.60, seniors £3, children/students £1.50. **Refreshments:** Cream teas and cakes.

map 5 H1

WYKEN HALL

Stanton, Bury St.Edmunds, Suffolk IP31 2DW
Tel: 01359 250287 Fax: 01359 252256

The garden, vineyard, country store and vineyard restaurant at Wyken are at the heart of an old Suffolk manor that dates back to Domesday. The garden, set among old flint walls and fine trees, embraces herb and knot gardens, an old-fashioned rose garden, maze, nuttery and gazebo set in a wild garden with spring bulbs. The Leaping Hare Vineyard Restaurant in the 400 year old barn serves Wyken's award-winning wines and is the 1998 Good Food Guide's 'Vineyard Restaurant of the Year'. The Country Store offers an unique collection of textiles, pottery and baskets from the Suffolk Craft Society. A walk through ancient woodland leads to the vineyard. **Open:** Thurs–Sun 10–6pm. Garden closed on Saturdays.

map 5 H1

ICKWORTH HOUSE, PARK & GARDEN

Ickworth, The Rotunda, Horringer, Bury St Edmunds IP29 5QE
Tel: Property Office 01284 735270

Open: 20 March to 31 Oct: daily except Mon & Thur (but open BH Mons) 1–5pm. Garden: 20 March to 31 Oct: daily; 1 Nov to end March 2000: daily except Sat & Sun 10–5pm; 1 Nov to end March 2000: 10–4pm. Park: daily 7–7pm.

LAVENHAM: THE GUILDHALL OF CORPUS CHRISTI

Market Place, Lavenham, Sudbury CO10 9QZ Tel: 01787 247646

Open: 27 March to 31 Oct: daily (closed Good Fri) 11–5pm. The building, or parts of it, may be closed ocassionally for community use.

MELFORD HALL

Long Melford, Sudbury CO10 9AH Tel: 01787 880286

Open: April & Oct: Sat, Sun & Bank Hol Mons; May to end Sept; daily except Mon & Tues (but open BH Mons) 2–5.30pm.

THEATRE ROYAL

Westgate Street, Bury St Edmunds, Suffolk IP33 1QR Tel: 01284 755127
Fax: 01284 706035

Open: Daily, except Sun & BHols 10.30–3.30pm. No access when theatrical activity in progress. Check in advance that theatre is open, tel. 01284 769505.

Surrey

A county of sandy heaths and spacious commons, Surrey commands wide views of the chequered Weald where oak and elm thrive.

Leafy lanes, steep and twisted, are an attractive feature of Surrey towns. The town planners seem to have determinedly built roads around both natural resources and old buildings, giving each town an intricate cobweb of infrastructure and genuine charm.

Surrey's verdant beauty was appreciated amongst some of the most prestigious literary figures of the past. Jane Austen, Sheridan, Keats and EM Forster gained inspiration from this county. Explore the cobbled charm of Surrey's Georgian capital, Guildford, or the tiny streets of hidden villages and you will feel equally as inspired.

River Wey, Guildford

ALBURY PARK

Albury, Guildford, Surrey, GU5 9BB.
Tel: 01483 202 964 Fax: 01483 205 013
(Country Houses Association)

Country mansion by Pugin. **Location:** 1.5 miles E of Albury, off A25 Guildford–Dorking Road. **Station(s):** Chilworth (2 miles), Gomshall (2 miles), Clandon (3 miles). **Bus Route:** Tillingbourne No. 25, Guildford–Cranleigh. **Open:** May–Sept, Wed & Thurs, 2–5pm. (Last entry 4.30pm). **Admission:** Adults £2.50, children free. Free car park. No dogs admitted. Groups by arrangement.

map 4
E5

CLAREMONT

Claremont Drive, Esher, Surrey, KT10 9LY
Tel: 01372 467 841 Fax: 01372 471 109
(The Claremont Fan Court Foundation Limited)

Excellent example of Palladian style. Built in 1772 by 'Capability' Brown for Clive of India. Henry Holland and John Soane were responsible for the interior decoration. It is now a co-educational school run by Christian Scientists. **Location:** ½ mile SW of Esher on A307, Esher-Cobham Road. **Open:** Feb–Nov, first complete weekend (Sat-Sun) in each month (except first Sat in July), 2–5pm. Last tour 4.30 pm. **Admission:** Adults £3, children/OAPs £2. Reduced rates for parties. Guided tours and souvenirs. **E-mail:** claremont@intonet.co.uk **Internet:** www.intonet.co.uk/~claremont

map 4
E5

CLANDON PARK

West Clandon, Guildford, Surrey, GU4 7RQ
Tel: 01483 222482 Fax: 01483 223479 (The National Trust)

An outstanding Palladian country house of dramatic contrasts; from the magnificent neoclassical marble hall to the Maori Meeting House in the garden; the opulent saloon to the old kitchen, complete with old range, below stairs. All this adds up to a fascinating insight into the different lifestyles of the ruling and serving classes in the 18th century. The house is rightly acclaimed for housing the famous Gubbay Collection of porcelain, furniture and needlework, as well as Onslow family pictures and furniture, the Mortlake tapestries and the Ivo Forde collection of Meissen Italian comedy figures. The garden has a grotto and parterre and there is a gift shop and licensed restaurant. **Location:** At West Clandon on the A247, 3 miles E of Guildford. B Rail Clandon 1 mile. **Open:** 28 Mar–31 Oct, Tue, Wed, Thur, Sun plus Bank Hols 11.30–4.30pm.

map 4
E5

CLAREMONT LANDSCAPE GARDEN

Portsmouth Road, Esher, Surrey
Tel: 01372 467806 (The National Trust)

One of the earliest surviving English landscape gardens, restored to its former glory. Features include a lake, island, grotto and extraordinary turf amphitheatre. Dogs: Not admitted Apr–October, admitted on leads Nov–Mar. Coach parties must pre-book. **Open:** All year, Nov–end Mar, Tues–Sun 10–5pm, or sunset if sooner. Apr–end Oct, Mon–Fri 10–6pm. Sat, Sun & Bank Hol Mons 10–7pm. Closed all day 25 Dec, 1 Jan, 13 July. Closed at 2pm 14–18 July. **Admission:** Adults £3, children £1.50, family ticket £7.50, pre-booked parties 15+ £2.50, pre-booked guided tours 15+ £1. Wheelchairs can be booked. Telephone for further details 01372 467806. **Events:** Fête Champêtre: 14–17 July. Sunday Concert: 18 July. Box office 01372 451596/457223.

map 4
E5

FARNHAM CASTLE

Farnham, Surrey GU7 0AG
Tel: 01252 721194 Fax: 01252 711283 (Church Commissioners)

Bishop's Palace built in Norman times by Henry of Blois, with Tudor and Jacobean additions. Formerly the seat of the Bishops of Winchester. Fine Great Hall re-modelled at the Restoration. Features include the Renaissance brickwork of Wayneflete's tower and the 17th century chapel. **Location:** ½ miles N of Town Centre on A287. **Station(s):** Farnham. **Open:** All year round, Weds 2–4pm; parties at other times by arrangement. All visitors given guided tours. Centrally heated in winter. **Admission:** Adults £1.50, OAPs/children/students 80p, reductions for parties. **Conferences:** Please contact Conference Organiser. Centrally heated in winter. Not readily accessible by wheelchair.

map 4
D5

CROYDON PALACE

Old Palace School, Old Palace Road, Croydon, Surrey, CR0 1AX
Tel: 0181 688 2027 / 01243 532717 Fax: 0181 680 5877
(The Whitgift Foundation)

Seat of the Archbishops of Canterbury since 871 AD. 15th century Banqueting Hall and Guardroom. Tudor Chapel. Norman Undercroft. **Location:** In Croydon Old Town, adjacent to the Parish Church. **Station(s):** East Croydon or West Croydon. **Open:** Conducted Tours only. Doors open 2pm. Last tour begins 2.30pm. 6–10 Apr & 31 May–4 June & 12–17 July & 19–24 July. **Admission:** Adults £4.00, children/OAPs £3, family £10. Includes tea served in the Undercroft. Parties catered for by prior arrangement (Tel: 01243 532717). Souvenir shop. Unsuitable for wheelchairs.

map 5
F4

GODDARDS

Abinger Common, Dorking, Surrey, RH5 6TH
Tel: The Landmark Trust: 01628 825920
(Leased to the Landmark Trust by the Lutyens Trust)

Built by Sir Edwin Lutyens in 1989–1900 and enlarged by him in 1910. Garden by Gertrude Jekyll. Managed and maintained by the Landmark Trust, which lets buildings for self-catering holidays. **Open:** By appointment only. Must be booked in advance, including parking, which is very limited. Visits booked for Wed afternoons from the Wed after Easter until last Wed of Oct between 2–6pm. **Admission:** Tickets £3, obtainable from Mrs Baker on 01306 730871, Mon–Fri, 9–6pm. Visitors will have access to part of the house and garden only. **Accommodation:** Available for up to 12 people for self-catering holidays. Tel: 01628 825925 for bookings. Full details of Goddards and 166 other historic buildings are featured in The Landmark Handbook (price £9.50 refundable against a booking) from The Landmark Trust, Shottesbrooke, Maidenhead, Berkshire, SL6 3SW.

map 4
E5

GREAT FOSTERS

Stroude Road, Egham, Surrey
Tel: 01784 433822 Fax: 01784 472455

Probably built as a Royal Hunting lodge in Windsor Forest, very much a stately home since the 16th century, today Great Fosters is a prestigious hotel. It is evident in the mullioned windows, tall chimneys and brick finials, while the Saxon moat – crossed by a Japanese bridge – surrounds three sides of the formal gardens complete with topiary, statuary and a charming rose garden. Within are fine oak beams and panelling, Jacobean chimney pieces, superb tapestries and a rare oakwell staircase leading to the Tower. Some guest bedrooms are particularly magnificent – one Italian styled with gilt furnishings and damask walls, others with moulded ceilings, beautiful antiques and Persian rugs. Close to M25, Heathrow and M3. London 40 minutes by rail.

map 4
E4

GREATHED MANOR

Dormansland, Lingfield, Surrey, RH7 6PA.
Tel: 01342 832 577 Fax: 01342 836 207
(Country Houses Association)

Victorian manor house. **Location:** 2.5 miles SE of Lingfield on B2028 Edenbridge road. Take Ford Manor road beside Plough Inn, Dormansland, for final one mile. **Station(s):** Dormans (1.5 miles), Lingfield (1.5 miles). **Bus Route:** No 429 to Plough Inn, Dormansland. **Open:** May–Sept, Wed & Thurs, 2–5pm. (Last entry 4.30pm). **Admission:** Adults £2.50, children free. Free car park. No dogs admitted. Groups by arrangement.

map 5
F5

GUILDFORD HOUSE GALLERY

155 High Street, Guildford, Surrey, GU1 3AJ
Tel: 01483 444740, Fax: 01483 444742 (Guildford Borough Council)

A beautifully restored 17th century town house with a number of original features including a finely carved staircase, panelled rooms and decorative plaster ceilings. Throughout the year, selections from the Borough's Collection are displayed including oil and pastel portraits by Guildford-born artist John Russell, RA (1745–1806), contemporary craft work, historical and modern paintings, drawings and prints. There is also a varied temporary exhibition programme including paintings, photography and craft work. Exhibition and events leaflet available. Lecture and workshop programme. Details on application. **Location:** Central Guildford on High Street. Public car parks nearby off pedestrianised High Street. **Open:** Tues–Sat 10–4.45. **Admission:** Free. **Refreshments:** Old kitchen tearoom. **Gallery Shop** with attractive selection of cards, craftwork and other publications.

map 4
E5

 ## HATCHLANDS PARK

East Clandon, Guildford, Surrey GU4 7RT
Tel: 01483 222482 Fax: 01483 223479

Built in 1758 for Admiral Boscawen and set in a beautiful Repton park offering a variety of park and woodland walks, Hatchlands contains splendid interiors by Robert Adam, his first commission in a country house in England. It houses the Cobbe Collection, the world's largest group of early keyboard instruments associated with famous composers, e.g. Purcell, JC Bach, Mozart, Chopin, Mahler and Elgar. Small garden by Gertrude Jekyll, gift shop, licensed restaurant. Audio Guide. Lunchtime recitals most Wednesdays. **Location:** 5 miles E of Guildford, on A246 Guildford–Leatherhead Road. **Open:** 1 Apr–31 Oct, walks daily 11.30–6pm. House: Tues, Wed, Thurs, Sun plus BH Mons and all Fris in Aug 2–5.30pm. **Events:** First Weekend in July 1999 Hatchlands Hat Trick Open Air Concerts Tel: 01372 451596.

 # LOSELEY PARK

Guildford, Surrey, GU3 1HS
Tel: 01483 304 440 Fax: 01483 302 036 (Mr & Mrs More-Molyneux)

Loseley House was built in 1562 by Sir William More, a direct ancestor of the present owner. It is a fine example of Elizabethan architecture, dignified and beautiful, set amid magnificent parkland. Inside are many fine works of art, including panelling from Henry VIII's Nonsuch Palace, paintings and tapestries. The 2.5 acre Walled Garden features a Rose Garden (with over 1,000 bushes, mainly old-fashioned varieties), a Herb Garden (divided into sections for culinary, medicinal, dyeing, cosmetic and ornamental purposes), a Flower Garden, a Fountain Garden and also Moat Walk. The Garden has been carefully planted to create interest and colour throughout the year. **Location:** 2 miles south of Guildford. (Take B3000 off A3 through Compton.) 2 miles north of Godalming (off B3100). OS Ref. SU975 471. **Station(s):** Farncombe

1.5 miles. Guildford 2 miles. **Admission: House & Gardens:** Adult £5, child £3, concession £4. **Gardens only:** Adult £2.50, child £1.50, concession £2. **Estate Trailer Tour:** Adult £3, child £1.50, concession £2.50. Group rates available. **Open: Garden, Shop & Tea Room:** 3 May–25 Sept, Wed–Sat & Bank Hol, 11–5pm. **House:** 31 May–30 Aug, Wed–Sat & Bank Hol, 2–5pm (last tour 4pm). **Estate Trailer Tour:** 31 May–30 Aug, Sat & Bank Hol, 12–4pm (dep. hourly). **Refreshments:** Courtyard Tea Room serves light lunches and teas. **Corporate:** The Tithe Barn is available for conferences, company days and wedding receptions. Both the House and Tithe Barn offer Civil wedding ceremonies. **Farm:** Booked school and group farm visits welcome all year.

PAINSHILL LANDSCAPE GARDEN

Portsmouth Road, Cobham, Surrey KT11 1JE
Tel: 01932 868113 Fax: 01932 868001 (Painshill Park Trust)

One of Europe's finest eighteenth century landscape gardens. Designed to surprise and mystify, leaving visitors spellbound at every turn. Walk around the huge lake. A Gothic temple, Chinese bridge, crystal grotto, Turkish tent, replanted shrubberies all disappear and reappear as the walk proceeds. **Location:** W of Cobham of A245; 200 metres E of A307 roundabout. Visitor entrance: Between Streets, Cobham. **Open:** April–Oct daily except Mon (open Bank Hols). 10.30–6.00pm (last entry 4.30pm). Nov–Mar daily except Mon & Fri, Christmas Day & Boxing Day. 11–4pm dusk if earlier. **Admission:** Adults £3.80, concessions £3.30, children 5–16 £1.50. School groups must arrange with Education Trust 01932 886743, prices vary. Adult groups of 10+ £3 (**must pre-book phone 01932 868113**). No dogs please.

RHS GARDEN WISLEY

Wisley, Woking, Surrey GU23 6QB
Tel: 01483 224234 E-Mail: sallyh@RHS.ORG.UK (Royal Horticultural Society)

A world famous garden which extends to 240 acres and provides a unique chance to glean new ideas and inspiration. The Alpine Meadow, carpeted with wild daffodils in spring, Battleston Hill, brilliant with rhododendrons in early summer, the heathers and autumnal tints together with the glasshouses, trials and model gardens are all features for which the garden is renowned. But what makes Wisley unique is that it is not just beautiful to look at. As the showpiece of the Royal Horticultural Society, the Garden is a source of not only practical advice but also over 9,000 plants available in the Plant Centre. **Location:** Wisley is just off M25 Jct 10, on the A3. **Open:** Every day of the year (except Christmas Day) though please note, Sundays are for Members only. **Further Information phone 01482 224234.**

map 4
E5

TITSEY PLACE AND GARDENS

Titsey Hill, Oxted, Surrey RH8 OSD
Tel: 01273 407056 (The Trustees of the Titsey Foundation)

Historic Mansion House. Situated outside Limpsfield, Surrey. Extensive formal and informal gardens containing Victorian Walled Garden, lakes, fountains and rose gardens. Outstanding features of this House include important paintings and object d'art. Home of the Gresham and Leveson Gower Family since the 16th century. **Location:** A25 Oxted to Westerham, at main traffic lights in Limpsfield turn left and then at the bottom of Limpsfield High Street on sharp bend, turn left in to Bluehouse Lane and then first right in to Water Lane. Under motorway and turn right in to Titsey Park. **Open:** Between 15 May–30 Sept on Weds and Suns. 1–5pm and Summer Bank Hols. Also Easter Mon (garden only). Guided tours of the House at 2pm, 3pm and 4pm. Private parties by prior arrangement. **Admission:** House and garden £4.50, garden only £2. Contact: Kate Moisson. Limited access to house, infinite capacity in garden.

map 5
F5

MILLAIS RHODODENDRONS

Crosswater Farm, Crosswater Lane, Churt, Farnham, GU10 2JN
Tel: 01252 792698, Fax: 01252 792526 (The Millais Family)

Six acre woodland garden and specialist nursery growing over 650 varieties of rhododendrons and azaleas. The nursery grows a selection of the best hybrids from around the world and also rare species collected in the Himalayas and available for the first time. Mail order catalogue 5 x 2nd class stamps. The gardens feature a plantsman's collection of rhododendrons and azaleas, with ponds, a stream and companion plantings. Trial garden displays hundreds of new varieties. **Location:** From Churt, take A287 ½ mile towards Farnham. Turn right into Jumps Road and after ½ mile left into Crosswater Lane. **Open:** Nursery: Mon–Fri 10–1pm, 2–5pm. Plus Saturdays in Spring and Autumn. Garden and nursery open daily in May. Teas available on National Gardens Scheme Charity Days 30 & 31 May 1999.

POLESDEN LACEY

Great Bookham, nr Dorking RH5 6BD Tel: Infoline: 01372 458203

Open: House: 27 March to 31 Oct: daily except Mon & Tues (but open BH Mons). 1.30–5.30pm; BH Mon 11–5.30pm. Garden daily 11–6pm or dusk if earlier.

WINKWORTH ARBORETUM

Hascombe Road, Godalming GU8 4AD Tel: 01483 208477

Open: All year: daily during daylight hours, but may be closed during bad weather (especially high winds). **Admission:** £2.70; family ticket £6.75 (2 adults, 2 children, additional family member £1.25). No reduction for groups. Coach groups must book in writing with Head of Arboretum to ensure parking space.

Sussex

Of all the counties Sussex is the easiest to visualise. Sussex lies in four parallel strips – the northern boundary being forest, the next strip the clay Weald, then the smooth green line of the downs and lastly, the coastline of chalk-cliff and low plain – each sublime in its own way.

East Sussex is dramatically beautiful. Inland, the rolling Downs provide a chalky background to the mysterious figure of the Long Man of Wilmington whilst on the coast lies Brighton, an intensely lively place which is often described as "London By The Sea".

West Sussex plays host to the historic town of Chichester where four atmospheric bustling streets meet at a central 16th century market cross. Chichester's cathedral is also worth a visit and its majestic spire dominates the surrounding countryside.

Lewes

ANNE OF CLEVES HOUSE

52 Southover High Street, Lewes, Sussex BN7 1JA
Tel: 01273 474 610 Fax: 01273 486 990 (Sussex Past)

This beautiful 16th century timber-framed Wealden hall-house contains wide-ranging collections of Sussex interest. Furnished rooms give an impression of life in the 17th and 18th centuries. Exhibits include artefacts from nearby Lewes Priory, Sussex pottery, Wealden ironwork and kitchen equipment. **Station(s):** Lewes (10 mins walk). **Bus route:** Adjacent. Bus station 15 mins walk away. **Open:** 1 Jan–21 Feb & 1–31 Dec, Tues, Thurs & Sat 10–5pm. 22 Feb–30 Nov, Mon–Sat, 10–5.30pm; Sun 12noon–5.30pm. **Admission:** Adults £2.30, children £1.10, OAP/Student £2.10, family (2+2) £6.20; combined ticket with Lewes Castle available. 50% discount to EH members. No dogs. **E-mail:** castle@sussexpast.co.uk

map 5 F6

BENTLEY HOUSE & GARDENS

Halland, Nr. Lewes, East Sussex, BN8 5AF
Tel: 01825 840573 (East Sussex County Council) Fax: 01825 841322

Bentley House dates back to early 18th century times and was built on land granted to James Gage by the Archbishop of Canterbury, with the permission of Henry VIII. The family of Lord Gage was linked with Bentley from that time until 1904. The estate was purchased by Gerald Askew in 1937 and during the 1960s he and his wife, Mary, added two, large, double height Palladian rooms to the original farmhouse. The architect who advised them was Raymond Erith, who had previously worked on 10 Downing Street. The drawing room in the East Wing contains mid 18th century Chinese wallpaper and gilt furniture. The Bird Room in the West Wing contains a collection of wildfowl paintings by Philip Rickman. The gardens at Bentley have been created as a series of 'rooms' divided by Yew hedges, one room leading into the next, specialising in many old-fashioned roses including the Bourbons, the Gallicas and the Damask. Nearby 6 stone sphinxes stand along a broad grass walk where daffodils bloom in spring. **Location:** 7 miles northeast of Lewes, signposted on A22, A26 & B2192. **Open:** 15 Mar–31 Oct, daily 10.30–4.30pm (last admissions). House opens 12noon daily 1 Apr–31 Oct. **Admission:** 1998 prices: Adults £4.20, senior/student £3.20, child (4–15) £2.50, family (2A+4C) £12.50, 10% discount for groups 11+. Special rates for disabled (wheelchairs available). Admission price allows entry to House, Gardens, Grounds, Wildfowl Reserve, Motor Museum, History of Bentley Exhibition, Woodland Walk, Children's Adventure Play Area. Picnic area, Gift shop, Education Centre with audio visual. **Refreshments:** Licensed tearooms. **Conferences:** Civil wedding ceremonies. Ample free parking. Dogs allowed in this area only. Please phone for group visits outside normal hours.

map 5 F6

ARUNDEL CASTLE

Arundel, West Sussex, BN18 9AB.
Tel: 01903 883136 Fax: 01903 884581(Arundel Castle Trustees Ltd)

A Castle has overlooked the picturesque South Downs town of Arundel and River Arun for almost 1000 years. The Castle is set in spacious and beautiful landscaped grounds and features a fully restored Victorian kitchen garden. The original Castle suffered some destruction by Cromwell's troops during the Civil War. With restoration and later additions, the Arundel Castle of today is quite magnificent and houses a very fine collection of furniture dating from the 16th century, tapestries, clocks and paintings by Canaletto, Gainsborough, Van Dyck and many other masters. There is such a wealth of treasures to see – the Library with its spectacular carved and vaulted ceiling, the Bedrooms including the suite refurbished for Queen Victoria and Prince Albert with its sumptuous gilt state bed, the Dining Room, the Picture Gallery and much, much more. **Open:** From 1 Apr until the last Friday in Oct, 12–5pm, the last admission on any day is at 4pm. The Castle is closed on Good Friday and Saturdays. Delicious home-made lunches and afternoon teas are served daily in the restaurant. Pre-booked parties are welcome and menus are available on request. Gifts and mementoes, chosen especially by the Countess of Arundel, can be purchased in the shop which is open at the same time as the Castle. For further information please contact: The Comptroller, Arundel Castle, West Sussex BN18 9AB. Tel: 01903 883136/882173. Fax: 01903 884581.

map 4
E6

BATTLE ABBEY

Battle, East Sussex
Tel: 01424 773792 (English Heritage)

Battle Abbey stands at one of the turning points in history, 1066 and the Battle of Hastings. A free interactive audio tour will lead you around the battlefield itself and you can even stand on the exact spot where King Harold fell. As the sounds of the battle ring in your ears you can retrace the lines of conflict and discover where the English army watched the advancing enemy. Explore the impressive abbey ruins then walk the abbey walls to the Great Gatehouse and climb the spiral staircase to the exhibition about abbey life in the Middle Ages. **Location:** At S end of Battle High Street. Battle is reached by road by turning off A21 onto the A2100. **Open:** 1 Apr–30 Sept: daily, 10–6pm, 1 Oct–31 Oct: daily, 10–5pm, 1 Nov–31 Mar: 10–4pm. (Closed 24–5 Dec) **Admission:** Adults £4, concs £3, child £2, family £10 (15% discount for groups of 11 or more).

`map 5 G6`

BORDE HILL GARDEN

Balcombe Road, Haywards Heath, West Sussex RH16 1XP
Tel: 01444 450326 Fax: 01444 440427 E-mail: info@bordehill.co.uk Internet: www.bordehill.co.uk

Spectacular Sussex garden with all year colour. Renowned botanical collection of specialist trees and shrubs planted at turn of the century. Areas of outstanding beauty include The Round Dell, with its subtropical atmosphere, and the Garden of Allah, home to a collection of rhododendrons, magnolias and camellias. For summer colour are the Rose and Herbaceous Garden and Italian Garden designed by RHS gold medallist, Robin Williams. **Location:** 1½ miles N of Haywards Heath on Balcombe Road. Brighton 15 miles; Gatwick 10 miles. **Station(s):** Haywards Heath 1½m. **Open:** All year 10–6pm. **Admission:** Adults £4, OAPs £3.75 (Mon–Fri), children £1.50, groups 20+ £3.50, family day ticket £10. **Refreshments:** Tearoom, restaurant. Bressingham Plant Centre. Wheelchair access and dogs on lead.

`map 5 F6`

CHARLESTON

Firle, Nr Lewes, East Sussex
Tel: 01323 811265 (Visitor Information) Fax: 01323 811628

Charleston was the home of Vanessa Bell, the sister of Virginia Woolf, and Duncan Grant from 1916 until Grant's death in 1978. The house became a 'Bloomsbury' outpost, full of intellectuals, artists and writers; walls, furniture and ceramics were decorated by the artists with their own designs, strongly influenced by post impressionism and interior decoration styles in France and Italy. The walled garden displays a vivid collection of contrasting plants and flowers **Location:** Signposted off the A27, 6 miles E of Lewes, between the villages of Firle and Selmeston. **Open:** 1 Apr–31 Oct, Weds to Sun & Bank Holiday Mons 2–5pm. Jul & Aug Wed–Sat 11.30–5pm, Sun & Bank Holiday Mons 2–5pm. Guided tours Weds–Sats; unguided Suns & Bank Holiday

Mons. Connoisseur Fridays; in-depth tour of the house including Vanessa Bell's studio and the kitchen, not July and Aug. **Admission:** House/Garden: Adult £5.50, children £3.50, Connoisseur Fridays £6.50, Concessions £3.50 Wed & Thurs only. Organised groups should telephone 01323 811626 for rates and information. **Refreshments:** Tea and cakes available Wed to Sun. **Events/Exhibitions:** The Charleston Festival 27–31 May. Literature, art and theatre. The Charleston Gallery; explores Charleston's history and influence on contemporary art. The shop is Craft's Council selected; applied art and books. No disabled access beyond ground floor. Disabled toilet. No dogs. No film, video or photography in the house.

`map 5 F6`

BRICKWALL HOUSE & GARDENS

Northiam, Rye, East Sussex, TN31 6NL
Tel: 01797 253388 Fax: 01797 252 567
(The Frewen Educational Trust)

Jacobean Manor House with magnificent 17th century Drawing Room and Grand Staircase. Superb plaster ceilings. Enchanting, well-planted gardens containing a formal Walled Garden with knot gardens and chess-board topiary, an Arboretum and extensive lawns for marquees for wedding receptions and functions. The Grand Drawing Room, which is licensed for Civil Marriage ceremonies, seats up to 60. There are conference and seminar facilities available for up to 120 delegates. <u>Open:</u> By appointment only. <u>Location:</u> 7 miles NW of Rye, on A28/B2088. Brickwall House is the home of Frewen College, a specialist school for dyslexic pupils. <u>Internet:</u> www.frewcoll.demon.co.uk

map 5 G6

CHICHESTER CATHEDRAL

West Street, Chichester, West Sussex, PO19 1PX
Tel: 01243 782595 Fax: 01243 536190 (The Dean and Chapter of Chichester)

In the heart of the city, this fine Cathedral has been a centre of Christian worship and community life for 900 years and is the site of the Shrine of St Richard of Chichester. Its treasures range from Romanesque stone carvings to 20th century works of art by Sutherland, Feibusch, Procktor, Chagall, Skelton, Piper and Ursula Benker-Schirmer. Treasury. <u>Location:</u> Centre of city, British Rail, A27, A286. <u>Open:</u> Summer 7.30–7pm; Winter 7.30–5pm. Choral Evensong daily (except Wed) during term time. <u>Admission:</u> Free; suggested donations adults £2, children 50p. <u>Conferences:</u> Medieval Vicars' Hall (for 100 people max). Loop system during Cathedral services; touch and hearing centre and braille guide for the blind. Guide dogs only. Parking in city car and coach parks. Contact: Mrs Jenny Thorn.

map 4 D6

DANNY

Hurstpierpoint, Hassocks, Sussex, BN6 9BB.
Tel: 01273 833 000 Fax: 01273 832 436
(Country Houses Association)

Elizabethan E-shaped house, dating from 1593. <u>Location:</u> Between Hassocks and Hurstpierpoint (B2116) – off New Way Lane. <u>Station(s):</u> Hassocks (1 mile). <u>Open:</u> May–Sept, Wed & Thurs, 2–5pm. (Last entry 4.30pm). <u>Admission:</u> Adults £2.50, children £1, groups £3.50 – including tea. Free car park. No dogs admitted.

map 5 F6

FIRLE PLACE

Nr Lewes, East Sussex BN8 6LP
Tel (Recorded Information): 01273 858335 Telephone/Fax: 01273 858188 Contact: Mrs Brig Davies, (Viscount Gage)

Discover the civilised atmosphere of Firle Place, the beautiful home of the Gage family for over 500 years. Admire and enjoy the magnificent collections of Old Master Paintings, the fine English and European Furniture; plus the notable collection of Sèvres Porcelain. Learn fascinating facts about the Gage family. This welcoming house which Connoisseurs will appreciate is set in parkland in an area of outstanding natural beauty at the foot of the South Downs. There is a delightful tea terrace and restaurant for lunch and cream teas. <u>Location:</u> 5 miles SE of Lewes on A27 Brighton/Eastbourne Road. <u>Station:</u> Lewes. <u>Open:</u> June–end Sept plus Bank Hols except Christmas. Wed, Thurs, Sun 2pm–last tickets at 4.30pm. House closes 5.30pm. Group Tours: May–end Sept by pre-arrangement with Curator. <u>Admission:</u> Adult £4, child £2, disabled £2.95. Connoisseur's Day first Wed June–Sept, £4.85. Car park adjacent to House. Restaurant. Shop. Wheelchair access to ground floor. General Information: 01273 858 335. Curator: Tel/Fax: 01273 858 188. Firle Place, Nr Lewes, East Sussex BN8 6LP.

map 5 F6

DENMANS GARDEN

Denmans Lane, Fontwell, Nr Arundel, West Sussex BN18 0SU
Tel: 01243 542808, Fax: 01243 544064 (Mr John Brookes)

Unique 20th century garden artistically planted forming vistas with emphasis on colours, shapes and textures for all year interest; glass areas for tender and rare species. John Brookes school of garden design in the Clock House where seminars are available. **Location:** Between Arundel and Chichester, turn off A27 into Denmans Lane (W of Fontwell racecourse). **Station(s):** Barnham (2 miles). **Open:** Daily from 1 March–31 October including all Bank Hols 9–5pm. Coaches by appointment. **Admission:** Adults £2.80, children £1.50, senior citizens £2.50. Groups of 15 or more £2.20 (1998 prices). **Refreshments:** Restaurant open 11–5pm. Plant centre. No dogs. National Gardens Scheme.

map 4 E6

MARLIPINS MUSEUM

High Street, Shoreham-by-Sea, Sussex BN43 5DA
Tel: 01273 462994

Shoreham's local and especially its maritime history are explored at Marlipins, itself an important historic Norman building believed to have once been used as a Customs House. It has a beautiful chequer-work facade of Caen Stone and inside, much of the original timberwork of the building is open to view. The maritime gallery contains many superb nautical models and fine paintings, while the rest of the museum houses exhibits dating back to Man's earliest occupation of the area. The development of Shoreham's airport and life in the town during the war years feature prominently in the displays. **Open:** 1 May–30 Sept, Tues–Sat, 10–1pm & 2–4.30pm, Sun 2–4.30 pm. **Admission:** Adults £1.50, children 75p, senior citizen/student £1.00.

map 4 E6

FISHBOURNE ROMAN PALACE

Salthill Road, Fishbourne, Chichester, Sussex PO19 3QR
Tel: 01243 785 859 Fax: 01243 539 266 (Sussex Past)

First occupied as a military base in AD43, Fishbourne's sumptuous palace was built around AD75. Remains include 20 spectacular mosaics and its story is told in the museum and by an audiovisual programme. The Roman garden has been replanted to its original plan and now features a Roman gardening museum. There is also an Education Centre and shop. **Station(s):** Fishbourne (5 mins walk). **Bus route:** 5 mins walk away. **Open:** 1 Jan–7 Feb & 14–31 Dec, Sat & Sun 10–4pm. 8 Feb–13 Dec daily 10–5pm (Mar–Jul & Sept–Oct) 10–6pm (Aug) 10–4pm (Feb, Nov–Dec) **Admission:** Adults £4.20, children £2.20. Students/OAP £3.50, disabled £3.30, family (2+2) £10.80. 50% discount to EH members. **Refreshments:** Cafeteria. Picnic area. Suitable for disabled. Parking and toilets. No dogs. **E-mail:** adminfish@sussexpast.co.uk

map 4 D6

GLYNDE PLACE

Glynde, Lewes, East Sussex, BN8 6SX
Tel: 01273 858 224 Fax: 01273 858 224 (Viscount & Viscountess Hampden)

Set below the ancient hill fort of Mount Caburn, Glynde Place is a magnificent example of Elizabethan architecture and is the manor house of an estate which has been in the same family since the 12th century. Built in 1569 of Sussex flint and Caen stone round a courtyard, the house commands exceptionally fine views of the South Downs. Amongst the collections of 17th and 18th century portraits of the Trevor family, a collection of Italian old masters brought back by Thomas Brand on his Grand Tour and a room dedicated to Sir Henry Brand, Speaker of the House of Commons 1872–1884. The house is still the family home of the Brands and can be enjoyed as such. **Location:** In Glynde village, 4 miles SE of Lewes, on A27. **Station(s):** Within easy walking distance of Glynde station, with hourly services to Lewes, Brighton and Eastbourne.

Open: Gardens only: Easter Day & Easter Mon and Sun in April. **House and gardens:** May, Sun and Bank Hols only; Jun–Sept, Wed, Sun & Aug Bank Hol only. July & Aug also Thurs. Guided tours for parties (25 or more) can be booked on a regular open day (£2.50 per person) or on a non-open day (£5 per person). Contact Lord Hampden on 01273 858 224. House open 2pm. Last admission 4.45pm. **Admission:** Adults £4, children £2. Free parking. **Refreshments:** Sussex cream teas in Georgian Stable block. Parties to book in advance as above. Exhibition of watercolours and prints by local artists and shop. **Exhibitions:** 'Harbert Morley and the Great Rebellion 1638–1660', the story of the part played by the owner of Glynde Place during the Civil War. **Weddings:** Glynde Place can be hired for a civil wedding.

map 5 F6

GOODWOOD HOUSE

Goodwood, Chichester, West Sussex PO18 0PX
Tel: 01243 755048 Fax: 01243 755005 (The Duke of Richmond)

In 1999 the BBC is screening <u>Aristocrats</u>, a real life drama about the Lennox sisters, daughters of the 2nd Duke of Richmond. Goodwood was their country home. The House is still lived in by the family and has been richly refurbished. <u>Location:</u> 3½ miles NE of Chichester. <u>Open:</u> Sundays, from 21 Feb, then Suns and Mons from Easter (4 Apr), until 27 Sept, and on Sun through to Thurs in Aug. 1–5pm. Closed on Special Event Days (18 & 19 Apr, 9 & 10 May, **the whole of June**, 22 & 23 Aug and 19 Sept. **Please check Recorded Information:** 01243 755040). Groups welcome on Open Days. All groups must book. Guided tours for groups on Mon mornings by arrangement and on Connoisseurs' Days. <u>Admission:</u> Adult £6, child (12–18) £3, groups (20–200) Guided £8. Open Days £5. <u>Refreshments</u> and teas. Free coach/car park.

map 4 D6

GREAT DIXTER HOUSE AND GARDENS

Northiam, Nr Rye, East Sussex TN31 6PH.
Tel: 01797 252 878 Fax. 01797 252 879 (Mr Christopher Lloyd)

Great Dixter, birthplace and home of gardening writer Christopher Lloyd, was built in 1460 and boasts one of the largest surviving timber–framed halls in the country. Lutyens was employed to restore both the house and gardens in 1910. The gardens are now the hallmark of Christopher Lloyd with an exciting combination of meadows, ponds, topiary and the famous Long Border and Exotic Garden. <u>Location:</u> signposted off the A28 in Northiam. <u>Open:</u> 1 Apr–31 Oct; Tues–Sun 2–5pm; open Bank Hol. Mon. <u>Admission:</u> House & Gardens: Adult £5, child £1.50. Gardens: Adult £4, child £1. <u>Refreshments & facilities:</u> Pre–packed refreshments, partial disabled access, free parking, plant nursery. All enquiries to Elaine Francis, Business Manager. <u>E-mail:</u> greatdixter@compuserve.com <u>Internet:</u> www. entertainnet.co.uk/attractions/greatdixter/index/html.

map 5 G6

HAMMERWOOD PARK

East Grinstead, Sussex, RH19 3QE.
Tel: 01342 850 594 Fax: 01342 850 864 (Mr & Mrs David Pinnegar)

Hammerwood Park is said by visitors to be the most interesting house in Sussex. Built in 1792 as a temple of Apollo, the house was the first work of Latrobe, the architect who designed both The White House and The Capitol in Washington, D.C., USA. Set in Reptonesque parkland on the edge of Ashdown Forest, the house is an early example of Greek Revival. Award winning restoration works have been completed including a trompe l'oeil decoration scheme in the staircase hall. Restoration of the gardens is now under way. Guided tours by the owner and his family, luscious cream teas. <u>Location:</u> 3.5m E of East Grinstead on A264 to Tunbridge Wells. 1m W of Holtye. <u>Station(s):</u> East Grinstead <u>Open:</u> Easter Mon–end Sept, Wed, Sat & BHol Mons 2–5.30pm. Guided tour starts just after 2pm. Coaches (21+) by appointment. <u>Admission:</u> Adult £4, child £1.50. Privilege card: 3 for 2, Apr–28 Jun (except BHol weekends). <u>Accommodation:</u> B&B in an idyllically peaceful location only 20 mins from Gatwick.

map 5 F5

HERSTMONCEUX CASTLE

Hailsham, East Sussex BN27 1RN
Tel: 01323 833816 Fax: 01323 834499 (Herstmonceux Castle Enterprises)

Set within 550 acres of beautiful parkland is the breathtaking 15th century moated Castle. The grounds are ideal for picnics and woodland walks. Don't miss the Rhododendron garden, Rose garden and Elizabethan garden! Seasonal Features: Spring – a wonderful display of daffodils and bluebells; Summer – extensive variety of herbaceous borders & roses, water lilies. Guided Castle tours (phone to confirm times and availability). Conference/function facilities available. New for 1999: nature trail. Natural Butterfly garden planted in 1998. Return of our Tercentenary Sundial. <u>Open:</u> Grounds & Gardens 27 Mar–31 Oct, 10–6pm (last entry 5pm). Closes one hour earlier during Oct. Group rates available. <u>Forthcoming Special Events:</u> Easter Sunday: Easter Egg Hunt. 12 June: Open Air Concert (tbc). 28, 29 & 30 Aug: Medieval Festival.

map 5 G6

HIGH BEECHES GARDENS

Handcross, West Sussex RH17 6HQ
Tel: 01444 400589 (High Beeches Gardens Conservation
Trust. Reg. non profit making Charity No. 299134)

Help us to preserve these twenty acres of enchanting landscaped woodland and water gardens recommended by Christopher Lloyd, with magnolias, rhododendrons and azaleas in Spring. In Autumn, one of the most brilliant gardens for leaf colour. Gentians and primulas are naturalised. Many rare plants. Tree trail. Four acres of natural wildflower meadows. **Location:** 1 mile E of A23 at Handcross, on B2110. **Open:** Gardens only: 1–5pm Apr 1–June 30, Sept 1–Oct 31 daily except Weds. July 1–Aug 31 Mon and Tues only 1–5pm. **Admission:** £3.50. Privilege Card admits 2 adults for the price of 1. Accompanied children free. **Refreshments:** Hot and cold drinks, ice cream and biscuits in Gate Lodge. Sadly, gardens not suitable for wheelchairs. Regret no dogs.

map 5 F6

LEWES CASTLE

Barbican House, 169 High Street, Lewes, Sussex, BN7 1YE
Tel: 01273 486 290 Fax: 01273 486 990 (Sussex Past)

Lewes' imposing Norman castle provides an invigorating climb rewarded by magnificent views. Adjacent Barbican House Museum follows the progress of Sussex people from their earliest beginnings. The Lewes Living History Model is a superb scale model of Victorian Lewes and an audio-visual presentation. There is also an Education Centre and shop. **Station(s):** Lewes (7 mins walk). **Bus route:** Adjacent. Bus station 10 mins walk away. **Open:** Daily (except Christmas & Boxing Day), 10–5.30pm. (Sun & Bank Hols 11–5.30pm). **Admission:** (1999) Adults £3.50, child £1.80, OAP/student £3, family (2+2) £10. 50% discount to EH members. Joint ticket with 'Anne of Cleves House': Adult £4.80, children £2.50. 50% discount to EH members. Audio tours 50p + deposit. No dogs. **E-mail:** castle@sussexpast.co.uk

map 5 F6

MERRIMENTS GARDENS

Hawkhurst Road, Hurst Green, East Sussex TN19 7RA
Tel: 01580 860666 Fax: 01580 860324 (Weeks Family with Mark Buchele)

"Gardened naturally, free from the restrictions of institute, experimenting continuously and always permitting nature to have its say." Set in 4 acres of gently sloping Wealden farmland, a naturalistic garden which never fails to delight. Deep curved borders richly planted and colour themed. An abundance of rare plants will startle the visitor with sheer originality. **Admission:** £2.50 **Open:** 2 April–end October. Daily 10–5pm. **E-mail:** merriments@msn.com **Website:** www.merriments.co.uk

map O

MICHELHAM PRIORY

Upper Dicker, Hailsham, Sussex, BN27 3QS
Tel: 01323 844 224 Fax: 01323 844 030 (Sussex Past)

Enclosed by a medieval moat, the remains of this beautiful Augustinian Priory are incorporated into a splendid Tudor mansion featuring a fascinating array of exhibits. Superb gardens are enhanced by a 14th century gatehouse, water mill, physic herb and cloister gardens, smithy, rope museum and dramatic Elizabethan Great Barn. **Location:** O.S. map ref: OS 198 TQ 558093. **Station(s):** Polegate (3 miles). Berwick (2 miles). **Buses:** Bus route (1.5 miles). **Open:** Wed–Sun. 15 Mar–31 Oct. Mar & Oct, 10.30–4pm. Apr–July & Sept, 10.30–5pm. Daily in Aug, 10.30–5.30pm. **Admission:** (1999 prices) Adults £4.20, children £2.20, OAP £3.50, family (2+2)£10.80. (50% discount to English Heritage members). **Refreshments:** Tearoom/restaurant. Picnic area. Museum, education centre and shop. Dogs are admitted in car park. **E-mail:** adminmich@sussexpast.co.uk

map 5 F6

LEONARDSLEE GARDENS

Lower Beeding, Nr Horsham RH13 6PP
Tel: 01403 891212 Fax: 01403 891305 (Mr Robin Loder)

Leonardslee Gardens, created and maintained by the Loder family since 1889, are set in a peaceful 240-acre valley. There are delightful walks around seven beautiful lakes, giving rise to glorious views and reflections. Camellias, magnolias and the early rhododendrons provide colour in April, while in May it becomes a veritable paradise, with banks of sumptuous rhododendrons and azaleas overhanging the paths which are fringed with bluebells. Also in May, the Rock Garden becomes a Kaleidoscope of colour with Japanese evergreen azaleas and ancient dwarf conifers. Superb flowering trees and interesting wild-flowers enhance the tranquillity of summer and the mellow seasonal tints of autumn complete the season. The fascinating Bonsai collection shows this oriental living art-form to perfection. Many visitors are surprised to see the wallabies, which have been used as environmentally–friendly mowing machines for over 100 years! Axis Fallow and Sika Deer roam in the parks and wildfowl are seen on the lakes. The Loder family collection of Victorian Motor Cars (1895–1900) has some fine examples–all in running order–from the dawn of motoring! There is a licensed restaurant and a café for refreshments, as well as a gift shop and a wide selection of plants for sale. **Open:** Daily 1 Apr–31 Oct, 9.30–6pm. **Admission:** May £5, all other times £4. Children (age 5–15) £2.50.

map 4
E6

PARHAM HOUSE & GARDENS

Parham Park, near Pulborough, West Sussex. Tel: 01903 742021
Info Line: 01903 744888 Fax: 01903 746557(Parham Park Ltd)

A much-loved family home, Parham opens its doors to visitors from April–October on Wednesday, Thursday, Sunday and Bank Holiday afternoons with private guided visits on Monday, Tuesday or Friday afternoons and Wednesday or Thursday mornings. Our Big Kitchen opens at 12 noon, for light lunches and delicious cream teas! Complementing the light panelled rooms full of beautiful furniture, paintings and needlework are fresh flower arrangements, the flowers having been grown in the award-winning walled garden. Spend a peaceful afternoon strolling through the greenhouse, orchard, potager and herbiary, try your hand at the brick and turf maze! Visit us in July when we have our annual garden weekend (17th & 18th).

map 4 E6

PASHLEY MANOR GARDENS

Pashley Manor, Ticehurst, E. Sussex
Tel: 01580 200888 Fax: 01580 200102 (Mr and Mrs J. Sellick)

Pashley Manor is a Grade I Tudor house standing in a well timbered park. The 9 acres of formal garden dating from the 18 century, created in true English romantic style, have many ancient trees and fine shrubs. New plantings add interest and subtle colouring throughout the year. Water features, a classical temple, walled rose gardens and new herbaceous borders. Home-made lunches and teas. Wine licence. **Admission:** £4.50, OAP's £4. **Open:** Tues, Wed, Thurs, Sat & Bank Hol Mons. 10 Apr–30 Sept 1998. **Location:** On the B2099, 1.5 miles southeast of Ticehurst, East Sussex. Tel: 01580 200888 for details. **Events:** Tulip Festival: 29 Apr–3 May. Summer Flower Festival: 17–20 June. Plant Fairs: 18 Apr & 15 Aug.

map 5 G6

PALLANT HOUSE GALLERY

9, North Pallant, Chichester, West Sussex, PO19 1TJ
Tel: 01243 774557

Meticulously restored Queen Anne town house with eight rooms decorated and furnished in styles from early Georgian to late Victorian. Also Georgian style gardens and important displays of Bow Porcelain (1747–1775) and Modern British Art (1920–1980). **Location:** Chichester City centre. **Open:** All year Tues–Sat 10–5pm (last admission 4.45) also open Sun 12.30–5pm. **Admission:** Adults £2.80, over 60s £2.20, students/ UB40 £1.50. **Refreshments:** Restricted availability. **Events/Exhibitions:** Call for details.

map 4 D6

PERRYHILL NURSERIES

Hartfield, East Sussex, TN7 4JP
Tel: 01892 770 377 Fax: 01892 770 929

Why not visit us and choose from the widest range of plants in the South East. We are not a garden centre but a genuine growing nursery offering over 5000 varieties of plants including the rare and unusual. Qualified staff available to answer your gardening questions. We will do our best to source plants you are looking for if we do not stock them. No mail order. Catalogues £1.65 incl. postage. **Location:** 1 mile N of Hartfield on B2026. **Open:** Mar–Oct, 9–5pm. Nov–Feb, 9–4.30pm. Seven days a week.

 map 5 F5

PRESTON MANOR

Preston Drove, Brighton BN1 6SD
Tel: 01273 292770 Fax: 01273 292771 (Brighton & Hove Council)

Experience the charms of this delightful Manor House which powerfully evokes the atmosphere of an Edwardian gentry home both 'Upstairs' and 'Downstairs'. There are more than twenty rooms to explore over four floors, from the superbly renovated servants' quarters and butler's pantry in the basement to the day nursery and attic bedrooms on the top floor. Situated adjacent to Preston Park, the Manor also comprises picturesque walled gardens and a pets' cemetery. **Location:** 2 miles north of Brighton on the A23 London Road. **Open:** Daily Tues–Sat 10–5pm, Sun 2–5pm, Mon 1–5pm (Bank Holidays 10–5pm). Closed 25 & 26 Dec and Good Friday. **Admission:** Adults £3, children £1.85, conc. £2.50. Please call for details of family and group tickets. (Prices valid until 31.3.99)

 map 5 F6

THE PRIEST HOUSE

North Lane, West Hoathly, Sussex RH19 4PP
Tel: 01342 810479

The Priest House nestles in the picturesque village of West Hoathly, on the edge of Ashdown Forest. Originally a 15th century timber-framed farmhouse with central open hall, it was modernised in Elizabethan times with stone chimneys and a ceiling in the hall. Later additions created a substantial yeoman's dwelling. Standing in the beautiful surroundings of a traditional cottage garden, the house has a dramatic roof of Horsham stone. Its furnished rooms, including a kitchen, contain a fascinating array of 17th and 18th century domestic furniture, needlework and household items. In the formal herb garden, there are over 150 herbs used in medicine and folklore. **Open:** 1 March–31 Oct, Mon–Sat, 11–5.30pm, Sun 2–5.30pm. **Admission:** Adults £2.30, children £1.10, OAP/student £2.10 (1999 prices).

ROYAL BOTANIC GARDENS, KEW AT WAKEHURST PLACE

Ardingly, Nr Haywards Heath, West Sussex RH17 6TN
Tel: 01444 894066 (Royal Botanic Gardens)

Managed by the Royal Botanic Gardens, Kew, Wakehurst Place near Ardingly is a garden for all seasons, set in 170 acres dating back to the 12th century. Set around a striking Elizabethan mansion with walled gardens, a winter garden and a wonderful spring border around the mansion pond, the vibrant ornamental plantings, providing year round colour and interest, blend into the beautiful natural landscape. Footpaths and trails lead through sweeping woodlands of native and exotic trees. **Open:** Wakehurst Place is open daily from 10am except Christmas Day and New Year's Day. Closing time vary. Please ring. **Admission:** Adult £5, concession £3.50, children (5–16) £2.50, under 5's free.

map 5
F5

THE ROYAL PAVILION

Brighton, East Sussex BN1 1EE
01273 290900, Fax: 01273 292871 (Brighton & Hove Council)

The Royal Pavilion, the famous seaside palace of King George IV, is one of the most exotically beautiful buildings in the British Isles. Originally a simple farmhouse, in 1787 architect Henry Holland created a neoclassical villa on the site. From 1815–1823, the Pavilion was transformed by John Nash into its current distinctive Indian style complete with Chinese-inspired interiors. Magnificent decorations and fantastic furnishings have been re-created in an extensive restoration programme. New for 1999 is the recently restored North Gallery, while throughout the year visitors will be able to see work in progress as the Banqueting Room ceiling undergoes major restoration. The Royal Pavilion is an ideal location for filming and photography and rooms are also available for corporate entertaining, private hire and wedding ceremonies. **Location:** In centre of Brighton (Old Steine). **Station(s):** Brighton (1/2 mile). **Open:** Daily (except 25 & 26 Dec) June–Sept 10–6pm, Oct–May 10–5pm. **Admission:** Adults £4.50, children £2.75 students/OAPs £3.25 (prices valid until 31.3.2000). **Refreshments:** Regency teas and refreshments in Queen Adelaide tearooms with balcony providing sweeping views over the restored gardens. **Events/Exhibitions:** A popular winter programme of events.

map 5
F6

ST MARY'S HOUSE & GARDENS

Bramber, West Sussex Tel/Fax: 01903 816 205
(P. F. Thorogood)

Magnificent historic house built in 1470 by Waynflete, Bishop of Winchester, founder of Magdalen College, Oxford. Fine panelled rooms. Unique trompe l'oeil 'Painted Room'. English costume-doll collection, family memorabilia and other exhibitions. Still a lived-in family home. "Warmest Welcome" Commendation. Charming gardens with amusing topiary. **Location:** Off A283, 10 miles NW of Brighton. **Station(s):** Shoreham-by-Sea from London (Victoria). **Open:** Easter Sun-last Sun in Sept, Sun & Thur & Bank Hol Mons, 2–6pm. Last tour 5pm. **Group bookings:** Other days by prior arrangement from Apr–Oct. **Admission:** Adults £4, children £2, Group rate £3.80, (groups of 25+). Parking in grounds. **Refreshments:** Teas in Music Room.

map 4
E6

SAINT HILL MANOR

Saint Hill Road, East Grinstead, West Sussex RH19 4JY
Tel: 01342 326711 (contact Liz Nyegaard)

Fine Sussex sandstone house built in 1792 and situated near the breathtaking Ashdown Forest. Saint Hill Manor's final owner, acclaimed author and humanitarian, L. Ron Hubbard, lived here for many years with his family. Under his direction extensive renovations were carried out uncovering exquisite period features hidden for over a century. Fine wood panelling, marble fireplaces, Georgian windows and plasterwork ceilings have been expertly restored to their original beauty. Outstanding features of this lovely house include a complete library of Mr. Hubbard's work, the elegant Winter Garden and the delightful Monkey Room, housing John Spencer Churchill's 100ft mural depicting many famous characters as monkeys, including his uncle Sir Winston Churchill. 59 acres of landscaped gardens, lake and woodlands. **Location:** Off A22, N of East Grinstead, down Imberhorne Lane. Straight into Saint Hill Road, 300 yds on right. Stations: East Grinstead. Owner: Church of Scientology. **Open:** All year. Daily, 2–5pm. Tours on the hour or by appointment. Group parties welcome. Parking for coaches and cars. **Admission:** Free. **Events/Exhibitions:** Classical concert in Winter garden, Sunday 11th April. Free admission. Outdoor production of Shakespeare's Comedy of Errors; Saturday 26th June. Telephone for details. Summer concerts on the terrace, musical evenings throughout the year. Conference and wedding reception facilities available in Saint Hill Castle. Seats up to 600 theatre style and 300 for dinner.

map 5
F5

SHEFFIELD PARK GARDEN

Sheffield Park, East Sussex TN22 3QX
Tel: 01825 790231 Fax: 01825 791264

A magnificent 120 acres (48 hectares) landscaped garden, laid out in the 18th century and extended with the advice of the famous landscape designers 'Capability' Brown and Humphrey Repton. Further developed in the early years of this century by it's owner, Arthur G. Soames, who planted on an ambitious scale much of what the visitor sees today including rare and exotic trees and shrubs. There are four lakes linked by cascades and waterfalls and the garden is renowned for stunning displays of daffodils, bluebells, rhododendrons and azaleas in Spring, and in Autumn the garden is transformed by a blaze of colour. The North American trees and shrubs produce a display of gold, orange and crimson that is reflected in the lakes.

THE WEALD & DOWNLAND OPEN AIR MUSEUM

Singleton, Nr Chichester, West Sussex
Tel: 01243 811348

The Museum is rescuing and re-erecting historic buildings from South-East England. The collection illustrates the history of vernacular architecture in the Weald and Downland area. Exhibits include a Medieval farmstead, garden and history of farming exhibition centred on Bayleaf Farmhouse (left), timber framed houses, a Tudor market hall, a 16th century treadwheel, farm buildings, a blacksmith's forge, plumber's and carpenter's workshops and a village school. A 'Hands On' gallery explores building materials and techniques. **Location:** 6 miles N of Chichester on A286 just S of Singleton. **Open:** 1 Mar–31 Oct daily 10.30–5pm, 1 Nov–28 Feb, Wed, Sat and Sun only 10.30–4pm, 26 Dec–1 Jan daily 10.30–4pm. **Admission:** Charged. Parties by arrangement (group rates available). **Refreshments:** Light refreshments during main season.

WEST DEAN GARDENS

The Edward James Foundation, Estate Office, West Dean, Chichester, West Sussex PO18 0QZ
Tel: 01243 818210 Fax: 01243 811342

Extensive downland garden with 300ft pergola, herbaceous borders and gazebo. Victorian Walled Kitchen Garden with unusual vegetables, herbs, cut flowers, fruit collection and 13 original glasshouses. Parkland Walk (2¼ miles). 45 acre St Roche's Arboretum. Visitor Centre houses restaurant. Garden shop. Plant sales. Group bookings/guided tours of garden arranged by appointment. **Location:** 6 miles N of Chichester on A286. **Open:** Mar–Oct incl. daily 11–5pm. Last admission 4.30pm. Parties by arrangement. **Admission:** Adults £4, over 60's £3.50, children £2, pre-booked parties 20+ £3.50 each. **Refreshments:** Restaurant. **Events:** Chilli Fiesta 14–15 Aug, Apple Day 17 October. Coach/car parking. No dogs. **E-mail:** westdean@pavilion.co.uk **Website:** http//www.westdean.org.uk/

UPPARK

South Harting, Petersfield, Hampshire GU31 5QR
Tel: 01730 825415 Fax: 01730 825873 (The National Trust)

National Trust's most ambitious restoration project: Georgian interior, paintings, ceramics, textiles, furniture and dolls house rescued from 1989 fire. Multimedia exhibition of restoration. Interesting servants' rooms with H G Wells connections. Garden restored to Repton's design. **Location:** 5 miles SE of Petersfield on B2146. **Open:** Sun–Thurs (closed Fri and Sat) 28 Mar–28 Oct. Tickets, grounds, garden, shop and tearoom: 11.30–5.30pm. House: 1–5pm (4pm in Oct). **Admission:** Timed tickets in operation. Adults £5.50; family ticket £13.75. Parties (weekends only – no reduction) must book in advance.

BODIAM CASTLE

Bodiam, nr Robertsbridge TN32 5UA Tel: 01580 830436

Open: 13 Feb to 31 Oct: daily 10–6 or dusk if earlier; 3 Nov to 2 Jan 2000: daily except Mon (closed 24–26 Dec), 10–4 or dusk if earlier. Last admission 1hr before closing.

PETWORTH HOUSE AND PARK

Petworth GU28 0AE Tel: 01798 342207; Infoline: 01798 343929

Open: House: 27 March to 31 Oct: daily except Thur & Fri (but open Good Fri) 1–5.30pm. Last admission to house 4.30pm; kitchens 5. Additional rooms shown weekdays (not BH Mon). Pleasure grounds and car park (for walks, picnics and access to tea-room, shop and Petworth town): daily except Thur & Fri (but open Good Fri). Park: daily 8 to sunset (closes noon 25–27 June).

Warwickshire

Of mountains, valleys and other natural beauties, Warwickshire has few. However, from a historical aspect, Warwickshire is the most fortunate of counties. The names of Warwickshire towns read like chapters in a history book: Stratford Upon Avon, Warwick, Kenilworth, Rugby and Coventry.

The town of Warwick retains some superb examples of medieval architecture, despite being partly destroyed by a huge fire in the late seventeenth century. Some of the finest buildings are to be found around the High Street and in Northgate Street.

The springs of Royal Leamington Spa, to the East of Warwick, were frequented by royalty when Queen Victoria visited the fashionable town in 1838. Nearby Kenilworth Castle

Kenilworth Castle

was constructed during Norman times and vastly altered by Elizabeth I's favourite, the Earl of Leicester. It then became renowned as a place of fine music and pageantry.

But it is for its association with William Shakespeare that Warwickshire is invariably best known. The town of Stratford-Upon-Avon stands central to "Shakespeare Country", with its many examples of Shakespearean heritage.

ARBURY HALL
Nuneaton, Warwickshire, CV10 7PT
Tel: 01203 382804, Fax: 01203 641147 (The Rt. Hon. The Viscount Daventry)

16th century Elizabethan House, Gothicised late 18th century, pictures, period furniture etc. Park and landscape gardens. Arbury has been the home of the Newdegate family since the 16th century. For a country house the Gothic architecture is unique, the original Elizabethan house being Gothicised by Sir Roger Newdigate between 1750 and 1800, under the direction of Sanderson Miller, Henry Keene and Couchman of Warwick. Beautiful plaster ceilings, pictures and fine specimens of period furniture, china and glass. Fine stable block with central doorway by Wren. Arbury Hall is situated in very large grounds and is about 1½ miles from any main road. Excellent carriage drives lined with trees. George Eliot's 'Cheveral Manor'. **Location:** 2 miles SW of Nuneaton off B4102. **Station(s):** Nuneaton. **Open:** All the year round for corporate functions and events.

Pre–booked visits to the Hall and Gardens for Parties/Groups of 25 and over from Easter to end of September. Hall and Gardens open from 2–5pm Sundays and Mondays or Bank Holiday Weekends only from Easter to September. **Admission:** Hall & Gardens: Adults £4.50, children £2.50. Gardens only: Adults £3, children £2, family ticket £10. Organised parties most days (25 or over) special terms by prior arrangement with Administrator. **Conferences:** Arbury is an ideal venue for corporate hospitality functions, promotions and as a film location etc. The Dining Room is also available for exclusive luncheons and dinners. **Events:** June 6 Arbury Motor Transport Spectacular. May 13–16 Birmingham Dog Show. June 26/27 Rainbow Craft Fair. July 3 "Shakespeare in the Garden". Wheelchair access ground floor only. Gravel paths. Free car park.

map 8
C7

BADDESLEY CLINTON HALL

Rising Lane, Baddesley Clinton Village, Knowle, Solihull, West Midlands
Tel: 01564 783294 Fax: 01564 782706 (The National Trust)

A romantic and atmospheric moated manor house dating from the 15th century and little changed since 1634. The interiors reflect the house's heyday in the Elizabethan era, when it was a haven for persecuted Catholics - there are no fewer than 3 priest-holes. There is a delightful garden, ponds, lake walk and nature trail. **Open:** House: 3 Mar–31 Oct, daily except Mon & Tues (closed Good Fri, open BH. Mon). Mar, Apr & Oct 1.30–5pm, May–end Sept 1.30–5.30pm. Grounds: 14 Feb–12 Dec daily except Mon & Tues (closed Good Fri, open BH. Mon). 14–28 Feb 12–4.30pm; Mar, Apr & Oct 12–5pm; May–end Sept 12–5.30pm and Nov–12 Dec 12–4.30pm. Licensed Restaurant: 14 Feb–12 Dec as shop. 12–2pm, 2.30–5.30pm (14–28 Feb closes 4.30pm, Mar, Apr & Oct 5pm, 3 Nov–12 Dec 4.30pm). Party lunches & dinners arranged. Picnic tables near entrance.

 map 4 B1

CHARLECOTE PARK

Warwick CV35 9ER
Tel: 01789 470 277, Fax: 01789 470 544

Home of the Lucy family since 1247. Present house built in 1550's. Queen Elizabeth I visited. Victorian interiors; objects from Fonthill Abbey. Park landscaped by Capability Brown. Jacob sheep. Red and fallow deer, reputedly poached by Shakespeare. **Open:** 20 Mar–31 Oct, Fri–Tues, 11–6pm. House open 12–5pm. Shop and restaurant 11–5.30pm. **Admission:** Adult £4.90, child (5–16) £2.45. Family ticket £12.20. Special group rate £3.90 (weekdays only for parties 15+). Evening guided tours for pre-booked parties £5.50 (including NT members; minimum charge £115 for party). Wheelchair facilities: All ground floor rooms accessible including Orangery and shop. Parking. Lavatories. **Refreshments:** Morning coffee, lunches, afternoon teas in restaurant (licensed). Picnic in deer park only. Changing and feeding room. No dogs allowed.

map 4 B2

THE HILLER GARDEN

Dunnington Heath Farm, Nr. Alcester,
Warwickshire, B49 5PD. Tel: 01789 490 991
Fax: 01789 490 439 (A. H. Hiller & Son Ltd)

Among gravelled walks, large beds display an extensive range of unusual herbaceous perennials providing colour and interest throughout the year in this two acre garden near Ragley Hall. The Rose Gardens, at the peak of their beauty from the end of June, hold a collection of some 200 old-fashioned, species, modern shrub, rugosa and English roses in settings appropriate to their characters. There is a well-stocked plant sales area, a garden gift shop, farm shop and licensed tearooms. **Location:** 3 miles S of Alcester on B4088 (formerly A435/A441 junction). **Open:** Daily (except Christmas and New Year), 10–5pm. **Admission:** Free. **Refreshments:** Morning coffee, light lunches, afternoon teas in the Garden Tea Rooms (licensed).

 map 4 B2

COUGHTON COURT

Alcester, B49 5JA, Warwickshire
Tel: 01789 400 777 Fax: 01789 765 544 Tel: 01789 762435(Visitor Information)

text Coughton Court has been the home of the Throckmorton family since the 15th century. The house contains one of the best collections of portraits and memorabilia of one family from Tudor times to the present day. There are two churches in the grounds to visit and magnificent ½ acre flower garden together with a lake and riverside walks, an orchard and bog garden. Gunpowder Plot Exhibition. **Location:** 2 miles north of Alcester, on A435. **Open:** Mid Mar– Mid Oct. Please contact Visitor Information Line for 1999 opening times & admission prices.

 C map 4 B2

HONINGTON HALL

Shipston-on-Stour, Warwickshire CV36 5AA
Tel: 01608 661434, Fax: 01608 663717 (Benjamin Wiggin Esq)

This fine Caroline manor house was built in the early 1680s for the Parker family. It was modified in the mid 18th century with the introduction within of exceptional and lavish plasterwork and the insertion of an octagonal saloon. It is set in 15 acres of grounds. **Location:** 10 miles S of Stratford-on-Avon; ½ mile E of A3400. **Open:** June, July, Aug, Weds & Bank Hol Mons 2.30–5pm. Parties at other times by appointment. **Admission:** Adults £3, children £1.50.

  map 4 B2

KENILWORTH CASTLE

Kenilworth, Warks CU8 1NE
Tel 01926 852078 (English Heritage)

Explore England's finest and most extensive castle ruins. Wander through rooms used to lavishly entertain Queen Elizabeth I. You can learn of the great building's links with Henry V, who retired here after his return from his victorious expedition to Agincourt. Today you can view the marvellous Norman keep and John of Gaunt's Great Hall, once rivalling London's Westminister Hall in palatial grandeur, as well as the beautiful reconstructed Tudor gardens. An audio–tour will guide you on a revealing journey around Kenilworth Castle. **Location:** Off A46. Follow A452 to Kenilworth town centre as signposted. **Open:** 1 Apr–30 Sept: daily, 10–6pm, 1 Oct–31 Oct: daily, 10–5pm, 1 Nov–31 Mar: daily, 10–4pm (closed 24/25 Dec). Open 1 Jan 2000. **Admission:** Adults £3.40, concs £2.60, child £1.70. (15% discount for groups of 11 or more).

map 4 **B1**

LORD LEYCESTER HOSPITAL

High Street, Warwick, Warwickshire, CV34 4BH
Tel: 01926 491 422 Fax: 01926 491 422 (The Governors of Lord Leycester Hospital)

In 1571, Robert Dudley, Earl of Leycester, founded his hospital for twelve 'poor' persons in the buildings of the Guilds, which had been dispersed in 1546. The buildings have been restored to their original condition: the Great Hall of King James, the Guildhall (museum), the Chaplain's Hall (Queen's Own Hussars Regimental Museum) and the Brethren's Kitchen. The recently restored historic Master's Garden is now open to the public (Easter–31 Sept £1 donation please). The Hospital, with its medieval galleried courtyard, featured in the TV serials 'Pride and Prejudice', 'Tom Jones', 'Moll Flanders'. **Location:** West Gate of Warwick (A429). **Station(s):** Warwick (¾m). **Open:** All year, Tues–Sun, 10–5pm (Summer) and 10–4pm (Winter). Open BH Mons, closed Good Fri and Christmas Day. **Admission:** Adult £2.75, children (under 14) £1.50, OAP/Student £2. Free car park.

map 4 **B1**

RAGLEY HALL

Alcester, Warwickshire B49 5NJ
Tel: 01789 762090 Fax: 01789 764791 (Marquess of Hertford)

RAGLEY HALL, home of the Marquess and Marchioness of Hertford and their family. The Hall was designed by Robert Hooke in 1680 and is one of the earliest and loveliest of England's great Palladian Houses. It contains some of the finest Baroque plasterwork by James Gibb, and contains Graham Rust's stunning mural 'The Temptation'. On show are some of the finest antique porcelain and furniture. Ragley is a working estate with more than 6,000 acres of land, The House is situated in 27 acres of gardens which were designed by Capability Brown, and include the beautiful Rose Garden. Near to The Hall are the working stables housing a carriage collection dating back to 1760 and a display of harnessess and assorted historical equestrian equipment. For children there is the adventure playground and maze situated by the lake. **Location:** 8 miles South of Stratford-upon-Avon. **Open:** 3 Apr–3 Oct. House: Thurs, Fri, Sun 12.30–5pm (last entry 4.30pm). Also open Bank Holiday Mons. Sat 11–3.30pm (last entry 3pm). Park and Gardens open Thurs–Sun 10–6pm (last entry 4.45pm) and everyday during July and Aug. **Admission:** Adults £5, children £3.50 includes entry into the house. Concessions available.

map 4 **B2**

Mary Arden's House

THE SHAKESPEARE HOUSES IN AND AROUND STRATFORD-UPON-AVON

The Shakespeare Centre, Henley Street, Stratford-upon-Avon, Warks CV37 6QW.
Tel: 01789 204016 Fax: 01789 296083

Five beautifully preserved Tudor houses, all associated with William Shakespeare and his family. In Town: **Shakespeare's Birthplace**, Henley Street. Half-timbered house where William Shakespeare was born in 1564. Visitor's centre showing highly acclaimed exhibition **William Shakespeare, His Life and Background**. **Nash's House and New Place**, Chapel Street. Nash's House was the home of Shakespeare's grand-daughter, Elizabeth Hall and contains exceptional furnishings. Upstairs there are displays about the history of Stratford. Also site and gardens of **New Place** (including Elizabethan style Knott Garden and Shakespeare's Great Garden), where Shakespeare lived in retirement. Discover why the house was demolished and see the foundations and grounds of his final Stratford home. **Hall's Croft**, Old Town. Impressive 16th century house and garden, with Jacobean additions. Owned by Dr John Hall who married Shakespeare's eldest daughter, Susanna. Includes exhibitions about medicine in Shakespeare's time and beautiful walled garden with mulberry tree and herb garden. Out of Town: **Anne Hathaway's Cottage**, Shottery. Picturesque thatched farmhouse cottage which belonged to the family of Shakespeare's wife. Contains the famous Hathaway bed and the other original furniture. Outside lies a beautiful English cottage garden, orchard and the Shakespeare Tree Garden. **Mary Arden's House** and **Shakespeare's Countryside Museum**, Wilmcote. This striking farmhouse was Shakespeare's mother's family home and offers a fascinating insight into rural farm life in the Tudor period. See also, falconry displays, working blacksmith, prize-winning livestock and Glebe Farm's kitchen of 1900. **Open:** Daily all year round except 23–26 Dec. Inclusive tickets available to three in-town, or all five houses. The Shakespeare Birthplace Trust is a Registered Charity, No. 209302.

map 4 B2

Shakespeare's Birthplace

Anne Hathaway's Cottage

WARWICK CASTLE
Warwick, Warwickshire, CV34 4QU
Tel: 01926 406 600 Internet: www.warwick–castle.co.uk

Warwick Castle reveals the secret life of England as you have never seen it before. From the days of William the Conqueror to the reign of Queen Victoria, the Castle has provided a backdrop for many turbulent times. Here you can join a mediaeval household in our Kingmaker attraction, watching them prepare for the final battle of the Earl of Warwick. Enter the eerie Ghost Tower, where it is said that the unquiet spirit of Sir Fulke Greville, murdered most foully by a manservant, still roams. Descend into the gloomy depths of the Dungeon and Torture Chamber, then step forward in time and marvel at the grandeur of the State Rooms. The 14th century Great Hall lies at the heart of the Castle and here you can see the death mask of Oliver Cromwell and Bonnie Prince Charlie's shield. Witness the perfect manners and hidden indiscretions of Daisy, Countess of Warwick and her friends at the Royal Weekend Party 1898 or stroll through the 60 acres of grounds and gardens which surround the Castle today. And besides the secrets, there are a host of special events to enjoy throughout the year, including Birds of Prey, Jousting and a Mediaeval Festival. The story of Warwick Castle is best told first hand, so come and hear it for yourself.

map 4 **B1**

BADDESLEY CLINTON
Rising Lane, Baddesley Clinton Village, Solihull B93 0DQ Tel: 01564 783294

Open: House: 3 March to 31 Oct: daily except Mon & Tues (closed Good Fri, but open BH Mons); March, April & Oct 1.30–5pm; May to end Sept 1.30–5.30pm. Grounds: 14 Feb to 12 Dec: daily except Mon & Tues (closed Good Fri, but open BH Mons). 14 to 28 Feb & Nov to 12 Dec, 12–4.30pm: March, April & Oct, 12–5pm; May to end Sept, 12–5.30pm. **Admission:** £5; family £12.50. Groups £4.20. Groups of 15+ and coaches are welcome by written arrangement. Grounds, restaurant & shop only £2.50. Free parking. Note: Admission to house is by timed ticket, but visitors may then stay as long as they wish. **Events:** tel. or send s.a.e for details. **Restaurant:** Licensed restaurant as grounds. 12–2pm & 2.30–5.30pm (closes 4.30pm, 14–28 Feb and Nov to 12 Dec, 5pm in March, April and Oct). Group lunches and dinners arranged. Picnic tables near entrance.

CHARLECOTE PARK
Warwick CV35 9ER Tel: 01789 470277 Fax: 01789 470544

Open: House & grounds: 20 March to 31 Oct: daily except Wed & Thur (closed Good Fri). House: 12–5pm, grounds 11–6pm. **Admission:** £4.90; family £12.20. Groups (max. 40) by arrangement. Group rate (£3.90) and introductory talk on weekdays only. Car and coach park 300m. Video film of life at Charlecote Park in the Victorian period. **Restaurant:** Licensed Orangery restaurant as grounds 11–5.30pm; last serving 5pm. Picnicking in deer park only.

FARNBOROUGH HALL
Banbury OX17 1DU Tel: 01295 690002

Open: House & grounds: April to end Sept: Wed & Sat 2–6pm, also 2 & 3 May 2–6pm. Terrace walk: April to end Sept, Thur & Fri 2–6pm. **Admission:** £3. Garden and terrace walk only £1.50. Terrace walk only (Thur & Fri) £1. Groups by written arrangement only, no reduction. Coach and car park. Strong shoes advisable for terrace.

PACKWOOD HOUSE
Lapworth, Solihull B94 6AT Tel: 01564 782024

Open: 27 March to 31 Oct: daily except Mon & Tues (closed Good Fri but open BH Mons). March to end Sept: 2–6pm, Oct 12.30–4.30pm. Note: On busy days entry may be by timed ticket. Garden: as house. March to end Sept: 1.30–6pm; Oct 12.30–4.30pm. Park and woodland walks: all year, daily. **Admission:** £4.40; family £11. Groups £4.20. Garden only £2.20. Car park £2, refunded on entry to house and garden (NT members free). **Events:** wide range, send s.a.e. for details. **Restaurant:** No tea room, but kiosk serving light refreshments (weekends and summer hols); picnic area in avenue opposite main gates.

UPTON HOUSE
Banbury OX15 6HT Tel: 01295 670266

Open: 27 March to 31 Oct: daily except Thur & Fri 2–6pm; last admission 5.30pm (5pm from 25 Oct). **Admission:** £5.20; family £13. Groups of 15+ by written arrangement; no reduction. Garden only £2.60. Free parking. **Events:** fine arts study tours, jazz concert and other events; send s.a.e. or tel. for details. **Restaurant:** Tea room as house. Last orders 5.30pm (5pm Sat to Wed, April & Oct and daily from 25 Oct).

West Midlands

The West Midlands are famously known as having been at the heart of The Industrial Revolution in the nineteenth century. The city of Birmingham was the base for a wide range of manufacturing trades and oversaw the vast growth in factories and associated housing for its workers.

Meriden

Today, Birmingham has established itself as a city of culture, with a thriving arts scene: The City of Birmingham Symphony Orchestra has a worldwide reputation for excellence and in recent times, The Royal Sadler's Wells have relocated their Ballet Company to Birmingham, in order to benefit from their excellent facilities. For lovers of Pre-Raphaelite art, the City Museum and Art Gallery offers the perfect opportunity to indulge in the works of, among others, Ford Maddox Brown and Sir Edward Burne-Jones.

On the outskirts of the city, the National Exhibition Centre is the venue for many of today's popular events. Indeed, in the last year it has hosted a wide variety of shows ranging from fashion exhibitions to car conventions. It is also a renowned music venue: various popular and classical artists have performed concerts at the Centre.

Britain's first completely modern cathedral, at Coventry, arose out of the ruins of the bombed city centre after the Second World War. Sir Basil Spence's fine building is adorned with superb sculptures by Jacob Epstein and Graham Sutherland.

ASTON HALL

Trinity Road, Aston, Birmingham, West Midlands, B6 6JD
Tel: 0121 327 0062 (Birmingham Museums & Arts)

A magnificent Jacobean mansion built by Sir Thomas Holte between 1618–1635, Aston Hall has period interiors from the 17th, 18th and 19th centuries, containing fine furniture, paintings, textiles and metalwork. Decorative highlights include the ceiling and frieze of the Great Dining Room, and the carved oak Great Stairs. On the staircase balustrade, sharp-eyed visitors will spot the traces of Roundhead cannon shot, fired during the Civil War siege. **Open:** Apr–Oct, daily, 2–5pm. **Guided** **Tours:** By appointment only. **Admission:** Free. Please quote Ref no. HHCG99.

map 8 **B7**

BIRMINGHAM BOTANICAL GARDENS & GLASSHOUSES

Westbourne Road, Edgbaston, Birmingham, West Midlands B15 3TR
Tel: 0121 454 1860 Fax: 0121 454 7835 E-Mail: admin@bham-bot-gdns.demon.co.uk

The Gardens are a 15 acre 'Oasis of Delight' with the finest collection of plants in the Midlands. The Tropical House, full of rainforest vegetation, includes many economic plants. Palms, tree ferns and orchids are displayed in the Palm House. The Orangery features citrus fruits and conservatory plants while the Cactus House conveys a desert scene. There is colourful bedding on the Terrace plus Rhododendron, Rose, Rock, Herb and Cottage Gardens, Trials Ground, Historic Gardens and the National Bonsai Collection. Children's Playgrounds and Aviaries. Gallery. The 'Shop at the Gardens' has a wide range of gifts, souvenirs and plants. Refreshments in the Pavilion. Bands play summer Sunday afternoons. Open daily.

map 4 **B1**

BLAKESLEY HALL

Blakesley Road, Yardley, Birmingham, West Midlands, B25 8RN.
Tel: 0121 783 2193 (Birmingham Museums & Arts)

A timber framed farmhouse in what was old Yardley village. Step over the threshold and back into time to meet staff in period costume. The hall itself was built in 1590 by Richard Smallbroke; today's furnishings date from an old inventory of 1684. All twelve rooms, from the Painted Chamber to Boulting House, tell their own story. **Open:** Apr–Oct. **Times:** Daily 2–5pm. **Admission:** Free. Please quote Ref no. HHCG99.

CASTLE BROMWICH HALL GARDENS

Chester Road, Castle Bromwich, Birmingham, West Midlands
Tel: 0121 749 4100

The gardens are a cultural gem and a unique example of early 18th century garden design. Succeeding generations developed and enhanced the gardens, including 'An Elegant Kitchen and Fruit Garden after a New and Grand Manner in the style of Batty Langley (1727); a 'Ladies Border' with plants of the period; a 'Wilderness' of mature trees underplanted with interesting specimen plants to provide a woodland atmosphere, plus a 'Holly Maze' of 19th century design. Major restoration of the original Orangery and Music Room, at either end of the long Holly Walk, together with the classic surrounding walls, enhance the beauty of the gardens. Guided tours. **Open:** pm, Easter–end Sept. Closed Mon & Fri.

COVENTRY CATHEDRAL

Coventry
Tel: 01203 227597

The remains of the blackened medieval Cathedral, bombed in 1940, stand beside the new Cathedral designed by Basil Spence, consecrated in 1962. Modern works of art include a huge tapestry by Graham Sutherland, a stained glass window by John Piper and a bronze sculpture by Epstein. **Location:** Coventry city centre. **Admission:** Donations for the Cathedral. **Open:** 9–5pm daily. Please phone for Sunday opening times.

SOHO HOUSE

Soho Avenue, Handsworth, Birmingham B18 5LB, West Midlands. Tel: 0121 554 9122 (Birmingham Museums & Arts)

The former home of industrial pioneer Matthew Boulton, who lived at Soho House from 1766 to 1809. It was also the meeting place of some of the most important scientists, engineers and thinkers of the time, The Lunar Society. Possibly the first centrally heated house in England since Roman times, Soho House has been carefully restored to its 18th century glory and contains some of Boulton's own furniture. **Open:** All year. **Times:** Tue–Sat, 10–5pm. Sun, 12 noon–5pm. Closed Mon except Bank Holidays. **Admission:** Adults £2.50, concessions £2, family ticket £6. 10% discount for groups of 10 or more. Please quote Ref no. HHCG99.

HAGLEY HALL

Stourbridge, West Midlands, DY9 9LG
Tel: 01562 882408 Fax: 01562 882632 (The Viscount Cobham)

The last of the great Palladian Houses, designed by Sanderson Miller and completed in 1760. The house contains the finest example of Rococo plasterwork by Francesco Vassali and a unique collection of 18th century furniture and family portraits including works by Van Dyck, Reynolds and Lely. **Location:** Just off A456 Birmingham to Kidderminster, 12 m from Birmingham within easy reach M5 (exit 3 or 4), M6 or M42. **Station(s):** Hagley (1 m) (not Suns); Stourbridge Junction (2 m). **Open:** Sun 3 Jan–Sun 28 Feb (excluding all Sats); Thurs 1–Tues 6 Apr; Sun 30 May–Tues 1 June; Sun 29–Tues 31 Aug; 2–5pm. **Admission:** Charges apply. **Refreshments:** Tea available in the house. **Conferences:** Specialists in corporate entertaining and conferences throughout the year.

WIGHTWICK MANOR

Wightwick Bank, Wolverhampton WV6 8EE
Tel: 01902 761108 Fax: 01902 764663

Open: House: 1 March to 31 Dec and March 2000: Thur & Sat (but open BHols for ground floor only) 2.30–5.30pm. Note: Viewing is by timed ticket, issued at front door from 2pm, and by guided tour only. Many of the contents are fragile and some rooms cannot always be shown, so tours vary. Garden: Wed & Thur 11–6pm; Sat, BH Sun & BHols Mon 1–6pm. Other days by appointment. Events: send s.a.e. for details. **Admission:** £5.40; students £2.70. No reduction for groups. Garden only: £2.40. Parking: only room for one coach in lay-by outside main gate; car park (120m) at bottom of Wightwick Bank (please do not park in Elmsdale opposite the property). **Restaurant:** Tea-room, Wed & Thur 11–5pm, Sat & BHols 1–5pm.

Wiltshire

Castle Combe

Wiltshire covers a vast and varied area. It remains largely unknown as a county and few visitors are intimate with its great bare sweeps of downland and the smooth lines of the uplands, where bygone tribes first trod the straight tracks and left their camps, dykes and burial mounds. Its gentle and limpid streams flow through the little hamlets and the scores of picturesque villages.

In 1220, Salisbury was founded. This tranquil city is the home to Salisbury Cathedral; a wonderful example of Gothic architecture which has the tallest spire in England. This majestic building dwarfs the charming streets that are strewn haphazardly at its foot and overlooks one of this country's most beautiful closes.

The open countryside of the Salisbury Plain made this area an important centre of prehistoric settlement and today there are many historic sites and relics to show its history. The most famous of these is Stonehenge, a monumental example of prehistoric enterprise that remains something of an enigma to this day.

Further afield, attractive villages lie waiting to be discovered, including charming Castle Combe, immortalised on television in the Doctor Doolittle stories.

CORSHAM COURT
Corsham, Wiltshire SN13 0BZ
Tel/Fax: 01249 701610 (J Methuen-Campbell Esq)

Home of the Methuen family since 1745, Corsham Court houses a collection of historic paintings and works of art influenced by extensive diplomatic travels to Europe. This includes many distinguished Old Master paintings and the surviving collection boasts works by Van Dyck and Carlo Dolci which hang alongside family portraits by Reynolds. The Georgian State Rooms were furnished by Thomas Chippendale and others during late 19th century. The Gardens contain magnificent views, particularly East, providing a tranquil aspect over the Park. The grounds comprise sweeping lawns and formal areas with a rose garden, lily pond and herbaceous borders. There are beautiful specimen trees including the Great Oriental Plane, cedars, beeches and oaks dating back to the original 18th century plantings by 'Capability' Brown and Repton. **Location:** Signposted 4 miles W of Chippenham from the A4 Bath Road. **Open:** Throughout the year to groups of 15 or more persons by appointment. Otherwise, open 20 Mar–30 Sept daily except Mondays (but including Bank Hols) from 11.00–5.30pm. 1 Oct–19 Mar open weekends from 2pm until 4.30pm. Closed December. Last entry 30 minutes before close. **Admission:** Adults £4.50, OAP's £3.50, child £1.00, group rates £3.50. **Refreshments:** Available at Johnsons Bakery nearby.

map 3 J2

177

BOWOOD HOUSE AND GARDENS

The Estate Office, Bowood, Calne, Wiltshire SN11 0LZ
Tel: 01249 812102 Fax: 01249 821757

Bowood is the family home of the Earl and Countess of Shelburne, the Earl being the eldest son of the Marquess of Lansdowne. Begun c.1720, the house was purchased by the 2nd Earl of Shelburne in 1754 and completed soon afterwards. Part of the house was demolished in 1955, leaving a perfectly proportioned Georgian home, much of which is open to visitors. Robert Adam's magnificent Diocletian wing contains a splendid library, the laboratory where Joseph Priestley discovered oxygen gas in 1774, the orangery, now a picture gallery, the Chapel and a sculpture gallery. Among the family treasures shown in the numerous exhibition rooms are Georgian costumes, including Lord Byron's Albanian dress; Victoriana; Indiana and superb collections of watercolours, miniatures and jewellery. The House is set in one of the most beautiful parks in England. Over 2,000 acres of gardens and grounds were landscaped by 'Capability' Brown between 1762 and 1768, and are embellished with a Doric temple, a cascade, a pinetum and an arboretum. The Rhododendron Gardens are open for six weeks during the flowering season, from late April to early June. All the walks have seats. For children, Bowood offers a truly outstanding Adventure Playground, complete with life–size pirate ship, giant slides, chutes and high level rope walks. **Admission:** Adults £5.50, senior citizens £4.50, children £3.20. Party rates: Adults £4.60, senior citizens £3.90, children £2.60. **Open:** daily from 27th March–31st October. Rhododendron Walks: Adults/OAPs £3, children free; cost per person £2 if combined with a visit to the House and Gardens on the same day. **Internet:** www.bowood-estate.co.uk

map 3 K2

CHARLTON PARK HOUSE

Malmesbury, Wiltshire SN16 9DG
(The Earl of Suffolk and Berkshire)

Jacobean/Georgian mansion, built for the Earls of Suffolk, 1607, altered by Matthew Brettingham the Younger, c.1770. **Location:** 1½ miles NE Malmesbury. Entry only by signed entrance on A429, Malmesbury/Cirencester road. No access from Charlton village. **Open:** May–Oct Mon & Thurs 2–4pm. Viewing of Great Hall. Staircase and saloon. **Admission:** Adults £1, children/OAP 50p. Car parking limited. Unsuitable for wheelchairs. No dogs. No picnicking.

map 3
K1

IFORD MANOR GARDEN

Bradford-on-Avon, Wiltshire, BA15 2BA
Tel: 01225 863 146 Fax: 01225 862 364 (Mrs Cartwright-Hignett)

Britannia guards the bridge over the River Frome and the entrance to Harold Peto's internationally influential garden. Mediterranean ideas and plants are grafted onto an English landscape and remnants of classical and renaissance periods complete the scene. **Location:** 7 miles S of Bath via A36. **Open:** Apr & Oct, Sun only. May–Sept, Sat–Sun & Tue–Thur, 2–5pm. **Admission:** Adults £2.50, children (10+) and OAPs £1.90. **Refreshments:** Saturdays and Sundays, May–Sept only. Children under 10 not admitted at weekends.

map 3
J2

HAMPTWORTH LODGE

Landford, Nr Salisbury, Wiltshire SP5 2EA
Tel: 01794 390215 (Mr N Anderson)

Rebuilt Jacobean Manor, with period furniture, including clocks. **Location:** 10 miles SE of Salisbury on the C44 road linking Downton on A338, Salisbury-Bournemouth to Landford on A36, Salisbury-Southampton. **Open:** House and garden daily, except Sundays. Monday March 30 to Thursday April 30 1998 (inclusive). Conducted parties only 2.30 and 3.45. Coaches by appointment only Apr 1–Sept 30. By appointment all year, 18 hole golf course 01794 390155. **Admission:** £3.50, under 11s free. No special arrangement for parties, but about 15 is the maximum. **Refreshments:** Downtown, Salisbury; nil in house. Car parking; disabled ground floor only.

map 4
B6

HEALE GARDEN & PLANT CENTRE

Middle Woodford, Salisbury SP4 6NT
Tel: 01722 782504 (Mr & Mrs Guy Rasch)

1st Winner of Christie's/HHA Garden of the Year award. Early Carolean manor house where King Charles II hid during his escape. The garden provides a wonderfully varied collection of plants, shrub, musk and other roses, growing in the formal setting of clipped hedges and mellow stonework, at their best in June and July. Particularly lovely in Spring and Autumn is the water garden, planted with magnificent Magnolia and Acers, surrounding an authentic Japanese Tea House and Nikko Bridge which create an exciting focus in this part of the garden. Stunning winter acoutes and snowdrops. **Location:** 4 m N of Salisbury on the Woodford Valley road between A345 and A360. Midway between Salisbury, Wilton and Stonehenge. **Open:** Garden, Plant Centre and shop open throughout the year, 10–5pm. **Refreshments:** Light refreshments tea and coffee, served in the shop.

map 4
B5

LUCKINGTON COURT

Luckington, Chippenham, Wiltshire SN14 6PQ
Tel: 01666 840205 (The Hon Mrs Trevor Horn)

Mainly Queen Anne with magnificent group of ancient buildings. Beautiful mainly formal garden with fine collection of ornamental trees and shrubs. Home of the Bennet family in the BBC TV adaptation 'Pride and Prejudice'. **Location:** 6 miles W of Malmesbury on B4040 Bristol Road. **Open:** All through the year Weds 2–5pm, garden only. Open Sun 2 May, 2.30–5pm. Collection box for National Gardens' Scheme. Inside view by appointment 3 weeks in advance. **Admission:** Outside gardens only £1, house £2. **Refreshments:** Teas in garden or house (in aid of Luckington Parish Church) on Sun 2 May only.

map 3
J2

PYTHOUSE

Tisbury, Salisbury, Wiltshire, SP3 6PB.
Tel: 01747 870 210 Fax: 01747 871 786
(Country Houses Association)

Palladian style Georgian mansion. **Location:** 2.5 miles W of Tisbury, 4.5 miles N of Shaftsbury. **Station(s):** Tisbury (2.5 miles). **Open:** May–Sept, Wed & Thurs, 2–5pm. (Last entry 4pm). **Admission:** Adults £2.50, children £1. Free car park. No dogs admitted. Groups by arrangement.

map 3
J3

LONGLEAT

Warminster, Wiltshire, BA12 7NW
Tel: 01985 844400 Fax: 01985 844885 (The Marquess of Bath)

Exactly 50 years ago, in 1949, Longleat House was the first stately home to be opened to the public on a fully commercial basis. The magnificent Elizabethan property, built by Sir John Thynne and substantially completed by 1580, has been the home of the same family ever since. The House contains many treasures including paintings by Tintoretto and Wootton, exquisite Flemish tapestries, fine French furniture, as well as elaborate ceilings by John Dibblee Crace incorporating paintings from the 'School of Titian'. The Murals in the family apartments in the West Wing were painted by Alexander Thynn, the present Marquess, and are fascinating and remarkable additions to the collections. Apart from the ancestral home, Longleat is also renowned for its Safari Park, the first of its kind in the UK. Here, visitors have the rare opportunity to see hundreds of animals in a natural woodland and parkland setting. Amongst the most magnificent sights are the famous pride of lions, a white tiger, wolves, gorillas and zebras. Also roaming free around the park are Longleat's giraffes, monkeys, rhinos and camels. New animals are constantly being introduced or born so each visit always brings new surprises. Other attractions that shouldn't be missed include the 'World's Longest Hedge Maze', the children's Adventure Castle, a tethered balloon ride, the Safari Boats (to view and feed sea lions and hippos) and the Needlecraft Centre. In fact there's so much to see and do for all the family, we recommend a second visit! The House is open all year, except Christmas Day, whilst the attractions are open from Mar–Oct. Please call 01985 844400 for further details. We look forward to seeing you in 1999 during our 50th year of welcoming guests.

map 3 J3

STOURHEAD

Stourton, Warminster, BA12 6QD, Wiltshire.
Tel: 01747 841 152 Fax: 01747 841 152 (The National Trust)

Stourhead combines Britain's foremost landscape garden with a fine Palladian mansion. Stourhead Garden is one of the most famous examples of the early 18th century English landscape movement. Planned in the belief that it was "Tiresome for the foot to travel, to where the eye had already been", the garden continually surprises the visitor with fresh glimpses of its enchanting lakes and temples. The House was designed in 1721 for Henry Hoare by Colen Campbell. Its contents include a collection of furniture designed by the younger Chippendale and many fine works of art. Interesting features of the estate include two Iron Age hill forts and King Alfred's Tower, a 160 ft high red brick folly. This tower offers magnificent views across the three counties of Wiltshire, Somerset and Dorset. **Location:** Stourton, off B3092, 3 miles NW of A303 (Mere). 2hrs from London, 1.5 hrs from Exeter. **Open:** Garden: All Year Daily, 9–7pm (or dusk if earlier), except 22–24 July (Fête Champêtre), when gardens close at 5pm (last admission 4pm). House: 27 Mar–31 Oct, Sat–Wed, 12–5.30pm or dusk if earlier (last admission 5pm). Plant Centre: Open Apr–Oct, 12–6pm. 01747 840 894. **Admission:** Garden or House: Adult £4.50, children £2.50, group (15 or more) £4, family £10. (2 adults & up to 3 children). Combined Garden and House: Adult £8, children £3.80, group £7.70, family £20. Large coach and car park. Guided Tours: Pre-booked garden tours are available on request throughout the year. **Events:** Held throughout the year. Please phone for leaflet.

map 3
J3

MALMESBURY HOUSE

The Close, Salisbury, Wiltshire SP1 2EB
Tel: 01722 327027 Fax: 01722 334414 (J.H. Cordle Esq.)

Malmesbury House was originally a 13th century canonry. It was enlarged in the 14th century and leased to the Harris family in 1660, whose descendant became the first Earl of Malmesbury. The west facade was added by Sir Christopher Wren to accommodate rooms displaying superb rococo plasterwork, including a superb 32ft high hall. Among the many illustrious visitors were King Charles II and the composer Handel, who used the chapel above the St Ann Gate for recitals. Francis Webb, a direct ancestor of Queen Elizabeth II lived here in the 1770's. The house is now the Cordle family home. Outside there is a charming garden, in which stands the orangery, which was built in 1629 and was used by fugitives, royalists and puritans as a hiding place. The house stands within 200 yards of the glorious Cathedral which was built in 1220 and remains open until 7pm each evening. Cars can be parked in The Close. **Location:** City of Salisbury, Cathedral Close, East end of North Walk by St Ann Gate. Coaches go to St John's Street. **Open:** Groups from 4 – 40 by prior arrangement. Meals can be served. **Admission:** Adults £5, students £3. Prices include entrance to the garden. Letters to the Administrator.

map 3 K3

 # WILTON HOUSE

The Estate Office, Wilton, Salisbury SP2 0BJ
Tel: 01722 746720 Fax: 01722 744447

From 9th century nunnery to the present day home of the 17th Earl of Pembroke, Wilton House provides a fascinating insight on British history. Marvel at Inigo Jones' magnificent State Rooms, including the Double Cube Room. Admire the world famous art collection. Relax in 21 acres of landscaped parkland, water and rose gardens beside the River Nadder and Palladian Bridge. The modern interpretative displays, include the introductory film, Tudor Kitchen and Victorian Laundry. Enjoy the 'Wareham Bears' – 200 miniature costumed teddies. 1999 Featured **Exhibition:** Sir Anthony Van Dyck. **Open:** 27 Mar–31 Oct 1999 (House closed 21–23 May 99) 10.30–5.30pm. (last admission 4.30pm).

map 4 B5

AVEBURY MANOR AND GARDEN

Nr Marlborough SN8 1RF Tel: 01672 539250

Open: House: 4 April to 31 Oct: Tues, Wed, Sun & BH Mons 2–5.30pm; last admission 5pm or dusk if earlier. Garden: 2 April to 31 Oct: daily except Mon & Thur (but open BH Mons) 11–5.30pm.

GREAT CHALFIELD MANOR

Nr Melksham SN12 8NJ Tel: 01225 782239

Open: 1 April to 29 Oct: Tues, Wed, Thur by guided tours only at 12.15pm, 2.15pm, 3pm, 3.45pm & 4.30pm. The tours take 45min and numbers are limited to 25. Visitors arriving during a tour can visit the adjoining parish church and garden first. Note: Groups are welcome on Fri & Sat (not BHols) by written arrangement with Mrs Robert Floyd. Organisers of coach groups should allow 2hrs because of limits on numbers in house.

LACOCK ABBEY

Lacock, Nr Chippenham SN15 2LG Tel: Abbey 01249 730227

Open: Museum, cloisters & grounds: 28 Feb to 31 Oct: daily (closed Good Fri) 11–5.30pm. Abbey: 28 March to 31 Oct: daily, except Tues, 1–5.30pm. Museum open some winter weekends, but closed 25 Dec to 7 Jan 2000; tel. for details. **Events:** send s.a.e. for leaflet.

MOMPESSON HOUSE

The Close, Salisbury SP1 2EL Tel: 01722 335659

Open: 27 March to 31 Oct: daily except Thur & Fri 12–5.30pm. **Restaurant.**

WESTWOOD MANOR

Bradford-on-Avon BA15 2AF Tel: 01225 863374

Open: 4 April to 29 Sept: Sun, Tues & Wed 2–5pm. At other times groups of up to 20 by written application with s.a.e. to the tenant.

Yorkshire

Yorkshire nowadays is sub-divided into various administrative areas. Pleasure-seekers can happily forget this contemporary arrangement.

North Yorkshire hosts two national parks, an excellent spa town in Harrogate, Knaresborough – the oldest town mentioned in the Doomsday book and enchanting small cities such as Ripon.

Between the Lake District and the North York Moors lie the Yorkshire Dales with their farming landscape.

The capital of the whole region – York – has retained so much of its medieval structure that walking into its centre is like entering a museum. Home to England's largest medieval church, the wonderfully gothic York Minster houses the largest collection of medieval stained glass in Britain and embodies history, with its 18 medieval churches, 2 mile long medieval city walls, elegant Jacobean and Georgian architecture and fine museums.

Mount Grace Priory, English Heritage

The town and country landscapes of West and South Yorkshire are striking. The powerful landscape of the Moors and the Pennine Moors, which have been a source of inspiration to a number of artists including the Brontë family, have withstood all attempts to tarnish their glory.

Leeds is the third largest of Britain's provincial cities. Productions at The Grand by Opera North and the impressive collection of British 20th century art at the City Gallery have helped to give Leeds a thriving and prosperous cultural scene.

In the 16th century, neighbouring Bradford was a market town and the opening of its canal in 1774 boosted trade. By 1850, it was the world's capital for the manufacture of wool. Today, Bradford and the entire area east of the Pennines have found new ways to achieve prosperity.

Yorkshire traditionally is England's greatest county and home to a large variety of historic houses and monuments.

ASKE HALL

Aske, Richmond, North Yorkshire DL10 5HJ
Tel: 01748 850391 Fax: 01748 823252 (The Marquess of Zetland)

The Hall – a Georgian gem – nestles in Capability Brown parkland with lake, follies, meadows, woods and a new terraced garden, the visionary creation of Lady Zetland described as the most ambitious gardening scheme of the day! It has been the family seat of the Dundas family for over 200 years and boasts an impressive collection of 18th century furniture, paintings and porcelain. **Location:** 2 m from A1 on the Richmond/Gilling West Road (B6274) **Stations:** Darlington 13 m away. **Admission:** £5.50 – for groups of 15+ by appointment only. "A Taste of Gentility", a tour followed by Yorkshire afternoon tea in the Regency dining room on Weds in July & Aug £15pp. Booking essential Tel: 01748 850391 for further details. **Events/Exhibitions:** Telephone for programme. **Conferences:** Suitable for up to a capacity of 100.

map 11 H5

THE BAR CONVENT

17 Blossom Street, York YO24 1AQ
Tel: 01904 643238 Fax: 01904 631792

The Bar Convent is an elegant Georgian building (1787) located on the corner of Blossom St and Nunnery Lane. It houses a beautiful neo-classical chapel (1769); both were designed by Thomas Atkinson. The Bar Convent Museum outlines the early history of Christianity in the North of England and also tells the story of Mary Ward, the foundress of the Institute of the Blessed Virgin Mary (IBVM). There are guided museum tours on Mon-Fri at 10.30am and 2.30pm. There is a cafe which serves coffee, tea and wine as well as hot meals (9.30–5.00pm Mon–Sat). There is a small souvenir and gift shop. Conference and residential facilities are available to groups; please contact the Business manager on 01904 643238.

map 8 D2

BOLTON ABBEY

Skipton, North Yorkshire, BD23 6EX. Tel: 01756 710 227
Fax 01756 710 535 (Trustees of the Chatsworth Settlement)

The Yorkshire Estate of the Duke and Duchess of Devonshire. The Augustine Bolton Priory was founded in 1154 and is now partly parish church. Other historic buildings include the 13th century Barden Tower – formerly owned by the Cliffords of Skipton. The Estate offers spectacular walks in some of the most beautiful countryside in England – along the riverside, on the heather moors and Nature Trails in Strid Wood (S.S.S.I.) renowned for its bird life and rare plants. **Location:** On B6160, N from the roundabout junction with the A59 Skipton-Harrogate Road, 23 miles from Leeds. **Station(s):** Skipton & Ilkley. **Open:** All year. **Admission:** £3.00 car park charge. £1.50 car park charge for disabled. No charge for coaches. Motorised chairs available. **Refreshments:** Restaurant and 2 tearooms. **Accommodation:** Farmhouse B&B, self-catering cottage, hotel.

map 8 B2

BOLTON CASTLE

Leyburn, North Yorkshire, DL8 4ET
Tel: 01969 623 981 Fax: 01969 623 332
(Hon. Mr & Mrs Harry Orde-Powlett)

Completed in 1399, Bolton Castle celebrates its 600th anniversary this year. Originally the stronghold of the Scrope family, the castle has a wealth of history. Mary, Queen of Scots was imprisoned here for 6 months shortly after her arrival in England. Medieval garden and vineyard also open to the public. Also tearoom and gift shop. **Location:** Just off A684, 6 miles W of Leyburn. **Open:** Daily, Mar–Nov. (Mar–Apr, 10–4pm; May–Nov, 10–5pm). **Admission:** Guided tour by arrangement for groups of 15+. Adults £4, OAP/children £3, family ticket £10 (2 adults & 2 children). **Refreshments:** Tearoom – meals available, picnic area. Wedding licence. **Internet:** www.yorkshirenet.co.uk/boltoncastle/

map 8 B1

BRAMHAM PARK

Wetherby, West Yorkshire, LS23 6ND
Tel: 01937 844 265 Fax: 01937 845 923 (G. F. Lane Fox)

The house was created at the end of the 17th century and affords an opportunity to enjoy a beautiful Queen Anne mansion containing fine furniture, pictures and porcelain – set in magnificent grounds with ornamental ponds, cascades and tall beech hedges – unique in the British Isles for its grand vista design stretching into woodlands. **Location:** 5 miles S of Wetherby, on A1. **Open:** Grounds only: Easter Weekend, May Day Weekend, Spring Bank Hol Weekend. House & grounds: 20 Jun–5 Sept, Tues, Wed, Thurs, Sun 1.15–5.30pm. Last admission 5pm. Also Bank Hol Mon. **Admission:** The Estate Office, Bramham Park, Wetherby, LS23 6ND, West Yorkshire. Tel: 01937 844 265. **Refreshments:** Picnics in grounds permitted.

map 11 H7

BRODSWORTH HALL

Brodsworth, Nr. Doncaster, South Yorkshire
Tel: 01302 722598 Fax: 01302 337165 (English Heritage)

Brodsworth Hall is an outstanding example of a Victorian country house. Within its grand Italianate exterior, visitors can glimpse a vanished way of life as they progress through over 30 rooms ranging from the sumptuous family reception rooms to the plain but functional servants' wing. A pervasive sense of faded grandeur and of time past adds an element of enchantment to the Hall. The restored Victorian gardens form the ideal setting. **Location:** 5 miles NW of Doncaster, A635 from Junction 37, A1(M). **Open:** 1 Apr–31 Oct, Tues–Sun & Bank Hols, 1–6pm. Last admission 5pm. Gardens, tearoom and shop from noon. Pre-booked guided tours from 10am. 6 Nov– 26 Mar 2000 Winter weekends, garden, shop and tearoom 11–4pm. **Admission:** Hall & Gardens: Adults £4.70, concs £3.50, child £2.40. Gardens: Adults £2.60, concs £2, child £1.30.

map 8 B3

BROCKFIELD HALL

Warthill, York, North Yorkshire YO19 5XJ
Tel: 01904 489298 (Lord and Lady Martin Fitzalan Howard)

A fine late Georgian house designed by Peter Atkinson, whose father had been assistant to John Carr of York, for Benjamin Agar Esq. Begun in 1804, its outstanding feature is an oval entrance hall with a fine cantilevered stone staircase curving past an impressive Venetian window. It is the happy family home of Lord and Lady Martin Fitzalan Howard. He is the brother of the 17th Duke of Norfolk and son of the late Baroness Beaumont of Carlton Towers, Selby. There are some interesting portraits of her old Roman catholic family, the Stapletons, and some good furniture. **Location:** 5 miles east of York, off A166 or A64 **Open:** August 1–31st 1999, 1pm–4pm except Mondays, other times by appointment. **Admission:** Adults £3.50, children £1.

map 11 J7

BROUGHTON HALL

Skipton, North Yorkshire BD23 3AE
Tel: 01756 792267 Fax: 01756 792362 (H. R. Tempest)

Broughton Hall was built in 1597 and remains the home of the Tempest family. It has since been enlarged on three occasions. The gardens were laid out by **Nesfield** in 1854 and are a fine example of his work. The house was largely refurbished in the 19th century and contains much documented **Gillow** furniture. There is also a fine 18th century **Catholic chapel**, still in regular use. **Open:** The house is open to the public on the summer bank holidays and for guided groups **by appointment**. Individuals wanting to see the house should contact the Estate office (Tel: 01756 799608). **Admission:** £5 per person with no concessions. The house and grounds are also available for **Events and Corporate entertainment** by arrangement.

map 8 B2

BURTON AGNES HALL

Burton Agnes, Diffield, East Yorks YO25 0ND
Tel: 01262 490 324 Fax: 01262 490 513 (Burton Agnes Hall Preservation Trust Ltd).

The Hall is a magnificent example of late Elizabethan architecture - still lived in by descendants of the family who built it in 1598. There are wonderful carvings, lovely furniture and a fine collection of modern French and English paintings of the Impressionist Schools. The walled garden contains a potager, maze, herbaceous borders, campanula collection, jungle garden and giant games set in coloured gardens. Also woodland gardens and walk, children's corner, Norman manor house, donkey wheel and gift shop. **Location:** 6 miles SW of Bridlington on Driffield/Bridlington Rd (A166). **Open:** Apr 1–Oct 31 daily 11–5pm. **Admission:** Adults £4.50, OAPs £4, children £2.25. **Gardens only:** Adults £2.25, OAPs £2, children £1. **Refreshments:** Licensed cafeteria. Teas, light lunches & refreshments.

map 9 F2

CANNON HALL

Cawthorne, Barnsley, South Yorkshire, S75 4AT
Tel: 01226 790 270
(Barnsley Metropolitan Borough Council)

18th century house by Carr of York. Collections of fine furniture, paintings, glassware, art nouveau pewter and pottery. Also the Regimental Museum of the 13th/18th Royal Hussars. 70 acres of parkland. Walled garden with historic fruit trees. Gift shop. **Location:** 5 miles W of Barnsley, off A635. 1 mile N of Cawthorne. **House Open:** Apr–Oct. Tue–Sat: 10.30–5pm. Sun: 12 noon–5pm. Closed Mon, except Bank Hol Mons. Winter opening subject to change. Please confirm before your visit. Small admission charge. Park open all year round. **Refreshments:** Victorian kitchen cafe open Summer and Sun pm. Limited disabled access.

C

CASTLE HOWARD

Nr York, North Yorkshire YO60 7DA
Tel: 01653 648444 Fax: 01653 648462 (The Hon. Simon Howard)

Magnificent palace designed by Vanbrugh in 1699. One of Britain's most spectacular stately homes. Impressive Great Hall and beautiful rooms are filled with fine furniture, paintings and objets d'art. Extensive grounds with lakes and colourful woodland. Rose garden, plant centre, adventure playground. 1999 is the Tercentenary year of Castle Howard and there will be a host of events and activities to celebrate this special anniversary. **Location:** 15 m NE of York; 3 m off A64; 6 m W of Malton; 22 m from Scarborough. **Open:** Daily 12 Mar–31 Oct. Grounds from 10am, house from 11am. Last admission 4.30pm. **Admission:** Adult £7, child £4.50, OAP £6.50. Groups (min. 12 people): Adult £6.50, child £4, OAP £6. Grounds only: Adult £4.50, child £2.50 **Refreshments:** Licensed cafeteria in House, Lakeside Café. Café and shops facilities in Stable Courtyard.

map 8 D2

CONSTABLE BURTON HALL

Constable Burton, Leyburn, North Yorkshire DL8 5LJ
Tel: 01677 450428 Fax: 01677 450622 (Mr Charles Wyvill)

Situated 3 miles east of Leyburn on the A684 and 6 miles west of the A1. A large romantic garden surrounded by 18th century parkland with a superb John Carr house (not open). Fine trees, woodland walks, garden trails and nature trails, rockery with an interesting collection of alpines and extensive shrubs and roses. Set in beautiful countryside at the entrance to Wensleydale. **Open:** Gardens Mar 25–Oct 17 daily 9–6pm. **Admission:** Please phone for details. Group tours of the house and gardens available by Phil Robinson, The Dales Plantsman. Tel: 01677 460225.

map 8 G1

DUNCOMBE PARK

Helmsley, Ryedale, York, North Yorks YO62 5EB
Tel: 01439 770213 Fax: 01439 771114

Visit Lord and Lady Feversham's restored family home in the North York Moors National Park. Built on a virgin plateau in 1713 overlooking both Norman Castle and river Valley it is surrounded by 35 acres of 'spectacularly beautiful' 18th century landscaped gardens and 400 acres of rolling, Arcadian parkland with National Nature Reserve and veteran trees. **Location:** Just off Helmsley Market Place, along A170 (Thirsk–Scarborough road). **Open:** 7 Apr–31 Oct 1999, Apr/Oct: Sun–Thurs, May–Sept: Sun–Fri. House & Garden: 11–6pm (last admission 4pm) tearoom, shop and walks (open to non-visitors to the house) 10.30–5.30pm. **Admission:** House & Garden: adult £5.75, concession £4.75, child (10–16yrs) £2.75, family £13. Gardens and parkland: adult £3.75, child £1.75. Discount for groups.

C map 8 D1

FAIRFAX HOUSE

Castlegate, York, YO1 9RN, North Yorkshire
Tel: 01904 655 543 Fax: 01904 652 262 (York Civic Trust)

An 18th century house designed by John Carr of York, and described as a class architectural masterpiece of its age. Certainly one of the finest town houses in England and saved from near collapse by the York Civic Trust who restored it to its former glory during 1982/84. In addition to the superbly decorated plaster work, wood and wrought iron, the house is now home for an outstanding collection of 18th century furniture and clocks, formed by the late Noel Terry. Described by Christie's as one of the finest private collections of this century, it enhances and complements the house and helps to create a very special 'lived in' feeling. The gift of the entire collection by Noel Terry's Trustees to the Civic Trust has enabled it to fill the house with appropriate pieces of the period and has provided the basis for what can now be considered a fully furnished Georgian Town house. **Location:** Centre of York, follow signs for Castle Area and Jorvik Centre. **Station(s):** York (10 mins walk). **Open:** 21 Feb–6 Jan, Mon–Thurs & Sat, 11am–5pm, Sun 1.30–5pm. Last admission 4.30pm. Closed Fri, except during Aug. Special evening tours, connoisseur visits and private dinners welcomed by arrangement with the Director. **Admission:** Adults £3.75, children £1.50, OAPs/students £3.00. Adult parties (pre-booked 15+) £3, children £1.25. Events and exhibitions. **Conferences:** By arrangement with the Director. Public car park within 50 yards. Suitable for disabled persons only with assistance (by telephoning beforehand, staff can be available to help). A small gift shop offers selected antiques, publications and gifts. Opening times are the same as the house.

map 8
D2

Elsham Hall Country and Wildlife Park and Elsham Hall Barn Theatre

Brigg, North Lincolnshire DN20 OQZ
Tel: 01652 688698 Fax: 01652 688240 (Capt Jeremy Elwes and Robert Elwes)

Beautiful lakes and gardens; miniature zoo; giant carp; falconry centre; wild butterfly walkway; adventure playground; mini–beast talks, garden and working craft centre: Granary tearooms and restaurant; animal farm, museum and art gallery; caravan site; ten National Awards. Also excellent new theatre with indoor winter and new outdoor summer programme with various festivals. **Location:** Near Brigg M180 Jct 5, near Humberside Airport. **Station(s):** Barnetby. **Open:** Times and prices on application. Contact Manager. **Refreshments:** Granary Tearooms, ice cream shop, restaurant, banqueting. **Conferences:** Conference facility. Licensed for civil weddings, medieval banquets and corporate entertainments/paintballing.

map 8 E3

The Grand Assembly Rooms

Blake Street, York, North Yorkshire
Tel: 01904 637 257

Georgian Ballroom, fully restored, scheduled monument status. Operates as cafe/restaurant/function room. Available for hire in part or as a whole for weddings, dinner dances, functions etc. Refreshments, light meals, disabled access. Live entertainment.

Harewood House

The Harewood Estate, Leeds, West Yorkshire, LS17 9LQ
Tel: 0113 288 6331 Fax: 0113 288 6467 E-mail: business@harewood.org (Earl & Countess of Harewood)

Award-winning Harewood is renowned for its stunning architecture, exquisite interiors and outstanding collections; beautiful gardens and 'Capability' Brown landscape, fascinating Bird Garden and wide variety of special events throughout the year. Recently accorded *'Designated Museum Status'*. **Location:** A61, between Leeds and Harrogate. **Open:** 9 Mar–31 Oct, daily. Grounds & Bird Garden: 10am. House: 11am, last admissions 4pm. **Admission:** Adult £6.95, OAP £6.25, Children £4.75, Family £22.50. **Events/Exhibitions:** The **Watercolour Rooms** and contemporary **Terrace Gallery** again reflect Harewood's diverse exhibition programme with 'Girtin in the North' and 'The Flower Show'. Outdoor events range from concerts to car rallies, and inside the House, by appointment, are 'behind the scenes' and specialist guided tours. Telephone for details.

map 8 C2

Harlow Carr Botanical Gardens

Crag Lane, Harrogate, North Yorkshire HG3 1QB
Tel: 01423 565418 Fax: 01423 530663 (Northern Horticultural Society)

Sixty-eight acre headquarters of the Northern Horticultural Society. Vegetable, fruit and flower trials. Rock, foliage, scented, winter and heather gardens. Alpines, herbaceous beds, display houses, fern house, streamside, woodland and arboretum. National collections, Museum of Gardening, Model Village, library, childrens' play area. Fully licensed restaurant, plant and gift centre. Picnic area. Courses, exhibitions, displays, walks and talks held on a regular basis throughout the year. Ample free coach parking, shelters, seating and hard surface pathways. Driver facilities vouchers. **Location:** 1½ miles W of town centre on B6162 Otley road. **Open:** Daily from 9.30am. Last admission 6pm or dusk if earlier. **Admission:** Adults £3.60, OAPs and groups of 20+ £2.70. **Internet:** www.stressweb.com/harlow

map 8 C2

Hovingham Hall

Hovingham, York, North Yorkshire YO62 4LU
Tel: 01653 628206 Fax: 01653 628668 (Sir Marcus Worsley)

Palladian House built c.1760 by Thomas Worsley to his own design. Unique entry by huge riding school. Visitors see family portraits and rooms in everyday use; also the extensive garden with magnificent yew hedges and dove-cot and the private cricket ground, said to be the oldest in England. **Location:** 20 miles N of York on Malton/Helmsley Road (B1257). **Open:** Open for parties of 15 or more *by written appointment* only Apr–end Sept 1999. Tues, Wed and Thurs 11–7pm. **Admission:** £3.50, children £1.50. **Refreshments:** At the Hall by arrangement. Meals at the Worsley Arms Hotel, Hovingham. **Conferences:** Facilities for up to 140.

map 8 D1

Ledston Hall

Hall Lane, Ledston, Castleford, WF10 2BB, West Yorkshire
Tel: 01423 523 423 Fax: 01423 521 373 (G. H. H. Wheler)

17th century mansion with some earlier work. **Location:** 2 miles N of Castleford, off A656. **Station(s):** Castleford (2 ¼ miles). **Open:** Exterior only: May–Aug, Mon–Fri, 9–4pm. Other days by appointment. **Refreshments:** Chequers Inn, Ledsham (1 mile).

map 8 D3

LINDLEY MURRAY SUMMERHOUSE

The Mount School, Dalton Terrace, York
Tel: 01904 667500 Fax: 01904 667524

The Summerhouse dated from 1774 and was situated in the grounds of Holgate House, York (now the Collingwood Hotel). Holgate House was the home of Lindley Murray (1795–1826). When the house was sold to the North Eastern Railway Company in 1901, William Wilberforce Morrell, the owner, presented the Summerhouse to the Mount School. Originally positioned adjacent to the boundary wall of the school grounds, it was moved to its present position in 1966. The building is listed Grade II*. A major refurbishment was carried out during 1997. Grants towards the cost of the work undertaken were received from – English Heritage, Mount Old Scholars' Association, York Civic Trust and York Georgian Society. The Grant from the Noel G Terry Charitable Trust was made in memory of the Terry Family, Scholars of The Mount School from 1901–1909.

NEWBURGH PRIORY

Coxwold, York, North Yorkshire, YO6 4AS
Tel: 01347 868 435 (Sir George Wombwell, Bt.)

One of the North's most interesting historic houses. Originally built in 1145 with alterations in 1568 and 1720–1760, the Priory has been the home of one family and its descendants since 1538. The house contains the tomb of Oliver Cromwell (his third daughter, Mary, was married to Viscount Fauconberg, the owner from 1647–1700). In the grounds there is a really beautiful water garden full of rare alpines, other plants and rhododendrons. **Location:** 5 miles from Easingwold, off A19, 9 miles from Thirsk. **Open:** **House & Grounds:** 4 Apr–30 June, Sun & Wed & Bank Hol Mons Easter and Aug. House open 2.30–4.45pm. Grounds open 2–6pm. Open at other times for parties of 25+ by appointment with the Administrator. **Admission:** **House & Grounds:** Adults £3.50, children £1. Grounds only: Adults £2, children free. **Refreshments:** Afternoon tea is served in the original Old Priory Kitchens.

NORTON CONYERS

Ripon, North Yorkshire, HG4 5EQ
Tel: 01765 640333 Fax: 01765 692772 (Sir James and Lady Graham)

Visited by Charlotte Brontë, Norton Conyers is an original of 'Thornfield Hall' in 'Jane Eyre' and a family legend was an inspiration for the mad Mrs Rochester. Another visitor was James II when Duke of York, in 1679. The room and the bed he and his wife traditionally used are still to be seen. 375 years of occupation by the Grahams (they bought it in 1624) have given the house a noticeably friendly atmosphere. Family portraits, furniture, ceramics and costumes. The paintings in the Great Hall include a celebrated John Ferneley, 'The Quorn Hunt', painted in 1822. The 18th century walled garden, with Orangery and herbaceous borders, includes a plant sales area, specialising in unusual hardy plants. Pick your own fruit in season; please check beforehand. **Location:** Near Wath, 4 miles N of Ripon, 3 miles from A1. **Open:** (House and garden) Bank Hol Suns and Mons, Suns 6 Jun–12 Sept, daily 12–17 Jul, 2–5pm. **Admission:** Adults £3, children (10–16) and OAPs £2.50. Prices for parties on application. Garden is free (donations welcome); a charge is, however, made at charity openings. **Refreshments:** Teas are available at garden charity openings. Dogs (except guide dogs) in grounds and garden only and must be on a lead. Photography by owners' written permission only. No high-heeled shoes in house, please. Wheelchair access ground only.

NEWBY HALL & GARDENS

Ripon, North Yorkshire, HG4 5AE
Tel: 01423 322 583 Fax: 01423 324 452 (R. E. J. Compton)

The family home of Mr and Mrs Robin Compton is one of Yorkshire's renowned Adam houses. It is set amidst 25 acres of award-winning gardens full of rare and beautiful plants. Famous double herbaceous borders with formal compartmented gardens, including a species rose garden, water and rock garden, the Autumn Garden and the tranquillity of Sylvia's Garden – truly a 'Garden for all Seasons'. Also holds National Collection of genus Cornus. The contents of the house are superb and include a unique Gobelins Tapestry Room, a gallery of classical statuary and some of Chippendale's finest furniture. Other attractions include railway rides beside the river, an adventure garden for children and a woodland discovery walk. There is a shop and plant stall and a picnic area. **Location:** 4 miles SE of Ripon on Boroughbridge Road (B6265). 3 miles W of A1. Harrogate (14 miles). York (20 miles). Leeds (35 miles). Skipton (32 miles). **Station(s):** Harrogate or York. **Open:** House & Garden: 1 Apr– 30 Sept, Tues–Sun and Bank Hol Mons. **Admission: House & Garden:** Adults £6.30, OAPs £5.20, children/disabled £3.80. Group: Adult/OAPs £5, children/disabled £3.40. **Garden Only:** Adult £4.50, OAPs £3.90, children/disabled £3. Group: Adult/OAPs £3.70, Child/Disabled £2.60. **Refreshments:** Lunches and teas in the licensed Garden Restaurant. **Events/Exhibitions:** 9 May: Spring Plant Fair; 12–13 Jun & 4–5 Sept: Rainbow Craft Fair; 18 July: Historic Vehicle Rally; 19 Sept: Autumn Plant Fair. **Conferences:** Function room for about 100.

map 8
C2

LOTHERTON HALL

Aberford, Yorkshire, LS25 3EB
Tel: 0113 281 3259 Fax: 0113 281 2100 (Leeds City Council)

Modest late Victorian and Edwardian country house of great charm and character, formerly the home of the Gascoigne family. Fine collections of furniture, silver, pottery and porcelain, paintings, sculpture and costume, including many family heirlooms. Famous period gardens with a deer park and bird garden. **Location:** 1mile E of A1 at Aberford, on the Towton Road (B1217). **Open:** 1 Apr–31 Oct, Tues–Sat 10–5pm, Sun 1–5pm. 1 Nov–31 Mar, Tues–Sat 10–4pm, Sun 12–4pm Closed Jan & Feb, closed Mons. **Admission:** Please contact for details of admission prices. **Refreshments:** Cafe in stable block.

map 8 D3

NUNNINGTON HALL

Nunnington, York, North Yorkshire YO62 5UY
Tel: 01439 748283 Fax: 01439 748284

Sheltered in a lovely walled garden on a quiet riverbank is this delightful 17th century manor house. It is easy to see why it has remained a much lovely family home for over 400 years. A magnificent oak panelled hall leads to cosy family living rooms, the nursery and maid's room. Explore the attics and discover the amazing Carlisle Collection of miniature rooms each exquisitely furnished to one eighth life size. **Open:** 27 Mar–31 Oct 1999. April, May, Sept & Oct, daily except Mon and Tues 1.30–6pm. (5.30 Apr & Oct). June–Aug, daily except Mon 1.30–6pm Good Fri and Bank Hol Mons. Last admission 1 hour before house closes. **Admission:** Adult £4, child £2, family £10 (2 adults and up to 3 children). Garden: Adult £1.50, children free, Group per person £3 (minimum 15 paying). **Tearooms:** Seating 72, plus 60 in the Tea Garden. Not licensed. Open 12.30pm.

map 8 D1

OAKWELL HALL

Birstall, Nr. Batley, West Yorkshire, WF19 9LG
Tel: 01924 326 240 (Kirklees Metropolitan Council)

This beautiful Elizabethan manor house, set in period gardens, has delighted visitors for centuries. Charlotte Brontë visited it in the 19th century and used it as a model for Fieldhead – the home of the heroine in Shirley. Built in 1583, the hall is now set out as it would have been in the 1690s and is surrounded by 100 acres of the original estate – now a country park. The site boasts excellent visitor facilities including a café, a well-stocked shop and an adventure playground. In addition, the innovative and unique 'Discover Oakwell' exhibition introduces children to the environment of a country park. Events range from period candlelight evenings to lively family activities. **Open:** 11–5pm, Mon–Fri, 12–5pm Sat and Sun.

map 8 C3

THE ORANGERY

Settrington House, Settrington, Malton, North Yorkshire YO17 8NP
Tel: 01944 768345 Fax: 01944 768484 (Sir Richard & Lady Storey)

"A UNIQUE VENUE FOR ANY OCCASION." This beautifully converted 18th century listed building, standing in the magnificent grounds of Settrington House, the home of Sir Richard and Lady Storey is the most superb environment for any event. Be it corporate entertaining, seminars, concerts, civil ceremonies, receptions or parties. With a choice of excellent caterers, fully licensed bar, seating for 40–400, disabled access and ample car parking. We guarantee first class attention and service. Enquires please telephone Mandy Ostick–King (manager) 01944 768440 or 01944 768345.

map 8 E2

RED HOUSE

Oxford Road, Gomersal, Cleckheaton, West Yorkshire
Tel: 01274 335 100 (Kirklees Metropolitan Council)

Built in 1660 by the Taylor family, Red House gets its name from its unusual red brick construction which sets it apart from the surrounding houses of local stone. Mary Taylor, daughter of the House in the early 19th century, was a close and life-long friend of Charlotte Brontë who stayed there often and featured the House as Briarmains in Shirley. The House now looks very much as it would have done in Charlotte's time; with a mixture of original and reproduction furniture, each room brings you closer to the 1830s. The renovated barn is the setting for the new state-of-the-art Secret's Out Gallery which explores Charlotte's connection with the Spen Valley and her friendship with two local women. **Open:** Mon–Fri 11–5pm, Sat–Sun 12–5pm. **Admission:** Free.

map 8 C3

![Ripley Castle viewed across the lake]

RIPLEY CASTLE

Ripley Castle Estate, Harrogate, North Yorkshire.
Tel: 01423 770152   Fax: 01423 771745 (Sir Thomas and Lady Ingilby)

For almost 700 years, Ripley has been the domain of the Ingilby family. The Castle Gatehouse was built to keep the Scots out in 1450, the Old Tower in 1555 and the remainder in 1780. After his victory at Marston Moor, Oliver Cromwell sought shelter at this Royalist stronghold and was rather surprised to find himself held at gunpoint by 'Trooper' Jane Ingilby who, along with her brother, had fought against him at the battle. The Knight's Chamber contains a Priest's Hiding Hole, a relic of the days when Francis and David Ingilby were described as the most dangerous Papists in the North and the family's associations with the Gunpowder Plot. Guided tours take approx. 75 mins and are full of humour and historical anecdote. The Walled Gardens contain two massive Herbaceous Borders, the National Hyacinth Collection and rare vegetables from the HDRA; the hothouses display a collection of tropical plants and ferns. A walk around the lake and deer park, a stroll to the many interesting shops in the adjacent village of Ripley, or a cup of tea or meal at Cromwells (or something stronger at the Boar's Head) complete a lovely day for the family. **Open:** 10.30–3pm. Nov & Dec, Tues–Thurs, Sat & Sun. Jan–Mar, Tues, Thurs, Sat & Sun. Apr–Jun, Thurs–Sun. Jul–Aug, open daily. Groups any day by arrangement. Gardens open daily. <u>**Admission:**</u> Adults £4.50, children £2. Family ticket £1 (2 adults & 2 children). Gardens: Adults £2.25, children £1. OAPs and groups £3.50 castle and gardens, £1.75 gardens only. £1 extra garden conducted tour (min 10 persons)

map 8
C2

 # RIEVAULX ABBEY

Helmsley, North Yorks
Tel: 01439 798228 (English Heritage)

Visit the spectacular remains of the first Cistercian monastery in Northern England and experience the unrivalled peace and serenity of its setting in the beautiful wooded valley of the River Rye. Imaginations will be fired as you listen to our audio tour while exploring the extensive remains; the soaring graceful arches silhouetted against the sky will take the breath away. **Location:** In Rievaulx, 2¼ m W of Helmsley on minor road off B1257. **Open:** 1 Apr–30 Sept: daily, 10–6pm. Open 9.30–7pm, July–Aug. 1 Oct–31 Oct: daily, 10–5pm, 1 Nov–31 Mar: daily, 10–4pm. Closed 24–5 Dec). **Admission:** Adults £3, concs £2.30, child £1.50. (15% discount for groups of 11 or more).

 map 8 D1

RIEVAULX TERRACE & TEMPLE

Rievaulx, Helmsley, York, YO6 5LJ
Tel: 01439 748283 Fax: 01439 748284

A ½ mile long grass covered terrace and adjoining woodlands with vistas over Rievaulx Abbey (English Heritage) and Rye Valley to Ryedale and the Hambleton Hills. There are two mid-18th century temples: the Ionic Temples has elaborate ceiling paintings and fine 18th century furniture. **Note:** No access to Rievaulx Abbey from Terrace. No access to property Nov–end of March. **Open:** 27 Mar–31 Oct 1999. Apr & Oct: Daily 10.30–5pm. June, July, Aug & Sept: Daily 10.30–6pm. Open Good Fri and Bank Hol Mons. Last admission an hour before closing. **Admission:** Adult £3, child £1.50, family £7.50 (2 adults and upto 3 children), group rate £2 per person (minimum of 15 paying). **Refreshments:** Ice cream only. Teas at Nunnington Hall 7m (see entry for Nunnington).

 map 8 D1

 # ROCHE ABBEY

Maltby, Rotherham, South Yorkshire S66 8NW
Tel: 01709 812739 (English Heritage)

This Cistercian monastery, founded in 1147, lies in a secluded landscaped valley sheltered by limestone cliffs and trees. Some of the walls still stand to their full height and excavation has revealed the complete layout of the abbey. **Location:** 1 mile south of Maltby off A634. Please phone for details of opening times and admission charges.

SEWERBY HALL & GARDENS

Church Lane, Sewerby, Bridlington, YO15 1EA
Tel: Estate Office:01262 673 769 Hall: 01262 677 874
(East Riding of Yorkshire Council)

Sewerby Hall and Gardens, set in 50 acres of parkland overlooking Bridlington Bay, dates back to 1715. The Georgian House, with its 19th century Orangery, is now the Museum of East Yorkshire and contains history/archaeology displays, art galleries and an Amy Johnson Room with a collection of her trophies and mementos. The grounds include the magnificent walled Old English and Rose gardens and host many events all year round. Activities for all the family include a children's zoo and play areas, golf, putting, bowls, plus woodland and clifftop walks. **Location:** Bridlington, 2m NE. **Station:** Bridlington (2.5 miles). **Open:** Hall: 2 Apr–31 Oct, 10–6pm daily. Off peak 6 Mar–30 Mar and 1 Nov–19 Dec 1999, Sat–Tues. Gardens and zoo open throughout the year. **Refreshments:** Traditional tearooms.

map 9 F2

SHANDY HALL

Coxwold, York, North Yorkshire, YO61 4AD
Tel: 01347 868 465 (The Laurence Sterne Trust)

Here in 1760–1767 the witty and eccentric parson Laurence Sterne wrote 'Tristram Shandy' and 'A Sentimental Journey'. Shandy Hall was built as a timber-framed open-hall in the mid-15th century and added to by Sterne in the 18th century. Not a museum but a lived-in house where you are sure of a personal welcome. Surrounded by a walled garden full of old-fashioned roses and cottage-garden plants. Also one acre of wild garden in an old quarry. **Location:** 20 miles north of York. **Open:** June–Sept. Wed 2–4.30pm. Sun 2.30–4.30pm. Other times by appointment. Gardens open every day May–Sept, except Sat, 11–4.30pm. **Admission:** Adults £3.00, children half price. Garden only £2. **Refreshments:** In village. **Exhibitions:** June–Sept, paintings and pots, by local artists. Unusual plants for sale.

 map 8 D1

SHEFFIELD BOTANICAL GARDENS

Clarkhouse Road, Sheffield, S10 2LN. Contact: Sheffield City Council, Meersbrook Park. Tel: 0114 250 0500 Fax: 0114 255 2375

Designed in 1833 by Robert Marnock, the original curator, the Gardens (listed Grade II by English Heritage) are a fine example of the Victorian 'Gardenseque' style. Particularly impressive is the straight promenade up to the 'Paxton Pavilions', an important example of early metal and glass curvilinear structure. Occupying 7.6 hectares in the south-west of the city, the Gardens contain around 5,000 species of plants, including the national collections of Weigela and Diervilla. In addition to the Pavilions, the Gardens contain the highest concentration of listed structures in Sheffield. **Open:** Daily, except Christmas, Boxing & New Year's Days. **Admission:** Free. **Refreshments:** For pre-arranged guided tours. **Events/Exhibitions:** Frequently, held by the Friends of the Botanic Gardens and specialist horticultural societies. **Conferences:** Facilities for 80 people.

map 8
C4

SHIBDEN HALL

Lister's Road, Halifax, HX3 6XG, West Yorkshire
Tel: 01422 352 246 Fax: 01422 348 440(Calderdale M.B.C. Leisure Services)

Allow yourself to drift into 600 years of history ... a world without electricity ... where craftsmen worked in wood and iron ... a house where you sense the family has just gone out ... allowing you to enjoy a sense of the past at Shibden Hall, Halifax's Historic Home. Set in 90 acres of park, Shibden Hall provides a whole day of entertainment. **Location:** 2 km outside Halifax, on A58 Leeds Road. **Buses:** 548/549 Brighouse, 508 Leeds, 681/682 Bradford. **Open:** Mar–Nov, Mon–Sat, 10–5pm. Sun, 12–5pm. Last admission 4.30pm. Contact for winter opening hours. **Admission:** (From April 1999) Adults £1.90, children 95p, OAPs £1, family ticket £5. Group rate for pre-booked party. **Refreshments:** Tearoom. Shop, amusements, toilets, car park, disabled access.

map 8
B3

 # SCARBOROUGH CASTLE

Castle Road, Scarborough YO11 1HY
Tel: 01723 372451 (English Heritage)

Spectacular coastal views from the walls of this enormous 12th century castle. The buttressed castle walls stretch out along the cliff edge and the remains of the great rectangular stone keep, still stand to over three storeys high. There is also the site of a 4th century Roman signal station. The castle was frequently attacked, but despite being blasted by cannons of the Civil War and bombarded from the sea during World War 1, it is still a spectacular place to visit. **Location:** Castle road, east of town centre. **Open:** Please phone for opening times and admission charges.

SKIPTON CASTLE

Skipton, BD23 1AQ, North Yorkshire
Tel: 01756 792442 Fax 01756 796100

Keeper of the southern gateway to the Yorkshire Dales for over 900 years, this is one of the best-preserved castles in England. A stronghold of the Lancastrian Cliffords inside Yorkshire, – besieged for three years in the Civil War, the last Royalist bastion in the North – every age left marks visible to the attentive visitor today. Yet the Castle is still fully roofed, so that a visit is enjoyable at any season. Within the precincts is a delightful walled picnic area, tearoom and a shop selling souvenirs, gifts and books. **Location:** Skipton is an unspoilt, bustling town, with four market days a week. The Castle gateway stands at the head of the High Street. **Open:** Daily, 10am (Sun 12pm). Last admission at 6pm (Oct–Feb, 4pm). Closed Christmas Day. **Admission:** Adults £4, children (5–17) £2, children (under 5) free, OAPs and students £3.50. Family ticket, 2 adults and up to 3 children, £11. All under 18s receive a free Castle Explorer's badge. Free tour sheets available in 8 languages. Guides are provided for pre-booked parties at no extra charge. Large car & coach park off nearby High Street. **Internet:** www.skiptoncastle.co.uk

map 8
B2

SION HILL HALL

Kirby Wiske, Nr Thirsk, North Yorkshire YO7 4EU
Tel: 01845 587206 Fax: 01845 587486 (H.W. Mawer Trust)

Charming Edwardian Country Mansion by Brierley of York – the 'Lutyens of the North'. The last country house built before the Great War and of outstanding architectural merit. This award winning mansion now houses the Mawer Collection of period furniture, porcelain, paintings, clocks & memorabilia–probably the most eclectic collection in the North. 20 rooms open with 'Members of the Household' in Period Costume. Collection of dolls & costume displays. Birds of Prey & Conservation Centre in the Victorian walled garden. Free parking. Gift & Bygones Shop. Granary Tearoom. **Location:** Off A167; 6 miles S of Northallerton: 4 miles W of Thirsk, 8 miles E of A1 via A61. **Open:** Hall: 2 Apr–26 Sept: 1–4.30pm, Wed to Sun.Groups by arrangement any time Feb–Nov. Birds: Open all day Mar–Oct. **Admission:** Adult £4, child £2, concessions £3.50.

map 8 C1

SUTTON PARK

Sutton–on–the–Forest, York YO61 1DP
Tel: 01347 810249/811239 Fax: 01347 811251 (Sir Reginald & Lady Sheffield)

Sutton Park is a charming example of early Georgian architecture and has a warm lived-in feeling. Plasterwork by Cortese, fine paintings, lovely 18th century furniture, important collection of porcelain. Full of wonderful treasures put together with great style. Award–winning GARDENS. Herbaceous and rose borders are full of rare and interesting plants. Truly a gem of a garden. Georgian Ice House and Woodland Walks. **Open:** House: Good Fri–Easter Mon, 2–5 Apr 1.30–5pm & all Bank Hol Mons 1.30–5pm. Every Wed & Sun, 7 Apr–29 Sept 1.30–5pm. Coach Parties to book please. Private parties by appointment. Gardens: Daily 7 Apr–end Sept 11–5pm. **Admission:** House & Garden: Adults £4, OAP's £3.50, child £2.50. Garden only: Adults £2, OAP's £1.50, child 50p. Private parties £5 per person. Tearooms open on House open days for self–service. Disabled access to the grounds only.

map 11 J7

TEMPLE NEWSAM HOUSE

Leeds, West Yorkshire, LS15 0AE
Tel: 0113 264 7321 Fax: 0113 260 2285 (Leeds City Council)

The magnificent Tudor-Jacobean house was the birthplace of Lord Darnley, husband of Mary, Queen of Scots and later became the home of the Ingram family, Viscounts Irwin. There are over 30 historic interiors (many newly restored), including a spectacular Picture Gallery, with superlative paintings, furniture (including the Chippendale Society collection), silver and ceramics. The thousand acre Capability Brown park (free) contains a home farm with rare breeds of animals, sensational displays of rhododendrons and azaleas (May & June), national collections of delphiniums and phlox (July & Aug), chrysanthemums (Sept) and roses (all summer). Guided tours available. Gift shop. There is limited disabled access. **Open:** Please contact for details of 1998 opening times and admission charges.

map 8 C3

THORP PERROW ARBORETUM

Bedale, North Yorkshire, DL8 2PR
Tel: 01677 425 323 Fax: 01677 425 323 (Sir John Ropner, Bt.)

Thorp Perrow, the country home of Sir John and Lady Ropner, contains the finest arboretum in the north of England. A collection of over 1,000 varieties of trees and shrubs including some of the largest and rarest in the country. It is also the home of three National Collections – ash, lime and walnut – and is becoming a popular attraction for all the family. The arboretum comprises 85 acres of landscaped grounds with a lake, grassy glades, tree trails and woodland walks. Thousands of daffodils carpet the ground in spring, while the summer is noted for bold drifts of wild flowers and the autumn brings glorious and vibrant colour. Nature trail. Children's trail. Tearoom and information centre. Plant centre. Electric wheelchair available. **Location:** Well–Ripon Road, S of Bedale. O.S. map ref: SE258851. 4 miles from Leeming Bar on A1. **Open:** All year, dawn-dusk. Guided tours available. Tel: 01677 425 323. **Admission:** Please contact the Arboretum Office for admission prices. Free car and coach park. **Refreshments:** Tearoom. Picnic area. Dogs permitted on a lead.

map 8 C1

WILBERFORCE HOUSE

25 High Street, Kingston-upon-Hull, East Yorkshire, HU1 1EP
Tel: 01482 613 902 Fax: 01482 613 710 (Kingston-upon-Hull City Council)
Internet: www.hulcc.gov.uk/museums/index.htm

Hull's oldest and most famous museum is a brick-built 17th century merchant's house in the centre of the old town. The birthplace of William Wilberforce (1759–1833), known worldwide for his fight to abolish slavery. The main displays within the museum tell the horrific story of slavery and Wilberforce's fight to abolish it. Wilberforce House is much more than just a reminder of slavery. The building contains survivals of every stage in its history: the oak-panelled 17th century rooms on the first floor; the 18th century staircase with elaborate rococo plasterwork ceilings and the Victorian parlour. The famous collection of Hull silver is displayed in the adjoining Georgian house. **Location:** In the centre of Hull's Old Town. **Open:** All year. Mon–Sat, 10–5pm. Sun, 1.30–4.30pm. **Admission:** Telephone for details and group rates.

map 9 F3

GREAT DAYS OUT IN YORKSHIRE

The National Trust owns and protects all these places for you to enjoy

Treasures...

Interesting buildings...

Lovely gardens...

4.

3.

1.

2.

5.

Special places...

Curious things...

7.

8.

6.

1. & 3. Fountains Abbey & Studley Royal
2. Rievaulx Terrace & Temples
4. Beningbrough Hall and Gardens
5. Nostell Priory
6. Nunnington Hall
7. Treasurer's House
8. Ormesby Hall

THE NATIONAL TRUST
Registered charity no. 205846

To find out more about these places pick up our 1999 'Yorkshire Visitors' Guide' leaflet at a Tourist Information Centre or ring 01904 702021

TREASURER'S HOUSE

Chapter House Street, York YO1 2JD Tel: 01904 624247

Open: 27 March to 31 Oct: daily except Fri 10.30–5pm. Last admission 4.30pm. Events: contact Property Manager for details of function hire and full calendar of special events. Licensed for civil weddings.

RIEVAULX TERRACE & TEMPLES

Rievaulx, Helmsley, York YO6 5LJ Tel: 01439 798340 Fax: 01439 748284

Open: 27 March to 31 Oct: daily 10.30–6pm (closes at 5pm in April & Oct). Last admission 1hr before closing. Ionic Temple closed 1–2pm. Events: contact the Visitor Manager at Nunnington Hall for information (Tel. 01439 748283).

BENINGBROUGH HALL & GARDENS

Shipton-by-Beningbrough, York YO6 1DD Tel: 01904 470666

Open: 27 March to 31 Oct: Sat to Wed, Good Fri & Fri in July and Aug. House: 11–5pm. Last admission 4.30pm. Grounds: 11–5.30pm. Last admission 5pm. Events: 16 May, Spring Plant Fair; 12 Sept, Autumn Plant Fair. Licensed for wedding ceremonies and receptions; please contact Assistant Property Manager for details.

NUNNINGTON HALL

Nunnington, York YO6 5UY Tel: 01439 748283 Fax: 01439 748284

Open: 27 March to 31 Oct: daily except Mon & Tues (but open BH Mon & every Tues during June, July & Aug) 1.30–6pm (1.30–5.30pm April & Oct); last admission 1hr before house closes. Events: outdoor concert; other exhibitions and events through the year, contact Visitor Manager for details.

FOUNTAINS ABBEY & STUDLEY ROYAL WATER GARDEN

Fountains, Ripon HG4 3DY Estate Office tel: 01765 608888

Open: Abbey & water garden: open all year daily except Fri in Nov, Dec, Jan and 24/25 Dec. April to Sept: 10–7pm (closes at 4pm on 9/10 July & 7 Aug); Oct to March 2000: 10–5pm (dusk if earlier). Closed 1 Jan 2000. Last admission 1hr before closing. Deer park: open all year daily during daylight hours. Floodlighting: Abbey is floodlit on Fri & Sat evenings until 10pm, 27 Aug to 16 Oct. Fountains Hall & St Mary's Church: restoration in progress, apply to Estate Office for opening times. Charge may be reduced on and around event days (9/10 July) due to restricted access to parts of estate. Events: extensive programme of concerts, plays, walks & talks available all year, incl. Shakespeare theatre; Music by Moonlight; outdoor promenade entertainment. Details from Box Office (tel. 01765 609999). All outside events wheelchair-accessible.

ORMESBY HALL

Ormesby, Middlesbrough TS7 9AS Tel: 01642 324188 Fax: 01642 300937

Open: 28 March to 31 Oct: daily except Mon, Fri & Sat (but open Good Fri, & BH Mons) 2–5.30pm. Events: Telephone or send sae for full programme. Hall licensed for wedding ceremonies.

NOSTELL PRIORY

Doncaster Road, Nostell, nr Wakefield WF4 1QE
Tel: 01924 863892 Fax: 01924 865282

Open: 27 March to 30 June, 1–12 Sept: Thur–Sun 12–5pm. 1 July–31 Aug: Wed–Sun 12–5pm. Please telephone for full events programme.

Great Houses & Gardens of Yorkshire

The Great Houses & Gardens of Yorkshire are a group of over 30 fine houses and gardens, situated throughout the Yorkshire and Humberside region and open to visitors.

Discover the wonderfully rich and varied heritage of this rewarding area. Grand stately homes, elegant country houses and fascinating museums all of which lie waiting to be explored with their unrivalled collections of art and furniture. Many of their treasures were gathered during the Grand Tour of Europe, a cultural mecca and part of every nobleman's education during the eighteenth and nineteenth centuries. These enchanting objects are still a source of wonder for the modern day visitor and will continue to delight for generations to come.

The architectural splendour of these great houses is complemented further by the beauty of Yorkshire's famous gardens and landscapes. Those seeking peace and tranquillity will surely find it here.

This is a selection of the Great Houses and Gardens of Yorkshire that are featured in this guide

Brodsworth Hall (EH): *Map Index 1*
Nostell Priory (NT): *Map Index 2*
Temple Newsam: *Map Index 3*
Lotherton Hall: *Map Index 4*
Oakwell Hall: *Map Index 5*
Skipton Castle: *Map Index 6*
East Riddleston Hall (NT): *Map Index 7*
Harewood House: *Map Index 8*
Harlow Carr Gardens: *Map Index 9*
Ripley Castle: *Map Index 10*
Fountains Abbey (NT): *Map Index 11*
Duncombe Park: *Map Index 12*

Bolton Castle: *Map Index 13*
Constable Burton Hall Gardens: *Map Index 14*
Sion Hill Hall & Falconry UK: *Map Index 16*
Mount Grace Priory (EH): *Map Index 17*
Nunnington Hall (NT): *Map Index 21*
Helmsley Castle (EH): *Map Index 22*
Rievaulx Abbey (EH): *Map Index 23*
Rievaulx Terrace & Temples (NT): *Map Index 23*
Sewerby Hall: *Map Index 27*
Beningbrough Hall (NT): *Map Index 28*
The Treasurers House (NT): *Map Index 29*
Wilberforce House: *Map Index 30*

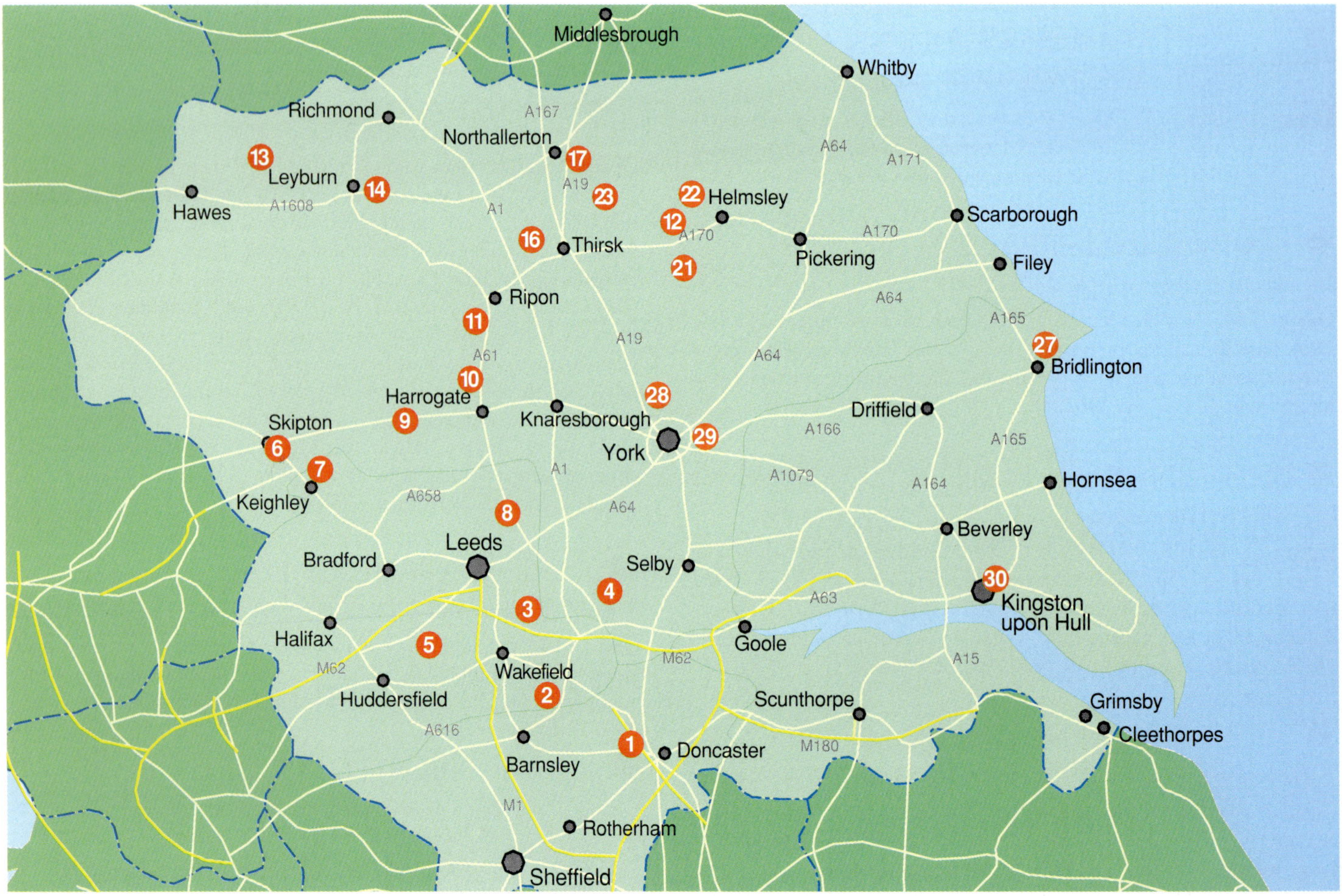

For further information on the Great Houses and Gardens of Yorkshire, please call 01423 770152

Wales

The North West landscape has a dramatic quality reflected in its history. In prehistoric times, Anglesey was a stronghold of the religious elite known as the Druids. Roman and Norman invasions concentrated on the coast, leaving the mountains to the Welsh. These wild areas are the centre of the Welsh language and culture.

The dominant feature of North Wales is Snowdon, the highest mountains in Wales. Snowdonia National Park extends dramatically from the Snowdonia massif south beyond Dolgellau, with thickly wooded valleys, mountain lakes, moors and estuaries. To the east are the softer Clywdian Hills and unspoilt coastlines can be enjoyed on Anglesey and the beautiful Llyn Peninsula, where the Welsh language is still spoken.

Above: Marloes. Right: Harlech Castle. Bottom: Nant Gwynant

South and mid Wales are less homogenous regions than North Wales. Most of the population live in the southeast corner. To the west is Pembrokeshire, the loveliest stretch of Welsh coastline. To the north the industrial valleys give way to the wide hills of the Brecon Beacons and the rural heartlands of Central Wales.

Magnificent coastal scenery marks the Pembrokeshire Coast National Park and cliff backed Gower Peninsula, while Cardigan Bay and Carmarten Bay offer quieter beaches. Walkers can enjoy grassy uplands in the Brecon Beacons and gentler country in the leafy Wye Valley. Urban life is concentrated in the southeast of Wales, where old mining towns line the valley north of Cardiff, the capital.

ABERGLASNEY GARDENS

East Bailiff's Lodge, Llangathen SA32 8QH
Tel & Fax: 01558 668998 (Aberglasney Restoration Trust)

Aberglasney is a 'garden lost in time'. Spectacularly set in the beautiful Towy valley of Carmarthenshire, the gardens have been an inspiration for poetry since 1477. Celebrated by John Dyer in his poem 'The Country Walk', this garden is a unique survival in Britain. Featured in a BBC TV series and the subject of a book commissioned by Weidenfeld and Nicolson, the gardens have first class horticultural and aesthetic qualities and a mysterious history. Set within eight acres are six different garden spaces, including three walled gardens, at its centre is the unique Elizabethan and Jacobean 'cloister' garden, from the parapet walk above there are views of an ornamental pond, walled gardens and ancient gatehouse. Rare specimen trees planted in the early 19th century still survive, although the greatest arboreal creation is the yew tunnel, which is claimed by one expert to be at least 1,000 years old. Its hauntingly beautiful and unspoiled pastoral landscape makes it one of the most fascinating gardens in the UK. The gardens are between Llandeilo and Carmarthen at the village of Llangathen. **Open:** Daily July–Sept 1999 and Apr–Oct 2000. **E-mail:** marketing@ aberglasney.org.uk

map 7
H4

BLAENAVON IRONWORK

North Street, Blaenavon
Enquiries Tel: 01495 792615
(Cadw: Welsh Historic Monuments)

This site is not only one of Europe's best-preserved 18th century ironworks, but a milestone in the history of the Industrial Revolution. Built in the 1780's, the ironworks were at the cutting edge of new technology. Visitors can still trace the entire process of production, which involved the harnessing of steam power to blow the blast furnaces, and the movement by water balance tower. The human side is represented at Stack Square, a community of small terrace dwellings built for pioneer ironworkers.

map 3
G1

CAERLEON ROMAN BATHS & AMPHITHEATRE

High Street, Caerleon NP6 1AE
Enquiries Tel: 01633 890104
(Cadw: Welsh Historic Monuments)

Caerleon is Britain's most fascinating and revealing Roman site. It was founded in AD75 as one of only three bases in Britain for the Roman's legionary troops. These elite soldiers enjoyed the conveniences of an entire township, complete with amphitheatre and bath house. The excavated remains of their barrack blocks – the only examples currently visible in Europe – stand in green fields near the fortress baths, a giant leisure complex equivalent to today's sports and leisure centre. The well-preserved amphitheatre, with seating for 6,000 was the setting for bloody combat involving wild beasts and gladiators.

map 7
J2

CAERPHILLY CASTLE

Caerphilly, Mid Glamorgan, CF83 1JD
Enquiries Tel: 01222 883143
(Cadw: Welsh Historic Monuments)

The largest castle in Wales, with extensive water defences and a famous leaning tower, was built by the De Clare family to defend their territory against the armies of Llewelyn, the last Welsh Prince of Wales. The effectiveness of the finished work is proved by the fact that throughout its long and colourful history, the castle has never been taken by attackers. Due to conservation work in 1776, a large amount of the castle remains undamaged, giving visitors a fascinating insight into medieval life. During the summer reconstructions of warfare, including working replica siege engines, provide an exhilarating and entertaining day out for all the family.

map 7
J3

CAREW CASTLE & TIDAL MILL

Carew, Nr. Tenby, Pembrokeshire, Wales
Tel/Fax: 01646 651 782
(Pembrokeshire Coast National Park)

A magnificent Norman castle and later an Elizabethan residence. Royal links with Henry Tudor, setting for Great Tournament of 1507. The Mill is the only restored tidal mill in Wales. Automatic talking points explaining milling process. Special exhibition 'The Story of Milling'. **Location:** 4 miles E of Pembroke. **Station(s):** Pembroke. **Bus:** Haverfordwest. **Open:** Easter-end Oct, daily. **Admission:** Please phone for details.

map 7
H6

CARREG CENNEN CASTLE

Trapp, Dyfed, SA19 6TS
Enquiries Tel: 01558 822291
(Cadw: Welsh Historic Monuments)

Spectacularly situated on a remote crag 300 feet above the River Cennen, this castle has for centuries been sought out by visitors who enjoy mystery and the dramatically picturesque. The site's origins are lost in ancient obscurity, but in the cave under the castle, which can be explored with torches, prehistoric human remains have been discovered. Other finds at the castle include Roman coins and it is believed that the existing castle is built on top of an Iron Age hill fort. The stone fortress we see today was started by a Norman knight, on top of a Welsh castle constructed by The Lord Rhys, the most famous Prince of South Wales.

 map 7 H4

THE CASTLE HOUSE

The Castle House, Usk, Monmouthshire
Tel: 01291 672563 (J.H.L. Humphreys)

Medieval Gatehouse with 19th century interior and 13th century castle ruins set in a series of gardens providing seasonal interest (Donations to N.G.S.). Location: OS Ref SO 376 011, off Monmouth Road in Usk, opposite Fire Station. **Open:** Castle on request and Gardens by appointment, throughout the year. House: Feb and Bank Hols., 2–5pm. Guided tours only, numbers limited to 5 – prior booking recommended. **Admission:** House & Garden: Adults £5, family £10. Castle & Garden: £2. Children free.

 map 7 H2

CASTELL COCH

Tongwynlais, Nr Cardiff, South Glamorgan, CF4 7JS
Enquiries Tel: 01222 810101
(Cadw: Welsh Historic Monuments)

One of the most distinctive and memorable castles in Wales, this spectacular building peeks out from the treetops of a cliff towering over the Taff valley near Cardiff. The original medieval castle was rebuilt by the third Lord Bute, who spared no expense on its reconstruction and decoration. From the exterior's re-creation of a medieval fortress complete with conical-roofed towers, the amazed visitor enters the breathtaking apartments of Lord and Lady Bute. Although the castle was intended only for occasional use as a country retreat, the interior is richly and exquisitely carved and painted with scenes from fables and fantasies, all of which are immaculately preserved.

  map 7 J3

CHEPSTOW CASTLE

Chepstow, Gwent NP6 5EZ
Enquiries Tel: 01291 624065
(Cadw: Welsh Historic Monuments)

It comes as quite a surprise to find a great castle in the pretty border town of Chepstow. But on a cliff overlooking the river Wye stands the earliest datable stone fortification in Britain; the great stone keep built by William the Conqueror's most trusted general. Since guarding the border was always an important task, Chepstow castle was developed and enlarged over the centuries in a series of modernisations and gives visitors the opportunity to trace centuries of history in its imposing stones. It was in use up to the Civil War and afterwards was used to keep Henry Marten under house arrest for signing the death warrant of Charles I.

 map 7 J4

CILGERRAN CASTLE

Cilgerran, Dyfed SA13 2SF
Enquiries Tel: 01239 615007 (Cadw: Welsh Historic Monuments)

Sitting on a high, rocky crag above the meeting-point of two rivers, Cilgerran Castle has the perfect defensive position and is so spectacular that it became a popular subject for romantic artists such as Turner. The earliest castle on this site was built by a Norman lord who married Princess Nest, a famous Welsh beauty. When raiders came to assassinate her husband in his bed, Nest helped him to escape, although she and her children were kidnapped. The castle has had a long and chequered history, passing from English to Welsh hands and back again many times during the long wars for the conquest of Wales. The Castle we see today was the work of the English Marshal family, who extended and strengthened the fortress over a period of two hundred years.

 map 7 G5

COLBY WOODLAND GARDENS

Stepaside, Narberth, Pembrokeshire.
Tel: 01834 811885 (National Trust)

Open: Colby Woodland Gardens open daily 10–5pm from 27 Mar–31 Oct. Walled garden 1 Apr 11–5pm. Daffodils and bluebells carpet this tranquil woodland valley in spring. Rhododendrons, azaleas, magnolias and camellias flower from Mar til the end of Jun followed by hydrangeas and eucryphias. A fine collection of rare trees and shrubs offers splendid autumn colour. Children's trail and regular guided walks. Events programme details, please telephone 01834 811885. **Admission:** Adult £2.80, child £1.40, family 2 + 2 £7, group rate £2.20. Coaches welcome group rate by appointment.

 map 7 H6

DINEFWR PARK

Llandeilo, Carmarthenshire
Tel: 01558 823902 Fax: 01558 822036 (The National Trust)

A fine country residence built in 1660, Newton House is set in over 450 acres of landscaped park in the outstanding Upper Towy Valley. Dinefwr Park is home to the ancient herd of Dinefwr White Park Cattle and fallow deer who roam the medieval Deer Park. Outstanding views of the Towy Valley can be seen from many vantage points. A Boardwalk through the Bog Wood and Mill Pond area of the Park allows access to all to experience the many species of plant and pond life in this virtually undisturbed corner of Dinefwr. A specially constructed Hide with views over the Oxbow lakes provides an ideal location to see many rare and unusual birds. **Open:** Open daily (except Tue & Wed) 11–5pm. **Admission:** Adult £2.80, child £1.40, group rates available.

 map 7 H4

KIDWELLY CASTLE

Kidwelly, Dyfed SA17 5BQ
Enquiries Tel: 01554 890104
(Cadw: Welsh Historic Monuments)

Perched high above the river Gwendraeth, looking out towards Laugharne across the Taf estuary, Kidwelly's early Norman earth and timber castle could be reached by boat, making it difficult to besiege. However, The Lord Rhys, Prince of South Wales, captured and burned the castle, which did not return to Norman hands until 1244 when the construction of a stone fortress was started. Over the following centuries, the castle and its walled town passed into different hands and was added to and modernised by the Dukes of Lancaster and then by the most powerful man in early Tudor Wales, Sir Rhys ap Thomas.

 map 7 H5

CRESSELLY

Kilgetty, Pembrokeshire SA68 0SP, Wales
Fax: 01646 687045 (HDR Harrison-Allen Esq.)

Home of the Allen family for 250 years. The house dates to 1770 with matching wings from 1869 and contains good plasterwork and fittings of both periods. The Allens are of particular interest for their close association to the Wedgwood family. **Location:** In the Pembrokeshire National Park, off the A4075. OS Ref SN0 606. **Open:** 28 days between May and September. Please write or fax 01646 687045 for details. **Admission:** Adults £3.50. No children under 12. Wedding receptions and functions in house or marquee for 20 to 300 persons. Dinners, private or corporate events in historic dining room. Guided tours only. Ample parking for cars (coaches by arrangement only). No dogs. Bed and breakfast and dinner by arrangement. Two double en suite with four-poster beds, single, twin and children by arrangement.

LAMPHEY BISHOP'S PALACE

Lamphey, Nr Pembroke SA71 5NT
Enquiries Tel: 01646 672224
(Cadw: Welsh Historic Monuments)

The medieval bishops of St David's built themselves a magnificent retreat away from the worries of Church and State. Here, amongst fish ponds, fruit orchards, vegetable gardens and sweeping parklands, they could enjoy the life of country gentlemen. The palace was improved over two centuries, though it is mainly the work of Henry De Gower, bishop of St Davids from 1328 to 1347, who built the splendid Great Hall. Later additions include a Tudor chapel with a fine, five-light east window.

LAUGHARNE CASTLE

Laugharne, Dyfed
Enquiries Tel: 01994 427906 (Cadw: Welsh Historic Monuments)

Looking out over the estuary that Dylan Thomas was to make famous for its beauty, is Laugharne's "castle, brown as owls". Like its neighbours at Kidwelly and Llansteffan, Laugharne is built on the site of an early Norman earth and timber fort, and was rebuilt in stone during the Middle Ages by the local Lord, Guy de Brian. As the castle passed down through succeeding generations of the family, it was added to and strengthened. By the reign of Elizabeth I, the castle had fallen into disrepair, and it was modernised in the Tudor style by Sir John Perrot, who was tried for treason. In this century, the castle was rented out to author Richard Hughes who wrote his novel "In Hazard" in the castle's gazebo, where Dylan Thomas later wrote "Portrait of the Artist as a Young Dog."

DYFFRYN GARDENS

St. Nicholas, Cardiff, SF5 6SU, The Vale of Glamorgan, Wales
Tel: 01222 593328 Fax: 01222 591966

'A Garden for all Seasons' describes Dyffryn, one of Wales' finest landscaped gardens. The beautifully laid out grounds offer an endless variety of colour and form with many small theme gardens, recently restorored with the aid of a Heritage Lottery Grant, heather bank, glasshouse ranges and arboretum. Dyffryn Gardens offer a different visual treat at every turn, with easy access, plentiful free parking and calendar of special events. Some areas may be closed in '99 for on-going restoration work. **Location:** Just off M4 Junction 33. **Open:** 10am to Dusk. **Admission:** Adult: £3; OAP/Children: £2 (under 4's free); Family: (2 Adults + 2 children) £6.50.

LLANVIHANGEL COURT

Nr Abergavenny, Monmouthshire, NP7 8DH
Tel: 01873 890 217 (Mrs Julia Johnson)

A Grade 1 listed Tudor Manor of 15th century origins. Beautiful early 17th century plaster ceilings and panelling and magnificent yew staircase, leading to a bedroom where Charles I is reputed to have stayed during the Civil War. Remodelled during the 1650s by John Arnold. The main entrance overlooks 17th century terraces and steps. Unusual stables from the same period with turned wood pillars. **Location:** 4 miles north of Abergavenny on A465. **Open:** 8 Aug–1 Sept inclusive, or by appointment. **Admission:** Adults £4, children (5–15) and OAPs £2.50.

map 7 H2

OXWICH CASTLE

Oxwich, Nr Swansea, West Glamorgan
Enquiries Tel: 01792 390359 (Cadw: Welsh Historic Monuments)

On a headland overlooking Oxwich Bay in the beautiful Gower peninsula, stands Oxwich Castle. A Tudor mansion, rather than a medieval fortress, its impressive gatehouse emblazoned with the Mansel family's coat of arms was added more as a show of pride than for military purposes. Like many successful gentlemen, Sir Rice Mansel remodelled his ancestral home in the modern Tudor style, with his son continuing the building programme by adding a stupendous multi-storey wing during Queen Elizabeth's reign. During conservation work on the castle, a magnificent gold and jewelled brooch was discovered, which may once have been part of King Edward II's lost royal treasure. How it came to be at Oxwich remains an intriguing mystery.

map 7 J4

RAGLAN CASTLE

Raglan, Gwent, NP5 2BT
Enquiries Tel: 01291 690228
(Cadw: Welsh Historic Monuments)

A monument to medieval family pride, this imposing fortress-palace was built by the Herbert family. The water-moated Great Yellow Tower was built by Sir William, "The Blue Knight of Gwent", a veteran of Agincourt. His son, William Herbert continued the construction of the majority of the existing castle, using profits he made by importing French wine. William was one of the leading Yorkist supporters in the Wars of the Roses and was so well trusted by King Edward IV that he was given custody of young Henry Tudor, later King Henry VII, who was brought up at Raglan. William's loyalty as the King's right-hand man in Wales brought a string of titles and estates, but Raglan remained the family's stronghold.

map 7 H2

 # ST DAVIDS BISHOP'S PALACE

St Davids SA62 6PE
Enquiries Tel: 01437 720517
(Cadw: Welsh Historic Monuments)

Even in ruin, this imposing palace, standing next to St Davids Cathedral, still conveys the affluence and power of the medieval church. Largely the work of Bishop De Gower, no expense was spared in creating a grand residence fit for a major figure of both Church and State. De Gower's palace boasted two sets of state rooms ranged around a courtyard, one for his own use, the other for ceremonious entertainment. The palace is richly embellished with lavish stone carvings. Particularly fine are its arcaded parapets, decorated with chequered stonework.

map 7 G7

PENHOW CASTLE

Nr Newport, South Wales NP6 3AD
Tel: 01633 400800 Fax: 01633 400990 (Stephen Weeks)

Wales' Oldest Lived-in Castle holds 8 awards for its careful restoration and interpretation. First home in Britain of the Seymour family, this enchanting Knight's border fortress now presents a glimpse into eight centuries of changing Castle life. Visitors cross the drawbridge to explore restored period rooms from battlements to kitchens, guided by acclaimed Walkman audio tours included free (also French & German). **Location:** A48 midway b/w Chepstow and Newport; M4 Jct 24. **Open:** Good Friend Sept, Wed–Sun incl. & Bank Hols, 10–5.15pm (last admission). Aug–open daily. Winter, Wed only 10–4pm and selected Sun pm's 1–4pm. Open all year for groups, Evening Candlelit Tours and school visits. Special Christmas Tours 15 Nov–5 Jan. **Admission:** Adult £3.60, child (5-16) £2.30, family (2+2) £9.50. Group discount 10% for 20+.

map 7 J2

 # PICTON CASTLE & WOODLAND GARDENS

Haverfordwest, Pembrokeshire, Wales, SA62 4AS
Tel/Fax: 01437 751 326 (Picton Castle Trust)

New for 1999 Castle open five days a week. Built in the 13th century, home of the Philipps family, the Castle retains it external appearance but was remodelled inside, above the undercroft in the 1750's and extended around 1800. The woodland and walled gardens cover 40 acres and are part of The Royal Horticultural Society access scheme for beautiful gardens. Events include art exhibitions and spring and summer horticultural shows. **Location:** OS Ref. SN011 135. 4 m E of Haverfordwest just off A40. **Open: Castle:** April–Sept. Closed Mon & Sat except Bank Hol, open all other afternoons for guided tours. **Garden & Gallery:** April-Oct. Tues–Sun inclusive. 10.30–5pm. **Admission: Castle, Garden & Gallery:** Adults £4, OAPs £3.50, children £1. **Garden & Gallery:** Adults £2.75, OAPs £2.50, children £1. Reduced prices for groups of 20 or more by prior appointment.

map 7 H6

ST. DAVIDS CATHEDRAL

The Deanery, The Close, St. Davids, Pembrokeshire, Wales
Tel: 01437 720 199 Fax: 01437 721 885 (The Dean and Chapter)

This cathedral, begun in 1181, is at least the fourth church to have been built on a site reputed to be that on which St. David himself founded a monastic settlement in the 6th century. The outstanding features of the building are the magnificent ceilings – oak in the Nave, painted in the Choir and Presbytery – and the sloping floor. The stalls of the Chapter of the cathedral contain medieval misericords and the Chapter is unique in having the reigning Sovereign as a member. The cathedral has been an important place of pilgrimage for nearly fourteen centuries. In 1124, Pope Calixtus II declared that two pilgrimages to St. Davids were equal to one to Rome and that three were equal to one to Jerusalem itself.

map 7
G7

STRATA FLORIDA ABBEY

Ystrad Meurig, Pontrhydfendigaid SY25 6BT
Enquiries Tel: 01974 831261
(Cadw: Welsh Historic Monuments)

None of the Cistercians' Welsh abbeys preserves that original spirit of remoteness more strongly than Strata Florida. There is much to captivate the visitor at this evocative, historically important site. The abbey, founded in the 12th century, grew to become a powerhouse of Welsh culture, patronised by princes and poets. Although in ruin, Strata Florida displays much evidence of its former status, including a wonderful carved doorway and beautiful medieval tiles.

map 7
F4

TINTERN ABBEY

Tintern NP6 6SE
Enquiries Tel: 01291 689251
(Cadw: Welsh Historic Monuments)

Founded by Cistercian monks in 1131 and largely rebuilt by Roger Bigod, Lord of nearby Chepstow Castle in the 13th century, Tintern Abbey encompasses grand design and architectural detail of great finesse. The shell stands open almost to its full height, an outstanding example of the elaborate 'decorated' style of Gothic architecture. Visitors are captivated by the vast windows, with their delicate tracery and the wealth of detail on the walls, doorways and soaring archways. Tintern has inspired artists and poets like JMW Turner and William Wordsworth.

map 7
H1

TRETOWER COURT AND CASTLE

Crickhowell, Powys NP8 2RF
Enquiries Tel: 01874 730279 (Cadw: Welsh Historic Monuments)

In the quiet foothills of the Black Mountains stands a unique example of a family's building through the centuries. Alongside the castle which had protected them for 300 years, the Vaughan family built a manor house which was later extended and enlarged into a medieval mansion with elaborately timbered roofs and a galleried courtyard. During the Wars of the Roses, the house was fortified to enable the family to live there in safety. They continued to do so until the seventeenth century, when the great poet Henry Vaughan drew inspiration from his wonderfully well-preserved family home and its beautiful surroundings. Now visitors can also enjoy the re-created medieval garden that was featured in the television programme "Geoff Hamilton's Paradise Gardens."

map 7
H2

TREDEGAR HOUSE & PARK

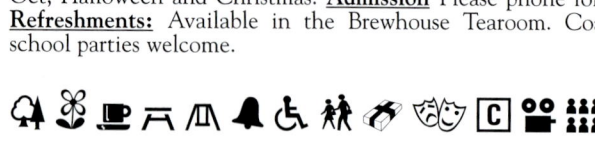

Newport, South Wales, Tel: 01633 815 880, NP1 9YW
Fax: 01633 815895. (Newport County Borough Council)

Set in 90 acres of award winning gardens and parkland, Tredegar House is one of the architectural wonders of Wales. For over five hundred years it was the ancestral home of the Morgans, later Lord Tredegar. Visitors can now discover what life was like for those who lived 'above' and 'below' stairs in thirty restored rooms. The intriguing tours explore the lavish staterooms and the curious servant's quarters, uncovering the Morgan stories and mysteries. <u>Location:</u> SW of Newport, signposted from M4, junction 28, A48. <u>Open:</u> From Good Friday–end Oct, Halloween and Christmas. <u>Admission</u> Please phone for details. <u>Refreshments:</u> Available in the Brewhouse Tearoom. Coach and school parties welcome.

map 7
J2

WEOBLEY CASTLE

Llanrhidian, Nr Swansea, West Glamorgan SA3 1HB
Enquiries Tel: 01792 390012
(Cadw: Welsh Historic Monuments)

This fortified manor house perches above the wild northern coast of the beautiful Gower peninsula, looking over the marshes towards the Loughor estuary. It dates from the medieval thirteenth and fourteenth centuries, a rare survivor from those wild and often troubled times. Weobley was designed to be a comfortable home for the knightly de la Bere family, but its defensive tower and turrets provided a safe shelter in times of trouble. In Tudor times, Sir Rhys ap Thomas, the most powerful man in Wales added the two-storey porch block, providing a more stately entrance to the hall and private apartments.

map 7
J5

WHITE CASTLE

Llantilio Crossenny, Gwent NP7 8UD
Enquiries Tel: 01600 780380
(Cadw: Welsh Historic Monuments)

One of a trio of castles built by the Normans to protect the route into Wales from Hereford, White Castle is the classic medieval castle. Standing on a low hill, its six towers and curtain wall are surrounded by a water-filled moat with drawbridge. It was built to house a garrison which, along with troops from Grosmont and Skenfrith castles, was responsible for the defence of the border against the rebellious Welsh. During Llewelyn the Last's attacks into the established Marcher lands of South Wales, the Three Castles were repaired and readied for war, but never saw action. After Henry Bolingbroke became King Henry IV, the castles, which were part of his Duchy of Lancaster, became the property of the Crown.

map 7
H2

BEAUMARIS CASTLE

Beaumaris, Anglesey, Gwynedd, LL58 8AP
Enquiries Tel: 01248 810361
(Cadw: Welsh Historic Monuments)

This lovely castle overlooks the Menai Straits between Anglesey and the North Wales mainland, guarding an important medieval trade route. It was built by Edward I to complete his chain of coastal fortresses and served as Anglesey's garrison, protecting the island and its precious grain stores against invaders. The castle was ingeniously designed to use the straits' tides to both fill the defensive moat and to enable large ships to sail right up to the castle gate at high tide. The castle's picturesque setting and unusual design have drawn visitors for centuries, including Princess Victoria, later to be Queen, who visited for a Royal Eisteddfod in 1832.

map 6
C4

BODELWYDDAN CASTLE

Bodelwyddan, Denbighshire, Wales
Tel: 01745 584 060 Fax: 01745 584 563 (Bodelwyddan Castle Trust)

Set against the magnificent background of the Clwydian Hills, this imposing Victorian mansion has been authentically restored and houses a major collection of 19th century portraits and photography from the National Portrait Gallery, furniture from the Victoria & Albert Museum and sculpture from the Royal Academy. Fascinating 'hands-on' galleries of Victorian amusements and inventions feature parlour games, puzzles and optical illusions – an extravaganza of Victorian fun. A varied programme of temporary exhibitions takes place throughout the year. Amid the Castle's grounds, gardens and parkland are picnic areas, a woodland trail and children's play facilities. The Castle is a winner of the 'Museum of the Year' Award. **Open:** Throughout the year. Please telephone for details.

map 6
C3

BODNANT GARDEN

Tal Y Cafn, Nr Colwyn Bay, Conwy LL28 5RE
Tel: 01492 650460 Fax: 01492 650448 (The National Trust)

Eighty acres of magnificent garden in the beautiful Conwy Valley. Rhododendrons, camellias and magnolias in Spring, with the famous Laburnum Arch and azaleas flowering mid May-mid Jun. The summer months give a show of herbaceous plants, water lilies, hydrangeas and roses, followed by superb autumn colour. **Open:** 13 Mar–31 Oct, daily 10–5pm. Adult £4.60, child £2.30. **Refreshments:** Pavilion. Ample parking.

map 6
C4

CAERNARFON CASTLE

Caernarfon, Gwynedd, LL55 2AY
Enquiries Tel: 01286 677617
(Cadw: Welsh Historic Monuments)

This most impressive of Edward I's Welsh defences was built near the Roman fort of Segontium, mentioned in the ancient tales of the Mabinogion. Its unique polygonal towers with decorative coloured stone bands echo the walls of the great city of Constantinople and marked the castle as a special place. Indeed, it was intended to be the official residence of the King's chief representative in the Principality and is inextricably linked with the Princes of Wales since it is the birthplace of Edward's heir, Edward Caernarfon, first English Prince of Wales. The twentieth century has seen it rise again to prominence as the site of the Investiture of both this century's Princes of Wales.

map 6
C5

BODRHYDDAN

Rhuddlan, Denbighshire
Tel: 01745 590414 Fax: 01745 590155 (Lord Langford)

The home of Lord Langford and his family. Bodrhyddan is basically a 17th century house with 19th century additions by the famous architect William Eden Nesfield, although traces of an earlier building exist. The house has been in the hands of the same family since it was built over 500 years ago. There are notable pieces or armour, pictures, period furniture, a 3000 year old mummy, a formal parterre, a woodland garden and attractive picnic areas. Teas are available. Bodrhyddan is a Grade I listing making it one of few in Wales to remain in private hands. **Location:** OS Ref. SJ045 788. On the A5151 midway between Dyserth and Rhuddlan, 4 miles SE of Rhyl. **Open:** Jun–Sept inclusive, Tue & Thur, 2–5.30pm. **Admission:** Adult £4, child £2. Coach parties and receptions by special arrangement. Partially suitable for disabled. Tearoom. Guided tours only. Ample parking.

map 6
C2

CONWY CASTLE

Conwy, Gwynedd, LL32 8AY
Enquiries Tel: 01492 592358
(Cadw: Welsh Historic Monuments)

This finest and most complete example of a fortified town and castle was constructed after the second Welsh war of independence by Edward I, whose apartments are in the castle's Inner Ward. Edward believed in building walled towns alongside his castles to create small pockets of English dominance in Wales. The town not only housed the community needed to supply the castle, but increased local prosperity and acted as the focal point of local government. Conwy is a classic example of this philosophy, cleverly designed to have 21 "circuit-breaker" towers along the town walls which enabled defenders to isolate an attacking force and ward them off effectively.

map 6
C4

CRICCIETH CASTLE

Criccieth, Gwynedd LL52 0DP
Enquiries Tel: 01766 522227
(Cadw: Welsh Historic Monuments)

Set high on a rocky headland overlooking Cardigan Bay, this is the most striking of the castles built by the native Welsh Princes. Llewelyn the Great built the first castle here, during his long campaign against the English annexation of Wales. When his grandson, Llewelyn the Last continued the struggle, he extended and strengthened Criccieth's defences. Over a century later, during the revolt of Owain Glyndwr, the rebel army was besieged in the castle, but were able to hold out due to the castle's position overlooking the sea, since provisions could be brought in by boat.

map 6
D5

CYMER ABBEY

Dolgellau, Gwynedd LL40 2HE
Enquiries Tel: 01341 422854
(Cadw: Welsh Historic Monuments)

The serene ruins stand in a lovely setting beside the River Mawddach. Even by the austere standards of the Cistercians, life must have been hard at Cymer – the abbey suffered badly during the troubled 13th century, the wars between England and Wales probably accounting for the failure to complete the original plan of the church. Cymer rewards visitors with a telling insight into the way of life of this enterprising order of monks. Particularly impressive are its great windows, arches and an unusual tower.

map 6
E4

DENBIGH CASTLE

Denbigh, Clwyd
Enquiries Tel: 01222 500200
(Cadw: Welsh Historic Monuments)

Encircling a rocky outcrop overlooking the Vale of Clwyd, Denbigh Castle is built on the site of a traditional Welsh court. At the end of Llewelyn the Last's wars of Welsh independence against Edward I, the English king gave Denbigh to his campaign commander, Henry de Lacy. Together they planned a castle and walled town similar to Edward's own fortresses along the north Welsh coast. Sadly, Henry never finished building the finely decorated gatehouse, the castle's final crowning glory, due to the death of his son in the castle well. In later years, as Denbigh passed into the hands of several powerful owners, the castle saw many famous visitors, including King Charles I.

DOLWYDDELAN CASTLE

Dolwyddelan, Gwynedd
Enquiries Tel: 01690 750366
(Cadw: Welsh Historic Monuments)

Tradition claims Dolwyddelan as the birthplace of Llewelyn ap Iorwerth, Llewelyn the Great; the Prince who united Wales. However, the stone keep that now stands was probably re-built by Llewelyn to guard the road into the heart of the stronghold of Snowdonia and Gwynedd through the strategically important Lledyr Valley. The castle would also have watched over Llewelyn's precious cattle pastures, since this was a time of war when cattle were essential battle supplies that were easily moved to support hungry armies. When Edward 1st took the castle during the Welsh wars for independence under Llewelyn the Last, he outfitted the garrison in white snow camouflage and made some additions to the existing structure.

map 6
D4

GWYDIR CASTLE

Gwydir Castle, Llanrwst, Gwynedd.
Tel: 01492 641687 Fax: 01492 641687 (Mr and Mrs Welford)

Gwydir Castle is situated in the beautiful Conwy Valley and is set within a romantic 10 acre garden. Built by the illustrious Wynn family c.1500, Gwydir is a fine example of a Tudor courtyard house, incorporating re-used medieval material from the dissolved Abbey of Maenan. Further additions date from c.1600 and c.1826. Both house and gardens are undergoing a phased programme of restoration most notably the re-installation of the important 1640's dining room panelling, recently repatriated from the New York Metropolitan Museum. **Location:** ½ mile W Of Llanrwst on A5106. **Open:** 1 Mar–31 Oct, daily 10–5pm. Limited opening at other times. **Admission:** Adults £3, children £1.50. Group discount 10%.

map 6
C4

ERDDIG HALL, GARDEN & COUNTRY PARK

Erddig, Nr Wrexham LL13 0YT
Tel: 01978 355314 Fax: 01978 313333 (Owner)

One of the most fascinating houses in Britain, not least because of the unusually close relationship between the family and their servants. The range of outbuildings includes: joiner's shop, smithy, sawmill, stables, bakehouse, laundry and kitchen, while the stunning state rooms display 18th and 19th century furniture and furnishings. The large walled garden has been restored to its 18th century formal design with Victorian parterre and yew walk. **Open:** 20 Mar–31 Oct daily, except Thurs & Fri but open Good Fri. Garden: 11–6pm. House: 12–5pm. July & Aug Garden: 10–6pm. 2 Oct–31 Oct Garden: 11–5pm. House: 12–4pm. Last admission to House an hour before closing. **Admission:** All inclusive ticket: Adult £6, child £3, family £15. Belowstairs (incl. outbuildings & garden) ticket: Adult £4, child £2, family £10. **E-mail:** PERMSN@SMT.NTRUST.ORG.UK

map
0

HARLECH CASTLE

Harlech, Gwynedd LL46 2YH
Enquiries Tel: 01766 780552
(Cadw: Welsh Historic Monuments)

Famed in song and story, Harlech is enshrined in the history of Wales. This is the "castle of lost causes" where a handful of defenders could hold off an army; a fortress which has been the last refuge for defiant, valiant men and women who have refused to compromise their principles. Built by Edward I, it had a clever channel connecting it to the sea, with a water gate and protected walkway to the castle allowing supplies to be brought in by boat. The castle was besieged in the 15th century when it was the headquarters and court of rebel leader, Owain Glyndwr; and again during the Wars of the Roses when it was the last Lancastrian stronghold in Wales to fall to the Yorkists.

map 6
D4

PLAS BRONDANW GARDENS

Llanfrothen, Nr. Penrhyndeudraeth, Gwynedd, Wales.
Tel: 01766 771 136 (The Second Portmeirion Foundation)

Created by Sir Clough Williams-Ellis, architect of Portmeirion, below his ancestral home. Italian inspired gardens with spectacular mountain views, topiary and folly tower. **Location:** 2 miles north of Penrhyndeudraeth. ¼ mile off the A4085 on Croesor Road. **Open:** All year, daily, 9–5pm. **Admission:** Adults £1.50, children 25p.

map 6
D4

PLAS MAWR, CONWY

Conwy, Gwynedd LL32 8DE
Tel: 01492 580167 (Cadw: Welsh Historic Monuments)

Within the town of Conwy, best-known for its great medieval fortifications of castle and walls, hides a perfect Elizabethan jewel. Plas Mawr is the best-preserved Elizabethan town house in Britain, famous for the quality and quantity of its plasterwork decoration. Plas Mawr is a fascinating and unique place which gives visitors a chance to peek into the lives of the Tudor gentry and their servants. This was the fast moving time, when the creation of increased wealth among merchants and the gentry meant that private homes such as Plas Mawr could be decorated and furnished lavishly. Cadw gives visitors the opportunity to enjoy all of this through an audio tour which also explains the amazing process of restoration the house has been through.

RHUDDLAN CASTLE

Rhuddlan, Clwyd
Tel: 01745 590777
(Cadw: Welsh Historic Monuments)

One of the first castles built by Edward I in his programme to fortify the North Wales coast, a man-made channel three miles long linked Rhuddlan to the sea, giving supply ships access to the castle. This was reputed to be Queen Eleanor's favourite castle and indeed, it seems that she and King Edward spent a large amount of time here. It was in Rhuddlan that Edward made a treaty with the Welsh Lords and persuaded them to accept his baby son, recently born in Caernarfon Castle, as the Prince of Wales by promising them that their new Lord would be born in Wales, with an unblemished character and unable to speak a word of English.

map 6
C3

RUG CHAPEL & LLANGAR CHURCH

C/o Coronation Cottage, Rug, Corwen LL21 9BT
Enquiries Tel: 01490 412025
(Cadw: Welsh Historic Monuments)

Rug is a rare example of a little altered 17th century private chapel. Carved angels appear as part of an elaborate roof, decorated from end to end. The skills of local artists and wood carvers can even be seen in the bench ends, which are decorated with fantastic carvings. Nearby Llangar Church is even older. The small, idyllically located medieval building retains many ancient features, including extensive 15th century wall paintings, a 17th century figure of death, old beams, box pews, pulpit and minstrels gallery.

map 6
D3

VALLE CRUCIS ABBEY

Llangollen
Enquiries Tel: 01978 860326
(Cadw: Welsh Historic Monuments)

The Cistercian abbey founded in the 13th century, lies in green fields beneath Llangollen's deep sided mountains. Many original features remain including the glorious west front complete with richly carved doorway and a beautiful rose window. Other well preserved features include the east end of the abbey (which still overlooks the monks' original fishpond) and lovely chapter house with its striking rib-vaulted roof. Valle Crucis, the "Abbey of the Cross", is named after Eliseg's Pillar, a nearby 9th century Christian memorial cross.

map 6
D2

CHIRK CASTLE

Chirk, Wrexham LL14 5AF Tel: 01691 777701 Fax: 01691 774706

Open: 27 March to 30 Sept: daily except Mon & Tues (but open BH Mon); 2 Oct to 31 Oct: Sat & Sun 12–5pm. Garden: as house 11–6pm; last admission 4.30pm. **Events:** send s.a.e for details of programme, which includes open–air plays, family fun days and snowdrop walks.

PENRHYN CASTLE

Bangor LL57 4HN Tel: 01248 353084 Infoline: 01248 371337

Open: 24 March to 31 Oct: daily except Tues. March to June, Sept to Oct 12–5pm, July & Aug 11–5pm (last audio tour 4pm). Grounds and stable block exhibitions: March to June, Sept to Oct 11–5.30pm, July & Aug 10–5.30pm; last admission to house & grounds 4.30pm. **Events:** send s.a.e. for details or tel. Infoline.

PLAS NEWYDD

Llanfairpwll, Anglesey LL61 6DQ Tel: 01248 714795

Open: House: 27 March to 31 Oct: daily except Thur & Fri 12–5pm. Garden: as house 11–5.30pm. Rhododendron Garden 27 March to early June only; woodland walk and marine walk open all year. **Events:** send s.a.e for full details of varied programme.

POWIS CASTLE & GARDEN

Welshpool SY21 8RF Tel: 01938 554338 Fax/Infoline: 01938 554336

Open: Castle & Museum: 27 March to 30 June, 1 Sept to 31 Oct: daily except Mon & Tues; July & Aug: daily except Mon (but open all BH Mons). Castle & Museum: 1–5pm. Garden: as castle & museum, 11–6pm. Last admission to castle, garden & museum each 30mins before closing. **Events:** varied programme, tel. for details.

Scotland

Southeast of the Highland boundary fault line lies a part of Scotland very different in character from its northern neighbour. If the Highlands embody the romance of Scotland, the Lowlands are the powerhouse. Lowlanders have always prospered in agriculture and more recently, in industry and commerce.

The Lowlands are traditionally all the land south of the fault line stretching northeast from Loch Lomond to Stonehaven. Confusingly, they include plenty of wild upland country. The region illustrates best the diversity of Scotland's magnificent scenery. The wooded valleys and winding rivers of the border give way to the stern moorland hills of the

Above: River Tweed. Below: Forth Bridge. Bottom: Isle of Skye

Cheviots and Lammermuirs.

Lively little fishing villages cling to the rocky east coast, while the Clyde coast and its islands are dotted with cheerful holiday towns. Inland lie the Trossachs: these romantic mountains surrounding Loch Lomond are a magnet for walkers and well within reach of Glasgow.

Scotland is renowned for its rich and diverse selection of the arts. The National Museum of Scotland displays both international collections of human and cultural history, archaeology, geology and the decorative arts whilst in the Western Isles of Scotland lies An Lanntair, an arts centre devoted to local artists and musicians.

 # ABBOTSFORD HOUSE

Melrose, Borders, Scotland, TD6 9BQ.
Tel: 01896 752 043 Fax: 01896 752 916

The house of Sir Walter Scott, containing many historical relics collected by him. **Location:** 3 miles W of Melrose; S of A72; 5 miles E of Selkirk. **Station(s):** No railway. **Open:** Third Monday in March–31 Oct: Mon–Sat, 10–5pm. Jun–Sept: Sun, 10–5pm. Mar–May & Oct: Sun, 2–5pm. **Admission:** Adults £3.50, children £1.80. Coach Party: Adults £2.50, children £1.30. **Refreshments:** Tea shop. Gift shop. Cars with wheelchairs or disabled enter by private entrance.

map 13 **H6**

AMISFIELD MAINS

Nr. Haddington, East Lothian, Scotland
Tel: 01875 870 201 Fax: 01875 870 620
(The Wemyss & March Estates Management Co. Ltd)

Georgian farmhouse with 'gothick' barn and cottage. **Location:** Between Haddington and East Linton on A1 Edinburgh-Dunbar Road. **Open:** Exteriors only. By appointment, Wemyss & March Estates, Estate Office, Longniddry, EH32 0PY, East Lothian, Scotland.

map 13 **H5**

ARTHUR LODGE

60 Dalkeith Road, Edinburgh, Scotland EH16 5AD
Tel: 0131 667 5163 (S. Roland Friden)

A Neo-Grecian dream of a country gentleman's residence in town (Thomas Hamilton 1827). Set in a beautiful garden and imaginatively restored and decorated, an exquisite and surprising private residence. **Open:** Jun–Jul, Wed & Sat. Aug–Sept, Wed only. Tours by appointment, at 12noon, 1pm & 2pm **Admission:** £3. Concessions £2

map 13 **G5**

 # AYTON CASTLE

Eyemouth, Berwickshire, Scotland, , TD14 5RD.
Tel: 018907 81212 Fax: 018907 81550
(Ayton Castle Maintenance Fund)

A Victorian castle built in red sandstone in 1846, which has been fully restored and is now lived in by the family owners. **Open:** 10 May–13 Sept: Sun, 2–5pm. At other times by appointment. **Admission:** £3, Children (under 15) free. **Events/Exhibitions:** Occasionally.

map 13 **J6**

BEANSTON

Nr. Haddington, East Lothian, Scotland
Tel: 01875 870 201 Fax: 01875 870 620
(The Wemyss & March Estates Management Co. Ltd)

Georgian farmhouse with Georgian orangery. **Location:** Between Haddington and East Linton on A1 Edinburgh-Dunbar Road. **Open:** Exteriors only. By appointment, Wemyss & March Estates, Estate Office, Longniddry, EH32 0PY, East Lothian, Scotland.

map 13 **H5**

BLAIRQUHAN CASTLE & GARDENS

Straiton, Maybole, KA19 7LZ, Ayrshire, Scotland
Tel: 016557 70239 Fax: 016557 70278 (James Hunter Blair)

Magnificent Regency Castle approached by a 3 mile long private drive beside the River Girvan. Walled gardens and pinetum. Picture gallery. Shop. Tree Trail. **Location:** 14 miles S of Ayr, off A77. Entrance Lodge is on B7045, 1/2 mile S of Kirkmichael. **Open:** 17 July–15 Aug, daily except Mons, 2–4.45pm. **Admission:** Adults £4, children £2, OAPs £3. Parties by arrangement any time of the year. **Refreshments:** Tearoom. Car parking. Wheelchair access – around gardens and principal floor of the Castle. **Internet:** www.blairquhan.co.uk **E-mail:** enquiries@blairquhan.co.uk

map 10 **B2**

BOWHILL

Selkirk, Borders TD7 5ET
Tel: 01750 22204 Fax: 01750 22204 (Buccleuch Heritage Trust)

Scottish Borders home of the Scotts of Buccleuch. Paintings by Guardi, Canaletto, Claude, Gainsborough, Reynolds and Raeburn. Superb furniture, porcelain. Monmouth, Sir Walter Scott, Queen Victoria relics. Victorian kitchen. Audiovisual. Theatre. Adventure Woodland. Nature trails. **Location:** 3 miles west of Selkirk, on A708. Edinburgh, Carlisle and Newcastle approx 1.5 hours by road. **Open:** House: 1–31 Jul, daily 1–4.30pm. Open by appointment at additional times for educational groups. Country park: 24 Apr–30 Aug daily except Fri, 12 noon–5pm. Open on Fridays in July with House. Last entry 45 mins before closing. **Admission:** House & Country Park: Adults £4.50, children £2, OAP and groups £4. Wheelchair users and children under 5 free. Country Park £2. **Refreshments:** Gift shop, tearoom.

map 13 H6

CRAIGDARROCH HOUSE

Moniaive, DG3 4JB Dumfries & Galloway, Scotland
Tel: 01848 200 202 (J. H. A Sykes)

William Adam house built for Annie Laurie. **Location:** 2 miles W of Moniaive, on B729. **Open:** All July, 2–4pm. **Admission:** £2. Please note: no public conveniences.

map 10 C3

HARELAW FARMHOUSE

Nr. Longniddry, East Lothian, Scotland
Tel: 01875 870 201 Fax: 01875 870 620
(The Wemyss & March Estates Management Co. Ltd)

Early 19th century 2-storey farmhouse built as an integral part of the steading. Dovecote over entrance arch. **Location:** Between Longniddry and Drem on B1377. **Open:** Exteriors only. By appointment, Wemyss & March Estates, Estate Office, Longniddry, EH32 0PY, East Lothian, Scotland.

map 13 H5

DALMENY HOUSE

South Queensferry, Edinburgh, Scotland, EH30 9TQ.
Tel: 0131 331 1888 Fax: 0131 331 1788 (Earl of Rosebery)

Home of the Earls of Rosebery, set in beautiful parkland on the Firth of Forth. Scotland's first gothic revival house. Rothschild Collection of 18th century French furniture and decorative art. Portraits by Reynolds, Gainsborough, Raeburn and Lawrence. Goya tapestries. Napoleonic Collection. **Location:** 7 miles N of Edinburgh, signposted off A90. **Buses:** St. Andrew Square Bus Station to Chapel Gate (1 mile from house). **Open to public:** July & August, Sun 1–5.30pm. Mon & Tues, 12–5.30pm. Special parties at other times by arrangement. **Admission:** Adults £3.80, children (10–16) £2, children under 10–free, OAPs £3.30, students £2.80, groups (min. 20) £3. Corporate events welcome throughout the year including product launches, dinners, outdoor activities. **Internet:** www.edinburgh.org

map 13 G5

GOSFORD HOUSE

Longniddry, EH32 0PY, East Lothian, Scotland Tel: 01875 870 201 Fax: 01875 870 620 (The Wemyss & March Estates Management Co. Ltd)

Robert Adam designed the Central block and Wings, which were later demolished. Two Wings rebuilt in 1890 by William Young. The 1800 roof was part burnt (military occupation) in 1940, but was restored in 1987. North Wing now roofless. South Wing is family home and contains famous Marble Hall (Staffordshire Alabaster). Parts of South Wing are open. Fine collection of paintings and works of art. Surrounding gardens redeveloping. Extensive policies, artificial ponds; geese and other wildfowl breeding. **Location:** On A198 between Aberlady and Longniddry. NW of Haddington. **Station(s):** Longniddry (2.5 miles). **Open:** June-July, Wed, Sat-Sun, 2–5pm. **Admission:** Adults £2.50, children 75p. **Refreshments:** Hotels in Aberlady.

map 13 H5

DRUMLANRIG CASTLE, GARDENS & COUNTRY PARK

Nr Thornhill, Dumfries & Galloway, DG3 4AQ
Tel: 01848 330248 (His Grace The Duke of Buccleuch & Queensberry K.T.)

Exquisite pink sandstone castle built by William Douglas, 1st Duke of Queensberry. 1679–91. Renowned art collection, including work by Holbein, Leonardo and Rembrandt. Versailles furniture, relics of Bonnie Prince Charlie. Douglas family historical exhibition. Working forge. Extensive gardens and woodlands superbly landscaped. Craft centre. Cycle museum. **Open:** Castle: 1 May–15 Aug inclusive. 7 days, weekdays 11–4pm, Sun 12–4pm. Limited tours 9, 10, 11 July. 16 Aug–30 Sept by appointment. Gardens and country park: 1 May–30 Sept inclusive. 7 days, 11–5pm. For further details telephone: 01848 330248. Countryside Service: 01848 331555. **Admission:** Adults: Castle and country park £6, country park £3. Child: Castle and country park £2. Senior citizens: Castle and country park £4, country park £3. Family (2 adults, 4 children) £14. Pre-booked parties (minimum 20) Normal time £4, outwith normal time £8. Wheelchairs free. **E-mail:** bre@drumlanrigcastle.org.uk

map 13 F7

LENNOXLOVE HOUSE

Haddington, East Lothian, Scotland, EH41 4NZ
Tel: 01620 823 720 Fax: 01620 825 112 (Duke of Hamilton)

Lennoxlove House, home of the Duke of Hamilton, dates from the 14th century and is set in 600 acres of woodland about 20 minutes drive from Edinburgh. The original Tower with its splendid Great Hall was known as Lethington Tower, but later renamed Lennoxlove after Frances Stewart, Duchess of Lennox, a favourite of Charles II. The house is home to the Hamilton Palace collection of furniture, paintings and porcelain as well as historic mementoes of Mary, Queen of Scots, including her silver casket, sapphire ring and a death mask. **Open: House & Grounds:** Easter Weekend-end Oct. Guided tours – Wed, (Most Saturdays – please check), Sun, 2–4.30pm. Private groups by arrangement. **Refreshments:** Garden Cafe serves morning coffee, lunch and afternoon tea. **E-mail:** lennoxlove@compuserve.com

map 13 H5

MANDERSTON

Duns, TD11 3PP, Berwickshire, Scotland.
Tel: 01361 883 450 Fax: 01361 882 010 (Lord & Lady Palmer)

Manderston, the home of Lord and Lady Palmer is an Edwardian mansion set in 56 acres of formal gardens (Scottish Borders).The only silver staircase in the world, insights into life at the turn of the century both 'upstairs' and 'downstairs'. Formal and woodland gardens, stables, Racing Room, Biscuit Tin Museum, Marble Dairy, lakeside walks. Tearoom serving cream teas on open days and gift shop. **Location:** 12 miles W of Berwick-upon-Tweed. **Open:** 13 May–26 Sept: Thurs & Sun, 2–5.30pm. Also Mons 31 May & 30 Aug 2–5.30pm. Group visits any time of year by appointment. **Admission:** Please phone 01361 883450 for details. **Refreshments:** Tearoom serving cream teas on open days. **Conferences:** Available as a corporate and location venue. **E-mail:** palmer@manderston .demon.co.uk **Internet:** http://www.manderston.demon.co.uk

map 13 J5/6

HOPETOUN HOUSE

South Queensferry, West Lothian, Scotland, EH30, 9SL
Tel: 0131 331 2451 Fax: 0131 319 1885 (Hopetoun House Preservation Trust)

Hopetoun House is a unique gem of Europe's architectural heritage and undoubtedly 'Scotland's Finest Stately Home' and in 1999 celebrates its 300th anniversary. Situated on the shores of the Firth of Forth, it is one of the most splendid examples of the work of Scottish architects Sir William Bruce and William Adam. The Bruce House has fine carving, wainscoting and ceiling painting, while in contrast the Adam interior, with opulent gilding and classical motifs reflect the aristocratic grandeur of the early 18th century. The House is set in 100 acres of rolling parkland including woodland walks, the Red Deer Park, the Spring Garden with a profusion of wild flowers, and numerous picturesque picnic spots. Panoramic views can be seen from the rooftop platform. **Location:** 2 miles from Forth Road Bridge. 10 miles from Edinburgh. **Open:** 2 Apr–26 Sept daily then weekends only in Oct 10–5.30pm. Last admission 4.30pm. **Admission:** Adults £5, children £2.80, OAPs/students/groups £4.50, family £15. **Refreshments:** Delicious meals and snacks served in the recently converted Stables Restaurant.

map 13
G5

210

LAURISTON CASTLE

Edinburgh, Lothian, Scotland
Tel: 0131 336 1921

A 1590s Scottish tower house with substantial additions from 1824 by the architect William Burn, the castle stands in 30 acres of parkland and tranquil gardens which enjoy a spectacular view across the Firth of Forth. The remarkably complete Edwardian interior was designed by the castle's last owner, William Robert Reid, who was the proprietor of the important Edinburgh cabinet making business, Morison & Company. Reid was both a connoisseur and a collector. Between 1903, when he purchased Lauriston and his death in 1919, he filled the castle with superb collections of eighteenth century Italian furniture (principally from Naples and Sicily), Derbyshire Blue John, Sheffield Plate, Caucasion carpets and rugs, clocks, porcelain, Mezzotint prints, tapestries, textiles and items of decorative art. There are also many items of fine furniture made by Morison & Co during the 1890s. The Castle is preserved exactly as left in 1926 at the death of Reid's widow, Margaret Johnston Reid, who gave it in Trust to the Nation. To enter Lauriston is to step across a threshold in time into the home of a wealthy and cultured family in the years before the Great War. **Located:** Cramond Road South, Davidson's Mains some three miles from the centre of Edinburgh. **Open:** April–October daily, except Friday, 11–1pm, 2–5pm, November–March, Saturday and Sunday only 2–4pm. Visit is by guided tour only. Tours take about 50 minutes. Last admission 40 minutes before each closing time. **Cost:** Admission charge (concessions available). Tel: 0131 336 2060. Free admission to grounds and car parking.

map 13
G5

PALACE OF HOLYROODHOUSE

Edinburgh EH8 8DX, Scotland
Tel: 0131 556 7371 (Her Majesty The Queen)

The Palace of Holyroodhouse, Buckingham Palace and Windsor Castle and are the Official residences of the Sovereign and are used by The Queen as both home and office. The Queen's personal standard flies when Her Majesty is in residence. Furnished with works of art from the Royal Collection, these buildings are used extensively by The Queen for State ceremonies, and official entertaining. They are opened to the public as much as these commitments allow. At the End of the Royal Mile stands the Palace of Holyroodhouse. Set against the spectacular backdrop of Arthur's Seat, Holyroodhouse has evolved from a medieval fortress into a baroque residence. The Royal Apartments, an extensive suite of rooms, epitomise the elegance and grandeur of this ancient and noble house, and contrast with the historic tower apartments of Mary, Queen of Scots' which are steeped in intrigue and sorrow. These intimate rooms where she lived on her return from France in 1561, witnessed the murder of David Rizzio, her favourite secretary, by her jealous husband, Lord Darnley and his accomplices. **Open:** Every day, except Good Friday, Christmas Day, Boxing Day and during Royal Visits. 9.30–5.15pm Apr–Oct, 9.30–3.45pm Nov–Mar. **Admission:** Adults £5.50, senior citizens (over 60) £3.90 and children (under 17) £2.70.

map 13
G5

MAYBOLE CASTLE

High Street, Maybole, Ayrshire KA19 7BX
Tel: 01655 883765 (The Trustees of The Seventh Marquess of Ailsa)

Historic 16th century town house of the Kennedy family. **Location:** High Street, Maybole on A77. **Open:** May–Sept. Sun, 3–4pm. At other times by appointment. **Admission:** Adult £2, concs. £1.

map 10
B2

 ## RAMMERSCALES

Lockerbie, Dumfriesshire, Scotland, DG11 1LD
Tel: 01387 811 988 Fax: 01387 810 940
(M. A. Bell Macdonald)

Georgian manor house dated 1760 set on high ground with fine views over Annandale. Pleasant policies and a typical walled garden of the period. There are Jacobite relics and links with Flora Macdonald retained in the family. There is also a collection of works by modern artists. **Location:** 5 miles W of Lockerbie (M6/A74). 2.5 miles S of Lochmaben on B7020. **Open:** Last week of July–first 3 weeks of August (except Sats) 2–5pm. **Admission:** Adults £5, children/OAPs £2.50.

map 10
D3

MELLERSTAIN HOUSE

Gordon, Berwickshire, Borders, Scotland, TD3 6LG
Tel: 01573 410 225 Fax: 01573 410636 (The Mellerstain Trust)

Scotland's famous Adam mansion. Beautifully decorated and furnished interiors. Terraced gardens and lake. Gift shop. **Location:** 9 miles NE of Melrose. 7 miles NW of Kelso. 37 miles SE of Edinburgh. **Open:** Easter (4 days), then May–Sept, daily except Sats. 12.30–5pm. (Last admission 4.30pm). Groups at other times by appointment. **Admission:** Adults £4.50, seniors £3.50, child £2.00. Groups (20+) £3.50 prior booking required. Apply Administrator. Free parking. **Refreshments:** Tearooms. **Events/Exhibitions:** 6 June: Vintage Car Rally. Permanent exhibition of Antique Dolls and Toys. Wheelchair access to principal rooms. **E-mail:** mellerstain.house@virgin.net **Internet:** http://muses.calligrafix.co.uk/mellerstain

map 13
J6

 ## PAXTON HOUSE & COUNTRY PARK

Paxton, Nr Berwick upon Tweed, Scottish Borders TD15 1SZ
Tel: 01289 386291 Fax: 01289 386660 (The Paxton Trust)

Award-winning 18th century Palladian Country House built in 1758 to the design of John and James Adam for a Prussian Princess. The largest Picture Gallery in a Scottish Country House, an outstation for the National Galleries of Scotland plus the greatest collection of Chippendale Furniture in Scotland. 80 acres of woodland, parkland, gardens and riverside walks include picnic areas, adventure playground, croquet, children's 'nature detective trails', highland cattle, shetland ponies and an observation hide from which you can watch the red squirrels. **Location:** Just 4 miles from the A1 Berwick upon Tweed bypass. **Open:** Daily 1 Apr–31 Oct, House 11.15–5pm, last tour 4.15pm. Shops, Tearoom and Exhibitions, 10–5pm, Grounds 10–Sunset. **Admission:** Adults £4.50, children £2.25.

map 13
K6

ROSSLYN CHAPEL

Rosslyn Chapel Trust, Roslin, Midlothian EH25 9PU
Tel: 0131 440 2159 Fax: 0131 440 1979 (The Earl of Rosslyn)

This most remarkable of churches was founded in 1446 by William St Clair, Prince of Orkney. Set in the woods of Roslin Glen and overlooking the River Esk, the Chapel is renowned for its richly carved interior and world famous apprentice pillar. Visitors to the chapel can enjoy a walk in some of Scotland's most romantic scenery. As Sir Walter Scott wrote: 'A morning of leisure can scarcely be anywhere more delightfully spent than in the woods of Rosslyn'. The chapel is available for weddings throughout the year. **Location:** OS Ref. NT275 630. 6m S of Edinburgh off A701. Follow B7006. **Open:** All year: Mon–Sat 10–5pm. Sun 12–4.45pm.

map 13
G5

ROYAL BOTANIC GARDEN

20a Inverleith Row, Edinburgh EH3 5LR
Tel: 0131 552 7171 Fax: 0131 552 0382

Scotland's premier garden. Discover the wonders of the plant kingdom in over 70 acres of beautifully landscaped grounds including the world famous Rock Garden, the Pringle Chinese Collection and the amazing Glasshouse Experience featuring Britain's tallest palmhouse. **Location:** Off A902, 1 mile north of the city centre. **Open:** Daily. January & November: 9.30–4pm. February & October: 9.30–5pm. March & September: 9.30–6pm. April–August: 9.30–7pm. **Admission:** Free, donations welcome.

SORN CASTLE

Sorn, Mauchline, Ayrshire.
Tel: Cluttons 01505 612 124 (R. G. McIntyre's Trust)

Dating from 14th century, the Castle stands on a cliff on the River Ayr. The 18th and 19th century additions are of the same pink sandstone quarried from the river banks. The woodlands and grounds were laid out in the 18th century with fine hardwood trees, rhododendrons and azaleas. The Castle is essentially a family home with fine examples of Scottish paintings and artefacts. **Location:** 4 miles E of Mauchline, on B743. **Open:** Castle: Sat 17 July–14 Aug, 2–5pm or by appointment. Grounds: 1 Apr–30 Oct. **Admission:** Adults £3.50.

map 12
E6

STEVENSON HOUSE

Haddington, East Lothian, Scotland, EH41 4PU. Tel: 0162 082 3217
(A. C. H. Dunlop, Brown Dunlop Country Houses Trust)

A family home for four centuries of charm and interest, dating from the 13th century when it belonged to the Cistercian Nunnery at Haddington, but partially destroyed on several occasions and finally made uninhabitable in 1544. Restored about 1560, the present house dates mainly from this period, with later additions in the 18th century. Fine furniture, pictures, etc. **Location:** 20 miles from Edinburgh, 1.5 miles from A1, 2 miles from Haddington. (See Historic House direction signs on A1 and in Haddington). **Open:** 3 Jul–1 Aug daily except Fri. Guided tour (1 hour) at 3pm. **Admission:** £2.50. Other times by arrangement only. Gardens open daily Apr–Oct, entrance £1 payable into box. **Refreshments:** Appointment parties coffees and teas by arrangement at Stevenson. Car parking. Suitable for wheelchairs in garden only.

map 13
H5

TRAQUAIR HOUSE

Innerleithen, Peeblesshire, Scotland EH44 6PW
Tel: 01896 830 323 Fax: 01896 830 639 (Mrs F. Maxwell Stuart)

Traquair is Scotland's oldest inhabited and most romantic house, spanning over 1000 years of Scottish history. Once a pleasure ground for Scottish kings in times of peace, then a refuge of Catholic priests in times of terror, the Stuarts of Traquair supported Mary, Queen of Scots and the Jacobite cause without counting the cost. Imprisoned, tried and isolated for their beliefs, their home, untouched by time, reflects the tranquillity of their family life. In one of the 'modern' wings (completed in 1680) visitors can also see an 18th century working brewery, which was resurrected by the 20th Laird and now produces the world renowned Traquair House Ale. In the grounds there is also a maze, craft workshops, 1745 Cottage Restaurant and extensive woodland walks. **Open:** 3 April–30 Sept, daily. Oct, Fri–Sun only. 12.30–5.30pm. Jun–Aug, 10.30–5.30pm. **E-mail:** traquair.house @scotborders.co.uk **Website:** www.traquair.co.uk

map 13
H6

THIRLESTANE CASTLE

Lauder, Berwickshire, Scottish Borders TD2 6RU
Tel: 01578 722 430 Fax: 01578 722 761 (Thirlestane Castle Trust)

One of the oldest and finest castles in Scotland, Thirlestane was the seat of the Earls and Duke of Lauderdale. It has unsurpassed 17th century ceilings, a restored picture collection, Maitland family treasures, historic toys and a country life exhibition. Woodland picnic tables, tearoom and gift shop. **Location:** Off A68 at Lauder, 28 miles south of Edinburgh. **Open:** 2–9 Apr inc. 11–5pm, 1 May–31 Oct Daily except Sat 11–5pm. Last admission 4.15pm each open day. **Admission:** Adults £4.50. Family (parents and own school age children) £11. Grounds only £1.50. Party discounts available, also booked tours at other times by arrangement. Free parking. Visit us on the World Wide Web at www.great–houses–scotland.co.uk **E-mail:** thirlestane@great–houses–scotland.co.uk

map 13
H6

BALCARRES

Colinsburgh, Fife, Scotland
Tel: 01333 340 206 (Balcarres Trust)

16th century house with 19th century additions by Burn and Bryce. Woodland and terraced garden. **Location:** ½ mile N of Colinsburgh. **Open:** Woodlands and Lower Garden: 8–24 Feb & 29 Mar–19 June, daily except Suns. West Garden: 7–19 Jun, daily except Suns. 2–5pm. House not open except by written appointment and 19 Apr–4 May **Admission:** Gardens only – Adults £2.50, children £1.50. House – £4.50. Car park. Suitable for disabled persons, no wheelchairs provided.

map 13
H4

BOLFRACKS GARDEN

Aberfeldy, Perthshire PH15 2EX
Tel: 01887 820207 (M. J. D. Hutchison)

The Garden, approximately four acres, overlooks the upper Tay Valley with splendid views over the river to the hills beyond. A walled garden of an acre contains a wide variety of flowering trees, shrubs and perennials including a good collection of old fashioned rambler and shrub roses. A less formal garden with a burn and lots of peat wall arrangements contains very many ericaceous plants including rhododendrons particularly dwarf, heaths, dwarf conifers. Primulas, moeonopisis, celmisias and gentians all do well. Masses of bulbs in spring and good autumn colour. **Open:** Apr–Oct, 10–6pm. **Admission** £2.50.

map 13
F3

BLAIR CASTLE

Blair Atholl, Pitlochry, Perthshire PH18 5TI Scotland.
Tel: 01796 481 207 Fax: 01796 481 487

Scotland's most visited historic house is home of the Atholl Highlanders, Britain's only private army. The Castle boasts 32 fascinating rooms containing a unique collection of beautiful furniture, fine paintings, arms and armour, china, costumes, lace and other treasures. Explore extensive grounds with walks, nature trails, deer park and enjoy the rare wildlife that exists in its natural habitat. 18th century walled garden restoration project. **Location:** 8 miles NW of Pitlochry, off A9. **Station:** Blair Atholl (half a mile). **Open:** Castle & Grounds: 1 Apr–29 Oct, daily 10–6pm. Last admission 5pm. **Admission:** Castle: Adults £6, children £4, OAP's £5. Grounds £2, children £1. Family tickets. Reduced rates and guided tours for parties by prior arrangements.

map 13
F2

CASTLE MENZIES

Weem, Aberfeldy, PH15 2JD, Perthshire, Scotland.
Tel: 01887 820 982 (Menzies Charitable Trust)

Magnificent example of a 16th century 'Z' plan fortified house, seat of Chiefs of Clan Menzies for over 400 years and now nearing completion of its restoration from an empty ruin. It was involved in the turbulent history of the Central Highlands. 'Bonnie Prince Charlie' was given hospitality here on his way north to Culloden in 1746. Visitors can explore the whole of the 16th century building, together with part of the 19th century addition. Small clan museum and gift shop. **Location:** 1.5 miles from Aberfeldy, on B846. **Open:** 1 Apr–16 Oct 1999, Mon–Sat, 10.30–5pm. Sun, 2–5pm. Last admission 4.30pm. **Admission:** Adult £3, OAPs £2.50, children £1.50 (reduction for groups). **Refreshments:** Tearoom.

map 13
F3

BRANKLYN GARDEN

Dundee Road, Perth PH2 7BB
Tel: 01738 625535 (The National Trust for Scotland)

Small but magnificent garden with an impressive collection of rare and unusual plants. Among the most breathtaking is the Himalayan blue poppy, *Meconopsis x sheldonii*. There is a rock garden with purple maple and the rare golden *Cedrus*. Seasonal highlights in May and June are the alpines and rhododendrons and in autumn the fiery red *Acer palmatum*. **Location:** On A85 at 116 Dundee Road, Perth. **Open:** Daily, 9.30–Sunset. 1 Mar–31 Oct. **Admission:** Adult £2.50, concession: £1.70, Adult group of 18 or more £2. Family groups £6.70.

DRUMMOND CASTLE GARDENS

Muthill Crieff, Tayside, Scotland, PH5 2AA
Tel: 01764 681 257/433 Fax: 01764 681 550

The gardens of Drummond Castle, first laid out in the early 17th century by John Drummond, 2nd Earl of Perth, are said to be among the finest formal gardens in Europe. A spectacular view can be obtained from the upper terrace, overlooking a magnificent example of an early Victorian parterre in the form of a St. Andrew's Cross. The gardens you see today were renewed by Phyllis Astor in the early 1950's, preserving features such as the ancient yew hedges and the copper beech trees planted by Queen Victoria to commemorate her visit in 1842. The multi-faceted sundial by John Mylne, Master Mason to Charles I, has been the centrepiece since 1630. The gardens recently featured in United Artists 'Rob Roy'. **Location:** Entrance 2 miles S of Crieff, on A822 Muthill Road. **Open:** May–Oct & Easter Weekend, daily, 2–6pm. (Last admission 5pm). **Admission:** Adults £3, children £1.50, OAPs £2.

map 13
F4

SCONE PALACE

Scone, Perth, PH2 6BD, Perthshire.
Tel: 01738 552300 (The Earl of Mansfield) Fax: 01738 552588

Situated 2 miles outside Perth, Scone was the ancient crowning place of the Kings of Scotland and the home of the Stone of Destiny. The present Palace was remodelled in the early nineteenth century, using the structure of the 1580 Palace and remains the home of the Earl and Countess of Mansfield. The State Rooms house unique collections of ivories, paintings, clocks, furniture, porcelain and Vernis Martin. The grounds contain magnificent collections of shrubs with woodland walks through the famed pinetum; many species were first introduced by David Douglas (of Douglas Fir fame). The magnificence of the Palace and its contents are complemented by an attractive gift shop, restaurants and adventure playground. New for 1998 is the Murray Star Tartan Maze. Scone is ideal for any family visit and can also provide a exciting venue for corporate and incentive hospitality, both in the Palace or outside in the grounds or Parklands running down to the River Tay. **Open:** 2 Apr–25 Oct, 9.30–5.15pm (last admission 4.45pm). **Admission:** Adults £5.40, children £3.20, OAPs £4.60, family £16.50. Groups: Adults £4.90, children £2.70, OAPs £4.20. **E-mail:** Sconepalace@cqm.co.uk

map 13
G3

 ## GLAMIS CASTLE

Glamis, Angus, Scotland, DO8 1RJ
Tel: 01307 840 393 Fax: 01307 840 733

Family home of the Earls of Strathmore and Kinghorne and a royal residence since 1372. Childhood home of H.M. Queen Elizabeth, The Queen Mother and the legendary setting of Shakespeare's play 'Macbeth'. Five-storey L-shaped tower block dating from 15th century, remodelled in 1606, containing magnificent rooms with wide range of historic pictures, furniture and porcelain, etc. **Location:** Glamis, 6 miles W of Forfar, A94. **Open:** 27 Mar–31 Oct, daily 10.30–5.30pm (Jul & Aug open from 10am). Last admission 4.45pm **Admission:** Adults £5.40, children (5–16) £2.80, OAPs £4.20, family £14.50. Grounds only: Adults £2.50, children/OAP £1.40. Party rates (min 20), adult £4.90, OAP £3.70, child £2.50. **Facilities:** Licensed self-service restaurant, seating for 96. Picnic area, four shops, magnificent grounds, garden and nature trail. Ample parking.

 map 13 H3

  ## STOBHALL

Guildtown, Perthshire, Scotland, (Earl of Perth)

Gardens and policies. Chapel with 17th century painted ceiling. **Location:** 8 miles N of Perth on A93. **Open:** Mid May–mid June, 1–5pm. **Admission:** Adults £2, children £1.

 map 13 G3

YESTER HOUSE

Gifford, East Lothian EH41 4JH
Tel: 01620 810241 Fax: 01620 810650 (Francis Menotti)

Splendid neoclassical House designed by James Smith, set on the edge of the Lammermuir Hills. For centuries the seat of the Marquesses of Tweedale. Fine 18th century interiors by William and Robert Adam, including the Great Saloon which is a perfect example of their style. Formal gardens were laid out in the 17th century and provide a beautiful natural setting to this day. The House has been extensively restored and sumptuously furnished by the current owner. **Open:** House and Chapel: 30 & 31 Oct, 2–5pm. **Admission:** House & Garden: Adults £4, children £1.50, OAPs £2.50. Garden only £1. Chapel only £1.

map 13 H5

BRAEMAR CASTLE

Braemar, Grampian, AB35 5XR, Scotland.
Tel/Fax:013397 41219 (Braemer Castle)

Built in 1628 by the Earl of Mar. Attacked and burned by the celebrated Black Colonel (John Farquharson of Inverey) in 1689. Repaired by the government and garrisoned with English troops after the rising of 1745. Later transformed by the Farquharsons of Invercauld, who had purchased it in 1732, into a fully furnished private residence of unusual charm. L-plan castle of fairy tale proportions, with round central tower and spiral staircase. Barrel-vaulted ceilings, massive iron 'Yett' and underground pit (prison). Remarkable star-shaped defensive curtain wall. Much valuable furniture, paintings and items of Scottish historical interest. **Location:** Half a mile NE of Braemar on A93. **Open:** Easter-late Oct, daily (except Fri), 10–6pm. **Admission:** Adults £2.50, children £1. Groups/OAPs/students £2. Free car and bus park. **E-mail:** invercauld@aol.com

 map 4 C5

CAWDOR CASTLE

Nairn, Scotland, IV12 5RD (The Dowager Countess Cawdor)
Tel: 01667 404615 Fax: 01667 404674

The most romantic castle in the Highlands. The 14th century keep, fortified in the 15th century and impressive additions, mainly 17th century, form a massive fortress. Gardens, nature trails and splendid grounds. Shakespearean memories of Macbeth. **Location:** S of Nairn, on B9090 between Inverness and Nairn. **Station(s):** Nairn (5m) and Inverness (14m). **Open:** 1 May–10 Oct, daily, 10–5.30pm. Last admission 5pm. **Admission:** Adults £5.40, children (5–15) £2.80, OAPs & disabled £4.40. Groups: Adult (20+) £4.90, children (5–15, 20+) £2.40, family (2 adults + up to 5 children) £14.50. Gardens, grounds and nature trails only: £2.80. **Refreshments:** Licensed restaurant, snack bar. Gift shop, bookshop and wool shop. Picnic area, 9-hole golf course and nature trails. No dogs allowed in Castle or Grounds. **E-mail:** cawdor.castle@btinternet.com

 map 15 F5

 CRAIGSTON CASTLE

Turriff AB5 7PX, Aberdeenshire
Tel: 01888 551228 (William Pratesi Urquhart of Craigston)

Built between 1604–1607 by John Urquhart, Craigston Castle is still owned and lived in, by the Urquhart family. Few changes have been made to the castle's exterior of which the main feature is the sculptured balcony, unique in Scottish architecture. The interior decoration dates mainly from the 19th century but features unique carved wooden panels from the 17th century. The drawing room contains mirrors from the Palace of Versailles. Open by appointment for parties: contact Mrs Morrison on 01888 551640. **Open:** 31 July–15 Aug 1999 (excl Mon–Tues) and 21–29 Aug (excl Mon–Tues). **Admission:** Adults £3, OAPs £2, children £1.

DOCHFOUR GARDENS

Dochfour, Inverness IV3 8GY
Tel: 01463 861218 Fax: 01463 861366 (Dochfour Estate)

Victorian garden near Inverness, with grassed terraces and panoramic views over Loch Dochfour. Magnificent specimen trees, naturalised daffodils, rhododendrons and azaleas, water garden, extensive yew hedges, walled kitchen garden. 6 miles SW of Inverness on A82 to Fort William. **Open:** Mon–Fri Apr–Sept 10–5pm Garden Walk. **Admission:** £1.50. Parking free. HOUSE NOT OPEN. Coaches by prior arrangement only.

THE DOUNE OF ROTHIEMURCHUS

Rothiemurchus Estate, By Aviemore, Inverness-shire PH22 1QH.
Tel: 01479 812345 Fax: 01479 811778 (J.P. Grant of Rothiemurchus)

The family home of The Grants of Rothiemurchus was nearly lost as a ruin and has been under an ambitious repair programme since 1975. This exciting project may be visited on selected Mondays throughout the year. Book with the Information Desk for a longer 2 hour "Highland Lady" tour which explores the haunts of Elizabeth Grant of Rothiemurchus, born 1797, author of "Memoirs of a Highland Lady" who vividly described the Doune and its surroundings from the memories of her childhood. **Location:** 2 m S of Aviemore on E bank of Spey river. **Open:** Grounds: May-Aug, Mon 10–12.30pm and 2–4.30pm. Also first Monday of the month in winter. **Admission:** Doune Grounds: £1. Guided Highland Lady Tour: £5, min. charge of £20. Booking essential. **E-mail:** rothie@enterprise.net **Internet:** www.aviemore.co.uk/rothiemurchus.htm

 # DUFF HOUSE COUNTRY HOUSE GALLERY

Banff, Banffshire, Scotland, AB45 3SX.
Tel: 01261 818 181 Fax: 01261 818 900

Duff House is one of the most imposing and palatial country houses in Scotland, with a classical façade and a grand staircase leading to the main entrance. It remained in the hands of the Duffs, Dukes of Fife, until 1906 when the family presented the house and park to Banff and Macduff, consigning its contents to the saleroom. Set in acres of parkland, by the banks of River Deveron, Duff House is one of the glories of the North East. Designed by William Adam for William Duff (1st Earl Fife), it is situated between the Royal burgh of Banff and the fishing port of Macduff and is a splendid example of Scottish baroque architecture. Duff House is now the premier outstation of the National Galleries of Scotland. **Location:** Banff. 47 miles NE of Aberdeen on A947. **Open:** 1 Apr–31 Oct, daily, 11–5pm. 1 Nov–31 Mar, Thur–Sun, 11–4pm. **Admission:** Adults £3, concessions £2. Free admission to shop, tearoom, grounds and woodland walks. **Refreshments:** Tearoom. **E-mail:** cjb@duffhouse.demon.co.uk

DUNROBIN CASTLE

Golspie, Sutherland KW10 6SF Scotland
Tel: 01408 633177 Fax: 01408 634081 (The Sutherland Trust)

Dunrobin Castle is the most northerly of Scotland's Great Castles and seat of the Earls of Sutherland (Earldom created c.1235). The keep dates from c.1300 and there are additions from the 17–19th centuries, the biggest being in 1845 when the castle was remodelled by Sir Charles Barry, who had just completed the Houses of Parliament. A serious fire in 1915 caused a lot of damage and gave Sir Robert Lorimer a chance to re-design and re-decorate all the major rooms. The Castle is filled with fine furniture, superb paintings, fine china and family memorabilia. The rooms and corridors are decorated with flowers from the garden which is overlooked by most of them. The Dining room contains the outstanding family silver. The whole building has a friendly, 'lived in' atmosphere. The beautiful gardens were laid out by Barry at the same time as he re-modelled the castle and are of French formal design. In recent years, they have been improved and restored and are one of the few remaining formal gardens in Scotland. The castle and gardens are set next to the sea and there are lovely walks along the beach and the surrounding woodlands. The garden contains an eccentric museum, unlike anything else in the UK. This must be seen, even by those who disapprove of the activities it displays! Regular falconry displays also in the garden. **Location:** OS Ref: NC850 010.50m N of Inverness on A9. 1m NE of Golspie. **Open:** 1 Apr–31 May & 1–15 Oct: Mon–Sat 10.30–4.30pm. Sun 12–4.30pm. Last entry 4pm. 1 Jun–30 Sept; Mon–Sat 10.30–5.30pm. Sun, 12–5.30pm. Last entry 5pm. **Admission:** Adult £5.50, child £4, OAP £4. Groups–Adult £5, child £4, OAP £4. Family (2 adults and 2 children) £16. Open all year round for pre-booked groups. **Refreshments:** Tearooms seating 90. **Events**: 15 Aug Vintage Car Rally. A variety of evening and lunchtime functions can be arranged on request. All functions are accompanied by good quality local music.

map 13
F3

Scottish THISTLE AWARDS 1997 FINALIST

SKYE'S MOST FAMOUS LANDMARK

Romantic & HISTORIC

DUNVEGAN CASTLE

WELCOME TO THE ISLE OF SKYE

THE HOME OF THE CHIEFS OF MACLEOD FOR NEARLY 800 YEARS

Any visit to this enchanted Isle must be deemed incomplete without savouring the wealth of history offered by Dunvegan Castle.

LICENSED RESTAURANT

TWO CRAFT AND SOUVENIR SHOPS

CASTLE WATER GARDENS

AUDIO-VISUAL THEATRE

PEDIGREE HIGHLAND CATTLE FOLD

CLAN EXHIBITION

ITEMS BELONGING TO BONNIE PRINCE CHARLIE

LOCH BOAT TRIPS

FAMOUS SEAL COLONY

ST KILDA CONNECTION WOOLLEN SHOP

MACLEOD OF DUNVEGAN QUALITY CLOTHES AND KILT SHOP

OPENING TIMES
22nd March - 31st October 1999
Castle, Gardens, Craft Shop & Restaurant Monday - Sunday 10.00am - 5.30pm (last entry into Castle - 5.00pm)
Telephone: 01470 521206 Website: http://www.dunvegancastle.com

INVERARAY CASTLE

Cherry Park, Inveraray, Argyll, Scotland, PA32 8XE
Tel: 01499 302 203 Fax: 01499 302 421
(Home of the Duke and Duchess of Argyll)

Since the early 15th century Inveraray Castle has been the Headquarters of the Clan Campbell. The present Castle was built in the third quarter of the 18th century by Roger Morris and Robert Mylne. The Great Hall and Armoury, the State Rooms, tapestries, pictures and the 18th century furniture and Old Kitchen are shown. Those interested in Campbell Genealogy and History will find a visit to The Campbell Room especially enjoyable. **Location:** ¼ mile NE of Inveraray by Loch Fyne. 61 miles NW of Glasgow. **Open:** 3 Apr–10 Oct.

map 12 D4

MOUNT STUART HOUSE & GARDENS

Mount Stuart, Isle of Bute, Scotland, PA20 9LR
Tel: 01700 503877 Fax: 01700 505313 Internet: www.mountstuart.com

Award winning Mount Stuart, one of Britain's most spectacular High Victorian Gothic houses, is the magnificent architectural fantasy of the 3rd Marquess of Bute (1847–1900) and the Scottish architect Robert Rowand Anderson. The scale and ambition of Mount Stuart is equalled only by Bute's collaboration with William Burges to restore Cardiff Castle and Castell Coch. The profusion of astrological designs, stained glass and marble is breathtaking, and all combine to envelop the visitor in the mystique and history of the house. Fabulous interiors and architectural detail. Set in 300 acres of stunning woodlands, mature Victorian pinetum, arboretum and exotic gardens. Facilities include shop, tearoom, adventure play and picnic areas, audio-visual, cycle hire, assisted wheelchair access, guided tours of house and gardens. Mount Stuart is easily accessible and can be reached by frequent ferry service from Wemyss Bay, Renfrewshire or Colintraive in Argyll. Regular bus service from Rothesay to Mount Stuart. **Open:** Easter and 1 May–mid October, daily except Tue & Thurs. Gardens: 10–5pm, House: 11–4.30pm. **Admission:** Adults: £6, Child: £2.50, Family: £15, Season: £15. Senior Citizen/Student/Group rates given. **Internet:** www.mountstuart.com

map 12 D6

CALLENDAR HOUSE

Callendar Park, Falkirk, Scotland, FK1 1YR
Tel: 01324 503 770 (Falkirk Council)

Imposing mansion within attractive parkland with a 900 year history. Facilities include a working kitchen of 1825 where costumed interpreters carry out daily chores, including cooking based on 1820's recipes. **Exhibition area:** 'Story of Callendar House', plus two temporary galleries, with regularly changing exhibitions. Permanent Exhibition 'William Forbes Falkirk' with working 1820's general store, clockmaker and printer. There is also a history research centre, gift shop and the Georgian tea shop at the Stables. **Location:** E of Falkirk town centre, on A803 Callendar Road. **Open:** Jan–Dec: Mon–Sat, 10–5pm. Apr–Sept: Sun, 2–5pm. Open all public hols. **Admission:** Adults £2.50, children £1, OAPs £1. Last admission 4pm.

map 13 F5

FASQUE

Fettercairn, Laurencekirk, AB30 1DN, Kincardineshire,
Tel: 01561 340 202/ 340 569 Fax: 01561 340 569(Charles Gladstone)

Fasque is a spectacular example of a Victorian 'Upstairs-Downstairs' stately home. Bought by Sir John Gladstone in 1829, it was home to William Gladstone, four times Prime Minister, for much of his life. In front of the house red deer roam in the park and behind the hills dramatically towards the Highlands. Inside, very little has changed since Sir John's days. Fasque is not a museum, bur rather an unspoilt old family home. Visit the kitchen, laundry, bakery, knives hall and buttery. You'll find a wealth of domestic articles from a bygone age. Climb the famous double cantilever staircase and wander through the magnificent drawing room, library and bedrooms. Explore a Victorian gamekeeper's hut, complete with man trap, or discover our exhibition of William Gladstone memorabilia. Groups and Coach Parties welcome.

map 13 J2

The National Trust for Scotland

The National Trust for Scotland

Please note that opening times are subject to change. For current details please telephone 0131 226 5922

ALLOA TOWER, Alloa, Clackmannanshire. Open: Good Fri–Easter Mon and 1 May–30 Sep, daily 1.30–5.30.

ANGUS FOLK MUSEUM, Kirkwynd, Glamis, Forfar, Angus DD8 1RT. Open: Good Fri–Easter Mon and 1 May–30 Sep, daily 11–5.

ARDUAINE GARDEN, Arduaine, By Oban, Argyll PA34 4XQ. Open: all year, daily 9.30–sunset.

BACHELORS' CLUB, Sandgate Street, Tarbolton KA5 5RB. Open: Good Fri–30 Sep, daily 11.30–5; weekends in Oct, 11.30–5

BANNOCKBURN, Glasgow Road, Stirling FK7 0LJ. Open: site, all year, daily. Heritage Centre and shop, 1–31 Mar and 1 Nov–23 Dec, daily 11–3; 1 Apr–31 Oct, daily 10–5.30.

BARRIE'S BIRTHPLACE, 9 Brechin Road, Kirriemuir, Angus DD8 4BX. Open: Good Fri–Easter Mon and 1 May–30 Sep, Mon–Sat 11–5.30 Sun 1.30–5.30.

BARRY MILL, Barry, Carnoustie, Angus DD7 7RJ. Open: Good Fri–Easter Mon and 1 May–30 Sep, daily 11–5.

BRANKLYN GARDEN, 116 Dundee Road, Perth PH2 7BB. Open: 1 Mar–31 Oct, daily 9.30–sunset.

BRODICK CASTLE AND GOATFELL, Isle of Arran, KA27 8HY. Open: castle, 1 Apr (or Good Fri if earlier)–31 Oct, daily 11.30–5.

BRODIE CASTLE, Brodie, Forres IV36 0TE. Open: castle, 1 Apr (or Good Fri if earlier)–30 Sep, Mon–Sat 11–5.30, Sun 1.30–5.30.

BROUGHTON HOUSE AND GARDEN, 12 High Street, Kirkcudbright DG6 4JX. Open: 1 Apr (or Good Fri if earlier)–31 Oct, daily 1–5.30.

CARLYLE'S BIRTHPLACE, The Arched House, Ecclefechan, Lockerbie DG11 3DG. Open: 1 May–30 Sep, Fri–Mon 1.30–5.30.

CASTLE FRASER, Sauchen, Inverurie AB51 7LD. Open: castle, Good Fri–Easter Mon, 1 May–30 Jun and 1–30 Sep, daily 1.30–5.30; 1 Jul–31 Aug, daily 11–5.30; weekends in Oct, 1.30–5.30 (last admission 4.45).

CRATHES CASTLE AND GARDEN, Banchory AB31 3QJ. Open: castle, Visitor Centre, shop and licensed restaurant, 1 Apr (or Good Fri if earlier)–31 Oct, daily 11–5.30 (last admission–castle 4.45).

CULLODEN, NTS Visitor Centre, Culloden Moor, Inverness IV1 2ED.

Open: site, all year, daily. Visitor Centre, 1 Feb–31 Mar and 1 Nov–30 Dec (except 25/26 Dec), daily 10–4; 1 Apr–31 Oct, daily 9–6.

CULROSS, Fife, off A985, 12M West of Forth Road Bridge. Open: Palace, 1 Apr (or Good Fri if earlier)–30 Sep, daily 11–5 (last admission 4). Town House and Study, same dates, 1.30–5 and weekends in Oct, 11–5.

CULZEAN CASTLE AND COUNTRY PARK, Maybole KA19 8LE. Open: castle, Visitor Centre, licensed restaurant and shops, 1 Apr (or Good Fri if earlier)–31 Oct, daily 10.30–5.30 (last admission 5)

DRUM CASTLE, Drumoak, By Banchory AB31 3EY. Open : Good Fri–Easter Mon and 1 May–30 Sep, daily 1.30–5.30; weekends in Oct, 1.30–5.30 (last admission 4.45). Garden, same dates, daily 10–6. Grounds, all year, daily 9.30–sunset.

FALKLAND PALACE, GARDEN AND TOWN HALL, Falkland, Cupar, Fife KY15 7BU. Open: palace and garden, 1 Apr (or Good Fri if earlier)–31 Oct, Mon–Sat 11–5.30, Sun 1.30–5.30 (last admission–palace 4.30,–garden 5).

FYVIE CASTLE, Fyvie, Turriff AB53 8JS. Open: castle, 1 Apr (or Good Fri if earlier)–30 Jun and 1–30 Sep, daily 1.30–5.30; 1 Jul–31 Aug daily 11–5.30; weekends in Oct, 1.30–5.30 .

THE GEORGIAN HOUSE, 7 Charlotte Square, Edinburgh EH2 4DR. Open: 1 Apr (or Good Fri if earlier)–31 Oct, Mon–Sat 10–5, Sun 2–5

GLADSTONE'S LAND, 477B Lawnmarket, Edinburgh EH1 2NT. Open: 1 Apr (or Good Fri if earlier)–31 Oct, Mon–Sat 10–5, Sun 2–5

GLENCOE, NTS Visitor Centre, Glencoe, Ballachulish PA39 4HX. Open: site, all year, daily. Visitor Centre and snack-bar, 1 Apr (or Good Fri if earlier) to 18 May and 1 Sep–31 Oct, daily 10–5; 19 May–31 Aug, daily 9.30–5.30 .

GLENFINNAN MONUMENT, NTS Information Centre, Glenfinnan PH37 4LT. Open: site, all year, daily. Visitor Centre and snack-bar, 1 Apr (or Good Fri if earlier)–18 May and 1 Sep–31 Oct, daily 10–1 and 2–5; 19 May–31 Aug, daily 9.30–6 (snack-bar 10–6).

GREENBANK GARDEN, Flenders Road, Clarkston, Glasgow G76 8RB. Open: all year, daily 9.30–sunset, except 25/26 Dec and 1/2 Jan. Shop and tearoom, 1 Apr (or Good Fri if earlier)–31 Oct, daily 11–5; 1 Nov–31 Mar, Sat/Sun 2–4. House open 1 Apr–31 Oct, Suns only 2–4 and during special events (subject–functions in progress). No dogs in garden, please.

HADDO HOUSE, Ellon, Aberdeenshire AB41 0ER. Open: house, Good Fri–Easter Mon and 1 May–30 Sep, daily 1.30–5.30; weekends in Oct, 1.30–5.30 (last admission 4.45); shop and Stables.

THE HILL HOUSE, Upper Colquhoun Street, Helensburgh G84 9AJ. Open 1 Apr (or Good Fri if earlier)–31 Oct, daily 1.30–5.30 (last admission 5); tearoom, 1.30–4.30.

HILL OF TARVIT MANSIONHOUSE, Cupar, Fife KY15 5PB. Open: house, Good Fri–Easter Mon and 1 May–30 Sep, daily 1.30–5.30; weekends in Oct, 1.30–5.30 (last admission 4.45). Garden and grounds, all year, daily 9.30–sunset.

HOUSE OF THE BINNS, Linlithgow, West Lothian EH49 7NA. Open: house, 1 May–30 Sep, daily except Fri, 1.30–5.30 (last admission 5). Parkland, 1 Apr–31 Oct, daily 9.30–7; 1 Nov–31 Mar, daily 9.30–4.

HOUSE OF DUN, Montrose, Angus DD10 9LQ. Open: house and shop, Good Fri–Easter Mon and 1 May–30 Sep, daily 1.30–5.30; weekends in Oct, 1.30–5.30 (last admission 5).

HUGH MILLER'S COTTAGE, Cromarty, IV11 8XA. Open: 1 May–30 Sep, Mon–Sat 10–1 and 2–5.30, Sun 2–5.30.

INVEREWE GARDEN, Poolewe IV22 2LQ. Open: garden, 15 March–31 Oct, daily 9.30am–9pm; 1 Nov–14 Mar, daily 9.30–5. Visitor Centre and shop, 15 Mar–31 Oct, daily 9.30–5.30. Licensed restaurant, same dates, daily 10–5. Guided garden walks, 15 Mar–30 Sep, Mon–Fri at 1.30. No dogs in garden please. No shaded car parking.

KELLIE CASTLE AND GARDEN, Pittenweem, Fife KKY10 2RF. Open castle, Good Fri–Easter Mon and 1 May–30 Sep, daily 1.30–5.30; weekends in Oct, 1.30–5.30 (last admission 4.45). Garden and grounds, all year, daily 9.30–sunset. .

KILLIECRANKIE, NTS Visitor Centre, Killiecrankie, Pitlochry PH16 5LG. Open: site, all year, daily. Visitor Centre, shop and snack-bar, 1 Apr (or Good Fri if earlier)–31 Oct, daily 10–5.30.

LEITH HALL AND GARDEN, Huntly AB54 4NQ. Open: house and tearoom, Good Fri–Easter Mon and 1 May–30 Sep, daily 1.30–5.30; weekends in Oct, 1.30–5.30 (last admission 4.45). Garden and grounds all year, daily 9.30–sunset.

PITMEDDEN GARDEN, Ellon AB41 0PD. Open: garden, Visitor Centre, museum, tearoom, grounds and other facilities, 1 May–30 Sep, daily 10–5.30 (last admission 5).

PRESTON MILL AND PHANTASSIE DOOCOT, East Linton, East Lothian, EH40 3DS. Open: Good Fri–Easter Mon, 1 May–30 Sep, Mon–Sat 11–1 and 2–5, Sun 1.30–5; weekends in Oct, 1.30–4.

PRIORWOOD GARDEN AND DRIED FLOWER SHOP, Melrose TD6 9PX. Open: 1 Apr (or Good Fri if earlier)–30 Sep, Mon–Sat 10–5.30, Sun 1.30–5.30; 1 Oct–24 Dec, Mon–Sat 10–4, Sun 1.30–4.

ROBERT SMAIL'S PRINTING WORKS, 7/9 High Street, Innerleithen EH44 6HA. Open: Good Fri–Easter Mon and 1 May–30 Sep, Mon–Sat 10–1 and 2–5, Sun 2–5; weekends in Oct, Sat 10–1 and 2–5, Sun 2–5 (last admission 45 mins before closing, morning and afternoon).

SOUTER JOHNNIE'S COTTAGE, Main Road, Kirkoswald KA19 8HY. Open: Good Fri–30 Sept, daily 11.30–5; weekends in Oct, 11.30–5 (last admission 4.30).

THE TENEMENT HOUSE, 145 Buccleuch Street, Glasgow G3 6QN. Open 1 Mar–31 Oct, daily 2–5 (last admission 4.30) Very restricted parking.

THREAVE GARDEN AND ESTATE, Castle Douglas DG7 1RX. Open: estate and garden, all year, daily 9.30–sunset. Walled garden and glasshouses, all year, daily 9.30–5.

TORRIDON, N of A896, 9M SW of Kinlochewe. Open: Countryside Centre, 1 May–30 Sep, Mon–Sat 10–5, Sun 2–5. Estate, Deer Park and Deer Museum (unstaffed), all year, daily.

WEAVER'S COTTAGE, The Cross, Kilbarchan PA10 2JG. Open: Good Fri–30 Sep, daily 1.30–5.30; weekends in Oct, 1.30–5.30

Ireland

Ireland is fast becoming one of most popular places to visit. For such a tiny island it has a vast history steeped in romanticism, valour, poverty, poetry and music.

From the stark craggy cliffs on the west coast of Galway to the calm running waters of the River Liffey in Dublin, Ireland offers contrasting territory that is both breathtaking and serene. Looking out on the barren lands of Connemara is to view a

Top: Glin Castle. Above: Powerscourt. Left: Mount Usher.

land still untouched by the modern world.

Music is an integral part of Irish life and can be heard on the streets drifting from the bars – another integral part of Irish life! The joviality and talk in the pubs is mingled with the live music that is played by the locals. It would also serve music lovers who visit Ireland to attend where possible a 'Fleadh' (pronounced 'Fla') which is a festival of music offering the opportunity to find great 'craic' (fun!)

The weather can be contrary but this is a secondary concern when you discover all that Ireland has to offer.

ANTRIM CASTLE GARDENS

Randalstown Road, Antrim (Antrim Borough Council)
Tel: 01849 428000 Fax: 01849 460 360

Antrim Castle Gardens boasts ownership of one of the earliest examples of an Anglo-Dutch water garden within the British Isles. It contains exceptional examples of ornamental canals, an ancient motte and a parterre garden. The parterre garden has preserved the timeless atmosphere of the 17th century formal garden. It has been planted with fine examples of 17th century plants which were originally used for culinary and medicinal purposes. An interpretative display in the foyer of Clotworthy Arts Centre outlines the process of the gardens' restoration. **Open:** Mon–Fri, 9.30am–9.30pm, Sat 10am–5pm. Jul–Aug, Sun 2–5pm. Admission: Free access to gardens. Guided tours available for groups; rates available on request.

BENVARDEN GARDENS

Benvarden Dervock, Co Antrim, N. Ireland.
Tel: 012657 41331 Fax: 012657 41955 (H.J. Montgomery)

Benvarden House is situated on the banks of the River Bush where the river is crossed by the Coleraine-Ballycastle road (B67). The Walled Garden, about 2 acres in area, appears on a map dated 1788 and has been cultivated since then without interruption, although with alterations to the layout from time to time. The Garden is one of the finest and best maintained in the North of Ireland and ranges from beautiful rose beds to a well stocked kitchen garden. The extensive pleasure grounds stretch down to the banks of the river which is spanned by a splendid iron bridge 90 feet long, erected by Robert Montgomery in 1878. **Open:** 1 Jun–31 Aug 2–6pm. Tues–Sun. Bank Hol Mons. **Admission** £2.

BANTRY HOUSE

Bantry, Co. Cork, Ireland
Tel: 00 353 2 750 047 Fax: 00 353 2 750 795 (Egerton Shelswell-White)

Partly Georgian mansion standing at edge of Bantry Bay, with beautiful views. Seat of family of White, formerly Earls of Bantry. Unique collection of tapestries, furniture, etc. Terraces and statuary in the Italian style in the grounds. Restoration work in progress. **Location:** In outskirts of Bantry (1/2 mile). 56 miles SW of Cork. **Open:** Daily, 9–6pm, 1 March–31 Oct. **Admission: House & Grounds:** Adults £6, children (up to 14) accompanied by parents free, OAPs £4.50, students £4. **Grounds only:** £2. **Groups (20+) House & Grounds:** £4. **Refreshments:** Tearoom, Bed & Breakfast and dinner. **Events/Exhibitions:** 1796 Bantry French Armada (permanent exhibition). West Cork Chamber Music Festival 26 June for ten days. **Accommodation:** B&B and dinner. Nine rooms en suite. **Conferences:** Facilities available. Shop.

map 16
B6

CASTLE COOLE

Enniskillen, Co. Fermanagh, Northern Ireland
Tel: 01365 322690 Fax: 01365 325665

Castle Coole is credited with being the finest neo-classical house in Ireland. Its interior was created by some of the leading craftsmen of the 18th century. Marble chimneys pieces were carved by Westmacott, plasterwork created by Rose and scagliola columns, the work of Bartoli. Magnificent state rooms, include the State Bedroom prepared for a visit by George IV. The surrounding 700 acre estate is a fitting setting for the mansion. Visitors can also enjoy walks through The Grand Yard, Servants Quarters and view the original Belmore Coach. Gift shop and tearoom available. **Open:** Apr–Sept: Sat, Sun, Bank Hols 1–6pm; Easter (Good Fri–Easter Mon) 1–6pm. May–Aug: daily except Thurs 1–6pm. Last tour 5.15pm. **Admission:** Estate £2. Guided tours of mansion: Adult £2.80, child £1.40, family £7, adult party £2.50, child party £1.25.

map 16
3C

DUBLIN WRITERS MUSEUM

18 Parnell Square, Dublin 1, Ireland
Tel: 00 353 1 872 2077 Fax: 00 353 1 872 2231
(Dublin Tourism Enterprises)

The Dublin Writers Museum is located in a splendidly restored 18th century house. It uniquely represents that great body of Irish writers – in prose, poetry and drama – which has contributed so much to the world of literature over the years. **Location:** Dublin city centre – 5 mins. walk from O'Connell St. **Open:** All year except 24/25/26 Dec. Mon–Sat 10–5pm. Sun & Public Hols 11–5pm. Late opening Jun–Aug, Mon–Fri 10–6pm. **Admission:** Adults £3, children £1.40, concessions £2.55, family £8.25. Group rates (20+): Adults £2.55, children £1.20, concessions £2.15.

map 16
D4

GLIN CASTLE

Glin, Co Limerick, Ireland
Tel: 00 353 68 34173 Fax: 00 353 68 34364 (Bob Duff)

Glin Castle, one of Ireland's most historic properties and home to the FitzGerald family, hereditary Knights of Glin. The castle, with its superb interiors, decorative plasterwork and collections of Irish furniture and paintings stands on the banks of the River Shannon surrounded by formal gardens and parkland and in the middle of 500 acres of dairy farm and woodland. The beautiful walled kitchen garden supplies the castle with fresh vegetables and fruit. Castle & Gardens open to the public 1 May–30 June 10–noon and 2–4pm daily. Castle rentals and overnight accommodation available. Glin Castle is a member of Ireland's Blue Book. **E-mail:** knight@iol.ie

map 16
B5

HAMWOOD

Hamwood, Dunboyne, Co Meath
Tel: (01) 8255210 (Major C.R.F. Hamilton)

Situated 3km from Dunboyne on Maynooth Road (beside Ballymacoll Stud). **Open:** House: 1 Mar–31 Aug 2–6pm. Gardens: Open 3rd Sun of each month Mar–Sept 2–6pm. Groups by arrangements. Hamwood is an 18th century house built in the Palladian style in 1779 by Charles Hamilton, wine importer and later Land Agent for the Duke of Leinster. The house was built at a cost of £2,500 with all the timber used in the construction coming from Memel in Russia and was one of the first in Ireland to be roofed with dry slating. The house contains a fine collection of 18th century furniture, mirrors and pictures of historical interest. Hamwood was also the home of Eva and Letitia Hamilton, artists of the 1920–1960 period and now the home of their nephew. The garden is one of the least known in Meath but is among the most fascinating.

map 16
D4

THE JAMES JOYCE MUSEUM

The Joyce Tower, Sandycove, Co. Dublin, Ireland
Tel: 00 353 1 280 9265 Fax: 00 353 1 280 9265
(Dublin Tourism Enterprises)

The Joyce Tower is a Martello tower, one of 26 built around Dublin in 1804 as defence against Napoleon. The building was lived in by James Joyce in 1904 and is described in his novel 'Ulysses'. It now houses the James Joyce Museum, a modern exhibition devoted to the life and works of the famous writer. The living room upstairs, described in 'Ulysses', has recently been reconstructed. **Location:** Sandycove Point on sea front, 1 mile from Dun Laoghaire. **Station(s):** DART to Sandycove. **Buses:** 8 (to Sandycove). **Open:** Apr–Oct, Mon–Sat, 10–1pm & 2–5pm. Suns and public hols, 2–6pm. **Admission:** Adults £2.60, children £1.30, concessions £2.10, family £7.75. Groups prices: Adults £2.10, children £1, concessions £1.85, by prior arrangement.

map 16
D4

KYLEMORE ABBEY & GARDENS

Connemara, Co Galway, Ireland
Tel: 00 353 95 41146 Fax: 00 353 95 41145

Set in the heart of the Connemara mountains is the renowned **KYLEMORE ABBEY ESTATE**. Its fame to date is derived from its status as a premier tourist attraction, international girls' boarding school, magnificent Gothic church, tranquil surrounds, superb restaurant, pottery and one of the finest craft shops in Ireland. Easter 1999 sees the opening to the public of the six acre Victorian Walled Garden, under restoration. This garden was the most impressive in Ireland. The walls stretch for over half a mile to enclose: the kitchen garden, the flower garden, gardener's cottage, bothy and the impressive glass (hot) house complex. All of these features and

more are being restored in phases over the next few years. The Benedictine Nuns at Kylemore continue to work tirelessly at restoring the estate and opening it to the education and enjoyment of all who visit, carrying on the unique Benedictine tradition, spanning over 1,500 years of warmth and hospitality. **A VISIT TO THE WEST OF IRELAND IS NOT COMPLETE WITHOUT VISITING KYLEMORE ABBEY AND GARDEN. Open:** Abbey, Grounds & Gothic Church: All year (Closed Good Friday and Christmas Week). Shop & Restaurant: Mar–Nov (Closed Good Friday). Garden Gate: Easter–Oct. **E-mail:** enquiries@kylemoreabbey.ie

map 16
B4

JAPANESE GARDENS & GARDEN OF ST FIACRE

Tully, Co. Kildare, Ireland. Tel: 00 353 45 521 617
Fax: 00 353 45 522 964 (Irish National Stud)

New for 1999 – The Commemorative Garden of St Fiacre. This garden is within a natural setting of woodland, wetland, lakes and islands. The Japanese Gardens were created between 1906–1910, the Gardens symbolise the Life of Man from the Cave of Birth to the Gateway to Eternity. Special features include the Tea House, Bridge of Life and some very old bonsai trees. **Location:** 1 mile from Kildare Town. 30 miles from Dublin, off N7. **Open:** 12 Feb–12 Nov, daily, 9.30–6pm. **Admission:** Adults £6, children (under 12) £3, students/OAPs £4.50, family (2 adults & 4 children under 12) £14. Please note that it is one ticket for the Irish National Stud, Japanese Gardens & Garden of St. Fiacre. **Refreshments:** Restaurant and Craft shop. **Events/Exhibitions:** The 'Path of Life' in the Japanese Gardens is unsuitable for disabled. However, the Irish National Stud is suitable.

map 16
D4

LISMORE CASTLE GARDENS

Lismore, Co. Waterford, Ireland
Tel: 00 353 58 54424 Fax: 00 353 58 54896 (Lismore Estates)

Lismore Castle has been the Irish home of the Dukes of Devonshire since 1753 and at one time belonged to Sir Walter Raleigh. The gardens are set in seven acres within the 17th century outer defensive walls and have spectacular views of the castle. There is also a fine collection of specimen magnolias, camellias, rhododendrons and a remarkable yew walk where Edmund Spenser is said to have written the "Faerie Queen". Throughout the open season there is always plenty to see in this fascinating and beautiful garden. **Location:** Lismore, 45 miles W of Waterford. 35 miles NE of Cork (1 hour). **Open:** Early Apr–end Sept. **Admission:** Adults £3, children (under 16) £1.50. Reduced rates for groups of 20⁺: Adults £2.50, children £1.30.

map 16
C6

LARCHILL ARCADIAN GARDENS

Kilcock, Kildare
Tel: 00 351 1 628 4580 Fax: 00 351 1 628 7354 (Michael & Louisa de las Casas)

"The most fashionable garden in all of Ireland". (Ordnance Survey 1830) 30 minutes from Dublin, this unique 18th century ornamental parkland is a Rococo fantasy in an Irish Pastoral setting. Larchill is Europe's only remaining Ferme ornée, set in 63 acres of landscaped garden with breathtaking views of the Dublin Mountains, 10 gothic and castellated follies. Romantic island fortress and temple on 8 acre lake. Exquisite shell lined tower in formal walled garden. The notorious Foxes Earth, a refuge for the 18th century Mr Watson's reincarnation as a fox. The parkland has the largest selection of Rare Breeds in Ireland. **Open:** May–end Sept 12–6pm. **Admission:** Adults £3.25, children £1.50, family £10.

map O

MALAHIDE CASTLE

Malahide, Co Dublin
Tel: 00 353 1 846 2184 Fax: 00 353 1 846 2537
(Dublin Tourism Enterprises)

Malahide Castle, set on 250 acres of parkland in the pretty seaside town of Malahide, was both a fortress and a private home for nearly 800 years and is an interesting mix of architectural styles. The Talbot family lived here from 1185 to 1973, when the last Lord Talbot died. The house is furnished with beautiful period furniture together with an extensive collection of Irish portrait paintings, mainly from the National Gallery. **Open:** Apr–Oct: Mon–Sat 10–5pm, Sun & Public Hols 11–6pm. Nov–Mar: Mon–Fri 10–5pm, Sat, Sun & Public Hols 2–5pm. Closed for tours daily 12.45–2pm. **Admission:** Adults £3.10, children £1.70, concs £2.60, family £8.50. Group: Adults £2.60, children £1.50, concs £2.20.

map 16 D4

MOUNT USHER

Ashford, Co Wicklow
Tel: 00 353 404 40205/40116 Fax: 00 353 404 4025 (Mrs Madelaine Jay)

Laid out along the banks of the river Vartry, Mount Usher represents the Robinsonian style, i.e. informality and natural design. Trees and shrubs introduced from many parts of the world are planted in harmony with woodland and shade loving plants. The river, with its weirs and waterfalls, is enchanted by attractive suspension bridges from which spectacular and romantic views may be enjoyed. The Gardens cover 20 acres and comprise of over 5000 different species of plants, most serving as host to a variety of birds and other wildlife. To the professional gardener, the lover of nature or the casual tourist, a visit to Mount Usher is sure to be a memorable one. **Location:** Ashford, 1 mile from Wicklow on Dublin-Bray Rd. **Open:** Mid Mar–end of Oct. **Admission:** Adults £3.50, OAP, students, children £2.50 (Special group rates for 20 or more).

map 16 D5

NEWBRIDGE HOUSE

Donabate, Co. Dublin, Ireland
Tel: 00 353 1 8436534 Fax: 00 353 1 8462537 (Dublin Tourism Enterprises)

This delightful 18th century mansion is set on 350 acres of parkland, 12 miles north of the city centre and boasts one of the finest Georgian interiors in Ireland. The house appears more or less as it did 150 years ago. It was built in 1737, to a design by Richard Castle, for the Archbishop of Dublin and contains elaborate stucco plasterwork by Robert West. The grounds contain a 29 acre traditional farm complete with farmyard animals, a delight to any young visitor and perfect for school tours and large groups. **Open:** Apr–Sept: Tues–Sat 10–5pm, Sun & Public Hols 2–6pm, closed Mons. Oct–Mar: Sat, Sun, Public Hols 2–5pm. Closed for tours daily 1–2pm. Coffee shop remains open **Admission:** Adult £2.95, children (under 12) £1.60, concs £2.55, family £7.95. Group: Adult £2.55, children £1.40, concs £2.15.

map 16 D4

NEWMAN HOUSE

85–86 St Stephen's Green, Dublin 2
Tel: 00 353 706 7422 Fax: 00 353 706 7211 (University College Dublin)

Numbers 85 and 86 St Stephen's Green are two of the finest Georgian houses in the city of Dublin. Each house contains a series of spectacular 18th century stucco interiors. By good fortune these remarkable buildings were united in common ownership in the 19th century when they were acquired by the Catholic University of Ireland, the precursor of modern University College Dublin. The building was named in honour of John Henry Newman, the University's first rector. The great English poet Gerard Manley Hopkins spent the last years of his life at Newman House and James Joyce was a student here from 1899–1902. Recently restored to its former grandeur, Newman House offers the visitor a unique combination of visual splendour and evocative literary associations. **Open:** June, July &Aug only, Tues–Fri 12–5pm, Sat 2–5pm, Sun 11–2pm. The rest of the year tours by appointment only.

map 16 D4

POWERSCOURT GARDENS & WATERFALL

Enniskerry, Co. Wicklow, Ireland
Tel: 00 353 204 6000 Fax: 00 353 286 3561

Just 12 miles south of Dublin, in the foothills of the Wicklow Mountains, lies Powerscourt Estate. Its 20 hectares of gardens are famous the world over. It is a sublime blend of formal gardens, sweeping terraces, statuary and ornamental lakes, together with secret hollows, rambling walks, walled gardens and over 200 variations of trees and shrubs. The shell of the 18th century house gutted by fire in 1974 has an innovative new use: incorporating a terrace restaurant overlooking the spectacular gardens, speciality shops and an exhibition on the Estate and Gardens. Powerscourt Waterfall (5km from Gardens) is Ireland's highest.

map 16 D4

MUCKROSS HOUSE, GARDENS & TRADITIONAL FARMS

National Park, Killarney, Kerry
Tel: 00 353 64 31440 Fax: 00 353 64 33926 (Trustees of Muckross)

Muckross House is a magnificent Victorian mansion, situated on the shores of Muckross Lake and set amidst the splendid and spectacular landscape of Killarney National Park. The exquisitely furnished rooms portray the lifestyles of the gentry, including Queen Victoria's boudoir and bedroom as it was when she visited in 1861. The basement depicts the lifestyles of the servants and today is home to Muckross Craft Workshops. The Gardens of Muckross are famed for their beauty worldwide. Muckross Traditional Farms is an exciting outdoor representation of the lifestyles and farming traditions of a rural community of the 1930s. Three separate working farms, complete with animals, poultry and traditional farm machinery will help you relive the past when all work was carried out using traditional methods. Muckross Vintage Coach, visitors to the Farms can enjoy a Free trip around the site on a beautiful Vintage Coach. Location: 3.5m from Killarney, on the Kenmare road. **Open:** Daily, all year. 9–5.30pm, 9–7pm Jul/Aug (Farms Mar–Oct) **Admission:** Adult Ir£3.80, students Ir£1.60. Group rate for 20+ Ir£2.70. Family Ir£9. Ditto for Muckross Traditional Farms. Substantial savings on joint tickets. Gardens free. **Website:** www.muckross–house.ie

map 16 B6

SEAFORDE GARDENS

Seaforde, Downpatrick, Co. Down, BT30 8PG, Northern Ireland
Tel: 01396 811 225 Fax: 01396 811 370 (Patrick Forde)

Over 600 trees and shrubs, container grown. Many camellias and rhododendrons. National collection of Eucryphius. Tropical butterfly house with hundreds of free flying butterflies. The 18th century walled gardens and pleasure grounds contain a vast collection of trees and shrubs. Many very rare. Huge rhododendrons. The Hornbeam maze is the oldest in Ireland. **Location:** On A24, Ballynahinch–Newcastle road. **Open:** Easter–end Sept, Mon–Sat 10–5pm. Sun 1–6pm.

map 16 E3

TULLYNALLY CASTLE & GARDENS

Castlepollard, Co. Westmeath, Ireland.
Tel: 00 353 44 61159/61289 Fax: 00 353 44 61856
(Thomas & Valerie Palceham)

Home of the Pakenhams (later Earls of Longford) since the 17th century. The original house is now incorporated in a huge rambling neo-gothic castle. Thirty acres of romantic woodland and walled gardens are also open to the public. **Location:** 1.5 miles outside Castlepollard on Granard Road. **Station(s):** Mullingar. **House open:** 15 June–30 July & 1–15 Sept, 2–6pm. Pre-booked groups admitted at other times. **Gardens:** May–Sept, 2–6pm. **Admission:** House & Gardens: Adults £4.50, children £2.50, groups £4. Gardens only: Adults £3, children £1. **Refreshments:** Tearoom open May–1 Sept at weekends and Bank Hols.

map 16 C4

STROKESTOWN PARK HOUSE & GARDENS

Strokestown, Co Roscommon, Ireland
Tel: 00 353 78 33013 Fax: 00 353 78 33712 **E-mail:** info@strokestownpark.ie

Strokestown Park was the home of the Pakenham Mahon family from the 1660's to 1979. The house retains most its original furnishings and is viewed by guided tour. The Famine Museum uses original documents and letters relating to the time of the Famine on the Strokestown Park Estate to explain the history of The Great Irish Famine and to draw parallels with the occurrence of famine in the Developing World today. The 4½ acre walled pleasure garden has been faithfully restored to its original splendour. Home of the longest herbaceous border in Ireland & UK. **Open:** House, gardens & Famine Museum 1 Apr–31 Oct, every day, 11–5.30pm (flexible for groups). **Admission:** House £3.25, museum £3.25, garden £3.25. All three £8.50. Reduced rates for families, senior citizens, unemployed and groups. Parking. Wheelchair access to museum and garden.

map 16 C4

SHANNON HERITAGE 'A COMMON CELTIC PAST'

Central Reservations Bunratty Castle & Folk Park, Bunratty, Co. Clare, Ireland
Tel: 00 353 61 360 788   Fax: 00 353 61 361 020

'A Common Celtic Past' is a concept which links each of the products in the Shannon Heritage portfolio together in a time line. The story which is thereby created brings the visitor into the magic and mystery of the Prehistoric, Celtic, Viking, Anglo Norman, Anglo and native Irish societies starting 5000 years ago and continuing to the present day. **Lough Gur** – Bruff, Co. Limerick – One of Ireland's most important prehistoric sites. Interpretation Centre (Open May–Sept). **Craggaunowen** – Quin, Co. Clare. 'The Living Fast' – Reconstruction of Bronze Age site. Costumed Characters. (Open daily Easter–Oct). **Killaloe Heritage Centre** – Co. Clare – Visitors Centre and Tourist Information Office. (Open May–Sept). **King John's Castle** – Limerick – Military Castle, imaginative historical exhibition. Multi-visual show and archeological excavations. (Open April–Oct). **Castle Lane Tavern** – Limerick – 18th/19th century style Tavern. Contemporary Irish evening entertainment. (April–Oct subject to demand) & Tavern open all year. **Bunratty Castle & Folk Park** – Co. Clare – 15th century Castle and Folk Park depicting Irish life during the 19th century (Open all year). Medieval banquets held in castle, traditional Irish Nights in Folk Park (Open all year – subject to demand). **Knappogue Castle** – Quin, Co. Clare – 15th century Castle with 19th century additions. Medieval banquets (summer season). Wedding requests welcome (Open April–Oct). **Cliffs Of Moher – O'Brien's Viewing Tower** – Co. Clare – Spectacular views of the Atlantic Ocean and visitors centre (Open all year). **Dunguaire Castle** – Kinvara, Co. Galway – 15th century Castle on the shores of Galway Bay. Medieval banquets (summer season). (Open mid-April–Oct). **MacCloskeys Gourmet Restaurant** – Bunratty House Mews (Tues–Sat). Unique corporate and incentive events available – requests welcome.

map 16
B5

Belgium

Belgium is the uncut diamond of Europe. Thankfully the Channel Tunnel is gradually revealing this undiscovered gem to a wider audience than those who travel only to its capital for parliamentary purposes.

Dukes, counts and lesser lords have built many a feudal castle on Belgian land and abbots and cardinals have constructed towering religious edifices. It was the merchants who built the cities and commissioned the works of art we admire today.

Brussels stands in the very centre of the country. It is booming city which has established itself as the capital of Europe. Here the European Community has its headquarters.

The south of the country is a wild, wooded area, with mountains rising to more than 2000

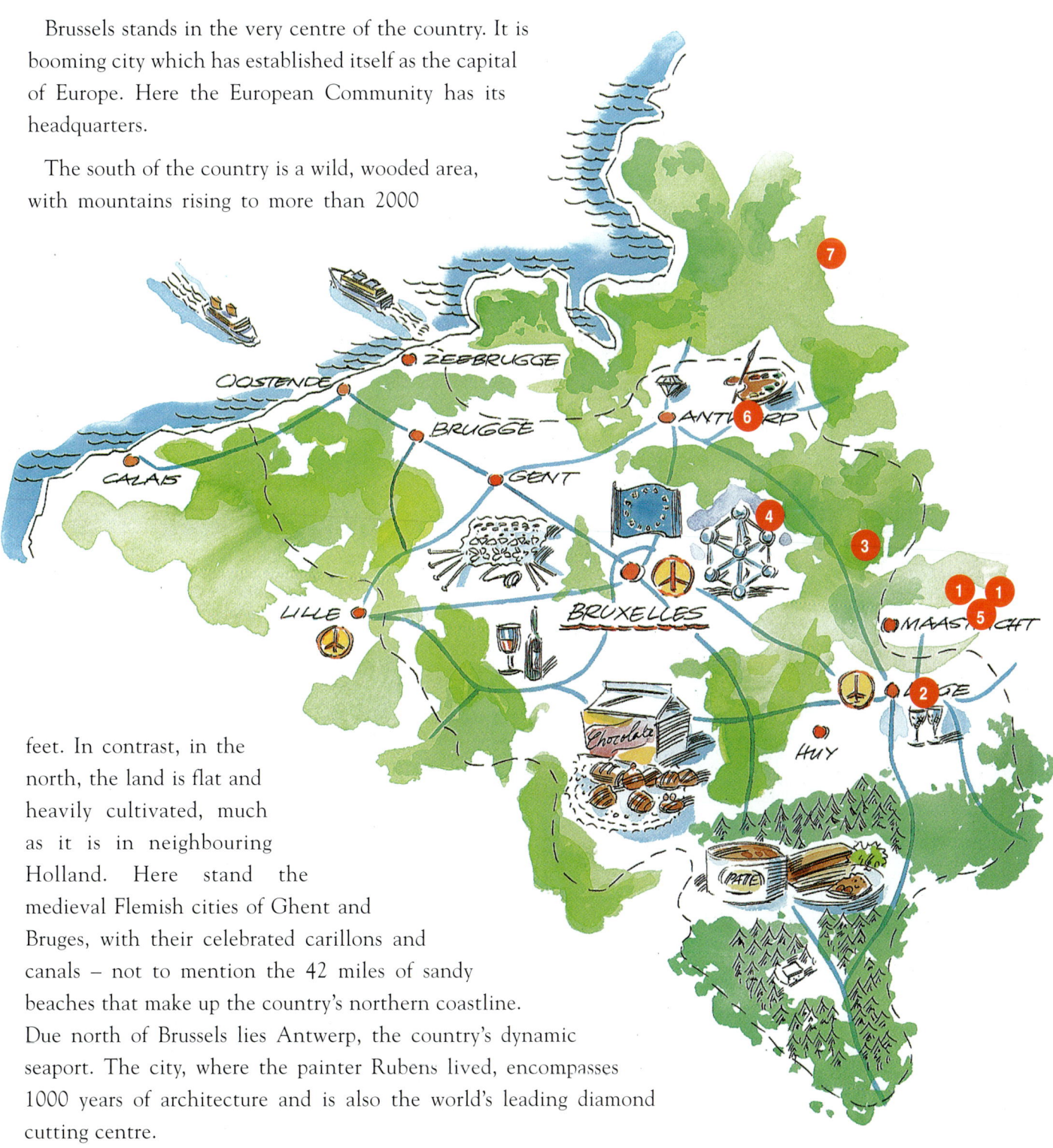

feet. In contrast, in the north, the land is flat and heavily cultivated, much as it is in neighbouring Holland. Here stand the medieval Flemish cities of Ghent and Bruges, with their celebrated carillons and canals – not to mention the 42 miles of sandy beaches that make up the country's northern coastline. Due north of Brussels lies Antwerp, the country's dynamic seaport. The city, where the painter Rubens lived, encompasses 1000 years of architecture and is also the world's leading diamond cutting centre.

CASTLES OF AIGREMONT & WARFUSEE

Aigremont – Les Awirs, 4400 Flemalle, Belgium　　　**Warfusee – 4470 St Georges s/Meuse, Belgium**

Tel: 0032 4 3361687　Fax: 0032 4 3370801 (Mme Renard-Ortmans)

Château D'Aigremont: Aigremont lies on the river Meuse and was built in 1715 by a wealthy canon. The house features classic architecture of the Mosane region and terraced gardens. The interior is beautifully decorated with remarkable examples of eighteenth century panelling and a collection of paintings and trompe l'oeil . There is also a collection of furniture, tapestries, paintings, painted ivory miniatures and small wooden objects from Spa. Meals and teas held within the rooms of the house (Groups only by pre-booking). **Location:** On Liege-Namur motorway (E42), exit 4, towards Flemalle, drive 2km and take signposted route to the right. **Open:** 1 April to 31 October, Sundays 10–12noon, and 2–6pm. 1st July to 31st August: every day except Monday. OPEN THROUGHOUT THE YEAR TO GROUPS BY PRIOR ARRANGEMENT.

Château De Warfusee: A major part of Wallonie's heritage. One of the most beautiful buildings in the Mosane region, built in 1754 by the architect Jean Gilles Jacob. Former residence of the prince-bishop Charles Nicolas d'Oultremont, the rooms at Warfusee remain decorated as they were at the time. Magnificent rooms decorated with tapestries. Also features a collection of furniture, paintings, porcelain, silverware, bookshelves and family treasures. The house is still occupied by the same family to this day. A superb park surrounds the house. After your visit, it is possible to have lunch in the rooms at Aigremont house. **Location:** Between Liege and Huy, on the E42 motorway. **Open:** Throughout the year by prior arrangement only for groups (min 25 people). Guided tours. Closed on Sundays.

map 229
1

CHATEAU-FORT (CASTLE OF BOUILLON)

Bte Postale 13, B6830 Bouillon, Belgium

Tel: 00 32 61 466 257　Fax: 00 32 61 468 285

The most interesting feudal castle in Belgium, this fortress probably goes back to 8C, but the first records date from 988. Its existence was made immortal by heroic Godfrey of Bouillon, leader of the First Crusade in 1096 and proclaimed King of Jerusalem. **Open:** Jan, Feb, Dec weekdays 1–5pm, weekends 10–5pm. Mar, Oct, Nov, 10–5pm. Apr–Jun, Sep, 10–6pm. Jul & Aug 9.30–7pm on Mon and Thurs. 9.30–10pm the other days. During the Christmas holidays and Spring holiday, 10–5pm weather permitting. Closed 25 Dec and 1 Jan. Possibility to combine with the museums and the archeoscope. **Admission:** Adult BF150, child BF80. Seniorcard BF140 . Studentcard BF120. Groups (20 pers.): Adult BF130, child (6–12yrs) BF70, student (13–18yrs) BF100. English guide BF30. **Events:** Night visit of the castle by torch. BF150 & BF70 for compulsory torch.

map 229
2

CHÂTEAU DE CORROY-LE-CHATEAU

Rue du Chateau de Corroy, 5032 Gembloux, Namur

Tel: 00 32 81 63 3232 Fax: 00 32 81 63 33 75 (Marquesses of Trazegnies)

Corry-le-Chateau represents the most impressive 13th century open-country stronghold in Belgium. It was built by the Counts of Vianden to defend the south of the Duchy of Brabant. This fortress has passed down by succession, from the Sponheim, Bavarian and Nassau families, to the Marquesses of Trazegnies who currently live there. The interior has been perfectly restored, and contains a spectacular neo-gothic hall, a chapel dating from 1270, salons featuring canvas paintings and numerous family belongings. **Location:** 5km West of Gembloux, N29. **Open:** Weekends and holidays from 1 May–3 Oct, from 10–12pm, and from 2–6pm. **Admission:** Adults 150BF, children (aged 6–10) 80BF, OAPs (groups) 100BF. **Events:** Music festival and summer theatre.

map 229
3

CHÂTEAU FORT ECAUSSINNES LALAING

1, rue de Seneffe–B7191 Ecaussinnes Lalaing, Belgium
Tel & Fax: 00 32 67 44 24 90

From the 11th and 12th century, transformed into a residence in the 15th century, this castle preserves the memory of the family of the counts van der Burch, who lived there from 1624 to 1854. Furnished rooms: grand salon, bedroom, oratory. Medieval part: armoury, ancient kitchen, chapel, dungeon. Collections: portraits of the counts van der Burch; paintings, sculptures, glasses, porcelain, furniture, ancient weapons. **Location:** 7km from exit 20 on E19 (direction Ronquieres). **Open:** 10–12pm, 2–6pm. 1 Apr–1 Nov–weekends and holidays. Jul–Aug, everyday except Tues and Weds. Groups by appointment 1 Apr–2 Nov (guided tours on request).

map 229
4

CHATEAU DE MODAVE

B–4577 Modave, Belgium
Tel: 32 85 411 369   Fax: 32 85 412 676

Dating back to 13C, the castle owes its architectural appearance to the restoration by Count de Marchin from 1652–1673. Modave had many distinguished owners, before it was bought in 1941 by the 'Compagnie Intercommunale Bruxelloise des Eaux', in order to protect the impounded water. Twenty richly decorated and furnished rooms are open to the public and include remarkable ceilings, stucco works by Jean-Christian Hansche, sculptures, paintings, Brussels tapestries and 18C furniture. In 1667 Rennequin Sualem built the hydraulic wheel that was used as a pattern for the machine at Marly, bringing the water from the Seine to Versailles Palace. This technical achievement is illustrated in one of the rooms with several documents, plans and an accurate replica of the wheel, made to scale. **Open:** 1 Apr–15 Nov, 9–6pm. 16 Nov–31 Mar, by appointment.

map 229
5

NATIONAL BOTANIC GARDEN OF BELGIUM

Domein Van Bouchout–B1860 Meise, Belgium
Tel: 00 32 22 69 39 05 Fax: 00 32 2 27 015 67

At only a stones throw from Brussels, the centre of European activity, lies the National Botanic Garden of Belgium in the domain of Bouchout, Meise. The domain is closely interwoven with Belgian history. The earliest remains of the castle date back to the 12th century. In more recent times it was the refuge of the former Empress of Mexico, Charlotte, sister of King Leopold II. She died in 1927. Apart from the castle there are various smaller features. There are ice cellars, small ornamental buildings, an exquisite greenhouse by Alphonse Balat, ancient trees and wide sweeping lawns. The Botanic Garden was located to the site in 1939 and added extensive living collections. The immense Plant-Palace houses the tropical and subtropical collections and covers more than 1 hectare. The temperate collections are grouped in several locations in the park. During summer the old Orangery functions as a restaurant and the castle houses a small shop. **Open:** Easter, 30 Oct, from 1pm onwards. Closing times vary according to season and weather conditions. Call: 00 32 (0) 2 269 39 05 for details. **Admission:** Adult BF200, child/student BF100. **Internet:** http//www. BR.fgov.be.

map 229
6

Provinciaal Museum Sterckshof – Silver Centre

Hooftvunderlei 160–B 2100 Antwerp (Deurne)
Tel: 00 32 3 360 5250   Fax: 00 32 3 360 5253

The Provinciaal Museum Sterckshof –Silver Centre is a museum in a park on the edge of the city of Antwerp. It is a journey of discovery that leads through a picturesque castle to the treasures of Belgian silver production from the 16th to the 20th centuries inclusive. At the end of the 18th century little remained of the castle built in the 16th century. On the basis of the original foundation and iconographic material, a reconstruction emerged during the thirties. The library with public reading room (Internet: www.cipal.be/digibib/home.htm), many exhibitions and the museum workshop throw further light on the art of the silversmith. The garden was relaid in 1994. The Sterckshof Museum is situated in the Provinciaal Domain Rivierenhof (Castle Rivierenhof, now a restaurant). **Location:** Provinciaal Domein Rivierenhof, entrance Cornelissenlaan, Antwerp (Deurne). Antwerp expressway (E 19) exit 3 and motorway Antwerp-Liège (E 313) exit 18. **Stations:** Antwerpen-Centraal and bus 18 (Collegelaan), 41 (Cogelsplein) or tram 10 (Cogelsplein), 24 (Waterbaan). Antwerpen-Berchem and bus 18 (Collegelaan). **Open:** 10–5.30pm. Closed on Mon and 25 Dec–2 Jan. **Admission:** Museum and garden free. Exhibition hall: BF250–100. **Events/Exhibition:** 1999 – Silver for Sir Anthony, 15 May–15 Aug.

map 224
4

France

France is a nation of contrasting landscapes, from high mountain plateaux to lush farmland, traditional villages to chic boulevards, where heritage is set against a backdrop of ever changing vistas. This country belongs to both northern and southern Europe, encompassing Britanny with its Celtic maritime heritage, the Mediterranean sunbelt, Germanic Alsace-Lorraine and the rugged mountain resorts of the Auvergne and the Pyrénées.

Artists have always been inspired by France, especially since landscape became a highly popular subject for art in the 19th century. Art and tourism have been closely linked for over a century, when the establishment of artists' colonies in the forest of Fontainbleau, Brittany and the South of France did much to make these areas attractive to visitors. Today, one of the pleasures of touring the countryside is the recognition of landscapes made famous in paintings by artists such as Monet, Van Gogh and Cezanne.

In the North, the River Seine winds its way across the gentle landscapes of the Ile de France towards Paris – a city of stately palaces – where the tradition of the classical French garden began. Moving onwards, the rich soils of Normandy provide a favourable climate where gardens thrive. It is here especially, that the influence of the English Garden is felt.

Nowhere in the world is a country more synonymous with wine than France. Each of the principal wine producing regions reveals its own identity, based on grape varieties, climate and local culture. The range, quality and reputation of the fine wines of Bordeaux, Dordogne, The Loire and Champagne in particular make them role models to the world, where the realm of chateaux and vineyards are inexorably linked.

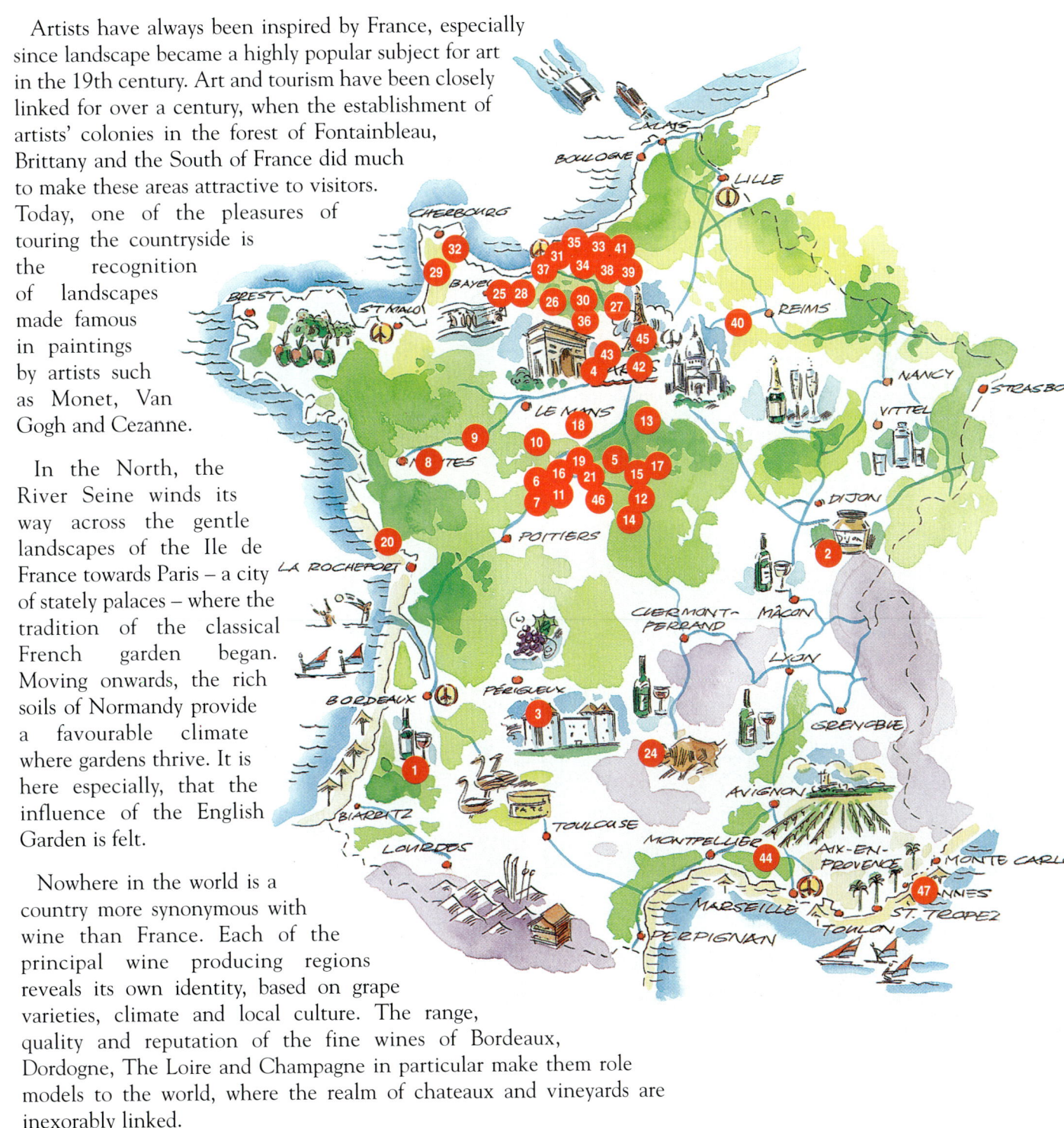

An area of green valleys and majestic Chateaux, The Loire is the setting for artistic towns such as Chartres, Tours and Poitiers. Southern France, however, is steeped in an Italianate balminess where villas perch on rocky clifftops amongst beautifully tended formal gardens filled with colour.

CHÂTEAU DE MALLE

33210 Preignac, France
Tel: 00 33 5 56 62 36 86 Fax: 00 33 5 56 76 82 40 (Comtesse De Bournazel)

Bordeaux area. Magnificent residence surrounded by Italian style gardens, in the heart of Sauternes vineyard, Malle built by Jacques de Malle, direct ancestor of the Comte de Bournazel, dates from the early 17 C. The castle is tile-roofed, dominated by a Mansard one-storied slate covered central pavillion with two round towers at each end, topped with slate domes. The chapel is in one of the towers. Ceilings, furniture and paintings have remained as they were. The vineyard encompasses the region of Sauternes (Malle is a great classified vintage under the famous Imperial classification of 1855) and Graves (red & white wines). **Open:** 1 Apr–31 Oct, 10–12noon & 2–6.30pm. Every day. Free parking. Groups by appointment. Possibility of tasting. **Location:** 35 m S Bordeaux by R.N. 113 or A62 to Langon. **Internet:** http//www.château–de–malle:fr **E-mail:** chateaudemalle@wanadoo.fr

map 233
1

CHÂTEAU D'ARLAY

39140 Arlay
Tel: 00 33 3 84 85 04 22 Fax: 00 33 3 84 48 17 96 (M et Mme R de Laguiche)

The castle was built in 1774 by the Countess of Lauraguais on the site of a Minime Convent, the only remains of which are the vaulted cellar. It was refurnished during the Restoration (1819–1835). A romantic park laid out inside the medieval ruins of the old fortress of the Princes of Orange, is an illustration of the spirit of playfulness of the late 18th century. The theme of play is also evoked by the garden created in 1996: hoops with roses on croquet lawn, with a central bell-hoop and a box-tree "ball". You can also see the four aces: hearts, spades, diamonds and clubs. Flowers, fruit and vegetables are brought together in harmony. **Open:** From 15 June–15 Sept.

map 233
2

CHÂTEAU DE LOSSE

24290 Thonac par Montignac-Lascaux, Dordogne (Périgord), France
Tel/Fax: 00 33 553 50 80 08 Internet: http://www.bestofPerigord.fr

The medieval stronghold overlooks the Vézère river, it is defended by the largest gatehouse in SW France, curtain walls linked by five towers and is surrounded by deep ditches. Within the Renaissance Hall's (1576) elegant architecture lies fine décor and exceptional period furniture (16th and 17th century). These bear witness to the way of life during the reign of the last Valois and first Bourbon kings. A walk through the green bowers in the gardens, terraced above the splendid valley and on the rose lined ramparts is a delightful conclusion to an evocative tour. **Open:** Easter–30 Sept, daily. Groups by appointment at other times. **Admission:** Adult FF32, child FF15. Group rates available. **Location:** On D706, 5km from Montignac-Lascaux to Les Eyzies. Disabled access (free access to 80% of tour), guided tours in English or with English texts.

map 233
3

LE CHÂTEAU D'ANET

28260 Anet, Ile De France, France.
Tel: 00 33 2 37 41 90 07 Fax: 00 33 2 37 41 96 45

In 1547, Diane de Poitiers, the mistress of Henry II of France, ordered the construction of The Château d' Anet. The castle is a masterpiece, a result of the work of the celebrated architect, Philbert de l'Orme and of many other artists. In the 17th century, the castle underwent numerous refurbishments including the grand staircase and the construction of the canal, built according to maps drawn up by Le Notre. The castle was considerably altered in the nineteenth century, with several generations of owners continually improving the castle, a true gem of French architecture. **Open:** 1–30 Nov and 1 Feb–31 Mar 1998, Sat and Sun, 2–5pm. 1 Apr–to 31 Oct, (every day except for Tues), 2–6.30pm. Closed in Dec and Jan. **Admission:** Adults FF37, groups (20 people or more)FF28, primary school children FF15, secondary school children FF20.

map 233
4

Photograph: F. Vallom – Kipa Press

CHÂTEAU DE CHEVERNY

41700 Cheverny, France
Tel: 00 33 2 54 79 96 29 Fax: 00 33 2 54 79 25 38 (Charles Antoine de Vibraye)

Travelling along the Loire Valley is like opening a book of the history of France. The principal jewels in this rich inheritance are: Chambord, Blois, Chenonceau and Cheverny. The Chateau of Cheverny, with its immaculate façade, is noted for its architecture which is both classical and majestic. For 7 centuries Cheverny has been the home of the very distinguished Hurault family, councillors to Kings Louis XII, Francois I, Henri III and Henri IV. Today their descendants preside over the fortunes of the Domaine de Cheverny. The chateau welcomes several hundred thousand visitors per year, enchanted by the richness of its decoration and the abundance of its superb furnishings. Cheverny is the most magnificently furnished chateau in the Loire Valley. In the park, the world's largest captive balloon lifts you to the height of 150 metres in complete silence, from the gondola, which holds up to 25 passengers, there is an unforgettable 360° view. In the distance, the Loire Valley can be seen on one side and the mysterious Sologne on the other. After, you can explore the park and canal by electric car and boat, in complete silence. **Location:** 13km south from Blois (D765). **Open:** daily, throughout the year. And from Apr–Nov for the balloon and the park and the canal. **Admission:** Adult FF34, child (under 14) FF17. **Internet:** www.chateau–cheverny.fr **E-mail:** chateau.cheverny @wanadoo.fr

map 233
5

CHÂTEAU DE CINQ MARS

Route de Pernay, 37130 Cinq-Mars-La-Pile, France
Tel: 00 33 2 47 96 4049 Fax: 00 33 2 47 96 4049

Cinq-Mars, with its towers, moat and fortification, is a classical feudal castle. Each of the two towers contains large vaulted rooms, two of which are available to rent out for receptions, lunch and special events. The owner and his children live in the last surviving wing of the 'Logis des Gardes'. The other wings were destroyed in 1840 to make way for a romantic garden. The 'Logis des Gardes' contains three bedrooms ('Chambres d'Hôte'). They occupy a wonderfully peaceful location in the middle of the park and provide the perfect location for a relaxing stay. **Open:** Daily (except Tue), 9–dusk. **Admission:** FF15. Rooms FF400/440 per night. Price is for two people and includes breakfast. **Location:** Between Tours (20 mins) and Langeais.

map 233
6

CHÂTEAU DE LA GUERCHE

37350 La Guerche
Tel: 00 33 2 47 91 02 39 Fax: 00 33 1 46 51 47 73 (Bernard de Crouy-Chanel)

La Guerche, which controlled an important bridge on the river Creuse, was fortified since the 1000s. In 1203, the marriage of the lady to a friend of the King of France urged John Lackland to take military control of the castle. The present castle was built in two stages during the 15th century (1450–1500). This ambitious construction reflects, like major castles of the Loire Valley, a concern for security (modern use of artillery), comfort and prestige. **Open:** 26 Jun–19 Sept, Mon–Sat, 10–12pm & 2–7pm. Sun 1–7pm. **Admission:** FF20, groups FF10. Low season groups only – advance notice phone/fax: 00 33 1 46 51 47 73. **Events:** 12–13 June special opening for exhibition of collectors.

map 233
7

CHÂTEAU DE GOULAINE

44115 Haute-Goulaine, France
Tel: 00 33 2 40 54 91 42 Fax: 00 33 2 40 54 90 23 (Marquis de Goulaine)

For over a thousand years, the Goulaine family have lived at the château, located some 11 miles south of Nantes. It was rebuilt during the 15th century and in spite of its location, belongs to the great "Châteaux de la Loire". The lavishly decorated upstairs apartments are almost unique in the entire Loire Valley. Close to the castle, a large green house shelters, in natural environment, hundreds of tropical butterflies, flying in freedom among their visitors. **Open to the public:** Easter–early November, 2–6pm: Sats, Suns and holidays. 15 June–15 Sept, every day pm, except Tues. Groups all year round, on special appointment, 10–6pm.

map 233
8

CHÂTEAU DE LA LORIE

49500 Segré, France
Tel: 00 33 2 41 92 10 04

The Château de La Lorie is situated near Angers, and 2km from Segré. Surrounded by formal French gardens, the château has kept it's charm of XVIIIth century. The highlight of La Lorie, is the marble drawing room which was entirely built by Italian artists in 1779. The château is lived in. **Open:** to the public daily, except Tuesday, from 3–6pm.

map 233
9

CHÂTEAU DU LUDE

72800 Le Lude, Sarthe, France
Tel: 00 33 243 94 60 09 Fax: 00 33 243 45 27 53

An old fortress of the Anjou dukedom dominating the Loir, transformed in the Renaissance into a country retreat by King Louis XI's chamberlain. The Château du Lude is a remarkable illustration of the way French architecture has evolved, from the Renaissance to the late 18th century. Lived in by the same family for the past 200 years, the Château contains a rich interior arrangement. Formal gardens on several terraces, rose garden, kitchen garden. **Location:** 30 miles S of Le Mans and N of Tours. **Open:** 1 Apr–30 Sept (all year on request for groups). Outside 10–12am, 2–6pm. Inside guided tour 2.30–6pm. **Admission:** FF40, reduction for children and groups. **Events:** Garden Fair, 5, 6 June, 2, 3 Oct. 'Cooking days' in the old kitchen and visit of the kitchen garden: 10, 11, 14 Jul, 14, 15 Aug, 18, 19 Sept.

map 233
10

CHÂTEAU DE LUYNES

Avenue du clos Mignot - BP34 37230 Luynes
Tel/Fax: 00 33 2 47 55 67 55 (Duke of Luynes)

Recently open to the public, the Château de Luynes is an exceptional property in the Touraine Region because it has always been inhabited throughout its 1000 years history. Whilst the fortress has retained its medieval structure (for defensive purposes, particularly during the Hundred Years War), it has gradually been turned into a pleasant private residence which has been owned by the Luynes family since 1619. Beautiful gardens overlooking the Loire Valley. Superb inner decoration and rich furnishings. Steeped in history as many of the great kings including Richard Coeur de Lion, Philippe Auguste, Louis XI and Louis XIII have stayed in this lovely place. More recently, the Queenmother and Prince Charles have visited the area and admired the charm of the Château de Luynes. **Open:** 1st week-end in Apr–30 Sept (every day). 10–6pm. For groups (upon request).

map 233
11

CHÂTEAU DE MAUPAS

Morogues 18220, France
Tel: 00 33 2 48 64 41 71 Fax: 00 33 2 48 64 19 82

The Château de Maupas was built in the 15th century by Jean Dumesnil Simon, bailiff and governor of the Berry. It was erected on the ancient site of a previous dwelling which first belonged to the Sullys (1284) then to the Mathefelons (14th century) and to the Rochechouarts. In 1682, the château became the property of Antoine Agard for the sum of 36 000F, paid in gold. Antoine Agard was ennobled by Louis XV in 1725. You may visit the different drawing rooms, a state bedroom with its games room, an old kitchen, etc... **Open:** Palm Sunday–1 Oct, daily, 2–7pm. On Sun and Bank Hols, 10–12noon. Open for groups in the morning on request. 14 Jul–1 Oct, daily, 10–12noon. 1 Oct–15 Oct, daily 2–6pm. 15 Oct–15 Nov, open Sun 2–6pm. **Location:** From Bourges the D955 (25km) then the C.D 46 or the C.D 59 (50 km).

map 233
12

CHATEAU DE MEUNG SUR LOIRE

45130 Meung Sur Loire, France
Tel: 00 33 2 38 44 36 47 Fax: 00 33 2 38 44 29 37

The oldest chateau of the Loire Valley with over 16 centuries of history. Entirely furnished–130 rooms–plus undergrounds open to the public. The only castle in the Loire Valley with an underground chapel, prisons, torture chamber and apparatus, dungeon and prison of Villon (a 15th century poet). Headquarters of the English armies during the 100 years war. Episcopal residence of the bishops of Orleans for 6 centuries, who were administrators of the crown. Centre of justice for central France. First castle of the Loire Valley south of Paris. British owned. **Open:** Jan–Mar & Nov – Dec: 10–12 noon & 2–4.30pm. Apr–Jun & Sept–Oct: 10–12.30pm & 2–5pm. Jul–Aug, 9–12.30pm & 1.30–6pm. **Location:** Situated on border of river Loire off A10 Paris to Bordeaux, outlet Meung, the medieval village immediately after Orleans.

map 233
13

CHÂTEAU DE SAGONNE

18600 Sagonne, France
Tel: 00 33 2 48 80 01 27 (M. Spang–Babou)

The Château de Sagonne stands overlooking a listed medieval village. Sagonne, with its prestigious history, occupies an area of Gallo-Roman origin. In AD832, the site was the stronghold of Agane, the daughter of Wicfred, Count of Bourges. Owned first by her descendants, the Counts of Sancerre and by the 'Amboise' family, it then belonged to: Jean Babou, General Commander of Ordnance; Charles de l'Aubespine, Saint-Simon's uncle; J.H. Mansart, architect of Versailles Palace and finally the Duchess of Mouchy, Marie Antionette's governess. The castle is still partly surrounded by defence walls and an impressive keep, adorned by a tower with a fine staircase. The castle displays medieval and 17C frescoes, tapestries, furnished rooms, weapons, portraits and historic mementoes. **Open:** 1 Jun–30 Sep, 10–12 noon & 2–6pm. **Location:** On RN76, 40km from Bourges.

map 233
14

CHATEAU DE LA VERRERIE

Oizon, 18700 Aubigny, s/Nère
Tel: 00 33 2 48 81 51 60 Fax: 00 33 2 48 58 21 25 (Comte Beraud de Vogüé)

A breathtakingly lovely Renaissance castle nestled alongside a romantic lake and surrounded by a large forest, between Sancerre and the Loire Valley. It was built by Beraud Stuart of Darnley at the end of the XVth century. Souvenirs by Robert Stuart of Lennox upon his return from Italy. The beautiful Duchess of Portsmouth, mistress of Charles II lived there between 1672 and 1734. Her descendants, the Dukes of Richmond, sold the castle in 1842 to the Marquis de Vogué. It is still the property of the family. The Château also offers 12 large comfortable bedrooms filled with antiques together with excellent modern bathrooms. There is also an extensive menu selection in the authentic and warm surroundings of the 17th century half timber cottage, converted into a restaurant. Rooms are open all year. Restaurant 1 Mar–1 Nov. Guided tours, 15 Mar–1 Nov.

map 233
15

CHÂTEAU & JARDINS DE VILLANDRY

37510 Villandry, France
Tel: 00 33 2 47 50 02 09 Fax: 00 33 2 47 50 12 85 (M.Carvallo)

The castle at Villandry is renowned for its architecture. Built during the reign of Francois I, the castle is constructed around an attractive courtyard and stands reflected in its surrounding moat. But it is Villandry's gardens, above all, that have won worldwide acclaim. The gardens are planted in layers, rising to a level of 30 metres: At the peak, high terraces have been cut into the hillside overlooking the castle. The next layer down comprises a huge expanse of water, which helps replenish the network of moats and fountains. At the base, you will find the ornamental gardens featuring vast box-hedges shaped into symbolic forms and edged with flowers. The castle itself, overlooks the kitchen garden. This, without doubt is the most original feature of the garden. Surrounded by vines, the garden is divided into nine squares, each of a different design. The vegetable borders are edged with dwarf box and are interspersed with fruit trees and standard roses, creating the image of a truly charming and colourful draught board. **Open:** Gardens: open every day, all year – unguided visits with leaflet. 1–27 Mar, 9–6pm. 28 Mar–30 Apr & 20 Sept–23 Oct, 9–7pm. 1 May–30 June & 1–19 Sept, 9–7.30pm. 1 July–31 Aug, 8.30–8pm. 24 Oct–28 Feb 2000, 9–5.30pm. Château: every day, 6 Feb–14 Nov 99 – Guided tours in French at set times (except Suns: 4 Apr–19 Sept & 14–15 May 99). 6 Feb–28 Feb, 9.30–5pm. 1–27 Mar, 9–5.30pm. 28 Mar–30 Jun & 1 Sept–24 Oct, 9–6pm. 1 July–31 Aug, 9–6.30pm. 25 Oct–14 Nov, 9–5pm. **Admission:** Children under 10: free. Gardens: FF32. Château & Gardens: FF45. Groups: (min. 15 paying visitors for 1 free ticket per coach) Students, large families & children 10+: Gardens FF26, Château & Gardens FF38.

JARDINS DU CHÂTEAU DE VILLIERS

18800 Chassy, France
Tel: 00 33 2 48 77 53 20 Fax: 00 33 2 48 77 53 29

A Berry manor house dating back to the 15 C, the Château de Villiers has been a family home for 350 years. Although the house itself is closed, the gardens are open to the public. After passing the dovecote upon entering and crossing a series of courtyards, your journey takes you to the beautiful secret garden, with its flowering shrubs, clematis and hardy perennials. The large lake awaits you, dominated by an old, recently restored, windmill. In springtime, enjoy the lilacs growing in the orchard, the rose-filled clearing and rows of Medlar trees. **Location:** 38km E of Bourges by D976 to Nérondes. Then 5km N by D6. **Station:** Nérondes. **Open:** 1 May–19 Sept, 10–7pm. **Admission:** FF35, child under 7 free, half price for under 18s. FF45 for groups by written arrangement, guided visit by owner. **Refreshments:** Tea and drinks. Home-made cakes are available in the afternoon.

PARC BOTANIQUE DE LA FOSSE

41800 Fontaine les Coteaux
Tel: 00 33 2 54 85 38 63 Fax: 00 33 2 54 85 20 39 (Jacques Gérard)

The park at La Fosse is one of the oldest arboretums in France. Thousands of trees and shrubs have been planted around the chateau-complex, since the end of the 18th century, winding through 25 rolling hectares of the Val du Loir. The perseverance and application of seven generations of the Gerard family, nurturing worldwide botanical discoveries of the past two centuries, have sustained, improved and enriched this exceptional collection. La Fosse was the first arboretum in France to be listed in the Inventory of Historic Monuments because of its botanical and aesthetic qualities. **Open** for guided visits only: From Easter–30 Sept: at 2.30 and at 4.30pm Sat, Sun and Bank Hols. July–August: also on Wed, Thurs and Fri (non Public Hols) at 3pm. From 1 Oct–All Saint's Day: at 3pm, Sat, Sun and Public Hols. Tours last approx. 1½ hrs. **Location:** Access is from the D917 between Montoire–sur–le–Loir and Troo. **Admission:** Adults 9 Euros.

CHÂTEAU DE CHENONCEAU

37150 Chenonceaux, Indre-et-Loire
Tel: 00 33 2 47 23 90 07 Fax: 00 33 2 47 23 80 88

The Château at Chenonceau is a wonderful example of the French Renaissance architecture. Situated in the heart of the Touraine, the castle is surrounded by a 70 Hectare park, and its two famous gardens created by Diane de Poitiers and Catherine de Medici. Diane de Poitiers was also responsible for adding the stunning galleried bridge which spans the River Cher. **Open:** 16 Mar–15 Sept, 9–7pm. 16–30 Sept, 9–6.30pm. 1–15 Oct & 1–15 Mar, 9–6pm. 16–31 Oct & 16–28 Feb, 9–5.30pm. 1–15 Nov & 1–15 Feb, 9–5pm. 16 Nov–31 Jan, 9–4.30pm. **Admission:** Adults FF45, students FF35, children (7–15yrs) FF35. Groups (20 or more) FF35.

PARC FLORAL CHÂTEAU DE LA COURT D'ARON

85540 St Syr en Talmondais
Tel: 00 33 2 51 30 86 74/00 33 2 51 30 84 82 Fax: 00 33 2 51 30 87 37 (Monsieur Johannes Matthysse)

Floral park situated 15 minutes away from the golden beaches of the Atlantic coast. Between May and October, visit the beautiful floral park which covers 10 hectares around the Château de la Court d'Aron. Castle open to the public in July and August. Take romantic walks amongst waterfalls and scented, floral canals as well as water and exotic gardens. The rose garden, bamboo plants, banana trees and Eucalyptus, provide the backdrop to the extraordinary floral spectacle provided by lakes covered with water lilies and Asian Lotus plants. Take a shady picnic, children's games provided. Animals include Japanese Carp, Australian Swans and deer. Exhibitions and orchid, lotus and ancient plant festivals during the season. **Open:** Floral Park open daily 10–7pm. **Admission:** Adults FF33 & FF44. Child 5–12 years FF12 & FF15. During the season, make the 'Domaine de Lotus' your second home.

map 233 **20**

PARC ET JARDIN DU DOMAINE DE SASNIERES

41310 Sasnieres, Loir-et-Cher
Tel: 00 33 2 54 82 92 34 (Domaine de Sasnieres)

A delightful and charming garden planted and maintained by a family on an estate dating back to the 16th century, located North of the Loire valley. As you climb the paths along the hills bordering a romantic valley you will discover a wide variety of trees and shrubs selected for their unusual barks, lovely spring flowers or autumn colours. A peaceful walk around a spring fed pond will lead you to the former walled kitchen garden where mixed borders filled with perennials are being planted. **Open:** Easter–1 Nov, 10–6pm, except Tues & Wed. **Admission:** FF35 (free for children). **Refreshments:** Tea, drinks and home-made pastries. **Location:** 15km south of Vendôme. On the N10, take the D108 towards Montoire.

map 233 **21**

CHÂTEAU DU COLOMBIER

12330 Mondalazac, Salles la Source, France
Tel: 00 33 5 65 74 99 79 Fax: 00 33 5 65 749978 (Annabelle Vicomtesse de la Panouse)

The medieval garden of Eden at the Château du Colombier is a lively depiction of the history of gardens from Charlemagne to the fifteenth century. As in times past, play croquet or chess in the flowering mead covered with violets, primroses, poppies and marguerites. Imagine maidens and their knights kissing in the folly or dancing around the May tree. Come and relive the times of yesteryear and sample moments of serenity and calm in this enchanted garden. There is a singing fountain amongst the lilies and shady walkways adorned with creeping vines. Sit on grassy banks of camomile and thyme amid a wealth of roses. The Garden of Eden will fill your senses with a thousand fragrances reminiscent of the past, and fill you with a desire to return soon. Every day an audiovisual presentation on "Man and the Animals in the Middle Ages" will entertain you. It is hoped that 1999 will see the opening of a fantastic animal park, complete with lions, wolves, bears and birds of prey. **Open:** 6 Feb–14 Nov 1999. Every day from 10–6pm or 7pm, depending on the day of the week and season. **Admission:** Château and medieval gardens: Adult FF30 (4.57 Euros), child FF15 (2.28 Euros). Château and Bestiary: Adult FF49 (7.46 Euros), child FF29 (4.42 Euros). Special group prices on request. Please note, the Bestiary subject to opening authorisation.

map 233 **24**

CHÂTEAU DE BALLEROY

14490 Balleroy, France
Tel: 00 33 1 231 216 061 Fax: 00 33 1 231 215 177 (Forbes Inc.)

Balleroy, an early work of the famous architect François Mansart, was built in 1631, and remains unspoiled and unaltered to this day. The village itself was laid out at the same time and is an essay in town planning which inspired the later work at Versailles. In 1970, Malcolm S Forbes purchased Balleroy for the family's media company and created the first international Balloon museum established in the Château's outer court. A very popular International balloon festival, the 20th one, will be held on June 18–19, 1999. Near Balleroy is the Normandy Coasts with nearby are Mont Saint Michel, Bayeux Tapestry and D. Day beaches. **Open:** 15 Mar–15 Oct, daily from 9–12am & 2–6pm. Closed on Tuesday. Open 10–6pm in Jul–Aug and all the year by appt for groups (20 persons min). **Admission:** Château: FF30, Museum: FF25, both FF37. **Website:** www.chateau–balleroy.com

map 233
25

CHÂTEAU DE BEAUMESNIL

Fondation Furstenberg-Beaumesnil, Beaumesnil, France
Tel/Fax: 00 33 2 32 444 009

Unique Louis XIII baroque style castle built from 1633–1640. Surrounded by 80 hectares landscaped by La Quintinie, who worked with Le Nôtre at Versailles. Furnished interiors and museum of ancient bookbindings. Video on book-binding and gold decoration. **Open:** Jul, Aug, daily (except Tues), 10–12noon & 2–6pm. Apr, May, Jun, Sept, Fri–Mon, 2–6pm. **Admission:** Adults FF35, children FF15. **Location:** 15km east of Bernay.

map 233
26

CHÂTEAU DE BIZY

27200 Vernon
Tel: 00 33 2 32 51 00 82 Fax: 00 33 2 32 21 66 54

Bizy was built in 1740, by Contant d'Ivry for the Marshal of Belle-Isle. It then belonged to the Duke of Penthièvre, Louis XIV and Madame de Montespan's grandson. Between 1822 and 1848, King Louis Philippe carried out some alterations to the castle and created a large English style park featuring lawns and large trees (beech, ash, lime, catalpa). The castle is surrounded by waterworks (under restoration) with famous sculptures depicting dolphins, sea horses and Gribouille as well as hedges and manicured yews. The large living rooms display 1st Empire relics collected by the current owners, the descendants of Marshal Suchet, Duke of Albufera. **Open:** 1 Apr–1 Nov, 10–12pm and 2–6pm. Closed on Mon. Nov, Feb, March: Sat & Sun, 2–5pm. Closed Dec & Jan. **Admission:** Adults FF38, groups FF30, child FF20. **Location:** 70km west of Paris (A13, Junction 16). 10 mins from Giverny.

map 233
27

CHÂTEAU DE FONTAINE–HENRY

14610 Fontaine–Henry, France
Tel: 00 33 2 31 80 00 42

Halfway between Caen and the D-Day beaches, the Château de Fontaine–Henry overlooks the lush green valley of the Mue. Its spectacular roofs, towering above the ancient trees of the garden, surmount a façade richly carved in the successive styles of the 15th and 16th centuries. The interior (guided tour) contains not only monumental fireplaces, carved doors and wonderful staircases, but also furniture, paintings and objets d'arts accumulated by successive generations. This family house frequently serves as a venue for cultural events. **Admission:** Adult FF30, child (12 yrs and over) FF20. Groups: Adults FF22 per person, children of school age FF15 per person. **Open:** Easter–15 Jun and 16 Sept–2 Nov: Sat, Sun & Bank Hols, 2.30–6.30pm. 16 June–15 Sept, afternoons (except Tues) 2.30–6.30pm. Open all year to groups by prior arrangement. **Location:** 10km from Caen.

map 233
28

CLAUDE MONET FOUNDATION

27620, Giverny, France
Tel: 00 33 2 32 51 28 21 Fax: 00 33 2 32 51 54 18

Claude Monet's property opened to the public in 1980 after completion of large-scale restoration work. Claude Monet's collection of Japanese wood prints is displayed in several rooms of the House. The water lily studio opened to visitors and Monet's flowers and water-garden are as they were in his time. **Open:** 1 Apr–31 Oct, 10–6pm. Closed on Mondays except Easter and Whit Mondays. **Admission:** FF35 per person. Groups by reservation only (minimum 20 Persons) FF25 per person.

map 233
29

JARDIN D'ART ET D'ESSAIS

76640 Normanville
Tel/Fax: 00 33 2 35 29 62 39 (Mr S Noel & Ms C Maitrot)

Set in a village bearing the name of an outstanding region renowned for its great achievements. The traditional tall beech curtain surrounding an 18thC gentleman farmer's house hides an exuberant treasure trove of plants, created with over 3000 flowering and fragrant species, planted in labyrinthine fashion on some of the best soil in Northern Europe. Four hands to garden two hectares – the result of a mutual bet between two artist/musicians – great fun for plant lovers! Collection of 125 rare bamboos. Musical film. **Internet:** http://ourworld.compuserve.com/homepages/jadade **Location:** Equidistant from Dieppe, Le Havre and Rouen or between Ourville and Fauville-en-Caux on the D50. **Open:** 15 Apr–15 Nov, Fri–Mon, 2.30pm–sunset. **Admission:** Adult FF30, child (7–14) FF15. "5 senses" guided tour (min. 8 people) FF50. Other groups please phone for details. **Refreshments:** Teas on rainy days.

map 233
30

NACQUEVILLE CHÂTEAU & GARDENS

50460 Urville-Nacqueville, France
Tel: 00 33 02 33 03 56 03 (Mr & Mrs F Azan)

Construction of the château began in 1510 as a fortified manor. Partly modified during the 18th and 19th centuries, it displays granite walls and stone roofs and is, therefore, characteristic of the finest Cotentin manors. The park, created in the 1830s by an English landscape gardener, is romantic and most delightful. A stream runs down to an enchanting lake in which the château is reflected. Many varieties of rhododendrons, azaleas, hydrangeas and ornamental trees are spread over the large lawns. **Open:** Easter–30 Sept, every day except Tuesday & Friday. Guided visits at 2, 3, 4 & 5pm only. **Admission:** Adults FF30, children FF10. **Location:** On North Cotentin coastal road, 5km West of Cherbourg.

map 233
31

PARC ET JARDINS DU CHÂTEAU DE CANON

14270 Mézidon-Canon, France
Tel: 00 33 2 31 20 05 07   Fax: 00 33 2 31 78 04 39

Situated between the 'Pays d'Auge' and the 'Plaine de Caen' in the heart of a country rich in Roman churches, manors and castles, Canon nestles amongst ancient trees and a cluster of bubbling springs. The château is graced with balusters, Italian statues, a Chinese kiosk, a temple and neoclassic ruins and park where the formal French garden harmonises with the more natural English garden: long sweeping avenues lead to the main courtyard. Canon still has its 'Chartreuses', an exception collection of walled herbaceous borders. Jean Baptiste Jacques Elie de Beaumont, a lawyer and treasurer of 'le comte d'Artois' (later became Charles X) designed the place and in 1775 created the famous feast of 'Bonnes Gens', a name once used by the village itself. **Open:** Easter–30 Jun, Sat, Sun and BHols, 2–6pm. 1 Jul–30 Sep, daily (except Tues), 2–7pm. Open to groups by prior arrangement.

map 233
32

THREE OUTSTANDING GARDENS AROUND DIEPPE

Le Bois des Moutiers, Le Domaine de Miromesnil and Les Jardins de Bellevue are three of the most beautiful complementary gardens in Normandy which are not to be missed. Three gardens with historical interest, botanical originality, most exceptional surrounding landscapes; Le Bois des Moutiers with its Lutyens house and its Jekyll gardens and park running down to the sea. Centenarian Rhododenrons, Azaleas... and the very first mixed borders in France.

Le Domaine de Miromesnil with a splendid beech planting shelters the 17th century château where Guy de Maupassant was born and its unique traditional floral kitchen garden surrounded by a splendid park.

Les Jardins de Bellevue, which were created 20 years ago, offer an incredible botanical trip through its national collection of Meconopsis and Helleborus in the most extraordinary landscape facing the Eawy forest.

CHÂTEAU DE MIROMESNIL

76 550 Tourville-sur-Arques, France
Tel & Fax: 00 33 2 35 85 02 80 (Comte T. de Vogüé)

Typical of Henri IV and Louis XIII "brick and stone" architecture, the Château was built (1590–1642) in the centre of a 25 acre beech grove, which hides a small chapel with lovely 18th century decoration. A 250 year old cedar tree dominates the park and the traditional "Potager", one of the best known in France, that still provides the family all the year round with fresh vegetables and flowers. A collection of clematis grows among roses and fruits on the 17th century brick walls and the strictly ordered rows of vegetables contrast with the profusion of the flowered borders. **Location:** 6 miles south of Dieppe, by RN27 or D915. Guided visits of Château, Chapel and garden. **Open:** 1 May–17 Oct, daily (except Tues) 2–6pm. **Admission:** FF35 (FF25 for 10–18). Special admission and opening conditions for pre-registered groups of 20 min. on request.

map 233
33

PARC DU BOIS DES MOUTIERS

76119 Varengeville-Sur-Mer, France
Tel: 00 33 2 35 85 10 02 Fax: 00 33 2 35 85 46 98 (Antoine Bouchayer-Mallet)

A unique garden of its kind in France. Arts and Crafts house built by Sir Edwin Lutyens (1869–1944) and still lived in by the family of Guillaume Mallet, creator of the walled gardens and of the park partly designed and influenced by Miss Gertrude Jekyll. An extensive collection of rare trees and shrubs coming from all over the world in a series of valleys running down to the sea. (Chinese magnolias and azaleas, Himalayan rhododendrons over 13 metres high, Japanese maples, hortensias...). **Location:** 2½ hours by boat from Newhaven to Dieppe only 8km from Dieppe by the cost (D25). **Open:** Daily from 15 Mar–15 Nov. Tickets from 10–12pm and 2–6pm. Visits from 10am–sunset. **Admission:** FF35/40 (May and June). **Facilities:** guided tour with a family member only by appointment.

map 233
34

JARDINS DE BELLEVUE

76850 Beaumont-le-Hareng, France
Tel: 00 33 2 35 33 31 37 Fax: 00 33 2 35 33 29 44 (Martine & Francis Lemonnier)

Hellebores, Prunus and Magnolias in winter, Meconopsis, Primulas and Peonies in spring, Viburnum, Roses and Hydrangeas in summer, gorgeous autumn colours together with a location is splendid: it faces the immense Eawy forest. The Stroller will seek out peace and delight. National collections: Hellebores and Meconopsis. Nursery specialised in perennials, and rare trees and shrubs (hardy for the coldest areas). **Location:** A28 or A29 exit 'Le Pucheuil', 1½ miles on N29 direction Tôtes (signposted). From Dieppe D915 Torcy turn right D154 up to Rosay (signposted). **Open:** All day May–31 Oct, everyday except Tuesdays, 10–7pm. **Admission:** FF30. **Refreshments:** Tearoom for groups (on require), B&B in the garden.

map 233
35

PARC DU CHÂTEAU D'ACQUIGNY
27400 Acquigny, France
Tel: 00 33 2 32 50 23 31 Fax: 00 33 2 32 40 46 68 (Bertrand d'Esneval)

Acquigny Castle, built in 1557 by Philibert Delorme for Anne de Montmorency Laval, Catherine of Médici's lady in waiting, is the epitome of Renaissance architecture. The main courtyard is graced with an ornate Italianate loggia which contrasts with the classicism of the south façade that opens out onto a large park. In its position below the wooded hills of the Eure region, and lying between the rivers Eure and Iton, the castle benefits from a favourable climate that allows Southern vegetation to prosper. Another remarkable particularity of the park is the presence of water canals, pools, waterfalls and a stone passage inspired by the works of Jean-Jacques Rousseau. Parts of the park dating from the 18th century include a large newly restored orangery featuring a collection of citrus plants, a walled former kitchen garden, canals and trees including the historic "Focus Sophora" that were planted in 1768. **Open:** 1st May–mid Oct: Sat, Sun and holidays. July & August: everyday 2–7pm. **Admission:** Adults FF30, children FF15, groups from 1 April–15 Nov. **Location:** 30 kms from Rouen. 15 kms from Evreux. Guided tours are available in English.

map 233
36

PARC ET JARDINS DU CHÂTEAU DE CANON
14270 Mézidon-Canon, France
Tel: 00 33 2 31 20 05 07   Fax: 00 33 2 31 78 04 39

Situated between the 'Pays d'Auge' and the 'Plaine de Caen' in the heart of a country rich in Roman churches, manors and castles, Canon nestles amongst ancient trees and a cluster of bubbling springs. The château is graced with balusters, Italian statues, a Chinese kiosk, a temple and neoclassic ruins and park where the formal French garden harmonises with the more natural English garden: long sweeping avenues lead to the main courtyard. Canon still has its 'Chartreuses', an exception collection of walled herbaceous borders. Jean Baptiste Jacques Elie de Beaumont, a lawyer and treasurer of 'le comte d'Artois' (later became Charles X) designed the place and in 1775 created the famous feast of 'Bonnes Gens', a name once used by the village itself. **Open:** Easter–30 Jun, Sat, Sun and BHols, 2–6pm. 1 Jul–30 Sep, daily (except Tues), 2–7pm. Open to groups by prior arrangement.

map 233
37

FORRIERRES DU BOSC
Route De Duclair, 76150 Saint Jean Du Cardonnay, France
Tel: 00 33 2 35 33 47 06 Fax: 00 33 2 35 33 70 53 (Dr. & Mrs D. Evrard)

Only 5 minutes from the centre of Rouen you will find this enticing 5 acre garden where hardy geraniums reign supreme. Designed, planted and maintained by its owners, it extends gracefully around a 17th/19th century house whose walls are covered by numerous roses rising from amongst shrubs and flowers. The many magnificent century-old trees add to the serenity of the site and are worth a visit in themselves. The French national collection of hardy geraniums is held here and has greatly contributed to the international reputation of the garden and its owners. **Location:** From Rouen A15 towards Le Havre, 1st exit 'Maromme' straight over the roundabout, follow D43 towards Duclair. **Open & Admission:** Please contact for details of opening times and admission charges. **E-mail:** dr.evrard@wanadoo.fr

map 233
38

LES JARDINS D'ANGÉLIQUE
Hameau du Pigrard. 76520 Montmain
Tel: 33 02 35 79 08 12 (Mr & Mrs Y. LeBellegard)

Yves and Gloria LeBellegard designed this romantic garden in 1989 in memory of their deceased daughter Angélique. Playing on different shapes and colour harmonies, the lawn pathway meanders over 2 1/2 acres in front of the 17th century manor patiently restored by the owners. Best known for its remarkable collection of roses, the garden also boasts many peonies, hydrangeas and perennials. In 1996 a new garden was opened on the front side of the house with boxwood parterres and topiary yews encasing a central fountain. **Location:** Leave Rouen towards Darnetal, exit the highway towards Lyons-la-Forêt. Follow D42 until the garden on your right after Montmain. **Open & Admission:** Please contact for details of opening times and admission prices. **Refreshments:** Teas.

map 233
39

CHÂTEAU DE CONDÉ
DEMEURE DES PRINCES
02330 Condé-en-Brie
Tel: 00 33 3 23 82 42 25 Fax: 00 33 3 23 82 86 66 (Madame Pasté de Rochefort)

Situated on the 'Route du Champagne', this private residence will enchant you. This is a real treasure trove, crammed with thousands of surprises and delights! The Prince of Condé, Savoie, Richelieu, Watteau, Oudry, Servandoni, have successively owned, lived in, decorated and loved the castle. We invite you to come and see for yourselves...... **Open:** Guided tours at 2.30, 3.30 and 4.30pm everyday throughout June, July, August and September. Sundays and Bank Holidays in May. Groups welcome throughout the year by appointment. Lunch is available for groups and only by appointment. **Internet:** http://perso.wanadoo.fr/chateaudeconde

map 233
40

CHÂTEAU FORT DE RAMBURES
80140 Rambures, France
Tel: 00 33 3 22 25 10 93 Fax: 00 33 3 22 25 07 88 (Comtesse de Blanchard)

A furnished, feudal, stronghold from the 15th century, where Henri IV once stayed, a jewel of military architecture from the end of the Middle Ages, built as a single flight of fancy to an original plan. The castle was built at a low level in order to reduce the chances of being damaged by firing. The walls are between three and seven metres thick and are pierced by 16 canon emplacements. The superb vaulted cellars were able to house the garrison. The 17th and 18th century outbuildings are still inhabited by descendants of the Rambures – La Roche Fontenilles. The construction of the interior beams bear witness to successive periods of time: very interesting Picardy furniture from the 15th, 16th and 17th centuries. An ancestral family associated with the most important fact in the history of France for a thousand years is linked to the Rambures estate. The name of Rambures first appeared in 1058 but came out into prominence from the 14th century when they occupied a high ranking position during the Hundred Years War, notably David de Rambures the Lord Rambures of Shakespeare's Henry V, Grand Master of Crossbowmen of France, who decided to build the actual castle in 1412. The Brave Rambures was the most famous from the 16th and 17th centuries. He received Henry IV as a guest whilst he was crossing Picardy to win his victory at Arques (1589) and he saved his life at the Battle of Ivry (1590). A great friendship united them. An English park and a wood planted with very old trees possessing rare oils, a true arboretum in the centre of the Vimeu Vert. **Open:** Castle & park open throughout the year (guided tours). 1 Mar–1 Nov, 10am–noon and from 2–6pm (except Weds), 2 Nov–28 Feb, 2–5pm, open Suns and Bank Hols (except 25 Dec and 1 Jan).

map 233
41

DOMAINE DE COURSON
91680 Courson–Monteloup
Tel: 00 33 1 64 58 90 12 Fax 00 33 1 64 58 97 00

Architecture typical of the majestic country houses built in the 17th century for the wealthy officers of the Crown around Paris. Napoleonic memorabilia. Spanish, Italian and French paintings. An early 19th century beautifully landscaped park with many rare species of trees and shrubs in 80 acres of woodland. **Open:** Sun & Public Hols. Park: 1 Jan–31 Dec. Château: 15 Mar–15 Nov. **Admission:** Adult FF42, child FF29. Reduced rates for groups and grounds only. **Events/Exhibitions:** Spectacular flower shows, third weekend of May and Oct. **Location:** Near Arpajon, 20 miles SW of Paris, 4 miles from the A10 and N20. Available for exclusive corporate entertainment. Weddings, receptions and seminars in 'Les Petites Ecuries du duc de Padoue'. Dogs allowed on lead. No access for dogs during flower shows. **E-mail:** COURSONDOM@AOL.COM

map 233
42

CHÂTEAU DE THOIRY

78770, Thoiry, France
Tel: 00 33 1 34 87 52 25 Fax: 00 33 1 34 87 54 12

The Château de Thoiry is a unique listed monument of esoteric Renaissance architecture built in 1559 by the great architect, Philibert de l'Orme. Conceived to be a transparent bridge of light, the sun rises or sets in the Castle's central arch at the summer and winter solstices. Family seat of the Counts of La Panoust for 440 years, Thoiry has fine furniture, tapestries, portraits and 950 years of family, national and international archives. The Castle's portraits, magically sonorized, reveal ancestors' secrets. The 300 acre gardens are graced by formal parterres by Le Nôtre, a bluebell wood with gigantic rhododendrons, magnolias, prunus, an Autumn Garden, flowering meadow, roses, peony border, a labyrinth and hortensias. Over 10,000 flowering trees and shrubs enhance the Botanical Gardens with many new garden creations every year. Rose Garden and Scented Garden. Thoiry's involvement in the conservation of endangered species is reinforced by "the first in France presentation" of rare Komodo dragons in a new Reptile House with hydrosaurus lizards and white crocodiles. A new river biotope of rare European otters, frogs, salamanders and fish is another big attraction. Kids "interactivate" along the new educational play circuit through the Zoological Gardens. With 'The Talking Trees' English audio guide, train tours, Giant Spiderweb Playground, and drive-through Wildlife Park, Thoiry offers hours of pleasure to all ages. **Open:** Every day of the year, 10–5/6.30pm following seasons. **Admission:** Castle only: Adult FF38, child (9+)/Student FF30. Castle, wildlife reserve, zoo and gardens: Adult FF133, child (3–12 yrs)/ student) FF101. Group prices please contact us. **Location:** 25m W of Paris by A13, A12, N12 to Pontchartrain, then D11 to Thoiry. 30mins from Versailles or Giverny, 1hr from Disneyland Paris. **Website:** www.thoiry.tm.fr

map 233
43

Les Monuments d'Exception

> *The 'Monuments d'Exception' offer all the comfort and qualities asscociated with British properties. These monuments, famous for their history, architecture, works of art and gardens, exude a unique style and charm. A visit any of these properties is bound to be a lively and interesting one.*

CHATEAU DES BAUX DE PROVENCE
13520 Les Baux de Provence
Tel: 00 33 4 90 54 55 56 Fax: 00 33 4 90 54 55 00

The Baux Château was constructed on one of the most beautiful sites in France, overlooking Provence as far as the sea. The Baux history museum retraces the turbulent history of this 1000yr old town, the imposing remains of the château and the ancient fortified town of Baux, (dungeon, fortified towers, columbarium, hospital, caves). Life-size medieval siege machines create a vivid impression of warfare in the middle ages. <u>Location:</u> 25km from Avignon, 15km from Arles, 40km from Nice. Off A7 at Avignon Sud or Salon de Provence exits. On A9 at Nimes exit, in direction of Arles. <u>Open:</u> Every day. Spring 9–7.30pm, Summer 9–8.45pm, Autumn 9–6.30pm. Winter 9–5pm.

map 233
44

MUSEE JACQUEMART-ANDRE
153 bd Haussmann, 75008 Paris
Tel: 33 01 42 89 04 91 Fax: 33 01 42 25 09 23

The Jacquemart-Andre Museum presents collections worthy of the greatest museums in a magnificent private mansion dating from the end of the 19th century, with all the atmosphere of a great residence. This sumptuous palace, property of Institut de France, allows the visitor to discover magnificent, intimate areas which are characteristic of Edouard André and his wife, Nélie Jacquemart: large function rooms, monumental staircase, winter garden, 'Italian Museum', private apartments. United by their passion for art, they created together one of the most beautiful collections in France, particularly for the Italian Renaissance, the Great Flemish Masters and the 18th century French School. <u>Location:</u> In the heart of Paris, 5 minutes from the Champs Elysées. <u>Open:</u> Every day, throughout the year, 10–6pm.

map 233
45

CHÂTEAU DE VALENCAY
36600 Valencay
Tel: 33 02 54 00 15 69   Fax: 33 02 54 00 02 37

The Valencay Chateau, one of the most beautiful French Renaissance monuments, was the residence of the Prince of Talleyrand, one of Napoleon Bonaparte's ministers. The castle guarantees a fascinating visit for all the family. The most remarkable architectural feature is undoubtedly the imposing Keep. The Great Function Rooms and furnished private suites retain the memories of Talleyrand and his illustrious guests. The castle is surrounded by magnificent gardens and a park featuring wild animals. Special events. <u>Location:</u> 220km from Paris, 50km from Blois, 70km from Tours on the D956 and the D960. <u>Open:</u> Every day, throughout the year: 1–31 Mar, 2–5pm. 1 Apr–30 Jun, 9.30–6pm. 1 Jul–31 Aug 9.30–7.30pm. 1 Sept–10 Nov, 9.30–6pm. 1 Nov–28 Feb, Weekends and holidays 2–5pm.

map 233
46

VILLA EPHRUSSI DE ROTHSCHILD
06230 Saint Jean Cap Ferrat
Tel: 33 04 93 01 33 09 Fax: 33 04 93 01 33 09

Built by Baroness Ephrussi de Rothschild during the Belle Epoque, the villa is surrounded by seven glorios gardens, decorated with ornamental lakes, waterfalls, patios, flower beds, shady paths and rare types of trees. Overlooking the sea and offering a unique view over the French Riveria, this palace has retained all the atmosphere of an inhabited residence. The Villa, inspired by the great residences of the Italian Renaissance, houses private function rooms and apartments with high quality works of art, collected by Beatrice Ephrussi throughout her life. A free English guide book is given to each visitor. In the summer, a series of concerts enlivens the gardens. <u>Location:</u> Between Nice and Monaco, on the coast road (N 98). <u>Open:</u> Everyday throughout the year, 15 Feb–1 Nov, 10–6pm and 2 Nov–14 Feb 1998. Weekends and school hols 10–6pm. Weekdays 2–6pm.

map 233
47

Germany

The Deutsche Burgenvereinigung (German Castles Association) would like to congratulate Historic Houses, Castles and Gardens on its 45th anniversary.

It was the travellers from England who started the first wave of tourism to German castles some 200 years ago. Paintings and poetry are a lasting testimony to the fascination that German rivers, vineyards and castles exercised on the early British tourist. Romanticism in Germany is closely associated with names like William Turner or Lord Byron. Our castles enjoyed a new revival. Prussian kings and their royal relations launched a reconstruction campaign and soon bankers and steel barons followed the trend.

In 1899 our association was founded not only to prevent the further destruction of historic sites but also to rectify inappropriate concepts and methods of restoration, which were the obvious result of a purely romantic approach to conservation. Celebrating our centenary this year we are proud to be the oldest national and, together with the National Trust, one of the oldest European heritage organisations.

Our "Marksburg", situated above the Rhine and a wonderful variety of other German castles and palaces keep their doors open to visitors. Income from tourism has become essential in maintaining our historic properties.

We would be delighted to see a revival of cultural tourism from Britain and feel certain that this publication will play a successful part.

Alexander Fürst zu Sayn-Wittgenstein-Sayn
President of The Deutsche Burgenvereinigung e.V.

247

ANHOLT CASTLE

Wasserburg Anholt, Postfach 2226, 46417 Isselburg
Tel: 00 49 2874 45353 4 Fax: 00 49 2874 45356

Moated Anholt Castle, set in the Rhine downstream landscape. Residence of the Princes of Salm-Salm. Unique setting with museum, park (35 acres), hotel-restaurant, golf course (18 holes) and rock-garden of 1894 (60 acres). Main castle with 'Broad Tower' from the 12th century. Enlarged into a barrack house in 1700. Since 1966, museum with historic furniture and the Princes' art gallery (700 works of art): Rembrandt, Van Goyen, Murillo, Breughel, Teniers, Terborch. Tapestries, porcelain collection, library, dining rooms, medieval kitchen, coinage, armour and weapons, rooms with fine plasterwork. French gardens with baroque ornaments, maze, tea house, arboretum and rose garden. English landscape gardens by Weyhe (1835) and Edward Milner (1858). The economic building, built in 1700, has been used as a hotel restaurant since 1968.

map 247
1

BRANITZ CASTLE

Kastanienallee 11, 03042 Cottbus
Tel: 00 49 355 751 521 Fax: 00 49 355 713 179

Branitz Castle stands in a historic English garden. The park (approx. 100 hectares) was laid by Herman Furst of Puckler–Muskau (1785–1871), a landscape gardener of the European circle. With its ponds, small water ways, hills, ornamental trees and bushes, the gardens have a very distinctive character. Rather unique pyramids lie deep within the garden. Inside the late Baroque-style castle and stable are the historically furnished rooms (from 19th century) which contain different exhibitions depicting the life and work of the Princes of Puckler. From June 1998 the Cottbus collection of the romantic painter, Carl Blechen, will be exhibited in the restored castle rooms. **Locations:** Cottbus, around 100km S of Berlin on A15. **Open:** Summer, daily 10–6pm. Winter, daily except for Mons, 10–5pm. Special events include theatre, concerts and readings.

map 247
2

DETMOLD CASTLE

D–32756 Detmold, Germany
Tel: 00 495231 70020 Fax: 00 495231 700249 (The Prince of Lippe)

The Castle in the centre of the town of Detmold has been used as the governing offices of the ruling Nobles and Princes of Lippe for hundreds of years. Indeed, it is still the home of the Noble Family. The state of Lippe was one of the small German Monarchy states up until 1918. The façade that encloses a rectangular courtyard is built in the 'Weser Renaissance' style. The old fortifications are still partly intact. The most noteworthy part of the historic furnishings are the tapestries dating from 1675, depicting in glowing colours, the military campaigns of Alexander the Great. **Admission:** Adults DM6, children DM3 and group DM4.50 per person. **Events:** Tours of the castle are between 10–12am, 2–5pm daily.

map 247
3

EHRENBURG

56332 Brodenbach/Mosel
Tel: 00 49 2605 2432 Fax: 00 49 2605 3079 (Thomas Schulz-Anschütz)

Ehrenburg Castle was built in the early 12th century by the Archbishops of Trier. Strongest castle of the Mosel River. Huge circular Renaissance bastion. Attacked and burnt by the soldiers of Louis XIV in 1689. The magic medieval castle is hidden in a secret wooded valley near Koblenz. **Open:** Apr–Oct, daily except Tues, 10–4pm. **Admission:** Adults DM7, children DM5. **Refreshments:** Served by Ehrenburg staff in medieval costumes, home-made hot and cold dishes. Catering for weddings and groups, medieval banquets in the original Knights Hall. Five romantic hotel rooms inside the castle, special medieval candle-light dinners for hotel guests can be arranged. **Events/Exhibitions:** Special events and medieval castle-fair Apr–Oct, every Sun. **E-mail:** kontakt@ehrenburg.de **Internet:** www.ehrenburg.de

map 247
4

ELTZ CASTLE

Burg Eltz, 56294 Münstermaifeld
Tel: 00 49 (26 72) 95 05 00 Fax: 00 49 (26 72) 950 50 50

Burg Eltz, perhaps the best known medieval castle in Germany, with its towering buildings reaching up to 10 storeys and its picturesque half-timbering, offers nearly 900 years of history to its visitors. Throughout these centuries it has been formerly, the stronghold, today, the much beloved ancestral home of the Lords and Counts of Eltz. The castle, looking down at the little Elz river from which it took its name, and cradled by the forest that surrounds it, seems very distant from the world today. Still, it is only a few miles away from some of Germany's busiest rivers and highways. It has been the favourite subject to many artists and particularly to William Turner and Edward Lear. Since it has never been destroyed or looted, it contains an interesting display of furniture and armament, reaching back to the 14th century, and some remarkable Old Masters including Lucas Cranach and Michael Pacher.

The treasury holds an impressive collection of gold and silverware, arms and pieces de vertu, all of which were in actual use of the family, some as early as the thirteenth century many bearing the Eltz coat-of-arms. **Location:** Lower Moselle river area, nearby Koblenz/Cochem; **Directions:** Car/coach by motorway A48, exit Polch, or by Federal roads B416/B49, both via Münstermaifeld. Train and boat: stop Moselkern. **Open:** 1 Apr–31 Oct, 9.30–5.30pm. **Admission:** Guided Tour: Adults: DM9 (4,60 Euro), children: DM6 (3,10 Euro), family DM27 (13,80 Euro). Treasury Vault: Adults DM4 (2 Euro), children DM2 (1 Euro). Groups of 20 or more: Adults DM8 (4,10 Euro), children DM5 (2,60 Euro). **E-mail:** kastellanei@burg-eltz.de **Website:** http://www.burg-eltz.de

map 247
5

CASTLES OF THE PRINCE OF HOHENLOHE – OEHRINGEN

Wald & Schlosshotel – 74639 Friedrichsruhe / Zweiflingen, Germany Tel: 00 49 7941 60870 Fax: 00 49 7941 61468
Schloss Neuenstein – 74632 Neuenstein, Germany Tel: 00 49 7942–2209/49 7941–60990 Fax: 00 49 7941–609920

Wald & Schlosshotel: This graceful hunting castle, once the summer residence of Prince Johann-Friedrich of Hohenlohe-Oehringen, is now part of an elegant hotel in a magnificent park. Visitors will appreciate the handsome reception rooms, with their splendid family portraits and gilt mirrors. The guest rooms are decorated in harmonious colours and extremely comfortable. The Michelin star restaurant, decorated with candles and chandeliers providing attractive lighting, offers a sensational international menu and first-class wines. Leisure facilities include indoor and outdoor pools, tennis, fishing, riding and an 18-hole golf course. **Directions:** BAB 6, Exit Öhringen, follow signs towards Zweiflingen; find signs to the Wald & Schlosshotel at Friedrichsruhe.

Schloss Neuenstein: Schloss Neuenstein, a water castle from the 11th century, was developed 500 years later into a noble residence in the Renaissance style. The castle houses the Hohenlohe Museum which has an extensive historic collection which reflects the art and culture of the Hohenlohe region. One can, amongst other things, visit the splendid Knights Hall, the Kaiser Hall with its rich collection of weapons and the art and rarity cabinet containing finely crafted goldsmiths work and ivory carvings. A special attraction is the fully functioning castle kitchen from 1485, which remains in its original condition. **Location:** BAB 6, exit Neuenstien, B19 Burgenstrasse. **Open:** 16 Mar–15 Nov, daily except Monday (when it is not a Bank Holiday), 9–12am and 1–6pm.

map 247
6

HOHENZOLLERN CASTLE

Burg Hohenzollern–Verwaltung, 72379 Hechingen, Germany
Tel: 00 49 7471 2428 Fax: 00 49 7471 6812

The majestic castle with its fantastic view is the ancestral seat of the Hohenzollern Dynasty, the Prussian Royal Family (Frederick the Great) and the German Emperors. Guided tours, showing a valuable collection of artwork and treasures, including the Prussian King's Crown, offer an insight into 19th century architecture and into Prussian and German history. **Location:** 5km from Hechingen town centre. **Open:** Daily all year except 24 Dec, 16 Mar–15 Oct. 9–5.30pm. 16 Oct–15 Mar, 9–4.30pm. Guided tours every 15 to 30 minutes, English tours on prior arrangement. **Admission:** Castle grounds and house: Adults DM9, groups DM6, children DM3. Castle grounds DM4. **Refreshments:** Snack bar, and restaurant open daily in summertime. **Internet:** www.burg–hohenzollern.com

map 247
7

KRONBURG CASTLE

Burgstrasse 1, 87758 Kronburg, Bavaria
Tel: 00 49 8394/271 Fax: 00 49 8394/1671 Internet: http://www.schloss-kronburg.de

Built on a picturesque hill in the Allgäu, Kronburg Castle has been the property of Baron of Vequel-Westernach for 375 years. This fine four-winged Renaissance style castle is mentioned first in documents from 1227. Part of the building is open to visitors from May–Oct (if booked in advance). The Baron and Baroness guide you personally through some superb rooms. (The German Master Hall, with rich stucco work, the Red drawing room with its original Renaissance ceiling, the Hunting room, Visionary gallery, many rooms with 300 yr old linen wallpaper and the Rococo style chapel).There are chamber and castle-yard concerts during the summer. A newly built guesthouse houses exclusive holiday apartments. **Location:** Nr Memmingen, 5km W on A7 (direction of Konigsschlossern), taking the exit Woringen. **Admission:** Adult DM7, child DM3.50.

map 247
8

LANGENBURG CASTLE

Fürstliche Verwaltung, Schloss Langenburg, 74595 Langenburg
Tel: 00 49 7905 1041 Fax: 00 49 7905 1040

With parts of the castle dating back to the 12C it is remarkable that this castle is still home to the noble family Hohenlohe-Langenburg. Offering one of the nicest Renaissance courtyards in Germany, a chapel and a Baroque garden, the former stables also house a classic car museum. In an area almost 2,000m², there are approx. 80 legendary cars from 1899 up to the modern Formula 1 racing car. The castle tour displays the superb Baroque hall, different museum rooms with fine stucco ceilings and the equally splendid furnishings of the Langenburg family. <u>Castle Tours:</u> Good Fri–1 Nov, daily, 10–5pm. Tours every hour on the hour. Groups should contact the castle for advance bookings. Groups can also visit at times outside the hours above and tours can also be in English. Castle concerts, stately rooms for weddings and events. Attractive walk, museum shop and cafe situated in rose garden.

map 247
9

LEMBECK CASTLE

46286 Dorsten-Lembeck, Nordrhein–Westfalen, Germany
Tel: 00 49 23697167 Fax: 00 49 236977391 (Ferdinand Graf von Merveldt)

A fine example of an early Baroque Westphalian moated castle built in 1692 on the foundations of a medieval fortress. The northwest wing was re-modelled in 1730 by the eminent architect Johann-Conrad Schlaun who worked extensively on other important houses in the region. The home of Graf Merveldt, whose family and ancestors have owned Lembeck since the Middle Ages, the castle is now a museum and hotel. It contains a substantial collection of Chinese porcelain, Flemish tapestries, Dutch furniture and items of local cultural and historic interest and stands in extensive grounds which include a fine rhododendron park. <u>Location:</u> From Autobahn 43 Haltern exit or Autobahn 31 Lembeck exit. Station: Lembeck, <u>Open:</u> Daily Mar–Nov from 10–6pm. <u>Admission:</u> Adult DM7, child DM4.50.

map 247
10

MARKSBURG CASTLE

56338 Braubach, Germany
Tel: 00 49 26 27 206 Fax: 00 49 26 27 88 66 E-mail: DBV.Marksburg@burgen.org

The imposing Marksburg, known as the jewel of the Rhine Valley, is the only castle on the cliffs of the Rhine that has never been destroyed. Dating back to the 12th century, the castle has maintained its medieval character. The high Keep is surrounded by the Romanesque Palace and the Gothic Hall with the Chapel Tower. Of special interest are the horse steps carved out of the rock, the Great Battery and the medieval Herb Garden with its spectacular view, the Gothic Kitchen, Knights' Hall, Armoury Chamber and collection of torture instruments. The Marksburg is the seat of the German Castles Association. <u>Location:</u> Braubach, 12 km south of Koblenz on B42. <u>Open:</u> Daily from 10–5pm, Nov–Easter 11–4pm. <u>Admission:</u> Adult DM8, families DM24, child DM6. Children under 6 years free. (guided tours also in English).

map 247
11

MILDENSTEIN CASTLE

Burglehn 6, 04703 Leisnig
Tel: 00 49 34321 / 12652

A Medieval castle in the heart of Sachsen. The Romanesque chapel with its late Gothic sculptures and the powerful central keep which provides a wonderful view of the surrounding countryside are worth seeing. Possibly the nicest room is the Knight's Hall which houses a collection from the castle museum. <u>Open:</u> Apr–Oct, Tues–Sun 9–5pm. Nov–Mar, Tue–Fri 9–4pm, Sat–Sun 9–5pm. <u>Admission:</u> Adults DM4, concs DM2.

map 247
12

PAPPENHEIM CASTLE

Neues Schloß, 91788 Pappenheim, Germany
Tel: 00 49 9143 83 890   Fax: 00 49 9143 6445 (Gräfliche Verwaltung)

An imposing 12th century castle, extension 300m long, overlooking the picturesque former residence city of the Hereditary Marshals of the Holy Roman Empire, the Marchesses Pappenheim, with important historic buildings, enlarged during the following centuries; partly destroyed since the 30-years-war, an economical building and the arsenal of the 15th century contain a small museum, torture chamber, keep, long fortification walls, falconry, twice a day demonstrations, herb garden, aboretum with collection of trees, shrubs and plants of the area, (more than 700 species), medieval tournament last weekend in June. Cafeteria. **Location:** 35 miles W of Eichstaett. **Open:** Easter–5 Nov, Tues–Sun, 10–5pm. **Admission:** Adults DM5, children DM3,50. Separate admission for falconry demonstration.

map 247
13

POSTERSTEIN CASTLE

04626 Posterstein/Thuringia Germany
Tel/Fax: 00 49 34496 22595

Going to Saxony's capital Dresden on the busy motorway A4 you will pass Burg Posterstein which is situated halfway between Thuringia's capital Erfurt and Dresden. Burg Posterstein is located in Eastern Thuringia, bordering on the classical Thuringia, marked by Goethe. The first information about the castle dates from 1191. The first owner, Knight Stein, got his landed property from King Friedrich I; Barbarossa. In the 16th and 17th century the old castle was rebuilt and became a little palace. The last restoration work took place from 1984 to 1991. **Museum Open:** Tues–Sat, 10–5pm; Sun 10–6pm. Nov–Feb: Tues–Fri 10–4pm; Sat–Sun 10–5pm. **Admission:** Adults: DM5, pupils, students: DM2, children under 14: free.

map 247
14

QUERFURT CASTLE

06268 Querfurt, Germany
Tel: 00 49 34771/5219 0 Fax: 00 49 34771/5219 99

Gracing the southern slope of the Quernebach Valley, the castle is one of the oldest in Germany. Its first documented mention occurred in the Hersfeld tithe register (866–899). In fact, this is also one of the largest castle compounds in the land, with an area almost seven times as large as that of the Wartburg. Presumably, Querfurt Castle served as a haven for refugees in Carolingian times. Evidence of stone buildings exists from the late 10th century onwards. The most conspicuous features of the castle are its three towers: 'Dicker Heinrich', 'Marterturm' and 'Pariser Turm'. At the centre is the Romanesque church built in the latter half of the 12th century, a crosshoped edifice with three semicircular apses and an octagonal crossing tower. **Open:** Tues–Sun, 9–5pm. Closed Mon. **Admission:** DM5, concessions DM3.

map 247
15

RITTERGUT HAUS LAER

Höfestrasse 45, 44803 Bochum (Ruhrgebiet, Nordrhein–Westfalen), Germany
Tel: 00 49 234 383044 Fax: 00 49 234 385375

Founded in 940, it is the oldest secular building existing in the middle Ruhrgebiet. A picturesque moated castle. The reliefs of the local sovereign Henry the Lion and his spouse Mathilde, who was the daughter of King Henry II and the sister of Richard Lionheart (Robin Hood, Nottinghamshire), are situated in two Suites of Haus Laer that can be rented. In 1704 and 1709 Haus Laer fought under John Churchill, Duke of Marlborough (Blenheim Palace Woodstock), successfully against King Ludwig XIV. Reservations for the suites "Madame Pompadour" and "Prince Soubise" possible. Guest house. Long and short stays in the Apartments/ suites are possible. The Hall of the Knights can be hired. **Location:** 4½km from the main station of Bochum; 2km from exit "Querenburg" of the A43; 1.6km from the Exit "Steinkuhl" of the urban motorway "Nordhausenring".

map 247
16

SAYN CASTLE & BUTTERFLY GARDEN

56170 Bendorf-Sayn Germany
Tel: 00 49 2622 15478 (The Prince & The Princess zu Sayn-Wittgenstein-Sayn)

Burg Sayn, built before 1200 by the Counts of Sayn, was destroyed in 1633 and recently restored. Spectacular view on romanesque Sayn abbey, Rhine Valley and Eifel mountains. A Turmuhrenmuseum contains fine collection of tower clocks. Castellated terraces descend to Schloss Sayn, where a museum for cast iron art will open in 2000. Landscaped park with rare trees, ponds, playgrounds and Garten der Schmetterlinge, an exotic dreamland with hundreds of live tropical butterflies. **Location:** Bendorf-Sayn, 10km NE of Koblenz on A48 and B42. **Open:** Mid Mar–early Nov. Butterfly garden daily from 9–6pm. **Admission:** Butterfly garden: Adult DM8, Child DM5. **Refreshments:** Burgschanke open 11–8pm (closed Mons). Cafeteria at butterfly garden. **Internet:** www.sayn.de

map 247 **17**

SIGMARINGEN CASTLE

F.H. Schlossverwaltung, 72488 Sigmaringen
Tel: 00 49 7571 729 230   Fax: 00 49 7571 729 105

Sigmaringen Castle is, to this day, the home of the descendants of the Princes of Hohenzollern. The castle majestically overlooks the town of Sigmaringen and its surrounding countryside. There are many fascinating things to see in the castle; the Hubertus hall houses a large collection of hunting trophies and over 3,000 historic weapons of all types (one of the largest private collections of its kind in Europe). Art is indestructible, but it has found a safe hiding place here in Hohenzollern's castle; valuable tapestries and paintings, priceless porcelain pieces, elegant and tasteful furniture, which capture a calm and still ambience, can be found here. **Open:** For guided tours: Nov, Feb–Apr, daily, 9.30–4.30pm; May–Oct, daily, 9–4.45pm; Dec–Jan, only organised tours with prior bookings, until 4pm. **E-mail:** rossero@hohenzollern.com

map 247 **18**

SONDERSHAUSEN CASTLE

Box 83 99702 Sonderhausen (Siftung Thüringer Schlösser und Gärten)
Tel: 00 49 36 32 6630

The former residence of the Counts (since 1697 Princes) of Schwarzburg-Sonderhausen is the many-sided and in historical and artistical terms, the most interesting building in the north of Thuringia to experience about 600 years of architecture. The castle is situated on a rise above the town, surrounded by a 19C park covering 30 hectares. **Location:** 60km N of Erfurt on B4, parking near castle; railway-line: Intercity to Erfurt, regional-line to Sondershausen. **Open:** Residence-museum Tues–Sun 10–4pm, closed Mon; guided tours 10am & 2pm and by arrangements; special tours by arrangement (contact museum Tel: 00 49 3632 663 120). **Admission:** Adult DM6, seniors/student DM4, child (under 6) free, groups (min 15 pers.) DM3. Restaurants in historical rooms daily 11–12pm. Concerts in historic rooms (symphonic and chamber music, organ recitals) and exhibitions.

map 247 **19**

STOLPEN CASTLE

Schlossstrasse 10, 01833 Stolpen
Tel: 00 49 35973 2340 Fax: 00 49 35973 23419

30km E of Dresden, this Medieval castle was once the secondary residence of the Bishops of Meissen and the Saxon electoral princes. The building beautifully complements the natural monument the 'Stolpener Basalt'. Stolpen castle with its striking towers dominates the landscape between the 'Lausitz' and the 'Elbsandsteingebirge'. The castle is linked with the tragic fate of Countess Cosel, the most famous of Augustus the Strong's mistresses. He was the electoral prince of Saxony and King of Poland. She was a prisoner in the castle for 49 years (1716–1765) and is buried in the chapel. The medieval character is preserved through prisons, cellars, a torture chamber and the deepest well in the world. The castle museum and events programme make Stolpen one of the liveliest historic places in Saxony. **Open:** Daily, Summer 9–5pm. Winter 10–4pm (weather permitting).

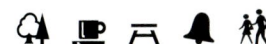

map 247 **20**

THE PRINCELY CASTLE OF THURN UND TAXIS

Emmeramsplatz 5, 93047 Regensburg, Bavaria
Tel: 00 49 0941 5048133 Fax: 00 49 0941 5048256

Since 1812, this has been the home of the Princes of Thurn und Taxis, who reconstructed parts of the former Benedictine monastery of St. Emmeram as their residence. Besides the palace staterooms, furnished in different styles (rococo, neo-rococo, classic, historic), you can visit the medieval cloister (11–14th centuries) with the mortuary chapel (19th century) and the carriage museum (carriages, sleighs, sedan chairs, harnesses) in the former princely stables and riding hall. **Location:** A93, Exit Regensburg-Konigswiesen, then direction "Regensburg centre" **Open:** Apr–Oct daily 11am, 2, 3, 4pm, on Sats and Suns also 10am, Nov–Mar, Sats, Suns, Bank Hols 10, 11, 2, 3pm (guided tours only), tours for groups by appointment. **Admission:** Adults DM12, reduced fee DM10.

map 247
21

CASTLES OF THE PRINCE OF OETTINGEN – WALLERSTEIN

Baldern Castle – 73441 Bopfingen, Germany Tel 00 49 7362 9688 0 **E-mail:** schloesser@fuerst–wallerstein.de
Harburg Castle – 86655 Harburg, Germany Tel: 00 49 9080 9686 0 **Internet:** www.fuerst–wallerstein.de

Baldern Castle: Baldern Castle, rebuilt in the early 18th century on the ground plans of the original fortress, houses one of the most extensive private collections of Arms and Armour in Germany from the 16th to 18th century, all still in good working order. Further highlights of the tour are the precious drawing rooms, a dining room and particularly the Ballroom with exceptional stucco decoration. Baldern offers a spectacular view over the surrounding countryside. **Location:** Just off the Romantic Road (leave B25 in Wallerstein) close to A7 Exit Ellwangen or Nordlingen. **Open:** Mid Mar–Oct 9–5pm (closed Mons) **Admission:** Adult DM7, child DM4, group DM6. **Refreshments:** Schloss-Schenke zum Marstall in the baroque stables. **Weddings:** Chapel can be hired for weddings (100–200 persons).

map 247
22

Harburg Castle: At Harburg visitors enter one of the earliest and best-preserved fortresses in southern Germany, built before 1100 and owned by the Counts and then the Princes of Oettingen since 1299. From the height of an imposing rock, it defends the entrance to the most researched meteor crater in the world, the 'Ries'. A tour around the fine Inner Court is a rendezvous with history. Along the wall walk visitors pass through a medieval world of prison cells, courtroom, keeps and towers. The highlight of every tour is the Great Ballroom and the Fortress Church. **Location:** On Romantic Road (B25) between Nördlingen and Donauwörth. **Open:** Mid Mar–Oct, 9–5pm (closed Mon). **Admission:** Adult DM7, child DM4, group DM6. **Refreshments:** Burgschenke in historic ambience. **Accommodation:** Hotel in the castle. Church can be hired for weddings (150 people).

map 247
23

WALLERSTEIN CASTLE

D–86757 Wallerstein, Germany
Tel: +49 9081 782 300

The 'New Castle' in Wallerstein arose after the thirty year war when the Fortress on the Wallerstein Cliffs was destroyed by Swedish troops. In its stately and private rooms (i.e. bedroom chamber, dining room, banquette hall) a fine Porcelain and Glass Collection as well as a unique exhibition of family uniforms of the Princes of Oettingen is on show. The adjacent english stlye park invites you to a relaxing stroll to the Orangerie and the impressive riding school. **Location:** On the Romantic Road (B25) between Dinkelsbühl and Nördlingen. **Open:** mid Mar–Oct, 9–5pm (closed Mons). **Admission:** Adult DM7, child DM4, Group DM6. **Refreshments:** Restaurant of Prince Oettingen–Wallerstein's brewery at the Wallerstein Cliff. **Weddings:** Chapel can be hired for weddings (80 persons). **E-mail:** schloesser@fuerst–wallerstein.de **Internet:** www.fuerst–wallerstein.de

map 247
24

WARTBURG CASTLE

99817 Eisenach, Germany
Tel: 00 49 3691 2500 Fax: 00 49 3691 203342

The Wartburg, situated on a 410m high hill in the heart of Germany, is one of the best preserved German medieval castles. Founded in 1067 and gradually enlarged through the years, it became an enormous castle complex, containing Romanesque, Gothic and 19th century buildings. When the visitor enters the Romanesque Palace, he opens a 900-year old history book: Medieval courtly culture, life and charity work of St. Elizabeth – one of the most remarkable female figures of the Middle Ages – and Martin Luther's translation of the New Testament. The Wartburg Art Collection includes artistic treasures from the Renaissance to the 19th century. **Location:** A4 Frankfurt/Main – Dresden. **Open:** Daily from 8.30–5pm; Nov–Feb 9–3.30pm. (guided tours also in English).

map 247 / 25

WERNIGERODE CASTLE

Schloss Wernigerode GmbH, Am Schloss 1, 38855 Wernigerode
Tel: 00 49 39 43 55 30 30 Fax: 00 49 39 43 55 30 55

The original Romanesque castle dating from the 12th century, extensively altered over the years, was up to 1945 the residential palace of the Earls of Stolberg, who took the name 'von Stolberg-Wernigerode' from their principality, the earldom of Wernigerode. The grand turreted stone and half-timber castle with magnificent views over the medieval town of Wernigerode today ranks as a major example of the North German "Historismus" building style. The remarkable rise to political power of Earl Otto, who became Vice Chancellor of Germany under Bismarck, gave impetus to the sumptuous late 19th century remodelling seen today, including the original staterooms of Europe's highest ranking nobility of that day. Changing exhibits, a variety of events and scientific symposiums fulfil the Schlossmuseum's aim to become a centre of artistic and cultural history of the 19th century. Weddings in the Chapel, banquets in the Dining Hall, receptions, conferences and parties in the grandly appointed staterooms by arrangement. **Location:** Above Wernigerode, 70km south of Brunswick. Transfer service every 20 minutes from the Town Centre. **Open:** May–Oct daily 10–6pm, last admission 5.30pm, Nov–Apr closed Mon. **Admission:** Adults DM8, children DM4. Gardens and panorama terrace free. **Refreshments:** Restaurant and tearoom open daily except Mondays. **Exhibitions/Events:** Open air opera, theatre, concerts and ballet on the central terrace, shop.

map 247 / 26

WILHELMSBURG CASTLE

Museum Castle Wilhelmsburg, Schlossberg 9, D–98574 Schmalkalden
Tel: 00 49 3683 403186 Fax: 00 49 3683 601682

Castle Wilhelmsburg was built between 1585 and 1590 by Landgrave Wilhelm IV of Hessen–Kassel. This unique monument to art and architecture, a mature example of Renaissance castle building is surrounded by well-preserved grounds and outer buildings. Renaissance ornamentation, wallpaintings and stucco are characteristic of the decor of the apartments and state-rooms. The castle's church provides an example of one of the most mature Protestant church buildings of the 16th centuries. Themes of the exhibitions are Renaissance, Reformation, history of the building and its use as well as contemporary art. **Events:** Recitals on the Renaissance organ (1589), Chamber music recitals. **Location:** A4, Exit Eisenach, 40km S on B19. **Open:** (not Mons) Feb–Oct: 9–5pm, Nov–Jan: 10–4pm. **Admission:** Adults DM6, child DM4, groups DM5. Tours by appointment DM30.

map 247 / 27

The Netherlands

Girls in clogs dancing under a windmill beside a tulip field. This stereotypical image of The Netherlands, also known as Holland, has been preserved as the country has kept many of its traditional aspects alive. The windmills still turn at the Zaanse Schans, the tulip gardens at Keukenhof explode in a riot of colour every Spring and the beautiful Dutch costumes are still daily wear for some people in the former fishing villages around the Ijsselmer.

However, much as the traditional aspects of the country are cherished, The Netherlands has many other attractive features such as its mixed culture, impressive architecture and art. The land of Rembrandt, Hals and Vermeer has more museums per square foot than any other country in the world. One of the most frequented galleries is the Van Gogh Museum, currently being refurbished. Some of the artist's 206 paintings may be seen at a special exhibition at the Rijksmuseum in Amsterdam.

The capital of The Netherlands, Amsterdam, is a fusion of both the past and present. Since the 16th century, when the diamond trade was first introduced to the city, Amsterdam has remained one of the world's most important diamond centres. The 'Koh-I-Noor' Mountain of Light diamond was cut and polished here for the British Crown Jewels in 1852. The city is striking with architectural masterpieces lining the narrow streets and tall trees forming a canopy along the beautiful canals, filled with houseboats. The beauty of the city contrasts strongly with the more permissive side of Amsterdam and its coffee-shop culture.

Situated further south along the coast is the town of Delft, famous for its Delft blue pottery. The historical walk, which uncovers the birthplace of the painter Vermeer, the old market square and the beautiful convent Het Prinsenhof, is an ideal way in which to explore the town.

Dutch cuisine, although largely influenced by Germanic flavours, incorporates much of its local produce such as the exquisite oysters and mussels from Zeeland. The country's dairy farms are a source of national pride, producing the world-famous Edam cheese. Indeed, such is the country's love of dairy products that the picturesque town of Gouda with its beautiful late Gothic architecture and lively markets gave its name to a cheese.

Nearby Rotterdam, with its impressive skyline, is an international business centre which hosts many trade fairs and conferences. The city on The Meuse combines centuries of architectural splendour with modern properties. This juxtapositioning of the very old with the brand new buildings is represented in the Rotterdam ArchiCentre. The city is currently preparing for the year 2001, when Rotterdam will become the Cultural Capital of Europe.

The Limburg province situated towards Belgium and Luxembourg is the essence of natural beauty with its dramatic landscape and rolling hills. The convivial ambience of the folk dancers and marching bands must be enjoyed from one of the lively pavement cafés. This is considered to be the most continental part of The Netherlands and like the rest of the country, its cultural diversity, rich heritage and traditions are truly quintessential.

MUIDERSLOT

Herengracht 1, 1398 AA Muiden
Tel: 00 31 (0) 294 261325 Fax: 00 31 (0) 294 261056 (Stichting Rijksmuseum Muiderslot)

The history of Muiden castle begins about 1280 when Floris V, Count of Holland, erected a stone fortress at the mouth of the river Vecht. The castle was destroyed in 1296 and rebuilt about 100 years later. The man who made the castle famous is the poet, playwright and historian Pieter Cornelisz Hooft (1581–1647). Hooft was bailiff of Muiden and reeve of Gooiland. For 39 years he summered at the castle, which he endowed with the splendour of Holland's Golden Age. Recently refurbished, the castle has regained its pristine elegance. The herb and kitchen gardens and the plum orchard also recall the sumptuous life of the castle's 17th century residents. During summer there is live falconry.

map 256
1

KEUKENHOF

Stationsweg 166a, 2161 AM Lisse, The Netherlands
Tel: 00 31 252 465 555

Keukenhof is known as the Spring Garden of Europe. In 1949 the area was developed as a permanent showcase for the bulb and flower industry. Today, Keukenhof is the world's largest bulb flower garden, with acres of tulips, daffodils, hyacinths and other flowering bulbs, flowering shrubs, ancient trees and beautiful ponds and fountains. Keukenhof also has changing indoor flower exhibitions or parades, theme gardens and a special 'Bollebozen' route for children. **Open:** 25 Mar–19 May 1999. Also open for a special summer exhibition between 19 Aug–19 Sept. Please call for further details of opening times and admission prices.

map 256
2

RIJKSMUSEUM

Stadhouderskade 42, Amsterdam
Tel: 00 31 20 6747000

The museum ranks as one of the most important art galleries in Europe. It was designed in the 19th century by the architect P.J.H Cuypers and features numerous works by the old masters. Works on show at the museum include works by Rembrandt, Vermeer and Frans Hals. **Open:** Daily 10–5pm. Closed 1st January. **Admission:** children: 6–18yrs, FL7.50, adults (aged 19 and over) FL15. Groups of fifteen or more, 20% discount.

map 256
3

PALEIS HET LOO NATIONAL MUSEUM

Koninklijk Park 1, NL–7315 JA Apeldoorn, The Netherlands
Tel: 00 31 55 577 2400 Fax: 00 31 55 521 9983

Built around 1686 by William III of Orange, favourite summer residence of the Royal Family until 1975. Palace and gardens restored to their seventeenth century state. Interiors from William & Mary-Wilhelmina (died 1962). Museum of the Chancery of The Netherlands Orders of Knight-hood; Royal stables. **Location:** Follow road signs; Bus 102 and 104 near Railway Station. **Open:** Palace and gardens open all year, Tue–Sun, 10–5pm; closed Christmas Day & Mon unless Bank Holidays. **Admission:** 6–17 years & 65+: Fl 10, Adults: FL 12,50; surcharge of FL 2,50 per person during exhibitions. **Guided Tours:** In English by appointment. **Refreshments:** Tea House, Ballroom. Banquets, Meetings: 00 31 55 577 2408. **E-mail:** paleis.het.loo@wxs.nl

map 256
4

SPAENSWEERD GARDENS

Bronkhorsterweg 18,6971 JA Brummen
Tel: 00 31 575 561104 Fax: 00 31 575 566160 (Diana Hummelen)

Spaensweerd dates back to the 17th century, but was altered in 1835 creating a lovely empire style. It is set in 3 acres of beautiful listed gardens with formal and informal elements. Old topiary, monumental trees and an astonishing number of rare and unusual plants in the herbaceous borders, which provides interest throughout the season. Splendid views from the garden overlooking the countryside. **Location:** 5 km south of Zutphen. **Open:** 5–6 & 19–20 June; 10, 11 & 25 July, 10–5pm. Groups by appointment. **Admission:** Adults FL 7,50. Children under 12 free. **Refreshments** and accommodation available.

map 256
5

VALKENBURG

Grendelplein 13, Valkenburg, (Limberg), The Netherlands
Tel: 00 31 43 6090110

Visit the only castle in The Netherlands to have been built on a mountain side – these magnificent ruins are situated on the 'Falcon's Mount' – a site occupied by the castle since 1100. The castle once belonged to the ducal house of Cleves and was the setting for the marriage between Beatrice of Valkenburg and Richard of Cornwall (brother of Henry III of England) in 1269. In 1329 the castle was destroyed and rebuilt in its current shape. It was conquered by the Duke of Brabant in 1365 and was subsequently beseiged on a number of occasions until being blown up by the armies of William III in 1672. Today, it is possible to visit the network of secret passages leading to the Velvet Cave. **Open:** Contact for details of opening times. **Admission:** Castle Ruins & Cave Tours: Adult FL10, children 4–12 yrs FL7, OAP's FL9. Family card FL30 (incl 2 adults & children aged 4–16).

map 256
6

SMOKING DAMAGES THE HEALTH OF THOSE AROUND YOU
Chief Medical Officers' Warning

AGED CIGARS

Supplementary List of Properties

The list of houses in England, Scotland and Wales printed here are those which are usually open 'by appointment only' with the owner, or open infrequently during the summer months. These are in addition to the Houses and Gardens which are open regularly and are fully classified. Where it is necessary to write for an appointment to view, see code (WA). * denotes owner/address if this is different from the property address. The majority of these properties have received a grant for conservation from the Government given on the advice of the Historic Buildings Councils. Public buildings, almshouses, tithe barn, business premises in receipt of grants are not usually included, neither are properties where the architectural features can be viewed from the street.

ENGLAND

AVON

Birdcombe Court, (Mr & Mrs P. C. Sapsed.) (WA), Wraxall, Bristol

Eastwood Manor Farm, (A. J. Gay), East Harptree

Partis College, (The Bursar.) (WA), Newbridge Hill, Bath, BA1 3QD Tel: 01225 421 532

The Refectory, (Rev. R. Salmon), The Vicarage Tel: 01934 833 126

Woodspring Priory, (WA), Kewstoke, Weston-Super-Mare.*The Landmark Trust.

BEDFORDSHIRE

The Temple, (The Estate Office) (WA), Biggleswade

Warden Abbey, (WA), Nr. Biggleswade
* The Landmark Trust.

BERKSHIRE

High Chimneys, (Mr & Mrs S. Cheetham) (WA), Hurst, Reading Tel: 01734 34517

St. Gabriel's School, (The Headmaster), Sandleford Priory, Newbury Tel: 01635 40663

BUCKINGHAMSHIRE

Bisham Abbey, (The Director), Marlow Tel: 01628 476 911

Brudenell House, (Dr H. Beric Wright) (WA), Quainton, Aylesbury, HP22 4AW

Church of the Assumption, (Friends of Friendless Churches), Harmead, Newport Pagnell Tel: 01234 39257
* For Key: Apply to H. Tranter, Manor Cottage, Hardmead, by letter or phone on 01234 39257.

Iver Grove, (Mr & Mrs T. Stoppard) (WA), Shreding Green, Iver

Repton's Subway Facade, (WA), Digby's Walk, Gayhurst Tel: 01908 551 564* JH Beverly, The Bath House, Gayhurst.

CAMBRIDGESHIRE

The Chantry, (Mrs T. A. N. Bristol) (WA), Ely, Cambridge

The Church of St. John the Baptist, (Friends of Friendless Churches), Papworth St. Agnes * For Key: Apply to Mrs P. Honeybane, Passhouse Cottage, Papworth St. Agnes, by letter or phone on 01480 830 631.

The King's School, Ely, (WA), Bursars Office, The King's School, Ely, CB7 4DB Tel: 01353 662 837, Fax: 01353 662 187

Leverington Hall, (Professor A. Barton) (WA), Wisbech, PE13 5DE

The Lynch Lodge, (WA), Alwalton, Peterborough
* The Landmark Trust

CHESHIRE

Bewsey Old Hall, (The Administrator) (WA), Warrington

Crown Hotel, (Proprietor: P. J. Martin), High Street, Nantwich, CW5 5AS Tel: 01270 625 283, Fax: 01270 628 047

Charles Roe House, (McMillan Group Plc) (WA), Chestergate, Macclesfield, SK11 6DZ

Shotwick Hall, (Tenants: Mr & Mrs G. A. T. Holland), Shotwick Tel: 01244 881 717
* R. B. Gardner, Wychen, 17 St. Mary's Road, Leatherhead, Surrey. By appointment only with the tenants, Mr & Mrs G. A. T. Holland.

Tudor House, Lower Bridge Street, Chester Tel: 01244 20095

Watergate House, (WA), Chester Tel: 01352 713353 * Ferry Homes Ltd, 49 High Street, Holywell, Clywd, Wales, CH8 9TF.

CLEVELAND

St. Cuthbert's Church & Turner Mausoleum, (Kirkleatham Parochial Church Council), Kirkleatham Tel: Contact Mrs R. S. Ramsdale on 01642 475 198 or Mrs D. Cook, Church Warden on 01642 485 395

CORNWALL

The College, (WA), Week St. Mary
* The Landmark Trust.

Town Hall, (Camelford Town Trust), Camelford

Trecarrel Manor, (N. H. Burden), Trebullett, Launceston Tel: 01566 82286

CUMBRIA

Coop House, (WA), Netherby
* The Landmark Trust.

Preston Patrick Hall, (Mrs J. D. Armitage) (WA), Milnthorpe, LA7 7NY Tel: 01539 567 200, Fax: 01539 567 200

Whitehall, (WA), Mealsgate, Carlisle, CA5 1JS
* Mrs S. Parkin-Moore, 40 Woodsome Road, London, NW5 1RZ.

DERBYSHIRE

Elvaston Castle, (Derbyshire County Council), Nr. Derby, DE72 3EP Tel: 01332 571 342

10 North Street, (WA), Cromford
* The Landmark Trust.

Swarkestone Pavilion, (WA), Ticknall
* The Landmark Trust.

DEVON

Bindon Manor, (Sir John & Lady Loveridge) (WA), Axmouth

Bowringsleigh, (Mr & Mrs M. C. Manisty) (WA), Kingbridge

Endsleigh House, (Endsleigh Fishing Club Ltd), Milton Abbot, Nr. Tavistock Tel: 01822 870 248, Fax: 01822 870 502

Hareston House, (Mrs K. M. Basset), Brixton, PL8 2DL Tel: 01752 880 426

The Library, (WA), Stevenstone, Torrington
* The Landmark Trust.

Sanders, (WA), Lettaford, North Bovey
* The Landmark Trust.

The Shell House, (Endsleigh Fishing Club Ltd), Milton Abbot, Nr. Tavistock Tel: 01822 870 248, Fax: 01822 870 502

Shute Gatehouse, (WA), Shute Barton, Nr. Axminster
* The Landmark Trust.

Town House, (Tenant: Mr & Mrs R. A. L. Hill), Gittisham, Honiton Tel: 01404 851 041
* Mr & Mrs R. J. T. Marker

Wortham Manor, (WA), Lifton
* The Landmark Trust.

DORSET

Bloxworth House, (Mr T. A. Dulake) (WA), Bloxworth

Clenston Manor, Winterborne, Clenston, Blandford Forum

Higher Melcombe, (M. C. Woodhouse) (WA), Dorchester, DT2 7PB

Moignes Court, (A. M. Cree) (WA), Owermoigne

Smedmore House, Kimmeridge, BH20 5PG

Stafford House, (Mr & Mrs Richard Pavitt), West Stafford, Dorchester Tel: 01305 263 668

Woodsford Castle, (WA), Woodsford, Nr. Dorchester
* The Landmark Trust.

COUNTY DURHAM

The Buildings in the Square, (Lady Gilbertson) (WA), 1 The Square, Greta Bridge, DL12 9SD Tel: 01833 27276

ESSEX

Blake Hall, Battle of Britain Museum & Gardens, (Owner: R. Capel Cure), Chipping Ongar, CM5 0DG Tel: 01277 362 502

Properties by Appointment Only

Church of St. Andrews and Monks Tithe Barn, (Harlow District Council), Harlow Study & Visitors Centre, Netteswellbury Farm, Harlow, CM18 6BW Tel: 01279 446 745, Fax: 01279 421 945

Grange Farm, (J. Kirby), Little Dunmow, CM6 3HY Tel: 01371 820 205

Great Priory Farm, (Miss L. Tabor), Panfield, Braintree, CM7 5BQ Tel: 01376 550 944

The Guildhall, (Dr & Mrs Paul Sauven), Great Waltham Tel: 01245 360 527

Old All Saints, (R. Mill), Old Church Hill, Langdon Hills, SS16 6HZ Tel: 01268 414 146

Rainham Hall, (The National Trust. Tenant: D. Atack), Rainham

Rayne Hall, (Mr & Mrs R. J. Portwee) (WA), Rayne, Braintree

The Round House, (M. E. W. Heap), Havering-atte-Bower, Romford, RM4 1QH Tel: 01708 728 136

GLOUCESTERSHIRE

Abbey Gatehouse, (WA), Tewksbury
* The Landmark Trust.

Ashleworth Court, (H. J. Chamberlayne), Gloucester Tel: 01452 700 241

Ashleworth Manor, (Dr & Mrs Jeremy Barnes) (WA), Ashleworth, Gloucester, GL19 4LA Tel: 01452 700 350

Bearland House, (The Administrator) (WA), Longsmith Street, Gloucester, GL1 2HL, Fax: 01452 419 312

Castle Godwyn, (Mr & Mrs J. Milne) (WA), Painswick

Chaceley Hall, (W. H. Lane), Tewkesbury Tel: 01452 28205

Cheltenham College, (The Bursar), The College, Bath Road, Cheltenham, GL53 7LD Tel: 01242 513 540

The Cottage, (Mrs S. M. Rolt) (WA), Stanley Pontlarge, Winchcombe, GL54 5HD

East Banqueting House, (WA), Chipping Camden
* The Landmark Trust.

Minchinhampton Market House, (B. E. Lucas), Stroud Tel: 01453 883 241

The Old Vicarage, ('Lord Weymyss' Trust), The Church, Stanway Tel: 01386 584 469
* Apply to Stanway House, Stanway, Cheltenham:

St. Margaret's Church, (The Gloucester Charities Trust), London Road, Gloucester Tel: 01452 23316
By appointment with the Warden on 01831 470 335.

Tyndale Monument, (Tyndale Monument Charity), North Nibley, GL11 4JA Tel: 01453 543 691
For Key: See notice at foot of Wood Lane.

GREATER MANCHESTER

Chetham's Hospital & Library, (The Feoffees of Chetham's Hospital & Library), Manchester, M5 1SB Tel 0161 834 9644, Fax: 0161 839 5797

Slade Hall, (Manchester & District Housing Assn.) (WA), Slade Lane, Manchester, M13 0QP

HAMPSHIRE

Chesil Theatre (formerly 12th century Church of St. Peter Chesil), (Winchester Dramatic Society), Chesil Street, Winchester, SO23 0HU Tel: 01962 867 086

The Deanery, (The Dean & Chapter), The Close, Winchester, SO23 9LS Tel: 01962 853 137, Fax: 01962 841 519

Greywell Hill, near Hook (PR FitzGerald, Wilsons)(WA) Steynings House, Fisherton Street, Salisbury SP2 7RJ

Manor House Farm, (S. B. Mason), Hambledon Tel: 01705 632 433

Moyles Court, (Headmaster, Moyles Court School) (WA), Moyles Court, Ringwood, BH24 3NF Tel: 01425 472 856

HEREFORD & WORCESTER

Britannia House, (The Alice Ottley School), The Tything, Worcester. Apply to the Headmistress.

Church House, (The Trustees), Market Square, Evesham

Grafton Manor, (J. W. Morris, Lord of Grafton), Bromsgrove Tel: 01527 31525

Newhouse Farm, (The Administrator) (WA), Goodrich, Ross-on-Wye

The Old Palace, (The Dean & Chapter of Worcester) (WA), Worcester.

Shelwick Court, (WA), Hereford * The Landmark Trust.

HERTFORDSHIRE

Heath Mount School, (The Abel Smith Trustees), Woodhall Park, Watton-at-Stone, Hertford, SG14 3NG Tel: 01920 830 286, Fax: 01920 830 357

Northaw Place, (The Administrator), Northaw Tel: 01707 44059

KENT

Barming Place, (Mr J. Peter & Dr Rosalind Bearcroft), Maidstone Tel: 01622 727 844

Bedgebury National Pinetum, (Forestry Enterprise), Nr. Goudhurst Tel: 01580 211 044, Fax: 01580 212 523

Foord Almshouses, (The Clerk to the Trustees) (WA), Rochester

Mersham-le-Hatch, (The Hon. M. J. Knatchbull), Nr. Ashford, TN25 5NH Tel: 01233 503 954, Fax: 01233 611 650. Apply to the tenant: The Directors, Caldecott Community.

Nurstead Court, (Mrs S. M. H. Edmeades-Stearns), Meopham Tel: 01474 812 121

Old College of All Saints, Kent Music Centre, Maidstone Tel: 01622 690 404
Apply to the Regional Director.

The Old Pharmacy, (Mrs Peggy Noreen Kerr), 6 Market Place, Faversham, ME13 7EH

Prospect Tower, (WA), Belmont Park, Faversham
* The Landmark Trust.

Yaldham Manor, (Mr & Mrs J. Mourier Lade) (WA), Kemsing, Sevenoaks, TN15 6NN Tel: 01732 761 029

LANCASHIRE

The Music Room, (WA), Lancaster
* The Landmark Trust.

Parrox Hall, (Mr & Mrs H. D. H. Elletson) (WA), Preesall, Nr. Poulton-le-Fylde, FY6 0NW Tel: 01253 810 245, Fax: 01253 811 223

LEICESTERSHIRE

Launde Abbey, (Rev. Graham Johnson), East Norton

The Moat House, (Mrs H. S. Hall), Appleby Magna Tel: 01530 270 301

Old Grammar School, Market Harborough Tel: 01858 462 202

Staunton Harold Hall, (Ryder-Cheshire Foundation), Ashby-de-la-Zouch Tel: 01332 862 798

LINCOLNSHIRE

Bede House, Tattershall

The Chateau, (WA), Gate Burton, Gainsborough
* The Landmark Trust.

East Lighthouse, (Cdr. M. D. Joel R.N.) (WA), Sutton Bridge, Spalding, PE12 9YT

Fulbeck Manor, (J. F. Fane) (WA), Grantham, NG32 3JN Tel: 01400 272 231

Harlaxton Manor, (University of Evansville) (WA), Grantham. *Group Visits by appointment only*

House of Correction, (WA), Folkingham
* The Landmark Trust.

The Norman Manor House, (Lady Netherthorpe) (WA), Boothby Pagnell

Pelham Mausoleum, (The Earl of Yarborough), Limber, Grimsby

Scrivelsby Court, (Lt. Col. J. L. M. Dymoke M.B.E. DL.) (WA), Nr. Horncastle, LN9 6JA Tel: 01507 523 325

LONDON

All Hallows Vicarage, (Rev. R. Pearson), Tottenham, London, N17

69 Brick Lane, (The Administrator) (WA), London, E1

24 The Butts, 192, 194, 196, 198, 202, 204-224 Cable Street, (Mrs Sally Mills) (WA), London

11-13 Cavendish Street, (Heythrop College) (WA), London

Celia & Phillip Blairman Houses, (The Administrator) (WA), Elder Street, London, E1

Charlton House, (London Borough of Greenwich) (WA), Charlton Road, Charlton, London, SE7 8RE Tel: 0181 856 3951

Charterhouse, (The Governors of Sutton Hospital), Charterhouse Square, London, EC1

17-27 Folgate Street, (WA), London, E1

36 Hanbury Street, (WA), London, E1

Heathgate House, (Rev. Mother Prioress, Ursuline Convent), 66 Crooms Hill, Greenwich, London, SE10 8HG Tel: 0181 858 0779

140, 142, 166 168 Homerton High Street, (WA), London, E5

House of St. Barnabas-in-Soho, (The Warden of the House) (WA), 1 Greek Street, Soho, London, W1V 6NQ Tel: 0171 437 1894

Kensal Green Cemetery, (General Cemetery Company), Harrow Road, London, W10 4RA Tel: 0181 969 0152, Fax: 0181 960 9744

69-83 Paragon Road, (WA), London, E5

Red House, (Mr & Mrs Hollamby) (WA), Red House Lane, Bexleyheath

Sunbury Court, (The Salvation Army), Sudbury-on-Thames Tel: 01932 782 196

Vale Mascal Bath House, (Mrs F. Chu), 112 North Cray Road, Bexley, DA5 3NA Tel: 01322 554 894

Wesley's House, (The Trustees of the Methodist Church), 47 City Road, London, EC1Y 1AU Tel: 0171 253 2262, Fax: 0171 608 3825

MERSEYSIDE

The Turner Home, (R. A. Waring RGN., CGN), Dingle Head, Liverpool Tel: 0151 727 4177

NORFOLK

All Saints' Church, (Norfolk Churches Trust) , Barmer Keyholder – No 5, The Cottages.

All Saints' Church, (Norfolk Churches Trust) , Cockthorpe. Keyholder - Mrs Case at farmhouse.

All Saints' Church, (Norfolk Churches Trust) , Dunton Key of Tower at Hall Farm.

All Saints' Church, (Norfolk Churches Trust) , Frenze Keyholder - Mrs Alston at farmhouse.

All Saints' Church, (Norfolk Churches Trust) , Hargham Keyholder – Mrs Clifford, Amost, Station Road, Attleborough.

All Saints' Church, (Rector, Churchwardens and PCC) , Weston Longville, NR9 5JU Keyholder - Rev. J. P. P. Illingworth.

All Saints' Church, (Norfolk Churches Trust) , Snetterton Keyholder - at Hall Farm.

Billingford Mill, (Norfolk County Council), Scole

6 The Close, (The Dean & Chapter of Norwich Cathedral) (WA), Norwich

Fishermen's Hospital, (J. E. C. Lamb F.I.H., Clerk to the Trustees), Great Yarmouth Tel: 01493 856 609

Gowthorpe Manor, (Mrs Watkinson) (WA), Swardeston, NR14 8DS Tel: 01508 570 216

Hales Hall, (Mr & Mrs T. Read) (WA), London, NR14 6QW Tel: 0150 846 395

Hoveton House, (Sir John Blofeld), Wroxham, Norwich, NR12 8JE

Lattice House, (Mr & Mrs T. Duckett) (WA), King's Lynn Tel: 01553 777 292

Little Cressingham Mill, (Norfolk Mills & Pumps Trust), Little Cressingham, Thetford Tel: 01953 850 567

Little Hautbois Hall, (Mrs Duffield) (WA), Nr. Norwich, NR12 7JR Tel: 01603 279 333, Fax: 01603 279 615

The Music House, (The Warden), Wensum Lodge, King Street, Norwich Tel: 01603 666 021/666022, Fax: 01603 765 633

Norwich Cathedral Close, (WA), The Close, Norwich Apply to the Cathedral Steward's Office, Messrs. Percy Howes & Co, 3 The Close, Norwich.

The Old Princes Inn Restaurant, 20 Prince Street, Norwich Tel: 01603 621 043

The Old Vicarage, (Mr & Mrs H. C. Dance), Crown St. Methwold, Thetford, IP25 ANR

St. Andrew's Church, (Norfolk Churches Trust), Frenze Keyholder - Mrs Altston at farmhouse opposite.

St. Celia's Church, West Bilney Keyholder - Mr Curl, Tanglewood, Main Road, West Bilney.

St. Margaret's Church, (Norfolk Churches Trust), Morton-on-the-Hill, NR9 5JS Keyholder - Lady Prince-Smith at the Hall.

St. Mary's Church, (Norfolk Churches Trust), Dunton

St. Peter's Church, (Norfolk Churches Trust), The Lodge, Millgate, Aylsham, NR11 6HX Keyholder - Lord & Lady Romney at Wesnum Farm or Mrs Walker at Pocklethorpe Cottages.

Stracey Arms Mill, (Norfolk County Council), Nr. Acle Tel: 01603 611122 Ext 5224

The Strangers' Club, 22, 24 Elm Hill, Norwich Tel: 01603 623 813

Thoresby College, (King's Lynn Preservation Trust) (WA), Queen Street, King's Lynn, PE30 1HX

Wiveton Hall, (D. MacCarthy) (WA), Holt

NORTHAMPTONSHIRE

Courteenhall, (Sir Hereward Wake Bt. MC) (WA), Northampton

Drayton House, (L. G. Stopford Sackville) (WA), Lowick, Kettering, NN14 3BG Tel: 01832 732 405

The Monastery, (Mr & Mrs R. G. Wigley) (WA), Shutlanger, NN12 7RU Tel: 01604 862 529

Paine's Cottage, (R. O. Barber) (WA), Oundle

Weston Hall, (Mr & Mrs Francis Sitwell) (WA), Towcester

NORTHUMBERLAND

Brinkburn Mill, (WA), Rothbury
* The Landmark Trust.

Capheaton Hall, (J. Browne-Swinburne) (WA), Newcastle-upon-Tyne, NE19 2AB

Causeway House, (WA), Bardon Mill

Craster Tower, (Col. J. M. Craster, Miss M. D. Craster & F. Sharratt) (WA), Alnwick

Netherwitton Hall, (J. C. R. Trevelyon) (WA), Morpeth, NE61 4NW Tel: 01670 772 219 Fax: 01670 772 332

NOTTINGHAMSHIRE

Winkburn Hall, (R. Craven-Smith-Milnes), Newark, NG22 8PQ Tel: 01636 636 465, Fax: 01636 636 717

Worksop Priory Church & Gatehouse, The Vicarage, Cheapside Tel: 01909 472 180

OXFORDSHIRE

26-27 Cornmarket Street & 26 Ship Street, (Home Bursar), Jesus College, Oxford Shop basement by written appointment to: Laura Ashley Ltd, 150 Bath Road, Maidenhead, Berks, SL6 4YS.

Hope House, (Mrs J. Hageman), Woodstock

The Manor, (Mr & Mrs Paul L. Jacques) (WA), Chalgrove, OX44 7SL Tel: 01865 890 836, Fax: 01865 891 810

Monarch's Court House, (R. S. Hine) (WA)Benson

Ripon College, (The Principal) (WA), Cuddesdon

30-43 The Causeway, (Mr & Mrs R. Hornsby), 39-43 The Causeway, Steventon

SHROPSHIRE

Bromfield Priory Gatehouse, (WA), Ludlow Tel: 01628 825 925* The Landmark Trust.

Halston, (Mrs J. L. Harvey) (WA), Oswestry

Hatton Grange, (Mrs P. Afia) (WA), Shifnal

Langley Gatehouse, (WA), Acton Burnell Tel: 01628 825 925 * The Landmark Trust, Shottesbrooke, nr. Maidenhead, Berks, SL6 3SW.

Oakley Manor, (Shrewsbury & Atcham Borough Council), Belle Vue Road, Shrewsbury, SY3 7NW Tel: 01243 231 456, Fax: 01243 271 598

St. Winifred's Well, (WA), Woolston, Oswestry * The Landmark Trust, Shottesbrooke, nr. Maidenhead, Berks, SL6 3SW.

Stanwardine Hall, (P. J. Bridge), Cockshutt, Ellesmere Tel: 01939 270 212

SOMERSET

Cothelstone Manor & Gatehouse, (Mrs J. E. B. Warmington) (WA), Cothelstone, Nr. Taunton, TA4 3DS Tel: 01823 432 200

Fairfield, (Lady Gass), Stogursey, Bridgwater, TA5 1PU Tel: 01278 732 251 Fax: 01278 732277

Gurney Manor, (WA), Cannington Tel: 01628 825 925 * The Landmark Trust, Shottesbrooke, nr. Maidenhead, Berks, SL6 3SW.

The Old Drug Store, (Mr & Mrs E. D. J. Schofield) (WA), Axbridge

The Old Hall, (WA), Croscombe * The Landmark Trust, Shottesbrooke, nr. Maidenhead, Berks, SL6 3SW.

The Priest's Hole, (WA), Holcombe Rogus, Nr. Wellington * The Landmark Trust, Shottesbrooke, nr. Maidenhead, Berks, SL6 3SW.

Stogursey Castle, (WA), Nr. Bridgwater * The Landmark Trust, Shottesbrooke, nr. Maidenhead, Berks, SL6 3SW.

West Coker Manor, (Mr & Mrs Derek Maclaren), West Coker, BA22 9BJ Tel: 01935 862 646

Whitelackington Manor, (E. J. H. Cameron), Dillington Estate Office, Illminster, TA19 9EQ Tel: 01460 54614

Properties by Appointment Only

STAFFORDSHIRE

Broughton Hall, (The Administrator) (WA), Eccleshall

Dunwood Hall, (Dr R. Vincent-Kemp FRSA), Longsdon, Nr. Leek, ST9 9AR Tel: 01538 385 071

The Great Hall in Keele Hall, (The Registrar, University of Keele) (WA), Keele

Ingestre Pavilion, (WA), Nr. Stafford
* The Landmark Trust, Shottesbrooke, nr. Maidenhead, Berks, SL6 3SW.

Old Hall Gatehouse, (R. M. Eades), Mavesyn Ridware Tel: 01543 490 312

The Orangery, (Mrs M Philips), Heath House, Tean, Stoke-on-Trent, ST10 4HA Tel: 01538 722 212

Park Hall, (E. J. Knobbs) (WA), Leigh

Tixall Gatehouse, (WA), Tixall, Nr. Stafford
* The Landmark Trust, Shottesbrooke, Nr. Maidenhead, Berks, SL6 3SW.

SUFFOLK

The Deanery, (The Dean of Bocking), Hadleigh, IP7 5DT Tel: 01473 822 218

Ditchingham Hall, (The Rt. Hon. Earl Ferrers), Ditchingam, Bungay

The Hall, (Mr & Mrs R. B. Cooper) (WA), Great Bricett, Ipswich

Hengrave Hall Centre, (The Warden), Bury St. Edmunds, IP28 6LZ Tel: 01284 701 561

Martello Tower, (WA), Aldeburgh
* The Landmark Trust.

Moat Hall, (J. W. Gray), Woodbridge, IP13 9AE Tel: 01728 746 317

The New Inn, (WA), Peasenhall
* The Landmark Trust.

Newbourne Hall, (John Somerville) (WA), Woodbridge

Worlingham Hall, (Viscount Colville of Culross) (WA), Beccles

SURREY

Crossways Farm, (Tenant: C. T. Hughes) (WA), Abinger Hammer

Great Fosters Hotel, (Manager: J. E. Baumann), Egham, TW20 9UR Tel: 01784 433 822

St. Mary's Home Chapel, Church Lane, Godstone Tel: 01883 742 385

SUSSEX

Ashdown House, (The Headmaster), Ashdown House School, Forest Row, RH18 5JY Tel: 01342 822 574, Fax: 01342 824 380

Chantry Green House, (Mr & Mrs G. H. Recknell), Steyning Tel: 01903 812 239

The Chapel, Bishop's Palace, (Church Commissioners), The Palace, Chichester

Christ's Hospital, (WA), Horsham Tel: 01403 211 293

Laughton Tower, (WA), Lewes * The Landmark Trust.

WARWICKSHIRE

Bath House, (WA), Walton, Stratford-upon-Avon
* The Landmark Trust, Shottesbrooke, nr. Maidenhead, Berks, SL6 3SW.

Binswood Hall, (North Leamington School) (WA), Binswood Avenue, Leamington Spa, CV32 5SF Tel: 01926 423 686

Foxcote, (C. B. Holman) (WA), Shipton-on-Stour

Nicholas Chamberlain's Almshouses, (The Warden), Bedworth Tel: 01203 312 225

Northgate, (R. E. Phllips) (WA), Warwick, CV34 4JL

St. Leonard's Church, (WA), Wroxall
Apply to Mrs J. M. Gowen, Headmistress, Wroxall Abbey School, Warwick, CV35 7NB.

War Memorial Town Hall, (The Secretary, D. R. Young), 27 Henley Street, Alcester, B49 5QX Tel: 01789 765 198

WILTSHIRE

Bradley House, Maiden Bradley, Warminster Tel: 01803 866633 (The Estate Office)

Chinese Summerhouse, Amesbury Abbey, Amesbury Tel: 01980 622 957

Farley Hospital, (The Warden), Church Road, Farley, SP5 1AH Tel: 01722 712 231

Milton Manor, (Mrs Rupert Gentle), The Manor House, Milton Lilbourne, Pewsey, SN9 5LQ Tel: 01672 563 344, Fax: 01672 564 136

Old Bishop's Palace, (The Bursar, Salisbury Cathedral School), 1 The Close, Salisbury Tel: 01722 322 652

The Old Manor House, (J. Teed) (WA), 2 Whitehead Lane, Bradford-upon-Avon

Orpins House, (J. Vernon Burchell) (WA), Church Street, Bradford-upon-Avon

The Porch House, (Tim Vidal-Hall) (WA), 6 High Street, Potterne, Devizes, SN10 5NA

YORKSHIRE

Beamsley Hospital, (WA), Skipton
* The Landmark Trust.

Busby Hall, (G. A. Marwood) (WA), Carlton-in-Cleveland

Calverley Old Hall, (WA), Nr. Leeds
* The Landmark Trust.

Cawood Castle, (WA), Nr. Selby
* The Landmark Trust.

Chapel & Coach House, Aske, Richmond

The Church of Our Lady & St. Everilda, (WA), Everingham Tel: 01430 860 531

The Culloden Tower, (WA), Richmond
* The Landmark Trust.

The Dovecote, (Mrs P. E. Heathcote), Forcett Hall, Forcett, Richmond Tel: 01325 718 226

Home Farm House, (G. T. Reece) (WA), Old Scriven, Knaresborough

Moulton Hall, (The National Trust. Tenant: The Hon. J. D. Eccles) (WA), Richmond

The Old Rectory, (Mrs R. F. Wormald) (WA), Foston, York

The Pigsty, (WA), Robin Hood's Bay
* The Landmark Trust.

Fulneck Boys' School, (I. D. Cleland, BA, M. Phil, Headmaster) (WA), Pudsey

Grand Theatre & Opera House, (General Manager: Warren Smith), 46 New Briggate, Leeds, LS1 6NZ Tel: 0113 245 6014, Fax: 0113 246 5906

Horbury Hall, (D. J. H. Michelmore), Horbury, Wakefield Tel: 01924 277 552

Town Hall, (Leeds City Council), Leeds Tel: 0113 247 7989

Weston Hall, (Lt. Col. H. V. Dawson) (WA), Nr. Otley, LS21 2HP

WALES

CLWYD

Fferm, (Dr M. C. Jones-Mortimer), Pontblyddyn, Mold, CH7 4HN Tel: 01352 770 876

Golden Grove, (N. R. & M. M. J. Steele-Mortimer) (WA), Llanasa, Nr. Holywell, CH8 9NE Tel: 01745 854 452, Fax: 01745 854 547

Halghton Hall, (J. D. Lewis) (WA), Bangor-on-Dee, Wrexham

Lindisfarne College, (The Headmaster) (WA), Wynnstay Hall, Ruabon Tel: 01978 810 407

Pen Isa'r Glascoed, (M. E. Harrop), Bodelwyddan, LL22 9D745 583 501D Tel: 01 45 583501

DYFED

Monkton Old Hall, (WA), Pembroke
* The Landmark Trust.

Taliaris Park, (J. H. Spencer-Williams) (WA), Llandeilo

University of Wales Lampeter, (Prof. Keith Robbins), Lampeter, SA48 7ED Tel: 01570 422 351, Fax: 01570 423 423

West Blockhouse, (WA), Haverfordwest, Dale
* The Landmark Trust.

SOUTH GLAMORGAN

Fonmon Castle, (Sir Brooke Boothby, Bt.), Barry, CF6 9ZN Tel: 01446 710 206, Fax: 01446 711 687

GWENT

Blackbrook Manor, (Mr & Mrs A. C. de Morgan), Skenfrith, Nr. Abergavenny, NP7 8UB Tel: 01600 84453, Fax: 01600 84453

Castle Hill House, (T. Baxter-Wright) (WA), Monmouth

Clytha Castle, (WA), Abergavenny
* The Landmark Trust.

Great Cil-Lwch, (J. F. Ingledew) (WA), Llantilio Crossenny, Abergavenny, NP7 8SR Tel: 01600 780 206

Kemys House, (I. S. Burge) (WA), Keyms Inferior, Caerleon

Llanvihangel Court, (Mrs D. Johnson) (WA), Abergavenny, NP7 8DH

Overmonnow House, (J. R. Pangbourne) (WA), Monmouth

3-4 Priory Street, (H. R. Ludwig), Monmouth

Treowen, (John Wheelock), Wonastow, Monmouth, NP5 4DL Tel: 01600 712 031

GWYNEDD

Cymryd, (Miss D. E. Glynne) (WA), Cymryd, Conwy, LL32 8UA

Dolaugwyn, (Mrs S. Tudor) (WA), Towyn

Nannau, (P. Vernon) (WA), Dolgellau

Penmynydd, (The Rector of Llanfairpwll) (WA), Alms House, Llnafairpwll

Plas Coch, (Mrs N. Donald), Llanedwen, Llanfairpwll Tel: 01248 714272

POWYS

Abercamlais, (Mrs J. C. R. Ballance) (WA), Brecon

Abercynrig, (Mrs W. R. Lloyd) (WA), Brecon

1 Buckingham Place, (Mrs Meeres) (WA), 1 Buckingham Place, Brecon, LD3 7DL Tel: 01874 623 612

3 Buckingham Place, (Mr & Mrs A. Whiley) (WA), 3 Buckingham Place, Brecon, LD3 7DL

Maesmawr Hall Hotel, (Mrs M. Pemberton & Mrs I. Hunt), Caersws Tel: 01686 688 255

Newton Farm, (Mrs Ballance. Tenant: D. L. Evans), Brecon

Pen Y Lan, (J. G. Meade), Meifod, Powys, SY22 6DA Tel: 01938 500 202

Plasdau Duon, (E. S. Breese), Clatter

Poultry House, (WA), Leighton, Welshpool * The Landmark Trust..

Rhydycarw, (M. Breese-Davies), Trefeglwys, Newton, SY17 5PU Tel: 01686 430 411, Fax: 01686 430 331

Ydderw, (D. P. Eckley) (WA), Llyswen

SCOTLAND

BORDERS

Old Gala House, (Ettrick & Lauderdale District Council), Galashiels Tel: 01750 20096

Sir Walter Scott's Courtroom, (Ettrick & Lauderdale District Council)), Selkirk Tel: 01750 20096

Wedderlie House, (Mrs J. R. L. Campbell) (WA), Gordon, TD3 6NW Tel: 0157 874 0223

DUMFRIES & GALLOWAY

Bonshaw Tower, (Dr J. B. Irving) (WA), Kirtlebridge, Lockerbie, DG11 3LY Tel: 01461 500 256

Carnsalloch House, (The Leonard Cheshire Foundation), Carnsalloch, Kirkton, DG1 1SN Tel: 01387 254 924, Fax: 01387 257 971

Kirkconnell House, (F. Maxwell Witham), New Abbey, Dumfries Tel: 0138 785 276

FIFE

Bath Castle, (Angus Mitchell), Bogside, Oakley, FK10 3RD Tel: 0131 556 7671

The Castle, (J. Bevan) (WA), Elie

Castle of Park, (WA), Glenluce, Galloway * The Landmark Trust.

Charleton House, (Baron St. Clair Bonde), Colinsburgh Tel: 0133 334

GRAMPIAN

Balbithan House, (J. McMurtie), Kintore Tel: 01467 32282

Balfluig Castle, (Mark Tennant) (WA), Grampian Apply to 30 Abbey Gardens, London, NW8 9AT

Barra Castle, (Dr & Mrs Andrew Bogdan) (WA), Old Meldrum

Castle of Fiddes, (Dr M. Weir), Stonehaven Tel: 01569 740 213

Church of the Holy Rude, St. John Street, Stirling

Corsindae House, (R. Fyffe) (WA), Sauchen by Inverurie, Inverurie, AB51 7PP Tel: 01330 833 295, Fax: 01330 833 629

Drumminor Castle, (A. D. Forbes) (WA), Rhynie

Erskine Marykirk - Stirling Youth Hostel, St. John Street, Stirling

Gargunnock House, (Gargunnock Estate Trust) (WA), Stirling

Gordonstoun School, (The Headmaster) (WA), Elgin Moray

Grandhome House, (D. R. Patton), Aberdeen Tel: 01224 722 202

Guildhall, (Stirling District Council), Municipal Buildings, Stirling Tel: 01786 79000

Old Tolbooth Building, (Stirling District Council), Municipal Buildings, Stirling Tel: 01786 79000

Phesdo House, (J. M. Thomson) (WA), Laurencekirk

The Pineapple, (WA), Dunmore, Airth, Stirling * The Landmark Trust.

Tolbooth, (Stirling District Council), Broad Street, Stirling Tel: 01786 79400

Touch House, (P. B. Buchanan) (WA), Stirling, FK8 3AQ Tel: 01786 464 278

HIGHLANDS

Embo House, (John G. Mackintosh), Dornoch Tel: Dornoch 810 260

LOTHIAN

Cakemuir, (M. M. Scott) (WA), Parthhead, Tynehead, EH3 5XR

Castle Gogar, (Lady Steel-Maitland), Edinburgh Tel: 0131 339 1234

Ford House, (F. P. Tindall ,OBE) (WA), Ford

Forth Road Bridge, (The Bridgemaster), South Queensferry Tel: 0131 319 1699

Linnhouse, (H. J. Spur(wa)y) (WA), Linnhouse, Livingstone, EH54 9AN Tel: 01506 410 742, Fax: 01506 416 591

Newbattle Abbey College, (The Principal), Dalkeith, EH22 3LL Tel: 0131 663 1921, Fax: 0131 654 0598

Penicuik House, (Sir John Clerk, Bt.), Penicuik

Roseburn House, (M. E. Sturgeon) (WA), Murrayfield

Townhouse, (East Lothian District Council), Haddington Tel: Haddington 4161

SHETLAND ISLES

The Lodberrie, (Thomas Moncrieff), Lerwick

STRATHCLYDE

Ascog House, (WA), Rothsa* The Landmark Trust.

Barcaldine Castle, (Roderick Campbell) (WA), Benderloch

Craufurdland Castle, (J. P. Houison Craufurdland), Kilmarnock, KA3 6BS Tel: 01560 600 402

Dunstrune Castle, (Robin Malcolm of Poltallock) (WA), Lochgilphead

Kelburn Castle, (The Earl of Glasgow) (WA), Fairlie, Ayrshire, KA29 0BE Tel: Country Centre: 01475 568 685 Kelburn Castle: 01475 568 204, Fax: Country Centre: 01475 568 121 Kelburn Castle: 01475 568 328

New Lanark, (New Lanark Conservation Trust), New Lanark Mills, Lanark, ML11 9DB Tel: 01555 661 345, Fax: 01555 665 738

The Place of Paisley, (Paisley Abbey Kirk Session), Paisley Abbey, Abbey Close, Paisley, PA1 1JG Tel: 0141 889 7654

Saddell Castle, (WA), Campbeltown, Argyll * The Landmark Trust.

Tangy Mill, (WA), Campbeltown, Kintyre, Argyll * The Landmark Trust.

Tannahill Cottage, (Secretary, Paisley Burns Club), Queen Street, Paisley Tel: 0141 887 7500

TAYSIDE

Ardblair Castle, (Laurence P. K. Blair Oliphant), Blairgowrie, PH10 6SA Tel: 01250 873 155

Craig House, (Charles F. R. Hoste), Montrose Tel: 01674 722 239

Kinross House, (Sir David Montgomery, Bt.) (WA), Kinross

Michael Bruce Cottage, (Michael Bruce Trust), Kinnesswood

The Pavilion, Gleneagles, (J. Martin Haldane of Gleneagles) (WA), Gleneagles, Auchterarder, PH3 1PJ

Tulliebole Castle, (The Lord Moncrieff), Crook of Devon

Bowring Countryside
Insurance Services

An Englishman's home is his castle - We want you to keep it that way

In association with Johansens

Bowring Countryside Insurance Services provide advice and insurance to those who want to enjoy their possessions secure in the knowledge that their 'castle' is always adequately insured.

With over 40 years' experience in managing insurance for Historic Houses, Farms and Estates, Bowring Countryside is ideally placed to ensure that your part of England's Heritage is protected properly. Their expertise, experience and competitive premiums have earned them the reputation as the UK's leading rural insurance broker.

They also have the support of the Country Landowners Association, who recommend the services of Bowring Countryside to its membership. The CLA appreciate the benefits that a specialist broker can bring to its members who include a large proportion of country house owners.

Are your property and valuables as well protected as you think?
Are your risks managed to keep your premiums down in the long term?
Would you like the leading rural insurance broker to assess your risks with no obligation?

The following are the main areas of insurance expertise:

- Historic Houses
- Estates
- Liabilities

- Fine Art
- Farms
- All Vehicles

- Houses open to the public
- Travel
- Legal Expenses

...... and all buildings from a Cottage to a Castle

If you would like some advice or a quotation please contact the Estates Department today and ask for Michael Portman or Cheryl Machen

01462 428043 or 01462 428207

Bowring Countryside Insurance Services
FREEPOST HI 182, Garden House, 42 Bancroft, Hitchin, Herts SG5 1DD
Part of J&H Marsh & McLennan, the world's leading insurance broker and Preferred Insurance Provider to Johansens members worldwide.

Universities

CAMBRIDGE

Note: Admission to the Colleges means to the Courts, not to the staircases and students' rooms. All opening times are subject to closing for College functions etc. on occasional days. Halls normally close for lunch (12–2pm) and many are not open during the afternoon. Chapels are closed during services. Libraries are not usually open, special arrangements are noted. Gardens do not usually include the Fellows' garden. Figures denote the date of foundation and existing buildings are often of later date. Daylight hours – some colleges may not open until 9.30am or later and usually close before 6pm – many as early as 4.30pm. All parties exceeding 10 persons wishing to tour the college between Easter and October are required to be escorted by a Cambridge registered Guide. All enquires should be made to the Tourist Information Centre, Wheeler Street, Cambridge CB2 3QB. Terms: Lent: Mid-January to Mid-March. Easter: April to June. Michaelmas: 2nd week October to 1st week December. Examination Period closures which differ from one college to another now begin in early April and extend to late June. Notices are usually displayed. Admission charges vary from college to college. **Visitors and especially guided parties should always call at the Porters' Lodge before entering the College.**

CHRIST'S COLLEGE (1505)
Porter's Lodge, St.Andrew's Street CB2 3BU
Tel:(01223) 334900 Fax: (01223) 334967

CLARE COLLEGE (1326)
Trinity Lane

CORPUS CHRISTI COLLEGE (1352)
Porter's Lodge, Trumpington Street CB2 1RH
Tel: (01223) 338000 Fax: (01223) 338061

DOWNING COLLEGE (1800)
Downing College, Regent Street CB2 1DQ
Tel: (01223) 334800 Fax: (01223) 467934

EMMANUEL COLLEGE (1584)
Porter's Lodge, St. Andrew's Street CB2 3AP
Tel: (01223) 334200 Fax: (01223) 334426

GONVILLE & CAIUS COLLEGE (1348)
Porter's Lodge, Trinity Street CB2 1TA
Tel: (01223) 332400

JESUS COLLEGE (1496)
Porter's Lodge, Jesus Lane CB5 8BL
Tel: (01223) 339339

KING'S COLLEGE (1441)
Porter's Lodge, King's Parade CB2 1ST
Tel:(01223) 331212 Fx:(01223) 331315

MAGDALENE COLLEGE (1542)
Porter's Lodge, Magdalene Street

NEWNHAM COLLEGE (1871)
Sidgewick Avenue

PEMBROKE COLLEGE(1347)
Trumpington Street

PETERHOUSE (1284)
Porter's Lodge, Trumpington Street CB2 1RD
Tel: (01223) 338200 Fax: (01223) 337578

QUEENS' COLLEGE (1448)
Porter's Lodge, Silver Street CB3 9ET
Tel: (01223) 335511 Fax:(01223) 335566

SIDNEY SUSSEX COLLEGE (1596)
Porter's Lodge, Sidney Street CB2 3HU
Tel: (01223) 338800 Fax: (01223) 338884

ST. CATHARINE'S COLLEGE (1473)
Porter's Lodge, Trumpington Street

ST. JOHN'S COLLEGE (1511)
Tourist Liaison Office, St. John Street CB2 1TP

TRINITY COLLEGE (1546)
Porter's Lodge, Trinity Street

TRINITY HALL (1350)
Porter's Lodge, Trinity Lane

Conducted Tours in Cambridge: Qualified badged, local guides may be obtained from: Tourist Information Centre, Wheeler Street, Cambridge CB2 3QB. Tel: (01223) 322640 or Cambridge Guide Service, 2 Montague Road, Cambridge CB4 1BX. We normally obtain the Passes and make all negotiations regarding these with the Tourist Office, so separate application is not needed. We have been providing guides for English, Foreign language and special interest groups since 1950. We supply couriers for coach tours of East Anglia, visiting stately homes etc. As an alternative to the 2 hour walking tour we can now offer half hour panoramic in clients' coach (providing there is an effective public address system) followed by a 1.5 hour tour on foot, or 1 hour panoramic only, special flat rate for up to 55 people.

OXFORD

NOTE: Admission to Colleges means to the Quadrangles, not to the staircases and students' rooms. All opening times are subject to closing for college functions etc., on occasional days. Halls normally close for lunch (12–2pm). Chapel usually closed during services. Libraries are not usually open, special arrangements are noted. Gardens do not usually include the Fellows' garden. Figures denote the date of foundation and existing buildings are often of later date. Terms: Hilary: Mid-January to Mid-March. Trinity: 3rd week April to late June. Michaelmas: Mid October to 1st week December. **Visitors and especially guided parties should always call at the Porter's Lodge before entering the College.**

ALL SOULS COLLEGE (1438)
Porter's Lodge, High Street OX1 4AL
Open: College Weekdays: 2–4.30. (2–4pm Oct–Mar).

BALLIOL COLLEGE (1263)
Porter's Lodge, Broad Street
Open: Hall Chapel & Gardens Daily 2–5. Parties limited to 25.

BRASENOSE COLLEGE (1509)
Radcliffe Square
Open: Hall Chapel & Gardens Tour parties: Daily 10–11.30 2–5 (summer) 10–dusk (winter). Individuals 2–5. College closed 11.30–2.

CHRIST CHURCH (1546)
St. Aldate's , Enter via Meadow Gate OX1 1DP
Tel: (01865) 276499
Open: Cathedral daily 9–4.30 (winter) 9–5.30 (summer). Hall daily 9.30–12,2–5.30. Picture Gallery weekdays 10.30–1, 2–4.30. Meadows daily 7–dusk. Tourist Information-(01865) 276499.

CORPUS CHRISTI COLLEGE (1517)
Porter's Lodge, Merton Street
Open: College, Chapel & Gardens Term and vacations – daily.

EXETER COLLEGE (1314)
Porter's Lodge, Turl Street OX1 3DP
Tel: (01865) 279600 Fax:(01865) 279630
Open: College & Chapel, Fellows' Garden term and vacations daily 2–5. (Except Christmas and Easter).

HERTFORD COLLEGE (1284, 1740 & 1874)
Porter's Lodge, Catte Street OX1 3BW
Tel: (01865) 279400 Fax: (01865) 279437
Open: Quadrangle & Chapel Daily 10–6

JESUS COLLEGE (1571)
Turl Street
Open: College, Hall & Chapel Daily 2.30–4.30.

KEBLE COLLEGE (1868)
Porter's Lodge, Parks Road
Open: College & Chapel Daily 10–7 (or dusk if earlier)

LADY MARGARET HALL (1878)
Porter's Lodge, Norham Gardens
Open: College & Gardens Daily 2–6 (or dusk if earlier). The chapel is also open to the public.

LINCOLN COLLEGE (1427)
Porter's Lodge, Turl Street
Open: College & Hall weekdays 2–5. Suns 11–5. Wesley Room All Saints Library Tues & Thurs 2–4.

MAGDALEN COLLEGE (1458)
High Street OX1 4AU
Tel: (01865) 276000 Fax:(01865) 276103
Open: College Chapel Deer Park & Water Walks daily 2–6 June–Sept 11–6.

MANSFIELD COLLEGE (1886)
Porter's Lodge, Mansfield Road
Open: College, May–July, Mon–Sat, 9–5.

MERTON (1264)
Merton Street OX1 4JD
Tel: (01865) 276310 Fax:(01865) 276361
Open: Chapel & Quadrangle Mon–Fri 2–4 Oct–June: Sat & Sun 10–4. Mon–Fri 2–5. Jul–Sept: Sat & Sun 10–5. Library not open on Sat Nov–Mar.

NEW COLLEGE (1379)
New College Lane
Open: Hall, Chapel, Cloister, Gardens daily. Oct–Easter in Holywell Street Gate 2–4. Easter – Early Oct, in New College Lane Gate (11–5)

NUFFIELD COLLEGE (1937)
Porter's Lodge, New Road
Open: College only, daily 9–5

ORIEL COLLEGE (1326)
Oriel Square OX1 4EW
Tel: (01865) 276555 Fax:(01865) 276532
Open: College daily 2–5.

PEMBROKE COLLEGE (1624)
Porter's Lodge, St.Aldate's
Open: College, Hall & Chapel & Gardens Term – daily on application at the Porter's Lodge.

THE QUEEN'S COLLEGE (1340)
High Street OX1 4AW
Tel: (01865) 279120 Fax:(01865) 790819
Open: Hall Chapel Quadrangles & Garden Open to public by apt.

ST. EDMUNDS HALL (1270)
Queen's Lane OX1 4AR
Tel: (01865) 279000
Open: On application to Porter

ST. JOHN'S COLLEGE (1555)
St. Giles' OX1 3JP
Tel: (01865) 277300 Fax:(01865) 277435
Open: College & Garden, Term & Vacation, daily 1–5. Hall & Chapel summer 2.30–4.30.

TRINITY COLLEGE (1554)
Main Gate, Broad Street OX1 3BH
Tel: (01865) 277300 Fax: (01865) 279898
Open: Hall, Chapel & Gardens daily during daylight hours.

UNIVERSITY COLLEGE (1249)
Porter's Lodge, High Street OX1 4BH
Open: College, Hall & Chapel Term 2–4.

WADHAM COLLEGE (1610)
Parks Road, Oxford

WORCESTER COLLEGE (1714)
Porter's Lodge, Worcester Street OX1 2HB
Tel: (01865) 278300 Fax:(01865) 278387
Open: College & Gardens Term daily, 2–6. Vacation daily 9–12 &2–6. Hall & Chapel Apply Lodge.

GUIDED WALKING TOURS OF THE COLLEGES & CITY OF OXFORD. Tours conducted by the Oxford Guild of Guides. Lectures are offered by The Oxford Information Centre, mornings for much of the year, afternoons, tours daily. For tour times please ring (01865) 726871. Tours are offered for groups in English, French, German, Spanish, Russian, Japanese, Polish and Serbo-Croat. Chinese by appointment. The most popular tour for groups, Oxford Past and Present, can be arranged at any time. The following special interest tours are available in the afternoon only: Alice in Oxford; Literary Figures in Oxford; American Roots in Oxford; Oxford Gardens; Modern Architecture in Oxford; Architecture in Oxford (Medieval, 17th century and Modern); Oxford in the Civil War and 17th century. Further details are available from the Deputy Information Officer.

HILDON LTD.
Hildon House, Broughton, Hampshire SO20 8DG
☏ 01794-301 747, Fax 01794-301 718

Properties Used As Film Locations

ENGLAND

BERKSHIRE

Dorney Court, Dorney, Nr. Windsor, Berkshire SL4 6QP. Tel: 01628 604638 Fax: 01628 665772 – *Children of the New Forest / Sliding Doors / The Jump / Vanishing Man*

BUCKINGHAMSHIRE

Claydon House, Middle Claydon, Nr. Buckingham, Bucks MK18 2EY. Tel: 01296 730349 – *Emma / Vanity Fair*

Stowe (Stowe School), Stowe MK18 5EH. Tel: 01280 813650 – *The Avengers*

CAMBRIDGESHIRE

King's College, King's Parade, Cambridge CB2 1ST Tel: 01223 331212

CHESHIRE

Arley Hall and Gardens, Arley, Northwich, Cheshire CW9 6NA. Tel: 01565 777353 Fax: 01565 777465 – *Good Living - Jane Asher / Brookside / Out & About*

Peckforton Castle, Stonehouse Lane, Nr. Tarporley CW6 9TN. Tel: 01829 260930 Fax: 01829 261230. – *Robin Hood*

Tabley House, Knutsford, Cheshire. Tel: 01565 750151 Fax: 01565 653230 – *Sherlock Holmes*

CORNWALL

Godolphin House, Godolphin Cross, Helston, Cornwall TR13 9RE. Tel: 01736 762409 – *Poldark / Wycliffe / Empty House*

Lanhydrock House, Bodmin, Cornwall. Tel: 01208 73320 Fax: 01208 74084 – *Twelfth Night*

CUMBRIA

Holker Hall & Gardens, Cark-in-Cartmel, Nr Grange-over-Sands LA11 7PL. Tel: 015395 58328 Fax: 015395 58776 – *The English Country Garden*

DERBYSHIRE

Haddon Hall, Bakewell, Derbyshire DE45 1LA. Tel: 01629 812855 Fax: 01629 814379 – *Jane Eyre / Prince & The Pauper / Moll Flanders / Elizabeth I*

Lea Gardens, Lea, Matlock, Derbyshire ED4 5GH. Tel: 01629 534380 Fax: 01629 534260 – *Gardeners World*

DEVON

Bickleigh Castle, Bickleigh, Nr. Tiverton, Devon EX16 8RP. Tel: 01884 855363 – *One Foot in the Past*

Cadhay, Ottery St Mary, Devon EX11 1QT. Tel: 01404 812432 – *Miss Marple - Sleeping Murder*

DORSET

Forde Abbey and Gardens, Forde Abbey, Chard, Somerset TA20 4LU. Tel: 01460 221290 Fax: 01460 220296

Lulworth Castle, The Lulworth Estate, East Lulworth, Wareham, Dorset BH20 5QS. Tel: 01929 400352 – *Inspector Morse / Tess of the D'Urbervilles / Red Violin*

Parnham House & Gardens, Parnham, Beaminster, Dorset. Tel: 01308 862204 Fax: 01308 863494 – *Jane Austen*

CO DURHAM

Durham Castle, Durham DH1 3RW. Tel: 01913 743863 Fax: 01913 747470 – *Ivanhoe*

Raby Castle, Staindrop, Darlington, Co. Durham DL2 3AY. Tel: 01833 660202 Fax: 01833 660169 – *Elizabeth I*

ESSEX

Layer Marney Tower, Nr Colchester, Essex CO5 9US. Tel/Fax: 01206 330784 – *Canterbury Tales*

The Sir Alfred Munnings Art Museum, Castle House, Dedham CO7 6AZ. Tel/Fax: 01206 322127 – *Liza's Country / Collectors Lot / Treasure Hunt*

GLOUCESTERSHIRE

Chavenage, Tetbury, Gloucestershire GL8 8XP. Tel: 01666 502329 Fax: 01453 836778 – *Cider With Rosie / Berkeley Square*

Frampton Court, Frampton-on-Severn, Gloucester. Tel: 01452 740698 – *Charge of the Light Brigade / Rocking Horse Winner / Animal Ark*

HAMPSHIRE

Avington Park, Winchester, Hampshire SO21 1DB. Tel: 01962 779260 Fax: 01962 779864 – *Jewels / Ruth Rendell*

Breamore House, Nr. Fordingbridge, Hampshire SP6 2DF. Tel: 01725 512468 – *Woodlanders / Florence Nightingale / Children of the New Forest / Barchester Towers*

Houghton Lodge Gardens, Stockbridge, Hampshire SO20 6LQ. Tel: 01264 810177 – *Grass Roots*

HEREFORD & WORCESTER

Moccas Court, Moccas, HR2 9LH. Tel: 01981 500381

Worcester Cathedral, College Green, Worcester, Worcestershire WR1 2LA. Tel: 01905 28854 Fax: 01905 611139 – *The Choir*

HERTFORDSHIRE

Cathedral & Abbey Church of Saint Alban, St Albans, Herfordshire AL1 1BY. Tel: 01727 860780 Fax: 01727 850944 – *First Knight*

Knebworth House, Knebworth, Hertfordshire. Tel: 01438 812661 – *Batman / Jane Eyre / Canterville Ghost*

KENT

Finchcocks, Goudhurst, Kent TN17 1HH. Tel: 01580 211702 Fax: 01580 211007 – *Collectors Lot / French & Saunders / The Making of Pride & Prejudice*

Penshurst Place and Gardens, Penshurst, Nr Tonbridge, Kent TN11 8DG. Tel: 01892 870307 Fax: 01892 870866 – *Love on a Branch Line / Little Lord Fauntleroy / Prince & The Pauper / Young Sherlock Holmes / The Mirror Cracked / Secret Garden*

LANCASHIRE

Dalemain, Nr Penrith, Cumbria Tel: 017684 86450 Fax: 017684 86223 – *Jane Eyre / Border TV Sir Harry Secombe 'Music Is My Life'*

Towneley Hall Art Gallery & Museums, Burnley, Lancashire BB11 3RQ. Tel: 01282 424213 Fax: 01282 436138 – *Whistle Down The Wind*

LEICESTERSHIRE

Stanford Hall, Lutterworth, Leicestershire LE17 6DH. Tel: 01788 860250 Fax: 01788 860870 – *Lost without Trace / The Deep Concern / The Canal Children*

OXFORDSHIRE

Broughton Castle, Banbury, Oxfordshire OX15 5EB. Tel/Fax: 01295 276070 – *Shakespeare In Love*

SHROPSHIRE

Ironbridge Gorge, Ironbridge, Telford, Shropshire TF8 7AW. Tel: 01952 433522 – *Feast of July / Home & Away / Dr Who / Anna of the Town / Fred Dibnah / Bill Bryson*

STAFFORDSHIRE

Tamworth Castle, The Holloway, Tamworth, Staffordshire. Tel: 01827 63563 Fax: 01827 56567 – *Out & About*

SUFFOLK

Somerleyton Hall & Gardens, Somerleyton, Lowestoft, Suffolk NR32 5QQ. Tel: 01502 730224 Fax: 01502 732143 – *Garden without Borders / Lovejoy / Watercolour Challenge*

SURREY

Albury Park, Albury, Guildford, Surrey GU5 9BB. Tel: 01483 202964 Fax: 01483 205013 – *Four Weddings & A Funeral / Underworld / Unsuitable Job For A Woman*

Clandon Park, West Clandon, Guildford, Surrey, GU4 7RQ. Tel: 01483 222482 Fax: 01483 223479 – *Fashion Shoots (Hello Magazine)*

Loseley Park, Guildford, Surrey GU3 1HS. Tel: 01483 304440 Fax: 01483 302036 – *The Worst Witch / Jonathan Creek / Spice Girls Movie / The Student Prince*

SUSSEX

Brickwall House & Gardens, Northiam, Rye, East Sussex TN31 6NL. Tel: 01797 253388 Fax: 01797 252567 – *Cold Comfort Farm*

Firle Place, Nr. Lewes, East Sussex BN8 6LP. Tel/Fax: 01273 858188 – *Return of Soldier / Firelight*

Parham House & Gardens, Parham Park, Nr. Pulborough, West Sussex. Tel: 01903 742021 Fax: 01903 746557 – *Prince & The Pauper / To Be The Best / Haunted*

The Royal Pavilion, Brighton, East Sussex BN1 1EE. Tel: 01273 290900 Fax: 01273 292871 – *Richard III*

WARWICKSHIRE

Arbury Hall, Nuneaton, Warwickshire CV10 7PT. Tel: 01203 382804 Fax: 01203 641147 – *Angels and Insects*

Lord Leycester Hospital, High Street, Warwick, Warwickshire CV34 4BH. Tel: 01926 491422 Fax: 01926 491422 – *Dangerfield / Songs of Praise / Surprise Gardens / Travels with Pevsner / Pride & Prejudice / Tom Jones / Moll Flanders*

WEST MIDLANDS

Baddesley Clinton Hall, Knowle, Solihull, West Midlands B93 0DZ. Tel: 01564 783294 Fax: 01564 782706 – *Sherlock Holmes*

WILTSHIRE

Longleat, Warminster, Wiltshire BA12 7NW. Tel: 01985 844400 Fax: 01985 844885 – *Barry Lyndon / The Missionary / Adventure of a Lady*

Luckington Court, Luckington, Chippenham, Wilshire SN14 6PQ. Tel: 01666 840205 – *Pride & Prejudice*

Wilton House, The Estate Office, Wilton, Salisbury SP2 0BJ. Tel: 01722 746720 Fax: 01722 744447 – *Madness of King George / Mrs Brown / Sense & Sensibility / Bounty*

YORKSHIRE

Aske Hall, Aske, Richmond, North Yorkshire DL10 5HJ. Tel: 01748 850391 Fax: 01748 823252 – *Collectors Lot*

Bolton Castle, Leyburn, North Yorkshire DL8 4ET. Tel: 10969 623981 Fax: 01969 623332 – *Elizabeth I / Ivanhoe*

Bramham Park, Wetherby, West Yorkshire LS23 6ND. Tel: 01937 844265 Fax: 01937 845923 – *Life & Crimes of William Palmer*

Elsham Hall Country and Wildlife Park and Elsham Hall Barn Theatre, Brigg, East Yorkshire DN20 0Q. Tel: 01652 688698 Fax: 01652 688240 – *History of Folk*

Ripley Castle, Ripley Castle Estate, Harrogate, North Yorkshire. Tel: 01423 770152 Fax: 01423 771745 – *Jane Eyre / The Cater Street Hangman / Duchess of Duke Street / Frankenstein*

IRELAND

Benvarden Gardens, Benvarden, Dervock, Co. Antrim, N Ireland. Tel: 012657 41331 Fax: 012657 41955 – *Beyond The Pale*

The James Joyce Museum, The Joyce Tower, Sandycove, Co. Dublin, Ireland. Tel/Fax: 00 353 1 280 9265 – *My Friend Joe / Ulysses*

Strokestown Park House & Gardens, Strokestown, Co. Roscommon, Ireland. Tel: 00 353 78 33013 Fax: 00 353 78 33712 – *Ann Devlin*

University College Dublin, Newman House, 85-86 St Stephen's Green, Dublin 2. Tel: +353 1 706 7422 / 706 7419 Fax: +353 1 706 7211 – *Aristocrats / Moll Flanders / Some Mothers Son*

SCOTLAND

Drummond Castle Gardens, Muthill Crieff, Tayside, Scotland PH5 2AA. Tel: 01764 681257/433 Fax: 01764 681550 – *Rob Roy*

Scone Palace, Scone, Perth PH2 6BD. Tel: 01738 552300 Fax: 01738 552588 – *Antiques Road Show*

WELL... DE GUSTIBUS
NON EST DISPUTANDUM

HILDON

AN ENGLISH
NATURAL MINERAL WATER
OF EXCEPTIONAL TASTE

DELIGHTFULLY STILL

Composition in accordance with the results of the officially
recognized analysis 26 March 1992.
Hildon Ltd., Broughton, Hampshire SO20 8DG. ☎ 01794-301 747

"FOR BEST BEFORE DATE SEE CAP"
Bottled at source, Broughton, Hampshire

Bottled at source, Broughton, Hampshire
"FOR BEST BEFORE DATE SEE CAP"

750 ml ℮

Garden Specialists

If you have been inspired by some of the wonderful gardens contained in this guide, why not recreate some of their beauty in your own garden? Whether you seek to create the traditional elegance of the English Rose Garden, the mass of glorious colour associated with Herbaceous Borders or perhaps are looking for particular varieties, the following specialists offer a range of plants and decorative garden ornaments to enhance gardens everywhere.

Right: Hodnet Hall Gardens, Shropshire

APULDRAM ROSES

Apuldram Lane, Dell Quay, Chichester, West Sussex
Tel: 01243 785 769 Fax: 01243 536 973 (Mrs D. R. Sawday)

Specialist Rose Nursery growing over 300 varieties of Hybrid Teas, Floribundas, Climbers, Ramblers, Ground Cover, Miniature and Patio Roses. Also a large selection of shrub roses, both old and new. Mature Rose Garden to view. Field open during summer months. Suitable for disabled, but no special toilet. **Location:** 1 mile SW of Chichester. A286 Birdham–Wittering Road from Chichester. Turn right into Dell Quay Road and then right again into Apuldram Lane. **Open:** 11 Jan–23 Dec, daily. Mon–Sat, 9am–5pm. Sun & Bank Hols, 10.30am–4.30pm. Parties can be taken around by prior arrangement with guided tour of roses, June–Sept. **Refreshments:** Ice creams.

map 4 D6

AYLETT NURSERIES LTD

North Orbital Road, St. Albans, Herts
Tel: 01727 822255 Fax: 01727 823024 (Mr and Mrs R S Aylett)

Aylett Nurseries of St Albans is a well-known family business with a reputation of high quality plants and service. Famous for dahlias– having been awarded a Gold Medal by the Royal Horticultural Society every year since 1961. In the spring our greenhouses are full of all popular bedding plants. Facilities also include spacious planteria, garden shop, coffee and gift shop, house-plants, florist, garden furniture. From the middle of October do not miss our Christmas Wonderland. **Location:** 2 miles out of St Albans, 1 mile from M10, M1, M25 & A1. **Open:** Daily (excl. Christmas and Easter day). Mon–Sat 8.30–5 Sun 10–4. **Admission:** Free. **Events:** Dahlia Festival–end Sept. **E-mail:** Aylett_Nurseries@compuserve.com **Internet:** www.martex.co.uk/hta/aylett

map 4 E3

BURNCOOSE NURSERIES & GARDEN

Gwennap, Redruth TR16 6BJ
Tel: 01209 861112 Fax: 01209 860011 (C H Williams)

The Nurseries are set in the 30 acre woodland gardens of Burncoose. Some 12 acres are laid out for nursery stock production of over 3000 varieties of ornamental trees, shrubs and herbaceous plants. Specialities include camellias, azaleas, magnolias, rhododendrons and conservatory plants. The Nurseries are widely known for rarities and for unusual plants. Full mail order catalogue £1.50 (posted). **Location:** 2 miles southwest of Redruth on the main A393 Redruth to Falmouth road between the villages of Lanner and Ponsanooth. **Open:** Mon–Sat 9–5pm, Sun 11–5pm. Gardens and tearooms open all year (except Christmas Day). **Admission:** Nurseries free, gardens £2.00.

map 2 C6

DEACONS NURSERY (H.H)

Moor View, Godshill, PO38 3HW, Isle of Wight
Tel: 01983 840 750 Fax: 01983 523 575 (G. D. Deacon & B. H. Deacon)

Specialist national fruit tree growers. Trees and bushes sent anywhere so send NOW for a FREE catalogue. Over 250 varieties of apples on various types of root stocks from M27 (4ft), M26 (8ft) to M25 (18ft). Plus pears, peaches, nectarines, plums, gages, cherries, soft fruits and an unusual selection of family trees. Many special offers. Catalogue always available (stamp appreciated). Many varieties of grapes; dessert and wine, plus hybrid hops and nuts of all types. **Location:** The picturesque village of Godshill. Deacons Nursery is in Moor View off School Crescent (behind the only school). **Open:** Winter – Mon–Fri, 8–4pm. Summer – Mon–Fri, 8–5pm. Sat, 8–1pm.

map 4 C7

FAMILY TREES

Sandy Lane, Shedfield, Hampshire, SO32 2HQ
Tel: 01329 834 812
(Philip House)

Wide variety of fruit for the connoisseur. Trained tree specialists; standards, espaliers, cordons etc. Other trees, old roses and climbing roses. Free catalogue of trees of good size from Family Trees (as above). **Location:** See map in free catalogue. **Station(s):** Botley (2.5 miles). **Open:** Mid Oct–end Apr, Wed & Sat, 9.30am–12.30. **Admission:** No charge. No minimum order. Courier dispatch for next day delivery.

map 5 V20

HADDONSTONE SHOW GARDEN

The Forge House, Church Lane, East Haddon, Northampton, NN6 8DB
Tel: 01604 770711 Fax: 01604 770027 (Haddonstone Limited)

See Haddonstone's classic garden ornaments in the beautiful setting of the walled manor gardens – including urns, troughs, fountains, statuary, bird baths, sundials and balustrading. Featured on BBC Gardeners' World, the garden is on different levels with shrub roses, ground cover plants, conifers, clematis and climbers. As part of Haddonstone's Silver Jubilee Celebrations, the garden was substantially expanded to allow a temple, pavilion and Gothic Grotto to be displayed. **Location:** 7 miles NW of Northampton off A428. **Open:** Mon–Fri 9–5.30pm closed weekends, Bank Hols and Christmas period. **Admission:** Free. Groups must apply in writing for permission to visit.

map 4 D1

KAYES GARDEN NURSERY

1700 Melton Road, Rearsby, Leicester, Leicestershire LE7 4YR
Tel: 01664 424578 (Mrs Hazel Kaye)

Set in the lovely rural Wreake Valley, the garden houses an extensive collection of interesting and unusual hardy plants. A long pergola leads the visitor into the garden and forms a backdrop to the double herbaceous borders. Mixed beds beyond are filled with a wide range of herbaceous plants, shrubs and shrub roses in subtle colour coordinated groups. A stream dissects the garden and ends in a large wild life pond alive with a myriad of dragonflies. Aromatic herbs surround a much favoured seat which looks out across one of the garden ponds towards flower beds shaded by old fruit trees, where hellebores, ferns and many other shade loving plants abound. **Open:** Mar–Oct inclusive Tues–Sat 10–5pm Sun 10am–noon. Nov–Feb inclusive Fri and Sat 10–4.30. Closed Dec 25–Jan 31 inclusive. **Admission:** Entrance to garden £2. Coach parties welcome by appointment.

 map 8 D6

LANGLEY BOXWOOD NURSERY

Rake, Nr Liss, Hampshire GU33 7JL
Tel: 01730 894467 Fax: 01730 894703 (Elizabeth Braimbridge)

This small nursery, in a beautiful setting, specialises in box-growing, offering a chance to see together a unique range of old and new varieties, hedging, topiary, specimens and rarities. Some taxus also. Descriptive list available (4 x 1st class stamps). **Location:** Off B2070 (old A3) 3 miles south of Liphook. Ring for directions. **Open:** Mon–Fri 9–4.30pm, Sat – enquire by telephone first. National Collection – Buxus. **E-mail:** langbox@msn.com.uk

 map 4 D6

MILLAIS RHODODENDRONS

Crosswater Farm, Crosswater Lane, Churt, Farnham, GU10 2JN
Tel: 01252 792698, Fax: 01252 792526 (The Millais Family)

Six acre woodland garden and specialist nursery growing over 650 varieties of rhododendrons and azaleas. The nursery grows a selection of the best hybrids from around the world and also rare species collected in the Himalayas and available for the first time. Mail order catalogue 5 x 2nd class stamps. The gardens feature a plantsman's collection of rhododendrons and azaleas, with ponds, a stream and companion plantings. Trial garden displays hundreds of new varieties. **Location:** From Churt, take A287 ½ mile towards Farnham. Turn right into Jumps Road and after ½ mile left into Crosswater Lane. **Open:** Nursery: Mon–Fri 10–1pm, 2–5pm. Plus Saturdays in Spring and Autumn. Garden and nursery open daily in May. Teas available on National Gardens Scheme Charity Days 30 & 31 May 1999.

PERHILL PLANTS

Perhill Nurseries, Worcester Road, Great Witley, Worcestershire
Tel: 01299 896 329 Fax: 01299 896 990 (Perhill Plants)

Specialist growers of 2,500 varieties of alpines, herbs and border perennials. Many rare and unusual. Specialties include penstemons, salvias, osteospermums, dianthus, alpine, phlox, alliums, campanulas, thymes, helianthemums, diascias, lavenders, artemesias, digitals and scented geraniums. **Location:** 10 miles NW of Worcester, on main Tenbury Wells Road (A443). **Open:** 1 Feb–15 Oct, daily, 9–5pm. Sun 10–4pm. Closed 16 Oct–31 Jan except by appointment.

  map 4 A1

PERRYHILL NURSERIES

Hartfield, East Sussex, TN7 4JP
Tel: 01892 770 377 Fax: 01892 770 929

Why not visit us and choose from the widest range of plants in the South East. We are not a garden centre but a genuine growing nursery offering over 5000 varieties of plants including the rare and unusual. Qualified staff available to answer your gardening questions. We will do our best to source plants you are looking for if we do not stock them. No mail order. Catalogues £1.65 incl. postage. **Location:** 1 mile N of Hartfield on B2026. **Open:** Mar–Oct, 9–5pm. Nov–Feb, 9–4.30pm. Seven days a week.

  map 5 F5

Garden Specialists

Plants for Sale

ENGLAND

BEDFORDSHIRE

Woburn Abbey, Woburn, MK43 OTP. Tel: 01525 290666
Fax: 01525 290271

BERKSHIRE

Dorney Court, Windsor SL4 6QP. Tel: 01628 604638
Fax: 01628 665772

The Savill Garden, Windsor Great Park. Tel: 01753 847518

BUCKINGHAMSHIRE

Waddesdon Manor, The Dairy, Nr Aylesbury, HP18 OJW.
Tel: 01296 651211 Fax: 01296 651142

CAMBRIDGESHIRE

Elton Hall, Elton, Peterborough, PE8 6SH. Tel: 01832 280468
Fax: 01832 280584

The Manor Hemingford Grey PE18 9BN. Tel: 01480 463134 Fax:
01480 465026

CHESHIRE

Arley Hall, nr Great Budworth, Northwich, CW9 6NA.
Tel: 01565 777353

Cholmondeley Castle Gardens, Malpas SY14 8AH.
Tel: 01829 720383 & Fax

Dunham Massey Hall, Altrincham WA14 4SJ. Tel: 0161 9411025
Fax: 0161 929 7508

Little Moreton Hall, Congleton CW12 4SD. Tel: 01260 272018

Ness Botanic Gardens, Ness, Nesston L64 4AY. Tel: 0151 3530123
Fax: 0151 353 1004

Norton Priory Museum, Tudor Road, Manor Park, Runcorn,
WA7 1SX. Tel: 01928 569895

Rode Hall, Church Lane, Scholar Green, ST7 3QP.
Tel: 01270 873237 Fax: 01270 882962

Tatton Park, Knutsford, Cheshire WA16 6QN. Tel: 01625 534400

CORNWALL

Bosvigo House, Bosvigo Lane, Truro, TR1 3NH.
Tel: 01872 275774 Fax: 01872 275774

Burncoose Nurseries and Garden, Gwennap, Redruth, TR16 6BJ.
Tel: 01209 861112

Caerhays Castle And Gardens, Gorran, St Austell PL26 6LY.
Tel 01872 501310 Fax: 01872 501870

Godolphin House, Godolphin Cross, Helston, TR13 9RE.
Tel: 01736 762409

Lanhydrock House, Bodmin, PL30 5AD. Tel: 01208 73320
Fax: 01208 74084

St. Michael's Mount, The Manor Office, Marazion, nr Penzance,
TR17 OEF. Tel: 01736 710507/710265

Pencarrow, Washway, Bodmin, PL30 5AG. Tel: 01208 841369

Tatton Park, Knutsford, WA16 6QN. Tel: 01565 654822
Fax: 01625 534403

Trelowarren House & Chapel, Mawgan-in-Meneage, Helston,
TR12 6AD. Tel: 01326 221366

Trevarno Estate & Gardens, Trevarno Manor, Helston,
TR13 ORU. Tel: 01326 574274 Fax 01326 574282

COUNTY DURHAM

Raby Castle, Staindrop, Darlington,, DL2 3AH. Tel: 01833
660202 Fax: 01833 660169

CUMBRIA

Acorn Bank Garden, Temple Sowerby, Penrith, CA10 1SP.
Tel: 017683 61893

Dalemain, nr Penrith, CA11 OHB. Tel: 017684 86450
Fax: 017684 86223

Holker Hall and Gardens, Cark-in-Cartmel, nr Grange-over-
Sands, LA11 7PL. Tel: 015395 58328 Fax: 015395 58776

Levens Hall, Kendal, LA8 OPB. Tel: 015395 60321
Fax: 015395 60669

Muncaster Castle, Ravenglass, CA18 1RQ. Tel: 01229 717614
Fax: 01229 717010

DERBYSHIRE

Chatsworth, Bakewell, DE45 1PP. Tel: 01246 582204
Fax: 01246 583536

Lea Gardens, Lea, Matlock, DE4 5GH. Tel: 01629 534 380
Fax: 01629 534 260

Renishaw Hall, Nr Sheffield, S31 9WB. Tel: 01246 432310

DEVON

Bickleigh Castle, Bickleigh, Tiverton, EX16 8RP.
Tel: 01884 855363

Cadhay, Ottery St Mary, EX11 1QT. Tel: 01404 812432

Hartland Abbey, Hartland, Nr Bideford, EX39 6DT.
Tel: 01237 441 264/234 Fax: 01884 861134

Killerton House, Broadclyst, nr Exeter, EX5 3LE.
Tel: 01392 881345 Fax: 01392 883112

Tiverton Castle, Tiverton, EX16 6RP. Tel: 01884 253200
Fax: 01884 253200

DORSET

Athelhampton House & Gardens, Athelhampton, Dorchester,
DT2 7LG. Tel: 01305 848363 Fax: 01305 848135

Chiffchaffs, Chiffeymoor, Bourton, Gillingham, SP8 5BY.
Tel: 01747 840841

Compton Acres Gardens, Canford Cliffs, Poole BH13 7ES.
Tel: 01202 700778 Fax: 01202 707537

Cranborne Manor Gardens, Cranborne, BH21 5PP.
Tel: 01725 517248 Fax: 01725 517862

Deans Court Garden, Deans Court, Wimborne, BH21 1EE.

Forde Abbey and Gardens, nr Chard, TA20 4LU.
Tel: 01460 220231 Fax: 01460 220296

Mapperton, Beaminster, DT8 3NR. Tel: 01308 862645

GLOUCESTERSHIRE

Barnsley House Garden, Nr Cirencester GL7 5EE.
Tel: 01285 740561 Fax: 01285 740628

Batsford Arboretum, Batsford Estate Office, Moreton-in-Marsh,
GL56 9QF. Tel: 01608 650722 Fax: 01608 650290

Berkeley Castle, Berkeley, GL13 9BQ. Tel: 01453 810332

Hodges Barn Gardens, Shipton Moyne, Tetbury, GL8 8PR.
Tel: 01666 880202 Fax: 01666 880373

Kiftsgate Court, Mickleton, nr Chipping Campden, GL55 6LW.
Tel: 01386 438777 Fax: 01386 438777

Lydney Park Gardens, Estate Office, Lydney GL15 6BU.
Tel: 01594 842844 Fax: 01594 842027

Painswick Rococo Garden, The Stables, Painswick House,
Painswick, GL6 6TH. Tel: 01452 813204 Fax: 01452 813204

Sudeley Castle, Winchcombe, GL54 5JD. Tel: 01242 602308

HAMPSHIRE

Broadlands, Romsey, SO51 9ZD. Tel: 01794 505010
Fax: 01794 505040

Gilbert White's House & Garden and the Oates , The Wakes,
Selborne, GU34 3JH. Tel: 01420 511275

Highclere Castle, Newbury, RG20 9RN. Tel: 01635 253210
Fax: 01635 255315

Houghton Lodge Gardens, Stockbridge, SO20 6LQ.
Tel: 01264 810177 Fax: 01794 388072

Langley Boxwood, Rake, Nr Liss, Hampshire GU33 7JL.
Tel: 01730 894467 Fax: 01730 894703

Mottisfont Abbey Garden, Mottisfont, Nr Romsey, SO51 OLP.
Tel: 01794 340757 Fax: 01794 341492

Sir Harold Hillier Gardens and Arboretum, Ampfield, nr Romsey
SO51 0QA. Tel: 01794 368787

Stratfield Saye House, Reading, RG7 2BT. Tel: 01256 882882

HEREFORD & WORCESTER

Dinmore Manor, nr Hereford, HR4 8EE. Tel: 01432 830332

Eastnor Castle, nr Ledbury, Hereford HR8 1RL. Tel: 01531 633160
Fax: 01531 631776

Harvington Hall, Harvington, Kidderminster, DY10 4LR.
Tel: 01562 777846 Fax: 01562 777190

Hergest Croft Gardens, Kington, HR5 3EG. Tel: 01544 230160
Fax: 01544 230160

How Caple Court Gardens, How Caple, HR1 4SX.
Tel: 01989 740612 Fax: 01989 740611

Perhill Nurseries, Worcester Road, Great Witley, WR6 6JT.
Tel: 01299 896329 Fax: 01299 896 990

HERTFORDSHIRE

Aylett Nurseries Ltd, North Orbital Road, St. Albans.
Tel: 01727 822255 Fax: 01727 823024

Knebworth House, Knebworth. Tel: 01438 812661

The Gardens of the Rose, Chiswell Green, St. Albans, AL2 3NR.
Tel: 01727 850461 Fax: 01727 850360

St. Pauls Walden Bury, Hitchin, SG4 8BP.
Tel: 01438 871218/871229

Hatfield House, Hatfield, AL9 5NQ. Tel: 01707 262823
Fax: 01707 275719

ISLE OF WIGHT

Deacons Nursery H.H. Moor View, Godshill, PO38 3HW.
Tel: 01983 840750 Fax: 01983 523575

KENT

Belmont, Throwley, nr Faversham, ME13 OHH. Tel: 01795 890202
Fax: 01795 890042

Doddington Place Gardens, Sittingbourne, ME9 OBB.
Tel/Fax: 01795 886101

Finchcocks, Goudhurst, TN17 1HH. Tel: 01580 211702
Fax: 01580 211007

Great Comp Garden, Borough Green, TN15 8QS.
Tel: 01732 886154/882 669

Great Maytham Hall, Rolvendon, Cranbrook, TN17 4NE.
Tel: 01580 241346 Fax: 01580 241038

Groombridge Place Gardens, Groombridge, TN3 9QG.
Tel: 01892 863999 Fax: 01892 863996

Hall Place, Bourne Road, Bexley DA5 1PQ. Tel: 01322 526574
Fax: 01322 522 921

Hever Castle & Gardens, Hever, nr Edenbridge TN8 7NG.
Tel: 01732 865224 Fax: 01732 866796

Ladham House, Ladham Road, Goudhurst. Tel: 01580 211203 Fax:
01580 212596

Leeds Castle, Maidstone ME17 1PL. Tel: 01622 765400
Fax: 01622 735616

Lullingstone Castle, Eynsford, DA14 0JA. Tel: 01322 862114 Fax:
01322 862115

Penshurst Place, Penshurst, Tunbridge Wells, TN11 8DG.
Tel: 01892 870307 Fax: 01892 870866

LANCASHIRE

Towneley Hall Art Gallery, Burnley, BB11 3RQ.
Tel: 01282 424213 Fax: 01282 436138

LEICESTERSHIRE

Kayes Garden Nursery, 1700 Melton Rd, Rearsby, Leicester,
LE7 4YR. Tel: 01664 424578

LINCOLNSHIRE

Marston Hall, Grantham. Tel: 01400 250225

LONDON

Chelsea Physic Garden, 66 Royal Hospital Road, Chelsea,
SW3 4HS. Tel: 0171 352 5646 Fax: 0171 376 3910

Museum of Garden History, Lambeth Palace Road, SE1 7LB.
Tel: 0171 401 8865 Fax: 0171 401 8869

Syon Park, Brentford, TW8 8JF. Tel: 0181 560 0881
Fax: 0181 568 0936

NORFOLK

The Fairhaven Garden, 2 The Woodlands, Wymers Lane, South
Walsam, Norwich, NR13 6EA. Tel: 01603 270449

Holkham Hall, Holkham Estate Office, Wells-next-the-Sea,
NR23 1AB. Tel: 01328 710227 Fax: 01328 711707

Houghton Hall, Kings Lynn, PE31 6UE. Tel: 01485 528569

Hoveton Hall, Norwich NR12 8RJ. Tel: 01603 782798
Fax: 01603 784 564

Mannington Hall, Saxthorpe, Norwich, NR11 7BB.
Tel: 01263 584175 Fax: 01263 761214

Sandringham House, Grounds & Museum, The Estate Office,
Sandringham PE35 6EN. Tel: 01553 772675 Fax: 01485 541571

Plants for Sale

NORTHAMPTONSHIRE

Boughton House, Kettering, NN14 1BJ. Tel: 01536 515731 Fax: 01536 417255

Coton Manor Garden, Coton, Nr Guilsborough, NN6 8RQ. Tel: 01604 740219 Fax: 01604 740838

Cottesbrooke Hall and Gardens, nr Northampton, NN6 8PF. Tel: 01604 505808 Fax: 01604 505619

Haddonstone Show Garden, The Forge House, CHurch Lane, East Haddon, NN6 8BD. Tel: 01604 770711 Fax: 01604 770027

Holdenby House Gardens & Falconry Centre, Holdenby, Northampton NN6 8DJ. Tel: 01604 770074 Fax: 01604 770962

The Menagerie - Horton, Horton, Northampton, NN7 2BX. Tel: 01604 870957

NORTHUMBERLAND

Chipchase Castle, Wark on Tyne, Hexham. Tel: 01434 230203 Fax: 01434 230740

OXFORDSHIRE

Blenheim Palace Woodstock OX20 1PX. Tel: 01993 811325 24hr information Fax: 01993 813527

Buscot Park, Buscot, Nr Faringdon, SN7 8BU. Tel: 01367 240786 Fax: 01367 241794

Waterperry Gardens, Waterperry Horticultural Centre, nr Wheatley, OX33 1JZ. Tel: 01844 339226 Fax: 01844 339 883

SHROPSHIRE

Burford House Gardens, Tenbury Wells, WR15 8HQ. Tel: 01584 810777 Fax: 01584 810673

Hodnet Hall Gardens, Hodnet, Nr Market Drayton, TF9 3NN. Tel: 01630 685202 Fax: 01630 685 853

Walcot Hall, Nr Bishops Castle, Lydbury North SY7 8AZ. Tel: 0171-581 2782 Fax: 0171 589 0195

Wollerton Old Hall, Wollerton, Market Drayton TF9 3NA. Tel: 01630 685760 Fax: 01630 685583

SOMERSET

East Lambrook Manor Garden, South Petherton TA13 5HL. Tel: 01460 240328 Fax: 01460 242 344

Gaulden Manor, Tolland, nr Taunton, TA4 3PN. Tel: 01984 667213

Hestercombe House Gardens, Cheddon Fitzpaine, Taunton, TA2 8LG. Tel: 01823 413923 Fax: 01823 413747

Milton Lodge Gardens, Milton Lodge, Wells BA5 3AQ. Tel: 01749 672168

Orchard Wyndham, Williton, nr Taunton, TA4 4HH. Tel: 01984 632309 Fax: 01984 633526

Sherborne Garden (Pear Tree House), Litton BA3 4PP. Tel: 01761 241220

STAFFORDSHIRE

Dunwood Hall, Longsdon, Nr. Leek ST9 9AR. Tel: 01538 385071

SUFFOLK

Helmingham Hall Gardens, The Estate Office, Helmingham Hall, Stowmarket, IP14 6EF. Tel: 01473 890363 Fax: 01473 890776

Hengrave Hall Centre, Hengrave Hall, Bury St Edmunds, IP28 6LZ. Tel: 01284 701561 Fax: 01284 702950

Somerleyton Hall, nr Lowestoft NR32 5QQ. Tel: 01502 730224 Fax: 01502 732143

Wingfield Old College & Gardens, Wingfield, Nr Stradbroke, IP21 5RA. Tel: 01379 384888 Fax: 01379 384034

Wyken Hall, Stanton, Bury St. Edmunds, IP31 2DW. Tel: 01359 250287 Fax: 01359 252256

SURREY

Clandon Park, West Clandon, Guildford GU4 7RQ. Tel: 01483 222482 Fax: 01483 223479

Loseley Park, Estate Office, Guildford, GU3 1HS. Tel: 01483 304440 Fax: 01483 302036

Millais Rhododendrons, Crosswater Farm, Churt, Farnham, GU10 2JN. Tel: 01252 792698

RHS Garden Wisley, Woking, GU23 6QB. Tel: 01483 224234

SUSSEX

Borde Hill Garden, Balcombe Road, Haywards Heath, RH16 1XP. Tel: 01444 450326

Charleston Farmhouse, Firle, nr Lewes. Tel: 01323 811626 Fax: 01323 811628

Waddesdon Manor, Buckinghamshire

Denmans Garden, Clock House, Denmans, Fontwell BN18 0SU. Tel: 01243 542808 Fax01243 544064

Fishbourne Roman Palace, Salthill Road, Fishbourne, Chichester, PO19 3QR. Tel: 01243 785859 Fax: 01243 539 266

Glynde Place, Glynde, nr Lewes, BN8 6SX. Tel: 01273 858224 Fax: 01273 858224

Great Dixter House, Northiam, Nr Rye, TN31 6PH. Tel: 01797 252878 Fax: 01797 252879

Leonardslee Gardens, Lower Beeding, Horsham, RH13 6PP. Tel: 01403 891212 Fax: 01403 891305

Michelham Priory, Upper Dicker, Hailsham BN27 3QS. Tel: 01323 844224 Fax: 01323 844030

Merriments Gardens, Hawkhurst Road, Hurst Green TN19 7RA. Tel: 01580 860666 Fax: 01580 860324

Parham House and Gardens, Parham Park Ltd, Pulborough, RH20 4HS. Tel: 01903 742021 Fax: 01903 746557

Pashley Manor Gardens, Ticehurst, Wadhurst, TN5 7HE. Tel: 01580 200692 Fax: 01580 200102

Perryhill Nurseries, Hartfield, TN7 4JP. Tel: 0892 770377

Royal Botanic Gardens, Kew at Wakehurst Place, Ardingly, Haywards Heath RH17 6TN. Tel: 01444 894066 Fax: 01444 894069

West Dean Gardens, West Dean Estate, nr Chichester, PO18 0QZ. Tel: 01243 818210 Fax: 01243 811342

WARWICKSHIRE

The Hiller Garden, Dunnington Heath Farm, Alcester, B49 5PD. Tel: 01789 490991

Lord Leycester Hospital, High Street, Warwick, CV34 4BH. Tel: 01926 491422 Fax: 01926 491 422

Shakespearian Properties, Henley Street, Stratford-upon-Avon CV37 6QW. Tel: 01789 204016 Fax: 01789 269083

WEST MIDLANDS

Baddesley Clinton Hall, B93 0DQ. Tel: 01564 783294 Fax: 01564 782706

Birmingham Botanical Gardens and Glasshouses, Westbourne Road, Edgbaston, Birmingham B15 3TR. Tel: 0121 454 1860 Fax: 0121 454 7835

Castle Bromwich Hall Gardens, Chester Road, Castle Bromwich, Birmingham. Tel: 0121 749 4100

WILTSHIRE

Bowood House and Gardens, The Estate Office, Bowood, Calne, SN11 0LZ. Tel: 01249 812102

Longleat, The Estate Office, Warminster, BA12 7NW. Tel: 01985 844400 Fax: 01985 844885

Stourhead, Stourton, nr Mere BA12 6QD. Tel: 01747 841152 Fax: 01747 841 152

YORKSHIRE

Burton Agnes Hall, Burton Agnes, Diffield, YO25 0ND. Tel: 01262 490324 Fax: 01262 490513

Castle Howard, York YO6 7DA. Tel: 01653 648444

Elsham Hall Country and Wildlife Park, The Estate Office, Brigg DN20 0QZ. Tel: 01652 688698 Fax: 01652 688240

Harewood House and Bird Garden, The Estate Office, Harewood, Leeds, LS17 9LQ. Tel: 0113 288 6331 Fax: 0113 288 6467

Harlow Carr Botanical Gardens, Crag Lane, Harrogate, HG3 1QB. Tel: 01423 565418 Fax: 01423 530663

Newby Hall & Gardens, Ripon HG4 5AE. Tel: 01423 322583 Fax: 01423 324 452

Norton Conyers, Ripon HG4 5EQ. Tel: 01765 640333 Fax: 01765 692772.

Nunnington Hall, Nunnington, York YO62 5UY. Tel: 01439 748283 Fax: 01439 748284

Ripley Castle, Ripley HG3 3AY. Tel: 01423 770152 Fax: 01423 771745

Sewerby Hall and Gardens, Church Lane, Sewerby, Bridlington, YO15 1EA. Tel: Estate Office: 01262 673 769 Hall :01262 677874

Shandy Hall, The Laurence Sterne Trust, Coxwold, York, YO6 4AD. Tel: 01347 868465

Skipton Castle, Skipton, BD23 1AQ. Tel: 01756 792442 Fax: 01756 796100

Thorp Perrow Arboretum, Bedale DL8 2PR. Tel: 01677 425323 Fax: 01677 425 323

IRELAND

Bantry House, Bantry, Co. Cork. Tel: 00353 2 750 047 Fax: 00353 2 750 795

Benvarden Gardens, Benvarden Dervock, Co Antrim, N. Ireland. Tel: 012657 41331 Fax: 012657 41955

Hamwood House, Hamwood, Dunboyne. Tel: 00353 1 8255210

Larchill Arcadian Gardens, Kilcock, Kildare. Tel: 00 3511 628 4580 Fax: 003511 628 7354

Powerscourt Gardens & Waterfall, Enniskerry, Co. Wicklow. Tel: 00353 1 204 6000 Fax: 00353 1 286 3561

Seaforde Gardens, Seaforde, Downpatrick BT30 3PG. Tel: +441396 811225 Fax:+441396 811370

Strokestown Park House & Gardens, Strokestown, Co. Roscommon. Tel: 00353 78 33013 Fax: 00353 78 33712

SCOTLAND

Blairquhan Castle and Gardens, Straiton,, Maybole KA19 7LZ. Tel: 016557 70239 Fax: 016557 70278

Bolfracks Garden, Aberfeldy PH15 2EX. Tel: 01887 820207

Bowhill House & Country Park, Bowhill, nr Selkirk TD7 5ET. Tel: 01750 22204 Fax: 01750 22204

Glamis Castle, Estate Office, Glamis DD8 1RT. Tel: 01307 840393 Fax: 01307 840 733

Mount Stuart House and Gardens, Mount Stuart, Isle of Bute PA20 9LR. Tel: 01700 503877 Fax: 01700 505 313

Paxton House & Gardens, Paxton, nr Berwick-upon-Tweed TD15 1SZ. Tel: 01289 386291

Traquair House, Innerleithen EH44 6PW. Tel: 01896 830323 Fax: 01896 830639

WALES

Aberglasney Gardens, East Bailiff's Lodge, Llangathen. Tel: 01558 668998 Fax: 01558 668998

The Castle House, Usk NP5 1SD. Tel: 01291 672563

Colby Woodland Gardens, Stepaside, Narberth SA67 8PP. Tel: 01834 811885

Dyffryn Gardens, St Nicholas, Cardiff CF5 6SU. Tel: 01222 593 328 Fax: 01222 591966

Erddig Hall, Gardens & Country Park, Nr Wrexham LL13 0YT. Tel: 01978 355314 Fax: 01978 355314

Picton Castle, Picton Castle Trust, Haverfordwest SA62 4AS. Tel: 01437 751326

Art Collections

Many properties throughout the guide contain notable works of art. The properties listed here have special collections.

ENGLAND

BEDFORDSHIRE

Woburn Abbey, Woburn, MK43 0TP
Tel: 01525 290666 – *Canaletto, Van Dyck, Reynolds*

BERKSHIRE

Dorney Court, Dorney, Nr Windsor, SL4 6QP
Tel: 01628 604638, Fax: 01628 665772

Eton College, Windsor, SL4 6DW
Tel: 01763 671177, Fax: 01753 671 265 – *Brew House Gallery, Exhibitions change*

Highclere Castle, Nr Newbury, RG20 9RN
Tel: 01635 253210. Old masters including Van Dyck

BUCKINGHAMSHIRE

Windsor Castle, Windsor, Berkshire SL4 1NJ
Tel: 01753 568286

CHESHIRE

Capesthorne Hall, Capesthorne, Siddington,
Nr. Macclesfield, SK11 9JY. Tel: 01625 861221.
Fax: 01625 861619

Norton Priory Museum & Gardens, Tudor Road,
Manor Park, Runcorn, WA7 1SX. Tel: 01928 569895 –
Contemporary sculpture

Tabley House, Knutsford, WA16 OHB
Tel: 01565 750151, Fax: 01565 653230 – *Lely,
Lawrence, Opie, Ward, Owen, Devis, Turner*

Tatton Park, Knutsford, WA16 6QN
Tel: 01565 750 250, Fax: 01565 654 822

CORNWALL

Mount Edgcumbe House & Country Park, Cremyll,
Torpoint PL10 1HZ Tel: 01752 822236

Pencarrow, Washway, Bodmin PL30 5AG.
Tel: 01208 841369 – *Sir Joshua Reynolds*

COUNTY DURHAM

Auckland Castle, Bishop Auckland DL14 7NR.
Tel: 01388 601627 Fax:01388 609323 – *Zurbaran*

Raby Castle, Staindrop, Darlington, Co Durham
DL2 3AY Tel: 01833 660 202

CUMBRIA

**Abbot Hall Art Gallery & Museum of Lakeland Life
& Industry,** Kirkland, Kendal LA9 5AL. Tel: 01539
722464 Fax: 01539 722494

Appleby Castle, Boroughgate, Appleby-In-Westmorland
CA16 6XH. Tel: 017683 51402, Fax: 017683 51082 –
Clifford Family Portraits

Dalemain, nr Penrith CA11 0HB. Tel: 017684 86450
Fax 017684 86223

Hutton-in-the-Forest, Skelton, Penrith CA1 9TH. Tel:
017684 84449 Fax:017684 84571 – *Furniture / Portraits
/ Ceramics / Tapestry*

DERBYSHIRE

Calke Abbey, Ticknall, Derby DE73 1LE. Tel: 01332
86382 Fax: 01332 865272

Kedleston Hall, Derby, DE22 5JH. Tel: 01332 842191
Fax: 01332 841972 – *17th & 18th century Italian / Dutch
collection*

Renishaw Hall, Nr Sheffield S31 9WB.
Tel: 01246 432310

DORSET

Athelhampton House & Gardens, Athelhampton,
Dorchester. Tel: 01305 848363 Fax: 01305 848135 –
A.W.Pugin

Parnham House, Parnham, Beaminster DT8 3NA.
Tel: 01308 862204 Fax 01308 863444

Wolfeton House, Dorchester DT2 9QN.
Tel: 01305 263500

DEVON

Powderham Castle, Kenton, Exeter EX6 8JQ. Tel: 01626
890 243 Fax: 01626 890729 – *Cosway, Hudson,
Reynolds*

Torre Abbey, The Kings Drive, Torquay TQ2 5JX
Tel: 01803 293593 Fax: 01803 201154 – *Pre-
Raphaelites; 19th century*

ESSEX

The Sir Alfred Munnings Art Museum, Castle House,
Dedham CO7 6AZ Tel: 01206 322127

GLOUCESTERSHIRE

Berkeley Castle, Gloucestershire GL13 9BQ Tel: 01453
810332

Frampton Court, Frampton-on-Severn GL2 7EU. Tel:
Home 01452 740 267 Office 01452 740 698

Owlpen Manor, Owlpen, nr Uley GL11 5BZ. Tel: 01453
860261 Fax 01453 860819

Sudeley Castle, Winchcombe, Gloucs. GL54 5JD
Tel: 01242 602308 – *Van Dyck, Ruben*

HAMPSHIRE

Breamore House, Breamore, nr Fordingbridge SP6 2DF.
Tel: 01725 512233 Fax: 01725 512858

Mottisfont Abbey Garden, Mottisfont, Nr Romsey SO51
0LP. Tel: 01794 340757 Fax:01794 341492 – *Derek
Hill's 20th Century picture collection*

Stratfield Saye House, Stratfield Saye, Reading,
Hampshire RE7 2BT. Tel: 01256 882882

HEREFORD & WORCESTER

Eastnor Castle, Eastnor, Nr Ledbury, HR8 1RL
Tel: 01531 633160 Fax 01531 631776

HERTFORDSHIRE

Hatfield House, Hatfield, Hertfordshire AL9 5NQ.
Tel: 01707 262823, Fax: 01707 275719

KENT

Cobham Hall, Cobham, Nr Gravesend, Kent DA12 3BL.
Tel: 01474 824319 Fax: 01474 822995

Finchcocks, Goudhurst, Kent TN17 1HH.
Tel: 01580 211702 Fax: 01580 211007 – *18th century,
musical theme*

Squerryes Court, Westerham TN16 1SJ. Tel: 01959
562345/563118 Fax:01959 565949 – *Old Masters /
Italian / 17th Century Dutch / 18th Century English
Schools*

LANCASHIRE

Heaton Hall, Heaton Park, Prestwich, Manchester M25
2SW. Tel: 0161 773 1231/236 5244 Fax 0161 236 7369

**Towneley Hall Art Gallery & Museum and Museum of
Local Crafts & Industries,** Burnley BB11 3RQ, Tel:
01282 424213 Fax: 01282 436138 – *18th Century &
19th Century*

LEICESTERSHIRE

Belvoir Castle, Nr Grantham, Lincolnshire. NG32 1PD
Tel: 01476 870262

LINCOLNSHIRE

Grimsthorpe Castle, Grimsthorpe, Bourne.
Tel 01778 591205 – *Family portraits*

LONDON

Apsley House, The Wellington Museum, 149
Piccadilly, Hyde Park Corner, London SW1.
Tel: 0171 499 5676 Fax: 0171 493 6576

Boston Manor House, Boston Manor Road, Brentford
TW8 9JX. Tel: 0181 560 5441 Fax: 0181-862-7602

Buckingham Palace, London SW1A 1AA.
Tel: 0171 839 1377

Greenwich Observatory, Queens House, National
Maritime Museum, Romney Road, Greenwich SE10
9NF. Tel: 0181-312 6565 Fax:0181 312 6632 – *Maritime
/ Seascapes / Royal Portraits*

Leighton House Museum & Art Gallery, 12 Holland
Park Road, London W14 8LZ. Tel: 0171 602 3316
Fax: 0171 371 2467 – *Pre-Raphaelite*

Museum of Garden History, Lambeth Palace Road,
Lambeth SE1 7LB. Tel: 0171-261 1891
Fax 0171 401 8869

Orleans House Gallery, Riverside, Twickenham, TW1
3DJ. Tel: 0181-892 0221 Fax: 0181 744 0501

Osterley Park, Jersey Road, Isleworth TW7 4RB.
Tel: 0181 568 7714

St. John's Gate, St John's Lane, Clerkenwell EC1M
4DA. Tel: 0171-253 6644, Fax: 0171 336 0587

Syon Park, Brentford, Middlesex TW8 8JF.
Tel: 0181 560 0881

NORFOLK

Holkham Hall, Wells-next-the-Sea, Norfolk NR23 1AB
Tel: 01328 710227 Fax: 01328 711707 – *Rubens, Van
Dyck, Claude, Poussin and Gainsborough*

Norwich Castle Museum, Norwich NR1 3JU.
Tel: 01603 223674

Wolterton Park, Erpingham, Norfolk. Tel: 01263 584175
Fax: 01263 761214

NORTHAMPTONSHIRE

Boughton House, Kettering NN14 1BJ. Tel: 01536
515731 Fax: 01536 417255 – *Van Dyck*

Castle Ashby House, Castle Ashby, Northampton NN7 1LQ. Tel: 01604 696696 Fax: 01604 696516 – *Reynolds, Van Dyck*

Cottesbrooke Hall & Gardens, Nr Northampton, NN6 8PF. Tel: 01604 505808 Fax: 01604 505619 – *Munnings, Gainsborough, Lionel Edwards*

Lamport Hall & Gardens, Northampton, NN6 9HD Tel: 01604 686272 Fax: 01604 686224

NORTHUMBERLAND

Alnwick Castle, Alnwick, Northumberland NE66 1NQ Tel: 01665 510777 Fax: 01665 510876 – *Titian, Van Dyck, Canelleto*

OXFORDSHIRE

Blenheim Palace, Woodstock, Oxon OX20 1PX Tel: 01993 811325 Fax: 01993 813527

Buscot Park, Buscot, Nr Faringdon SN7 8BU. Tel: 01367 240786 Fax:01367 241794

Fawley Court - Marian Fathers Historic House & Museum, Marlow Road, Henley-On-Thames RG9 3AE. Tel: 01491 574917 Fax: 01491 411587

Waterperry Gardens, Nr. Wheatley, Oxon. Tel: 01844 339226/254 – *Art Gallery*

SHROPSHIRE

Burford House Gardens, Tenbury Wells WR15 8HQ. Tel: 01584 810777 Fax 01584 810673 – *Botanical, contemporary*

Ironbridge Gorge Museum, Ironbridge, Telford TF8 7AW. Tel: 01952 433522 Fax:01952 432204 – *History of Industrial Revolution*

Rowleys House Museum, Barker Street, Shrewsbury SY1 1QH. Tel: 01743 361196 Fax: 01743 358411

STAFFORDSHIRE

Sandon Hall, Sandon, Stafford. Tel: 01889 508004 Fax: 01889 508586

The Shugborough Estate, Milford, Nr. Stafford ST17 Tel: 01889 881388

SUFFOLK

Christchurch Mansion, Christchurch Park, Ipswich Tel: 01473 253246 Fax: 01473 281274

Gainsborough's House, 46 Gainsborough Street, Sudbury, Suffolk CO10 6EU Tel: 01787 372958

Somerleyton Hall & Gardens, Somerleyton, Lowestoft, Suffolk NR32 5QQ. Tel: 01502 730224

Wingfield Old College, Wingfield, Nr Eye, Suffolk IP21 5RA. Tel: 01379 384888 Fax: 01379 384034

SURREY

Clandon Park, West Clandon, Guildford GU4 7RQ Tel: 01483 222 482 – *Gubbay Collection, Porcelain, Needlework & Furniture*

Guildford House Gallery, 155, High Street, Guildford GU1 3AJ. Tel: 01483 444740 Fax 01483 444742 – *John Russell R A / Henry J Sage / Edward Wesson*

SUSSEX

Arundel Castle, Arundel. West Sussex. Tel: 01903 883136

Bentley House & Gardens, Halland, Nr Lewes BN8 5AF. Tel: 01825 840573 – *Philip Rickman*

Charleston Farmhouse, Firle, nr Lewes. Tel: 01323 811265 Fax: 01323 811628

Firle Place, Nr Lewes, East Sussex, BN8 6LP Tel/Fax: 01273 858188. – *Van Dyck, Reynolds, Rubens, Gainsborough, Guardi, Seargeant, Tenniers, Puligo, Larkin plus many others*

Goodwood House, Goodwood, Chichester PO18 0PX. Tel: 01243 755048 Fax 01243 755005

Pallant House, 9 North Pallant, Chichester PO19 1TJ Tel: 01243 774557 – *Modern British*

Parham House and Gardens, Parham Park Ltd, Pulborough RH20 4HS. Tel: 01903 742021/ Info line 01903 744888 Fax: 01903 746557

Royal Pavilion, Brighton BN1 1EE. Tel: 01273 290900 Fax 01273 292871 – *Chinoiserie, Regency Silver Gilt*

West Dean Gardens, West Dean Estate, nr Chichester PO18 0QZ. Tel: 01243 818210 Fax: 01243 811342 – *Tapestry studio*

WARWICKSHIRE

Arbury Hall, Nuneaton CV10 7PT. Tel: 01203 382804 Fax 01203 641147

Coughton Court, Alcester, B49 5JA. Tel: 01789 400777 Fax: 01789 765544

WEST MIDLANDS

Baddesley Clinton Hall, Rising Lane, Baddesley Clinton Village, Knowle, Solihull, West Midlands. Tel: 01564 783294 Fax: 01564 782706

Birmingham Botanical Gardens & Glasshouse, Westbourne Road, Edgbaston, Birmingham B15 3TR. Tel: 0121 454 1860 Fax: 0121 454 7835

WILTSHIRE

Corsham Court, Corsham, Wilts SN13 0BZ Tel: 01249 701610/701611. – *Van Dyck, Carlo Dolei*

Longleat, The Estate Office, Warminster BA12 7NW. Tel: 01985 844400 Fax: 01985 844885 – *Alexander Thynn / Portraits*

Malmesbury House, The Close, Salisbury SP1 2EB Tel: 01722 327027, Fax: 01722 334414

Wilton House, Wilton, Salisbury SP2 0BJ. Tel: 01722 746720 Fax: 01722 744447 – *Van Dyck*

YORKSHIRE

Aske Hall, Aske, Richmond, North Yorkshire DL10 5HJ Tel: 01748 850391 , Fax: 01748 823252

Elsham Hall Country and Wildlife Park, The Estate Office, Brigg DN20 0QZ. Tel: 01652 688698 Fax 01652 688240

Bramham Park, Wetherby LS23 6ND. Tel: 01937 844265 Fax:01937 845 923

Burton Agnes Hall, Buton Agnes, Driffield, nr Bridlington YO25 0ND. Tel: 01262 490324 – *Impressionists*

Cannon Hall, Cawthorne, Barnsley S75 4AT. Tel: 01226 790 270

Harewood House and Bird Garden, The Estate Office, Harewood, Leeds LS17 9LQ. Tel: 0113 288 6331 Fax: 0113 288 6467 – *Renaissance / Turner / Reynolds / Contemporary*

Lotherton Hall, Aberford, Yorkshire L25 3EB. Tel: 0113 281 3259 Fax: 0113 281 2100

Norton Conyers, Ripon HG4 5EQ. Tel: 01765 640333 Fax: 01765 692772 – *17th & 18th Century portraits, 19th Century hunting pictures*

Sewerby Hall & Gardens, Church Lane, Sewerby, Bridlington, East Yorks YOQT 1EA. Tel: Estate Office: 01262 673769

Temple Newsam House, Leeds LS15 OAE. Tel: 0113 264 7321, Fax: 0113 260 2285

WALES

Bodelwyddan Castle, Bodelwyddan, St Asaph, Bodelwyddan LL18 5YA. Tel: 01745 584060 Fax 01745 584563 – *National Portrait Gallery, 19th Century Collection*

Bodrhyddan Hall, Rhuddlan LL18 5SB. Tel: 01745 590414 Fax:01745 590155

Colby Woodland Gardens, Stepaside, Narbeth SA67 8PP. Tel: 01834 811885

Dinefwr Park, Llandeilo, Carmarthenshire. Tel: 01558 823902

Picton Castle, Picton Castle Trust, Haverfordwest SA62 4AS. Tel: 01437 751326

SCOTLAND

Bowhill House & Country Park, Bowhill, Nr. Selkirk, TD7 5ET Scottish Borders. Tel/Fax: 01750 22204 – *Gainsborough, Canaletto*

Dalmeny House, South Queensferry, Edinburgh, EH30 9TQ. Tel: 0131 331 1888, Fax: 0131 331 1788

Glamis Castle, Estate Office, Glamis DD8 1RT. Tel: 01307 840393 Fax: 01307 840 733

Gosford House, Longniddry EH32 0PY. Tel: 01875 870201 Fax:01875 870620

Lennoxlove, Haddington EH41 4NZ. Tel: 01620 823720 Fax:01620 825 112

Mount Stuart House & Gardens, Mount Stuart, Isle of Bute, PA20 9LR. Tel: 01700 503877 Fax: 01700 505 313

Scone Palace, Perth PH2 6BD. Tel: 01738 552300 Fax:01738 552588 – *Vernis Martin, ivories, porcelain*

Thirlestane Castle, Lauder, Berwickshire TD2 6RU. Tel: 01578 722430 Fax 01578 722761

IRELAND

Bunratty Castle and Folk Park, Bunratty, Co. Clare. Tel: 00353 61 360 788 Fax:00353 61 361 020 – *Medieval*

Glin Castle, Glin. Tel: 00353 68 34173 Fax: 00353 68 34364

Malahide Castle, Malahide, Co. Dublin. Tel: 00353 1 846 2184 Fax:00353 1 846 2537 – *Collection of Irish portrait paintings mainly from the National Gallery*

Strokestown Park House & Gardens, Strokestown, Co. Roscommon. Tel: 00353 78 33013 Fax: 00353 78 33712

Properties Licensed for Civil Marriages

ENGLAND

BEDFORDSHIRE

Woburn Abbey, Woburn, MK43 OTP.
Tel: 01525 290666 Fax: 01525 290271

BUCKINGHAMSHIRE

Stowe Landscape Gardens, Buckingham, MK18 5EH.
Tel: 01280 822850 Fax: 01280 822437

Stowe (Stowe School), Stowe, MK18 5EH.
Tel. 01280 813650

Waddesdon Manor, The Dairy, Nr Aylesbury, HP18
OJW. Tel: 01296 651211 Fax: 01296 651142

CAMBRIDGESHIRE

Kimbolton Castle, Kimbolton School, Kimbolton,
PE18 OAE. Tel: 01480 860505 Fax: 01480 861763

CHESHIRE

Arley Hall, nr Great Budworth, Northwich, CW9 6NA.
Tel: 01565 777353

Bramall Hall, Bramhall Park, Stockport, SK7 3NX.
Tel: 0161 485 3708 Fax: 0161 486 6959

Capesthorne Hall, Siddington, Macclesfield, SK11 9JY.
Tel: 01625 861221 Fax: 01625 861619

Ness Botanic Gardens, Ness, Nesston, L64 4AY.
Tel: 0151 3530123 Fax: 0151 353 1004

Peckforton Castle, Stonehouse Lane, Peckforton,
Tarporley, CW6 9TN. Tel: 01829 260930
Fax: 01829 261230

Tabley House, Knutsford, WA16 OHB. Tel: 01565
750151 Fax: 01565 653230

Tatton Park, Knutsford, WA16 6QN. Tel: 01565 654822
Fax: 01625 534403

CORNWALL

Trevarno Estate & Gardens, Trevarno Manor, Helston
TR13 0RU. Tel: 01326 574274 Fax: 01326 574282

CUMBRIA

Appleby Castle, Appleby-in-Westmorland, CA16 6XH.
Tel: 017683 51402 Fax: 017683 51082

Muncaster Castle, Ravenglass CA18 1RQ.
Tel: 01229 717614 Fax: 01229 717010

Naworth Castle, The Gatehouse, Naworth, Brampton
CA8 2HE. Tel: 016977 3229 Fax: 016977 3679

DERBYSHIRE

Kedleston Hall and Park, Quarndon, Derby DE22 5JH.
Tel: 01332 842191 Fax: 01332 841972

Renishaw Hall, Nr Sheffield S31 9WB. Tel: 01246
432310

DEVON

Bickleigh Castle, Bickleigh, Tiverton EX16 8RP.
Tel: 01884 855363

Buckfast Abbey, Buckfastleigh, TQ11 0EE.
Tel: 01364 642519 Fax: 01364 643891

Kingston House, Staverton, Totnes TQ9 6AR.
Tel: 01803 762235 Fax: 01803 762444

Powderham Castle, Kenton, EX6 8JQ.
Tel: 01626 890243 Fax: 01626 890729

Tiverton Castle, Tiverton, EX16 6RP. Tel: 01884
253200/255200 Fax: 01884 254200

ESSEX

Layer Marney Tower, Nr Colchester, CO5 9US.
Tel: 01206 330784

GREATER MANCHESTER

Heaton Hall, Heaton Park, Prestwich, M25 2SW.
Tel: 0161 773 1231/236 5244 Fax: 0161 236 7369

HAMPSHIRE

Avington Park, Winchester, SO21 1DB.
Tel: 01962 779260 Fax: 01962 779864

Highclere Castle, Newbury RG20 9RN.
Tel: 01635 253210 Fax:01635 255315

Mottisfont Abbey Garden Mottisfont, Nr Romsey,
SO51 0LP. Tel: 01794 340757 Fax: 01794 341492

HEREFORD & WORCESTER

Avoncroft Museum of Buildings, Stoke Heath,
Bromsgrove, B60 4JR. Tel: 01527 831886 or 831363
Fax: 02527 876934

Eastnor Castle, nr Ledbury, Hereford, HR8 1RL.
Tel: 01531 633160 Fax: 01531 631776

*Getting married in costume at
Bickleigh Castle, Devon*

Hopton Court, Cleobury Mortimer, Kidderminster,
DY14 0HH. Tel: 01299 270734 Fax: 01299 271132

Worcester Cathedral, College Green, Worcester,
WR1 2LH. Tel: 01905 28854 Fax: 01905 611139

HERTFORDSHIRE

Hatfield House, Hatfield ,AL9 5NQ. Tel: 01707 262823
Fax: 01707 275719

Knebworth House, Knebworth. Tel: 01438 812661

KENT

Cobham Hall, Cobham, nr. Gravesend, DA12 3BL.
Tel: 01474 824319

Down House, Downe, BR6 7JT. Tel: 01689 859119

Finchcocks, Goudhurst, TN17 1HH. Tel: 01580 211702
Fax: 01580 211007

Gad's Hill Place, Gads Hill School, Higham, Rochester
ME3 7PA. Tel: 01474 822366 Fax: 01478 822977

Groombridge Place Gardens, Groombridge, TN3 9QG.
Tel: 01892 863999 Fax: 01892 863996

Mount Ephraim Gardens, Hernhill, nr Faversham,
ME13 9TX. Tel: 01227 751496 Fax: 01227 750940

Penshurst Place, Penshurst, Tunbridge Wells,
TN11 8DG. Tel: 01892 870307 Fax: 01892 870866

Tonbridge Castle, Tonbridge TN9 1BG.
Tel: 01732 770929 Fax: 01732 770449

LONDON

Burgh House, New End Square, Hampstead, NW3 1LT.
Tel: 0171 431 0144 Fax: 0171 435 8817

Chiswick House, Burlington Lane, Chiswick W4.
Tel: 0181 995 0508

Greenwich Observatory, Queens House, National
Maritime Museum, Romney Road, Greenwich, London
SE10 9NF. Tel: 0181 312 6565 Fax: 0181 312 6632

Kew Gardens - Royal Botanic Gardens, Richmond,
TW9 3AB. Tel: 0181 940 1171 Fax: 0181 332 5197

Orleans House Gallery, Riverside, Twickenham,
TW1 3DJ. Tel: 0181 892 0221 Fax: 0181 744 0501

Osterley Park, Jersey Road, Isleworth, TW7 4RB.
Tel: 0181 568 7714

St. John's Gate, St John's Lane, Clerkenwell,
EC1M 4DA. Tel: 0171 253 6644 Fax: 0171 336 0587

Syon Park, Brentford ,TW8 8JF. Tel: 0181 560 0881
Fax: 0181 568 0936

NORTHAMPTONSHIRE

Castle Ashby House, Castle Ashby, Northampton,
NN7 1LQ. Tel: 01604 696696 Fax: 01604 696516

Lamport Hall and Gardens, Northampton, NN6 9HD.
Tel: 01604 686272 Fax: 01604 686 224

NORTHUMBERLAND

Chillingham Castle, Chillingham, Alnwick, NE66 5NJ.
Tel: 01668 215359 Fax: 01668 215643

NOTTINGHAMSHIRE

Norwood Park, Southwell, NG25 0PF.
Tel/Fax: 01636 815649

OXFORDSHIRE

Ardington House, Wantage, OX12 8QA.
Tel: 01235 821566 Fax: 01235 821151

SHROPSHIRE

Burford House Gardens, Tenbury Wells, WR15 8HQ.
Tel: 01584 810777 Fax: 01584 810673

Old Colehurst Manor, Colehurst, Market Drayton, TF9
2JB. Tel: 01630 638833 Fax: 01630 638647

Shrewsbury Castle & Shropshire Regimental Museum,
Castle Street, Shrewsbury, SY1 2AT.
Tel: 01743 358516 Fax: 01743 358411

Walcot Hall, Nr Bishops Castle, Lydbury North,
SY7 8AZ. Tel: 0171-581 2782 Fax: 0171 589 0195

Weston Park, Weston under Lizard, nr Shifnal
TF11 8LE. Tel: 01952 850207 Fax: 01952 850430

STAFFORDSHIRE

Ford Green Hall, Ford Green Road, Smallthorne, Stoke-
on-Trent, ST6 1NG. Tel: 01782 233195
Fax: 01782 233 194

The Shugborough Estate, Milford, Stafford, ST17 0XB.
Tel: 01889 881388 Fax: 01889 881323

SUFFOLK

Somerleyton Hall, nr Lowestoft, NR32 5QQ.
Tel: 01502 730224 Fax: 01502 732143

SURREY

Clandon Park, West Clandon, Guildford, GU4 7RQ.
Tel: 01483 222482 Fax: 01483 223479

Great Fosters Hotel, Stroude Road, Egham TW20 9UR.
Tel: 0784 433822

Loseley Park, Estate Office, Guildford GU3 1HS.
Tel: 01483 304440 Fax: 01483 302036

SUSSEX

Anne of Cleves House, 52 Southover High Street,
Lewes, BN7 1JA. Tel: 01273 474610 FX 01273 486990

Bentley House & Gardens, Halland, Nr Lewes,
BN8 5AF. Tel: 01825 840573

Brickwall House and Gardens, Northiam, Rye,
TN31 6NL. Tel: 01797 253388 Fax: 01797 252567

Glynde Place, Glynde, nr Lewes, BN8 6SX.
Tel: 01273 858224 Fax: 01273 858224

Goodwood House, Goodwood, Chichester, PO18 0PX.
Tel: 01243 755048 Fax: 01243 755005

Herstmonceux Castle, International Study Centre,
Queens University, Hailsham BN27 1RN.
Tel: 01323 833816 Fax: 01323 834499

Royal Pavilion, Brighton, BN1 1EE. Tel: 01273 290900
Fax: 01273 292871

Eastnor Castle, Hereford & Worcester

WARWICKSHIRE

Ragley Hall, Alcester B49 5NJ. Tel: 01789 762090
Fax: 01789 764791

WEST MIDLANDS

Birmingham Botanical Gardens and Glasshouses,
Westbourne Road, Edgbaston, Birmingham B15 3TR.
Tel: 0121 454 1860 Fax: 0121 454 7835

Hagley Hall, nr Stourbridge DY9 9LG. Tel: 0562 882408

WILTSHIRE

Longleat, The Estate Office, Warminster BA12 7NW.
Tel: 01985 844400 Fax: 01985 844885

YORKSHIRE

Bolton Castle, Leyburn, DL8 4ET. Tel: 01969 623981
Fax:01969 623332

The Bar Convent, 17 Blossom Street, York, Y02 2AH.
Tel: 01904 643238 Fax: 01904 631792

Bolton Abbey Estate, Bolton Abbey, Skipton,
BD23 6EX. Tel: 01756 7110227 Fax: 01756 710535

Duncombe Park, Helmsley, York, YO62 5EB.
Tel: 01439 770213 Fax: 01439 771114

Elsham Hall Country and Wildlife Park, The Estate
Office, Brigg, DN20 0QZ. Tel: 01652 688698
Fax: 01652 688240

Harewood House and Bird Garden, Harewood, Leeds
LS17 9LQ. Tel: 0113 288 6331 Fax: 0113 288 6467

Newburgh Priory, Coxwold, YO6 4AS.
Tel: 01347 868435

Oakwell Hall, Birstall, WF19 9LG. Tel: 01924 326 240

Ripley Castle, Ripley HG3 3AY. Tel: 01423 770152
Fax: 01423 771745

Sewerby Hall and Gardens, Church Lane, Sewerby,
Bridlington YO15 1EA.
Tel: Estate Office: 01262 673 769 Hall :01262 677874

WALES

Gwydir Castle, Llanrwst. Tel: 01492 641 687
Fax: 01492 641687

Tredegar House, Newport NP1 9YW. Tel: 01633 815880
Fax: 01633 815895

SCOTLAND

Braemar Castle, Braemar, AB35 5XR.
Tel/Fax: 013397 41219

Dalmeny House, Charisma, South Queensferry,
EH30 9TQ. Tel: 0131-331 1888 Fax: 0131 331 1788

Duff House Country House Gallery, Banff AB45 5SX.
Tel: 01261 818181 Fax: 01261 818900

Lennoxlove, Haddington, EH41 4NZ. Tel: 01620 823720
Fax: 01620 825 112

Paxton House & Gardens, Paxton, nr Berwick-upon-
Tweed, TD15 1SZ. Tel: 01289 386291

Rosslyn Chapel, Roslin EH25 9PU. Tel: 0131 448 2948

Scone Palace, Perth PH2 6BD. Tel: 01738 552300
Fax: 01738 552588

Traquair House, Innerleithen, EH44 6PW.
Tel: 01896 830323 Fax: 01896 830639

IRELAND

Antrim Castle Gardens, Antrim.
Tel: 01849 428000 Fax: 01849 460360

Strokestown Park House & Gardens, Strokestown, Co.
Roscommon. Tel: 00353 78 33013 Fax: 00353 78
33712

Properties offering Top Teas!

ENGLAND

BEDFORDSHIRE
Woburn Abbey, Woburn MK43 0TP. Tel: 01525 290666

BERKSHIRE
Basildon Park, Lower Basildon, Reading RG8 9NR. Tel: 0118 984 3040
Dorney Court, Windsor SL4 6QP. Tel: 01628 604638
Savill Garden, Crown Estate Office, Windsor Great Park, Windsor SL7 2HT. Tel: 01753 860222

BUCKINGHAMSHIRE
Claydon House, Middle Claydon, Buckingham MK18 2EY. Tel: 01296 730349
Cliveden, Taplow, Maidenhead SL6 0JA. Tel: 01628 605069
Hughenden Manor, High Wycombe HP14 4LA. Tel: 01494 532580
Stowe Landscape Gardens, Buckingham MK18 5EH. Tel: 01280 822850

CAMBRIDGESHIRE
Ely Cathedral, The Chapter House, The College, Ely CB7 4DL. Tel: 01353 667735

CHESHIRE
Arley Hall and Gardens, Nr Great Budworth, Northwich CW9 6NA. Tel: 01565 777353
Dunham Massey, Altrincham WA14 4SJ. Tel: 0161 9411025
Little Moreton Hall, Congleton CW12 4SD. Tel: 01260 272018
Ness Botanic Gardens, Ness, Nesston L64 4AY. Tel: 0151 3530123
Tabley House Collection, Tabley House, Knutsford WA16 0HB. Tel: 01565 750151
Tatton Park, Knutsford WA16 6QN. Tel: 01565 654822

CORNWALL
Burncoose Nurseries and Garden, Gwennap, Redruth TR16 6BJ. Tel: 01209 861112
Pencarrow Washway, Bodmin PL30 5AG. Tel: 01208 841449
Trevarno Estate & Gardens, Trevarno Manor, Helston TR13 0RU. Tel: 01326 574274
Lanhydrock, Bodmin PL30 5AD. Tel: 01208 73320

CUMBRIA
Appleby Castle, Appleby-in-Westmorland, CA16 6XH. Tel: 017683 51402
Dalemain, nr Penrith CA11 0HB. Tel: 017684 86450
Hutton-in-the-Forest, Skelton, Penrith CA1 9TH. Tel: 017684 84449
Muncaster Castle, Ravenglass CA18 1RQ. Tel: 01229 717614

DERBYSHIRE
Haddon Hall, Estate Office, Bakewell DE45 1LA. Tel: 01629 812855
Lea Gardens, Lea, Matlock DE4 5GH. Tel: 01629 534 380
Renishaw Hall, Nr Sheffield, S21 3WB. Tel: 01777 860755

DEVON
Bickleigh Castle, Bickleigh, Tiverton EX16 8RP. Tel: 01884 855363
Buckfast Abbey, Buckfastleigh TQ11 0EE. Tel: 01364 643891
Killerton House, Broadclyst, nr Exeter EX5 3LE. Tel: 01392 881345
Powderham Castle Kenton, Exeter EX6 8JQ. Tel: 01626 890243
Torre Abbey, The Kings Drive, Torquay TQ2 5JX. Tel: 01803 293593

DORSET
Athelhampton House & Gardens, Athelhampton, Dorchester DT2 7LG. Tel: 01305 848363
Compton Acres Gardens, Canford Cliffs, Poole BH13 7ES. Tel: 01202 700778
Deans Court Garden, Wimborne BH21 1EE.
Lulworth Castle, The Lulworth Estate, East Lulworth, Wareham BH20 5QS. Tel: 01929 400352
Purse Caundle Manor, Purse Caundle, nr Sherborne DT9 5DY. Tel: 01963 250400
Sherborne Castle, Sherborne DT9 3PY. Tel: 01935 813182
Forde Abbey and Gardens, nr Chard TA20 4LU. Tel: 01460 220231
Wolfeton House, Dorchester. Tel: 01305 263500

COUNTY DURHAM
Raby Castle, Staindrop, Darlington DL2 3AH. Tel: 01833 660202

ESSEX
Hedingham Castle, Castle Hedingham, nr Halstead CO9 3DJ. Tel: 01787 460261
Ingatestone Hall, Ingatestone CM4 9NR. Tel: 01277 353010
Layer Marney Tower, Colchester CO5 9US. Tel: 011206 330784

GLOUCESTERSHIRE
Berkeley Castle, Berkeley GL13 9BQ. Tel: 01453 810332
Chavenage, Tetbury GL8 8XP. Tel: 01666 502329
Kiftsgate Court, Mickleton, nr Chipping Campden GL55 6LW. Tel: 01386 438777
Owlpen Manor, Uley, nr Dursley GL11 5BZ. Tel: 01453 860261
Painswick Rococo Garden, The Stables, Painswick House, Painswick GL6 6TH. Tel: 01452 813204
Sudeley Castle, Winchcombe GL54 5JD. Tel: 01242 602308

HAMPSHIRE
Avington Park, Winchester SO21 1DD. Tel: 01962 779260
Breamore House, Breamore, nr Fordingbridge SP6 2DF. Tel: 01725 512233
Gilbert White's House & Garden and the Oates Museum, The Wakes, Selborne GU34 3JH. Tel: 01420 511275
Mottisfont Abbey Garden, Mottisfont, SO51 0LP. Tel: 011794 341220

HEREFORD & WORCESTER
Burton Court, Eardisland, Leominster HR6 9DN. Tel: 01544 388231
Eastnor Castle, Nr Ledbury, Hereford HR8 1RD. Tel: 01531 633160
Harvington Hall, Harvington, Kidderminster DY10 4LR. Tel: 01562 777846
Hergest Croft Gardens, Kington. Tel: 01544 230160
How Caple Court Gardens, How Caple HR1 4SX. Tel: 01989 740612
Kentchurch Court, Nr Pontrilas, Hereford. Tel: 01981 240228

HERTFORDSHIRE
Gardens of the Rose, Chiswell Green, St. Albans AL2 3NR. Tel: 01727 850461
Hatfield House, Hatfield AL9 5NQ. Tel: 01707 262823
Knebworth House, Knebworth. Tel: 01438 812661

KENT
Belmont, Throwley, Nr Faversham ME13 0HH. Tel: 01795 890202
Cobham Hall, Cobham, Nr Gravesend DA12 3BL. Tel: 01474 824319/823371
Doddington Place Gardens, Doddington, Sittingbourne ME9 0BB. Tel: 01795 886101
Gad's Hill Place, Gad's Hill School, Rochester ME3 7AA. Tel: 01474 822366
Groombridge Place Gardens, Groombridge TN3 9QG. Tel: 01892 863999
Ladham House, Goudhurst. Tel: 01580 211203
Lullingstone Castle, Eynsford DA14 0JA. Tel: 01322 862114
Penshurst Place, Penshurst, Tunbridge Wells TN11 8DG. Tel: 01892 870307
Squerryes Court, Westerham TN16 1SJ. Tel: 01959 562345

LANCASHIRE
Gawthorpe Hall, Padiham, Nr Burnley BB12 8UA. Tel: 011282 770353
Towneley Hall Art Gallery, Burnley BD11 3RQ.Tel: 01282 424213

LEICESTERSHIRE
Kayes Garden Nursery, 1700 Melton Rd, Rearsby, Leicester LE7 4YR. Tel: 01664 424578
The Manor House, Donington-le-Heath.
Stanford Hall, Stanford Park, Lutterworth LE17 6DH. Tel: 01788 860250

LONDON
Burgh House, New End Square, Hampstead NW3 1LT. Tel: 0171 431 0144
Chelsea Physic Garden, 66 Royal Hospital Road, Chelsea SW3 4HS. Tel: 0171 352 5646
Museum of Garden History, Lambeth Palace Road, Lambeth SE1 7LB. Tel: 0171 261 1891
Osterley Park, Jersey Road, Isleworth TW7 4RB. Tel: 0181 568 7714

NORFOLK
Hoveton Hall Gardens, Wroxham NR11 7BB.

NORTHAMPTONSHIRE
Coton Manor Garden, Coton, Nr Guilsborough NN6 8RQ. Tel: 01604 740219
Lamport Hall and Gardens, Northampton NN6 9HD. Tel: 01604 686272

NOTTINGHAMSHIRE
Norwood Park, Holme Pierrepont, Nr Southwell NG12 2LD.

OXFORDSHIRE
Buscot Park, Buscot, Nr Faringdon SN7 8BU. Tel: 01367 240786
Waterperry Gardens, Waterperry Horticultural Centre, Nr Wheatley OX9 1SZ. Tel: 01844 339226/339254

SHROPSHIRE
Burford House Gardens, Tenbury Wells WR15 8HQ. Tel: 01584 810777
Hodnet Hall Gardens, Nr Market Drayton TF9 3NN. Tel: 01630 685202
Ironbridge Gorge Museum, Ironbridge, Telford TF8 7AW. Tel: 01952 433522
Walcot Hall, Nr Bishops Castle, Lydbury North SY7 8AZ. Tel: 0171-581 2782
Wollerton Old Hall, Wollerton, Market Drayton TF9 3NA. Tel: 01630 685760

SOMERSET
Gaulden Manor, Tolland, Nr Taunton TA4 3PN. Tel: 019847 213
Hestercombe House Gardens, Cheddon Fitzpaine, Taunton TA2 8LQ. Tel: 01823 413923

STAFFORDSHIRE
Dunwood Hall, Longsdon, Nr. Leek ST9 9AR. Tel: 01538 385071
Sandon Hall, Sandon ST18 0BZ. Tel: 01889 508004

SUFFOLK
Helmingham Hall Gardens, The Estate Office, Helmingham Hall, Stowmarket IP14 6EF. Tel: 01473 890363
Kentwell Hall. Long Melford, Nr. Sudbury CO10 9BA. Tel: 01787 310207
Somerleyton Hall, nr Lowestoft. Tel: 011502 730224
Wingfield Old College, Wingfield, Eye IP21 5RA. Tel: 011379 384888

SURREY
Clandon Park, West Clandon, Guildford GU4 7RQ. Tel: 01483 222482

Claremont Landscape Garden, Portsmouth Road, Esher KT10 9JG. Tel: 01372 469421
Hatchlands Park, West Clandon, Guildford GU4 7RT. Tel: 01483 222482
Loseley House, Estate Office, Guildford GU3 1HS. Tel: 01483 304440
RHS Garden Wisley, Woking GU23 6QB. Tel: 01483 224234

SUSSEX
Bentley House & Gardens, Halland, Nr Lewes BN8 5AF. Tel: 01825 840573
Borde Hill Garden, Haywards Heath RH16 1XP. Tel: 01444 450326
Denmans Garden, Clock House, Denmans, Fontwell BN18 0SU. Tel: 01243 542808
Firle Place, Nr Lewes BN8 6LP. Tel: 01273 858188
Fishbourne Roman Palace, Salthill Road, Fishbourne, Chichester PO19 3QR. Tel: 01243 785859
Glynde Place, Nr Lewes BN8 6SX. Tel: 01273 858224
Goodwood House, Goodwood, Chichester PO18 0PX. Tel: 01243 755048
Hammerwood Park, East Grinstead RH19 3QE. Tel: 01342 850594
Leonardslee Gardens, Lower Beeding, Horsham RH13 6PP. Tel: 01403 891212
Merriments Gardens, Hawkhurst Road, Hurst Green TN19 7RA. Tel: 01580 860666
Michelham Priory, Upper Dicker, Hailsham BN27 3QS. Tel: 01323 844224 FX- 844030
Parham House and Gardens, Parham Park Ltd, Pulborough RH20 4HS. Tel: 01903 742021
Pashley Manor Gardens, Ticehurst, Wadhurst TN5 7HE. Tel: 01580 200692
Royal Pavilion, Brighton BN1 1EE. Tel: 01273 290900
The Weald & Downland Open Air Museum, Singleton, nr Chichester PO18 0EL. Tel: 01243 811363
West Dean Gardens, West Dean Estate, Nr Chichester PO18 0QZ. Tel: 01243 818210

WARWICKSHIRE
Arbury Hall, Nuneaton CV10 7PT. Tel: 01203 382804
Lord Leycester Hospital, High Street, Warwick CV34 4BH. Tel: 011926 492797

WEST MIDLANDS
Baddesley Clinton Hall, B93 0DQ. Tel: 01564 783294

WILTSHIRE
Longleat, The Estate Office, Warminster BA12 7NW. } Tel: 01985 844400

YORKSHIRE
Aske Hall, Aske, Rickmond DL10 5HJ. Tel: 01748 823222
The Bar Convent, 17 Blossom Street, York Y02 2AH. Tel: 01904 643238
Bolton Castle, Leyburn DL8 4ET. Tel: 01969 623981
Brodsworth Hall, Brodsworth. Tel: 01302 722598
Elsham Hall Country and Wildlife Park, The Estate Office, Brigg DN20 0QZ. Tel: 01652 688698
Oakwell Hall, Birstall WF19 9LG. Tel: 01924 474926
Sewerby Hall and Gardens, Church Lane, Sewerby, Bridlington YO15 1EA. Tel: Estate Office: 01262 673 769

WALES
Colby Woodland Garden, Amroth, Narberth SA67 8PP. Tel: 01558 822800/01834 811885
Dinefwr Park, Llandeilo SA19 6RT. Tel: 011558 823902
Picton Castle, Picton Castle Trust, Haverfordwest SA62 4AS. Tel: 01437 751326
Tredegar House, Newport, Newport NP1 9YW. Tel: 01633 815880

SCOTLAND
Cawdor Castle, Nairn, Inverness IV12 5RD. Tel: 01667 404615
Dalmeny House, Charisma, South Queensferry EH30 9TQ. Tel: 031-331 1888
Manderston, Duns, Berwickshire TD11 3PP. Tel: 011361 882636

IRELAND
Bantry House, Bantry, Co. Cork. Tel: 00353 2750047
Benvarden Garden, Dervock, Ballymoney, CO. Antrim. Tel: 012657 41331
Dublin Writer's Museum, 18 Parnell Square, Dublin 1. Tel: 00353 1 872 2077
Kylemore Abbey, Kylemore, Connemara. Tel: 0195 41146
Malahide Castle, Malahide, Co. Dublin. Tel: 00353 1 846 2184
Mount Usher Gardens, Ashford. Tel: 00353 404 40205 /40116
Newbridge House, Donabate, Co. Dubin. Tel: 00353 1 8436534
Powerscourt Gardens & Waterfall, Enniskerry, Co. Wicklow. Tel: 00353 1 204 6000
Seaforde Gardens, Seaforde, Downpatrick BT30 3PG. Tel: +441396 811225
Strokestown Park House & Gardens, Strokestown, Co. Roscommon. Tel: 00353 78 33013
Tullynally Castle, Castlepollard, Co. Westmeath. Tel: 00353 44 61159

Properties Open All Year

ENGLAND

BERKSHIRE

Dorney Court, Windsor SL4 6QP. Tel: 01628 604638
Fax: 01628 665772
The Savill Garden, Windsor Great Park, Tel: 01753 860222 Crown
Property.
Windsor Castle, Windsor, SL4 INJ Tel: 01753 868286

BUCKINGHAMSHIRE

Cliveden, Taplow, Maidenhead SL6 OJA. Tel: 01628 605069
Fax: 01628 669461
Stowe Landscape Garden, Buckingham, Buckinghamshire MK18 5EH
Tel: 01280 822850

CAMBRIDGESHIRE

Ely Cathedral, The Chapter House, The College, Ely CB7 4DL.
Tel: 01353 667735 Fax: 01353 665658
King's College, Cambridge CB2 1ST. Tel: 01223 331212
Fax: 01223 331315
The Manor, Hemingford Grey PE18 9BN. Tel: 01480 463134
Fax: 01480 465026
Oliver Cromwell's House, 29 Mary Street, Ely CB7 4DF
Tel: 01353 665555 ext.294 Fax: 01353 668518

CHESHIRE

Adlington Hall, Macclesfield SK10 4LF. Tel: 01625 820875
Fax: 01625 828756
Ness Botanic Gardens, Ness, Nesston L64 4AY.
Tel: 0151 3530123 Fax: 0151 353 1004
Norton Priory Museum, Tudor Road, Manor Park, Runcorn WA7
1SX. Tel: 01928 569895

CORNWALL

Burncoose Nurseries & Garden, Gwennap, Redruth
TR16 6BJ Tel: 01209 861112
Trevarno Estate & Gardens, Trevarno Manor, Helston TR13 0RU.
Tel: 01326 574274 Fax: 01326 574282

CUMBRIA

Hutton-In-The-Forest, Penrith Tel: 017684 84449
Muncaster Castle, Ravenglass CA18 1RQ. Tel: 01229 717614
Fax: 01229 717010. Gardens Only
Naworth Castle, Brampton CA8 2HF Tel: 0169 773229

DEVON

Buckfast Abbey, Buckfastleigh TQ11 OEE. Tel: 01364 642519
Fax: 01364 643891
Killerton House, Broadclyst, nr Exeter EX5 3LE. Tel: 01392 881345
Fax: 01392 883112. Gardens Only

DORSET

Athelhampton House & Gardens, Athelhampton, Dorchester
Tel: 01305 848363 Fax: 01305 848135
Christchurch Priory, Quay Road, Christchurch, BH23 1BU.
Tel: 01202 485804 Fax: 01202 488645
Forde Abbey, Chard Tel: 01460 220231
Lulworth Castle, The Lulworth Estate, East Lulworth, Wareham BH20
5QS. Tel: 01929 400352

GLOUCESTERSHIRE

Barnsley House Garden, The Close, Barnsley,
Nr Cirencester GL7 5EE.
Frampton Court, Frampton-on-Severn
Gloucester GL2 7EU Tel: 01452 740267

HAMPSHIRE

Beaulieu, Brockenhurst, SO42 7ZN Tel: 01590 612345
Langley Boxwood Nursery, Rake, Nr. Liss, GU33 7JL
Tel: 01730 894467 Fax: 01730 894703
Gilbert White's House & Garden & The Oates Museum, 'The
Wakes' Selborne, Nr Alton, GU34 3JH
Sir Harold Hillier Gardens and Arboretum, Ampfield, nr Romsey
SO51 0QA. Tel: 01794 368787 Fax:

HERTFORDSHIRE

Cathedral & Abbey Church Of St. Alban, St. Albans, Hertfordshire
AL1 1BY.

HEREFORD & WORCESTER

Burford House Gardens, Tenbury Wells, WR15 8HQ.
Tel: 01584 810777 Fax: 01584 810673
Dinmore Manor, nr Hereford HR4 8EE. Tel: 01432 830332
How Caple Court Gardens, How Caple HR1 4SX.
Tel: 01989 740612 Fax: 01989 740611
Worcester Cathedral, College Green, Worcester WR1 2LH.
Tel: 01905 28854 Fax: 01905 611139

KENT

Hall Place, Bourne Road, Bexley, DA5 1PQ.
Tel: 01322 526574 Fax: 10322 522921
Ladham House, Gouldhurst, Tel: 01580 212674
Leeds Castle, Maidstone, Tel: 01622 765400
Lullingstone Castle, Eynsford, Kent DA14 OJA.
Tel: 01322 862114
The New College Of Cobham, Cobham, Nr Gravesend, DA12 3BX
Tel: 01474 812503
Owl House Gardens, Lamberhurst, Tel: 01892 890962

Pattyndenne Manor, Goudhurst TN17 2QU. Tel: 01580 211361
The Theatre Royal, 102 High Street, Chatham, ME4 4BY
Tel: 01634 831028
Tonbridge Castle, Tonbridge TN9 1BG. Tel: 01732 770929
Fax: 01732 770449

LANCASHIRE

Towneley Hall Art Gallery & Museums, Burnely, BB11 3RQ
Tel: 01282 424213

LEICESTERSHIRE

Kayes Garden Nursery, 1700 Melton Road, Rearsby, Leicester LE7 4YR.
Tel: 01664 424578

LONDON

Buckingham Palace, The Queens Gallery, SW1A 1AA
Tel: 0171 839 1377
Burgh House, New End Square, Hampstead,
Tel: 0171 431 0144
College Of Arms, Queen Victoria Stret Tel: 0171 248 2762
Greenwich – Observatory, National Marime Museaum,
Romney Road, Greenwich SE10 9NF. Tel: 0181 858 4422
Kew Gardens, Royal Botanic Gardens, Kew, Richmond
Tel: 0181 940 1171
Orleans House Gallery, Riverside, Twickenham, TW1 3DJ.
Tel: 0181-892 0221 Fax: 0181 744 0501
Osterley Park, Jersey Road, Isleworth TW7 4RB. Tel: 0181 568 7714
Pitshanger Manor Museum, Percival House, Mattock Lane, Ealing W5
5EQ. Tel: 0181-567 1227 Fax: 0181-567 0595
Syon House, Brentford TW8 8JF. Tel: 0181 560 0881
St. John's Gate, St John's Lane, Clerkenwell EC1M 4DA.
Tel: 0171-253 6644 Fax: 0171 336 0587
Tower of London, Tower Hill Tel: 0171 709 0765
Wallace Collection, Hertford House, Manchester Square
Tel: 0171 935 0687 Fax: 0171 224 2155

NORFOLK

Mannington Hall, Saxthorpe, Norwich NR11 7BB. Tel: 01263 584175
Fax: 01263 761214
Norwich Castle Museum, Norwich NR1 3JU
Tel: 01603 223624
Walsingham Abbey Grounds, Walsingham, NR22 6BP.
Tel: 01328 820 259
Wolterton Park, Erpingham Tel: 01263 584175

NORTHAMPTONSHIRE

Castle Ashby House, Castle Ashby, Northampton NN7 1LQ.
Tel: 01604 696696 Fax: 01604 696516

NOTTINGHAMSHIRE

Norwood Park, Southwell, Nottingham NG25 OP
Tel: 01636 815649 Fax: 01636 815649

OXFORDSHIRE

Broughton Castle, Banbury, OX15 5EB Tel: 01295 262624
Rousham House, Rousham, Steeple Aston, OX6 3QX.
Tel: 01869 347110
University Of Oxford Botanic Gardens, Rose Lane, Oxford OX1 4AX.
Wallingford Castle Gardens, Castle Street, Wallingford
Tel: 01491 835373
Waterperry Gardens Ltd, Nr Wheatley, Oxfordshire
Tel: 01844 339226/254

SHROPSHIRE

Burford House Gardens, Tenbury Wells WR15 8HQ.
Tel: 01584 810777 Fax: 01584 810673
Ironbridge Gorge Museum, Ironbridge, Telford TF8 7AW.
Tel: 01952 433522 Fax: 01952 432204
Ludlow Castle, Castle Square, Ludlow
Tel – Custodian: 01584 873947.
Shipton Hall, Much Wenlock TE13 6JZ. Tel: 01746 785 225
Walcot Hall, Lydbury North, Nr. Bishops Castle, SY7 8AZ
Tel: 0171 581 2782

SOMERSET

Hestercombe Gardens, Cheddon Fitzpain, Taunton,
TA2 8LG Tel: 01823 423923

STAFFORDSHIRE

Dunwood Hall, Longsdon, Nr. Leek ST9 9AR
Tel: 01538 385071
Ford Green Hall, Ford Green Road Smallthorne,
Stoke-on-Trent. Tel: 01782 233195
Sandon Hall, Sandon, Stafford Tel: 01889 508004
Stafford Castle, Newport Road, Stafford ST16 1DJ. Tel: 01785 257 698
Tamworth Castle, The Holloway, Tamworth B79 7LR. Tel: 01827
709626 Fax: 01827 709630

SUFFOLK

Christchurch Mansion, Christchurch Park, Ipswich
Tel: 01473 253246 Fax: 01473 281274
Gainsborough's House, 46 Gainsborough Street, Sudbury CO10 6EU
Iel: 01787 372958 Fax: 01787 376991
Ipswich Museum, Ipswich IP1 3QH Tel: 01473 213761

SURREY

Claremont Landscape Garden, Portsmouth Road, Esher
Tel: 01372 467842
Great Fosters Hotel, Stroude Road, Egham TW20 9UR.
Tel: 0784 433822

Guildford House Gallery, 155, High Street, Guildford GU1 3AJ.
Tel: 01483 444740 Fax: 01483 444742
Painshill Landscape Gardens, Portsmouth Road, Cobham KT11 1JE.
Tel: 01932 868113 Fax: 01932 868001
RHS Garden Wisley, Woking GU23 6QB. Tel: 01483 224234

SUSSEX

Anne Of Cleves House, 52 Southover High Street, Lewes BN7 1JA.
Tel: 01273 474610 Fax: 01273 486990
Borde Hill, Balcombe Road, Haywards Heath S16 1XP.
Tel: 01444 450326
Chichester Cathedral, West Street, Chichester PO19 1PX.
Tel: 01243 782595 Fax: 01243 536190
Lewes Castle, Barbican House, 169 High Street, Lewes
BN7 1YE. Tel: 01273 486290 Fax: 01273 486990
Pallant House,, 9 North Pallant, Chichester PO19 1TJ
Tel: 01243 774557
Perryhill Nurseries, Hartfield TN7 4JP. Tel: 0892 770377
Preston Manor, Preston Drove, Brighton BN1 6SD
Tel: 01273 290900 Fax: 01273 292871
Royal Botanic Gardens, Kew At Wakehurst Place, Ardingly, Nr
Haywards Heath RH17 6TN Tel: 01444 894066
The Royal Pavilion, Brighton, East Sussex BN1 1EE
Tel: 01273 290900 Fax: 01273 292871
Saint Hill Manor, Sant Hill Road, East Grinstead
RH19 4JY Tel: 01342 326711

WARWICKSHIRE

Lord Leycester Hospital, High Street, Warwick, CV34 4BH.
Shakespeare Birthplace Trust, 38/39 Henley Street, Stratford upon
Avon, Tel: 01789 204016
Warwick Castle, Warwick, CV34 4QU. Tel: 01976 406600

WEST MIDLANDS

Birmingham Botanical Gardens & Glasshouses, Westbourne Road,
Edgbaston, Birmingham, B15 3TR. Tel: 0121 454 1860
Fax: 0121 454 7835
Soho House, Soho Avenue, Handsworth, Birmingham
B18 5LB Tel: 0121 554 9122

WILTSHIRE

Longleat, The Estate Office, Warminster BA12 7NW.
Tel: 01985 844400 Fax: 01985 844885
Stourhead, Stourton, Mere BA12 6QH Tel: 01747 841152

YORKSHIRE

Aske Hall, Aske, Richmond DL10 5HJ. Tel: 01748 850391
Bolton Abbey, Skipton, North Yorkshire BD23 6EX.
Tel: 01756 710227 Fax: 01756 710535
Elsham Hall Country and Wildlife Park, The Estate Office, Brigg
DN20 0QZ. Tel: 01652 688698 Fax: 01652 688240
Harlow Carr Botanical Gardens, Crag Lane, Harrogate HG3 1QB.
Tel: 01423 565418 Fax: 01423 530663
Oakwell Hall, Nutter Lane, Birstall, Batley
Tel: 01924 326240
Red House, Oxford Road, Gomersal, Cleckheaton
Tel: 01274 335100
Sewerby Hall & Gardens, Church Lane, Sewerby, Bridlington, YO15
1EA. Tel: 01262 673769
Skipton Castle, Skipton, North Yorkshire BD23 1AQ.
Tel: 01756 792442 Fax: 01756 796100
Wilberforce House, 25 High Street, Kingston-upon-Hull, HU1 1EP.
Tel: 01482 613902

IRELAND

Antrim Castle Gardens, Antrim Tel: 01849 428000
Dublin Writers Museum, 18 Parnell Square, Dublin 1.
Kylemore Abbey, Conemara, Co. Galway.
Tel: 00 353 95 41146 Fax: 00 353 95 41123
Malahide Castle, Malahide, Co. Dublin.
Tel: 00 353 1 846 2184 Fax: 00 353 1 846 2537
Powerscourt Gardens & Waterfall, Enniskerry, Co. Wicklow. Tel: 00
353 204 6000 Fax: 00 353 28 63561
Newbridge House, Donabate, Co Dublin.
Tel: 00 353 1 8436534 Fax: 00 353 1 8462537

SCOTLAND

Ayton Castle, Eyemouth, Berwickshire TD14 5RD.
Tel: 018907 81212 Fax: 018907 81550
Dalmeny House, South Queensferry, Edinburgh EH30 9TQ Tel: 0131
331 1888 Fax: 0131 331 1788
The Doune of Rothiemurchus, Rothiemurchus Estate Office, Aviemore
PH22 1QH. Tel: 01479 810858 Fax: 01479 811778
Duff House Country House Gallery, Banff AB45 5SX. Tel: 01261
818181 Fax: 01261 818900
Palace Of Holyroodhouse, Edinburgh, EH8 8DY
Tel: 0131 556 7371.

WALES

Bodelwyddan Castle, Bodelwyddan, St Asaph, Bodelwyddan LL18 5YA.
Tel: 01745 584060 Fax: 01745 584563
Penhow Castle, Nr Newport NP6 3AD. Tel: 01633 400800 fax: 01633
400990
St. Davids Cathedral, The Deanery, The Close, St. Davids,
Pembrokeshire. Tel: 01437 720202 Fax: 01437 721 885

Properties with Conference Facilities

ENGLAND

BEDFORDSHIRE

Woburn Abbey, Woburn MK43 OTP. Tel: 01525 290666
Fax: 01525 290271

BERKSHIRE

Dorney Court, Windsor SL4 6QP. Tel: 01628 604638
Fax: 01628 665772

Eton College, The Visits Office, WIndsor SL4 6DW.
Tel: 01753 671177 Fax: 01753 671265

Highclere Castle, Nr Newbury, RG20 9RN.
Tel: 01635 253210 Fax: 01635 255315

BUCKINGHAMSHIRE

Stowe Stowe School, Stowe MK18 5EH.
Tel: 01280 813650

Waddesdon Manor, The Dairy, Nr Aylesbury HP18 OJW.
Tel: 01296 651211 Fax: 01296 651142

CAMBRIDGESHIRE

Elton Hall, Elton, Peterborough PE8 6SH. Tel: 01832 280468
Fax: 01832 280584

Kimbolton Castle, Kimbolton School, Kimbolton PE18 OAE.
Tel: 01480 860505 Fax: 01480 861763

King's College, Cambridge CB2 1ST. Tel: 01223 331212
Fax: 01223 331315

CHESHIRE

Adlington Hall, Macclesfield SK10 4LF. Tel: 01625 820875
Fax: 01625 828756

Arley Hall, nr Great Budworth, Northwich CW9 6NA.
Tel: 01565 777353

Bramall Hall, Bramhall Park, Stockport SK7 3NX.
Tel: 0161 485 3708 Fax: 0161 486 6959

Capesthorne Hall, Siddington, Macclesfield SK11 9JY.
Tel: 01625 861221 Fax: 01625 861619

Ness Botanic Gardens, Ness, Nesston L64 4AY.
Tel: 0151 3530123 Fax: 0151 353 1004

Peckforton Castle, Stonehouse Lane, Nr. Taporley CW6
9TN. Tel: 01829 260930 Fax: 01829 261230

Tabley House Stately Home, Tabley House, Knutsford WA16
OHB. Tel: 01565 750151 Fax: 01565 653230

Tatton Park, Knutsford, Cheshire, WA16 6QN.
Tel: 01625 534400 fax: 01625 534402

CUMBRIA

Appleby Castle, Appleby-in-Westmorland, CA16 6XH.
Tel: 017683 51402 Fax: 017683 51082

Dalemain, nr Penrith CA11 0HB. Tel: 017684 86450
Fax: 017684 86223

Muncaster Castle, Ravenglass CA18 1RQ. Tel: 01229 717614
Fax: 01229 717010

Naworth Castle, The Gatehouse, Naworth, Brampton CA8
2HE. Tel: 016977 3229 Fax: 016977 3679

DERBYSHIRE

Chatsworth, Bakewell DE45 1PP. Tel: 01246 582204
Fax: 01246 583536

DEVON

Bickleigh Castle, Bickleigh, Tiverton EX16 8RP.
Tel: 01884 855363

Buckfast Abbey, Buckfastleigh, TQ11 0EE.
Tel: 01364 642519 Fax: 01364 643891

Hartland Abbey, Hartland, Nr Bideford EX39 6DT.
Tel: 01237 441 264/234 Fax: 01884 861134

Kingston House, Staverton, Totnes TQ9 6AR.
Tel: 01803 762235 Fax: 01803 762444

Powderham Castle, Kenton, Exeter EX6 8JQ.
Tel: 01626 890243 Fax: 01626 890729

Tiverton Castle, Tiverton EX16 6RP. Tel/Fax: 01884 253200

Torre Abbey, The Kings Drive, Torquay TQ2 5JX.
Tel: 01803 293593 Fax: 01803 215948

Ugbrooke House, Chudleigh TQ13 OAD. Tel: 01626 852179
Fax: 01626 853322

Chatsworth, Derbyshire

DORSET

Athelhampton House & Gardens, Athelhampton, Dorchester
DT2 7LG. Tel: 01305 848363 Fax: 01305 848135

Forde Abbey, Chard, TA20 4LU. Tel: 01460 221290
Fax: 01460 220296

Lulworth Castle, The Lulworth Estate, East Lulworth,
Wareham BH20 5QS. Tel: 01929 400352

Parnham House, Parnham, Beaminster DT8 3NA.
Tel: 01308 862204 Fax: 01308 863444

Sherborne Castle, Sherborne DT9 3PY. Tel: 01935 813182
Fax: 01935 816727

COUNTY DURHAM

Auckland Castle, Bishop Auckland DL14 7NR.
Tel: 01388 601627 Fax: 01388 609323

Durham Castle, University of Durham, Durham DH1 3RW.
Tel: 0191 374 3800 Fax: 0191 374 7470

ESSEX

Gosfield Hall, Halstead, CO9 1SF. Tel: 01787 472914
Fax: 01787 479551

Hylands House, Park & Gardens, Writtle, Chelmsford CM1
3HW. Tel: 01245 606812

Layer Marney Tower, Nr Colchester CO5 9US.
Tel: 01206 330784

GLOUCESTERSHIRE

Chavenage, Tetbury GL8 8XP. Tel: 01666 502329
Fax: 01453 836778

Owlpen Manor, Owlpen, nr Uley GL11 5BZ. Tel: 01453
860261 Fax: 01453 860819

Sudeley Castle, Winchcombe GL54 5JD. Tel: 01242 602308

HAMPSHIRE

Avington Park, Winchester SO21 1DB. Tel: 01962 779260
Fax: 01962 779864

Beaulieu, Brockenhurst, SO42 7ZN. Tel: 01590 612345
Fax: 01590 612624

Gilbert White's House & Garden and the Oates Museum,
The Wakes, Selborne GU34 3JH. Tel: 01420 511275

Mottisfont Abbey Garden, Mottisfont, Nr Romsey SO51 0LP.
Tel: 01794 340757 Fax: 01794 341492

St Agatha's Church, 9 East Street, Fareham PO16 OBW.
Tel: 01329 230330 Fax: 01329 230330

Sir Harold Hillier Gardens and Arboretum, Ampfield, nr
Romsey SO51 0QA. Tel: 01794 368787

Somerley, Ringwood BH24 3PL. Tel: 01425 480819

HEREFORD & WORCESTER

Avoncroft, Stoke Heath, Bromsgrove, B60 4JR.
Tel 01527 831363 Fax: 01527 876934

Burton Court, Eardisland, Leominster HR6 9DN.
Tel: 01544 388231

Dinmore Manor, nr Hereford HR4 8EE. Tel: 01432 830332

Eastnor Castle, nr Ledbury, Hereford HR8 1RL.
Tel: 01531 633160 Fax: 01531 631776

Harvington Hall, Harvington, Kidderminster DY10 4LR.
Tel: 01562 777846 Fax: 01562 777190

Hopton Court, Cleobury Mortimer, Kidderminster DY14
0HH. Tel: 01299 270734

HERTFORDSHIRE

Knebworth House, Knebworth. Tel: 01438 812661

The Gardens of the Rose, Chiswell Green, St. Albans AL2
3NR. Tel: 01727 850461 Fax: 01727 850360

Hatfield House, Hatfield AL9 5NQ. Tel: 01707 262823
Fax: 01707 275719

KENT

Cobham Hall, Cobham, nr. Gravesend DA12 3BL.
Tel: 01474 824319

Finchcocks, Goudhurst TN17 1HH. Tel: 01580 211702
Fax: 01580 211007

Hever Castle & Gardens, Hever, nr Edenbridge TN8 7NG.
Tel: 01732 865224 Fax: 01732 866796

Ladham House, Goudhurst. Tel: 01580 211203
Fax: 01580 212596

Leeds Castle, Maidstone ME17 1PL. Tel: 01622 765400
Fax: 735616

Mount Ephraim Gardens, Hernhill, nr Faversham ME13 9TX.
Tel: 01227 751496 Fax: 01227 750940

Penshurst Place, Penshurst, Tunbridge Wells TN11 8DG.
Tel: 01892 870307 Fax: 01892 870866

Riverhill House Gardens, Riverhill, Sevenoaks TN15 0RR.
Tel: 01732 458802/452557

Squerryes Court, Westerham TN16 1SJ.
Tel: 01959 562345/563118 Fax: 01959 565949

LANCASHIRE

Towneley Hall, Burnley, BB11 3RQ. Tel: 01282 424213
Fax: 01282 436138

LEICESTERSHIRE

Belvoir Castle, Nr Grantham, NG32 1PD. Tel: 01476 870262

Stanford Hall, Stanford Park, Lutterworth LE17 6DH.
Tel: 01788 860250 Fax: 01788 860870

LONDON

Banqueting House, Whitehall Palace. Tel 0171 930 4179

Boston Manor House, Boston Manor Road, Brentford TW8 9JX. Tel: 0181 560 5441 Fax: 0181 862 7602

Chelsea Physic Garden, 66 Royal Hospital Road, Chelsea SW3 4HS. Tel: 0171 352 5646 Fax: 0171 376 3910

Greenwich Observatory, Queens House, National Maritime Museum, Romney Road, Greenwich SE10 9NF. Tel: 0181 312 6565 Fax: 0181 312 6632

Kenwood House, Hampstead. Tel: 0181 348 1286

Museum of Garden History, Lambeth Palace Road, SE1 7LB. Tel: 0171 401 8865 Fax: 0171 401 8869

Orleans House Gallery, Riverside, Twickenham, TW1 3DJ. Tel: 0181 892 0221 Fax: 0181 744 0501

Pitshanger Manor & Gallery, Mattock Lane, Ealing, W5 5EQ. Tel: 0181 567 1227 Fax: 0181 567 0595

St. John's Gate, Clerkenwell, EC1M 4DA. Tel: 0171 253 6644 Fax: 0171 336 0587

Strawberry Hill House, Waldegrave Road, Strawberry Hill, Twickenham. Tel: 0181 240 4114 Fax: 0181 255 6174

Syon Park, Syon House & Gardens, Brentford, TW8 8JF. Tel: 0181 560 0883 Fax: 0181 568 0936

Meols Hall, Churchtown, Southport PR9 7LZ. Tel: 01704 228326 Fax: 01704 507185

NORFOLK

Wolterton Park, Erpingham NR11 7BB. Tel: 01263 584175 Fax: 01263 761214

NORTHAMPTONSHIRE

Castle Ashby House, Castle Ashby, Northampton NN7 1LQ. Tel: 01604 696696 Fax: 01604 696516

Holdenby House Gardens & Falconry Centre, Holdenby, Northampton NN6 8DJ. Tel: 01604 770074 Fax: 01604 770962

Lamport Hall and Gardens, Northampton NN6 9HD. Tel: 01604 686272 Fax: 01604 686 224

NORTHUMBERLAND

Alnwick Castle, Estate Office, Alnwick NE66 1NQ. Tel: 01665 510777 Fax: 01665 510876

Chillingham Castle, Chillingham, Alnwick NE66 5NJ. Tel: 01668 215359 Fax: 01668 215643

NOTTINGHAMSHIRE

Norwood Park, Southwell NG25 0PF. Tel: 01636 815649

Papplewick Hall, Nr Nottingham, NG15 8FE. Tel: 0115 963 3491 Fax: 0115 964 2767

OXFORDSHIRE

Ardington House, Wantage OX12 8QA. Tel: 01235 821566 Fax: 01235 821151

Blenheim Palace, Woodstock, OX20 1PX. Tel: 01993 811325 Fax: 01993 813527

Fawley Court - Marian Fathers Historic House & Museum Marlow Road, Henley-On-Thames RG9 3AE. Tel: 01491 574917 Fax: 01491 411587

Kelmscott Manor, Kelmscott, nr Lechlade GL7 3HJ. Tel: 01367 252486 Fax: 01367 253 754

SHROPSHIRE

Burford House Gardens, Tenbury Wells, Worcestershire WR15 8HQ. Tel: 01584 810777 Fax: 01584 810673

Hawkstone Hall and Gardens, Weston-U-Redcastle, Shrewsbury SY4 5LG. Tel: 01630 685242 Fax: 01630 685565

Hawkstone Historic Park & Follies, Weston-under-Redcastle, Shrewsbury SY4 5UY. Tel: 01939 200611 Fax: 01939 200 311

Ironbridge Gorge Museum, Ironbridge, Telford TF8 7AW. Tel: 01952 433522 Fax: 01952 432204

Old Colehurst Manor, Colehurst, Market Drayton TF9 2JB. Tel: 01630 638833 Fax: 01630 638647

Walcot Hall, Nr Bishops Castle, Lydbury North SY7 8AZ. Tel: 0171-581 2782 Fax: 0171 589 0195

Weston Park, Weston under Lizard, nr Shifnal TF11 8LE. Tel: 01952 850207 Fax: 01952 850430

SOMERSET

Maunsel House, North Newton, nr Bridgwater TA7 0SU. Tel: 01278 663413/661076

The Bishop's Palace, Wells BA5 2PD. Tel: 01749 678691

STAFFORDSHIRE

Sandon Hall, Sandon ST18 0BZ. Tel: 01889 508004 Fax: 01889 508586

The Shugborough Estate, Milford, Stafford ST17 0XB. Tel: 01889 881388 Fax: 01889 881323

SUFFOLK

Hengrave Hall Centre, Hengrave Hall, Bury St Edmunds IP28 6LZ. Tel: 01284 701561 Fax: 01284 702950

Kentwell Hall, Long Melford, nr. Sudbury CO10 9BA. Tel: 01787 310207 Fax: 01787 379318

Otley Hall, Otley, nr Ipswich IP6 9PA. Tel: 01473 890264 Fax: 01473 890803

Somerleyton Hall, nr Lowestoft NR32 5QQ. Tel: 01502 730224 Fax: 01502 732143

Wingfield Old College & Gardens, Wingfield, Nr Stradbroke IP21 5RA. Tel: 01379 384888 Fax: 01379 384034

SURREY

Clandon Park, West Clandon, Guildford GU4 7RQ. Tel: 01483 222482 Fax: 01483 223479

Farnham Castle, Farnham GU7 0AG. Tel: 01252 721194 Fax: 01252 711283

Great Fosters Hotel, Stroude Road, Egham TW20 9UR. Tel: 0784 433822

Loseley Park, Estate Office, Guildford GU3 1HS. Tel: 01483 304440 Fax: 01483 302036

Painshill Landscape Garden, Portsmouth Road, Cobham KT11 1JE. Tel: 01932 868113 Fax: 01932 868001

SUSSEX

Borde Hill Garden, Balcombe Road, Haywards Heath, RH16 1XP. Tel: 01444 450326 Fax: 01444 440427

Brickwall House and Gardens, Northiam, Rye TN31 6NL. Tel: 01797 253388 Fax: 01797 252567

Chichester Cathedral, Cathedral Cloisters, West Street, Chichester PO19 1PX. Tel: 01243 782595 Fax: 01243 536190

Firle Place, Nr Lewes BN8 6LP. Tel: 01273 858188

Goodwood House, Goodwood, Chichester PO18 OPX. Tel: 01243 755048 Fax: 01243 755005

Herstmonceux Castle, International Study Centre, Queens University, Hailsham BN27 1RN. Tel: 01323 833816 Fax: 01323 834499

Pallant House, 9 North Pallant, Chichester PO19 1TY. Tel: 01243 774557

Preston Manor, Preston Drove, Brighton BN1 6SD. Tel: 01273 292770 Fax: 01273 292871

Royal Pavilion, Brighton, East Sussex BN1 1EE. Tel: 01273 290900 Fax: 01273 292871

Saint Hill Manor, Saint hill Road, East Grinstead, RH19 4JY. Tel: 01342 325711

West Dean Gardens, West Dean Estate, nr Chichester PO18 0QZ. Tel: 01243 818210 Fax: 01243 811342

WARWICKSHIRE

Arbury Hall, Nuneaton CV10 7PT. Tel: 01203 382804 Fax: 01203 641147

Lord Leycester Hospital, High Street, Warwick CV34 4BH. Tel: 01926 491422 Fax: 01926 491 422

Ragley Hall, Alcester B49 5NJ. Tel: 01789 762090 Fax: 01789 764791

Warwick Castle, Warwick CV34 4QU. Tel: 01926 406600 Fax: 01926 401692

WEST MIDLANDS

Birmingham Botanical Gardens and Glasshouses, Westbourne Road, Edgbaston, Birmingham B15 3TR. Tel: 0121 454 1860 Fax: 0121 454 7835

Hagley Hall, nr Stourbridge DY9 1LG. Tel: 0562 882408

WILTSHIRE

Longleat, The Estate Office, Warminster BA12 7NW. Tel: 01985 844400 Fax: 01985 844885

Wilton House, Wilton, Salisbury SP2 OBJ. Tel: 01722 746720 Fax: 01722 744447

YORKSHIRE

Aske Hall, Aske, Richmond DL10 5HJ. Tel: 01748 850391 Fax: 01748 823252

The Bar Convent, 17 Blossom Street, York YO2 2AH. Tel: 01904 643238 Fax: 01904 631792

Bolton Abbey Estate, Bolton Abbey, Skipton BD23 6EX. Tel: 01756 7110227 Fax: 01756 710535

Bolton Castle, Leyburn, DL8 4ET. Tel: 01969 623981. Fax: 01969 623332

Duncombe Park, Helmsley, York YO62 5EB. Tel: 01439 770213 Fax: 01439 771114

Elsham Hall Country and Wildlife Park, The Estate Office, Brigg DN20 0QZ. Tel: 01652 688698 Fax: 01652 688240

Harewood House and Bird Garden, The Estate Office, Harewood, Leeds LS17 9LQ. Tel: 0113 288 6331 Fax: 0113 288 6467

Hovingham Hall, Hovingham, York YO6 4LU. Tel: 01653 628206 Fax: 01653 628668

Newby Hall, Ripon, HG4 5AE. Tel: 01423 322583. Fax: 01423 324452

Ripley Castle, Ripley HG3 3AY. Tel: 01423 770152 Fax: 01423 771745

Sewerby Hall and Gardens, Church Lane, Sewerby, Bridlington YO15 1EA. Tel: Estate Office: 01262 673 769 Hall :01262 677874

WALES

Cresselly, Cresselly, Kilgetty SA68 0SP. Tel: 01646 651992

Dinefwr Park, Llandeilo SA19 6RT. Tel: 01558 823902 Fax: 01558 822036

Picton Castle, Picton Castle Trust, Haverfordwest SA62 4AS. Tel: 01437 751326

Tredegar House, Newport NP1 9YW. Tel: 01633 815880 Fax: 01633 815895

SCOTLAND

Ayton Castle, Estate Office, Eyemouth TD14 5RD. Tel: 0189 07 81212 Fax: 018907 81550

Blairquhan Castle and Gardens, Straiton,, Maybole KA19 7LZ. Tel: 016557 70239 Fax: 016557 70278

Bowhill House & Country Park, Bowhill, nr Selkirk TD7 5ET. Tel: 01750 22204 Fax: 01750 22204

Dalmeny House, Charisma, South Queensferry EH30 9TQ. Tel: 0131-331 1888 Fax: 0131 331 1788

Doune of Rothiemurchus, By Aviemore, Inverness-shire, PH22 1QH. Tel: 01479 812345 Fax: 01479 811778

Drummond Castle Gardens, Muthill, Crieff PH5 2AA. Tel: 01764 681257/433 Fax: 01764 681 550

Duff House Country House Gallery, Banff AB45 5SX. Tel: 01261 818181 Fax: 01261 818900

Dunrobin Castle, Golspie, Sutherland KW10 6SF. Tel: 01408 633177 Fax: 01408 634081

Lennoxlove House, Haddington, East Lothian, EH41 4NZ. Tel: 01620 823720 Fax: 01620 825112

Manderston, Duns, Berwickshire TD11 3PP. Tel: 01361 883450 Fax: 01361 882010

Paxton House & Gardens, Paxton, nr Berwick-upon-Tweed TD15 1SZ. Tel: 01289 386291

Traquair House, Innerleithen EH44 6PW. Tel: 01896 830323 Fax: 01896 830639

IRELAND

Antrim Castle Gardensm, Antrim. Tel: 01849 428000 Fax: 01849 460360

Bantry Housem, Bantry, Co. Cork. Tel: 00353 2 750 047 Fax: 00353 2 750 795

Dublin Writer's Museum, 18 Parnell Square, Dublin 1. Tel: 00353 1 872 2077 Fax: 00353 1 872 2231

Glin Castlem, Glin. Tel: 00353 68 34173 Fax: 00353 68 34364

Newman House, 85/86 St. Stephens Green, Dublin 2. Tel: +353 7067422 Fax: +353 7067211

Shannon Heritage, Bunratty Castle & Folk Park, Bunratty, Co. Clare, Ireland. Tel 00 353 61 360788 Fax: 00 353 61 361020

Strokestown Park House & Gardens, Strokestown, Co. Roscommon. Tel: 00353 78 33013 Fax: 00353 78 33712

Tullynally Castle, Castlepollard, Co. Westmeath. Tel: 00353 44 61159/ 61289 Fax: 00353 44 61856

Properties Offering Accommodation

ENGLAND

BERKSHIRE

Swallowfield Park, Swallowfield, RG7 1TG. Tel: 01734 883815
Welford Park, Newbury RG20 8HU. Tel: 01488 608203 Fax: 01488 608853

BUCKINGHAMSHIRE

Waddesdon Manor, Nr. Aylesbury, HP18 OJW. Tel: 01296 651236, Fax: 01296 651 142

CAMBRIDGESHIRE

The Manor, Hemingford Grey PE18 9BN. Tel: 01480 463134 Fax: 01480 465026

CHESHIRE

Adlington Hall, Macclesfield SK10 4LF. Tel: 01625 820875 Fax: 01625 828756

CORNWALL

Tregrehan, Par, PL24 25J Tel: 01726 814 389/812 438.
Accommodation: Self-catering cottages available

CUMBRIA

Appleby Castle, Boroughgate, Appleby-in-Westmorland, CA16 6XH Tel: 01763 51402
Castletown House, Rockcliffe, Carlisle CA6 4BN. Tel: 01228 74792 Fax: 01228 74464
Dalemain, Nr. Penrith, CA11 0HB Tel: 017684 86450
Accommodation: B&B, Parkhouse Farm, Dalemain. Tel: 017684 86212
Naworth Castle, Brampton Castle, Brampton CA8 2HE Tel: 016977 3229 Accommodation: There are 10 bedrooms available for overnight parties.

DEVON

Buckfast Abbey, Buckfastleigh TQ11 OEE Tel: 01364 642519, Fax: 01364 643891
Flete, Ermington, Ivybridge, Plymouth, PL21 9NZ Tel: 01752 830 308, Fax: 01752 830 309
Kingston House, Staverton, Totnes,TQ9 6AR Tel: 01803 762235 Luxury accommodation in house and self-contained cottages.
Tiverton Castle, Tiverton EX16 6RP Tel: 01884 253200. Accommodation: 3 superb self-catering holiday apartments inside Castle available weekly, short breaks, or winter lettings. Graded 4 Keys Highly Commended.
Yarde, Malborough, Nr Salcombe TQ7 3BY Tel: 01548 842367

DORSET

Mapperton, Beaminster DT8 3NR. Tel: 01308 862645

COUNTY DURHAM

Durham Castle, Durham Tel: 0191 374 3863
Accommodation: Contact 0191-374 3863

ESSEX

Gosfield Hall, Halstead, CO9 1SF Tel: 01787 472 914

GLOUCESTERSHIRE

Frampton Court, Frampton-on-Severn GL2 7EU. Tel: Home 01452 740 267
Owlpen Manor, Uley, nr Dursley GL11 5BZ Tel: 01453 860261 Accommodation: Nine period cottages available, including listed buildings.
Sudeley Castle and Gardens, Winchcombe, GL54 5JD Tel: 01242 603197/602308 Accommodation: 14 romantic Cotswold Cottages on Castle Estate. Private guided tours of Castle Apartments and Gardens by prior arrangement. Schools educational pack available.

HAMPSHIRE

Gilbert White's House & Garden and the Oates Museum, The Wakes, Selborne GU34 3JH. Tel: 01420 511275
Hall Farm House, Bentworth, Alton GU34 5JU. Tel: 01420 564010
Houghton Lodge Gardens, Stockbridge SO20 6LQ. Tel: 01264 810177, Fax: 01794 388072

HEREFORD & WORCESTER

Bernithan Court, Llangarron
Accommodation: On application.
Brobury House & Garden, Borbury, Nr Hereford, HR3 6BS Tel: 01981 500 229
Burton Court, Eardisland HR6 9DN Tel: 01544 388231
Accommodation: Holiday flat, self contained – sleeps 7.
Eastnor Castle, Nr Ledbury, HR8 1RD Tel: 01531 633160/632302, Fax: 01531 631766
Luxury accommodation for select groups.
Hergest Croft Gardens, Kington Tel: 01544 230160
Accommodation: Self-catering house – nursery sleeps 7.
Kentchurch Court, Hereford Tel: 01981 240228
Accommodation: By appointment.
Moccas Court, Moccas HR2 9LH Tel: 01981 500381
Accommodation: Available at The Red Lion Hotel, Bredwardine.

KENT

Cobham Hall, Cobham, nr. Gravesend, DA12 3BL
Tel: 01474 824319/823371 Accommodation: The house, grounds, accommodation 250 beds and sports facilities are available for private hire, wedding receptions, business conferences, residential and non-residential courses and film and photographic location.

Down House, Downe BR6 7JT. Tel: 01689 859119
Great Maytham Hall, Rolvenden, Cranbrook, TN17 4NE. Tel: 01580 241 346, Fax: 01580 241 038
Goodnestone Park, Goodnestone, Canterbury CT3 1PL. Tel: 01304 840107
Ladham House, Ladham Road, Goudhurst. Tel: 01580 211203 Fax: 01580 212596
Pattyndenne Manor, Goudhurst TN17 2QU. Tel: 01580 211361

LONDON

De Morgan Foundation, Old Battersea House, 30 Vicarage Crescent, Battersea SW11 3LD.
Linley Sambourne House, 18 Stafford Terrace W8 7BH. Tel: 0171 937 0663 Fax: 0181 995 4895
Museum of Garden History, Lambeth Palace Road, Lambeth SE1 7LB. Tel: 0171 261 1891 Fax 0171 401 8869
The Traveller's Club, Pall Mall SW1Y 5EP. Tel: 0171-930 8688 Fax: 0171 930 2019

NORFOLK

Mannington Hall, Saxthorpe, Norwich NR11 7BB. Tel: 01263 584175 Fax: 01263 761214
Walsingham Abbey, Estate Office, Walsingham, NR22 6BP Tel: 01328 820259 Accommodation: Also available in the village Hotel, B&B etc..

NORTHAMPTONSHIRE

Castle Ashby House, Castle Ashby, Northampton NN7 1LQ Tel: 01604 696696
Accommodation: Holiday cottages.
The Menagerie, Horton, Horton, Northampton NN7 2BX. Tel: 01604 870957

NORTHUMBERLAND

Alnwick Castle, Alnwick, Northumberland NE66 1NQ Tel: 01665 510777 Accommodation: Holiday cottages.
Chillingham Castle and Gardens, Alnwick Tel: 01668 215359 Accommodation: Private family suites of rooms available.
Norwood Park, Southwell NG25 0PF. Tel: Tel/Fax: 01636 815649

NOTTINGHAMSHIRE

Carlton Hall, Carlton-On-Trent, Newark NG23 6NW Tel: 01636 821421 Accommodation: Self-catering by appointment.
Norwood Park, Southwell, Nottingham NG25 OPF Tel: 01636 815649
Papplewick Hall, Near Nottingham NG15 8FE Tel: 0115 9633491 Accommodation: Country House hospitality, full breakfast and dinner, prices on request.

OXFORDSHIRE

Ardington House, Wantage OX12 8QA. Tel: 01235 821566 Fax: 01235 821151
Aynhoe Park, Suite 10, Aynho, Banbury, Oxfordshire, OX17 3BQ Tel: 01869 810 636
Ditchley Park, Ditchley Foundation, Enstone OX7 4ER. Tel: 01608 677346 Fax: 01608 677399
Mapledurham House and Watermill, Mapledurham RG4 7TR Tel: 01734 723350 Accommodation: Eleven self catering holiday cottages.

SHROPSHIRE

Fairfield, Stogursey, Bridgwater TA5 1PU. Tel: 01278 732251 Fax: 01278 732272
Hawkstone Historic Park & Follies, Weston-under-Redcastle, Shrewsbury SY4 5UY. Tel: 01939 200611 Fax: 01939 200 311
Ironbridge Gorge Museum, Ironbridge, Telford TF8 7AW. Tel: 01952 433522 Fax:01952 432204
Ludford House, Ludlow SY8 1PJ. Tel: 01584 872542 Fax: 01584 875662
Old Colehurst Manor, Colehurst, Market Drayton TF9 2JB. Tel: 01630 638833 Fax: 01630 638647
Upton Cressett Hall, Bridgnorth Tel: 01746 714307, Accommodation: Self catering accommodation available in Gatehouse.
Walcot Hall, Lydbury North, Nr Bishops Castle SY7 8AZ Tel: 0171 581 2782 Accommodation: 3 flats and Ground Floor wing available all year.
Weston Park, Nr Shifnal TF11 8LE Tel: 01952 850207 Accommodation: Luxury rooms in the house.

SOMERSET

Barford Park, Enmore, nr Bridgwater TA5 1AG. Tel: 0278 671269
Barstaple House Trinity Almshouses, Old Market Street, Bristol BS2 OEU. Tel: 01179 265777 Warden
Barford Park, Enmore, nr Bridgwater TA5 1AG. Tel: 0278 671269
Maunsel House, North Newton, nr Bridgwater TA7 O8U. Tel: 01278 663413/661076

STAFFORDSHIRE

Dunwood Hall, Longsdon, Nr Leek, Staffordshire, ST9 9AR Tel: 01538 385071
Sandon Hall, Sandon ST18 0BZ. Tel: 01889 508004 Fax: 01889 508586
Shugborough, Stafford ST17 OXB Tel: 01889 881388
Accommodation: Details of group accommodation can be obtained from the booking office

SUFFOLK

Haughley Park, nr Stowmarket IP14 3JY. Tel: 01359 240701
Hengrave Hall Centre, Hengrave Hall, Bury St Edmunds IP28 6LZ. Tel: 01284 701561 Fax: 01284 702950

SURREY

Albury Park, Albury, Guildford GU5 9BB Tel: 01483 202 964, Fax: 01483 205 013
Goddards, Abinger Common, Dorking RH5 6TH. Tel: 01628 825920
Great Fosters Hotel, Stroude Road, Egham TW20 9UR. Tel: 0784 433822
Greathed Manor, Dormansland, Lingfield, RH7 6PA Tel: 01342 832 577, Fax: 01342 836 207

SUSSEX

Danny, Hurstpierpoint, Hassocks BN6 9BB Tel: 01273 833 000, Fax: 01273 832 436
Goddards, Abinger Common, Dorking RH5 6TH. Tel: 01628 825920
Goodwood House, Chichester PO18 OPX Tel: 01243 774107 Accommodation: Goodwood Park Hotel, Golf and Country Club- reservations 01345 123333/01243 775537
Hammerwood Park, nr East Grinstead RH19 3QE Tel: 01342 850594, Fax: 01342 850864 Accommodation: B&B with a difference in an idyllically peaceful location only 20 minutes from Gatwick.

WILTSHIRE

Malmesbury House, The Close, Salisbury SP1 2EB. Tel: 01722 327027 Fax: 01722 334 414
Pythouse, Tisbury, Salisbury SP3 6PB Tel: 01747 870 210, Fax: 01747 871 786

WILTSHIRE

Hopton Court, Cleobury Mortimer, Kidderminster DY14 0HH. Tel: 01299 270734

YORKSHIRE

Aske Hall, Aske, Richmond DL10 5HJ. Tel: 01748 850391 Fax: 01748 823252
The Bar Convent, 17 Blossom Street, York YO2 2AH Tel: 01904 643238
Bolton Abbey, Skipton, North Yorkshire, BD23 6EX Tel: 01756 710 535
Broughton Hall, Skipton BD23 3AE. Tel: 01756 792267 Fax: 01756 792362
Hovingham Hall, Hovingham, York YO6 4LU. Tel: 01653 628206 Fax: 01653 628668
Elsham Hall Country and Wildlife Park, The Estate Office, Brigg DN20 0QZ. Tel: 01652 688698 Fax 01652 688240
Lindley Murray Summerhouse, The Mount School, Dalton Terrace YO24 4DD. Tel: 01904 667500 Fax: 01904 667524
The Orangery at Settrington, Settrington, Malton YO17 8NP. Tel: 01944 768345 / 768440out of hours Fax: 01944 768484
Ripley Castle, Ripley HG3 3AY Tel: 01423 770152
Accommodation: 25 deluxe bedrooms at the Estate owned Boar's Head Hotel, 100 yards from the Castle in Ripley village. The hotel is rated RAC****.

IRELAND

Bunratty Castle and Folk Park, Bunratty, Co. Clare. Tel: 00353 61 360 788. Knappogue Castle appartment – sleeps up to 10 people.
Bantry House, Bantry, Co. Cork. Tel: 027 50047
Accommodation: Bed & Breakfast and dinner. Nine rooms en suite.
Benvarden Gardens, Dervock, Ballymoney, CO. Antrim . Tel: 012657 41331 Fax: 012657 41955
Glin Castle, Glin Tel: 068 34173/34112
Accommodation: Overnight stays arranged. Castle can be rented.
Powerscourt Gardens & Waterfall, Enniskerry, Co. Wicklow . Tel: 00353 1 204 6000

SCOTLAND

Ayton Castle, Eyemouth, Berwickshire TD14 5RD Tel: 01890 7 812812
Balcarres, Leven, Colinsburgh KY9 1HL. Tel: 01333 340206
Dalmeny House, Charisma, South Queensferry EH30 9TQ. Tel: 0131-331 1888 Fax: 0131 331 1788
The Doune of Rothiemurchus, Rothiemurchus Estate Office, Aviemore PH22 1QH. Tel: 01479 810858 Fax: 01479 811778
Dunvegan Castle, Isle Of Skye TD11 3PP Tel: 01470 521206 Accommodation: Self catering cottages within grounds.
Manderston, Duns, Berwickshire TD11 3PP Tel: 01361 883450 Accommodation: By arrangement.
Sorn Castle, Sorn, Mauchline Tel: 01505 612124
Accommodation: Available - contact Cluttons
Traquair, Innerleithen EH44 6PW Tel: 01896 830323, Accommodation: 2 rooms B&B and Holiday flat to rent.

WALES

Cresselly, Cresselly, Kilgetty SA68 OSP. Tel: 01646 651992
Gwydir Castle, Llanrwst, Gwynedd LL26 OPN. Tel: 01492 641 687
Llanvihangel Court, Abergavenny NP7 8DH. Tel: 01873 890217

285

Johansens Recommendations

Alphabetical list of Johansens Recommendations in Great Britain & Ireland

HOTELS

ENGLAND

BEDFORDSHIRE

Flitwick Manor	Woburn	01525 712242
Moore Place Hotel	Milton Keynes	01908 282000
Woodlands Manor	Bedford	01234 363281

BERKSHIRE

Chauntry House Hotel & Restaurant	Bray-on-Thames	01628 673991
Cliveden	Maidenhead	01628 668561
Donnington Valley Hotel & Golf Course	Newbury	01635 551199
Elcot Park Hotel & Country Club	Newbury	01488 658100
Fredrick's Hotel & Restaurant	Maidenhead	01628 635934
The French Horn	Sonning-On-Thames	01189 692204
Hollington House Hotel	Newbury	01635 255100
Monkey Island Hotel	Bray-on-Thames	01628 623400
Oakley Court	Windsor	01753 609988
Royal Berkshire	Ascot	01344 623322
Sir Christopher Wren's Hotel & Business Centre	Windsor	01753 861354
Swan Diplomat	Streatley-On-Thames	01491 873737
The Vineyard At Stockcross	Newbury	01635 528770

BRISTOL

Swallow Royal Hotel	Bristol	0117 9255200

BUCKINGHAMSHIRE

Danesfield House	Marlow-On-Thames	01628 891010
Hartwell House	Aylesbury	01296 747444
The Priory Hotel	Aylesbury	01296 641239
Stoke Park	Slough	01753 717171

CAMBRIDGESHIRE

The Haycock	Peterborough	01780 782223
The Old Bridge Hotel	Huntingdon	01480 452681

CHESHIRE

The Alderley Edge Hotel	Alderley Edge	01625 583033
The Bridge Hotel	Prestbury	01625 829326
Broxton Hall Country House Hotel	Chester	01829 782321
Carden Park	Chester	01829 731000
The Chester Grosvenor	Chester	01244 324024
Crabwall Manor	Chester	01244 851666
Mollington Banastre	Chester	01244 851471
Nunsmere Hall	Chester	01606 889100
Rookery Hall	Nantwich	01270 610016
Rowton Hall Hotel	Chester	01244 335262
Shrigley Hall Hotel Golf & Country Club	Macclesfield	01625 575757
The Stanneylands Hotel	Manchester	01625 525225
Willington Hall Hotel	Willington	01829 752321

CLEVELAND

Grinkle Park Hotel	Easington	01287 640515

CORNWALL

Budock Vean Golf & Country House Hotel	Falmouth	01326 250288
Fowey Hall Hotel & Restaurant	Fowey	01726 833866
The Garrack Hotel	St. Ives	01736 796199
Hotel Tresanton	St Mawes	01326 270055
The Lugger Hotel	Portloe	01872 501322
Meudon Hotel	Falmouth	01326 250541
Nansidwell Country House	Falmouth	01326 250340
The Nare Hotel	Veryan	01872 501279
Penmere Manor	Falmouth	01326 211411
Rose-in-Vale Country House Hotel	St Agnes	01872 552202
Talland Bay Hotel	Talland-By-Looe	01503 272667
Treglos Hotel	Padstow	01841 520727
The Well House	St Keyne	01579 342001

COUNTY DURHAM

Headlam Hall	Darlington	01325 730238
Lumley Castle Hotel	Durham	0191 389 1111
Redworth Hall Hotel & Country Club	Newton Aycliffe	01388 772442

CUMBRIA

Appleby Manor Country House Hotel	Appleby-in-Westmorland	017683 51571
The Borrowdale Gates Country House Hotel	Keswick	017687 77204
Farlam Hall Hotel	Brampton	016977 46234
Gilpin Lodge	Windermere	015394 88818
Graythwaite Manor	Grange-Over-Sands	015395 32001
Holbeck Ghyll Country House Hotel & Health Spa	Ambleside	015394 32375
Lakeside Hotel On Lake Windermere	Windermere	0541 541586
Langdale Chase	Windermere	015394 32201
Langdale Hotel & Country Club	Ambleside	015394 37302
Linthwaite House Hotel	Windermere	015394 88600
Lovelady Shield Country House Hotel	Alston	01434 381203
Michaels Nook	Grasmere	015394 35496
Miller Howe	Windermere	015394 42536
Nanny Brow Country House Hotel & Restaurant	Ambleside	015394 32036
Rampsbeck Country House Hotel	Lake Ullswater	017684 86442
Rothay Manor	Ambleside	015394 33605
Sharrow Bay Country House Hotel	Lake Ullswater	017684 86301
Tufton Arms Hotel	Appleby-In-Westmorland	017683 51593
The Wordsworth Hotel	Grasmere	015394 35592

DERBYSHIRE

Callow Hall	Ashbourne	01335 343403
The Cavendish Hotel	Baslow	01246 582311
Fischer's	Baslow	01246 583259
George Hotel	Hathersage	01433 650436
Hassop Hall	Bakewell	01629 640488
The Izaak Walton Hotel	Ashbourne	01335 350555
Makeney Hall Country House Hotel	Derby	01332 842999
Mickleover Court	Derby	01332 521234
The Palace Hotel	Buxton	01298 22001
The Priest House On the River	Derby	01332 810649
Riber Hall	Matlock	01629 582795
Risley Hall Country House Hotel	Derby	0115 939 9000
Riverside House Hotel	Ashford-In-The-Water	01629 814275
The Wind In The Willows	Glossop	01457 868001

DEVON

The Arundell Arms	Lifton	01566 784666
Bel Alp House	Dartmoor	01364 661217
Bolt Head Hotel	Salcombe	01548 843751
Brookdale House Restaurant & Hotel	North Huish	01548 821661
Buckland-Tout-Saints	Kingsbridge Estuary	01548 853055
Combe House Hotel	Honiton	01404 540400
The Edgemoor	Bovey Tracey	01626 832466
Gidleigh Park	Chagford	01647 432367
Holne Chase Hotel	Ashburton	01364 631471
Hotel Riviera	Sidmouth	01395 515201
Ilsington Country Hotel	Ilsington	01364 661452
Lewtrenchard Manor	Lewdown	01566 783 256
Northcote Manor	Burrington	01769 560501
Orestone Manor Hotel & Restaurant	Maidencombe	01803 328098
The Osborne Hotel & Langtry's Restaurant	Torquay	01803 213311
The Palace Hotel	Torquay	01803 200200
Percy's at Coombeshead	Launceston	01409 211236
Soar Mill Cove Hotel	Salcombe	01548 561566
St Olaves Court Hotel	Exeter	01392 217736
Watersmeet Hotel	Woolacombe	01271 870333
Woolacombe Bay Hotel	Woolacombe	01271 870388

DORSET

Bridge House Hotel	Beaminster	01308 862200
The Dormy	Bournemouth	01202 872121
The Mansion House Hotel and Dining Club	Poole	01202 685666
Moonfleet Manor	Weymouth	01305 786948
The Norfolk Royale Hotel	Bournemouth	01202 551521
Plumber Manor	Sturminster Newton	01258 472507
The Priory	Wareham	01929 551666
Summer Lodge	Evershot	01935 83424

EAST SUSSEX

Ashdown Park Hotel	Forest Row	01342 824988
Broomhill Lodge	Rye	01797 280421
Buxted Park Country House Hotel	Buxted,Near Uckfield	01825 732711
Dale Hill	Ticehurst	01580 200112
The Grand Hotel	Eastbourne	01323 412345
Horsted Place Hotel	Uckfield	01825 750581
Netherfield Place	Battle	01424 774455
PowderMills Hotel	Battle	01424 775511
Topps Hotel	Brighton	01273 729334
White Lodge Country House Hotel	Alfriston	01323 870265

EAST YORKSHIRE

Willerby Manor Hotel	Hull	01482 652616

ESSEX

Five Lakes Hotel Golf & Country Club	Colchester	01621 868888
Maison Talbooth	Dedham	01206 322367
Pontlands Park Country Hotel	Chelmsford	01245 476444
The White Hart Hotel & Restaurant	Colchester	01376 561654
Whitehall	Stansted	01279 850603

GLOUCESTERSHIRE

Calcot Manor	Tetbury	01666 890391
Charingworth Manor	Chipping Campden	01386 593555
Corse Lawn House Hotel	Tewkesbury	01452 780479
The Cotswold House	Chipping Campden	01386 840330
The Grapevine Hotel	Stow-On-The-Wold	01451 830344
The Greenway	Cheltenham	01242 862352
Hotel On The Park	Cheltenham	01242 518898
Lords Of The Manor Hotel	Upper Slaughter	01451 820243
The Manor House Hotel	Moreton-In-Marsh	01608 650501
The Painswick Hotel	Painswick	01452 812160
Stonehouse Court	Stonehouse	01453 825155
The Swan Hotel At Bibury	Bibury	01285 740695
Washbourne Court Hotel	Lower Slaughter	01451 822143
Wyck Hill House	Stow-On-The-Wold	01451 831936

GREATER MANCHESTER

Etrop Grange	Manchester Airport	0161 499 0500

HAMPSHIRE

Careys Manor Hotel	Brockenhurst	01590 623551
Esseborne Manor	Andover	01264 736444
Fifehead Manor	Middle Wallop	01264 781565
Hotel Du Vin & Bistro	Winchester	01962 841414
Lainston House Hotel	Winchester	01962 863588
The Master Builder's House	Beaulieu	01590 616253
The Montagu Arms Hotel	Beaulieu	01590 612324
New Park Manor	Brockenhurst	01590 623467
Old Thorns	Liphook	01428 724555
Parkhill Hotel	Lyndhurst	01703 282944
Passford House Hotel	Lymington	01590 682398
Rhinefield House Hotel	Brockenhurst	01590 622922
Stanwell House	Lymington	01590 677123
Tylney Hall	Basingstoke	01256 764881

HEREFORDSHIRE

The Chase Hotel	Ross-On-Wye	01989 763161
Pengethley Manor	Ross-On-Wye	01989 730211

HERTFORDSHIRE

Down Hall Country House Hotel	Bishop's Stortford	01279 731441
Hanbury Manor	Ware	01920 487722
Pendley Manor Hotel & Conference Centre	Tring	01442 891891
Sopwell House Hotel & Country Club	St Albans	01727 864477
Stocks	Hemel Hempstead	01442 851341
West Lodge Park	Hadley Wood	0181 440 8311

ISLE OF WIGHT

The George Hotel	Yarmouth	01983 760331

KENT

Brandshatch Place Hotel	Fawkham	01474 872239
Chilston Park	Maidstone	01622 859803
Eastwell Manor	Ashford	01233 219955
Hotel Du Vin & Bistro	Tunbridge Wells	01892 526455
Howfield Manor	Canterbury	01227 738294
Rowhill Grange	Dartford	01322 615136
The Spa Hotel	Tunbridge Wells	01892 520331

LANCASHIRE

The Gibbon Bridge Country House Hotel	Preston	01995 61456

LEICESTERSHIRE

Barnsdale Lodge	Rutland Water	01572 724678
Quorn Country Hotel	Leicester	01509 415050
Stapleford Park, An Outpost of The Carnegie Club	Stapleford	01572 787522

LINCOLNSHIRE

Belton Woods	Grantham	01476 593200
The George Of Stamford	Stamford	01780 750750

LONDON

The Ascott Mayfair	London	0171 499 6868
Basil Street Hotel	London	0171 581 3311
The Beaufort	London	0171 584 5252
Beaufort House Apartments	London	0171 584 2600
Blakes Hotel	London	0171 370 6701
The Cadogan	London	0171 235 7141
Cannizaro House	London	0181 879 1464
The Cliveden Town House	London	0171 730 6466
The Cranley	London	0171 373 0123
The Dorchester	London	0171 629 8888
Draycott House Apartments	London	0171 584 4659
The Halcyon	London	0171 727 7288
Harrington Hall	London	0171 396 9696
The Hempel	London	0171 298 9000
The Leonard	London	0171 935 2010
The London Outpost of the Carnegie Club	London	0171 589 7333
The Milestone	London	0171 917 1000
Number Eleven Cadogan Gardens	London	0171 730 7000
Number Sixteen	London	0171 589 5232
One Aldwych	London	0171 300 1000
Park Consul Hotel	London	0171 225 7500
Pembridge Court Hotel	London	0171 229 9977
The Royal Horseguards	London	0171 839 3400

NORFOLK

Congham Hall	King's Lynn	01485 600250
Park Farm Hotel & Leisure	Norwich	01603 810264
Petersfield House Hotel	Norwich	01692 630741
Sprowston Manor Hotel	Norwich	01603 410871

NORTH DEVON

Whitechapel Manor	South Molton	01769 573377

NORTH YORKSHIRE

The Balmoral Hotel	Harrogate	01423 508208
The Boar's Head Hotel	Harrogate	01423 771888
Crathorne Hall Hotel	Crathorne	01642 700398
The Devonshire Arms Country House Hotel	Bolton Abbey	01756 710441
The Grange Hotel	York	01904 644744
Grants Hotel	Harrogate	01423 560666
Hackness Grange	Scarborough	01723 882345
Hazlewood Castle Hotel	Hazlewood	01937 535353
Hob Green Hotel & Restaurant	Harrogate	01423 770031
Middlethorpe Hall	York	01904 641241
Monk Fryston Hall	Monk Fryston	01977 682369
Mount Royale Hotel	York	01904 628856
The Pheasant	Helmsley	01439 771241 /770416
Rudding Park House & Hotel	Harrogate	01423 871350
The Worsley Arms Hotel	Hovingham	01653 628234
Wrea Head Country Hotel	Scarborough	01723 378211
York Pavilion Hotel	York	01904 622099
Simonstone Hall	Hawes	01969 667255

NORTHAMPTONSHIRE

Fawsley Hall Hotel	Daventry	01327 892000

NORTHUMBERLAND

Linden Hall Hotel, Health Spa & Golf Course	Newcastle-Upon-Tyne	01670 516611
Marshall Meadow Country House Hotel	Berwick-Upon-Tweed	01289 331133
Slaley Hall Hotel International Hotel Golf Resort & Spa	Newcastle-Upon-Tyne	01434 673350
Tillmouth Park	Berwick-Upon-Tweed	01890 882255

NOTTINGHAMSHIRE

Langar Hall	Nottingham	01949 860559

OXFORDSHIRE

The Bay Tree Hotel & Restaurant	Burford	01993 822791
The Feathers Hotel	Woodstock	01993 812291
Le Manoir Aux Quat' Saisons	Oxford	01844 278881
Mill House Hotel	Kingham	01608 658188
Phyllis Court Club	Henley-On-Thames	01491 570500
The Plough at Clanfield	Clanfield	01367 810222
The Springs Hotel & Golf Club	Wallingford	01491 836687
Studley Priory	Oxford	01865 351203
Weston Manor	Oxford	01869 350621
Wroxton House Hotel	Banbury	01295 730777

RUTLAND

Hambleton Hall	Oakham	01572 756991
The Lake Isle	Uppingham	01572 822951

SHROPSHIRE

Albrighton Hall Hotel & Restaurant	Shrewsbury	01939 291000
Dinham Hall	Ludlow	01584 876464
Hawkstone Park Hotel	Shrewsbury	01939 200611
Madeley Court	Telford	01952 680068
The Old Vicarage Hotel	Wolverhampton	01746 716497

SOMERSET

The Bath Priory Hotel and Restaurant	Bath	01225 331922
Bindon Country House Hotel & Restaurant	Taunton	01823 400070
The Castle At Taunton	Taunton	01823 272671
Charlton House and The Mulberry Restaurant	Shepton Mallet	01749 342008
Combe Grove Manor & Country Club	Bath	01225 834644
Daneswood House Hotel	Bristol South	01934 843145
Homewood Park	Bath	01225 723731
Hunstrete House	Bath	01761 490490
The Mount Somerset Country House Hotel	Taunton	01823 442500
Periton Park Hotel	Middlecombe	01643 706885
The Queensberry	Bath	01225 447928
The Royal Crescent	Bath	01225 823333
Ston Easton Park	Bath	01761 241631

SOUTH YORKSHIRE

Charnwood Hotel	Sheffield	0114 258 9411
Whitley Hall Hotel	Sheffield	0114 245 4444
The Brookhouse	Burton upon Trent	01283 814188
Hoar Cross Hall Health Spa Resort	Lichfield	01283 575671
Swinfen Hall	Lichfield	01543 481494

SUFFOLK

The Angel Hotel	Bury St Edmunds	01284 753926
Cornwallis Arms	Diss	01379 870326
Hintlesham Hall	Ipswich	01473 652268
Ravenwood Hall	Bury St Edmunds	01359 270345
Seckford Hall	Woodbridge	01394 385678
Swallow Belstead Brook Hotel	Ipswich	01473 684241
The Swan Hotel	Southwold	01502 722186
Swynford Paddocks Hotel & Restaurant	Newmarket	01638 570234
Wentworth Hotel	Aldeburgh	01728 452312

SURREY

The Angel Posting House And Livery	Guildford	01483 564555
The Carlton Mitre Hotel	Hampton Court	0181 979 9988
Foxhills	Ottershaw	01932 872050
Grayshott Hall Health Fitness Retreat	Grayshott	01428 604331
Great Fosters	Egham	01784 433822
Langshott Manor	Gatwick	01293 786680
Lythe Hill Hotel	Haslemere	01428 651251
Nutfield Priory	Redhill	01737 822066
Oatlands Park Hotel	Weybridge	01932 847242
The Richmond Gate Hotel And Restaurant	Richmond-Upon-Thames	0181 940 0061
Woodlands Park Hotel	Cobham	01372 843933

SUSSEX

Ghyll Manor Country Hotel	Rusper	01293 871571
Newick Park	Lewes	01825 723633

WARWICKSHIRE

Billesley Manor	Stratford-Upon-Avon	01789 279955
Coombe Abbey	Coventry	01203 450450
Ettington Park Hotel	Stratford-Upon-Avon	01789 450123
The Glebe At Barford	Warwick	01926 624218
Nailcote Hall	Coventry	01203 466174
Nuthurst Grange	Hockley Heath	01564 783972
Welcombe Hotel & Golf Course	Stratford-Upon-Avon	01789 295252

WEST MIDLANDS

The Burlington Hotel	Birmingham	0121 643 9191
The Mill House Hotel & Lombard Room Restaurant	Birmingham	0121 459 5800
New Hall	Birmingham	0121 378 2442
The Swallow Hotel	Birmingham	0121 452 1144

WEST SUSSEX

Alexander House	Gatwick	01342 714914
Amberley Castle	Amberley	01798 831992
The Angel Hotel	Midhurst	01730 812421
Bailiffscourt	Arundel	01903 723511
Little Thakeham	Storrington	01903 744416
The Millstream Hotel	Chichester	01243 573234
Ockenden Manor	Cuckfield	01444 416111
South Lodge Hotel	Horsham	01403 891711
The Spread Eagle Hotel & Health Spa	Midhurst	01730 816911

WEST YORKSHIRE

42 The Calls	Leeds	0113 244 0099
Bagden Hall Hotel & Golf Course	Huddersfield	01484 865330
Chevin Lodge Country Park Hotel	Otley	01943 467818
Haley's Hotel and Restaurant	Leeds	0113 278 4446
Holdsworth House	Halifax	01422 240024
Linton Springs	Wetherby	01937 585353
Oulton Hall	Leeds	0113 282 1000
Rombalds Hotel	Ilkley	01943 603201
Wood Hall	Wetherby	01937 587271

WILTSHIRE

Beechfield House	Lacock	01225 703700
Bishopstrow House	Warminster	01985 212312
Crudwell Court Hotel	Malmesbury	01666 577194
Ivy House Hotel	Marlborough	01672 515333
Lucknam Park	Bath	01225 742777
The Manor House	Castle Combe	01249 782206
The Old Bell	Malmesbury	01666 822344
The Pear Tree at Purton	Swindon	01793 772100
Whatley Manor	Malmesbury	01666 822888
Woolley Grange	Bradford-On-Avon	01225 864705

WORCESTERSHIRE

Brockencote Hall	Chaddesley Corbett	01562 777876
The Colwall Park Hotel	Malvern	01684 540206
The Cottage In The Wood	Malvern Wells	01684 575859
Dormy House	Broadway	01386 852711
The Elms	Abberley	01299 896666
The Evesham Hotel	Evesham	01386 765566
Grafton Manor Country House Hotel	Bromsgrove	01527 579007
The Lygon Arms	Broadway	01386 852255
Salford Hall Hotel	Stratford-Upon-Avon	01386 871300
Wood Norton Hall	Evesham	01386 420007

IRELAND

CO ANTRIM (NORTHERN IRELAND)

Galgorm Manor	Ballymena	01266 881001

CO. CLARE

Dromoland Castle	Newmarket-On-Fergus	00 353 61 368144

CO CORK

Longueville House & Presidents' Restaurant	Mallow	00 353 22 47156

CO DOWN (NORTHERN IRELAND)

Culloden Hotel	Belfast	01232 425223
The McCausland Hotel	Belfast	01232 220200
Slieve Donard Hotel	Newcastle	013967 23681

CO DUBLIN

Portmarnock Hotel & Golf Links	Dublin	00 353 1 846 0611

CO GALWAY

Renvyle House Hotel	Connemara	00 353 95 43511

CO KERRY

Aghadoe Heights Hotel	Killarney	00 353 64 31766
Dunloe Castle	Killarney	00 353 64 44111
Muckross Park Hotel	Killarney	00 353 64 31938
The Park Hotel Kenmare	Kenmare	00 353 64 41200
Parknasilla Hotel	Parknasilla	00 353 64 45122
Randles Court Hotel	Killarney	00 353 64 35333
Sheen Falls Lodge	Kenmare	00 353 64 41600

CO KILDARE

Barberstown Castle	Dublin	00 353 1 6288157
Kildare Hotel & Country Club	Dublin	00 353 1 601 7200

CO LIMERICK

Adare Manor	Adare	00 353 61 396566

CO. MAYO

Ashford Castle	Cong	00 353 92 46003

CO MONAGHAN

Nuremore Hotel & Country Club	Carrickmacross	00 353 42 61438

CO WEXFORD

Kelly's Resort Hotel	Rosslare	00 353 53 32114
Marlfield House	Gorey	00 353 55 21124

CO WICKLOW

Humewood Castle	Kiltegan	00 353 508 73215
Hunter's Hotel	Rathnew	00 353 404 40106
Tinakilly Country House Hotel & Restaurant	Wicklow	00 353 40469274

DUBLIN

Brooks Hotel	Dublin	00 353 1 670 4000
The Merrion Hotel	Dublin	00 353 1 603 0600
The Hibernian	Dublin	00 353 1 668 7666

GALWAY

Connemara Coast Hotel	Furbo	00 353 91 592108

WEST CORK

The Lodge & Spa at Inchydoney Island	Clonakilty	00 353 23 33143

SCOTLAND

ABERDEENSHIRE

Ardoe House Hotel & Restaurant	Aberdeen	01224 867355
Darroch Learg Hotel	Ballater	013397 55443
Kildrummy Castle Hotel	Kildrummy	019755 71288
Pittodrie House	Inverurie	01467 681444
Thainstone House Hotel & Country Club	Aberdeen	01467 621643
Tor-na-coille Hotel	Banchory	01330 822242

ANGUS

Letham Grange Hotel & Golf Course	Angus	01241 890373

ARGYLL

Ardanaiseig	Kilchrenan by Taynuilt	01866 833333
Enmore Hotel	Dunoon	01369 702230
Isle Of Eriska	Isle Of Eriska,by Oban	01631 720371
Knipoch Hotel	Oban	01852 316251
Stonefield Castle Hotel	Tarbert	01880 820836
Western Isles Hotel	Isle Of Mull	01688 302012

AYRSHIRE

Montgreenan Mansion House Hotel	Irvine	01294 557733
Piersland House Hotel	Troon	01292 314747

BANFFSHIRE

Craigellachie Hotel	Craigellachie	01340 881204

DUMFRIES & GALLOWAY

Balcary Bay Hotel	Auchencairn	01556 640217
Cally Palace Hotel	Gatehouse Of Fleet	01557 814341
Corsewall Lighthouse Hotel	Stranraer	01776 853220

DUNBARTONSHIRE

Cameron House	Loch Lomond	01389 755565

EAST LOTHIAN

Greywalls	Gullane	01620 842144

FIFE

St. Andrews Golf Hotel	St. Andrews	01334 472611

INVERNESS-SHIRE

Arisaig House	Beasdale By Arisaig	01687 450622
Culloden House Hotel	Inverness	01463 790461
Glenspean Lodge Hotel	Fort William	01397 712223
Kingsmills Hotel	Inverness	01463 237166
Knockie Lodge Hotel	Fort Augustus	01456 486276
Loch Torridon Hotel	Torridon	01445 791242
Mansion House Hotel & Country Club	Elgin	01343 548811

KINCARDINSHIRE

Raemoir House Hotel	Banchory	01330 824884

LANARKSHIRE

Shieldhill	Biggar	01899 220035

MID LOTHIAN

The Bonham	Edinburgh	0131 226 6050
Borthwick Castle	Edinburgh	01875 820514
Channings	Edinburgh	0131 315 2226
Dalhousie Castle Hotel & Restaurant	Edinburgh	01875 820153
The Howard	Edinburgh	0131 557 3500
The Norton House Hotel	Edinburgh	0131 333 1275
Prestonfield House	Edinburgh	0131 668 3346

MORAYSHIRE

Rothes Glen	Elgin	01340 831254

Johansens Recommendations

PEEBLESHIRE
Cringletie House Hotel ... Peebles ... 01721 730233

PERTHSHIRE
Auchterarder House ... Auchterarder ... 01764 663646 / 7
Ballathie House Hotel ... Perth ... 01250 883268
Cromlix House ... Kinbuck Nr Stirling 01786 822125
Dalmunzie House ... Glenshee ... 01250 885224
Huntingtower Hotel ... Perth ... 01738 583771
Kinfauns Castle ... Perth ... 01738 620777
Kinloch House Hotel ... Blairgowrie ... 01250 884237
Pine Trees Hotel ... Pitlochry ... 01796 472121
Roman Camp Hotel ... Callander ... 01877 330003

RENFREWSHIRE
Gleddoch House ... Glasgow ... 01475 540711

ROSS-SHIRE
Coul House Hotel ... Strathpeffer ... 01997 421487
Mansfield House Hotel ... Tain ... 01862 892052

ROXBURGHSHIRE
Ednam House Hotel ... Kelso ... 01573 224168
Sunlaws House Hotel & Golf Course ... Kelso ... 01573 450331

SCOTTISH BORDERS
Dryburgh Abbey Hotel ... St Boswells ... 01835 822261
Philipburn Country House Hotel & Restaurant .. Selkirk ... 01750 720747

STIRLINGSHIRE
Airth Castle Hotel ... Falkirk ... 01324 831411

SUTHERLAND
Inver Lodge Hotel ... Lochinver ... 01571 844496

WEST LOTHIAN
Houstoun House ... Uphall ... 01506 853831

WIGTOWNSHIRE
Kirroughtree House ... Newton Stewart ... 01671 402141

WALES

CEREDIGION
Conrah Country House Hotel ... Aberystwyth ... 01970 617941

DENBIGHSHIRE
Bodidris Hall ... Llandegla ... 01978 790434
Bryn Howel Hotel & Restaurant ... Llangollen ... 01978 860331
Tyddyn Llan Country House Hotel ... Corwen ... 01490 440264

FLINTSHIRE
Soughton Hall ... Chester ... 01352 840811
St. David's Park Hotel ... Chester ... 01244 520800

GWYNEDD
Bodysgallen Hall ... Llandudno ... 01492 584466
Bontddu Hall ... Barmouth ... 01341 430661
Bron Eifion Country House Hotel ... Criccieth ... 01766 522385
Gwesty Seiont Manor Hotel ... Caernarfon ... 01286 673366
Hotel Maes-Y-Neuadd ... Harlech ... 01766 780200
The Hotel Portmeirion ... Portmeirion Village .. 01766 770228
Palé Hall ... Bala ... 01678 530285
Penmaenuchaf Hall ... Dolgellau ... 01341 422129
Porth Tocyn Country House Hotel ... Abersoch ... 01758 713303
St Tudno Hotel ... Llandudno ... 01492 874411
Trearddur Bay Hotel ... Anglesey ... 01407 860301
Tynycornel Hotel ... Tywyn ... 01654 782282
Ye Olde Bull's Head ... Beaumaris ... 01248 810329

HEREFORDSHIRE
Allt-Yr-Ynys Hotel ... Abergavenny ... 01873 890307

MID GLAMORGAN
Miskin Manor ... Cardiff ... 01443 224204
St. David's Spa ... Cardiff ... 01222 454045

MONMOUTHSHIRE
The Cwrt Bleddyn Hotel ... Usk ... 01633 450521
Llansantffraed Court Hotel ... Abergavenny ... 01873 840678

MONTGOMERYSHIRE
Lake Vyrnwy Hotel ... Lake Vyrnwy ... 01691 870 692

PEMBROKESHIRE
The Court Hotel & Restaurant ... Pembroke ... 01646 672273
Penally Abbey ... Tenby ... 01834 843033
Warpool Court Hotel ... St David's ... 01437 720300

POWYS
Gliffaes Country House Hotel ... Crickhowell ... 01874 730371
The Lake Country House ... Llangammarch Wells 01591 620202
Llangoed Hall ... Brecon ... 01874 754525
Ynyshir Hall ... Machynlleth ... 01654 781209

VALE OF GLAMORGAN
Coed-Y-Mwstwr Hotel ... Bridgend ... 01656 860621
Egerton Grey Country House Hotel ... Cardiff ... 01446 711666

WEST GLAMORGAN
Norton House Hotel & Restaurant ... Swansea ... 01792 404891

CHANNEL ISLANDS

St Pierre Park Hotel ... Guernsey ... 01481 728282
The Atlantic Hotel ... Jersey ... 01534 44101
Château La Chaire ... Jersey ... 01534 863354
Hotel L'Horizon ... Jersey ... 01534 43101
Longueville Manor ... Jersey ... 01534 725501

COUNTRY HOUSES
ENGLAND

CAMBRIDGESHIRE
Melbourn Bury ... Cambridge ... 01763 261151

CHESHIRE
Pear Tree Lake Farms & Equestrian Centre ... Crewe ... 01270 820307

CO.DURHAM
Grove House ... Hamsterley Forest .. 01388 488203

CORNWALL
Allhays Country House ... Looe ... 01503 272434
Boskerris Hotel ... St. Ives ... 01736 795295
Coombe Farm ... Looe ... 01503 240223
The Cormorant Hotel ... Golant by Fowey ... 01726 833426
The Cornish Cottage Hotel ... New Polzeath ... 01208 862213
The Countryman At Trink Hotel & Restaurant St Ives ... 01736 797571
Cross House Hotel ... Padstow ... 01841 532391
The Hundred House Hotel ... St Mawes ... 01872 501336
Nansloe Manor ... Helston ... 01326 574691
The Royal Hotel ... Truro ... 01872 270345
The St Enodoc Hotel ... Rock ... 01208 863394
Trebrea Lodge ... Tintagel ... 01840 770410
Trehellas House & Memories ... Wadebridge ... 01208 72700
Trelawne Hotel-The Hutches Restaurant ... Falmouth ... 01326 250226
Tye Rock Hotel ... Porthleven ... 01326 572695

CUMBRIA
Aynsome Manor Hotel ... Cartmel ... 015395 36653
Crosby Lodge Country House Hotel ... Carlisle ... 01228 573618
Dale Head Hall Lakeside Hotel ... Keswick ... 017687 72478
Fayrer Garden House Hotel ... Windermere ... 015394 88195
Hipping Hall ... Kirkby Lonsdale ... 015242 71187
The Old Vicarage Country House Hotel ... Witherslack ... 015395 52381
Quarry Garth Country House Hotel ... Windermere ... 015394 88282
Storrs Hall ... Windermere ... 015394 47111
Swinside Lodge Hotel ... Keswick ... 017687 72948
Temple Sowerby House Hotel ... Penrith ... 017683 61578
White Moss House ... Grasmere ... 015394 35295

DERBYSHIRE
The Beeches Farmhouse ... Ashbourne ... 01889 590288
Biggin Hall ... Biggin-By-Hartington 01298 84451
Dannah Farm Country Guest House ... Belper ... 01773 550273 / 630
East Lodge Country House Hotel ... Bakewell ... 01629 734474
The Manor Farmhouse ... Matlock ... 01629 534246
The Peacock Hotel at Rowsley ... Bakewell ... 01629 733518
Sheriff Lodge Hotel ... Matlock ... 01629 760760
Underleigh House ... Hope ... 01433 621372

DEVON
Ashelford ... Combe Martin ... 01271 850469
Bel Alp House ... Dartmoor ... 01364 661217
Broome Court ... Dartmouth ... 01803 834275
Coombe House Country Hotel ... Crediton ... 01363 84487
Easton Court Hotel ... Chagford ... 01647 433469
Foxdown Manor ... Clovelly ... 01237 451325
Hewitt's Hotel ... Lynton ... 01598 752293
Kingston House ... Staverton ... 01803 762 235
The Lord Haldon Hotel ... Exeter ... 01392 832483
The Lyndhurst Hotel ... Salcombe ... 01548 842481
Marsh Hall Country House Hotel ... South Molton ... 01769 572666
Moor View House ... Lydford ... 01822 820220
Nonsuch House ... Dartmouth ... 01803 752829
Preston House Hotel ... Saunton ... 01271 890472
Prince Hall Hotel ... Dartmoor ... 01822 890403
The Thatched Cottage Country Hotel ... Lifton ... 01566 784224
Venn Ottery Barton ... Ottery St. Mary ... 01404 812733
The White House ... Kingsbridge ... 01548 580580
Wigham ... Morchard Bishop ... 01363 877350
Yeoldon House Hotel ... Bideford ... 01237 474400

DORSET
Beechleas ... Wimborne Minster .. 01202 841684
The Eastbury Hotel ... Sherborne ... 01935 813131
Kemps Country House Hotel & Restaurant ... Wareham ... 01929 462563
Rectory House ... Evershot ... 0193583 273
Thatch Lodge Hotel ... Lyme Regis ... 01297 560407
Yalbury Cottage Hotel ... Dorchester ... 01305 262382

EAST SUSSEX
The Granville ... Brighton ... 01273 326302
Hooke Hall ... Uckfield ... 01825 761578
White Vine House ... Rye ... 01797 224748

EAST YORKSHIRE
The Manor House ... Beverley ... 01482 881645

GLOUCESTERSHIRE
Bibury Court ... Bibury ... 01285 740337
Burleigh Court ... Minchinhampton ... 01453 883804
Charlton Kings Hotel ... Cheltenham ... 01242 231061
Halewell ... Cheltenham ... 01242 890238
Lower Brook House ... Blockley ... 01386 700286
The Malt House ... Chipping Campden 01386 840295
The Old Rectory ... Broadway ... 01386 853729
Owlpen Manor ... Owlpen ... 01453 860261
Tudor Farmhouse Hotel & Restaurant ... Clearwell ... 01594 833046
Upper Court ... Tewkesbury ... 01386 725351

HAMPSHIRE
The Beaufort Hotel ... Portsmouth ... 01705 823707
Langrish House ... Petersfield ... 01730 266941
Moortown Lodge ... Ringwood ... 01425 471404
Thatched Cottage Hotel & Restaurant ... Brockenhurst ... 01590 623090
Whitley Ridge & Country House Hotel ... Brockenhurst ... 01590 622354

HEREFORDSHIRE
The Bowens Country House ... Hereford ... 01432 860430
Glewstone Court ... Ross-On-Wye ... 01989 770367
Lower Bache House ... Leominster ... 01568 750304
The Steppes ... Hereford ... 01432 820424

HERTFORDSHIRE
Little Offley ... Luton ... 01462 768243
Redcoats Farmhouse Hotel & Restaurant ... Stevenage ... 01438 729500

ISLE OF WIGHT
Rylstone Manor ... Isle of Wight ... 01983 862806

KENT
Romney Bay House ... New Romney ... 01797 364747
Tanyard ... Maidstone ... 01622 744705
Wallett's Court ... Dover ... 01304 852424
The Woodville Hall ... Dover ... 01304 825256

LANCASHIRE
Quarlton Manor Farm ... Bolton ... 01204 852277

LEICESTERSHIRE
Abbots Oak ... Coalville ... 01530 832 328
The Old Manor Hotel ... Loughborough ... 01509 211228
White Wings ... Fenny Drayton ... 01827 716100
Washingborough Hall ... Lincoln ... 01522 790340

LONDON
Sandringham Hotel ... Hampstead Village 0171 435 1569

MIDDLESEX
Oak Lodge Hotel ... Enfield ... 0181 360 7082

NORFOLK
The Beeches Hotel & Victorian Gardens ... Norwich ... 01603 621167
Beechwood Hotel ... North Walsham ... 01692 403231
Broom Hall ... Saham Toney ... 01953 882125
Catton Old Hall ... Norwich ... 01603 419379
Felbrigg Lodge ... Holt ... 01263 837588
Norfolk Mead Hotel ... Norwich ... 01603 737531
The Old Rectory ... Great Snoring ... 01328 820597
The Old Rectory ... Norwich ... 01603 700772
Vere Lodge ... Fakenham ... 01328 838261

NORTH YORKSHIRE
Appleton Hall ... Appleton-Le-Moors 01751 417227
Dunsley Hall ... Whitby ... 01947 893437
Millers House Hotel ... Middleham ... 01969 622630
Newstead Grange ... Malton ... 01653 692502
The Parsonage Country House Hotel ... York ... 01904 728111
Rookhurst Georgian Country House Hotel ... Hawes ... 01969 667454
Ryedale Country Lodge ... Helmsley ... 01439 748246
The White House ... Harrogate ... 01423 501388

NORTHUMBERLAND
Eshott Hall ... Morpeth ... 01670 787777
Waren House Hotel ... Bamburgh ... 01668 214581

NOTTINGHAMSHIRE
The Cottage Country House Hotel ... Nottingham ... 01159 846882
Langar Hall ... Nottingham ... 01949 860559

OXFORDSHIRE
Conygree Gate Hotel ... Stow-On-The-Wold 01608 658389
Fallowfields ... Oxford ... 01865 820416
The Shaven Crown Hotel ... Shipton-Under-Wychwood 01993 830330
The Stonor Arms ... Stonor ... 01491 638866

SHROPSHIRE
Cross Lane House Hotel ... Bridgnorth ... 01746 764887
Delbury Hall ... Ludlow ... 01584 841267

Mynd House Hotel & Restaurant	Church Stretton	01694 722212
Overton Grange Hotel	Ludlow	01584 873500
Pen-y-Dyffryn Country Hotel	Oswestry	01691 653700

SOMERSET

Apsley House	Bath	01225 336966
Ashwick Country House Hotel	Dulverton	01398 323868
Bath Lodge Hotel	Bath	01225 723040
The Beacon Country House Hotel	Exmoor	01643 703476
Beryl	Wells	01749 678738
Bloomfield House	Bath	01225 420105
Channel House Hotel	Minehead	01643 703229
The Cottage Hotel	Porlock Weir	01643 863300
Coxley Vineyard	Wells	01749 670285
The Crown Hotel	Exford	01643 831554/5
Dukes' Hotel	Bath	01225 463512
Eagle House	Bath	01225 859946
Glencot House	Wells	01749 677160
Holbrook House Hotel	Wincanton	01963 32377
The Old Rectory	Ilminster	01460 54364
Oldfields	Bath	01225 317984
Paradise House	Bath	01225 317723
Periton Park Hotel	Middlecombe	01643 706885
The Pheasant Hotel	Seavington St Mary	01460 240502
Simonsbath House Hotel	Simonsbath	01643 831259
Woolverton House	Bath	01373 830415

SOUTH GLOUCESTERSHIRE

Petty France	Badminton	01454 238361

SOUTH YORKSHIRE

Staindrop Hotel & Restaurant	Sheffield	0114 284 6727

SUFFOLK

Chippenhall Hall	Diss	01379 588180 / 586733
Hope House	Yoxford	01728 668281
Lavenham Priory	Lavenham	01787 247404
The Priory	Bury St. Edmunds	01284 766181
Wood Hall Hotel & Country Club	Woodbridge	01394 411283

SURREY

Chalk Lane Hotel	Epsom	01372 721179
Chase Lodge	Hampton Court	0181 943 1862
Stanhill Court Hotel	Gatwick	01293 862166

WARWICKSHIRE

The Ardencote Manor Hotel & Country Club	Warwick	01926 843111
Arrow Mill Hotel And Restaurant	Alcester	01789 762419
Chapel House	Atherstone	01827 718949
Glebe Farm House	Stratford-upon-Avon	01789 842501

WEST SUSSEX

Burpham Country House Hotel	Arundel	01903 882160
Chequers Hotel	Pulborough	01798 872486
Crouchers Bottom Country Hotel	Chichester	01243 784995
Findon Manor	Worthing	01903 872733
Woodstock House Hotel	Chichester	01243 811666

WILTSHIRE

Widbrook Grange	Bath	01225 864750 / 863173

WORCESTERSHIRE

Collin House Hotel	Broadway	01386 858354
The Mill At Harvington	Evesham	01386 870688
The Old Rectory	Redditch	01527 523000

IRELAND

CO CLARE

Halpins Hotel & Vittles Restaurant	Kilkee	00 353 65 56032

CO CORK

Ballylickey Manor House	Bantry	00 353 27 50071
Liss Ard Lake Lodge	Skibbereen	00 353 28 40000

CO DONEGAL

Castle Grove Country House	Letterkenny	00 353 745 1118

CO FERMANAGH (NORTHERN IRELAND)

The Inishclare Restaurant	Killadeas	013656 28550

CO GALWAY

Ross Lake House Hotel	Connemara	00 353 91 550109

CO KERRY

Ard-na-Sidhe	Caragh Lake	00 353 66 69105
Caragh Lodge	Caragh Lake	00 353 66 9769115
Earls Court House	Killarney	00 353 64 34009

CO SLIGO

Coopershill House	Riverstown	00 353 71 65108
Markree Castle	Sligo	00 353 71 67800

CO TIPPERARY

Cashel Palace Hotel	Cashel	00 353 62 62707

CO WATERFORD

The Old Rectory - Kilmeaden House	Kilmeaden	00 353 51 384254

CO WICKLOW

The Old Rectory	Wicklow	00 353 404 67048

DUBLIN

Aberdeen Lodge	Dublin	00 353 1 2838155
Fitzwilliam Park	Dublin	00 353 1 6628 280

SCOTLAND

ABERDEENSHIRE

Balgonie Country House	Ballater	013397 55482
The Old Manse of Marnoch	By Huntly	01466 780873

ARGYLL

Ardsheal House	Kentallen Of Appin	01631 740227
Highland Cottage	Isle of Mull	01688 302030
Aldonaig	Rhu	01436 820863

ARGYLLSHIRE

Druimneil	Port Appin	01631 730228
Dungallan House Hotel	Oban	01631 563799
Killiechronan	Isle Of Mull	01680 300403
The Manor House Hotel	Oban	01631 562087

DUMFRIES & GALLOWAY

Longacre Manor	Castle Douglas	01556 503576
The Dryfesdale Hotel	Lockerbie	01576 202427
Well View Hotel	Moffat	01683 220184
Trigony House Hotel	Dunfries	01848 331211

INVERNESS-SHIRE

Boath House	Nairn	01667 454896
Culduthel Lodge	Inverness	01463 240089
Polmaily House Hotel	Drumnadrochit	01456 450343

ISLE OF SKYE

Bosville Hotel & Chandlery Seafood Restaurant	Isle of Skye	01478 612846

KINROSS-SHIRE

Nivingston Country House	Kinross	01577 850216

LOTHIAN

No 22 Murrayfield Gardens	Edinburgh	0131 337 3569

PERTHSHIRE

Dunfallandy House	Pitlochry	01796 472648
The Killiecrankie Hotel	Killiecrankie	01796 473220
The Lake Hotel	Port Of Menteith	01877 385258
Newmiln Country House	Perth	01738 552364
The Pend	Dunkeld	01350 727586
Queen's View Hotel	Strathtummel	01796 473291
The Royal Hotel	Comrie	01764 679200

ROXBURGHSHIRE

Clint Lodge	St. Boswell By Melrose	01835 822027

STIRLING & TROSSACHS

Culcreuch Castle Hotel & Country Park	Fintry	01360 860555

SUTHERLAND

The Kinlochbervie Hotel	Kinlochbervie	01971 521275
Navidale House Hotel	Helmsdale	01431 821 258

WESTERN ISLES

Ardvourlie Castle	Isle Of Harris	01859 502307

WALES

CONWY

The Old Rectory	Conwy	01492 580611
Tan-y-Foel	Betws-y-Coed	01690 710507

GWYNEDD

Berthlwyd Hall Hotel	Conwy	01492 592409
Plas Bodegroes	Pwllheli	01758 612363
Plas Dolmelynllyn	Dolgellau	01341 440273
Plas Penhelig Country House Hotel	Aberdovey	01654 767676
Ty'n Rhos Country House	Caernarfon	01248 670489

MONMOUTHSHIRE

The Crown At Whitebrook	Monmouth	01600 860254
Llanwenarth House	Abergavenny	01873 830289
Parva Farmhouse and Restaurant	Tintern	01291 689411
Penyclawdd Court	Abergavenny	01873 890719

PEMBROKESHIRE

The Pembrokeshire Retreat	Cardigan	01239 841387
Waterwynch House Hotel	Tenby	01834 842464

POWYS

Buttington House	Welshpool	01938 553351
Glangrwyney Court	Abergavenny	01873 811288
Old Gwernyfed Country Manor	Brecon	01497 847376

CHANNEL ISLANDS

Bella Luce Hotel & Restaurant	Guernsey	01481 38764
La Favorita Hotel	Guernsey	01481 35666
The White House	Herm Island	01481 722159
Hotel La Tour	Jersey	01534 43770
Sea Crest Hotel And Restaurant	Jersey	01534 46353

TRADITIONAL INNS, HOTELS & RESTAURANTS

ENGLAND

BERKSHIRE

The Bull at Streatley	Reading	01491 875231
The Christopher Hotel	Eton	01753 811677 / 852359
The Leatherne Bottel Riverside Inn	Goring-On-Thames	01491 872667
Stag & Hounds	Binfield	01344 483553
The Swan Inn	Newbury	01488 648271

BRISTOL

The Boars Head	Bristol	01454 632581
The Codrington Arms	Chipping Sodbury	01454 313145
The New Inn	Bristol	01454 773161

BUCKINGHAMSHIRE

The Different Drummer	Milton Keynes	01908 564733

CAMBRIDGESHIRE

The George Coaching Inn	Buckden	01480 810307
Olivers Lodge Hotel & Restaurant	St. Ives	01480 463252
Panos Hotel & Restaurant	Cambridge	01223 212958

CHESHIRE

Longview Hotel And Restaurant	Knutsford	01565 632119
The Pheasant Inn	Chester	01829 770434
The Plough Inn & Old Barn Restaurant	Congleton	01260 280207

CORNWALL

Jubilee Inn	Pelynt,Nr Looe	01503 220312
The Old Custom House Hotel	Padstow	01841 532359
The Port Gaverne Hotel	Port Gaverne	01208 880244
The Port William	Tintagel	01840 770230
Trengilly Wartha Country Inn & Restaurant	Falmouth	01326 340332
Tyacks Hotel	Camborne	01209 612424

CUMBRIA

The Mortal Man Hotel	Troutbeck	015394 33193
The New Dungeon Ghyll Hotel	Ambleside	015394 37213
The Pheasant	Bassenthwaite Lake	017687 76234
The Royal Oak Inn	Appleby-In-Westmorland	017683 51463
The Swan Hotel	Newby Bridge	015395 31681
The Tarn End House Hotel	Carlisle	016977 2340

DERBYSHIRE

Boar's Head Hotel	Burton Upon Trent	01283 820344
The Chequers Inn	Calver	01433 630231
Manor House Hotel & Restaurant	Dronfield	01246 413971
The Maynard Arms	Grindleford	01433 630321
The Old Vicarage	Sheffield	0114 247 5814
The Plough Inn	Hathersage	01433 650319
Red Lion Inn	Ashbourne	01335 370396
The Waltzing Weasel	Hayfield	01663 743402

DEVON

The Barn Owl Inn	Kingskerswell	01803 872130
The Dartbridge Inn	Buckfastleigh	01364 642214
The Fisherman's Cot	Bickleigh	01884 855237
Home Farm Hotel	Honiton	01404 831278
The Kings Arms Hotel	Kingsbridge	01548 852071
The New Inn	Coleford	01363 84242
The Rising Sun	Lynmouth	01598 753223
The Sea Trout Inn	Totnes	01803 762274
Thelbridge Cross Inn	Thelbridge	01884 860316
Tytherleigh Cot Hotel	Axminster	01460 221170
The Victoria Hotel	Dartmouth	01803 832572
The Watermans Arms	Totnes	01803 732214
The Acorn Inn Hotel	Evershot	01935 83228
The Manor Hotel	Bridport	01308 897616

EAST SUSSEX

The George Hotel	Rye	01797 222144
Winston Manor	Crowborough	01892 652772

EAST YORKSHIRE

The Londesborough	Market Weighton	01430 872214

ESSEX

The Cricketers	Clavering	01799 550442
The White Hart Hotel & Restaurant	Colchester	01376 561654

Johansens Recommendations

GLOUCESTERSHIRE

The Bear of Rodborough Hotel & Restaurant	Stroud	01453 878522
The Catherine Wheel	Bibury	01285 740250
The Close Hotel	Tetbury	01666 502272
Dial House Hotel	Bourton-On-The-Water	01451 822244
The Frogmill Hotel	Andoversford	01242 820547
The Horse and Groom Inn & Restaurant	Stow-on-the-Wold	01451 830584
Kingshead House Restaurant	Cheltenham	01452 862299
The New Inn at Coln	Cirencester	01285 750651
The Noel Arms Hotel & Restaurant	Chipping Campden	01386 840317
The Unicorn Hotel & Restaurant	Stow-on-the-Wold	01451 830257

HAMPSHIRE

Duke's Head	Romsey	01794 514450
The Hatchgate	Hartley Wintney	01189 32666
Hotel Gordleton Mill	Lymington	01590 682219
The Snakecatcher	Brockenhurst	01590 622348
The Woodfalls Inn	Fordingbridge	01725 513222

HEREFORDSHIRE

Cottage of Content	Ross-on-Wye	01432 840242
Feathers Hotel	Ledbury	01531 635266
Rhydspence Inn	Hay-On-Wye	01497 831262
Ye Olde Salutation Inn	Weobley	01544 318443

HERTFORDSHIRE

The Greyhound Inn	Aldbury	01442 851228

KENT

The Harrow At Warren Street	Maidstone	01622 858727
Ringlestone Inn	Maidstone	01622 859900
The Royal Oak	Sevenoaks	01732 451109
The White Lion Hotel	Tenterden	01580 765077
Ye Old Crown	Edenbridge	01732 867896

LANCASHIRE

Fence Gate Inn	Burnley	01282 618101
The Inn At Whitewell	Whitewell	01200 448222
The Old Bell Inn Hotel	Saddleworth	01457 870130
Tree Tops Country House Restaurant & Hotel	Southport	01704 879651
Ye Horn's Inn	Preston	01772 865230

LEICESTERSHIRE

The Rothley Court	Rothley	0116 237 4141

LINCOLNSHIRE

The Black Horse Inn	Grimsthorpe	01778 591247
The Hare & Hounds Country Inn	Lincoln	01400 272090

NORFOLK

The Barton Angler Country Inn	Wroxham	01692 630740
Elderton Lodge Hotel & Restaurant	North Walsham	01263 833547
Green Farm Restaurant And Hotel	Thorpe Market	01263 833602
The Hoste Arms Hotel	Burnham Market	01328 738777
The Lifeboat Inn	Thornham	01485 512236
The Rose & Crown	King's Lynn	01485 541382
The Stower Grange	Norwich	01603 860210
White Horse Hotel	Blakeney	01263 740574

NORTH YORKSHIRE

The Blue Lion	East Witton	01969 624273
The Boar's Head Hotel	Harrogate	01423 771888
The Dower House	Harrogate	01423 863302
The Feathers Hotel	Helmsley	01439 770275
The Feversham Arms Hotel	Helmsley	01439 770766
The George at Easingwold	York	01347 821698
The Kings Arms Hotel And Restaurant	Askrigg	01969 650258
The Low Hall Hotel	Harrogate	01423 508598
Mallyan Spout Hotel	Goathland	01947 896486
The Red Lion	Burnsall	01756 720204
The Wensleydale Heifer Inn	West Witton	01969 622322
The Wheatsheaf Inn	Egton	01947 895271

NORTHAMPTONSHIRE

The Falcon Hotel	Castle Ashby	01604 696200
The Windmill At Badby	Badby Nr Daventry	01327 702363
The Talbot	Oundle	01832 273621

NORTHUMBERLAND

The Blue Bell Hotel	Belford	01668 213543
The Tankerville Arms Hotel	Wooler	01668 281581

NOTTINGHAMSHIRE

Hotel Des Clos	Nottingham	01159 866566

OXFORDSHIRE

The George Hotel	Dorchester-On-Thames	01865 340404
The Golden Pheasant Hotel & Restaurant	Burford	01993 823417
Cotswold Gateway Hotel	Burford	01993 822695
Holcombe Hotel	Oxford	01869 338274
The Jersey Arms	Oxford	01869 343234
The Kings Head Inn & Restaurant	Stow-On-The-Wold	01608 658365
The Lamb Inn	Burford	01993 823155
The Lamb Inn	Shipton Under Wychwood	01993 830465
The Mill & Old Swan	Oxford	01993 774441
The Red Lion Inn	Adderbury	01295 810269
The Shaven Crown Hotel	Shipton Under Wychwood	01993 830330
The White Horse Inn	Duns Tew	01869 340272

RUTLAND

Normanton Park Hotel	Rutland Water	01780 720315

SHROPSHIRE

Crown At Hopton	Cleobury Mortimer	01299 270372
The Hundred House Hotel	Telford	01952 730353
Mr Underhill's	Ludlow	01584 874431
Naughty Nell's	Shifnal	01952 411412
The Redfern Hotel	Cleobury Mortimer	01299 270 395

SOMERSET

The Devonshire Arms Hotel	Long Sutton	01458 241271
The George Hotel	Castle Cary	01963 350761
The King's Arms Inn & Restaurant	Montacute	01935 822513
The Royal Oak Inn	Exmoor	01643 831506/7
The Royal Oak of Luxborough	Exmoor	01984 640319
The Talbot Inn at Mells	Mells	01373 812254
The Walnut Tree	Sherborne	01935 851292
The Woolpack Inn	Beckington Nr Bath	01373 831244

SOUTH YORKSHIRE

The Fountain Inn & Rooms	Penistone	01226 763125

STAFFORDSHIRE

The Dower House	Stafford	01889 270707
The George Hotel	Eccleshall	01785 850300
The Moat House	Acton Trussell	01785 712217
Old Beams Restaurant with Rooms	Ashbourne	01538 308254
The Three Horseshoes Inn & Restaurant	Leek	01538 300296
The Wheatsheaf Inn At Onneley	Onneley	01782 751581

SUFFOLK

The Bell Inn	Walberswick	01502 723109
The Bull Hotel	Sudbury	01787 378494
The Countrymen	Long Melford	01787 312356
Four Horseshoes	Thornham Magna	01379 678777
The Plough Inn	Clare	01440 786789
The White Horse Inn	Haverhill	01440 706081

WARWICKSHIRE

The Coach House Hotel & Cellar Restaurant	Stratford-upon-Avon	01789 204109
The Golden Lion Inn of Easenhall	Rugby	01788 832265

WEST SUSSEX

Badgers	Petworth	01798 342651
The Boathouse Brasserie	Amberley	01798 831059
The Chequers At Slaugham	Handcross	01444 400239/400996
The Old Tollgate Restaurant And Hotel	Worthing	01903 879494
The Stonemason's Inn	Petworth	01798 342510
White Horse Inn	Petworth	01798 869 221

WEST YORKSHIRE

Old White Lion Hotel	Haworth	01535 642313
The Rock Inn Hotel	Halifax/Huddersfield	01422 379721

WILTSHIRE

The Crown Inn	Chippenham	01249 782229
The Horse And Groom Inn	Malmesbury	01666 823904
The Lamb at Hindon	Hindon, Nr Salisbury	01747 820573
The Old Mill Hotel & Restaurant	Salisbury	01722 327517
The White Hart	Ford,Nr Bath	01249 782213
The White Horse	Salisbury	01725 510408

WORCESTERSHIRE

The Broadway Hotel & Restaurant	Broadway	01386 852401
The Old Schoolhouse	Worcester	01905 371368
Riverside Restaurant And Hotel	Evesham	01386 446200
The White Lion Hotel	Upton-Upon-Severn	01684 592551

SCOTLAND

ABERDEENSHIRE

Birse Lodge Hotel	Aboyne	01339 886253

BANFFSHIRE

The Seafield Arms Hotel	Cullen	01542 840791

CLACKMANNANSHIRE

The Gartwhinzean	Powmill	01577 840595

DUMFRIESSHIRE

Annandale Arms Hotel	Moffatt	01683 220013

FIFE

The Grange Inn	St Andrews	01334 472670

INVERNESS-SHIRE

The Foyers Hotel	Loch Ness	01456 486216
Grouse & Trout	Inverness	01808 521314

ISLE OF SKYE

Hotel Eilean Iarmain or Isle Ornsay Hotel	Isle Of Skye	01471 833332
Uig Hotel	Isle Of Skye	01470 542205

PERTHSHIRE

The Glenisla Hotel	Blairgowrie	01575 582223
The Kenmore Hotel	Kenmore	01887 830205
The Loft Restaurant	Blair Atholl	01796 481377
The Moulin Hotel	Pitlochry	01796 472196

STIRLINGSHIRE

The Black Bull	Killearn	01360 550215

WESTER ROSS

The Plockton Hotel & Garden Restaurant	Plockton	01599 544274
Pool House Hotel	Poolewe	01445 781272

WALES

CARMARTHENSHIRE

The Plough Inn	Llandeilo	01558 823431

DENBIGHSHIRE

The West Arms Hotel	Llanarmon Dyffryn Ceiriog	01691 600665

MONMOUTHSHIRE

The Castle View Hotel	Chepstow	01291 620349

MONTGOMERYSHIRE

The Lion Hotel And Restaurant	Welshpool	01686 640452

CHANNEL ISLANDS

Sea Crest Hotel And Restaurant	Jersey	01534 46353

EUROPE & THE MEDITERRANEAN

AUSTRIA

Grand Hotel Sauerhof	Baden bei Wien	00 43 2252 41251 0
Hotel Altstadt Radisson SAS	Salzburg	00 43 662 8485710
Hotel Auersperg	Salzburg	00 43 662 88944
Hotel im Palais Schwarzenberg	Vienna	00 43 1 798 4515
Hotel Klosterbräu	Seefeld in Tyrol	00 43 5212 26210
Hotel Palais Porcia	Klagenfurt	00 43 463 51 1590
Hotel Schloss Dürnstein	Dürnstein	00 43 2711 212
Hotel Schloss Leonstein	Pörtschach Am Wörther See	00 43 4272 28160
Hotel Schloss Mönchstein	Salzburg	00 43 662 84 85 55 0
Hotel & Spa Haus Hirt	Bad Gastein	00 43 64 34 27 97
Hotel Viktoria	Seefeld	00 43 52 12 44 41
Kur-Sport & Gourmethotel Moser	Bad Hofgastein	00 43 6432 6209
Landhaus Hubertushof	Altaussee	00 43 36 22 71 280
Landhaus Kellerwand	Kösthach-Mauthen	00 43 47 15 269
Romantik Hotel im Weissen Rössl	St Wolfgang am See	00 43 61 38 23 060
Romantik Hotel Schwarzer Adler	Innsbruck	00 43 512 587109
Romantik Hotel Tennerhof	Kitzbühel	00 43 53566 3181
Romantik-Hotel Gasthof Hirschen	Schwarzenberg im Bregenzerwald	00 43 55 12/29 44 0
Schloss Haunsperg	Salzburg	00 43 62 45 80 662
Schlossberg Hotel	Graz	00 43 316 80700
Schlosshotel Igls	Igls	00 43 512 37 72 17
Seeschlössl Velden	Velden	00 43 4274 2824
Sporthotel Igls	Igls	00 43 512 37 72 41
Sporthotel Kristiania	Lech	00 43 55 83 25 610
Thurnhers Alpenhof	Zürs	00 43 5583 2191

BELGIUM

Art Hotel Siru	Brussels	00 32 2 203 35 80
Château d'Hassonville	Marche-en-Famenne	00 32 84 31 10 25
Chateau de Palogne	Vieuxville	00 32 86 21 38 74
Die Swaene	Bruges	00 32-50- 34 27 98
Firean Hotel	Antwerp	00 32 3237 02 60
Hostellerie Le Prieuré De Conques	Florenville	00 32 61 41 14 17
Hostellerie Trôs Marets	Malmedy	00 32-80- 33 79 17
Hotel Acacia	Bruges	00 32 50 34 44 11
Hotel de Orangerie	Bruges	00 32 50 34 16 49
Hotel Hansa	Bruges	00 32 50 33 84 44
Hotel Jan Brito	Bruges	00 32 50 33 06 01
Hotel Manoir Du Dragon	Knokke-Heist	00 32 50 63 05 80
Hotel Montanus	Bruges	00 32 50 33 11 76
Hotel Prinsenhof	Bruges	00 32-50- 34 26 90
Hotel Rubens	Antwerp	00 32 32 22 48 48
L'Amigo	Brussels	00 32 2 547 47 47
La Butte Aux Bois	Lanaken	00 32 89 72 12 86
The Stanhope	Brussels	00 32 2 506 91 11

CYPRUS

The Four Seasons Hotel	Limassol	00 35 75 310 222

CZECH REPUBLIC

Hotel Hoffmeister	Prague	00 420 2 5731 0942
Sieber Hotel & Apartments	Prague	00 420 224 25 00 25

DENMARK

Hotel Hesselet	Nyborg	00 45 65 31 30 29
Steensgaard Herregårdspension	Faaborg	00 45 62 61 94 90

ESTONIA

Park Consul Schlössle	Tallinn	00 372 699 7700

FRANCE

Château de Candie	Chambéry-le-Vieux	00 33 47 99 66 300
Château de Coudrée	Sciez sur Leman	00 33 4 50 7262 33
Château de Danzay	Chinon	00 33 2 47 58 46 86
Château de la Bourdaisière	Montlouis-sur-Loire	00 33 2 47 45 16 31
Château de Vault de Lugny	Avallon	00 33 3 86 34 07 86
Château des Alpilles	Saint-Rémy-de-Provence	00 33 4 90 92 03 33
Château des Briottières	Champigné	00 33 2 41 42 00 02
Château des Vigiers	Monestier	00 33 5 53 61 50 00
Château Eza	Eze Village	00 33 4 93 41 12 24
Domaine de Rochebois	Sarlat-Vitrac	00 33 5 53 31 52 52
Ermitage de Corton	Beaune	00 33 3 80 22 05 28
Grand Hôtel du Domaine de Divonne	Divonne-les-Bains	00 33 4 50 40 3434
Grand Hôtel Vista Palace	Monaco	00 33 4 92 10 40 00
Hostellerie La Briqueterie	Épernay	00 33 3 26 59 99 99
Hostellerie les Bas Rupts et son Chalet Fleuri	Gérardmer	00 33 3 29 63 09 25
Hôtel Annapurna	Courchevel	00 33 4 79 08 04 60
Hôtel Buci Latin	Paris	00 33 1 4329 0720
Hôtel Byblos	Saint Tropez	00 33 4 94 56 68 00
Hôtel de Crillon	Paris	00 33 1 4471 1500
Hôtel de L'Arcade	Paris	00 331 533 0 60 00
Hôtel de Mougins	Mougins	00 33 4 92 92 17 07
Hôtel du Louvre	Paris	00 33 1 4458 3838
Hôtel du Palais	Biarritz	00 33 5 59 41 64 00
Hôtel le Saint-Grégoire	Paris	00 33 1 45 48 23 23
Hôtel Le Tourville	Paris	00 33 1 47 05 62 62
Hôtel Mont-Blanc	Megève	00 33 4 50 21 20 02
Hôtel Regent Petite France	Strasbourg	00 33 3 88 76 43 43
Hôtel Savoy	Cannes	00 33 4 92 99 72 00
Hôtel Square	Paris	00 33 1 44 14 91 90
Hôtel Sube	Saint Tropez	00 334 94973004
Hôtel Villa Belrose	Saint Tropez	00 33 4 94 55 97 97
Hôtel Westminster	Paris	00 33 1 4261 5746
L'Antarès	Méribel	00 33 4 79 23 28 23
L'Auberge du Choucas	Serre-Chevalier	00 33 4 92 24 42 73
L'Hôtel	Paris	00 33 1 43 25 27 22
L'Hôtel Pergolese	Paris	00 33 1 53 64 04 04
La Chaumière	Honfleur	00 33 2 31 81 63 20
La Domaine de Rochevilaine	Billiers	00 33 2 97 41 61 61
La Ferme Saint Siméon	Honfleur	00 33 2 31 89 23 61
La Réserve de Beaulieu	Beaulieu-sur-Mer	00 33 4 93 01 00 01
La Résidence de la Pinède	Saint Tropez	00 33 4 94 55 91 00
La Tour Rose	Lyon	00 33 4 78 37 25 90
Le Byblos des Neiges	Courchevel	00 33 4 79 00 98 00
Le Manoir de Gressy	Gressy-en-France	00 33 1 60 26 68 00
Le Manoir de Vaumadeuc	Pleven	00 33 2 96 84 46 17
Le Manoir du Butin	Honfleur	00 33 2 31 81 63 00
Le Moulin de Connelles	Connelles	00 33 2 32 59 53 33
Le Relais Saint-Germain	Paris	00 33 1 43 29 12 05
Lodge Park Hôtel	Megève	00 33 4 50 93 05 03
Mas d'Artigny	Saint Paul	00 33 4 93 32 84 54
Villa Saint Elme	Les Issambres	00 33 4 94 49 52 52

GERMANY

Burghotel Auf Schönburg	Oberwesel/Rhein	00 49 67 44 93 93 0
Hotel Burg Wassenberg	Wassenberg	00 49 2432 9490
Hotel Burg Wernberg	Wernberg-Köblitz	00 49 9604 9390
Hotel Cristall	Cologne	00 49 221 163 00
Hôtel Eisenhut	Rothenburg ob der Tauber	00 49 9861 70 50
Hotel Königshof	Munich	00 49 89 551 360
Hotel Schloss Waldeck	Waldeck	00 49 5623 5890
Mönchs Posthotel	Bad Herrenalb	00 49 70 83 74 40
Parkhotel Schlangenbad	Schlangenbad	00 49 61 29 420
Reindl's Partenkirchner Hof	Garmisch Partenkirchen	00 49 8821 58025
Romantik Hotel Goldene Traube	Coburg	00 49 9561 8760
RR Binshof Resort	Speyer	00 49 6232 6470
Schlosshotel Oberstotzingen	Niederstotzingen	00 49 7325 1030
Schweizer Stuben	Wertheim-Bettingen	00 49 9342 3070

GREECE

Elounda Bay Palace	Crete	00 30 841 41502
Elounda Beach	Crete	00 30 841 41 412/3
Hotel Bratsera	Hydra	00 30 298 53971
Hotel Pentelikon	Athens	00 30 1 62 30 650 6

HUNGARY

Danubius Hotel Gellért	Budapest	00 36 1 185 2200

ITALY

Albergo Annunziata	Ferrara	00 39 0532 20 11 11
Albergo Pietrasanta-Palazzo Bonetti-Barsanti	Pietrasanta	00 39 0584 793727
Albergo Quattro Fontane	Lido	00 39 041 5260227
Albergo San Lorenzo	Mantova	00 39 0376 220500
Albergo Terminus	Como	00 39 031 329111
Europa Palace Hotel	Capri	00 39 081 837 3800
Grand Hotel Cocumella	Sorrento	00 39 081 878 2933
Grand Hotel Excelsior Vittoria	Sorrento	00 39 081 80 71 044
Grand Hotel Fasano	Lake Garda	00 39 0365 290 220
Grand Hotel Tremezzo	Tremezzo - Lake Como	00 39 0344 40446
Grand Hotel Villa Balbi	Sestri Levante	00 39 0185 42941
Grand Hotel Villa Cora	Florence	00 39 055 22 98 451
Hellenia Yachting Hotel	Giardini Naxos	00 39 942 51737
Hotel Auriga	Milan	00 39 02 66 98 58 51
Hotel Bucaneve	Breuil-Cervinia	00 39 0166 949119
Hotel Farnese	Rome	00 39 06 321 25 53
Hotel Giulio Cesare	Rome	00 39 06 321 0751
Hotel Il Negresco	Forte Dei Marmi-Lucca	00 39 0584 787133
Hotel J &J	Florence	00 39 55 2345005
Hotel Lorenzetti	Madonna Di Campiglio	00 39 0 465 44 1404
Hotel Metropole	Venice	00 39 041 52 05 044
Hotel Miramare E Castello	Ischia	00 39 081 991333
Hotel Relais La Suvera	Pievescola	00 39 0577 960 300
Hotel Terme Di Saturnia	Saturnia	00 39 0 564 601061
Hotel Victoria	Torino	00 39 011 56 11 909
Hotel Villa Diodoro	Taormina	00 39 0942 23312
Hotel Villa Flori	Como	00 39 031 573105
Hotel Villa Michelangelo	Vicenza-Arcugnano	00 39 0444 550300
Hotel Villa Paradiso Dell' Etna	Etna	00 39 751 2409
Hotel Villa Sant' Andrea	Taormina Mare	00 39 0942 23125
Hotel Villa Sirio	Salerno	00 39 0974 960 162
Il Grand Hotel Di Rimini	Rimini	00 39 0541 56000
Il Pellicano	Porto Ercole	00 39 0564 858111
La Posta Vecchia	Rome-Palo Laziale	00 39 06 9949 501
La Villarosa Albergo E Terme	Isla d'Ischia	00 39 081 99 13 16
Le Silve di Armenzano	Assisi	00 39 075 801 90 00
Museo Albergo Atelier Sul Mare	Messina, Sicily	00 39 0921 334 295
Parkhotel Sole Paradiso	San Candino	00 39 0474 913120
Posthotel Weisses Rössl	Nova Levante	00 39 0 471 613113
Regency Hotel	Milan	00 39 02 39216021
Relais Villa Pomela	Novi Ligure	00 39 0143 329910
Ripagrande Hotel	Ferrara	00 39 0532 765250
Romantic Hotel Oberwirt	Marling-Méran	00 39 0473 22 20 20
Romantik Golf Hotel-Castello Formentini	San Floriano	00 39 0481 884051
Romantik Hotel Barocco	Rome	00 39 0 6 4872001
Romantik Hotel Locanda Dei Mai Intees	Malpensa	00 39 0332 457223
Romantik Hotel Miramonti	Cogne	00 39 0165 74030
Romantik Hotel Poseidon	Positano	00 39 089 81 11 11
Romantik Hotel Stafler	Mauls	00 39 0472 771136
Romantik Hotel Tenuta Di Ricavo	Castellina In Chianti	00 39 0577 740221
Romantik Hotel Turm	Südtirol-Völs am Schlern	00 39 0471 725014
Romantik Hotel Villa Cheta Elite	Maratea	00 39 0 973 878 134
Romantik Hotel Villa Ducale	Taormina	00 39 0942 28153
Romantik Hotel Villa Giustinian	Portobuffolé-Treviso	00 39 0422 850244
Villa Condulmer	Venice	00 39 041 45 71 00

LATVIA

Hotel de Rome	Riga	00 37 1 708 7600
Hotel Konventa Seta	Riga	00 371 708 7501

LUXEMBOURG

Hotel Saint Nicolas	Remich	00 352 69 8888
Parc Hotel	Berdorf	00 352 790195

NETHERLANDS

Ambassade Hotel	Amsterdam	00 31 20 626 2333
Hotel De Arendshoeve	Bergambacht	00 31 182 35 1000
Hotel De Duinrand	Drunen	00 31 416 372 498
Hotel de Wiemsel	Ootmarsum	00 31 541 292 155
Hotel Restaurant de Swaen	Oisterwijk	00 31 135 23 3233
Manoir Restaurant Inter Scaldes	Kruiningen	00 31 11338 1753
Restaurant-Hotel Savelberg	Voorburg	00 31 70 387 2081

NORWAY

Dalen Hotel	Dalen	00 47 35 07 70 00
First Hotel Bastion	Oslo	00 47 22 47 77 00
Fleischers Hotel	Voss)	00 47 56 51 11 55
Gloppen Hotel	Sandane	00 47 57 86 53 33
Grand Hotel Honefoss	Honefoss	00 47 32 12 27 22
Grand Hotel Terminus	Bergen	00 47 55 31 16 55
Hotel Union Oye	Norangsfjorden	00 47 70 06 21 00
Kronen Gaard Hotel	Sandnes/Stavanger	00 47 51 62 14 00
Kvikne's Hotel	Balestrand	00 47 57 69 11 01
Walaker Hotell	Solvorn	00 47 576 84 207

PORTUGAL

As Janelas Verdes	Lisbon	00 351 1 39 68 143
Casa Domilu	Carvoeiro	00 351 82 358 409
Hotel Palacio de Seteais	Sintra	00 351 1 923 32 00
Hotel Quinta das Lagrimas	Coimbra	00 351 39 44 16 15
Hotel Tivoli Lisboa	Lisbon	00 351 1 319 89 00
La Réserve	Faro	00 351 89 999474
Monte do Casal	Faro	00 351 89 91503
Quinta Da Bela Vista	Madeira	00 351 91 764144
Quinta de Sao Thiago	Sintra	00 351 1 923 29 23
Romantik Hotel Vivenda Miranda	Lagos	00 351 82 763 222
Vintage House Hotel	Pinhao	00 351 54 730 230

PRINCIPALITY OF LIECHTENSTEIN

Parkhotel Sonnenhof	Vaduz	00 41 75 232 1192

SLOVENIA

Hotel Vila Bled	Bled	00 386 64 7915

SPAIN

Casa De Carmona	Seville	00 34 954 19 10 00
Gran Hotel Bahia Del Duque	Tenerife	00 34 922 74 69 00
Hacienda Benazuza	Seville	00 34 95 570 33 44
Hacienda El Santiscal	Arcos De La Frontera	00 34 9 56 70 83 13
Hotel Botánico	Tenerife	00 34 922 38 14 00
Hotel Byblos Andalus	Mijas-Costa	00 34 95 246 0250
Hotel Claris	Barcelona	00 34 93 487 62 62
Hotel de la Reconquista	Oviedo	00 34 98524 1100
Hotel Jardin Tropical	Tenerife	00 34 922 746 000
Hotel La Costa	Pals	00 34 972 66 77 40
Hotel Puente Romano	Marbella	00 34 9 52 82 09 00
Hotel Rigat Park	Lloret de Mar	00 34 972 36 52 00
Hotel Rincon Andaluz	Marbella	00 34 9 5 281 1517
Hotel Termes Montbrío Resort, Spa & Park	Tarragona	00 34 9 77 81 40 00
Hotel Vistamar De Valldemosa	Mallorca	00 34 971 61 23 00
La Posada Del Torcal	Malaga	00 34 9 5 203 11 77
La Reserva Rotana	Mallorca	00 34 9 71 84 56 85
Las Dunas Suites	Marbella/Estepona	00 34 95 279 43 45
Marbella Club Hotel	Marbella	00 34 95 282 22 11
Monasterio de San Miguel	Santa Maria-Cádiz	00 34 956 54 04 40
Pikes	Ibiza	00 34 971 34 22 22
Read's	Mallorca	00 34 9 971 140 262
Residencia Rector	Salamanca	00 34 923 21 84 82
The San Roque Club	Sotogrande/San Roque	00 34 956 613 030
Trasierra	Cazalla De La Sierra	00 34 95 488 43 24
Villa Real	Madrid	00 34 91420 37 67

SWEDEN

Aspa Herrgård	Aspa Bruk	00 46 583 50210
Buena Vista	Bastad	00 46 431 760 00
Halltorps Gästgiveri	Borgholm	00 46 485 85000
Hotel Eggers	Gothenburg	00 46 31 80 60 70
Hotel Tanndalen	Tanndalen	00 46 684 22020
Hotell Åregården	Åre	00 46 647 178 00
Hotell Diplomat	Stockholm	00 46 8 459 68 00
Romantik Hotel Åkerblads	Tällberg	00 46 247 50800
Romantik Hotel Söderköpings Brunn	Söderköping	00 46 121 109 00
Svartå Herrgård	Svartå	00 46 585 500 03
Tanums Gestgifveri	Tanumshede	00 46 525 29010
Toftaholm Herrgård	Lagan	00 46 370 44055

SWITZERLAND

Hostellerie Bon Accueil	Chateau d'Oex	00 41 26 924 6320
Posthotel Engiadina	Zouz	00 41 81 85 41 021
Romantik Hotel Wilden Mann	Lucerne/ Luzern	00 41 41 210 16 66
Royal Hotel Bellevue	Kandersteg	00 41 33 675 88 88
Villa Principe Leopoldo & Residence	Lugano	00 41 91 985 8855

TURKEY

Bosphorus Pasha	Istanbul	00 90 216 422 0003
Club Savile	Kas	00 90 242 836 1393
Hotel Grand Kaptan	Alanya	00 90 242 514 0101
Hotel Villa Mahal	Kalkan	00 90 242 844 3268
Savile Residence	Kas	00 90 242 836 2300

Calendar of Events

Kew Gardens, London

Leeds Castle, Kent

Pashley Manor Gardens, Sussex

MARCH

4th	Kew Orchid Festival Event: Flower Arranging	Royal Botanic Gardens Kew, London (0181 332 5000)
6th	The 33rd Churchill Memorial Concert	Blenheim Palace, Oxfordshire (01993 811091)
6–14th	Garden Crafts	RHS Garden Wisley, Surrey (01483 224234)
7th	Bridal Fayre	Sandon Hall, Staffordshire (01889 508004)
10–14th	Baileys Antique Fairs	Tatton Park, Cheshire (01625 534400)
21st	Donington Merrels Championship	The Manor House, Leicestershire (01530 831259)
21–24th	Phillips Fine Art Sale	Powderham Castle, Devon (01626 890243)
24th	Sotheby's Valuation Day	Tredegar House and Park, Newport, Wales (01633 815880)
27–28th	Armada! Weekend	Penshurst Place & Gardens, Kent (01892 870307)
31–31st May	The Aristocrats – Costumes from the BBC Television Drama	Tredegar House and Park, Newport, Wales (01633 815880)

APRIL

2–5th	Easter Craft Festival	Duncombe Park, Yorkshire (01439 770213)
2–5th	Easter Egg Trail – in the Gardens	Erddig, Wrexham, Wales (01978 355314)
2–18th	Courtly Sports, Games and Pastimes	Hampton Court Palace, London (0181 781 9500)
2–5th	Easter Weekend	Hever Castle, Kent (01732 865224)
2–5th	Great Easter Egg Quiz & Re–creation of Tudor Life at Eastertide	Kentwell, Suffolk (01787 310207)
2–5th	Mediaeval Easter	Warwick Castle, Warwickshire (01926 495421)
3–5th	A Celebration of Easter	Leeds Castle, Kent (01622 815895)
3–5th	Ballooning and Kite Flying Festival	Longleat, Wiltshire (01985 844400)
4th	Easter Egg Trail	Baddesley Clinton, Warwickshire (01564 783294)
4th	Easter Egg Hunt	Herstmonceux Castle, Sussex (01323 833816)
4th	The Lulworth Easter Bunny Hunt	Lulworth Castle, Dorset (01929 400352)
4–5th	Garden Show	Elton Hall, Cambridgeshire (01832 280468)
4–5th	Victorian Easter	Holdenby House, Northamptonshire (01604 770074)
4–5th	Easter at Penshurst Place	Penshurst Place & Gardens, Kent (01892 870307)
4–5th	Easter Egg Hunt	Rievaulx Terrace & Temples, Yorkshire (01439 798340)
5th	Children's Treasure Hunt	Charlecote Park, Warwickshire (01789 470277)
5th	Daffodil Time	High Beeches Garden, Sussex (01444 400589)
10–11th	Rainbow Craft Fair	Capesthorne Hall, Cheshire (01625 861221)
10–11th	Gamekeepers' Fair	Shugborough Estate, Staffordshire (01889 881388)
11th	Classical Concert in Winter Garden	Saint Hill Manor, Sussex (01342 326711)
17–18th	Garden Festival	Borde Hill, Sussex (01444 450326)
17–18th	Craft Fair	Elton Hall, Cambridgeshire (01832 280468)
17–18th	The West Wales Open Spring Show & Garden Festival	Picton Castle, Dyfed, Wales (01437 751326)
18th	Spring Plant Fair	Pashley Manor Gardens, Sussex (01580 200692)
18th	Samhain Medieval Society	Peckforton Castle, Cheshire (01829 260930)
23–25th	Country Homes & Gardens Show	Highclere Castle, Berkshire (01635 253210)
25th	Craft Fair	Harvington Hall, Hereford & Worcester (01562 777846)
29th	Garden Festival Preview	Haddonstone, Northamptonshire (01604 770300)
29–3rd May	"Tulip Festival, with Bloms Bulbs"	Pashley Manor Gardens, Sussex (01580 200692)

MAY

1–2nd	Orchard open to the public, (this weekend only)	Waterperry Gardens, Oxfordshire (01844 339226)
1–3rd	Living Heritage Oxfordshire Craft Fair Blenheim Park	Blenheim Palace, Oxfordshire (01993 811091)
1–3rd	Pets, Pets, Pets	Harewood House, Yorkshire (0113 288 6331)
1–3rd	Bedfordshire Spring Craft Show	Woburn Abbey, Bedfordshire (01525 290666)
1–3rd	Craft Show	Penshurst Place & Gardens (01892 870307)
2nd	Ladham House Gardens Open to public	Ladham House, Kent (01580 211203)
2nd	Volkswagon Owners Club Rally (Warks. & Leics. Branch)	Stanford Hall, Leicestershire (01788 860250)
2–3rd	Food & Country Fair	Capesthorne Hall, Cheshire (01625 861221)
2–3rd	Spring Country Fair	Eastnor Castle, Hereford & Worcester (01531 633160)
2–3rd	Garden Festival	Haddonstone, Northamptonshire (01604 770300)
2–3rd	Falconry Weekend	Holdenby House, Northamptonshire (01604 770074)
3rd	Bluebell Time	High Beeches Garden, Sussex (01444 400589)
3rd	Flower Fair	Hergest Croft Gardens, Herefordshire (01544 230160)
6–9th	Living Crafts	Hatfield House & Gardens, Hertfordshire (01707 262823)
7–9th	Home Design and Interiors Exhibition	Elton Hall, Cambridgeshire (01832 280468)
8–17th June	Botanical Show	Burford House Gardens, Shropshire (01584 810777)
8–4th July	Contemporary Photography Exhibition	Orleans House Gallery, London (0181 892 0221)
9th	Spring Plant Fair	Newby Hall, N Yorkshire (01423 322583)
15–27th June	Victorian Valentine Cards	Torre Abbey, Devon (01803 293593)
16th	NWCD – Carriage Driving	Dalemain Estates, Cumbria (01768 486450)
16th	British Red Cross Garden Day	Chillingham Castle, Northumberland (01668 215359)
15–16th	Festival of English Food & Wine	Leeds Castle, Kent (01622 815895)
15–16th	County Antiques Fair	Sandon Hall, Staffordshire (01889 508004)
15–16th	Out of the Wood Show	The Weald & Downland Open Air Museum, Sussex (01243 811384)
16th	Spring Plant	Erddig, Wrexham, Wales (01978 355314)
16th	Ladham House Gardens Open to public	Ladham House, Kent (01580 211203)
16th	Plant Fair	Nunnington Hall, Yorkshire (01439 748283)
16th	Leicestershire Ford RS Owners Club Rally	Stanford Hall, Leicestershire (01788 860250)
22nd	Actors' Centre North East – Stars Night	Chillingham Castle, Northumberland (01668 215359)
24–28th	Special Chelsea Show Week Opening incl. Exhibition The Flowering of Botanical Art	Chelsea Physic Garden, London (0171 352 5646)
27–31st	Charleston Festival	Charleston, Sussex (01323 811626)

Chillingham Castle, Northumberland

Gilbert White's House, Hampshire

Claremont Landscape Garden, Surrey

29–31st	Craft Show	Breamore House, Hampshire (01725 512233)
29–30th	Arts & Craft Weekend	Cecil Higgins Art Gallery, Bedfordshire (01234 211222)
29–31st	Merrie England Weekend	Hever Castle, Kent (01732 865224)
29–31st	Red Wyvern Society re–enactment in Skipton Castle in the 15th century	Skipton Castle, N Yorkshire (01756 792442)
29–30th	Scottish Beer Festival	Traquair House, Peeblesshire, Scotland (01896 830323)
29–31st	Jousting	Warwick Castle, Warwickshire (01926 495421)
30–30th June	Sculpture in the Garden Exhibition	Deans Court Garden, Dorset
30–31st	Southern Countries Game & Country Fair	Highclere Castle, Berkshire (01635 253210)
30–31st	Lamport Country Festival	Lamport Hall, Northamptonshire (01604 686272)
30–31st	Civil War Weekend	Holdenby House, Northamptonshire (01604 770074)
30–31st	Wine Festival	Mount Ephraim Gardens, Kent (01227 751496)
30–31st	Classic Car Show	Penshurst Place & Gardens, Kent (01892 870307)
30–31st	Georgian Fun and Games	Tredegar House and Park, Newport, Wales (01633 815880)
31st	Country Fair	Duncombe Park, Yorkshire (01439 770213)
31st	Sherborne Castle Country Fair	Sherborne Castle, Dorset (01935 813182)

JUNE

4–6th	Much Ado About Nothing	Ingatestone Hall, Essex (01277 353010)
5th	'Top Brass at Stourhead' on the lawns	Stourhead, Wiltshire (01747 841152)
5–6th	Special Gardens Weekend	Cawdor Castle, Inverness–shire, Scotland (01667 404615)
5–6th	Rolls Royce Enthusiasts' Club Annual Rally	Cottesbrooke Hall & Gardens, Northamptonshire (01604 505808)
5–6th	Flower and Garden Show	Eastnor Castle, Hereford & Worcester (01531 633160)
5–6th	Classic Car Show	Tatton Park, Cheshire (01625 534400)
5–6th	Leicester Mercury Flower & Garden Festival	Stanford Hall, Leicestershire (01788 860250)
5–6th	Woburn Garden Show & Maze	Woburn Abbey, Bedfordshire (01525 290666)
6th	Medieval Music on the Terrace	Rievaulx Terrace & Temples (01439 798340)
6th	Heavy Horse Summer Spectacular	The Weald & Downland Open Air Museum, Sussex (01243 811384)
10–13th	Homes & Gardens Magazine Grand Summer Fair	Ripley Castle, Yorks (01423 770152)
11–13th	Antiques Fair	Duncombe Park, Yorkshire (01439 770213)
12th	Performing Arts Music for the Movies Outdoor concert with fireworks	Blenheim Palace, Oxfordshire (01993 811091)
12th	Open Air Concert	Herstmonceux Castle, Sussex (01323 833816)
12th	Bournemouth Orchestra – Open Air Concert with Fireworks	Lulworth Castle, Dorset (01929 400352)
12–13th	Rainbow Craft Fair	Newby Hall, Yorkshire (01423 322583)
12–13th	Steam Rally in Park	Parham Park, Sussex (01903 742021)
13th	Alfa–Romeo Owners Club National Rally	Stanford Hall, Leicestershire (01788 860250)
16th	Friends of Kew Plant Auction	Royal Botanic Gardens Kew, London (0181 332 5000)
17–20th	Summer Flower Festival	Pashley Manor Gardens, Sussex (01580 200692)
19th	Picnic to 'Jazz in June' in delightful parkland setting	Gilbert White's House, Hampshire (01420 511275)
19th	Fire Sculpture	Longleat, Wiltshire (01985 844400)
19–20th	Rose Weekend	Borde Hill, Sussex (01444 450326)
19–20th	Craft Show – Eastern Events	Erddig, Wrexham, Wales (01978 355314)
19–20th	Unusual Plants Fair	Gilbert White's House, Hampshire (01420 511275)
19–20th	Festival of Gardening	Hatfield House & Gardens (01707 262823)
19–20th	Medieval Fair	Tatton Park, Cheshire (01625 534400)
20th	Vintage Collectors Day (Ty–Hafan Charity Event)	Picton Castle, Dyfed, Wales (01437 751326)
20–11th July	Great Annual Re–creation of Tudor Life	Kentwell, Suffolk (01787 310207)
24th	Millennium Ball	Powderham Castle, Devon (01626 890243)
27th	Cumbrian Classic Car Caper	Dalemain, Cumbria (01768 486450)
26th	Opera Brava present Mozart's Don Giovanni	Baddesley Clinton, Warwickshire (01564 783294)
26th	The Music of the Night – Firework Finale	Charlecote Park, Warwickshire (01789 470277)
26th	Bournemouth Sinfonietta's Concert with Fireworks	Sherborne Castle, Dorset (01935 813182)
26–3rd July	The 21st Anniversary Leeds Castle Open Air Concerts	Leeds Castle, Kent (01622 815895)
26–27th	The Arley Garden Festival	Arley Hall, Cheshire (01565 777284)
26th	Outdoor Production of Shakespeare's Comedy of Errors	Saint Hill Manor, Sussex (01342 326711)
27th	Opera Brava present Rossini's Barber of Seville	Baddesley Clinton, Warwickshire (01564 783294)

JULY

2–18th	The Pergola Open Air Theatre	West Dean Gardens, Sussex (01243 818210)
3rd	Jazz Concert	Ingatestone Hall, Essex (01277 353010)
3rd	King's College Chapel Foundation Concert – 'Mozart – C Minor Mass'	King's College Chapel, Cambridge (01223 357851)
3rd	Longleat Outdoor Opera Concert	Longleat, Wiltshire (01985 844400)
3–4th	Powderham Horse Trials	Powderham Castle, Devon (01626 890243)
3–4th	American Car Show	Tatton Park, Cheshire (01625 534400)
4th	Lulworth 'Classic' Car Event	Lulworth Castle, Dorset (01929 400352)
4th	Samhain Medieval Society	Peckforton Castle, Cheshire (01829 260930)
6–18th	Craft Fortnight	Picton Castle, Dyfed, Wales (01437 751326)
8–11th	Hampton Court Palace Flower Show	Hampton Court Palace, London (0181 781 9500)
8–11th	The Jungle Book – promenade theatre	Harewood House, Yorkshire (0113 288 6331)
10th	Summer Ball	Borde Hill, Sussex (01444 450326)
10–5th Sept	20th Century Fine Art	Orleans House Gallery, London (0181 892 0221)
10–11th	Balloon Fiesta	Penshurst Place & Gardens, Kent (01892 870307)
10–11th	Victorian Weekend	Warwick Castle, Warwickshire (01926 495421)
11th	Samhain Medieval Society	Peckforton Castle, Cheshire (01829 260930)
11th	Open Gardens Day	Tredegar House and Park, Newport, Wales (01633 815880)
11th	Country Fair, 11am–5pm	Squerryes Court, Kent (01959 562345)
11–5th Sept	Summer Exhibition Rainforests for Health	Chelsea Physic Garden, London (0171 352 5646)
14–18th	Fête Champêtre	Claremont Landscape Gardens, Surrey (01372 451596)
15–18th	Art in Action – Arts, crafts and music	Waterperry Gardens, Oxfordshire (Info–0171 381 3192)
16–18th	Outdoor Play	Harvington Hall, Hereford & Worcester (01562 777846)
17–18th	13th Great Annual Dalemain Rainbow Craft Fair	Dalemain, Cumbria (01768 486450)
17–18th	A Tudor Revel	Hatfield House & Gardens, Hertfordshire (01707 262823)

Calendar of Events

Ironbridge Gorge Museum, Shropshire

Roman Baths, Somerset

Herstmonceaux Castle, Sussex

18th	NECPWA Car Rally	Newby Hall, N Yorkshire (01423 322583)
20th	Performing Arts Lakeside Concert	Ripley Castle, Yorkshire (01423 770152)
20–21st Nov	A Pot of Gold Exhibition	Cecil Higgins Art Gallery, Bedfordshire (01234 211222)
20–24th	Kew Gardens Jazz Festival (with fireworks)	Royal Botanic Gardens Kew, London (0181 332 5000)
22–24th	Fête Champêtre 'The Belle Époque' in the Garden	Stourhead, Wiltshire (01747 841152)
22–24th	A Midsummers Night's Dream'	Painswick Rococo Garden, Gloucestershire (01452 813204)
22–25th	Royal Horticultural Flower Show	Tatton Park, Cheshire (01625 534400)
23rd	Stowe Summer Ball	Stowe School, Buckinghamshire (01280 813650)
23–25th	Galloway Antiques Fair	Ripley Castle, Yorks (01423 770152)
24th	Jousting Tournaments	Hever Castle, Kent (01732 865224)
24th	Outdoor Orchestral Spectacular Concert	Mount Ephraim Gardens, Kent (01227 751496)
24th	Shakespeare Henry V by Oddsocks Theatre Co.	Nunnington Hall, Yorkshire (01439 748283)
24th	Fireworks & Laser Concert	Shugborough Estate, Staffordshire (01889 881388)
24–25th	Elizabethan Revelry	Penshurst Place & Gardens (01892 870307)
25th	Classic Car Show	Capesthorne Hall, Cheshire (01625 861221)
25th	Vintage Car Rally	Doddington Place Rally, Kent (01795 886101)
25th	Classic Car Rally	Ingatestone Hall, Essex (01277 353010)
25th	Powderham Food and Drink Festival	Powderham Castle, Devon (01626 890243)
25th	Vintage Motorcycle Club Founders Day Rally	Stanford Hall, Leicestershire (01788 860250)
25th	Show for Rare & Traditional Breeds	Weald & Downland Open Air Museum, Sussex (01243 811384)
27–7th Aug	Embroidery Exhibition	St Agatha's Trust, Hampshire (01329 230330)
28th	Teddy Bear's Picnic	Charlecote Park, Warwickshire (01789 470277)
28th	Sandringham Flower Show	Sandringham, Norfolk (01485 540860)
28th	Illyria's open air performance 'The Water Babies'	Sherborne Castle, Dorset (01935 813182)
30–1st Aug	CLA Game Fair	Harewood House, Yorkshire (0113 288 6331)
31st	Jousting Tournaments	Hever Castle, Kent (01732 865224)
31st	The Halle Firework Concert	Tatton Park, Cheshire (01625 534400)
31–1st Aug	Live Stream Model Show	Breamore House, Hampshire (01725 512233)
31–1st Aug	Hot Air Balloon Meet	Eastnor Castle, Hereford & Worcester (01531 633160)

AUGUST

1–31st	August evenings open until 9.30pm	Roman Baths, Somerset (01225 477789)
1st	Treasure Hunt around the garden	Doddington Place Gardens, Kent (01795 886101)
5–8th	English National Sheep Dog Trials	Powderham Castle, Devon (01626 890243)
6th	Jazz on a Summers Evening	Penshurst Place & Gardens, Kent (01892 870307)
6–8th	The Welsh Open Championship Show & Gardening Fayre	Picton Castle, Dyfed, Wales (01437 751326)
6–8th	Art in Clay	Hatfield House & Gardens, Hertfordshire (01707 262823)
7th	Proms Evening with fireworks	Erddig, Wrexham, Wales (01978 355314)
7th	Jousting Tournaments	Hever Castle, Kent (01732 865224)
7th	Open Air Concert	Highclere Castle, Berkshire (01635 253210)
7th	Ripley Show	Ripley Castle, Yorkshire (01423 770152)
7th	An Evening of Opera , Tosca	Pashley Manor Gardens, Sussex (01580 200692)
7th	Much Ado About Nothing' on the lawns	Stourhead, Wiltshire (01747 841152)
7–8th	Lulworth Horse Trials & Country Fair	Lulworth Castle, Dorset (01929 400352)
7–8th	Traquair Fair	Traquair House, Peebleshire, Scotland (01896 830323)
8th	Fuscia Show	Borde Hill, Sussex (01444 450326)
8th	Opera – Open-air performance	Erddig, Wrexham, Wales (01978 355314)
8th	Marie Curie Family Fun Day	Hartland Abbey & Gardens, Devon (01237 441264/234)
8th	Country House Fair	Tredegar House and Park, Newport, Wales (01633 815880)
14th	Performing Arts Fireworks and Laser Concert	Bowood House & Gardens, Wiltshire (01249 812102)
14th	Children's Society	Chillingham Castle, Northumberland (01668 215359)
14th	Jousting Tournaments	Hever Castle, Kent (01732 865224)
14th	Longleat Outdoor Proms Concert	Longleat, Wiltshire (01985 844400)
14th	The 1999 Music & Fireworks Spectacular	Stanford Hall, Leicestershire (01788 860250)
14–15th	Chilli Fiesta Weekend	West Dean Gardens, Sussex (01243 818210)
14–15th	Children's Activity Weekend	Weald & Downland Open Air Museum, Sussex (01243 811384)
15th	Rolls Royce Enthusiasts' Club Rally	Blenheim Palace, Oxfordshire (01993 811091)
15th	Fireworks & Laser Symphony Concert	Capesthorne Hall, Cheshire (01625 861221)
15th	Festival of Transport	Highclere Castle, Berkshire (01635 253210)
15th	Summer Plant Fair	Pashley Manor Gardens, Sussex (01580 200692)
16–20th	Childrens' Fun Week	Eastnor Castle, Hereford & Worcester (01531 633160)
20–22nd	Craft Show in Park	Parham Park, Sussex (01903 742021)
21st	Fireworks Concert	Hatfield House & Gardens, Hertfordshire (01707 262823)
21st	Jousting Tournaments	Hever Castle, Kent (01732 865224)
21–22nd	Antiques Fair	Elton Hall, Cambridgeshire (01832 280468)
21–23rd	The Victorian Love Story	Ironbridge Gorge Museum, Shropshire (01952 432166)
22nd	Theatre Set–Up 'Much Ado'	Penshurst Place & Gardens, Kent (01892 870307)
22nd	Irish & Vintage Car Rally	Powerscourt Gardens, Co Wicklow, Ireland (00 353 204 6000)
22nd	Commercial Vehicles Road Run	Woburn Abbey, Bedfordshire (01525 290666)
27–30th	Jazz Festival – Deer Park	Ripley Castle, Yorkshire (01423 770152)
28th	Jousting Tournaments	Hever Castle, Kent (01732 865224)
28–12th Sept	Exhibition by Torbay Guild of Artists	Torre Abbey, Devon (01803 293593)
28–30th	Living Heritage Oxfordshire Craft Fair Blenheim Park	Blenheim Palace, Oxfordshire (01993 811091)
28–30th	Medieval Festival	Herstmonceux Castle, Sussex (01323 833816)
28–30th	Live Craft Fair	Highclere Castle, Berkshire (01635 253210)
28–30th	Jousting and Birds of Prey	Warwick Castle, Warwickshire (01926 495421)
28–30th	Summer Craft Fair	Shugborough Estate, Staffordshire (01889 881388)
29th	Cumbrian Classic Car Show	Dalemain, Cumbria (01768 486450)
29th	Proms Concert in the Park	Penshurst Place & Gardens, Kent (01892 870307)
29th	Classic Car Show	Waterperry Gardens, Oxfordshire (01844 339226/254)
29–30th	Breamore Classic Car Show	Breamore House, Hampshire (01725 512233)
29–30th	The Berkeley Household: Living History in the Wars of the Roses	Eastnor Castle, Hereford & Worcester (01531 633160)
29–30th	Horse Trials	Highclere Castle, Berkshire (01635 253210)
29–30th	Medieval Weekend	Holdenby House, Northamptonshire (01604 770074)

Longleat, Wiltshire

West Dean Gardens, Sussex

Warwick Castle, Warwickshire

SEPTEMBER

4th	Erddig Country Day	Erddig, Wrexham, Wales (01978 355314)
4th	Laser & Firework Spectacular	Longleat, Wiltshire (01985 844400)
4th	Pride and Prejudice Ball	Tatton Park, Cheshire (01625 534400)
4–5th	Rainbow Craft Fair	Newby Hall, Yorkshire (01423 322583)
4–5th	Bedfordshire Craft Fair	Woburn Abbey, Bedfordshire (01525 290666)
5th	Last night of the Proms – Open Air Concert	Harewood House, Yorkshire (0113 288 6331)
5th	Samhain Medieval Society	Peckforton Castle, Cheshire (01829 260930)
9–12th	The Blenheim International Horse Trials	Blenheim Palace, Oxfordshire (01993 811091)
10–12th	Country Lifestyle Fair	Hatfield House & Gardens (01707 262823)
10–12th	Craft Show	Penshurst Place & Gardens, Kent (01892 870307)
10–13th	Torre Abbey Flower Festival	Torre Abbey, Devon (01803 293593)
11–12th	The Great Leeds Castle Balloon & Vintage Car Weekend	Leeds Castle, Kent (01622 765400)
11–12th	Country Show in Park	Parham Park, Sussex (01903 742021)
11–12th	Needlework Fair	Traquair House, Peebleshire, Scotland (01896 830323)
12th	Rare Plants Fair	Borde Hill, Sussex (01444 450326)
12th	Frampton Country Fair	Frampton Court, Gloucestershire (01452 740698)
12th	Samhain Medieval Society	Peckforton Castle, Cheshire (01829 260930)
12th	Mini Owners Club National Rally	Stanford Hall, Leicestershire (01788 860250)
18–19th	Dahlia Festival	Aylett Nurseries, Hertfordshire (01727 822255)
19	Autumn Plant Fair	Newby Hall, Yorkshire (01423 322583)
25–26th	Dahlia Festival	Aylett Nurseries, Hertfordshire (01727 822255)
26th	Churchtown Country Show	Meols Hall, Merseyside (01704 228326)

OCTOBER

2–3rd	Christmas Craft Fair	Eastnor Castle, Hereford & Worcester (01531 633160)
2–3rd	Living History Weekend	Royal Pavilion, Sussex (01273 290900)
2–3rd	Crafts at Stanford Hall	Stanford Hall, Leicestershire (01788 860250)
3rd	Plant Sale	Hergest Croft Gardens, Hereford & Worcester (01544 230160)
3rd	Ladham House Gardens Open to public	Ladham House, Kent (01580 211203)
9–10th	Erddig Apple Festival	Erddig, Wrexham, Wales (01978 355314)
9–10th	Christmas Craft Fair	Shugborough Estate, Staffordshire (01889 881388)
16–23rd	I can do that! Staff show	Burford House Gardens, Shropshire (01584 810777)
17th	Apple Day	Acorn Bank Garden, Cumbria (01768 361893)
17th	Apple Day	West Dean Gardens, Sussex (01243 818210)
18–21st	Apple Days	RHS Garden Wisley, Surrey (01483 224234)
20–24th	Apple Week	Nunnington Hall, Yorkshire (01439 748283)
23–24th	Apple Day Weekend	Waterperry Gardens, Oxfordshire (01844 339226)
23–24th	Gifts & Crafts Fair	Lamport Hall, Northamptonshire (01604 686272)
23–24th	4 Wheel Drive Family Safari	Longleat, Wiltshire (01985 844400)
25–26th	Ghostly Tales for adults and children	Charlecote Park, Warwickshire (01789 470277)
30th	Halloween Fireworks Party	Hatfield House & Gardens, Hertfordshire (01707 262823)
30th	Bonfire & Fireworks Spectacular	Sandon Hall, Staffordshire (01889 508004)
31st	Hallowe'en Stories	Penshurst Place & Gardens, Kent (01892 870307)
31st	Halloween	Tatton Park, Cheshire (01625 534400)

NOVEMBER

5–7th	Antiques Fair	Duncombe Park, Yorkshire (01439 770213)
6th	Bonfire Night & Fireworks	Ironbridge Gorge Museum, Shropshire (01952 432166)
6th	Grand Fireworks Spectacular	Leeds Castle, Kent (01622 815895)
6th	Grand Bonfire	Meols Hall, Merseyside (01704 228326)
12–14th	Galloway Antique Fair	Powderham Castle, Devon (01626 890243)
20–28th	Christmas at Wisley	RHS Garden Wisley, Surrey (01483 224234)
21st	Craft Fair	Harvington Hall, Hereford & Worcester (01562 777846)
26–28th	Christmas Craft Festival	Harewood House, Yorkshire (0113 288 6331)
28th	Mulled Wine & Christmas Shopping Day	Gilbert White's House, Hampshire (01420 511275)
28–24th Dec	Christmas at the Castle	Warwick Castle, Warwickshire (01926 495421)

DECEMBER

3–5th	Christmas Fair	Highclere Castle, Berkshire (01635 253210)
4th	St Etheldreda's Church Fair	Hatfield House & Gardens, Hertfordshire (01707 262823)
4th	Christmas Concert	Nunnington Hall, Yorkshire (01439 748283)
4th	Lancastrian Theatre Organ Christmas Concert	Tatton Park, Cheshire (01625 534400)
4–5th	Christmas Craft Festival	Duncombe Park, Yorkshire (01439 770213)
7–9th	Christmas at Shugborough	Shugborough Estate, Staffordshire (01889 881388)
6th,13th,20th	Christmas Days & Evenings at Arley	Arley Hall, Cheshire (01565 777284)
10–12th	Christmas at Tredegar House	Tredegar House and Park, Newport, Wales (01633 815880)
11th	Carols at Christmas in the Great Hall	Charlecote Park, Warwickshire (01789 470277)
11–12th	Wassail	Harvington Hall, Hereford & Worcester (01562 777846)
11–12th	Kew Gardens Christmas Events	Royal Botanic Gardens Kew, London (0181 332 5000)
13–24th	Christmas at the Castle	Leeds Castle, Kent (01622 815895)
16–19th	Christmas at Tredegar House	Tredegar House and Park, Newport, Wales (01633 815880)
18th	Stowe Christmas Carol Concert	Stowe School, Buckinghamshire (01280 813650)
18–19th	Kew Gardens Christmas Events	Royal Botanic Gardens Kew, London (0181 332 5000)

RAINBOW FAIR *presents*

RAINBOW FAIR

promoting the work of British craft workers at high quality venues throughout the Country.

All exhibitors are vetted to ensure a high standard of work and originality of design.

Demonstrations are encouraged to add to an interesting visit, and all goods are for sale to the public.

Beautiful settings, interesting venues and **BRITISH** crafts (no brought in goods) have made Rainbow the Country's leading promoters of events of this kind.

**Rainbow Fair, Navigation Wharf, Carre Street, Sleaford, Lincolnshire NG34 7TW
Telephone: (01529) 414793   Fax: (01529) 414985**

ORDER FORM

Call our 24hr credit card hotline FREEPHONE 0800 269 397

Simply indicate which title(s) you require by putting the quantity in the boxes provided. Choose your preferred method of payment and return this coupon (NO STAMP REQUIRED) to: Johansens, FREEPOST (CB264), 43 Millharbour, London E14 9BR. Your FREE gifts will automatically be dispatched with your order.
Fax orders welcome on 0171 537 3594

PRINTED GUIDES

	Qty	Total £
A Hotels – Great Britain & Ireland 1999 ....£19.95		
B Country Houses and Small Hotels – Great Britain & Ireland 1999 ....£10.95		
C Traditional Inns, Hotels and Restaurants – Great Britain & Ireland 1999 ......£10.95		
D Hotels – Europe & The Mediterranean 1999 ....£14.95		
E Hotels – North America, Bermuda, Caribbean 1999 ....£9.95		
F Historic Houses Castles & Gardens 1999 ....£4.99		
G Museums & Galleries 1999 *published & mailed to you in April '99* £8.95		
H Business Meeting Venues 1999 ....£20.00		
I Japanese Edition 1999 ....£9.95		
J Privilege Card 1999 ....£20.00 *You get one free card with your order, please mention here the number of additional cards you require*		
TOTAL 1		

CD-ROMs

	Qty	Total £
K The Guide 1999 – Great Britain & Ireland £29.95		
L The Guide 1999 – Europe & North America................£19.95		
M Business Meeting Venues 1999 ....£20.00		
TOTAL 2		

SPECIAL OFFERS

	Qty	Total £
SAVE £7.85 3 Johansens guides A+B+C £41.85 ..£34		
In a presentation box set add £5		
SAVE £12.80 4 Johansens guides A+B+C+D ....£56.80 ..£44		
In a presentation box set add £5		
SAVE £14.75 5 Johansens guides A+B+C+D+E ....£66.75 ..£52		
In a presentation box set add £5		
+*Johansens Suit Cover*	**FREE**	
+P&P	**FREE**	
SAVE £10.90 2 Johansens CD-ROMS K+L £49.90 ..£39		
SAVE £10 Business Meeting Pack H+M......£40 ..£30		
TOTAL 3		

Postage & Packing
UK: £4.50 or £2.50 for single orders and CD-ROMs
Ouside UK: Add £5 or £3 for single orders and CD-ROMs.

TOTAL 4 **FREE**

One Privilege Card
10% discount, room upgrade when available,
VIP service at participating establishments

TOTAL 1+2+3+4

Name (Mr/Mrs/Miss)

Address

Postcode

Prices Valid Until 31 August 1999
Please allow 21 days for delivery

Occasionally we may allow other reputable organisations to write to you with offers which may be of interest. If you prefer not to hear from them, tick this box. ☐

☐ I enclose a cheque for £ _____ payable to Johansens
☐ I enclose my order on company letterheading, please invoice (UK only)
☐ Please debit my credit/charge card account (please tick).
☐ MasterCard ☐ Diners ☐ Amex ☐ Visa ☐ Switch (Issue Number)

Card No

Signature

Exp date

J12

✂ ....

ORDER FORM

Call our 24hr credit card hotline FREEPHONE 0800 269 397

Simply indicate which title(s) you require by putting the quantity in the boxes provided. Choose your preferred method of payment and return this coupon (NO STAMP REQUIRED) to: Johansens, FREEPOST (CB264), 43 Millharbour, London E14 9BR. Your FREE gifts will automatically be dispatched with your order.
Fax orders welcome on 0171 537 3594

PRINTED GUIDES

	Qty	Total £
A Hotels – Great Britain & Ireland 1999 ....£19.95		
B Country Houses and Small Hotels – Great Britain & Ireland 1999 ....£10.95		
C Traditional Inns, Hotels and Restaurants – Great Britain & Ireland 1999 ......£10.95		
D Hotels – Europe & The Mediterranean 1999 ....£14.95		
E Hotels – North America, Bermuda, Caribbean 1999 ....£9.95		
F Historic Houses Castles & Gardens 1999 ....£4.99		
G Museums & Galleries 1999 *published & mailed to you in April '99* £8.95		
H Business Meeting Venues 1999 ....£20.00		
I Japanese Edition 1999 ....£9.95		
J Privilege Card 1999 ....£20.00 *You get one free card with your order, please mention here the number of additional cards you require*		
TOTAL 1		

CD-ROMs

	Qty	Total £
K The Guide 1999 – Great Britain & Ireland £29.95		
L The Guide 1999 – Europe & North America................£19.95		
M Business Meeting Venues 1999 ....£20.00		
TOTAL 2		

SPECIAL OFFERS

	Qty	Total £
SAVE £7.85 3 Johansens guides A+B+C £41.85 ..£34		
In a presentation box set add £5		
SAVE £12.80 4 Johansens guides A+B+C+D ....£56.80 ..£44		
In a presentation box set add £5		
SAVE £14.75 5 Johansens guides A+B+C+D+E ....£66.75 ..£52		
In a presentation box set add £5		
+*Johansens Suit Cover*	**FREE**	
+P&P	**FREE**	
SAVE £10.90 2 Johansens CD-ROMS K+L £49.90 ..£39		
SAVE £10 Business Meeting Pack H+M......£40 ..£30		
TOTAL 3		

Postage & Packing
UK: £4.50 or £2.50 for single orders and CD-ROMs
Ouside UK: Add £5 or £3 for single orders and CD-ROMs.

TOTAL 4 **FREE**

One Privilege Card
10% discount, room upgrade when available,
VIP service at participating establishments

TOTAL 1+2+3+4

Name (Mr/Mrs/Miss)

Address

Postcode

Prices Valid Until 31 August 1999
Please allow 21 days for delivery

Occasionally we may allow other reputable organisations to write to you with offers which may be of interest. If you prefer not to hear from them, tick this box. ☐

☐ I enclose a cheque for £ _____ payable to Johansens
☐ I enclose my order on company letterheading, please invoice (UK only)
☐ Please debit my credit/charge card account (please tick).
☐ MasterCard ☐ Diners ☐ Amex ☐ Visa ☐ Switch (Issue Number)

Card No

Signature

Exp date

J12

HIGHLAND.
An almost feminine charm and character all of its own. Light and aromatic, the Gentle Spirit is rich in body with a soft heather honey finish.

ISLE OF SKYE.
Assertive but not heavy. Fully flavoured with a pungent, peaty ruggedness. It explodes on the palate and lingers on. Well balanced. A sweetish seaweedy aroma.

SPEYSIDE.
Finely balanced with a dry, rather delicate aroma, good firm body and a smoky finish. A pleasantly austere malt of great distinction with a character all its own.

WEST HIGHLAND.
Oban is the West Highland malt. A singular, rich and complex malt with the merest suggestion of peat in the aroma, slightly smoky with a long smooth finish.

ISLE OF ISLAY.
Seaweed, peat, smoke and earth are all elements of the assertive Islay character. Pungent, an intensely dry 16 year old malt with a firm robust body and powerful aroma.

LOWLAND.
Typically soft, restrained and with a touch of sweetness. An exceptionally pale smooth malt which, experts agree, reaches perfection at 10 years maturity.

DALWHINNIE	TALISKER	CRAGGANMORE	OBAN	LAGAVULIN	GLENKINCHIE
15 YEARS OLD	10 YEARS OLD	12 YEARS OLD	14 YEARS OLD	16 YEARS OLD	10 YEARS OLD
HIGHLAND	SKYE	SPEYSIDE	WEST HIGHLAND	ISLAY	LOWLAND

Les grands crus de Scotland.

In the great wine-growing regions, there are certain growths from a single estate that are inevitably superior.

For the Scots, there are the single malts. Subtle variations in water, weather, peat and the distilling process itself lend each single malt its singular character. The Classic Malts are the finest examples of the main malt producing regions. To savour them, one by one, is a rare journey of discovery.

SIX OF SCOTLAND'S FINEST MALT WHISKIES

You'll also find that when your customers taste The Classic Malts, their appreciation will almost certainly increase your sales of malt whisky – in itself a discovery worth making.

To find out more, contact our Customer Services team on 0345 444 111, or contact your local wholesaler.

Index to Properties

Indexes

Indexes

T

U

V

W

Y

BELGIUM

C

N

S

Indexes

FRANCE

GERMANY

THE NETHERLANDS

Key to Map Pages

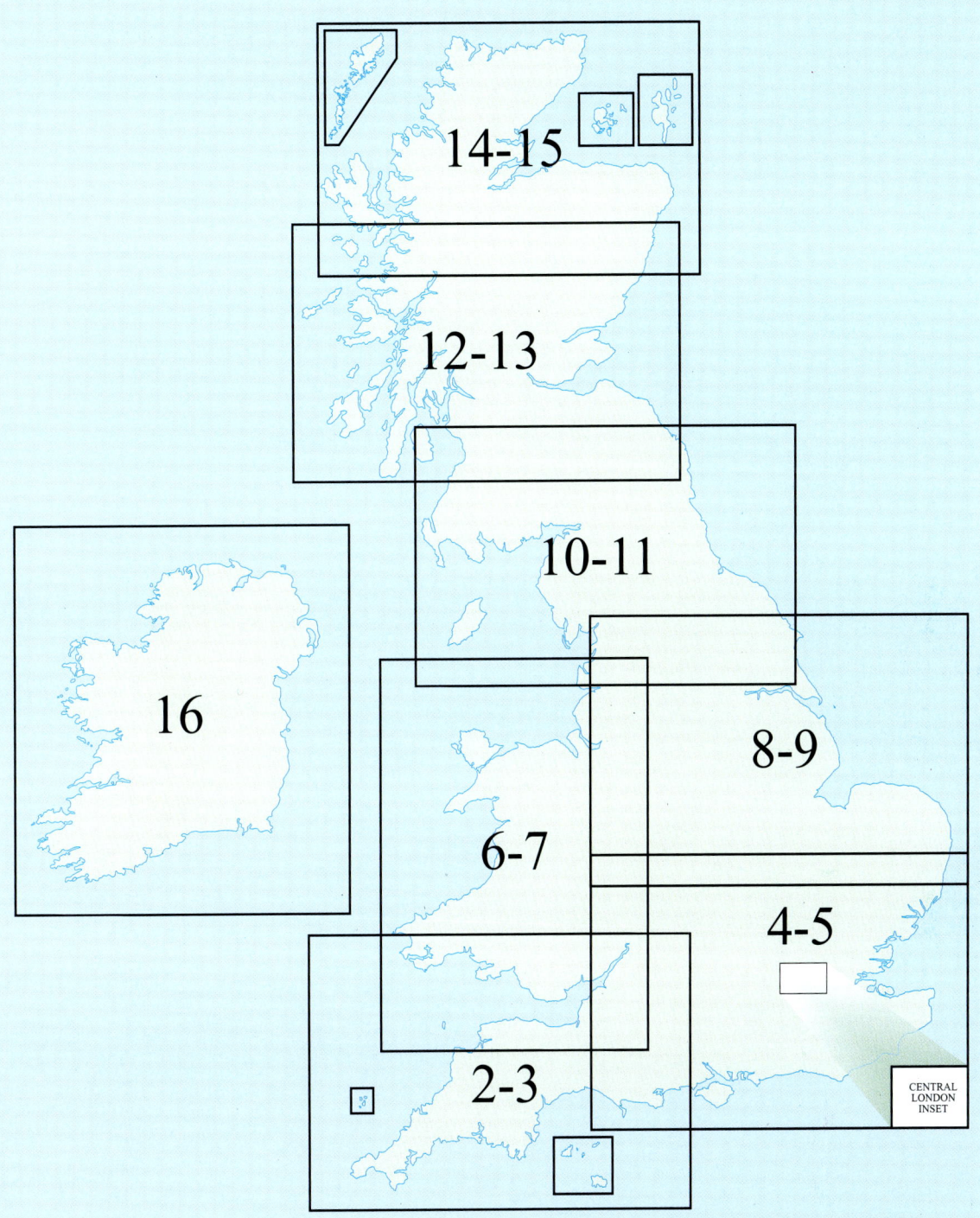

14-15

12-13

16

10-11

8-9

6-7

4-5

CENTRAL
LONDON
INSET

2-3

Key to Map Symbols

M62 12	Motorway	⊞	Property in the care of English Heritage	⌂	House with or without garden
A56	Primary Route	🦌	Property in the care of The National Trust	⛫	Castle with or without garden
	A Roads				
	B Roads	☗	Property in the care of The National Trust for Scotland	✽	Garden

CARTOGRAPHY BY AND MAP GRAPHICS LTD, COPYRIGHT © AND MAP GRAPHICS LTD 1998

Numbered Sites Within the M25

1. Fenton House
2. Burgh House
3. Keats House
4. Kenwood, The Iveagh Bequest
5. Capel Manor
6. Rose Cottage
7. Sutton House
8. Hall Place
9. The Old Palace
10. Southside House
11. Royal Botanic Gardens, Kew
12. Syon House
13. Syon Park Gardens
14. Strawberry Hill
15. Marble Hill House
16. Ham House
17. Hampton Court Palace
18. Osterley Park
19. Boston Manor
20. Claremont Landscape Garden
21. Claremont
22. Painshill Park
23. 2 Willow Road

Central London Inset

Scale 1 : 730 000

0   10   20 miles
0 10 20 30 kilometres

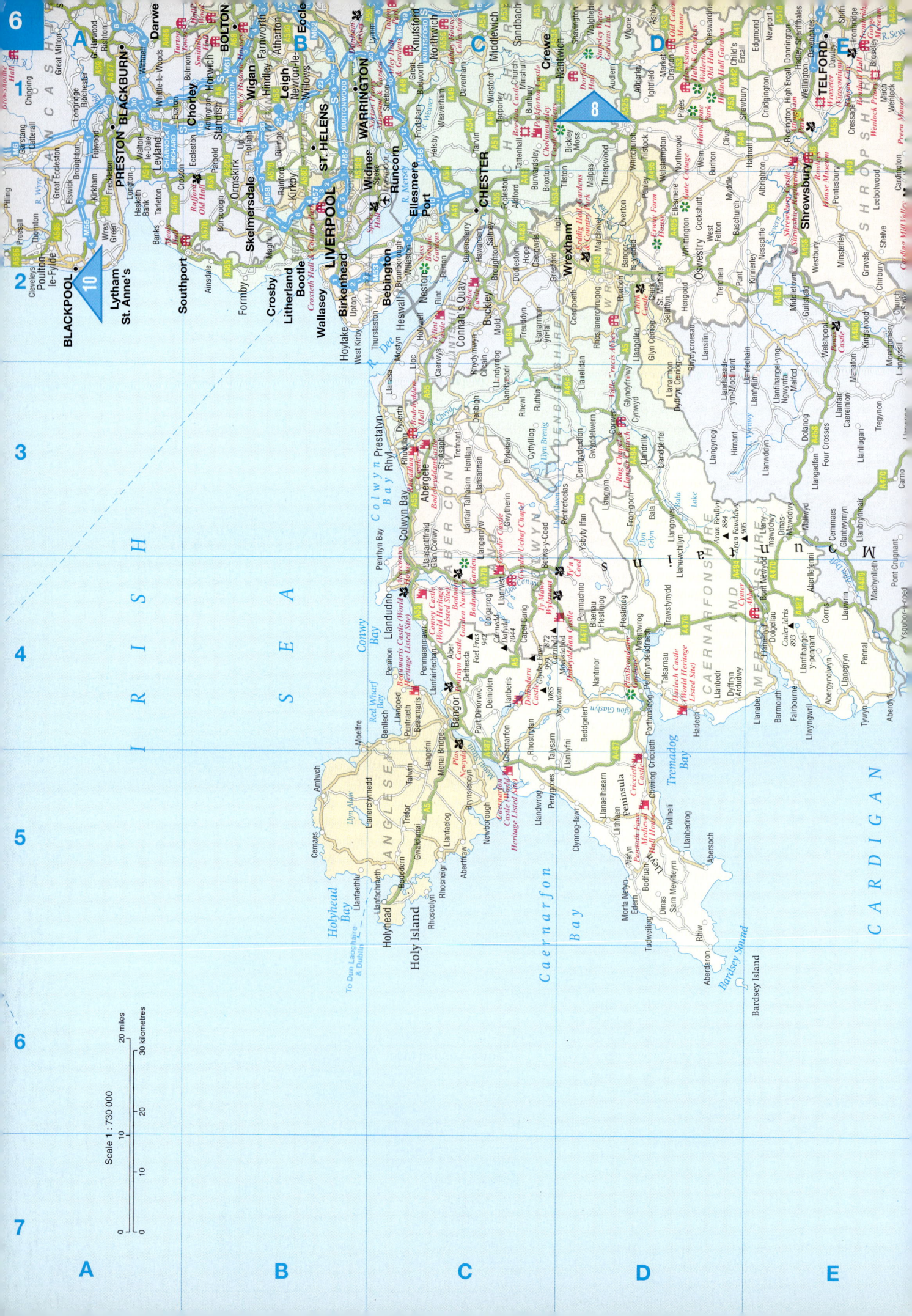

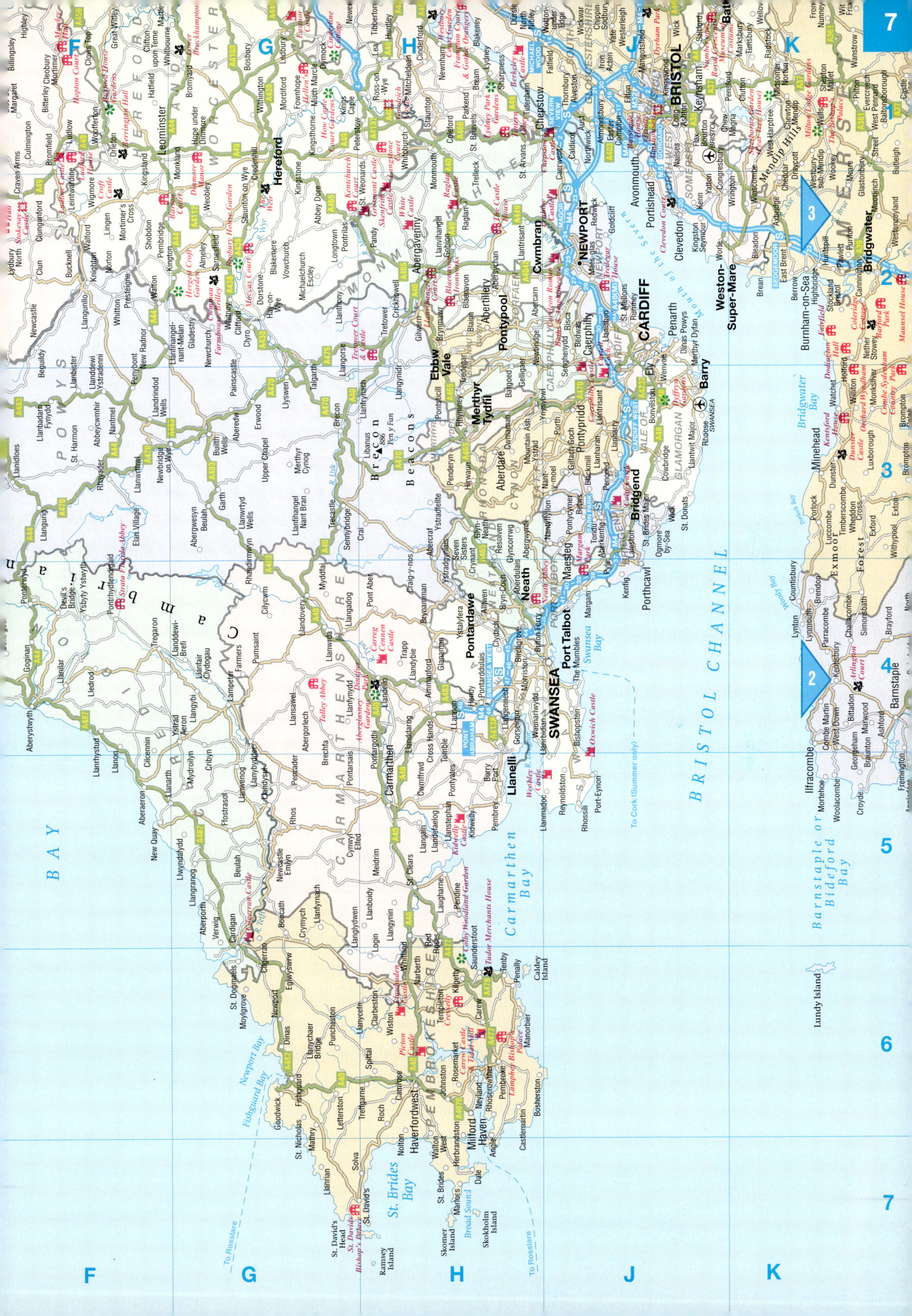

F G H J K

1

Scale 1 : 730 000

0   10   20 miles
0   10   20   30 kilometres

2

3

4

N O R T H

S E A

5

6

7